W9-CKK-156

MY PAMET

Cape Cod Chronicle

MY PAMET

Cape Cod Chronicle

TOM KANE

MOYER BELL LIMITED : MOUNT KISCO, NEW YORK

Dedicated to my child bride,

Anne

974,4
Kane
Aug. 8, 1989
Cape Cod

Published in the United States and Canada
by Moyer Bell Limited
Copyright © 1989 by Tom Kane
Cover and text illustrations copyright © 1989 by Hilarie Crosman.

All rights reserved. No part of this publication may be reproduced,
stored in a retrieval system or transmitted, in any form or by any
means, electronic, mechanical, photocopying, recording or otherwise,
without the prior written permission of Moyer Bell Limited, Colonial
Hill, Mt. Kisco, New York 10549.

First Edition

Library of Congress Cataloging-in-Publication Data

Kane, Tom, 1916–1989
    My Pamet : Cape Cod chronicle / Tom Kane.
        p.   cm.
    Includes index.
    1. Truro Region (Mass. : Town)—History.   2. Truro
Region (Mass. : Town)—Social life and customs.   3. Cape
Cod (Mass.)—History.   4. Cape Cod (Mass.)—Social life
and customs.   I. Cape Cod chronicle.   II. Title.
F74.T9K36   1989
974.4'92—dc19   88-37119
ISBN: 0-918825-91-1   CIP

Printed in the United States of America

INTRODUCTION

A popular feature of many small town newspapers is a column that chronicles social happenings: baptisms, graduations and anniversary celebrations; events held by various clubs and organizations; births, marriages and deaths. Here are reported activities that are part of the social fabric of the community, although not of the import to be placed among the "news worthy" items on page one. This is not journalism that wins Pulitzer prizes, nor is it usually of lasting value, except perhaps as an archival record.

It might seem strange, then, to be introducing a collective sampling from just such a column, one that ran for over forty years in two Cape Cod newspapers, *The Advocate*, of Provincetown, and *The Cape Codder*. But our author, Tom Kane, had the attributes of a natural writer, gifted with the ability to transform a standard formula, lifting it out of the dullness of routine, and creating a story that, taken altogether, is the universal one that brings Small Town America to life.

Kane started writing his column in the 1940's; it became a weekly feature in the 1950's, continuing until his final column in January, 1989. He produced more than two thousand separate pieces. E. J. Kahn, Jr., *New Yorker* staff writer, upon Kane's retirement as a columnist, said: "I can remember when his first column came out, and then more of them kept coming out every week, and I kept thinking, how can a young upstart writer like this go on writing every week when we professional writers struggle for a month to do it. Now it's more that 40 years he has been writing, while we are still sweating, and I think it is one of the most remarkable feats of non-stop writing that I know of."

Kane called his column "My Pamet" after the Pamet River, itself named for the tribe of Indians living in this part of Cape Cod at the time of the Pilgrim's landing. The river rises, seemingly in defiance of the usual laws governing sources for fresh water streams, at the foot of sand dunes a few hundred yards from the Atlantic Ocean. It courses its way west, towards Cape Cod Bay, cutting the "Narrow Land" of Truro (a favorite phrase of Kane's for this part of Cape Cod) in two. About mid-point in its journey it passes through Truro center—if a half dozen buildings clustered along a two lane highway can be called a town center. The river's run ends at Truro Harbor, now effectively closed to anything but small boats because the drifting sands of Cape Cod Bay have made the entrance to the harbor too shallow for larger vessels. But the Truro Harbor often referred to in Kane's chronicles was, in the first half of the nineteenth century, the busy center of nautical activity, home port to a large fleet of whaling and fishing vessels.

Kahn's summer house, an old Cape Codder, overlooks the Pamet River about a half mile from Kane's home. In 1970, Kahn was asked by his neighbor to write a quest column. With the kind permission of its author that column is quoted here. In gentle and effective parody, Kahn assumes Kane's format and colloquial language, and provides valued biographical information on Kane:

> A calm, clear day. Wind out of the east—but still hot enough to make a duck sweat. Lilacs cover the valley, and the first mosquitoes are darting at the arms.
>
> Talked with number three brother Tony, and had a chuckle over the times we used to rub poison ivy in each other's shoes. Mowed a peace sign in the lawn, then noticed the lights on at the Thomas Kanes', so I thought I'd head up for a chat.
>
> Drove into the driveway, saw number four son Geoff in the garden, then was attacked by the dog. Had teeth sharper than a razor clam. Shook hands with the Town Father (an old expression used in reference to town officials, he told me, and came out of one of Snowie's old columns in *The Advocate*) and sat down outside to chew the fat.
>
> Talked about the old days, and he recalled that he was in his 28th year as Town Clerk, Treasurer, and Tax Collector. "Been opposed once or twice," he chuckled, "but it's never been too close."
>
> "Beginning to think about retiring though," he went on. "Number four son Geoff is graduating this week, and that'll take the financial pressure off."
>
> He thought back to the time when he was born in Dorchester, son of an Irish streetcar operator. His father was going to "buy a little chicken farm and retire," but he died young, and the family came to Truro without him.
>
> Graduating from the old Wellfleet High School he went to Boston University on scholarship, but the Recession came, and the money ran out. "I was working at the Hotel Brunswick, and it had to close down. Darn near starved."
>
> About this time he decided to join the Maritime Service, and was

sent to Sheepshead Bay, Brooklyn. But then V-J Day rolled around, and he headed back to the Cape. Ambulance driving and liquor clerking followed, along with a mite of substitute teaching, and then in the late fifties he was offered a full-time job at the Provincetown Temple of Learning, which he took faster than a clam squirts.

"Teaching's getting more difficult now—modern math, the oral-aural technique for foreign languages—and the unrest in students has filtered down to the high school level. We have constant debate over demonstrations—they expect more freedom, more rights—and it's hard for me to keep in contact with them."

We thought back to the old one-room schoolhouse, where four grades would sit together. "Sure, with one teacher she was spread pretty thin, but I learned the table of equivalences and decimals when I was in the fifth grade, and even a little Shakespeare, just by overhearing what was going on in the higher grades."

Even the combination of town official and teacher couldn't satisfy the needs of a growing family, and he found he had to branch out to other areas—telegram delivery, real estate-agent, town lawn mower. Now he's ready to slow down and relax.

Still on his mind, though, is the future of the town.

"I'd like to see Truro stay just as it is, but that's impossible. The Master Plan wants to move the political center of town down to the Pamet Harbor, and they quote history in saying that that was where the original center was.

"But then it was a large, working harbor, and I doubt that it will ever be that functional again. Furthermore, the town would become involved with things like eminent domain and landfill, which would get quite complicated."

Finally talk turned to his column, which he's been writing since World War II.

"Yes, I have a set pattern," he chuckled. "First, a squib about the weather, then some local notes and finally an old tale. Apocryphal? Well, let's say I use poetic journalistic license.

"I can remember the time I wrote a story about Al Bettencourt having his false teeth locked in the ballot box—even the Christian Science Monitor reprinted part of it. Poor Al got mighty embarassed."

Then his child bride signaled from the window, and the Town Father sauntered into the house.

Another mark of the quality of the writing in this book is the subtle and effective way Kane's own character reveals itself. He seems to have made a conscious effort to shield himself from his readers. He chose for the by-line not his own name, but the anonymous sobriquet "Town Father." He studiously avoided using the first person singular pronoun. (It is used for the first time in his last column, and this sudden personal note makes his farewell to his readers all the more touching.) Yet I doubt there will be a reader who, finishing this book, won't have formed a clear image of its author, and love him as much as they do his other characters.

One finds revealed a person who lives in gentle harmony with family and friends and neighbors. A person of generosity, sharing his time and talents for the enrichment of his beloved Pamet. A person with the wisdom to know that yes, one finds humor in the foibles of fellow man, but portrays them with sympathetic understanding that avoids any hint of derision.

And one finds an uncommonly good writer.

Larry Peters
Truro, Cape Cod

NINETEEN FIFTIES

1950's

NINETEEN FIFTY-ONE

1951

High noon of a bright, sparkling day in Truro. A brisk cool breeze from the bay, and the sky, except for a fringe of clouds on the horizon, a brilliant clear blue. All that's left of last night's sudden, boiling snow squall is a faint powdering of white in the sheltered, frost-bound nooks, or a trickle of moisture from the crown of the blacktop to the sand shoulders of the road. The view from Town Hall is satisfying to the eye and the soul; the dense blue-green pine hills to the southeast, and the clear-etched Hogsbacks of South Truro, and the sun-washed bay, and the rugged, barren moorlands of the Corn Hill area. Back oceanward again, where the General Fields blend into the drab, gray-brown of the scrub oak copse, and the distant dunes of Long Nook stand bold and yellow in the noon sun. The Pamet below in the valley is making up for flood tide, and the noon signal has just sounded across the hills, and we to our chronicling.

Back in the twenties, our teachers at the Wilder School were healthy humans, sound of wind, strong of limb, and resistant to the sundry viruses which beset the pedagogues of today. On occasion, however, some affliction in the form of a fractured arm or a ruptured appendix would lay a teacher low, and for a period we'd have a substitute enthroned at the battered, golden oak desk. Mary Snow was always our favorite. Trained as a teacher, she could slip into the routine of the classroom schedule with little difficulty, and it therefore became a game involving considerable skill to outwit her. Mary's keen eye could spy out the usual crude schoolboy pranks—placing thumbtacks in a neighbor's seat, nailing Herb Gray's sheepskin coat to the dressing room wall—so a more subtle plan had to be worked out.

It was Robert "Dud" Meier who came up with the idea about the stove.

3

The "Big Part" or upper classroom of the school was heated by a huge, potbellied iron stove, connected to the chimney by a rickety length of rusty pipe. Dud, who was a mite slow in his school work in those days, took care of the fire during the day, and he knew all the peculiarities of the ancient Station Master. On certain days, for instance, when the wind was southeast, a peculiar downdraft would prevail in the school chimney, and unusual pains had to be taken with the stove to insure good combustion.

Fortune conspired one winter day to send Mary as a substitute when the heavy, damp breeze blew in over Holway's Hill, and, as we filed into school for the morning session there was already a faint odor of coal gas in the room. Naylor Hatch, the janitor, had fixed the drafts in accordance with weather conditions, but Dud soon made his adjustments. First a trip to the woodroom, there to pick up a hod of coal from the bottom of the bin, where the accumulated dust of years could be scraped in large quantities. After this had been dumped into the hot firebox, the pipe damper was opened wide to admit the downdraft, the ashpit door adjusted to permit air to get at the fire, and the feed door buttoned down tight. All through opening exercises the distressed stove gave out vague warnings that all was not well in its capacious middle. At one point, while the bible was being read, a faint muffled noise emanated from the Station Master, but the accumulated gas burned off with no further incident. During the five minutes allotted to a half chapter or so of *Nick Carter* there were further minor symptoms—the smell of gas grew stronger, and occasionally there'd be a paroxysm, starting in the stove and traveling up the smoke pipe, rather like a reverse peristalsis.

Exercises over, Mary threw herself into the business of seventh grade grammar. Armed with a pointer, she was explaining how to diagram a complex sentence when, with a frightening roar, the venerable stove blew open. The doors clanged and the entire pipe collapsed, giving off clouds of black soot. The result was so stupendous that we plotters were scared out of the full enjoyment of our prank. And, from our vantage point in the front seat close to Mary, we were almost sure that the language which issued briefly from our substitute had nothing to do with the diagramming of complex sentences.

No complete history of Truro will ever be written without some mention of one of Pamet's most colorful characters, Anthony Robert "Phat" Francis, onetime postmaster, general storekeeper, perennial political candidate, collector of automobiles, raconteur, newspaper correspondent, and dog fancier. Our earliest recollection of Phat would place him in the old Truro

4

Post Office, a sober, efficient government servant, busy sorting the mail, or stepping briefly into the lobby to sell from his assorted merchandise, a bathing cap, a mechanical pencil, or a mustard plaster. Several times each week, Phat would allow himself the luxury of a barber shop shave, administered by the expert hands of Charlie Myrick. The rotund postmaster would emerge from his doorway, shouting last minute instructions over his shoulder to some underling in the office, and pace down the path to his huge green Maxwell touring car, parked in the square. After some time the motor would roar to life, and Phat would make a grand tour of the parking space, grinding to a stop in front of the tonsorial parlor, a distance of some one hundred feet from the post office.

Somewhat later, we recall, the green Maxwell was replaced by a bright red Model T Ford, with special underslung springs, and mysterious gadgets on the engine reputed to make it outrun any car on the road. This stripped down vehicle was used for delivering telegrams to the outlying districts of Pamet. It was equipped with ropes and shovels to combat the sandy roads, and a jug of water was wedged firmly between the bucket seats, ready to replenish a leaky radiator. We had, at this point, become a staunch friend to Phat and on good summer days we'd help him deliver his yellow envelopes about town. In the process we picked up a good bit of homespun Francis philosophy, and smoked our first Peter Schuyler, which made us deathly sick.

We are cleaning out some old papers in the office today, and on many of them we sighted the familiar, bold signature of Manuel F. Corey, Truro's efficient Town Clerk for many years. Officially, we had no business transactions with Mr. Corey until the day we stood before him and nervously made application for a marriage license. However, we do remember him as a successful Pamet farmer: a big, burly man with a powerful bass voice and a penetrating eye. Laird of Corey Hill, he produced from his meadow garden the finest of vegetables, and his orchard in the pine clearing of Edgewood Farm yielded fabulous apple crops. Then too, he had large flocks of hens, and a cow or two in the big airy barn which boasted a collection of Massachusetts auto number plates tacked around the door frame dating back years into the past. Mr. Corey was at home in any company—presiding as master of the Wellfleet Grange, reading the warrant for the town meeting, officiating as a marrying justice of the peace in his front parlor, or haggling with a Provincetown customer over the price of MacIntosh apples.

East wind, the constant and unwelcome spring visitor, is in the valley today. Chill and searching and steady, the breeze moves in from the ocean, blanking out the sun with strata of gray clouds, tossing the scrub pines, and moaning gently in the eaves of venerable town hall. The coolness of the day belies the recent warm spell and the date of the calendar, twelfth day of April. But the high temperature of the weekend past and the mild southwest wind have done their work. The sod shows the fresh blackness of myriad wormcasts. The peewinks are in good voice in the swamps, and on Saturday last the State Dept. of Conservation stocked the Pamet River with several hundred trout. Since then local teenage nimrods have been haunting the banks of the creek, drooling over the darting, shadowy brownies, and our youngest son, Geoffrey, has turned over a huge patch of turf under the locusts in search of angle worms for the opening day of the season. Snowie of the Shell Station has inaugurated another pool for young fishermen of the Pamet, and intends to wet a line himself, before work mornings. This means the Snow oil painting will suffer for a spell, and the customers of the petroleum station will be subjected to tall, daily-repeated tales of the one that got away.

The good citizens of Wellfleet, when we last visited there, were incensed no end at the installation of a public pay station by the telephone company smack on the sidewalk in front of the office. With its gay red roof and classic simplicity of line, it resembled strongly what one of our lady teachers at the Wilder School used to delicately refer to as the "outie."

The new aerial photographs of Truro arrived the other day, and this afternoon, as we were glancing over the sheets with Squire Dyer, Pop Snow barged into the office in a cloud of acrid cigar smoke, and peered over our shoulder. We were tracing the course of the Little Pamet River from its source way up Long Nook Valley to its outlet at Pamet Harbor. Pop took advantage of a pause in the conversation to point a calloused, toil-worn index finger at a locus on the map which we identified as that curved section of Castle Road which crosses the Little Pamet between Tom's Hill and the Willows. "See that sharp bend in the road?" he queried, punctuating the question with a puff of smoke. "I'm responsible for that." We thought back through the years to the time when Pop's father, old C.W. Snow had been superintendent of streets for Pamet, and all the Snow sons had worked for him, in one capacity or another. Perhaps, we ventured, Pop had been layout man for his father and perhaps the transit had been faulty, or the steel tape a mite out of whack due to cold weather or some such?

"Hell no, boy," grunted Pop. "The road used to be straight as a string across Phil Ryder's Dyke—located about a hundred yards to the east'ard. It would still be there, too, if I hadn't gone after that cussed fish." We smelled a yarn, of course, and hastened to offer Pop a chair and a big ash tray.

"Phil Ryder (he lived right down in that section—Miss Link owns the house now) he come up street one day, early in the spring, and started tellin' a yarn in the post office about whoppin' great horned pout he'd seen in the Little Pamet. Claimed he didn't dast let his cows out to pasture on the bank of the creek fer fear that fish'd do 'em harm. Phil said he'd tried to spear the pout with everything from an eel spear to a boat gaff; the pout looked like a porcupine with shafts stickin' out of his back, but he was healthier'n ever. What bothered Phil most, though, was his prize swamp garden; he claimed that fish was so big, and drank so much water every day, that the crick was in danger of bein' dried up, and Phil's garden would parch away.

"Well sir, lots of the young fellers around town went down to the dyke, and tried to catch that monster. They had plenty of bites all right, but there warn't any gear heavy enough to hold the cuss. He'd snap off half-inch cod line like it was a thread, and manila rope, why he'd chew through that same's you'd eat a salt herrin'. Kind of got my dander up, it did, to think of that fish defyin' all us Truro folks, so one Saturday I went out in the workshop an' dragged out a big barge anchor, heated her up in the forge, cut off one of the flukes, and sharpened t'other one up to a point. Loaded the anchor on a truck wagon, together with a coil of wire rope and a dozen railroad sleepers, and a sheep that had died that morning.

"Then I drove over to Ryder's Dyke, and unloaded my gear; I speared the sheep on the anchor, and fastened the cable to the big hook. Then I dropped the bait into a big deep hole west'ard of the culvert that goes under the dyke, and threaded the wire rope back through the pipe to the east side, and wrapped the bitter end around the railroad ties, and made her fast. Well sir, sometime during the night I remember waking up because the house shook a mite. Next morning, bright and early, I saddled up a horse, and rode over to the Little Pamet. Just comin' daylight, it was, and as I rode over the crest of Tom's Hill and looked down into the valley . . ."

Pop's stogie expired at this point, and we waited with bated breath as he went through the ritual of lighting a fresh smoke. "Did you catch that horned pout, Pop?" we asked, unable to hold back the question. "No—not exactly. When I hauled up the anchor, I found about two hundred pounds of his upper lip on the hook. No fish, but in his struggles to get away, that pout had tugged the whole cussed dyke, road, willow trees, culvert, and fence, downstream. We measured it with instruments later—two hundred seventy-nine feet, three inches. . . ."

April is the month of showers, flowers, and dog licenses, and speaking of dogs, we are reminded of that eventful day in Truro when the law descended on Anthony R. Phat Francis to clean out his allegedly unlicensed dogs. Word of the proposed punitive expedition had gotten around, and by noon the hills of Truro were blackened with humanity, taking advantage of a beautiful day and the contour of the land, which made a natural amphitheater facing the Francis domicile, a combination dwelling/store in Pamet Square. At the appointed hour the law, in the persons of a deputy sheriff, the district agent for the Animal Rescue League, a state cop or two, and sundry other gentlemen, pressed through the crowd and mounted the steps of Phat's dwelling. Confronted by a securely locked door, they proceeded to read a long legal document, interspersed with such phraseology as "in the name of the Commonwealth" and "by the authority vested in me as. . . ."

When it appeared that admission would not be gained by the writ, the deputy sheriff produced a large hammer, and began to belabor the door. This had the effect of bringing Phat to face his accusers, and face them he did, his voice ringing on the mild spring air, to the delight of the vast audience. After some moments, Phat was persuaded to permit a search of his premises, and to the chagrin of the searchers no dogs could be found. At this point the prosecution rested, withdrawing across the square for a conference, their entire case threatened with collapse, due to lack of evidence while Phat posed on his door step, the picture of injured innocence.

The impasse lasted only a few moments, however, as over the hill from Castle Road appeared Al Paine's beagle, out for her afternoon walk. With the unerring skill of the true hunter, she made for the old unused blacksmith shop, across the square from Phat's store, and there she scratched and yelped at the big sliding door. Pandemonium broke loose as the entire pack of missing dogs, locked inside, aroused by the rabbit hound, broke into a chorus of barking. It was but a few moments' work for the law to gather up the canine criminals, and whisk them away to the kennels. As the crowd dispersed Phat was heard to observe, sadly, "They were done in by a female."

★ ★ ★

Already the lawns of Pamet are sere and crisped, as the dry weather stays with us, day after day. Last night a brief shower settled the dust, but again today the sun is hot, the wind strong from the southwest, and there is that unpleasant morning dampness in the air to make things sticky to the touch. Excellent swimming in bay, pond, or ocean, however, and fine for the vacationists. Honeysuckle is in full bloom, and gardens, where water is available, are doing well. Today there is a faint blue haze to replace the overcast, which is being swept away by a strong breeze and already the acrid smell of the scrub pine in the hot sun fills the air, and the strident call of the cicada comes up the valley to town hall.

Homeward bound up our road the other evening, we were shocked to note that the contractors, in a scorched earth policy associated with the new road construction, had stripped all the trees from the river bank below South Pamet. This includes, of course, the gnarled wild apple in which our friend, the kingfishers of Fratus' Bend, perched and we are incensed at the sacrilege.

On Tuesday we waited a decent interval for the old magneto telephone system to expire; then, at 7:30 a.m. we picked up the streamlined handset and shakily dialed the local filling station. As the mechanism clicked and buzzed, we thought of several facetious things to say: "Mr. Watson, come here, I want you," or, "What hath the Bell System wrought?" But when the irate voice of some summer lady, still heavy with sleep queried, "Yes?" we hastily mumbled that we had the wrong number, and dropped the instrument.

This would be a fine moment to pay a final, sincere compliment to the staff of operators who have given us such excellent service at the Wellfleet agency. In our multiple occupations we have more occasion than most to call on the services of the telephone company, and we have always appreciated the human touch of the girls at the switchboard. On many occasions they have gone far beyond the actual requirements of their duties in locating us when we were needed for the ambulance, or when a long-distance call could not reach us in our usual haunts. In time of emergency, accident, fire, hurricane, or even in response to lesser calls, such as the correct time, condition of the tide, or any of the host of other inquiries, we have always received a courteous answer from the operator on the board. To Chief Operator Helen Smith, then, and to her assistants, Doris White, Julia Allmon, Charlotte Curran, Marg Dalby, Jean Davis, Alma Taylor, and Miriam Webber, thanks, and good luck.

★ ★ ★

Recipe for the recent weather: sprinkle the sand spit with wild morning glories and sweet peas and sundry flowers to taste, add a dash of damp salt air direct from the ocean, cover with a thin, gray overcast, and place in the hot July sun. About mid-forenoon uncover, baste with essence of scrub pine, and just a smidgin of privet blossom, and expose to a strong, steady southwest wind. Top off with a glowing red sunset, and fetch back the cloud cover for the night.

Thoughts while posting taxes: oddest address in our tax files would be Wappingers Falls, New York, and in that town we have two property owners. Also, Dodie Captiva of the North village claims the town as her birthplace. Inks vary from standard royal blue to brown, red, black, and lurid green, and the handwriting presents an interesting study. In our humble opinion, Mrs. Victor Morris writes the prettiest hand, clear, flowing, and full of character. In the Marx envelope we always find a cheery greeting, and L. Thomas Hopkins usually finds time for a word or two. On the other hand, there are those perennial disgruntled taxpayers who put in a note with their tax bills beginning, "I can't understand the increase, etc., etc.," this despite a special slip enclosed with all notices from our office requesting that communications in re taxes be addressed to the board of assessors.

We miss, these past few years, the distinctive envelope from George Littlefield, bearing on its flap a cut of a man busily bucking wood. One time we queried the Beach Point man regarding this trade mark, and he told us it represented his family motto. "Saw wood, and say nothing." There is a handsome bird stamp on Rosalie Kramer's letter this year, and from Albert Cusson's check came a subtle, heady perfume which gave us pause for a moment. . . .

We reminisce about our first major encounter with tobacco which came at a tender age. We had sampled corn silk in a T.D. pipe, and several varieties of cigarettes—Sweet Caporals, Perfections, even a medicinal brand used to ease the symptoms of asthma (Cubebs, if memory serves us correctly). All these experiences had been fleeting, surreptitious, and unsatisfactory. Mostly, the session had been held in Ezra Hopkins' hayloft, and we were hampered by the fear of fire. Then, too, Ernie Snow kept insisting that we were, at best, nibbling at the edges of true smoking enjoyment—a cigar was the only satisfactory smoke, with plenty of volume, and the flavor of far-off Cuba in its filler. So one July day, we picked up our blueberry tin, and started off down the road for a real smoker. The affair was to be in the nature of a Roman feast, an orgy of uninterrupted pleasure behind the outdoor billboard on the sharp curve just north of Town Hall Road, with Ernie supplying the cigars, and Herbie Rose, Ralph Ormsby, and Tony Portlock completing the company. Once assembled, we spent some time in preparation for the actual business, admiring the huge brown stogies (Canadian Club was the brand name), swapping stories as to our past experiences with the weed. At last matches flared, and a we lighted up, drawing huge puffs, exhaling clouds of blue into the summer air. After some time the conversation lagged, and the puffing became less enthusiastic. Ernie was taken with a mild coughing spell which seemed to affect his color—his normal tan turned a pale green. As for us, we suddenly noticed that the clear, blue July sky was somewhat overcast. Copious quantities of saliva flooded our mouth, faster than we could expectorate; several butterflies in our stomach began to belabor our esophagus, and a general feeling of malaise obtained, from head to foot. The two South Pamet boys of a sudden found business elsewhere so that, once alone, we managed in good grace to discard the mangled stub of our cigar and give in completely to our illness, which, by now, was acute. It must have been hours later that we staggered home, chastened in spirit, swearing never to touch tobacco again. Of the quintet involved, four of us made clean breasts of the matter to our folks, but Ernie Snow, ever adroit with an alibi, told his father that he had been in the hot sun too long. Until the day that billboard was torn down, we experienced a queasy feeling in our middle each time we passed the spot.

Mr. Benjamin Waite, unofficial ambassador of goodwill between the parent city of Truro, England, and this Cape Cod town, arrived by bus on Saturday last, and was officially greeted by our own Grover Whalen. John R. Dyer, Jr. accepted from Mr. Waite a copy of the financial report of the city of Truro, together with a file of newspapers and a personal letter from his Honor, the Mayor. The cordial note says, in part, "Kindly convey my greetings to the Moderator, Wilfred G. Slade, whose office, I presume, corresponds to that of Mayor." In lieu of a public parade, Mr. Waite was then escorted through the cemeteries of Truro, and the Dyer car became stuck in the sand on the Old Bridge Road, necessitating a call to Mr. Selectman Tony Duarte. In the process of extricating John's car, Tony jammed his thumb in the tow chain, and still sports a swollen digit. Mr. Waite fortunately had his hearing aid turned down when the accident took place.

11

In our mail, a postcard from Frank Dickerson, on a junket to the Far West, who, to disprove our chuckling at what we considered the odd name of his home town, Wappingers Falls, offers, among others, Tintic Tooele, Rabbit Valley, and Dirty Devil River, all in the State of Utah.

Snowie has recently installed in his petrol emporium a big billed black and white toucan which interests the customers no end. The button-eyed bird can't sing, or fly, or talk, but he has a prodigious appetite for bananas and peanuts and cereal, and will even sip a spot of beer on Saturdays. He's extremely photogenic, too, and Snowie is planning to charge a small fee for the privilege of taking his picture next summer, despite cries of 'unfair' from Anthony R. Francis, who resents the competition.

In re Phat Francis, that gentleman has just emerged from the toils of the law. Held by the grand jury on a charge of maintenance of a public nuisance, to wit, several dogs, Phat was found guilty, ordered to dispose of all but two of the canines. The defense was ably handled by Charles E. Frazier, Jr. of Wellfleet. During the course of the trial, some unidentified newspaper man injected a bit of human interest into his story with the information that Mr. Francis was a wounded veteran of World War I. This is a point of which we had hitherto been in ignorance, and would be still if Mr. C. A. Slade had not cleared up the matter for us. Eying the enormous Francis waistline, Mr. Slade allowed, "Must have been World War II—Battle of the Bulge."

And while munching our standard New England breakfast this morning—soft boiled eggs, toast, and cocoa made with fresh goat milk, the milk donated, since we no longer have a herd of our own—we got to thinking about the unusual tastes in vittles for the morning meal. Mr. Manuel Corey, we recall, favored fried yams occasionally, and Ed Snow relished warmed-over clam chowder. Mr. George Barnes, a normal person in all other respects, used to drool in recounting the story of his last trip to England when he listed the breakfast menu: cold boiled bacon with English mustard, bloaters (lovingly called one-eyed steaks by the British) and tea.

Properly enough, this first day of November finds the weather cold and gray, with a steady wind from the nor'east, bringing a scattering of rain to the valley. The huckleberry patches on the farther hills have faded to an indeterminate shade of rust red, and the locusts are almost stripped of their foliage, long since shriveled and sere.

Chief Berrio reports little damage as the results of last night's Halloween pranks. The usual small building moved to the square, surrounded by sundry articles, a soaped window here and there, a sign or two removed, a daub of paint on the post office retaining wall, and little else of import. The party at town hall sponsored by the Community Club, judging by the noise and the costumes and the food consumed, and the enthusiastic witch hunt in adjoining Congregational Cemetery (where a gruesome, knife-butchered corpse was found prone outside the tomb) was a success. Among the little tykes, especially, the ingenuity of the costumes was amazing. We chuckled at the animated beer stein, the battered football player, and the mermaid and fisherman combination.

The call for volunteer observers for Truro's newly-formed civilian air craft warning service is still in effect. Chief Observer Horace "Pop" Snow tells us that, unlike the boring, full-time schedule of World War II, the present plan calls for alerts on certain 24-hour periods, with long rests between the tests. We glanced at the handbook recently, were astonished to note the change in the silhouettes of today's fighter planes, grown slimmer and more deadly, in direct contrast to our own personal anatomical outline.

On one of his recent trips to New York, Snowie, always the practical joker, picked up a small book titled, "All About Baseball." The volume actually is a miniature shocking machine, contains a small battery and condenser in its hollowed-out vitals, and connects with the foil cover so that when the lid is flipped open, a mild electrical impulse greets the reader. A prissy toy, indeed, as compared with the machine we rigged up during a long tedious winter at the Truro Liquor Emporium. It all started, we recall, when someone pointed out that Cal Stevens, of Depot Road, was able to short the spark plugs of his Chalmers car through his finger tips to the metal cowl, and stall the engine without blinking an eyelash. In an effort to determine just who among the loiterers in the back room possessed this remarkable power over voltage, or amperage, or whatever, we borrowed a bundle of dry cell batteries from Charlie Snow, and from Arthur Joseph the marine coil of the fisherman, Elsie G. Silva, lately wrecked at Ballston Beach. This infernal gadget was then wired, via a push button under the counter, to the heavy brass door knob of the back room. The first victim, and we apologize to him and to our readers, for so often using his name in the column, was none other than Anthony R. Phat Francis, chosen in the interests of science by a nonpartisan group. The day, we recall, was rainy, the sidewalk outside the store soaked with moisture providing a perfect ground, and the victim, at peace with the world, sauntered across the street with a set of nomination papers under his arm. (If memory serves us correctly, that was the year Phat was running for Representative in Congress.)

There was a theatrical pause as Mr. Francis stopped to knock the ashes from a new White Owl cigar, then the knob twisted in Phat's firm grasp. Quickly we jabbed the button, and the coil sang its high pitched squeal; simultaneously, the door flew open, one fervent malediction rent the peaceful Pamet air, and two hundred-odd pounds of humanity rolled on the floor. Herb Brown afterwards claimed that he saw blue sparks issuing from Phat's ears, the nails in his shoes, and his American Legion ring, but in any event, our victim was in a bad way. Several of us dragged the inert body out into the ozone, propped him against the nearby fence, and forced a dram or two of spirits down his throat. After a moment our politician victim revived, to the accompaniment of sighs of relief from the audience. As perpetrator of the foul deed, we leaned over and begged, "Say something, Phat." A brief pause, then, in a faint tenor Phat allowed, "Those damn Republicans will do anything to keep me off the ballot."

A fortnight ago we were rehearsing at the auditorium of the high school in Wellfleet, and there in a dark corner, we spied a battered, tarnished tuba. We examined it carefully, and on the bell, next to the trade name we found, deeply scratched into the metal, the initials TK-AD (Tom Kane-Anne deGroot). As the memories flooded over us, we thought back to the days when Pamet students went to Wellfleet High School, then a drab, gray, two story frame building standing gaunt on the skyline next to the "White Church," overlooking the harbor. In our freshman year at this venerable institution of learning, the school committee had made several stupendous concessions to the progressiveness of the times. Running water had been installed in the building, and the downstairs entry sported a sink and drinking fountain, from which trickled a stream of water. The committee however, would have no truck with indoor plumbing nor electricity (except for what could be generated in the physics lab) nor indeed with sundry other fancies.

That would be the year Thomas Nassi, beloved Albanian bandmaster appeared on the Cape scene, prepared to introduce school children to the beauties of instrumental music. His message fell on fertile soil in the music-starved shellfish town. Those were the darkest days of the depression—money was as scarce as registered Democrats—and many of the kids who yearned to play could not afford a horn. Mr. Nassi appeared at school with a B-flat bass horn, and asked for volunteers to learn the instrument. Several of the boys eyed the big silver tuba, hefted it experimentally, and walked away—thinking, no doubt, of the long, hot marches of the future, and the great quantities of wind required to force a note from the coiled tubes.

And so the horn became ours to play. Hour after hour we'd spend, those long winter evenings, Arban's "Method for the Bass" propped in the rays of the Alladin kerosene lamp, blowing sustained notes until our lips ached. Timidly at first, then asserting ourselves with more volume on the characteristic down beat notes, we listened for an imaginary after peck from the altos and even, in moments of occasional daring, added a brief run or a charming grace note when the music called for a rest.

The first public appearance of the Wellfleet High School Orchestra, we recall, was at the graduation exercises held in the Congregational Church. It was the typical secondary school commencement—the auditorium packed with humanity, hot, stuffy, the air perfumed with the sickly odor of cut flowers, many lengthy dry speeches to be endured, presentations, declamations given by tense, perspiring seniors in the trite style of all graduates—then thunderous music from the pipe organ, drowning out rather than accompanying the chorus of students. At long last Mr. Nassi beamed at the orchestra to assemble front and center, and we eagerly toted our horn to a position where friends and family could see us plainly. The number to be rendered, we remember, was "Amaryllis," a dainty, provoking piece we'd rehearsed for months. As the stick in Mr. Nassi's hand signalled ready, we puckered up and depressed the first valve for middle C, and as the baton descended, we put our very soul into that first note. The ensuing sound bore a startling and faithful resemblance to the bubbling of a plugged water closet. In response to frantic signals from the leader, we desisted from further efforts, and sat through the selection in an agony of redfaced embarrassment.

After the ceremonies, we dragged our tuba in hasty retreat to the cellar, secured a strong piece of wire, and proceeded to fish into the bell for whatever might be forthcoming. Out came a battered felt hat, a crumpled edition of the Cape telephone directory, several pieces of chalk, and four live Wellfleet fiddler crabs. By dexterous maneuvering, we then drained several quarts of water from the coils, and soon the basement was echoing to the mellow tones of the bass part of "Amaryllis"—late, but nonetheless beautiful. We afterwards learned that the deed had been done by a jealous schoolboy rival for the hand of a pretty Wellfleet freshman girl. His efforts to discredit us, however, were only temporarily successful, since we have been proud to list her, these many years since, as a charming helpmate and dependent on our federal income tax return. If the Wellfleet School committee should ever decide to get rid of that tuba, we shall make a serious bid for it.

NINETEEN FIFTY-TWO

1952

A thin white blanket of snow still covers Pamet's hills despite today's thaw, and tonight a full moon, riding between patches of jagged gray clouds, washes the town with a silvery light. The recent storm was brief and violent, with a whipping, nor'east wind to bring down sundry trees about town, and convert into twisted wreckage some TV antennas in exposed locations. But it was worth the damp feet and the shoveling to catch a glimpse of those beautiful evergreens at Dr. Lupien's, heavy-laden with snow as the early morning sun sparkled on the countryside. The roaring surf has stilled to a muted boom, and the wind is back in the warmer quarter of the bay. The valley is littered with the drift of the recent high tides.

Among other information to be gleaned from the town records at the year's end is the fact that only nine bounties for fox were paid out during 1951. This figure represents a substantial drop from the several years previous, and bears out the contention of the local hunters that some natural enemy or condition is killing off Brother Reynard. The fox population dwindled once before, we recall, back in the twenties, when the sight of the animal was a rarity. At one time Joe Peters, of North Truro, dug out a den of foxes near East Harbor, and for some time kept several caged animals on his property.

While the New Year arrived pretty much on schedule elsewhere on the Cape, not until 4 p.m. of January 1, was it officially admitted to the sacred confines of Pamet Point Valley, where Councillor and Mrs. Silas Clark gave their belated sanction in the form of an elegant party involving egg nog, and food, from dainty hors d'oeuvres to a masterful pot of beans, grown on Clark soil, and cooked in true New England style in the Clark oven. At the Clark party we talked briefly with Bill Wenneman and his charming wife, Ruth, who told us her lovely daughters and all their families are well.

Walter Horton of North Truro is busy these days at hog butchering. Cold weather makes for good storage conditions for the meat, and the average hog by now has reached a good size for slaughter. Besides, pocket books are lean, come January, and as John Adams used to say, it's better to eat off the pig than have him eating off you. We bemoan the lack of neighborliness and sociability which marks today's butchering practices. A telephone call to Mr. Horton, a few smothered squeals from your sty in the early, gray hours before the neighborhood is awake, and then, in a few days a trip to North Truro, there to pick up your neatly shaven, pink carcass, reduced to loin, shoulder, ham, and sundries by the expert knife of the butcher.

In our day, local butchering was a gala occasion. Take the year we raised that handsome white sow in partnership with Ernie Snow. Nothing but the choicest of grain with selected table scraps had ever entered Mabel's alimentary tract. She slept on the finest of sedge from the salt valley of the Pamet and she enjoyed the devotion of her owners. We entered her in the Wellfleet Town Fair that summer, but a group of prejudiced judges, influenced by the gross bulk and size of Earl Eldridge's entry, awarded the prize to his red boar. (Jack Hall, we've always felt, was responsible for this bit of perfidy.)

In any event, as cold weather approached, we began to steel ourself for the ordeal of the approaching slaughter of Mabel. Arthur Joseph agreed to perform the rite, and a crew consisting of Joe Williams, Ernie Snow, and O'Caghan himself were to assist. For several days in advance of the killing we gathered the necessary accessories: an ancient, four-legged bathtub for scalding, a kitchen door for the actual sacrificial altar, sundry pieces of stout rope to bind the victim, and utensils to heat great quantities of water. This was to be a deluxe butchering since Arthur opined that Mabel looked like a particularly full-blooded specimen, we were to make blood pudding or morcelas, rolled Portuguese style. Our own courage, come the day of the butchering, lasted only until poor Mabel was trussed and rolled onto the makeshift platform. At the sight of the wicked, gleaming knife in Arthur's hand we made a hasty excuse to the group and beat a retreat to the house. Even indoors the agonized screams of the dying pig reached us, and we were obliged to fortify ourself with the vision of fresh liver, frying in the pan. After the noise had abated somewhat, we glanced cautiously out the window and espied Joe Williams calmly stirring the contents of a dishpan which he held in a suggestive position just below Mabel's throat. Our own part in the whole affair was limited to carting water out to the tub, where the other men were busily scraping the remains, and we do recall tying up the casings after they had been stuffed to capacity with onions, and spices, and other unmentionable ingredients.

Time heals all things, however, and several days later, after a hearty breakfast of morcelas and eggs, we met John Adams at the post office. Our breath, we realized, was strong almost to the point of offensiveness, and hastened to apologize to neighbor Adams. "Tsk-tsk-boy," growled John, "you eat that every morning, you'll never catch cold. . . ."

From the yellowed bundle of papers loaned to us by Mr. Art Cobb we gleaned the following account of a near disaster off the Backside, as told by Mr. I. M. Small, marine observer for many years at the Highland.

The steamship Aguan, Adair Co., from Jamaica to Boston with a cargo of bananas consigned to the Boston Fruit Co., arrived off Highland last Thursday afternoon. When first sighted by the marine reporter at 2:15 p.m. she was going full speed. Suddenly, when directly opposite the telegraph station at 2:30 she stopped and immediately displayed the signal letters P.N., "We want a steam tug." The signal was understood as soon as shown, and in eight minutes from that time a tug, the William H. Sprague of the Boston Tow Boat Co., was preparing to leave her dock in Boston to go to the disabled steamer. The Marine Station here is unfortunately not provided with any kind of signals to communicate with vessels in distress, hence no reply could be given to the ship. Waiting a few moments, seeing no signal that they understood, and becoming impatient, a boat was launched from the ship, placed in charge of Mr. Jones, the first officer, with three seamen, and ordered to proceed as near to the shore as seemed safe and endeavor to telegraph for assistance. John Marshall on the day watch at Highland Life Savings Station discovered the ship, promptly reported the situation and the surfmen immediately repaired to the beach.

A heavy swell, the result of the strong southeast gale of the previous day, was rolling in and breaking on the bars. Fearing that an attempt might be made on the part of those on the ship to send a boat ashore, signal letters H. L. were displayed from the L. S. S. staff: "Do not attempt to land in your own boat." But the officers of the ship, not expecting signals in that direction did not observe them and the boat as before mentioned put off from the ship and pulled rapidly shoreward. The surfmen of Highland Station seeing the determination of those on the boat to attempt a landing, started on the run along the beach, as the boat, if she landed at all, would do so a mile below them. On came the boat, rising and falling on the swell. No one thought they would attempt a landing through such a dangerous surf, and when it was discerned that they really intended to try it, every effort was made by those on shore to warn them against such a foolhardy step. Too late, a great white comber caught the boat under her counter, whirled her around as if she were a chip, and turned her in an instant bottom up.

The mate, as he came to the surface, caught at the gunwale of the boat and clung desperately there. This was worse for him as it afterwards proved, since the water was so intensely cold that he was losing strength every moment he remained there. Finding the boat would not drive in towards the beach he left her and struggled as best he could towards shore, nearly a hundred yards away; the sailors meanwhile had struck out at once for land. Those on shore, realizing that every moment made the case more desperate, formed a line by joining hands and rushed boldly into the ice-cold surf to reach the sinking men. The sailors were pulled to safety and then every nerve was strained to reach the officer, who, by clinging to the boat so long was now almost exhausted; he was seized not a moment too soon, and dragged in a helpless condition from the water.

Among the rescuing party we particularly commend the heroic and successful efforts of surfmen Hiram Hatch, Isaiah Kelley, and William Paine of the Highland Station and Keeper Amasa Dyer of the lighthouse. Later in the day Capt. Worthen launched his boat through the high surf—the boat being thrown back on the beach on the first attempt—and carried the men back to their ship. Once clear of the outer line of breakers, they were safe, but on the return from the ship, beaching the boat became a hazardous proceeding. The bars showed an unbroken line of rushing foam-capped waves. There was no way but to pull strong and straight through them. A great wave following sharply; everyone bending with the strain, the boat flew onward with frightening velocity, as her bow struck the sand, the driving waves behind lifted her stem clear of the water and threw the captain headlong over the bow, scattered the crew in all directions, and landed the boat bottom up in the surf, drenching every man to the skin in the cold water.

The noon hour signifies to today's Pamet small fry the time to eat, but in our youth it denoted that period of hustle and activity that accompanied the arrival of the mail. As a special favor for chores done in the morning, we could earn a trip with Ezra Hopkins, the mailman, to Truro Depot. Ezra was a recent convert to the automobile, and he operated his Model T station wagon in a style reminiscent of many years at the reins of a spirited horse. The process of starting the beach wagon never varied. Ezra would grasp the crank, then signal us to flip the ignition to battery position, while he churned the motor over and pulled on the choke wire. After several musical buzzes from the coil box on the dash, the engine would come to life with a satisfying roar, clouds of blue smoke pouring from the exhaust. To the accompaniment of more frantic signals from Ezra, we would advance the spark lever, retard the hand throttle, flip the switch key to magneto, and give her a jab of choke on the inside control. Soon we'd be in the scattered line of moving traffic bound for the depot, with Ezra bearing down on the low gear pedal to bring us over Wilder School Hill.

At opportune places on the road we'd pass the horse-drawn traffic— Roger Burhoe driving Eben Paine's wagon, bound for his load of bread and groceries; Naylor Hatch with a cargo of eel traps or twine; John Adams just in from the morning clam tide; and Ed Snow homeward bound atop a load of salt hay. We always allowed a few minutes to fraternize on the station platform, and the summer kids from South Truro, the Bensons and the Olsens and the DeChamps would be there to whoop and dash around the freight house in a brief game of tag. About this time the motor car with its crew of section hands would come putting in from Corn Hill, just a few moments ahead of the northbound train, and, with a great bustle, the boys would swing their buggy off the rails, then break open their lunch buckets for a leisurely noon meal.

When the 12:05 had ground to a stop at the platform, our task was to receive the mail bags from Ezra or Ephie Hill, and stow them neatly in the Ford, saving space for a possible paying customer. The trip back to town was one of thrills and tension, as Ezra, aroused by the importance of his cargo and the time schedule involved, would jam the hand throttle to the bottom of the quadrant, passing everything we overhauled on the narrow blacktop. The climax of the trip came at Wilder's Hill, where the old gentleman would give her one last spurt of gas, then reach for the clutch to coast into Truro Square, horn blowing, tires scuffing on the last sharp turn into the parking space.

Up betimes, on a cold bright day, and to our chores. Pamet is in the grip of a real, old-fashioned nor'wester, the mercury hovering near twenty, and the ground frost bound under foot. A penetrating wind searches the valley, and howls with a banshee wail along the eaves of the town hall, and the frozen, winding river is filmed with dust from the cuts along the new road. Typical town-meetin' weather, to be followed, as Charlie Snow dourly predicts, by a real, snorting snow storm. But the hours of daylight are lengthening, and the post these days brings gaudy spring catalogs from the mail order houses. In local loafing spots the boys are discussing politics and the town warrant (40 articles this year, longest in the memory of our old timers) and folks are wondering if the business can be disposed of in the usual single afternoon session, as is customary.

This afternoon Horace "Pop" Snow, chief ground observer for the civilian air craft warning service, dashed up to the hall for a test call in connection with the civil defense program. At 3:46 a huge, silver plane roared through the sky to east'ard, and Pop sprinted to the extension phone in the lobby to make his report in concise, terse phrases. "Very successful test," allowed Pop, "except for that cussed stuffed muskellunge out there on the shelf—almost shoved my hand down his throat reachin' for the handset."

The newly devised voting lists show a total of 477 legal voters in town at the close of registration, February 8. Absentee ballots are coming in with each mail, and the vote, weather permitting, should be a sizable one. Tonight the Truro Neighborhood Association sponsors its annual pre-meeting sampler of the warrant, 8 p.m. at the town hall. . . .

Speaking of town meetings, they were reminiscing down at the Shell Station the other day about the fine orators of the past: Bert Ingraham, of North Truro, for many years an election officer, who would step on stage with his tellers upon completion of the tallying of votes to intone in a fine tenor voice, "You have elected . . ." and then proceed to list the successful candidates. The late Edward C. Morgan, one-time selectman, was recalled as a thin, earnest speaker, who wore a celluloid collar several sizes too large. Mr. Morgan, they say, would trumpet loudly in the heat of debate, working his neck up and down like an irate turkey.

Over in Truro, Richard Rich was acknowledged as a gifted speaker, and Phil Ryder, one-time constable, had such a pleasing voice that the voters were wont to have him repeat the lengthy reading of the warrant. For sheer fervor, however, we would vote for Br. Joe Cabral, a prosperous farmer from the Whitmanville section of town. Joe still retained strong traces of his native Portuguese tongue, despite many years in his adopted country, but that didn't prevent his speaking when he felt he had something to say. On one occasion, we recall, a special meeting had been called for the purpose of acting on a new county program for mosquito control. In order for the town to participate in the program, a modest appropriation would have to be voted, and the opposition bloc, headed by Joe Cabral, was present in goodly numbers on this sultry summer evening, to hamstring the article. After a good deal of debate the atmosphere became tense, tempers flared, and harsh words were spoken. The moderator's gavel pounded on the table with increased frequency, and finally Joe was recognized and rose to speak. "Why we want to kill the mosquitoes?" demanded Joe. This was followed by furtive applause, then by a long silence. About this time a huge winged specimen of the New Jersey variety flew in the window, alighted on Joe's bald head, and ran his stinger to the hilt. There was a loud smack as Cabral swatted the insect, a ripple of laughter ran through the auditorium, and the motion was quickly passed.

This column might well be entitled "Impression of Town Meeting Day." We digress from our usual style to bring to our out-of-town readers a factual account of the citizens of Truro exercising their democratic privilege. In the most exact tradition, Monday was a real Town Meetin' Day—the ground covered with slippery, drifting snow, a howling nor'east gale spilling more of the white stuff as the day progressed, traffic slowed to a crawl due to hazardous driving conditions, and, atop Town Hall Hill, the ancient seat of the government creaked in the teeth of the gale.

At 8:45 on this February morning, the appointed hour for the opening of the polls, a handful of citizens had gathered at the hall, and in the inner sanctum of the selectmen's office, Moderator Wilfred G. Slade was huddled over the bulky tomes of the General Laws, searching out the statute pertaining to postponement of such functions. At 9 a frantic telephone call was made to the state house in Boston, and the reply clearly indicated that, while the business meeting could be postponed, election of officers must go on, unless no voter could be persuaded to cast his vote. Tellers were sworn, and the opening formalities were observed, the first vote being cast at the tardy hour of 10. The rival candidates for office began their shuttling errands about town, picking up voters, and slowly the totals rang up on the ballot box set up on the stage.

Meanwhile, the ladies of the Christian Workers were busy as beavers in the kitchen, baking beans, brewing coffee, and unwrapping sliced ham and sundry delicious looking pies. Arthur Rose, the only male at the food table, was chopping away at a small mountain of cold slaw. At noon a small but appreciative number of townfolk sat down to a Herculean repast from which the only missing item appeared to be the rolls—marooned in Provincetown, according to Johnnie Perry, by the storm.

Since the weather showed no signs of moderating when the business session opened at 2 o'clock, a vote was passed to extend the balloting until four p.m., and further articles of business were adjourned to Tuesday, at 7 in the evening. Results of the voting in the contested offices gave the combined offices of selectman, assessor and member of the board of public welfare to the candidate for reelection, Irving A. Horton. Joseph W. Francis won the school committee race, and Vincent F. Benson defeated his opponent, Anthony R. Francis, for the post of town auditor. Mr. Benson's success was short lived, however, as his position was abolished by town vote scarcely a day later when the meeting approved the establishment of the office of town accountant.

Brevity was the watchword of the business session. Pamet voters, faced with the longest warrant in town history, appeared anxious to expedite the handling of the 39 articles, and the routine business of authorizing the treasurer to borrow money in anticipation of revenue, and authorization for the collector to use all means under the law were quickly granted.

Article 4 brought a motion from John S. Perry to increase several items under the schedule of elective officers' salaries which an economy-minded public found displeasing; after an amendment offering a ten per cent raise was generously turned down by the selectmen, the original salary schedule for the previous year was voted in.

Articles, 5, 6, 7, and 8, all dealing with roadwork and highway construction and maintenance brought queries from the voters, which were satisfactorily explained by Selectman Antone Duarte, Jr., who pointed out that the newly-enacted home rule law, so-called, required full appropriations from the town, subject to reimbursement in 1953. Hence the regrettable but unavoidable reflection in this year's tax rate.

Police Chief Harold M. Berrio expressed dissatisfaction with a 33 and one third per cent reduction in his budget, but was held to his appropriation of $2,000. In explaining an increase of $25 in the Memorial Day Account, John S. Perry volunteered that this year "each child in town would have a flag to carry."

Two items dealing with tax titles, sales and foreclosures, were rapidly passed by the voters, and the report of the Pamet Harbor Committee was read and accepted. From our vantage point on the stage we noted looks of joy on the most truculent faces as the next article, calling for authorization to use $10,000 from the surplus in the treasury to reduce the tax rate, was passed.

Considerable discussion centered over article 21, asking $1,500 to purchase the interest of William A. Joseph in the Great Hollow parking area. The piece of land in question is a small, triangular area with a very cloudy title, but it does represent an integral part of the important parking lot and beach at Great Hollow. This motion was rejected by the voters. Twinefield Road, from the site of the old railroad station at North Truro, running in a general northerly direction, was then accepted by the assembly, and an appropriation of $400 for its improvement was authorized, and a taking of Old King's Road, as shown by previous layout, was voted. Again pleased expressions filled the hall when the town accepted a bequest of $1,000 from the estate of Sheldon Dick for the purpose of buying books for the Cobb Library.

In another road layout article, the town accepted certain parcels of land from property owners to establish a road between Bay View Road and Hughes Road. The bicycle safety law, so-called, was accepted under article 37, a committee was authorized to work with committees of neighboring towns on the matter of a regional school, a renovation appropriation in the amount of $800 for the upper hall in town hall building met with favor, and, in the final business of the evening the selectmen were instructed to set the fees for rental of the town hall. Meeting adjourned at 9:50 p.m., and the adding machine tapes which were totted up by the assessors as the meeting progressed seem to indicate only a small raise in the tax rate for the current year.

Since early morning an easterly storm has been brewing. The wind has been raw, fitful, strong of the smell of the ocean, carrying the uneasy sound of the surf from the backshore. The pines on Storm Hill toss in ragged unison with the pulsing air, and overhead the sky is heavy, gray, sodden with the rain yet to come. Over the river at Monroe's Landing a slate-colored tern is circling endlessly above the water, occasionally plunging after some hapless minnow. And we glance at the calendar, reflecting that this might well be January, instead of the first day of spring. Even the kids at the central school, goaded into a premature attempt at baseball by the radio accounts of their Boston Red Sox in the Grapefruit League, have abandoned the national pastime pending the departure of frost from the ground, and the appearance of more positive signs of spring—perhaps the blossoming of daffodils, or the shrill whistle of the peewinks.

To scotch a rumor we heard last week, Mr. Selectman Tony Duarte did not recently bury a crop of marijuana on his premises; he had bought a weimaraner dog, which died shortly after he was brought home.

It's 10:55, and comes a call from Dr. Charles Hutchings, our esteemed North Truro neighbor, who interrupts our late snack of cold baked bean sandwich to inform us that the call of a peewink can be heard in the meadow near his house. A truthful man, say we, and to him goes, for the next year, a subscription to the Lower Cape's finest newspaper.

The Pamet River, blocked at the dyke while the Brothers Roach construct a headwall for the culvert, is a swollen stream, still luring the fishermen with promise of pink-fleshed trout. The local kids have finally discovered the secret, and this week Peewee Garry Ormsby proudly trotted up the road with his first catch, as did our nephew and namesake, Tommy Kane. Jackie Duarte also has been taking fish, and Sgt. Bishop of the Airforce is whipping the stream each evening with considerable success. The contractors on the new bridge overpass at South Pamet Road have raised a veritable forest of timbers across the roadbed, preparing for the forms which will carry the state highway overhead. Slow and particular work, this, each step to be supervised by the engineers in charge, and much trussing and bracing to carry the weight of the huge slabs of concrete and the steel beams.

Since we started our own chimney-fireplace project some weeks ago, we have been chimney conscious. Each time we travel the byroads of Pamet, we find ourself studying the brickwork on each rooftop, and, strangely enough, in many cases of the older structures, we have noted a similarity of work that is unmistakable. The chimneys all lean to the east. Our discovery prompted us the other day to pose a question to Mr. John Dyer, a man of keen memory and unimpeachable truth. We had just started to outline the case when John interrupted. "Oh, you mean those Obadiah Brown chimneys. Yep, they lean to east'ard, every one of them. Kind of a trade mark. And he used to shingle right cross the valley of a roof, used a board because he said flashing cost too much. Always boasted he could whittle a neater button for a woodhouse door than any carpenter in town. Used an old shaving mug for a level, he did, filled it almost full of water, and set it right on each course of brick; being left-handed, he'd set it down the same way every time, and sight the water level with the top of the mug. It wasn't until he'd used that mug for some ten years that he discovered the top was about a quarter inch out of line.

Our No. 3 son, Mike, goes today to the Central School for his pre-school examination, and already we feel a vague sympathy for the lad at the thought of his approaching vaccination, since this conjures up for us the memory of our immunization shots at the Maritime Training Station at Sheepshead Bay, New York, during the war. As part of the ragged, demoralized group of civilians we formed on the barracks street under the supervision of a leather-lunged ship's company petty officer in response to the eternal, tinny recorded bugle call. There was just time enough, we recall, to swap names with the man next in line (his name was LeCompte, undertaker from some little town on the Eastern Shore of Maryland) then off to the medical building, feebly chanting cadence as each rough cowhide shoe hit the pavement. After a block or so morale picked up; thoughts of a letter from home, the solid feeling of being with kindred souls, the sight of the American flag waving on the reservation flagstaff, or the heavy, salt odor of the Sound and the distant line of surf at Far Rockaway brought back a measure of courage. Then we marched by the huge drill building, Bowditch Hall, where a group of seasoned veterans was snatching morning smokes, and the heckling began. "Watch out for that one with the propellor on it, mate. Hope they can find your vein, Mac. Make 'em change the needle if it has a hook on it, Buddy," all to the accompaniment of a raucous laughter and fake calls of agony. This mental hazing proved an ideal introduction to our "shot" series.

Stripped to the waist, we steeled ourself to the ordeal, exposing first the left deltoid for typhus, the right for typhoid, again the left for smallpox, the right for yellow fever, and for the final indignity, the gluteus maximus for a final, Herculean dose of tetanus toxoid. For days afterward, we vividly recall, the portals of entry for all the little bugs administered by the pharmacist's mates burned like fire. We never did get around to stand by Bowditch Hall to shout at the "boots," but months later, at our graduation from the Hospital Corps School, we stood on the other side of the "shot" line, puncturing the civilians, asking the same question at intervals as the blue clad line weaved through M building: "Anybody here from Cape Cod?"

Spring, at long last, is here. Here in the warmth of a bright, sun-filled, lazy day, with a langorous southwest breeze sweeping wisps of clouds across the pale blue bowl of the sky. Here in the smell of green, growing things, and warm earth. We just took a brief constitutional up to Baldy Hill, as dusk filled the valley, and we heard our first whippoorwill of the season—his call a mite jerky and short-phrased, to be sure, but brave and full, nonetheless. A sunset solo offered on the background of the peewink chorus in the swamp below, with the atonal obligato of chipping sparrows in the oak brush, and the lilt of a bob white from the pines over Corey Hill way. On the far bank of the creek a pair of anglers stand motionless in the cattails and a pair of black ducks wing hurriedly up-river to their nesting place abreast Ma Gray's cottage. The molten, red ball of the sun drops reluctantly into the bay. From below comes the strident cries of the young fry at their evening baseball game, and the whine of distant traffic in the cut towards Long Nook. To the Good Weather Man we offer a silent apology for our complaints these past weeks, and thanks for the simple bounty of the day. It's good to be alive in Pamet on a May day like this.

On a recent rainy day at town hall we sat talking to old Art Cobb, one of our favorite people. The conversation turned to the youth of today, their shortcomings, their faults. "Don't know the value of a dollar, they don't," boomed Art, "and they don't respect a cussed thing. They'll walk all over my grass [Art's emerald green, close-shaven lawn is one of his chief prides] and steal my strawberries, and tease my dog. Don't know what the world's comin' to."

We were just clucking our tongue in wordless agreement when Wilfred "Red" Slade came in, shook the raindrops from his hat, and queried Art about some locations on a survey map. "Been working over South Truro way, near where you were born, Mr. Cobb. Ever hear tell of Parker Lombard's store?" Art caught the name second try, after he'd adjusted his hearing aid, and then, "Parkie Lombard's store? Well I sh'd say I do remember it. Wasn't rightly what you'd call a store, though. 'Twas a barn, located right in the fork of the road at Fisher Road and the spur that goes over to that artist feller's—Hopper? That's his name. Well sir, Parkie, he was a cripple, sort of; had club feet—toes turned right in to face each other. He used to buy up aigs, around South Truro from all the farmers, he'd cart 'em to his barn, there, and sort 'em out, and wash 'em and pack 'em in crates and ship 'em up to the city.

"Reason I remember Parkie and his barn and his aigs, is because me an' Irv Collins played a little joke on him once. Wasn't much doin' that spring in South Truro. The old skatin' rink had gone out of business, and there was a strong Methodist revival goin' on—no square dancin', or socials, or parties. Irv an' me, we got to itching for a bit of excitement, and as we were walkin' up the railroad track one day, we looked over at Parkie Lombard's barn, and cussed if Parkie didn't have his horses harnessed up to the truck wagon, with a big load of aigs all packed aboard. So I says to Irv, 'Let's go over to say hello to Parkie,' and we did. Only Parkie, he went inside the buildin' to fetch out the last case of aigs, and Irv went with him, and that left me all alone outside with the horse and wagon. First thing I knew, I had a piece of plank in my hands, and I pried up the wagon body, and slipped the king-pin out of the axle hole, and let 'er down easy-like so she just rested on the metal bearin'. And then Irv, he come out of the barn, and we scooted over the hill, and hid behind a beach plum bush. Pretty soon, out comes Parkie, shufflin' through the soft sand, and he climbed up into the wagon and fetched the horse a touch with the whip, and WHUP the horse trotted off with the shafts an' the whiffletree and the front wheels, and down come the wagon body, and old Parkie, he was sittin' in scrambled aigs up to his waist.

"Boys might've had high spirits, those days—but my gosh, they wasn't vicious. . . ."

A dubious day in Pamet, this. Lowering gray clouds in the western sky, and a pale sun faintly washes the valley. But the Josiah's pears are in full, glorious bloom, and the beach plums, despite the driving easterly rain of the past weekend, are snowy patches on the hillsides. The meadows on the river banks are a full, rich green, and, daily we see Sumner Horton chugging on his tractor about town, on his spring round of plowing.

And we to our task of cutting the cemetery lots, carrying with us the faint odor of fresh cut bluegrass. We find the work pleasant, as usual this year, and on one fine afternoon this past week we took our No. 3 son, Mike, to help us, and we even took a few moments to tell him a tale or two about the interesting stones in the beautiful, locust-rimmed Congregational burying ground: here the obelisk commemorating all those brave mariners lost in the memorable gale of 1842; there the plain marble stone which marks the resting place of legless Ambrose Snow, crusty and prosperous patriarch of his line.

In this corner the neat, mounded plots of neighbors Naylor Hatch (truant officer at the old Wilder School when we were young) and of Mr. Manuel Corey, for many years the able Town Clerk of Truro. Those unmarked graves near the east fence, of course, are the final resting places of sundry sailors, whose bodies were washed up on the Back Shore. Eben Paine, genial groceryman of Truro, sleeps here, north of the church, and near that clump of lilacs is the grave of Manuel House, last of the Pamet millers. Manuel plied his trade on that little knoll directly across the Bridge Road, and on windy days the creaking mill would grind out native corn; the track of the beam wheel used to face the blades into the breeze is still plainly visible in the hog cranberry patch.

Last week the good folk of Truro had their lungs X-rayed at Central School, courtesy of the Barnstable County Public Health Association. The first customer to appear at the deluxe trailer unit was none other than Anthony R. Phat Francis, stove pipe hat and all. Mr. Francis' generous girth posed somewhat of a problem to the technicians, since it prevented the Francis lungs from being positioned sufficiently close to the plates to develop a satisfactory picture. As a last resort, the patient was backed into position, and his plural cavity was explored from a posterior aspect. "I always was different from other people," sighed Phat, as he departed in his 1926 Chevy.

Our oldest son, Ran, has been camping out with Dennis Mooney in the wilds of Fox Bottom near the ocean. The boys are doing it prissy style, using Arthur Joseph's camp as their headquarters, cooking on a stove, and making frequent trips back to civilization for food and conversation with their fellow men. Which brings to mind a camping trip we once made with Phil Merriss, bosom companion of our early teens. Phil stayed at our house one spring when his mother traveled to Europe, and, as soon as school closed, we felt the irrepressible urge to commune with nature. Phil had a stout new pup tent and a shiny cooking outfit, so when the weather produced a series of fair, warm days, we packed up our gear and hiked down to Eben Paine's store to provision ourselves for the trip. Good Bond Bread in the green wrapper which looked like the engraving on U. S. currency, a flitch of lean bacon, cocoa, and sundry canned goods soon filled the knapsacks, and then we embarked on our journey.

Ostensibly, our itinerary was to take us to the far reaches of South Truro, but actually, we had picked out a spot less than a mile from the O'Caghan residence, about where the L. Thomas Hopkins home now stands—just in case, as we pointed out to Phil, one of us got sick during the night. Besides, we could extend our trip on the following night if the damp air did not prove harmful to us on first trial. We took the lower path by the swamp on the way to Hopkins Hill, and at one spot we came close enough to our house so that Tobey, the family dog, must have smelled us out, for he came bounding through the poverty grass to meet us. We managed to drive him away with loud shouts (a mistake we were to bitterly regret shortly) and soon arrived at our site, where the better part of the afternoon was used up in pitching the tent and preparing a camp fire location.

At dusk we ate a huge meal of bacon and eggs, and as night and the good Pamet mosquitoes settled over the land, we crawled into the pup tent. The conversation began spiritedly enough, we recall, with Phil telling of his experiences at the Cathedral School of St. John the Divine in New York. We, in turn, boasted of having recently driven Ezra Hopkins' Model T Ford under the supervision of Waldo "Buster" Brown, and then we compared the relative satisfaction to be gotten from Postmaster cigars as opposed to Piedmont cigarettes. There were interruptions at this point as we whacked at some pesty mosquitoes, then the talk resumed with a heated discussion on the merits of the recent Dempsey-Tunney fight and some conjecture as to this girl, Gertrude Elderly, who was to attempt to swim the English Channel, come full summer.

By now it was pitch dark, and outside our tiny tent the night chorus of tree frogs and crickets pressed in on us with a somewhat frightening oppressiveness each time a lull came into the conversation. We counted the mournful loops of a whippoorwill's call, and the strident squawk of a heron rose from the bottom of Arrowsmith's Swamp, below the hill. For a moment the tempting picture of our own living room, pleasant in the glow of the Alladin lamp on the round table, came to us. We thought of the stout walls of our Cape Cod house, the sturdy Yale lock on the back door, and the alert, dwarf collie, Tobey, ever ready to bark at strange sounds.

Phil was bundled close to us, by this time, and his body under the blankets, felt tense and uneasy. Suddenly, from the scrub thicket at our back, came the unsteady heavy thump of footsteps, heading straight for our tent. Then, the wrenching tearing sound of grass being torn up by the roots just outside the tent wall and the deep, stentorious breathing of some wild beast came against the canvas. Slowly the animal worked its way to the narrow flap of the opening, while Phil clasped us in an agony of fearful suspense. For a moment the feeding sounds continued, then gradually faded into the distance. As though by prearranged signal, the two brave campers bolted for the tent flap, and in record time the locked door of our house was echoing to the frantic beatings of the Pamet explorers.

It was much later we learned that our older brother Paul, in an excess of subtle mental torture, had perpetrated the scheme, aided and abetted by our dog, Tobey, who had followed our trail willingly enough from the spot where we had rebuffed him earlier in the day.

Ship captains of Pamet in the old days were a hardy lot, and because of their arduous life, they were allowed certain eccentricities not tolerated in the landlubber. Legless Ambrose Snow, for instance, would allow no women in the cabin of his packet, which made weekly trips across the Bay to Boston, and Capt'n Zoheth Rich, skipper of a mackerel fishing boat always carried a chip of marble from his late wife's footstone in his sea bag when he sailed. But it was Lewis Lombard, of Castle Point, who caught the fancy of the townsfolk with his odd habit of wearing a straw hat on board ship in direct contradiction to all established customs. Come squall or fair weather, Captain Lombard prowled the deck in his battered straw skimmer while the crew wore the conventional woolen watch caps, the oilskin sou'westers, or the peaked cap of the officer.

On one of his trips in the whaler "Enterprise" on a far off shipping lane in the South Seas, Captain Lombard was supervising the reading of the log at the taffrail when a sudden gust of wind whipped his straw hat from his head, and carried it far astern. The Lombard skimmer was reluctantly left to the mercy of the ocean and the Enterprise continued on her long voyage to the whaling grounds. Next day, the Truro schooner "White Wing," Charles Cooper, master, happened along that same spot in the sealane, and the lookout spied a familiar object in the water. The White Wing put about, a small boat was lowered, and Capt. Lombard's hat, with a good deal of reverence, was gaffed and brought aboard.

After a decent interval of search for signs of wreckage or possible survivors, Capt. Cooper continued his voyage, and subsequently returned to Truro. A delegation of men then made the sad trip to the Lombard home, bearing the sad news and the straw hat to widow Lombard. The good woman bore up well under the loss, as had so many of her ancestors, relatives, and friends in this tiny seaport town. The water-stained memento was hung on the hat-tree in the front hall, and various domestic adjustments were made in the Lombard family. The oldest boys left school and found work, a big garden was planted, an extra cow purchased, and the fancy gig sold to a neighbor. Up in Snow cemetery a new name was chipped into the Lombard monument by Mr. Nickerson, the stone cutter from Province-town.

A year passed, and then, one fine fall day, when the wind was making white caps on the bay off the harbor lighthouse, and poverty grass rippled over the bare hills which climb from the valley, the noon stage pulled into Truro and out climbed Captain Lombard and several members of his crew, hale, hearty, and reasonably prosperous after an uneventful voyage. The Enterprise lay in New Bedford harbor, her cargo of whale oil discharged, ready to be outfitted for yet another trip, and the seamen were looking forward to reunion with their families. Captain Lombard hired a wagon from the local livery stable, and touching the horse up to a smart pace, he set out, down the valley, up Castle Road, then across the hill to his handsome white house. The good captain, who realized by now that his wife had been misinformed concerning his untimely demise at sea, made all attempts to take the shock from the meeting, and his family, much in the manner they had absorbed the original news, bore up well. After the first excitement had died down, Elvirah Lombard, newly rejoined to her spouse, removed the straw hat from the hatrack and prepared to consign it to the kitchen fireplace, a fitting end for the object of all her anxiety. Here Captain Lombard spoke up, and taking the skimmer from her hand he allowed, "Now, now, Elviry, no use in throwing away a perfectly sound hat. I'll just give her a coat of spar varnish, and she'll be good as new."

Although the promised thundershowers did not arrive last evening, there has been a decided change in the weather. It's a real working day, today, with a brisk breeze from the southeast that tears shreds of white cloud from some distant bank on the ocean horizon to slip by overhead, casting fleeting shadows along the hillsides. In the valley the locust leaves toss and show their silvered undersides, and the rich new crop of cattails gracefully sway in the ocean breeze. To replace the faded crop of wild roses which, for the past few weeks has rimmed the river, there are clusters of milkweed buds, just about to blossom, and the wild morning glory at Fratus' Corner is in full bloom. But it's dust dry, these rainless days, and the lawns of Pamet are parched and sere, and we could stand a good old Atlantic soaker.

Square dances at town hall, each Tuesday night, are attracting many folks, young and old, native and summer visitor, to the hill. The selectmen have, in deference to this affair, changed their weekly sessions to Wednesday evenings, 7 to 10.

The blueberry crop, despite the recent dry weather, is bountiful. Town hall makes a good stopping off place for a cool drink as the kids of Castle Road cut across the hill for the patches near the cemeteries, and last week we checked with the young fry of the Bakelands, the Youngs and the Todds. After some time in the field, they had returned empty-handed, and we probed for their excuses. "Too many mosquitoes . . . got bit by a wild bee . . . awful hot out there." The Young boy, in a burst of frankness, showed his berry-dyed teeth in a grin and admitted, "They taste too good to carry home."

On Friday, we hear, the bridge crew will have completed their task on the handsome concrete structure which will carry Route 6 traffic over the South Pamet Road, and the Brothers Roach are spreading the clay to bring the approaches up to grade level of the ramp. Deep in our thoughts is the firm intention of being the first to cross the bridge (perhaps in our gay blue Model A) even before such traffic is officially condoned. Dave Kerr, handsome lieutenant of the Navy, who weekends in Pamet, has indicated his plans to do this also, and we reckon on an early morning trip these next few days, notarized by neighbor John Dyer, Jr., to anticipate the lad.

One of our chores, as a broth of a lad, was going for the milk, each evening. In those days no gaily painted trucks delivered the bovine product to the door. Milk had to be fetched from the farmers in the neighborhood, and the source of supply varied with local conditions. If Naylor Hatch's cow went dry, for instance, or Manuel Corey's herd got into the turnip patch with disastrous results to the flavor of the milk, we'd be obliged to make the trip down into the hollow to John Adams' house armed with our two empty bottles for the day's supply. Each place had its own hazards—the approach to Mr. Corey's neatly-kept property led through Newcomb's Hollow, where there were mosquitoes as big as woodpeckers lurking in the lilac clump, awaiting their prey; the meadow below Naylor Hatch's contained sinister, squirming black snakes; but John Adams had a dog—a vicious, snarling brute, part bull, balance of ancestry undetermined, whose sole purpose in life seemed to be the unprovoked attack of innocent bypassers. When complaints were made to John, he'd grin under his bushy black moustach and rumble, "He don't mean no harm, boy, just rubbing against you, that's all."

After several near encounters one summer, we made a deal with John's daughter, Marian, to place the milk in a box atop a post in the middle of an open field some distance from the Adams' domain. This scheme worked well for several days. Each morning we'd stealthily approach the milk box, a stout stick grasped firmly in our sweaty palm, exchange our empties for the full bottles, then sprint for the fence and safety. And each evening we'd hear Laddy as he was affectionately misnamed, bedeviling some poor cat on the Adams' premises, or barking at the wheels of a wagon bringing guests to John's house. Our odor had evidently escaped the beast, and we grew overconfident to the point that we neglected to carry our stick.

Came a night, when dusk was setting over the hollow, and the pleasant night sounds of the cricket and the whippoorwill, and the tree frog were blending in the swamp. We ducked under the fence by Archie Holden's, and traipsed across the open pasture to our milk box, leisurely removed the full bottles, still warm from the cow's body heat, and proceeded blithely back homeward, whistling an excerpt from "Collegiate," fresh from the crystal set. Without warning, a vicious growl came to us from the beachplum bushes astern, and the sunbaked sod gave off noises of Laddy in his mad scramble to overtake us before we reached the sanctuary of Holden's fence. Foolishly, we neglected to jettison our cargo of milk, and, unable to pump our arms in the approved style for sprinting, we rapidly lost ground to the angry bulldog. Agonizingly close to the fence, we stumbled on a clump of poverty grass, and Laddy had us—sounds of denim ripping, interspersed with yelps of triumph from the dog, of terror from ourself. Then, his pride satisfied, the good race run, Laddy made off homeward.

We met John next day in the post office, and made protest to him, showing the visible evidences of the attack.

"Sure rubbed you this time, didn't he," chuckled John. "Almost rubbed the pants right off'n you."

But next day Laddy was confined to his chain, and there propped against the milk post was a huge bag of sweet corn and summer squash, silent attrition for our attack.

On Saturday afternoon last we carefully steered our blue Ford into South Pamet Road, just as the final piece of the contractor's equipment growled slowly from the rough road bed. We sighted the course for stray pieces of lumber or rusty nails; then, at a given signal from contractor Ed Roach above us on the bridge, we gave a blast on the horn, and slowly drove under the overpass. Thus we were able to sneer a trifle at handsome young Ensign Dave Kerr, of the Navy, and inform him that we had beaten him at his own game.

Gone is the oppressive humidity from the air this morning in Pamet, only the sticky salt in the shakers reminding us of yesterday's dampness. The sky is a vault of bright blue overhead and a brisk breeze is blowing from the northwest. The foliage is alive and green again, and swamp blueberries are plentiful. There's grass to be cut, too, and late summer flowers bloom by the roadside: old maid's pink, and Queen Ann's lace, and milkweed. Since the past weekend Truro merchants have noted a slump in business, attributed in part to the opening of the new state highway, bypassing the town. However, further checking reveals that the recession has been general all over the Lower Cape, a sort of mid-August pause before the final plunge into Labor Day.

Henry S. Hutchings, late of North Truro, was a man of great versatility and uncommon skills. Henry lived in the nook west of the Christian Union Church, and in the fertile swamp soil below the old homestead, he grew the finest of vegetables to be trucked into Provincetown each week for sale. At various times in his life, the lean, wiry Cape Codder had tried his hand at fishing, and for one period he tended light for the old Lighthouse Service, up and down the coast. Mr. Hutchings was a licensed auctioneer, much in demand about the village, and in slack seasons he operated a feather bed renovating service in the spacious barn. In addition to this assortment of occupations, Mr. Hutchings was the local undertaker, fully qualified to take complete charge of a funeral, from embalming to digging the grave. In connection with his duties as funeral director, Henry was obliged to keep a horse, which was used to draw the shiny black, glass-paneled hearse, housed over the hills in Long Nook, for common usage by the two villages.

Chester was the beast's name, and a fine, glossy ebony horse he was, sleek, well-fed, and gentle, yet proud in manner, and a decided addition to any funeral. For years Chester performed his special task with complete satisfaction, and between sad trips to the Old North Cemetery on the hill, he browsed contentedly in the meadow. Then one summer, Chester, the hearse-horse, began to act up a mite: got off his feed, shied when his master came to fetch him in from pasture nights, and bared his teeth when the curry comb was run over his shiny hide. Mr. Hutchings blamed Chester's behavior on lack of exercise (there'd been very few funerals since spring, and folks scarcely ever died in summertime, too busy taking care of summer visitors) and paid little attention to the horse until the day Chester found a break in the pasture fence and ambled over to the flower beds near the house. He was daintily sampling some petunias when the good housewife, Mary Jane Hutchings, spied him from the kitchen ell, and appeared on the scene armed with a broom, with which she commenced to beat him about the head and shoulders.

Far from responding to this treatment in the accepted manner, Chester bared his teeth, and with flattened ears and flaring nostrils advanced on Mary Jane, herding her back to the safety of the kitchen doorway. Just as the housewife reached sanctuary of the house, the horse broke through her defense, and nipped her smartly on the arm. The ensuing piercing scream brought Henry to the scene from the garden. Pausing briefly to pick up a stout ash oar by the barn, the irate farmer braced his feet and took a mighty swing, delivering a stunning blow to Chester's temple which dropped the horse in his tracks. It required several buckets of well water to bring Chester back to consciousness, but the horse, once restored, profited by his lesson no end.

In fact, the far-reaching effects of the incident came to light several years afterward, when the hearse was drawn up to the platform at the North Truro Depot, prepared to fetch a body which had just arrived on the train up to the cemetery. The tailgate was fastened shut, Mr. Hutchings climbed up on the driver's seat, and clucked smartly to Chester. No response. "Giddup," said Henry. Still no answering tug at the shafts. "GIT-on," this time in a much sharper tone, usually reserved for emergencies by Henry, and accompanied by a twitch at the reins. This unprecedented situation seemed unsolvable until the undertaker, glancing about the small group of people who stood idly watching the hearse and its balky horse, noted that one of the rubber-booted fishermen seemed to have Chester's attention. "John," shouted Mr. Hutchings, "you mind puttin' thet oar you're carryin' back of the depot for a minute?" No sooner had the offending article disappeared from sight than Chester demurely stepped off from the platform, and the funeral went off, first rate.

We note with some interest that the new automobile models will soon be unveiled to an eager public. The industry has created somewhat of a suspenseful situation in a concentrated campaign involving radio, television, and the press, but we have a deep conviction that the new cars will offer only such minor changes as a fractional increase in horsepower, or a change in the sweep of body lines, or a prissy touch in interior upholstering for added decor—as the ads term it. In our day, we emphatically submit, the adventure of buying a new automobile was vastly greater than today.

In the first place, there was much more choice in the field. Looking back we can recall dozens of cars no longer manufactured nor on the road—and fine cars they were, too. Charlie Snow, for instance, always favored a Peerless, while his brother Dave drove a big Hudson (no more like today's undistinguished, bloated model than day is like night). Joe Curley Francis sported the lower Cape in his Maxwell touring, while Wallace Smith swore by (and sometimes at) his Dort two-door. The Hupmobile was a reliable car, as the North Pamet Lloyds would readily attest, and Cal Stevens boasted that his Chalmers could stay with anything on wheels. We remember that the Gengrass family, summer folks at Long Nook (T'other Hollow) always drove the sporty cars, at first the Stutz two seater, later the Blackhawk and the Auburn, which proudly advertised 115 horses under the hood. A plume of blue smoke was the trademark of Will Rose in his Willy-Knight.

Will always said the car was supposed to burn a mite of oil, sleeve valves, you know, but when the knock-off hubcaps occasionally allowed a wheel to drop off the Knight, Will had to trade her for a Chandler Six. Occasionally, we'd see a model which required some study, such as the Richenbacker, the Star, the Moon, or the Marmon, but at least the variety was a challenge to the powers of observation of the teenagers. Today the vast majority of the rolling stock consists of the small families of the so-called "Big Three," whereas in the twenties you could prowl through the parking space in front of the old post office and pick out a Velie, or a Kissel, a Pierce-Arrow, a Lexington, or a Locomobile.

And they looked like what they were, too, rugged, comfortable conveyances, with a running board to stand on when you climbed up into your genuine leather seat, and headlights that stood out by themselves, bold and brassy, and stout military wheels, with varnished oak spokes. Each shining hub cap proudly proclaimed the car's name, and the dashboard was a thing of beauty, usually satin-finished walnut with a goodly assortment of instruments you could read. The gas and spark levers occupied prominent places atop the steering wheel, chromed and notched to their quadrants, and when you choked your car, you did it by hand, no gadgets in the carburetor depriving you of the satisfaction of a healthy tug on the proper button.

It's mildly amusing for us to read in the papers about the so-called new plans adopted by industry to keep their employees occupied, and happy when they reach the age considered to be correct for retiring. Why, folks down here on Cape Cod have been doing just that since Colonial days, with no fanfare at all. Aman works, for instance, at fishing until he's 70-odd, and begins to feel his tasks a mite heavy. So he'll kind of retire, and take things easy; lay abed till six or so in the morning, and have a few acres of garden and a half a dozen cows and a horse to keep his mind occupied. They still tell the story, locally, of Elisha Atkins, from down Prince Valley way, who for years worked as a ship's carpenter down at Union Wharf, mouth of the Pamet River. Lishe noticed his eyes were getting poor shortly after his seventy-fifth birthday. Got so he'd miss strokes, sometimes, with his razor sharp adze, and once he pounded his thumb instead of a hickory peg in the deck planking of a new packet. So Lishe packed all his tools in his brass-bound chest, and trundled them back over into South Truro, there to enjoy the rest of his years in leisure.

Wasn't long, though, till boredom overtook the old craftsman—got so he couldn't stand the gossip in the post office, and the hands which had skillfully toiled with plane and augur found farming tools awkward and unsatisfying. He yearned for the satisfying sight of a vessel's hull on the ways, and the pungent odor of wood shavings, and tar, and the familiar sounds of the boatyard. And since he couldn't go back to the harbor, Lishe did the next best thing; he made a working agreement with Frank Pascal, the local undertaker, to build all the coffins to be used in the village, and soon he was established in his new business, in the back room of the California Store on Ryder Road. Business thrived from the very outset, and, more important than the small profit to be derived, Lishe found himself happy, occupied, and somewhat of a special figure in the community.

There was something personal, satisfying about the work of furnishing the final earthly possession for a neighbor. And the coffins were custom made too, from choice of woods to solid silver handles in all styles. About the only danger in the whole enterprise came when some grief stricken relative would insist on furnishing a bonus to Lishe in the form of a jug of spirituous liquor—then it required all the old man's will power to put the bonus aside until the job was completed.

Winter of '59 old John Cooper died, and the folks came over to the California Store to make arrangements for Lishe to build his coffin, a handsome cherry wood box, with handplowed molding and a German silver nameplate, heavily engraved. One of the Cooper brothers furnished all the measurements, together with two bottles of Jamaica rum, black, rich, and potent, and then the grieving family left Lishe at his work. The stove in the back room had gone out that night and Lishe, sensing a chill coming on, felt the need of one good, stiff drink to warm his blood, and make limber his stiff old fingers.

Three hours later the coffin was finished, and so were the two bottles of rum. Lishe had avoided his chill, and the finished coffin was a work of art, perfectly proportioned, hand-rubbed to a dull glow with boiled fish oil and the lid, as Lishe was wont to say, "fit like a hot coal in the snow." The Coopers were of course pleased no end when they returned at noon—that is, until one curious member of the family pried up the top cover to examine the inside. Hastily, he dropped the lid, and exclaimed to the other mourners, "Tarnation boys, we shouldn't have left thet rum with Lishe—he's gone and built an oak centerboard into this coffin."

The year in retrospect we find, on the whole pleasing. Concerning our own personal views, we find a little less on the top, and a bit more around the middle. New friends we made, at town hall, in the Blacksmith Shop, and about town. Among them we recall Bert Davy, the man who strung an antenna from the town hall spire, sat in his automobile talking to brother hams around the world on his short wave radio. Those nice folks we worked with in the Wellfleet Players, and the plays we helped to produce, with degrees of success varying from "The Bat" to "Light Up the Sky" and most recently, "You Can't Take It With You." We saw a new, broad road opened through our beloved Pamet, and a massive concrete bridge over-passing the river road. The venerable package store moved lock, stock and barrel to a new location.

Some of our good friends made the Long Journey: Amelia Holden, and Guy Borgarello, and Francis Small, Bill Scott, Mary Rich, John Morris, Josie Nickerson, Seraphine Steele and Fred Priest. On the other side of the ledger we welcomed into the town children of the Ray Days, and the Bobby Dutras, and the Fred Jacobs, the Carlton Fetners, James Avila, and the John Thomases. New faces, too, in town hall—Georgie Rose at the selectman's desk, and Vin Benson supervisor of the newly installed state system of accounting. In 1952 we saw our teenage daughter go out on her first date, found a new Syrian restaurant in Boston which almost weaned us away from our favorite spot in Chinatown. And, like many other Americans, we warmed to the story of Capt. Carlson and his "Flying Enterprise," lost with the Red Sox and the Gentleman from Illinois, and remained neutral in the matter of that popular song of the year's end, "I saw Mommy . . . etc."

NINETEEN FIFTY-THREE

1953

A strong northwest wind speaks with the voice of authority this March morning, moaning along the gables of our house, and whipping the locusts into a frenzied motion in our back yard. Shredded clouds hurry across the intense blue sky, bleaching pure white as they pass before the early bright sun, and tiny swirls of dust start by the roadside with each gust of wind. Unmistakable are the signs of a waning winter. Yesterday we saw a pert kingfisher at Fratus' Bend, and in the meadow the buds on the pussy willows are swollen, and the advance agent for the redwing blackbirds of the valley arrived last week to inspect their summer home. The meadow grass is at its drabbest, most bleached shade, waiting for the magic warm touch of spring.

As is our annual custom, we again this year offer a subscription to this paper for the first reader reporting the spring call of the tree frog (Peewinks, we call them here in Truro). Just drop a post card to Town Father, giving date, time and place and when and where you first heard the welcome treble piping of the peewink.

Mild winters like this one invariably cause comparisons to be drawn, and for our generation we draw on the winter of 1933–34 as the standard of measurement. That would be the year which saw several consecutive days of below zero temperatures; the ground rock-hard with a frost which came in late October and stayed for months—salt water ice formed early, first in the creeks, then the harbors of Wellfleet and Provincetown, and finally in Cape Cod Bay, where a huge crystal white ice floe slowly formed, as the bitter cold held, day after day. With the changing wind, the floe shifted from shore to shore, now piled along Beach Point and Provincetown shores, now drifting into Wellfleet Harbor (grinding at the pilings of the venerable, wharf-borne Chequessett Inn), now drifting along to Brewster. For a period of several days the floe built up off the Brewster coastline. There, one Sunday afternoon, a group of bored CCC boys, stationed at the Brewster Camp of that outfit, decided to explore the huge, jagged icefield, and soon a group of adventurers were crawling out toward open water. At this point the wind shifted to the easterly quarter. The floe began to give off ominous groanings and splitting noises, and soon a black, open void of water appeared between shore and the moving ice field, which still carried the now panic-stricken boys.

Word soon spread to the villages, and plans were made to rescue the unhappy lads. Several local fishermen made unsuccessful attempts to cross the widening gap of water, only to be turned back by floating ice. Word was sent to the Civil Air Patrol as the afternoon drew on, and a plane laden with canned soups and sundry other supplies came roaring down the coast to drop packages to the castaways, by now miles offshore. Daylight was on the wane, and the breeze was picking up. The floe carrying the boys was in a fair way to break up, and the situation was serious. The one bright spot appeared to be the delivery of the food, and cigarettes and supplies to the floating field. Word of the situation had by this time reached the Coast Guard, and after several attempts on the part of the surf station crews from nearby installations to rescue the boys had failed, a call was put in to Provincetown, where the good ship Harriet Lane, a 125 foot third class cutter lay at Town Wharf.

As soon as her skipper, Chief Warrant Officer Fedderson, USCG, had learned the approximate location of the floe carrying the CCC boys, messengers were sent about Provincetown to locate the members of the Lane's crew. Soon the powerful diesels of the Harriet were roaring as she tugged at her mooring lines, and, as the last crewman dashed down the ladder, Capt. Fedderson bawled out his orders, and the Lane cut through the black waters of Cape Cod Bay on her mission of mercy. Far off the Brewster coast, Fedderson encountered the edge of the floe. In the thickening dusk, Harriet met the drifting ice, brushing aside the smaller, floating cakes, until the solid body of the field rose white and jagged dead ahead. Nothing daunted, the ship rose to the occasion; bells jangled in the engine room, the diesels roared into top speed, and the cutter churned determinedly forward. Up on the ice floe rode the keen steel bow, and, as the weight of the hull bore down, the jagged floe gave way, and the craft settled back into black water, to reverse her engines and repeat the battering, crushing action.

Hours later the powerful spotlight of the Lane's pilot house picked out the huddled boys on the floe, and in jig time the warm lighted galley was crowded with the rescued youths. Cook Tommy Rogers politely offered food and boiling coffee, which was wolfed down at once. Cigarettes were passed around, much shaking of hands, and voluble thanks, and exchanging of addresses and telephone numbers, and then, in a lull in the conversation,

Gus Lundgren, coxwain, addressed the boy nearest him. "What kind of food they drop to you?"

"Oh, canned soups, and canned biscuits, and some canned cigarettes," was the reply.

"That so?" observed Gus. "How'd you heat the stuff up, out there on the ice?"

"We never got that far," ruefully replied the CCC boy. "You see, they forgot to drop a can opener."

For us, the story, like that told above, of a rescue at sea or on the storm-tossed back shore has a romance and an appeal without equal. Since the old timers of the original Lifesaving Service are a fast-disappearing breed, we welcome every opportunity to pick up a yarn from our good friend Art Cobb, of North Truro, a man of unimpeachable truth and reliable memory. We sat in Art's neat Cape Cod kitchen this afternoon, lulled by the patter of rain on the multi-paned windows, and pored through his yellowed clippings, as Art boomed out the story of the bark Harding, and we offer it to our readers herewith.

The date: November 30, 1889. A howling nor'easter lashed the backside, thick of snow, and bitter cold, and the mountainous surf piled up at the base of the Clay Pounds below the Highlands. Art Cobb, doing his trick as cook for the Highland Lifesaving Station, gave his yeast bread dough a final affectionate pat, wrapped it well in a heavy towel to rise, and stowed it behind the black iron Crawford stove. "Don't forget to call me early," he said to the outbound watch, Heman Smith, "so's I can get the bread started for breakfast." A final look at the worsening storm, a leisurely pull on his battered pipe, and off to bed, in the bunk chamber overhead. It seems but moments later when Art felt an urgent hand on his bunk, and he was aroused by the urgent voice of Smith, telling of a vessel ashore to the south'ard. "Can't tell for sure, it's so thick out, but she looks like a three-master."

In an instant the station was a beehive of ordered activity, each man doing his chore with the precision brought by long training. Capt. Ed Worthen hastily cranked the telephone, calling help from High Head Station; Antone Lucas dispatched to the Highland House Hotel for a pair of horses to haul the beach apparatus. George Bowley and John Francis break out the surfboat; Cobb and John Marshall assemble the Lyle gun and other necessary paraphernalia, and, just as the first gray of dawn lightens the horizon, the men pile out on the beach and stagger up shore to the wreck, bucking the terrific wind and the biting sand. Much later they were to learn that the stricken vessel was the bark Kate Harding, built in Thomaston, Maine, but of British registry, bound for Boston light, her Captain, Ed. B. Perry. The Harding lay hard up on the outer bar, almost head on, and the sea between was a maelstrom of wild foaming water.

Capt. Worthen, realizing that the surfboat could not live in such a sea, ordered the beach apparatus set up immediately, and the combined crews set to work with a will, mounting the cross-arms, burying the sand-anchor, making fast the whip line and hawser, and loading a capacity charge into the heavy iron Lyle gun. Worthen himself sighted the one-pounder, and his first shot carried fair over the topmast of the bark's main spar. Whip line and hawser were quickly rigged, and the breeches buoy dispatched to the stricken vessel. At this point the Harding commenced to roll so violently in the rising tide that the hawser was in grave danger of parting, so the line to the sand anchor was replaced by a block and falls, and a man was stationed nearby to pay off and take up slack as the ship's motion dictated. First man ashore was the colored cook, clutching to himself the pet parrot and canary, and a dog-eared Gideon bible, and then, in rapid succession, the members of the crew and the captain.

"We quick got 'em all back to the station," recounts Art, "and filled 'em up on black coffee and some spirits from the medicine chest, and bunked 'em down for the night on spare mattresses in the boat house. Ordered a half barrel of corned beef from Thompson's store and lots of extra grub to feed 'em and gathered up some clothing in the village.

"Well sir, the storm let up the next day, and we all tramped out to the Kate Harding to see what she looked like in broad daylight. Besides, someone had heard the Harding had ten gallons of Barbados rum in the skipper's cabin, and we thought we'd get it afore the salt water spoiled it. But them consarn Forty Thieves that used to salvage all the wrecks for the underwriters beat us to it, and stripped her clean."

We took this opportunity to ask Art if the Lifesaving men had gotten any medals or commendations or such for their brave deeds. "Hell no, boy," boomed Art. "Only way you ever got medals in them days was to lose a life or two, and then the Boston papers might mention the story. All we lost was a few night's sleep, and Heman Smith had his toes frostnipped."

(Ed. Note: What about the bread?)

An ocean storm still holds our Narrow Land in its tenacious grip. Each day the wind works steadily from an easterly quarter, bringing rain in varying quantities. Today the rain comes in a driving, silver-gray scud, out of a fog-lined cloud bank, on a steady, pressing breeze from the northeast.

By the roadside stand huge, swollen puddles, their surfaces windstirred and the grass is a lush, rich green, but the fresh beauty of the blossoming forsythia and the daffodils is lost in the storm. Lost, too, in the mournful sound of the wind is the pleasant sound of the peewinks in the swamps at night, and the spring call of the chicadee and the red-wing blackbird at sun down. We've probably had many Cape springs like this, but the bitter reality of yet another tardy season is no easier to take. And so we repair to the cellar, thinking on cemetery lots soon to be cut, there to clean and sharpen our machines, and to inspect the tools of our trade, musing, the while, and paraphrasing the words of Thomas the Doubter in Holy Scripture: "And until I shall savor the mild southwest wind, and smell the good green grass of April, and feel the warm sun on the hillside, I shall not believe."

We got to talking with George Rogers, custodian of the Provincetown High School today while that genial, gray-thatched gentleman was in a mood for reminiscing. George was reflecting on that period in his life when he left home and went up to the big city, in this case, Lowell, Mass. Time hung heavy on the country boy's hands, and money being scarce, George sought out places of entertainment which were inexpensive, or, if possible, free. "That would be about the time Carrie Nation, the great prohibitionist, was in full swing," mused George. "She'd been all over New England, raisin' havoc with every bar room she could get near, and danged if she didn't reach Lowell, come the weekend. How she ever kept out of jail, no one could figger—she did hundreds of dollars of damage to the drinkin' spots, including the corner spa I used to frequent.

"Well sir, t'was a Sunday night, and we heard that Carrie was goin' to give a lecture at the Lowell Civic Auditorium, so a bunch of the boys decided to go down to hear her speak. Good crowd, there, too; friend of mine, Irish boy name of Murphy, sat right up near the platform, and Murph had a mite too much aboard. Red-faced and talkative, he was, and Carrie had no sooner started to lecture when Murphy started hecklin'. Pretty soon there was a question and answer period, and Murph, he lurched to his feet and started queryin' her about this third party, the Prohibition Party that she was talkin' in favor of. 'Miz Nation,' he shouted, 'Can you tell me the difference between a Republican and a Democrat?' Quick as a wink she shot back, 'They're just the same as you, mister, both wet; but one is in, and the other is OUT.'"

A new moon over the weekend brought huge spring tides to the bay, and a gray flood filling the Pamet Valley, and on the ebb tides Truro folk swarmed out on the exposed bars offshore to harvest the wily seaclam. Today Truro kitchens will give off the heavenly aroma of baking seaclam pies, and golden, sizzling fritters, and creamy rich chowder and a dogwood itch to any cook who adulterates this latter dish with tomatoes, or pepper, or such. As a matter of fact, this would be a fine spot for the genuine New England seaclam chowder recipe, intended for men only, since we contend that every male should be able to turn out this famous dish. Here's what you'll need for ingredients: one pint of seaclams, finely ground, medium sized onion, diced, a slab of salt pork size of a cigarette package, scored with a knife to try out quicker, four small potatoes, diced, a pint of rich milk, salt, pepper, and butter. In an iron frying pan (Truro folks call it a spider) slowly brown the salt pork until a quantity of liquid has been tried out. In this liquid, lightly brown the onion—transfer the pork and onion to a kettle in which your diced potatoes nestle, just covered with enough water to simmer.

As the mixture reaches a hearty boil, add the chopped clams and salt to taste—you'll have a mite of clam juice to help with the flavor at this point. Pour it in! In a separate pan, bring the milk to a simmer point, and, when the clams are tender (fifteen minutes or so) add the hot milk. Float a big piece of butter on the chowder, dust with black pepper, and serve with pilot crackers. If some member of the family should be called away from the table (a grass fire, or some other unavoidable call to duty) you'll just possibly have a mite of this chowder left. Put it in the ice box, let it blend overnight, and heat it up for breakfast next morning. Hard to believe, but chowder can improve in flavor in this fashion.

Good fishing in the river these days, trout aplenty, and, for the first time in many years, pudgy white perch to be taken. There's a fishing pool at Snowie's Shell Station, where the lucky anglers take their wiggling trout to be carefully measured; so far Sgt. Earl Bishop of the Air Force leads with a rainbow just over 10 inches in length, hooked on a juicy worm at the culvert. Up in Wellfleet's Herring Brook the alewives are running, and last week our No. 1 son brought home a weird looking fish about the length and girth of a lead pencil, with a bill-like snout not unlike a soda straw, a faint brown diamond pattern on its dorsal side, and protruding eyes. We've not been able to identify the specimen by comparing it to the plates in our encyclopedia. Must be otter bait, since it came from the Pamet.

To Boston on the plane Wednesday week, our first trip in the air to fetch home a borrowed ambulance while our own vehicle was being repaired. Comforted not at all by the cheerful grin of Pilot John C. Van Arsdale, nor the seeming nonchalance of the other passengers (mostly blue-uniformed men from the 762 ACW base at North Truro) we forced ourself into the metal monster, legs atremble, palms dripping with perspiration. We had left a rather sentimental note to John Dyer Jr., on our desk at town hall, devising and bequeathing our worldly goods, and now it seemed proper to pick out a safe seat in the plane.

We debated the relative merits of the nose or the tail, finally settled into one in the midsection, and reviewed, mentally that breast stroke we used to do in the Wellfleet ponds, just in case we had to finish the trip on our own, across the bay.

Our tension increased as the plane paused before takeoff and John raced the motors in an obvious attempt to tear them from their mountings in the fragile wings. It seemed ages before the illuminated sign advised "No Smoking—Fasten Belts" and then we were off—into a blue haze which covered the Cape. As the land faded from view something cracked in our ears and we were stricken stone deaf, so that any faltering of the motors was mercifully spared us. At various points on the trip a strong wind alternately buffeted the frail craft, or slacked off into a dead calm, allowing the plane to plummet toward the rough sea below, and we had just become accustomed to this frightening motion when the familiar sight of the Custom House tower and the wharves and the water front of South Boston hove into view. By the time we had folded our magazine and snuffed out our cigarette, the plane was skimming into Bedford airport.

We looked up from our fumbling at the safety belt as John squeezed from his pilot's compartment in time to read the question on his lips (still deaf, we were). "Liked it fine, John," we shouted. "Why the old town hall shakes worse than that in a good nor'easter." The second leg of the trip into Logan airport found us calm and experienced, and we almost asked John to barrel-roll her into the runway, or land downwind, or some such of daring.

The weather man has an explanation for the beautiful day which greets Pamet this morning—via the wireless he tells of high pressure areas, and cool masses moving from the west, and low humidity conditions. For our part, we accept the perfect June day for what it is, and enjoy it for the cool sou'west breeze, and the cloudless, vaulted blue of the sky, and the clean smell of the valley. Yesterday a brief shower moistened the tip of the Cape, ending abruptly somewhere in Whitmanville, while our village saw only the unfulfilled promise of rain in a lowering black cloudbank.

Last night we glimpsed the first fireflies of the season in the nook at Fratus' Bend, and the whippoorwills contested, early in the evening, at their monotonous, repeated calls. And we to our chores in the cemeteries, cleaning up the withered flowers of the holiday, passing over the dried grass in a final cutting before hot weather parches the mounded lots. In the Congregational churchyard the smell of fermented locust blossoms blends with the aroma of freshly cut bunchgrass and the sickly-sweet smell of the Balm of Gilead tree by the west fence, and visitors drop by to read the stones, and it's peaceful on the hilltop.

We got to thinking, as we looked at the swollen, orange moon shining over the bay on the way home from band rehearsal last night, about street lights. Nowadays, except for four scattered lights in the two villages of Truro, the moon is the only illumination for the byroads of our town. Neighboring Wellfleet boasts a fine system of street lights, but we often wonder if the modern, automatic incandescent bulbs can ever replace the original lamps which graced the winding, elm-shaded streets of the little shellfishing town. Older Wellfleet folks will tell you that the lamp lighters making their rounds added a touch of personal interest to the daily chore. Despite the importance of the task, the lamp lighter could usually find time to chat a bit, or do an errand for a neighbor on his evening round.

Of the many men who held the town job as lamplighters, George Ephraim Pierce and Allen Higgins seem to stand out in the memories of folks as being the most colorful. Mr. Pierce tended the lamps from Kemps Corner down through Main Street to the Corner School house. He was a tall man, gifted with an extraordinary touch with flint and tinder, which he used to ignite his lamps, even long after sulphur matches came into general use.

And then there was, of course, Allen Higgins, a spare short Wellfleeter, who always affected a light duster when he made his rounds. Being of less than normal stature, Mr. Higgins was obliged to plan somewhat more carefully, and use considerably more equipment in his lamplighting job. First off, Mr. Higgins made for his wheelbarrow a spacious platform, fitted with a dozen or so stubby cedar posts, turned down to fit snugly into the sockets of the bases of the street lamps. In starting his rounds, the lamplighter would carefully place his lamps, all trimmed, filled and lighted, on the cedar pegs, and trundle them along lower Commercial Street from the town pump to Isaiah Doanes corner, placing them, with the aid of a stubby ladder, atop each post as he came to it.

Next morning, bright and early, he'd fetch in the lamps, and prepare them for the following night. Thus even the wildest northwest winter wind failed to slow the lighting of the lamps on the Higgins route, since they had already been lighted in the snug Higgins kitchen. In 1903, when the town of Wellfleet lowered the road in front of Oliver Linnell's house, Mr. Linnell approached the town fathers with the request that they install a street lamp at his corner, pointing out that the dark cut presented certain hazards to foot traffic. The town fathers pondered the request for a suitable period, then made the proposition that the light would be installed if Mr. Linnell would take care of the lamp. The agreement further bound Mr. Linnell's heirs and assigns forever to the task of trimming and filling and polishing the shade of the lamp.

"But they finally agreed to furnish the kerosene," states Mary Freeman, one of the aforesaid heirs, "so we took care of it until the town put in electric street lights in 1927. Used to let it burn all night, we did, since the fuel was found by the town. Never forget the time I bumped the lamp post when I was learning to drive a Model T Ford. Cost me 70¢ for a new chimney, and my folks wouldn't let me touch the wheel again for months."

We allowed about this time that Mr. Higgins' lamps must have consumed a good deal of kerosene, burning all night, too.

"Law, no," said Mary. "He only'd put in about a quarter of a tank. Always said that folks should be in bed by nine o'clock, and he fixed it so's his lamps would go out about that time."

The symptoms of summer are with us in the age old pattern; queues of customers at Mary Howard's grocery, and impatient drivers at Snowie's petrol pumps, where the bulletin board proclaims to the public the hours of high tide and prognostications on the weather; strange faces in the post office lobby, and baggage laden cars on the pike—and sightseers cautiously peering into our office door at town hall, inquiring as to whether the venerable building was ever a church. "Squire" John Dyer Jr., has the proper answer for the latter folks. He always says, "No . . . 'tisn't a church, and never was. We're reverent people, though, both of us."

To this day we find the refinements of the new dial phone somehow lacking in satisfaction. There's an absence of the personal touch personified by the mechanical buzzing tone of the dial replacing the friendly voice of the operator. Most of all, we miss the custom of listening in on the party lines. While our line still services eight subscribers at this time of year, the other folks are mostly summer people, and we hesitate to carry on a conversation with them if we should lift the receiver by accident while they are making a call. Then, too, most of our calls are made from town hall, on a private line; a sterile, untapped circuit which leads straight to the exchange.

In the old days, by common agreement, all the folks on Arthur Joseph's line would lift the receiver when Art's phone rang, especially late at night. Art was the fire chief, and this informal custom worked as a sort of alarm for the members of the department on South Pamet Road. Anthony Marshall tells the yarn about Sarah Farwell, one of the earliest subscribers on the first line to be run down Truro Depot Road and into South Truro. Sarah was an intrepid old soul, widow of a Civil War veteran, who lived beyond the Hogsbacks, across Lewis' Swamp in the house now owned by the Schumanns. She lived alone, except for a dozen or so cats, several canaries, and a flock of hens, and she relied for protection against any invasion of her privacy on a heavy, double barrel shotgun which she kept loaded behind the kitchen door.

Sarah learned the mysteries of the telephone in short order, and, in true neighborly fashion, when someone else's ring jangled on the line, she'd lift the receiver and listen in. Mostly folks didn't mind, but occasionally, when several receivers were lifted at once, the drain on the voltage of the old magneto system would prove too great, and the person to whom the call was made would be unable to hear his caller's voice. Then one by one, the subscribers would be politely requested to hang up.

Like the time, for instance, when John Marshall, Anthony's father, was expecting a call from the neighboring town of Wellfleet, where he had entered into negotiations with John Higgins for purchase of a heifer calf. It was a rainy Sunday afternoon, and all the Depot Road folks were housebound, bored by the weather, so that when the phone finally jangled the Marshall number, several receivers clicked open, and the Higgins voice faded into nothingness.

Mr. Marshall wiggled the hook patiently, shouting into the mouthpiece. "What color is she, John?" referring, obviously, to the calf. A pause, and then, as a surge of voltage coursed through the line, the voice of Dick Rich, conversing with Sarah Farwell, came faintly to the waiting Marshall ears. The Rich-Farwell conversation, however, had to do with some baby canaries recently hatched out in the Farwell house, and the reply came back, "Black and yellow, and just now featherin'." The astonished Mr. Marshall now posed another question, taking advantage of another surge of voltage in the line, "How big, is she, John?" More buzzing and fading, and a jumble of voices. More jiggling of the hook, and then a faint voice, "About the size of your thumb." Mr. Marshall hung up at this point, and, turning to his puzzled family, allowed, "Place for that calf is in the circus."

From the John B. Dyer historical address, 1909:

Our present Truro is 11 miles long, in a straight line, and the width of the Cape wide. Farming and fishing have always been the principal industries of the people. In the early days the stork was a frequent visitor to the home. 12 or 15 children being no unusual occurrence. In the old red kitchen around the open fireplace a large family of boys grew fat and chubby, played with toy boats, and afterwards navigated their ships around the world. As a rule the early generations married young. The woman was a veritable helpmate of the man. She assumed the marriage relation with no other idea than doing her own housework and rearing her own family. On the wedding ring was inscribed: "Let love abide until death divide," and true to that declaration they lived and died. With plenty to do they minded their own business. They found no time for the alienation of affection and the patronage of the divorce courts. Dame Fashion was little sought by the busy housewife, and while she wove and spun, scrubbed and baked year in and year out, she did not neglect the sterling principles which have come down to us as a legacy of thrift, and a good, practical common sense.

The story is told of a Dutch settler in Truro, on whom her minister called and found busy. She was churning butter, rocking the cradle, tending the fire, watching the cows, and reading a book. He congratulated her upon her thrift, enumerating the things he saw her doing, and she added, "Yes, and pressing the cheese."

The sons of Truro are said to be the first to adventure to the Falkland Islands in pursuit of whales. Voyages were undertaken by Captains David Smith and Gamaliel Collins in 1774 at the suggestion of an admiral of the British Navy and were successful. The business of seafaring continued to increase as the years went by, so that after 1800 business in the vicinty of Pamet Harbor began to promise a bright future.

The tide waters flowed in and out of the Long Nook meadows and in every nook, corner, and cove of the Pamet meadows, and out again into the Bay, making a good depth of water in the harbor. Shipbuilding was begun, and from 1845 to 1852, vessels were built in Truro, much of the timber being cut in our woods from the old white oak growth.

From 1849 to 1865, 111 vessels first and last, belonging to Truro, were sailed by Truro captains and manned by Truro crews. They included whalers, coasters, Grand Bankers, freighters and fishermen, the latter class being the greatest number. Hayward's Gazetteer of Massachusetts says that in 1837, 63 vessels were owned at Truro, employed in the cod and mackerel fishery, measuring 3,437 tons, the product of which in one year was 16,950 quintals of codfish and 15,750 barrels of mackerel valued at $145,350. The number of hands employed was 512. Pamet harbor was a busy place. Mackerel packing establishments, stores of all kinds, carpenters, riggers, and sailmakers, blacksmiths and mechanics of every sort, found plenty to do.

But the tide turned. The harbor began to grow shallow. Dykes across the nooks and coves lessened the run of water in and out of the harbor, and the fishing industry was doomed. The increase in the size of vessels helped to hasten the end.

★ ★ ★

Up, to the urgent jangling of the telephone, and out in the pre-dawn darkness on an ambulance trip to the city, and finding the scene beautiful on the Lower Cape. Banks of thick white mist on each of the ponds near Wellfleet, and rigid, wide-eyed rabbits by the roadside; pale golden sky lightly traced with cirrus clouds, and a faint breeze to toss the foliage as the light strengthens. Daylight shows the landscape clear-etched in the period following the recent dry easterly; in the Great Marshes of Barnstable an errant bird flock, and in the cold waters of the Canal a lone boat, plowing against the current at the apex of a long V. Cape towns are silent and clean and deserted, and the early morning sun reflects in the east windows of neat houses in Plymouth, and Kingston, and the Braintrees and when the city is reached, the traffic thickens. At the bus stops, knots of early morning risers glance at us with idle interest, and we at them. And our business done, we hie back to the native hearth, apprehensive of the approaching deadline, and endeavoring to woo the muse.

We're still atingle with the thrill of our first (and only) ride in a Stanley Steamer. We're referring, of course, to Frank Gardner's handsomely restored 1912 Stanley, which is seen on the Lower Cape roads this summer. A thing today of mechanical beauty, lustrous paint and burnished nickel, the Stanley was discovered by Frank in an old barn in Vermont, battered and dust-covered, and, over a period of years, Frank succeeded in restoring the car to factory newness. We were in conference with Town Accountant Vin Benson and Dr. Charles Hutchings at town hall when Frank glided to a stop before the door and invited us for a spin. Dr. Hutchings at first demurred, pleading an allergy to kerosene fumes, but we finally overcame his argument with the promise he might tote his black bag with him in the rear seat, and in we all climbed, settling comfortably into the soft, well-padded leather cushions. The doors, we recall, closed like the town vault, with a solid, reassuring thump. Frank threw off the parking brake, and advanced the throttle just a mite; with a slight hiss, the Stanley floated around the corner and down Town Hall Road. Nary a grinding of gears, or chattering of clutch, or roar of motor—just a pulsing power and a sound not much louder than what Jack Edwards makes when he blows through the spit-key of his sousaphone.

More from the Dyer historical address:
On February 24, 1723, occurred the Great Storm. The tide was four feet higher than ever known before. May 18, 1780, was the "Dark Day." At that

time considerable license was given to superstition, and many supposed it omened some great calamity. Others thought the world was coming to an end. It was so dark at noonday that the hens went to roost.

In January, 1806, occurred the "Cold Friday" the thermometer at that time being six degrees below zero. It was the coldest day then ever known in Truro. It was the time Mr. Ambrose lost his legs, and on cold days the saying still lives among the people, who comment on the weather by saying: "It hasn't been so cold since Ambrose lost his legs."

In 1816 the "Great Sickness" prevailed. It was called by various names, as malignant fever, putrid fever, spotted fever, and the cold plague. Thirty-six died in this town, from the ninth of March to the twenty-third day of May. Rev. Mr. Damon spread a very good account of it on the church record. Seventy-two died of it in Eastham, about one-eleventh of the population.

October 3, 1841, to which reference has been made, was the saddest event the town has ever known. The "October Gale" will never cease to live in the history of the town. June 27 and 28, 1872, was the occasion of the reunion of the Rich family on Hall Hill. The number present was estimated about 3,000 Riches coming from all parts of the country, among them being a Mormon from Utah. Riches are more numerous than any other name on the town records. Truro was selected as the place for the family reunion because of being the great breeding ground of the family.

Another and last event of our history is the celebration of the 200th anniversary of our incorporation. May it pass into history as an honorable and creditable event of our day and generation.

The war record of Truro would be long and interesting, but brevity is called for. In the Revolutionary War, 32 men, it is said, north of the Pond responded to the defense of home and country. The Civil War of 1861–1865 is yet fresh in the memory of many. Early in the war, Truro had 156 men liable to draft. Of that number all but 32 volunteered or were drafted.

In the old days a few slaves were owned in town. Toby and Violet, slaves of Ebenezer Dyer, were married Feb. 22, 1758, and duly recorded on the town records. Perhaps the largest slave owner in town was Mr. Jonathan Paine of Long Nook. He owned a slave named Pomp, who was brought from over the seas by some sea captain of a whaling vessel, and sold to Mr. Paine. One day, being homesick and longing for kith and kin, with a belief in the transmigration of the soul, he took a jug of water, a little food and a rope, and wandered to a thickly wooded spot in the eastern section of Long Nook. There he hung himself to a tree, where his lifeless body was found long afterwards. The woodlot of the suicide has since been known as Pomp's lot and is pointed out as such by the native Long Nooker.

★ ★ ★

It's interesting to compare the sales methods used nowadays in the automobile business as compared with those of the earlier days. We recall vividly, for instance, the first showing of the Model A Ford in Truro. It was a Sunday morning, and George Williams, Ford's crack salesman, natty and well-groomed as always, had been to early church in North Truro; now he had  parked the sensational new car in William Gray Square, and, as folks stopped for their papers at Phat Francis' store, George casually slipped out of the driver's seat and commenced dusting her off a bit. And a thing of beauty she was: a sleek, dark blue four door model, if memory serves correctly, with shiny headlights and radiator shell, and racy wire wheels. George had the motor idling, with the spark retarded, to show off the even, powerful firing of the motor, and, as folks gathered around, he obligingly lifted the hood so that a better look at the compact power plant could be had.

Ed Snow, we recall, remarked it would be a shame to get the upholstery soiled when gassin' her up, and George hastened to explain that in these here new ones, the tank was filled up here, near the hood; and Alec Francis, a devotee of the old Model T, shook his head doubtingly when it was pointed out to him that the reverse pedal of the planetary transmission was a thing of the past, replaced by the rugged gear shift, amidships. The questions came thick and fast, and George answered them all, aided by the handy booklet which he occasionally referred to; and later on groups of prospective customers or just plain joy riders climbed into the Ford and went for a spin with the salesman. Anthony "Cookie" DeLuze went along about the third trip, together with "Tooch" Gray and Charlie Joseph and Henry Hanson—a goodly load for any car. Cookie had always been partial to a rival small car, and he figured the way to discredit the Model A would be to give her the acid test: a trip up Perry's Hill, in South Truro, in high gear. And so he made the proposition to George, and George, with some misgivings, turned the Ford down Depot Road and around the Mill Pond. In the back seat, a hot argument was raging between Cookie and Charlie Joseph; Cookie pointed out that Charlie and Tooch and Henry Hanson were all well over two hundred pounds in weight, and besides, the Ford only had four cylinders.

"Yes, but look at the stroke and bore," Charlie kept insisting, "and remember how George scuffed rubber off those tires when he gave her the gas in the Square—lots of power under that hood." Well sir, we heard afterwards from George that there was an audible intake of breath from all the riders as they turned the corner from Mill Pond Road onto Old County, and the hill loomed up before them almost vertical. George tightened his grip on the wheel, and fed her the gas, easy-like so she wouldn't choke up; he titivated the spark lever on the quadrant until the four cylinders were firing perfectly, and, as the boys in the back seat (except for Cookie) rocked back and forth with body English designed to aid the little car over the grade, they passed the halfway mark, then Perry's driveway, and finally, with a burst of speed, the Ford slipped over the top. And that's how they used to sell cars in the old days.

Don't forget the Chili supper, open to the public, benefit of the Cub Scouts, town hall, Wednesday night, 6 p.m., November 18th, Tess Daisy at the range.

Wreck of the ship Jason, from the booklet by Isaac H. Small. Late in the afternoon of Dec. 5th, 1893, the patrol of the coast guard of Life Savers of Nauset Beach, a few miles south of Highland Light, during a momentary break in the furious storm driven snow, saw the outlines of a great ship, not more than two miles from the beach, heading towards the Port of Boston under close reefed sails struggling with the grasp of giant waves which threatened every moment to overwhelm her. Soon the increasing gale hid all the turbulent waters of the great sea. The winter night came on with rapid pace. All along shore each Life Saving Station had been warned by telephone to watch with increased vigilance for a disaster which their experience had taught them was inevitable. Not a Coast Guardsman slept that night. All the boats and beach apparatus were made ready for instant use; the patrol watches were doubled; the men at the stations stood ready, dressed, anxious, dreading but ever watchful and ready for the call which they expected to come at any moment.

At 7:15 a surfman of the Pamet River Station rushed breathlessly and excitedly into the station and shouted, "She is ashore, half a mile north of this station." All the stations were immediately notified. Then out into the storm and darkness and the blinding snow, along the galeswept beach where flying sand cut their faces like knives, toiling through yielding sand with their mortar guns and boats, hoping to reach the scene of the disaster ere it was too late, the Life Savers hurried. Chips and logs along the shore were gathered together and a huge bonfire kindled that those on the ship might know that every human effort was being exerted to aid them. By the glare of the light on the shore away over there in the awful night, the faint outlines of the doomed ship could be seen, her great white sails being torn to shreds by the savage fury of the winter storm. Great torrents of gale driven sea swept her decks every moment. Her masts fell with a crash to her decks. Soon her iron hull was twisted and wrenched asunder; through her rended decks and battered sides floated portions of her cargo to the shore. The cries of her drowning sailors could be heard above the fury of the storm. The mortar gun of the Life Savers thundered again and again. The shots sped true to their mark and the life lines fell across the ship's hull, but her men could not reach them, so madly rushed the waters between.

Eventually a surfman saw a dark object thrown up by the sea; it was a human being. He was quickly taken up by willing hands and hurried to the station, restoratives were applied, and soon he was able to tell the story of the wreck:

"Our vessel was the British ship Jason, Capt. McMillan. We were on a voyage from the East Indies to Boston with jute bales. We did not know our position until we saw land at 4 this afternoon. We tried, by crowding on every sail upon the ship, to weather Cape Cod; we failed. There were 27 officers and men in our ship's company. I am the only one that lives; I saw all my shipmates perish when the mizzen mast fell."

Like many another shipwreck the irony of fate pursued this ship's company; when her keel was driven into the sand bar by the force of the mighty waves which hurled her forward, the only spot upon the whole ship which seemed to offer a place of refuge from the boiling surf which tore across her deck was the mizzenmast. Into the rigging of this spar every man hurried except the one man who was saved. He was swept from the rail before he could gain a foothold with his shipmates; but what they had hoped would be their haven of safety was their doom. Scarcely had they climbed above the maelstrom of rushing waters when the mast went down with a crash into the sea, killing many of the sailors in its fall, and drowning the others in its wreckage. The foremast stood unmoved by the winter's storms for many weeks. Had this unfortunate crew reached this portion of the ship, many of them would have been rescued on the following day.

Out there today when the tide is low, protruding through the sands of the bar and the white caps that wash them, are the broken fragments of the sunken ship looking like tombstones in the village churchyard. All along the shores of this windswept sea washed coast those half submerged and silent sentinels remind us that up and down this sandy beach the ever moving sea has covered hundreds of those heroic men who have gone down in ships in the great ocean.

NINETEEN FIFTY-FOUR

1954

We deplore the lack of publicity which the office of truant officer suffers in recent years. As we recall, it has been the policy of the school committee for some time now to delegate the duties of that position to the school janitor. And not since the days of the late Will Hopkins has a janitor taken the duties seriously. Will used to wear a shiny badge inside his coat, and when one of the pupils of the Truro Central School was absent without good excuse from the building, why Will would climb into his Model A Ford, and search out the little rascal, deliver a brief lecture to the parents, and fetch him back to the temple of learning.

Snowie of the Shell Station remembers the truant officer of his days (the more vividly perhaps because of personal contact) as Phil Ryder, who lived on the Little Pamet River other side of Tom's Hill. Phil was a big, beefy man, wore a flourishing moustache, had a grain business on Depot Road, and always drove a sleek, black horse, hitched to a rubber-tired buggy. Mr. Ryder was also the constable, and the weighty combination of his two offices added a good deal of prestige to his position as an officer of the law. On town meeting days Phil used to stand at the head of the stairs, casting a baleful eye at the loiterers and the perennial wags, ready to pounce on an unruly voter at the slightest signal from the moderator.

"I remember one meetin' day I cut school and sneaked up to the hall. I kept out of old Phil's sight," says Snowie, "until a heated debate started, front of the hall, and Phil edged away from the head of the stairs, and I tiptoed up to the first landing. Gramp Snow, I could hear, was defending his work as town road surveyor, and all the other Snows was chimin' in. Uncle David, and Uncle Charlie, and Pop, and Isaiah and Norman. Just at the most exciting part of the argument, Mr. Ryder turned around to expectorate into the big terra-cotta cuspidor, and he caught sight of me. 'You git back to school fast's your legs'll carry you,' growled Phil, 'there's enough damn Snows up here already.'"

★ ★ ★

55

As typical of the whoppers told by Capt. Smith, the following story is quoted. Seems Capt. Smith, as a callow youth of 14, was left alone aboard ship while the other crew members went ashore. Seated by the galley stove, and catching an evening snack, his empty rubber boots beside him, the Truro man accidentally dropped a heel of bread into the sea boot. Shortly, a hungry rat came from a hole in the wall, scrambled into the boot, to be followed by another, and another, until in short order, the boot was filled. Smith then seized the slack of the boot top, went topside, and emptied the struggling rats overboard. Kept it up all night, he did, until the last rat was taken from the ship—1,905 of them in all.

A colorful and interesting story indeed. But for the gentle art of spoofing with all the other qualities of a good anecdote, including hyperbole, and a happy choice of adjectives and the indispensible ingredient of brevity, give us Pop Snow when he's in the mood. And he was in the mood this morning, when we stopped by the Shell Station. Income tax out of the way, so Pop allowed, and a hearty breakfast under his belt (corn beef hash and fried eggs and apple pie) and a fragrant cigar to drag on, and the beauties of the Pamet Valley to admire in the bright morning sun, "Hear they're havin' trouble with the water system up at town hall. Them deep well pumps, you can't tell about them after they're down, or while you're poundin' them." Here a huge blue cloud of smoke, which drifted into the toucan's cage and brought forth a sneeze from Tookie.

"I remember the time we took a contract to drive a well for Frank Sargent Small, over near Highland. Father bid $2.00 a foot, guaranteed to get water. The job looked jinxed to me from the very beginning—big veins of clay there, you know, and boulders in the ground. Nearest well there was somethin' over two hundred feet deep, and folks said they'd worked over a month drivin' that one. Well sir, we got a crew together, Charlie and me, and the two Souza brothers, Jesse and Barteez, (yep, that's what they called him, no matter if it is spelled Baptiste in the records) and Henry Hanson. We loaded the gear into the truck wagons at the barn, two inch pipe and a strainer, and a tripod, and a pair of blocks, and a cussed big driving-pounder must've weighed eighty pounds, or more.

"Got over there, we did, on the hottest dern day of the summer, sun pourin' down and not a mite of a breeze. We set up the tripod, and rigged the pulley, and started to pound, after we'd threaded the drivin' head on the pipe. Well, you never seen such hot weather—sweat pourin' off the men; the more they'd drink the more they'd sweat. Every one of us raised a crop of blisters on our hands from pullin' the rope on the pounder, and my, didn't that pipe go down slow. Most of the time it would take about a thousand blows to drive her down an inch. Second day we rigged up a tarpaulin over the tripod to keep some of the sun off, and started in before sunup, to see if we c'd get her down a bit before it got too hot. Thirty one inches we drove, and then the pipe broke off, and we couldn't haul up the well, so we started a new one.

Third day was hotter'n ever, and I remember the green flies started swarmin' up from the beach to add to the misery. Still that cussed well was goin' slower'n axle grease in January, and finally she seemed to bite up solid, against a rock or something. We heaved on that rope for three hours, and all of a sudden we could feel her give, and from then on, with each pound, that well would go down a couple of inches. About then a breeze came up from the eastard, the greenheads disappeared, and we knocked off for lunch. Charlie and me went over to a clump of locusts in the shade, and sat down, opened our dinner pails, and we both et hearty, and then we broke out cigars and started to smoke."

Here another capacity draw on the stogy, and an exhaled cloud of blue smoke aimed at the beagle, Spotty. "You won't believe this, but just as Charlie went to stretch out for a little nap, he felt something sharp in the grass, and when he cleared away with his hands, Jee-rusalem, there was the end of the cussed well-point, sticking up out of the ground. We figgered afterwards it must have struck a boulder, underground, bent that two inch pipe like a piece of wet spaghetti, U-shaped, and headed right back for the surface."

On our way to work this morning, we were invited to peek into the big black fish box in the back of Frankie Davis' truck, to find the box almost filled with beautiful, sleek, ten-pound striped bass. After making appropriate remarks of admiration, we casually asked Frankie how the price was, these days. "Twenty-five cents a pound on the wharf," quoted Frankie, and then, with a cautious look over his shoulder, in a lowered voice, "thirty cents to natives, dressed, and thirty-five to summer folks."

The Shell station these days is a hotbed of political intrigue. Pop Snow is armed to the teeth with brochures and slick-covered magazines extolling the virtues of the Republican party, supplied to him, no doubt, free of charge by the higher ups, since Pop is local chairman of the GOP. Consequently, we've been careful to keep our black briefcase tightly zipped lest Pop and his cohorts spy our own tattered copy of the Democratic Digest when we drop in for our morning chat. Dode Kimball was there today, occupying his usual seat of honor near the door: he'd been growling, according to Snowie, since six o'clock about the lateness of the morning paper, and his fawn boxer, Sonya, was echoing his sentiments. We managed to slip our sylph-like form past the savage beast and took a seat just as Dode began extolling the virtues of his dog. With Dode's usual profanity deleted, here's how it went.

"I've owned a good many blank-blank dogs in my day, but this boxer is the finest animal of 'em all. Goes everywhere with me, too. She likes the front seat, so my wife, Grace, always sits in back when we go for a ride. Sleep with me? Of course she does. Not a flea nor a woodtick on her, so why not? Only trouble is, winter time, I always sleep with the windows wide open, and last year poor Sonya used to get chilly when cool weather came on. I tried an electric blanket for her, but she didn't like being covered up, and I just about made up my mind to close the blank-blank windows, when I remembered about Martin Robbins' dog house. Brand new, it was, shingled, insulated, and Martin's blank-blank dog wouldn't sleep in it. So I bought it for Sonya. Had to take down part of the banister to get it up stairs, and rip the finish off the bedroom door, but there she sets, and when it's cold, why Sonya just jumps off the bed and sleeps in there."

And the boxer looked up at Dode, and twitched the stub of her blank-blank tail, and just then the papers came in, and the session was over; peace, complete peace, reigned in my Pamet.

Somewhere nature has gathered the ingredients for a superior summer day this hot Tuesday in late July. The sun is burning hot through a thin haze of smudge cloud, and the wind is southwest, steady and strong enough to toss the foliage on the glossy green locusts carrying the acrid tang of the scrub pines and the rich odor of the mudflats in the winding Pamet in the valley below. To south'ard the regimented conifers on the hills beyond the Hogsbacks are blended in the distance, and the view of the bay is foreshortened in the smoky afternoon air. Gone is the benzedrine effect of the recent easterly spell, and today is a day for the beach, and for loafing.

But few of the natives can loaf, and Snowie of the Shell Station, when we saw him at noon, was slaving over a flat tire which we consider meet justice for his having attempted to discredit the Provincetown Band by sucking on a lemon near the trumpet section last night at the concert in Wellfleet.

The polio emergency fund turned up richer to the tune of $31.40 as a result of the Cape Cod Ball held at Ballston Beach last Saturday afternoon. Ballet, skits, songs, food sale, white elephant sale, and just plain donations pushed the gross higher and higher. The biggest single sale (dash grabbit, how that man's name always seems to crop up) was $3.50 for a still life in oils—bottles, of course—donated by a local petroleum purveyor, name of

Snowie. The cast and promoters: Bonnie Sue and Duncan Ross, Susan and Jane Hartwig, and Marie Joseph.

Hello folks, Snowie speakin'. Town Father Tommy Kane come into the Shell Station this mornin', and he sez to me, "Up to my ears in work this week, friend, (he must have herd about the Quaker meetin' at Bill Merriss' last week) and I wuz wonderin' if yew would like to rite a guest column fer me. What say?" So I quick took him up on hiz ofer, and here goes. Bizness is quiet these days at the stashun, any how, and I bin spoilin' for months to get a chance to anser sum of the slurs an' insults T.F. has bin throwin' at me.

Mite begin by describin' the weather today, as seen through an artist's eye. The sky is a pale, kinda washed blue, with a few wisps uv cotton-white clouds out over the bay; do 'em with a light touch of the palette knife. Then you blend in the line of the bay with a mite more uv manganese blue an then yew wash the pines kind uv a potato brown with a smidgin uv red. Ended with venetian red and burnt sienna—make the tree trunks good an' bold, silver gray fer the locusts, and that's all the colors Cleve Woodward hez let me use, so far, except for white, and yew kin block out the houses in the valley with that. Make it all stand out good an' clear, because it's a dry northeaster today, an' yew kin see fer miles, almost like an etchin'.

I seen Pop polishin' up his best shoes today, and he had Maw pressin' his purple suit. I hadn't heard uv any funerals in town, so I asked him why he wuz dollin' up. "Primaries, tomorrow," he snapped, "an' you know I'm the warden at the polls." I waited until he got a cigar goin', and then I sez to him, "How come, Pop, you're such a strong Ree-publican?"

"Well, I'll tell you Horace," he sez, "father wuz a Ree-publican, an' hiz father before him, an' I s'pose HIZ father, too. Straight ticket men, all of 'em. Thet's why I can't fathom how come you ever drifted. I remember once, though, I wuz tempted, but I learned my lesson, good an' proper. Your mother an' me, we went out to Butte, Montana, where her folks lived, right after we wuz married. 1912 it wuz, the year Woodrow Wilson, an' Teddy Roosevelt, and Taft wuz all runnin' for president. I got a job, first off, workin' on the street cars. Liked the work first rate; all I did was sit on my stern, an' pull the controls, and collect fares. But then they started hirin' in the Anaconda Copper mines, an' I hed a chance to take a job as pay clerk, so I took it.

"Well sir, they had a strong union in the mines, and they wuz all Democrats. They also hed a trick they used to play on all the green help, kind of an initiation, and I hadn't bin to work more'n a week when they pulled it on me. The elevator operator come over to me this day, and he sez,

'Horace, you've got to go down in the shaft with me an take inventory of the mules, down in level sixty. We do it every year.' So I sharpened a half a dozen pencils an' grabbed som paper, an' stepped into the car. The door clanged shut, and this feller he pushed the lever over hard, and down we went, slow at first, an' then faster an' faster. I began to get a mite nervous, an' looked over at the operator, and cussed if he didn't have the control handle danglin' in his hand—twisted it right off, he had. And he just stood there lookin' foolish, an' then he commenced to fumble with the handle, tryin' to get it back where it belonged. All the time we kept a'droppin' faster and faster, an' still he was fussin' with the lever. Bells started ringin' in my ears, an' I got dizzier every time we shot by each landin'. Last I remember is droppin' to the floor, then everything turned black. Next thing I know, someone wuz throwin' water on me. 'Passed out coldern a well-digger's heel,' someone wuz chucklin' 'an' only half-way down, at that.' I opened my eyes, an' the first thing I saw was the Wilson buttons on the jackets of them cusses. Well sir, I mentally apologized to my ancestors for even thinkin' of goin' astray. Voted Ree-publican then, and every election ever since."

Never did get around to ribbin' Kane, did I? Well, mebbe he'll let me write another colyum sometime.

It's that quiet part of the mid-afternoon when the sounds of the valley have stilled to a pianissimo. The raucous starling fledglings, and the argumentative jay and the rusty sentinel crow who stands watch on the knoll of the Snow Cemetery, have been lulled by the heat of the afternoon sun into a brief siesta. In venerable town hall a buzzing fly aimlessly circles the office, and the Seth Thomas clock on the wall measures out the time with even beat, and next door Squire Dyer worries at his typewriter in bursts of speed. There's a distant, vague hum of traffic on the highway, and the staccato firing of a boat motor out on the bay, which glows a golden flood in the rising afternoon tide. Across the valley a pair of artists in the scanty shade of the locusts are putting the beautiful simple lines of the Congregational church on canvas. And the desultory bark of a dog somewhere across the river floats up on the breeze. Due east, the wind is, dry and light, and there's a faint tracing of cirrus smudge on the southern horizon.

Under the reciprocal agreement between the Lower Cape and the Orleans Ambulance Associations, we occasionally travel out of our territory to transport an up-Cape patient. We made such a trip yesterday when the Orleans dispatcher called to ask for our services: seems the new Orleans ambulance was having a radio installed, couldn't be used. So off we hied to Brewster, there to pick up a man named Ogden, who was going to fetch his wife home from the County Hospital at Pocassett. Turns out Mr. Ogden is a retired railway postal clerk, and, despite twenty-odd years out of harness, he still thrills to the melancholy call of the train whistle and the acrid smell of steam and oil and soft coal smoke. Traveled the Cape run for twenty years, did Mr. Ogden, knew every agent on the road, and most of the folks who frequented the depots at train time. We reminisced for a bit, and recalled the old timers—Ephie Hill and Ike Freeman and Harry McAnistan and Charlie Aydelotte—and then came a yarn.

"Good thing there's so few trains on the Cape nowadays," opined Mr. Ogden. "With all the cars on the roads, there'd be some terrible grade crossing accidents. I recollect the time we was rolling down grade to the Pleasant Lake crossing back in the early twenties, fine summer afternoon. Didn't see it myself, but the engineer, he told me afterwards he caught sight of two men in a buggy galloping down the road abreast of the track, tryin' to beat us to the crossing. Whistle started blasting the regular call—two shorts and two longs, and still that driver kept whipping up his horse.

Well sir, it was too late to put on the brakes, so the engineer just crossed his fingers, and turned his head, and there was a sound of wood busting up and then the brakes jammed on, and we ground to a stop. We grabbed the stretcher out of the mail car, jumped out and ran back to where the two men were lying on the ground. One of the fellows had been thrown against the bell house on the crossing, and he was in bad shape. Other man landed in a patch of cranberry swamp, and he didn't look so bad. Well sir, we wrapped them up with bandages from the first aid kit, and took them into the store on the crossing and left them. When we got to Harwich the station master, name of Cahoon, he pulled out his watch and told us we were almost an hour late. Course we told him about the accident. 'You say you hit old Hank Eldridge and Bert Bearse? Hank in bad shape?' We told him as how we didn't think Hank'd survive. Train was just pullin' out when Cahoon made his prediction. 'He'll live, all right. Hank's got more lives'n a cat.'

"And by gosh he did, too. Top it all off, he sued the railroad in court, won his case. First time I ever heard of gettin' $30,000 for losin' a race."

Up betimes, as day begins to touch the valley. And a poor day it is, what with a heavy overcast, a damp, strong breeze from the southwest, a chill in the air. In the locust thicket behind our house a hassle of bird calls, crows, and jays, and starlings—and the meadow, to our jaundiced eye, has the appearance of the outcropping on a small boy's head following his first baldy sour of the season, as the new cattails sprout above last year's dead growth. Our springer pup, Dolce, sits disconsolately on the porch, sniffing the fitful wind, with its last faint odor of decaying squid from the salt creek and we note that three of the maple saplings we planted last week have succumbed to the dry weather and the other hazards of transplanting.

Al Gengras, former Long Nook summer resident from Hartford, Conn., once told us a yarn about Snowie of the Shell Station which we promised to use only as a last resort. It now being 7:20 of press morning with our cerebrum devoid of any creative thoughts, we are going to tell all.

Seems back in the depressions days, Snowie went up to the big city to find work. The Cape lad ended up in Hartford, and, after pounding the pavement for weeks, he finally got a position as clerk in a clothing store. The salary was meager, the hours long, and the boss was a tight-fisted slave driver who set up quotas for his clerks which were next to impossible to meet.

On the occasion we speak of, an inventory of stock had produced a motley assortment of baggy, poorly-made suits which had been in the store for years. Snowie made the mild suggestion that they be given to the Salvation Army, or some other charitable organization—the boss, in a cruel bit of contrariness, promptly ordered Snowie to move the clothing within a week, or be fired. Well sir, by expert salesmanship, Yankee ingenuity, and horse trading ability inherited from a long line of Truro ancestry, our Pamet lad managed to unload all but one suit.

It was Saturday, and if the final baggy, moth-eaten item were not sold by closing time, Snowie's job ended. Middle of the afternoon, much selling effort expended, and still the suit hung on its rack. Snowie, desperate, offered it at cut prices, willing to make up the difference from his own pay check, but no takers. Just before closing time, the boss went out, briefly, for a delivery, and when he returned to the shop, prepared to terminate the services of his unlucky salesman, he found a bedraggled, bruised, lacerated Snowie, happily ringing up the cash from the sale of the shopworn suit. The boss grudgingly complimented Snowie on his sale, then added, "But what happened to you. Did the customer put up a struggle?" "Oh, no," said Snowie, "but his seeing-eye dog gave me a hard time."

It lacks a few moments before full dusk, and a pale golden afterglow, lacking in warmth, is on the western sky. Overhead the purple clouds, lemon-rimmed, stretch to the ocean in disorderly cirrus formation. The breeze has died to a dead calm, and the dark pines stand like sentinels on

Town Hall Hill. It's getting colder, too; skim ice forming on the puddles by the roadside, and a soiled patch of snow under the beachplum thicket the only trace of the recent snow storm. Down in the valley a pair of mackerel terns are poised over the river, and a flock of crows are winging to their nesting spot in Snow's pines. Life in the village, like the winding Pamet, is at low ebb this mid-December day.

Our first Christmas present arrived today—a montage done artfully and painstakingly by good friend Snowie of the Shell Station. From magazines and periodicals Snowie cut pictures and sketches showing the various things we do, pasting them on an oil-daubed background. Racing ambulances, a portly bartender, a flinty-eyed tax collector and a man tootling on a trombone. Here a begoggled piano player, and in one corner a pedagogue pointing out arithmetic examples on a blackboard. One figure on the montage we cannot explain: a photograph of the ample rear quarters of a horse—Snowie must be referring to that period in our life some years ago when we did a bit of horseback riding. But it's the sentiment behind the gift that counts, and we are deeply touched.

John Worthington showed up while we were in a nostalgic mood, and joined us in reminiscing about the fabulous cars of earlier days: the sporty Mercer, and the powerful Packard twin six, and the Locomobile, and the racy Stutz Bearcat. John used to race Stanley Steamers in competition with the other young bloods around Dedham, Mass. Not conventional races, you understand, but in reverse, no less (the Stanley had equal speed in either direction).

Those were the days when an operator's license could be had by merely writing to the Registry of Motor Vehicles. But John points out that a chauffeur's license required a road test which would put the demonstration of today to shame. "Went into Boston one day with a friend of mine to watch him try for his chauffeur's license. Driving a huge Peerless limousine, I remember, and after we picked up the inspector, it started to rain. We drove out to the Back Bay, turned down one of the narrow side streets, probably Ipswich, or Gloucester St., and the registry man said to my friend, 'I want you to turn around in the street without touching the curbs.' That lad just fed her the gas, twisted the wheel, and jammed on the brakes—the old Peerless skidded around in a 180 degree turn, and the inspector wrote out the chauffeur's license on the spot."

Editor, Provincetown Advocate:

THIS IS IT. He asked for it, Mr. Editor, and I'm going to give it to him. I'm referring, of course, to Horace H. Snow, Jr., and the scurrilous letter which he wrote, published in last week's *Advocate*. For several years I have been abused, vilified, degraded, and, humiliated by this purveyor of watered petroleum. My policy has always been one of tolerance, but I feel the time has come to abandon peaceful co-existence, as they say in world politics, and use the big stick.

May I state categorically to begin with, that I am in no way indebted to Snowie (sneer—as he playfully dubs himself) for any news used in my column. The few items of local interest which come from him have usually been riddled with errors, and were obviously offered to wheedle free advertising for his business. We all make mistakes, and one of my more serious ones was to let this self-same Snowie write a guest column for me one day last summer when I was pressed for time; ever since then he has fancied himself a journalist of the first water (imagine Snowie having anything to do with water, except to shave) and he has been trying to replace me in your fine weekly. I deeply resent Snowie's accusations anent the veracity of my yarns—I am a Democrat, sir—must I say more?

The paragraph I found most insulting, however, was the Snow parody on my opening columns—the weather report and description of the valley. I try to paint with words the scene as I see it; and I know the many faithful readers of my column will join me in condemning Snowie's pseudojuvenile takeoff on my style.

As for food, of course I enjoy it; perhaps I even show it by being a few ounces over weight. But I've never seen Grandma Moses refuse a box of Chinese food fetched by O'Caghan from Boston in the ambulance and remember, Shakespeare says, "Beware yon Cassius, he hath a lean and hungry look." Must've been thinking of the Snow-type physique.

Speaking of painting—we would never have revealed this secret had we not been goaded into it by the Snow letter—we have recently learned that the oils supposedly done by Snowie are actually the work of his Uncle Norman G. Snow, a talented artist. Horace fils, starts each picture in the Shell Station, then spirits the canvas in the dark of night to Uncle Norman's cellar, where Norm ghostpaints the work to completion—they split the selling price, fifty-fifty. Mr. Editor, I am by nature a forgiving man, and, in spite of the grievous wrong done me by Horace H. Snow, Jr., in his recent communication to The Advocate, I am willing to forgive (this being the Christmas season) and forget if the aforementioned gentleman will make a public retraction within a reasonable time. The apology must be written in correct English, of course, with proper spelling and with special attention to the points outlined above. I shall expect him to apologize to my pup, Dolce, my bantam rooster, and my BELOVED wife, mentioning each specifically. He must also write the following five hundred times: "Snowie is the Town Fathead, Tom Kane is Town Father." This latter must be publicly posted in the Shell Station for at least fourteen days.

Sincerely,

Town Father.

And Now . . . My Pamet

It's a reasonably peaceful Tuesday night in the O'Caghan menage. The last of the supper dishes are being stacked away by No. 2 son, and No. 1 son is gathering up his school books for a session with his homework; sons 3 and 4 are hassling over a parlor game, and the family parakeet is engaging in a debate with an oily-voiced TV news commentator. Dolce, the springer pup, wants out at the kitchen door, and mother is pondering over the crossword puzzle. As for T.F., he's seated at the faithful Royal, staring at the empty onion skin sheets, listening to the domestic noises and the burbling of an embolus in the heating pipes, and thinking of today's sudden snowstorm.

The gay cards strung above our fireplace remind us, at this year's end, of the many friends to whom we would like this column to be a personal expression of the season's greetings. To our friends of the Blacksmith Shop, staff and customers; to the fellow Thespians of the Wellfleet Players; to folks we have met in the ambulance; to the faculty and students of Provincetown High School, where we sometimes teach; to the boys and girls of the band; to the summer residents, bless 'em, of Corn Hill, and Tom's Hill, and Ballston Beach, and Long Nook, and the Hogsbacks, to the readers of our little squibs, and last but not least, to all our neighbors and friends of Pamet—may we take this opportunity of wishing you all a very Merry Christmas and a happy and prosperous New Year.

P.S. Yes, and Snowie, too.

NINETEEN FIFTY-FIVE

1 9 5 5

We got to thinking, as we watched the TV tonight, how poor Tooch Gray would have enjoyed this latest gift of science to the amusement world. Tooch was an inverterate movie-goer, and he used to throw himself whole-heartedly into the spirit of the picture, be it a dusty western or a spine-tingling mystery. Going to the movies was a big event in the old days. Folks didn't have cars in those times, and on Saturday nights Charlie Snow would put his big yellow school bus at the disposal of the public—25 cents for the round trip to Provincetown, meet at Truro Square at 7 in the evening. The kids would have their price of admission and an extra dime to buy candy or soda pop, and when the bus had loaded, off we'd roll to the Cape end, sneaking a smoke behind the seats in the back row. There'd be some impromptu group singing en route, and much horseplay as friends from North Truro boarded in the neighboring village.

When Charlie ground to a stop before the garishly lighted marquee of the theatre, there'd be a wild rush for the door, and a confused queuing of Truroites at the ticket window. The beefy special cop would cast a suspicious eye at the outlanders looking for contraband peanuts in the shell, and we'd press upstairs to the balcony and land down as far front as space would permit. In the few brief moments before the show began there'd be mild bedlam—tussles among the boys, catcalls, whistles, paper airplanes sailing down into the audience below. Then the piano player would take her seat at the battered upright, the lights would dim, and the stirring strains of "Connecticut March" would break through the din.

At this point Tooch would kick off his shoes and settle down for an evening of solid enjoyment. He'd peel the wrapper from a candy bar as the newsreel flashed on the screen. The chocolate would be gone as "Coming Features" flickered into view, and Tooch would break out a formidable plug of chewing tobacco and work up a satisfactory cud. They used to have serials in those days; endless, complicated thrillers to leave you tingling as the heroine slid helplessly into a stone crusher or the juvenile lead, his foot jammed into a railroad switch, waited for sure death under the wheels of an approaching locomotive. Tooch would live every second of the drama. "Look out behind you," he'd shout, when the hero was about to be ambushed by a knife-wielding villain. And when the love scenes bored him Tooch would expectorate a stream of tobacco juice at the floor.

They say neighbor Gray was ejected bodily from the movie house the night they played "Tale of Two Cities"; had to give the manager his word of honor he'd never let himself go like that again. Tooch managed to contain himself with reasonable decor until the guillotine scene. Then, as the helpless hero was dragged from the tumbril, strapped to the board, and the heavy, keen knife was hoisted to its position aloft, the Truro man was unable to look at the picture, closed his eyes and leaned forward in his seat. At that precise moment, someone behind reached forward and clipped Tooch smartly with the edge of a program, directly on the collar line. Quiet as the tomb, it was, and every cussword that Tooch emitted could be heard from one end of the movie hall to the other. "Make matters worse," Tooch said after the show, "I swallowed my cud, sat on my Sunday hat, and the cop wouldn't even give me time to find my shoes."

Notes on a northeaster. Our venerable old Cape Cod cottage is vibrating tonight in the elemental fury of a late winter storm of near-gale intensity. We watched the developing pattern of the storm from town hall between chores today. At mid-morning a perceptible thickening in the rolled clouds to eastward, and a freshening of the fitful ocean wind. By noontime the scattered rain drops had settled into a driving, steady rain, and the eaves of the building echoed the hollow sound of a breeze become half-gale in force. And now the night outside is black, and wet, and lit by sudden flashes of lightning, and in the occasional lulls of the blow the distant thunder of surf can be heard on the Back Shore. Somewhere on the house a loosened blind punctuates with sudden clarity the drumming of rain on the clapboards. And the wild sound of the wind in the locusts rises and falls in volume as the storm rushes down-valley.

This week's meeting of the Hook, Stitch and Chatter Club will be held on Thursday at the home of Mable Small in North Truro. The Shell Station these days is becoming a sort of gallery for sundry works of art. Last week, for instance, in addition to the usual Snow oil colors, we inspected a winter scene in water color medium by Dr. Gerald Hoeffel, a fine model whale boat fashioned by Walter Gonsalves, and a pair of miniature wooden ducks, expertly carved by Joe "Curley" Francis. In the near future, Snowie plans to show Johnny (Hillside Farm) Perry's collection of buttons (political, that is) all Republican, needless to say.

We are indebted to Tony Duarte, Pamet's insurance broker, for the following yarn. Tony has been spending a good deal of time in Orleans since last fall, in pursuit of a private flying license in order to coordinate his newly-purchased hotel business in Jackton, Maine, with his local real estate and insurance operations. On days not suitable for flying this winter, Tony has been passing the time of day at Sky Meadow Field, absorbing flying technique second hand, and listening to the yarns of the pilots and the ground crew. "They have a big moosehead hanging on the wall up there," said Tony, "and the expression on the animal's face attracted me from the first time I saw it. Kind of a pained, drawn look, and believe it or not, the poor cuss seems to be looking backwards, and sort of downwards. Didn't seem as though any competent taxidermist would've mounted the head that way, so I asked a fellow, name of Harris, who frequents the airport, what he knew about the beast. I certainly asked the right man.

"Seems this Harris had been chiefly responsible for capturing the moose, but not with a gun, nor a bow and arrow, or any conventional weapon. A party of Orleans men had gone up to Maine on a hunting trip a few years back, and were just making the final run of the journey to a lodge in some obscure, wilderness village in an ancient Model A Ford. They had stopped the car for lunch in an overgrown dirt road, and had just unwrapped their mashed Eastham turnip sandwiches, when Harris happened to look out the back window; lo and behold, there was the biggest blackest moose he'd ever seen, sniffing at the Massachusetts number plate of the Model A. Well sir, those Orleans men were in quite a predicament; every last rifle had been taken down and packed securely with the luggage, and they realized that by the time a firearm could be assembled, the old moose would be long gone.

"Harris was looking wildly around the car, and finally spied a can of turpentine and a brush in the midst of the gear (the boys had been planning to do a bit of painting at the lodge) and he quick grabbed the two items, slipped out of the door to leeward, sneaked up in back of the moose, and daubed a big brushfull of turps on the hind quarters of the unsuspecting beast. The moose let out a bellow of pain, dropped to his haunches, and started dragging himself off up the road by his forefeet, glancing back over his shoulder at his tingling tail-end." Tony says he interrupted Harris at this point to observe that the boys probably found time then to unlimber their rifles and shoot the animal. "'Shucks, no,' replied Harris, 'didn't have time to do that. We jammed the Ford in gear, and lit out after the moose. Caught up with him about a mile down the road. Good thing we made such fast time, too, because when we jumped out and grabbed him, he'd chafed himself on that gravel road right up to the shoulders. Taxidermist only had to trim off an inch or two. Another quarter of a mile, I figger, we'd a had nothing but a pair of horns.'"

At one period in our life our favorite reading consisted of the short stories of O. Henry, and memories of pleasant moments spent over his "Gentle Grafter" came back to us this morning as we sat in the Shell Station and listened to Charlie Snow tell of his adventures in the city with a confidence man. It all started when Chief Berrio came in with a fist full of mail, among which were several pictures of wanted criminals. Charlie was looking over his shoulder at the mug shots, and one of them evoked a grunt of recognition from Pamet's superintendent of streets.

"Harold, that feller's a dead ringer for a man tried to flim-flam me one day in Boston. I was up there on vacation—fall of the year—stayin' with my cousin Henry up on Beacon Hill. Henry told me when I left his rooms in the mornin' not to talk to strangers, and to keep my money in a safe place. I took his advice. I had my roll of bills—thirty-eight dollars—all fastened with elastic bands, pinned to my undershirt, and I had some coins in my pants pocket case I wanted to buy somethin' to eat. Well sir, soon's lunch time I was down by the Custom House, and I was leanin' back against a buildin' across the street, lookin' way up at that tower, when all of a sudden I felt someone nudge me in the ribs. I quick looked around, and there was this fancy Dan standin' right next to me. All dressed up, he was, with a pair of spats, and a striped suit, and a black derby. 'Stranger,' he sez to me, 'I wonder if you could change a twenty-dollar bill for me?' I got suspicious right away, and I asked him, 'Why don't you step into one of these stores?' 'Why, mister,' says the city slicker, 'I have an eye condition—can't see well indoors—and last time I passed paper money in a store, a dishonest clerk cheated me. But I can tell you're an honest man.'"

Charlie says he was so touched by the poor fellow's story that he unbuttoned his vest, pulled out his shirt tail, and started probing for his roll of paper money. Just got it unpinned and commenced to peel off the elastic band, when suddenly a big, red-faced individual came charging up the sidewalk and collared both Charlie and the man in the derby.

"Took us both down to the police station," said Charlie. "Never was so embarrassed in my life—people starin' at us in the street, me with my shirt tail still flapping—and finally he dragged us up before another policeman, sittin' at a bench. 'Well, well,' sez the sergeant, 'if it ain't Derby Dan—or what name are you usin' this week?' No time at all, they took him off to jail, and then they turned to me. They had quite a time makin' up their mind whether I was an accomplice or a victim, I guess, because they made me produce my money to see if it was counterfeit, like the stuff this Dan feller had been carryin'. I remember when I unwrapped the roll, one of them silver shiners flew out of a crease in the bills, and the cops started to laugh, and the sergeant said, 'O.K. boys, let him go. But keep away from Federal St., mister. There's a guy down there will sell you the South Station for fifty dollars.' I dunno what he said that for. All I had was thirty-eight dollars, anyhow."

It wants to clear; there's still a bank of sepia fog in the valley, and the dampness of last night's storm is in the beaded grass and the dripping foliage; but now and again the bright, warm sun finds a hole in the overcast, and the breeze is freshening from the southwest. From Town Hall Hill the visibility varies with tantalizing irregularity as the fog thickens and dissipates. Now the stones of the Snow Cemetery across the hill are wraithed in mist; comes a puff of wind and the rolling Hogsbacks to southard stand, clear-etched in a brilliant pool of sunlight. The birds, in the pine thicket below the hill, are in a riot of song, and from somewhere across the marsh comes the muffled, uneven thump of carpenters at work. Down the coast the fog-horn at Highland sends out its warning to ocean traffic, and the dank, briny smell of the sea gives way, as the day warms, to the lush, rich tang of growing things in the sunlight. The summer population is burgeoning as good weather hits the narrow land. Each week, as city schools close, the summer folks arrive, city-pale, luggage-laden, come to take the cure of Pamet sun and salt air.

To the many friends we have made during the past decade or so we have served as driver of the Lower Cape Ambulance: sincere thanks to all of you who have said nice things to us since we announced our intention of resigning the position. Ambulance driving is the kind of job that gets into your blood, and now that our term of duty is almost completed, we'd like to reminisce, for a bit, with our readers. We've been married to the big, white car for a long time, and, as is the case in most marriages, there have been trying moments. The pay has been small in proportion to the hours on call, but we've always felt that a large part of our compensation came in the form of intangibles—a warm handclasp from a grateful patient, a sincere blessing from a poor soul from Provincetown's West End (you don't have to know much Portuguese at a time like that) a packet of catfish, neatly skinned, a poem, even, from a grand old fellow we used to visit in the ward, at Cape Cod Hospital.

Oh certainly that's part of the job, along with emptying bed pans, and helping to prep a patient on the emergency table, and telling the big, white lie to the members of the family waiting in the accident room, when you know, from the attitude of the doctor as he feels for the thready, fluttering pulse, that the broken body is losing its life at every breath.

And you can't push your empty cot down the corridor, past the ward doors, without stopping in to say a word or two to patients you've brought in previously. Give 'em a big grin, and tell them how chipper they look, and spin the yarn for them about the doctor and the thermometers, and slip away while they're still laughing.

We've seen life begin and end on the gay red blankets of our ambulance, and when we've been close by at the birth of a baby, we've had the universal, foolish grin that comes to all men, and especially fathers, when the first wail comes from a living bundle. And when the sand runs out on the other end of the life line, we try to remember to do the decent things—call the priest, or break the news as gently as we can to the family. It's been a satisfying job, one that develops many qualities in a man, and before we become maudlin about the matter, we'll close the column.

Mr. Editor and gentle readers: We submit that today in Pamet is such a perfect one as to rate a few lines of description. Gone is the humidity and sultry heat of the week's opening days, swept from the Narrow Land by a brisk, steady northerly breeze. Nary a cloud in the sky, which is this morning, of an intense, crystalline blue. The landscape is clear-etched, from the scrub pine hills to the bare Hogsbacks to the poverty grass patches on the General Fields, to the lush green cattails on the valley. There's the spicy smell of wild honeysuckle on the meadows, and the pleasing acrid tang of pine needles in the early morning sun. Below the hill of town hall a quail breaks out into sudden song, and the cricket chorus forms background music for the rasping call of the cicada. Far off across the bay, the headlands of Manomet loom sepia-gray on the horizon, and a lone whitetail hawk soars above the bend in the river at Monroe's landing. But now a blue bottle fly zooms through the open door, and the ticking of our office clock reminds us that there are chores to be done, and we to our chronicling. We feel moved to turn the key in the door and spend a vagrant hour or so touring the byroads of Pamet on an informal junket. Care to come along?

Let's start across the Wellfleet line, and enter Truro by way of Pamet Point Road. We're heading westerly now, down-valley toward Old County Road. The white oak copse gradually thins, and soon we're passing the big locust stand that brings us in the clearing where Si Clark's house overlooks the road. Cape folks like locusts, by the way, since the nodules in the tree's roots fix nitrogen in the soil, and the grass is always green under them. Well sir, Si's gardens look as beautiful as ever, with neatly trimmed shrubbery and rich, weed free soil, and a riot of colors from the August flowers. Take it slowly around the hairpin turn onto Old County Road, and glance out on the meadow, where a fringe of pale old maid's pink frames the dark green of the cattails, and look for the big, faded blossoms of the marsh mallow. Better not pick them, because the mallow wilts rapidly as a cut flower.

Now here on your right, just past the town line, is the brushtangled entrance to Paradise Valley. Time was when several families lived up there, and the cellar holes can still be found, each with a clump of lilac or honeysuckle. Follow the old weed-green cartroad far enough, and you'll come to Johnson's Pond. With luck, we could still find the foundations of old George Richardson's cottage. George was the last of Truro's hermits; lived all alone in his dilapidated house, and, to save labor, he'd cut whole trees in the woods, feed them into his stove as they burned. Of course the house was a mite smoky, but people smoke tobacco, too, as George always used to say.

Now, as we make the turn to northward out of Ryder Beach Road, we're coming up onto the true Hogsbacks. The name originated in the days when the mariners of South Truro, returning from their trips to sea, first caught sight of the head lands of their beloved village. Seen from the bay, the barren, hog cranberry-covered hills look not unlike a litter of piglets feeding at a trough. Over that hill, there, is the home of Col. and Mrs. Dick Magee. Her father was Elisha W. Cobb, a local boy who went up to the city, borrowed the last dollar of his family's savings to buy a partnership in the infant leather firm which later became one of the largest in the world—Beggs and Cobb. Mr. Cobb remembered the town of his birth in later years with the donation of a beautiful library, and Mrs. Magee preserved the tradition of philanthropy when she gave to Truro, in the memory of her parents, the town clock atop Cobb Library and a set of Westminster chimes located in town hall belfry. The chimes, by the way, will be restored to good working order this summer.

As we come down off the Hogsbacks of South Truro, past Iselin's house on the left, and "Thousand Dollar Hill," so-called because the wealthy New York family paid this (at that time) fantastic price for the land. Down at the bottom of the hill here, where Snake Pond creek trickles under the road, is the driveway leading into Grove's Crossing. Phat Francis lives in there, and beyond his home is the cottage of Henry Varnum Poor, well-known artist, and his wife, Bessie Brewer Poor, novelist and short-story writer.

Now let's travel up Holsbery Road. The locust-shaded entrance, off Depot Road, gives onto the higher elevation of the open hills, and eventually runs down onto the meadow where Waldo Frank, famed author, lives. Up through the pines, on a small knoll near Powers' driveway is one of Truro's tiny smallpox cemeteries, located in this isolated location as a precautionary measure in connection with the dread disease.

As we browse around the entrance to Hatch Road, on our right, nestled below the hill is Arrowsmith's Swamp which boasts, each fall, one of the finest displays of autumn foliage to be seen hereabouts; in the spring you can usually hear the first peewink of the season at this same spot. This tiny bowl on your left used to be the "Hallow" playground used by the kids of Wilder School in the old days. We used to play baseball down there, and eat our lunches in the shelter of the gnarled apple tree. See those blue spruce along the fence line? Given to the school by the Grange some years ago, they were planted by the boys under the direction of Mr. Joe Peters, then, as now, the principal of Pamet's school. And here, in the fork of the road is Wilder School itself, built in the style of all public buildings of the period: severely plain and box-like, with heavy box trim and high studs, and painted, of course, traditional yellow with green finish.

When the town outgrew the two-room building in the early thirties, the new consolidated school was built over in Whitmanville, and the post office was moved into the Wilder building. Arthur Joseph, the new owner, made some changes, of course. He tore off the cloakroom, with its big dusty coal-bin, and the rows of hand wrought spikes where generations of Truro children had hung their clothes, and he replaced the venerable, creaking hand pump with a new-fangled electric pump. The blackboards were removed, and the pot-bellied stoves gave way to modern heating equipment, and the banks of mail boxes were installed; but we can still close our eyes and see the "Big Part" room exactly as it was when we have time to reminisce. It's a mite difficult, we'll admit, to conjure up the picture of the king-size privy that used to nestle in the clump of beach plum bushes off there to east'ard. Arthur should have kept that, we submit; would have made a good waiting room for the bus.

We're stopping for a breather atop the knoll overlooking the George Joseph property, and down on the left, we're pointing out the home of E.J. Kahn, star reporter for the New Yorker Magazine. In our day, this house has been known variously as the Atkins, the Joe King, and the Washburn cottage. We'd like to digress for a moment and spin a yarn they tell hereabouts concerning old Joe King. A Portuguese immigrant with scarce command of the language of his foster home, Joe went before the town clerk, a Yankee, of course, to register as an alien. Joe's real name was Joaquinho del Rica, and the clerk found it too difficult to spell, so he entered it simply as Joseph King; other branches of the family settled in New Bedford and apparently had similar difficulties, since they are now known as the Reesers. Joe might have found the language puzzling, but the soil responded to his green thumb; he was known as one of the best farmers in Truro.

Brother Kane stopped by the Shell Stashun this morning in an awful tizzy. "Snowie, ole pal," he sez to me, "I'm all druv up with chores, and I jest can't find time to rite my colyum, and I wuz wonderin' if you could help me out this week, and act as guest conducter." First off, I wuzn't gonner help hem, and then I thought uv the big bill he owes me, an I figgered maybe he'd be slow on payin' if i refoosed, so here goes nuthin'. I took out one uf Kane's old colyums, an' decided ter foller his formatt, I guess they call it, an' here t'is.

Mr. Editor, pleez correct the spellin' an puncktewashin' if necessary. Well sir, the weather is about the same. Fine October days, coolish in the mornings, shirt sleeve weather when it comes midday, and excellent for sleeping when the sun sets. And the town is pretty as a picture, as any artist like myself can testify. The valley has the mature loveliness of a woman in the prime of life. There are still patches of brilliant color, but the true outline of the hills shows as the foliage thins. You can see more browns and grays, and the cattails which were lush green yesterday are now drab, but natural as they stand on the banks of the limpid, meandering Pamet. Shucks, I could do better with my oils, and if you don't believe it, drop in to the station and see some of my work. I'm doing a sort of composite scene of South Truro, with a big oak tree the main figure, and the medium I'm using is ground brick dust, chiefly, mixed with lubricating oil from the store room, and it's too bad I can't give the brand name. The picture calls for bold strokes, so I'm applying the stuff with a tire iron. . . .

Today's weather has been fine enough to suit the most critical. It's been warm enough to fling wide the doors and windows to welcome the rich, earthy smell of fallen leaves in the mellow October sun, and the sky has worn on its perimeter the delicate smoke-blue haze of late autumn, which blends the distant dunes into the glistening waters of the bay, and masks the harshness of the pine hills. Frosts we've had lately, chill sheets of white that turn to myriad jewels in the early rays of the sun, and a goodly amount of ocean rain that keeps the grass lush and green while the withered foliage of the oaks and the locusts lose their brilliant colors and scatter before the fitful winds. This is the season when the black duck flies in precise formation up-valley, and the cock pheasant struts from his cover over freshly-harrowed garden plots, and the cottontail rabbit explodes from the clumped beachplum of the roadside.

Some prudent folks are starting to hang their storm sash, against the first, inevitable cold snap, and tomorrow taxes start to draw interest, and cider's on the market, and plans are being laid for family reunions at Thanksgiving, and term marks go out on report cards for the school kids the weekend, as we prepare for the eleventh month. This afternoon at town hall we queried Chief Berrio of Truro's finest as to his Halloween plans. "Don't anticipate much vandalism," allowed the chief, "but I'll have a skeleton crew on duty, just in case." We wondered if Harold could be working a pun on us, as we conjured up the vision of the department's second-in-command, 350-lb. Ray Enos.

And speaking of viands and such, we're reminded of Wannie Rich's yarn anent the first time he was assigned to a cooking chore at Highland Coast Guard Station, some years back. "Never had cooked so much as a boiled egg up to that time," reminisces the old timer. "A hungry crew waitin' for chow, and nothin' in the butt'ry but a half dozen rabbits that Hiram Hatch had shot the day before, I asked Hiram how to cook the cussed things, and he sez to me, 'Why you just take and stew 'em. Put in a turnip or two, an' half a dozen potatoes, an' some onions, an' some carrots.' I thought I'd serve up the stew real fancy-like, same's they do in first-class restaurants, so I dished it out in soup plates, and covered each one with another plate, tipped upside down. My, you should hev seen the expression on the crew's face when they uncovered that stew. Hiram, y'see had forgotten to tell me you had to skin the rabbits."

But let us hie off on the next leg of the O'Caghan guided tour of Pamet. You'll recall we're almost finished with the Pamet loop, making up grade on North Pamet to the hill overlooking Joe Duarte's handsome cottage to our left, overlooking the river, with the parsonage on our right. Just changed hands, has the parsonage, now belongs to Jack and Laurel Carleton, Ballston Beach colonists these many years. A few years back, North Pamet used to run close up against the bank through the alder swamp and out onto the state highway in the square, but now the new highway layout calls for you to drive down the service ramp, back under the bridge, and so onto Wilder's Dyke. Here on your left is a cluster of yellow-painted buildings which might be described as the focal point of social life in Truro.

We're referring of course, to Snow's Shell Station. Here's where folks get their newspapers, and things automotive, and good conversation, and convivial companionship. Here Horace Snow Sr., better known as Pop, is in his tiny office back of the candy counter. He's working on his books, wants everything in good shape before he sets out for Florida, end of the month. If you can see through the blue cloud of cigar smoke, perhaps you can make out some of Pop's keepsakes: a letter file made from wood from the bark Castagna, sunk in a furious gale off the back shore; a captain's bar from the steamer Portland; a collection of pictures showing various views of the ship Jason; a snap of the crack North Truro Baseball team; a bronze letter-box drop from the old South Truro post office, and a collection of Republican campaign buttons.

This handsome, be-moustached young gentleman who stands brooding before a crude oil painting abaft the toucan cage would be Snowie, and there are probably other members of the Snow clan, settin' a spell, and gossiping. We'll head north, now, across the Dyke, with a passing glance at the Pamet, where she turns salt at the tide gate. Over on the far end of the dyke there's a tiny mudhole (we've heard tell it's all that remains of an early salt water evaporator) where Curley Francis' horse almost drowned some years ago. It happened one afternoon just as school was letting out, and we kids had a ringside seat at the exciting event. The unfortunate nag had slipped out of his pasture, jogged along the highway, and evidently had been tempted by a clump of salt meadow grass on the edge of the sloughhole. By the time word got around, the poor beast was stuck fast to his withers.

A hasty call was put in to Arthur Joseph's house, and in jig time, Art appeared on the scene, clad in rubber boots, and toting a coil of heavy rope. Somebody fetched a long plank, and Art gingerly stepped out on the makeshift bridge, and slipped a noose over the horse's head. The free end of the line was made fast to Arthur's truck, we recall, and the ancient Reo ground into gear and slowly took up the slack. The rope stretched a good bit, and so did the horse's neck, but finally, with a soft, sucking noise, the animal was extricated from the mud and stood shivering, free, and not too much the worse for wear. Arthur said afterwards you could handle a horse's neck like a politician handles the truth: it'd stretch a-plenty before it would tear.

Bedtime in the O'Caghan menage. In the next room the TV wrings drama from the tortured lips of a gray-haired lady, "Is-is my boy badly hurt?" Comes the sudden, sobering punctuation of the toilet bowl flushing; the slam of the refrigerator door as one of the younger males forages for food; the uneven thumping rhythm of our pup Dolce, worrying at a flea. The clink of an air bubble threads its way through the baseboard radiators, and we hear the piping treble of the young fry saying their prayers in the farther bedroom. The family cat paces stiff-legged in to visit us, his tail a stiff question mark, reflecting the mild curiosity in his eyes. Outside on

Pamet Road a solitary car spins up the road, and some board in the side-chamber overhead creaks comfortingly. The mood of the TV program changes, crash of music, unctuous-tongued announcer, and we to our chronicling.

These days our schedule is so full we have little enough time to travel the byroads of Pamet, and our weather report must needs be done through the windows of a classroom (our homeroom at Wellfleet High School looks out on an uninteresting stretch of barren sand and scrub pine) or perchance from the window of our faithful vehicle as we wend our way late in the afternoon to chores at town hall. Our valley is still beautiful, in a bare, rugged fashion. The oaks and the locusts have surrendered to the frosts, and the slightest breeze serves to strip the drab remaining foliage from the alders and the choke cherries. The cattails are a solid carpet of sere withes, and only the huckleberries hold a faint, burned crimson color. At dusk, the telephone wires are strung with black birds, and bosky rabbits scurry along the roadsides, and the hunters say that foxes are plentiful this fall. Come the next moonlit night, and we'll hear the coon call in the valley, and see the skunk family foraging for beetles among the poverty grass. Pleasant enough is the weather, except for rainy weekends.

Joe and Ethel Duarte have returned from Boston with their daughter, Donna, and the young lady is much improved after observation at the Children's Hospital. Much excitement the weekend when Dotty Boyd and several of the neighborhood kids found what they thought was the wreckage of the missing jet plane in the surf off Ballston Beach. In no time the dunes were swarming with Air Force personnel (who landed in a helicopter) but the wreckage turned out to be that of a buzz plane (radio controlled plane used for target practice by the (A.F).

Ready for another installment of the O'Caghan guided tour of Pamet? We were in the tiny hamlet of Snowville, on Castle Road. We'll say a few words about old C.W. Snow's neighborhood water system, the source of which was that battered windmill that stands down in the bottom, next the Snow homestead. On the property you'll also find the famed Long Shop, where Mr. Snow used to do his carpenter work, and on occasion, try out blackfish "melons" when the big, oil-bearing fish came ashore on the Lower Cape. Over against the bank is the Snow barn, a big, well-built structure which housed for many years the Snow horses, and cows, and pigs. Down in the cellar you can still see the remnants of old C.W.'s concrete block machine— another first for Truro in the Snow enterprises. Son Charlie lives across the street. Charlie is the town supt. of streets, a title he inherited from his dad, and although folks are happy with Charlie's work on the roads, they miss the flowery reports that the old gentleman used to write for the annual town book.

Back from the deadend roadway then, onto Castle Road, and continuing towards Corn Hill we find Isaiah Snow's house, and, a mite further along, and high up on the pine hill, Alfred Smith's Mizzentop. There's a steep dip in the road here, and a dyked inlet where C. W. Snow used to raise the biggest potatoes ever. Son Horace "Pop" Snow says it only took three of 'em to fill a wheelbarrow. As we start to climb the grade going northerly, there's a level spot on our left where once stood Truro's poorhouse.

The poorhouse, so they say, was used for the accommodation not only of indigent persons, but for folks as wasn't quite right in the head. One yarn has it that when Josh Ryder was driving by one day with a wagon load of ripe barnyard manure (the natives still call it "dressing") one of the Knowles brothers, sunning himself in the poorhouse yard, called out to ask what Josh intended using the dressin' for. Josh tolerantly replied as how he was goin' to spread it on his strawberries. Knowles burst at once into laughter, and when Josh queried him as to the reason, he chuckled, "I-gorry. Here at the poorhouse we spread sugar an' milk on OUR strawberries."

It is with a touch of sadness that we report the sale, in the very near future, of the Shell Station in Truro by our sometime friend, Snowie, to Norman Lee. With the passing of the papers will pass one of Pamet's established institutions, and we know we voice the sentiment of all the patrons of the station when we say that we will miss the ministrations of the handsome, genial, gray-thatched Snowie. We understand Norm intends to remodel the buildings, using the establishment as a show room and nerve center for his contracting business, while continuing to dispense petrol and allied products. To Snowie, in whatever his plans for the future may be, good luck; and to Norm Lee, sincere best wishes for prosperity and success in the new venture.

These snow flakes in the valley, says Norm Snow, are too big and fluffy to make a real storm. Wind is almost due north, too, and the thermometer is down in the low twenties, and bird traffic is all off shore. Never heard of seagulls heading for the bay with bad weather brewing, did you? Now you take the way the clouds made up, early, with a kind of false dawn—that's a sure sign of clearing before noon. And so the prognostications ran as Norm made his pronouncements in the Shell Station. But it's almost noon now, and the snow is falling thicker, blowing in dry, powdery sprays across the blacktop parking space at town hall. The breeze has freshened and backed more into the northeast, rising in pitch and volume in its song in the eaves. It's probably a mite warmer, too, although we have no outside glass to check the temperature. And just now as we stared out at the swirling, flake-filled scene—gently tossing scrub pine, snow filled patches of red-brown poverty grass—we heard the mewing of seagulls returning with the tide.

Something of the vague restlessness of the day has transmitted itself to us, we note, as we prowl from window to window at town hall, studying the scene this late December day. Strikingly beautiful of nights is the Congregational Church, floodlighted this holiday season. Not since the days of Pamet's glory has the steeple glowed at night, and in those days the flickering light of whale-oil lamps served as a bearing for vessels making into Truro harbor.

There's an almost tangible aura of peace in the Snow Cemetery, across the hill; the geometric lines and angles of the stones softened by the snow veil; winding sand ruts slowly filling, harsh scars of a sunken grave blending under a sheet of white. Off to south'ard the grim scaffolding of the MIT radar towers looms through the storm only faintly, and the Hogsbacks are lost to sight in a sudden squall. Wish you were here, good summer folks, to visit for a spell, in this week between the holidays, and to set before a glowing fireplace, and walk a brisk bit on the moors, in the biting wind, and to smell, when the weather changes, the tang of the ocean as fog rolls up the valley.

The sad business of changing owners goes on at the Shell Station these days. Snowie has been clearing out his personal belongings while Norm Lee casts the practiced eye of a contractor over the buildings. A partition to be removed here, a new sill to be installed there, change in wiring, plumbing, painting. The genial artist-proprietor was a bit misty-eyed as we talked over how nice folks have been when they learned of his plans. "Got dozens of letters from all over," said Snowie, "tellin' me how they'd miss me. Gives you a kind of warm feelin' inside." For our part, we helped ourself to a tissue handkerchief from the showcase, and daubed surreptitiously at our eyes. "Remember when you used to have that sign in your window, nights? 'When the light's lit, I'm out. When the light's out, I'm lit.'" Snowie acknowledged our little contribution to the "remember-when" session.

"Can you ever forget that big Packard roadster I had, used to send it across the dyke, when you worked in Joe's package store," continued Snowie, "and it would come back across, all by itself, with a wee poteen?" Much slow head-shaking, and clucking of tongues. "And that mongrel pup, Penny, I had. Died under the wheels of a car when I went to work in

Connecticut, during the war; always wished I could've buried him in Truro where he belonged."

We swallowed a big lump in our throat, and managed to blurt out, "How about the time the practical joker dropped a pile of clothes above the tide clapper, with a suicide note saying the poor man had plunged into the Pamet? Dave Francis, the town constable, spent half a day probing the river with an eel spear, looking for the body—always figured those clothes came from the Shell Station."

Tuesday, December 20, 8:30 of the evening—and a bitter cold night it is. Not since the memorable town meeting day of 1943 have we seen it so cold. When last we looked at the thermometer on the back porch, the mercury stood at 8 above zero—and this is 8 above with a brisk, bitter wind out of the northwest. A brief glance at the sky confirms the fact that the cloud scud is still there, blotting out the brittle, flickering light of the stars. Comes the occasional rattle of a loose blind on our house to break the stillness, and a dry locust limb creaks mournfully in the breeze. But the scene in the O'Caghan menage is reasonably peaceful—a roaring blaze in the fireplace—muffled treble voices of the younger fry making much ado about retiring in the farther bedrooms. Dolce, the springer pup snoring near the warm hearth, and the family cat has crammed his bulk into a tiny discarded Christmas carton, his twitching tail indicating some sort of wild dream. Strung on the wall is our first batch of Christmas cards, and their gay, bright colors are good for the soul.

NINETEEN FIFTY-SIX

1956

A welcome break in the weather, this; since early morning the Narrow Land has been fog-wraithed, for sometime during the night a mass of warm air moved out from the mainland, raising the temperature to a moderate 40, and there she stands now, as the last of the melted snow drips from the gutter. The topsoil abaft our porch, iron hard with frost these past few days, is a small quagmire of black mud, bearing the tracks of the local young fry and the neighborhood dogs. The serpentine fresh Pamet still has in its coils the half-rotten ice of the recent cold spell, and out on the tide water side broken white cakes fill the river bed from bank to bank.

In the dark, damp night air, the smell of salt from the ocean is strong, and the sound of the fog horn booms along the back shore from Highland, and the friendly wraith moves in closer as the breeze freshens. The old timers had a phrase for a sudden warm spell like this. "January thaw," Ed Snow would allow, pleased-like, as he loosened a button or two of his Brown's Beach Jacket. "When the day's lengthen, cold'll strengthen" would be John Adams' sour retort. And, much as we dislike admitting it, John was more often right than not.

Take, for instance, the coldest spell recorded in recent times in Truro. Feb. 15, 1943, town meeting day, third Monday of the month, that would be. Readings on the glass varied about town from eleven to fifteen below zero at 10 in the forenoon—and this with a biting, strong northwest wind, straight from the bay. We know because we considered the information important enough to be included with our report of the business meeting, and so we set down the facts for some future Town Clerk to see and marvel at. Only 50 people voted at the polls that morning (couldn't heat the upstairs auditorium, so voting was adjourned to the downstairs dining room). And when the ballots were sorted and counted, we were privileged to record a unanimous vote for O'Caghan for clerk, treasurer and collector, a situation undoubtedly never to be repeated.

We've just finished reading Mary McCarthy's "Charmed Life," as cruel a caricature of Lower Cape life, native and summer colony, as ever we've seen. One of the best ways to break the conversational ice is to mention the book—you'll be deluged with positive statements as to the characters—and no two readers will list the same people. Although the ambulance driver was mentioned briefly in the novel, we disclaim any pleasure at having been identified, however anonymously, with midnight calls to a drunken orgy, promoted by summer folks. And the village idiots, and incompetent sales clerks—is this the way we really look to you, good summer people? As a matter of fact, we're so aroused by the McCarthy book that we've decided to collaborate with Snowie, and take a Sunday afternoon to put together a sort of rebuttal to "Charmed Life."

The outline for the first chapter goes something like this: scene opens with local real estate agent salting uranium deposit in sand bank of old Cape property. Neighborhood garage owner (he's really a second cousin to the realtor—these Truro folks are all related) drops by to service car of summer tenant in aforesaid old Cape property; just happens to have geiger counter in car, picks up radioactive impulses. Greedy summer tenant steals property for ten times its actual value. Summer tenant has huge house warming when papers are passed, but has difficulty hiring local help (the electrician, the plumber, the paperhanger would all prefer to go fishin' rather than make money) but the S. T. manages to hire the local idiot to tend bar, and they all sit around eating pickerel-weed sandwiches while the guests discuss the finer points of Portuguese folk dances. There has to be a touch of violence, of course, so we'll have our S. T. and two of his female guests, at whom he has been casting lecherous glances, fall through the floor which has been weakened by termites. The discussion upstairs, however, continues unabated, and corporatists (and since we lean to corporatism, we'll naturally have the latter win the argument). Comes time for the folks to go home, and they get all confused as they pile into their automobiles (musical cars, as it were) and spouses and souses become hopelessly mixed up. Now the second chapter has to do with the inevitable beach party; but you begin to see the picture, of course.

Pop Snow is still a-tingle over his first plane trip. We interviewed him at his home recently, and here are the highlights of the junket, according to our notes. "Left Florida at 7:30 a.m.," recounted Pop. "Don't know why in tarnation they wait until the middle of the day to get goin'." (Pop usually arises at 4:30, vacation or no.) "Purtiest stewardess I ever see come over to me after I settled in my seat. She asked me to put out my cigar until we got into the air, and wanted to know if I had my belt on. I kinda blushed, and told her I wore suspenders, and she said no, she meant my safety belt, and

I said where in tarnation is it, and she said I was settin' on it.

"Well sir, pretty soon the plane filled up, and the engines started up, and we jockeyed around the field, and off we went. Pretty soon I notice my ears was crackin', and I couldn't hear a thing. The stewardess come by, and asked if everything was all right, and when she noticed I couldn't hear her, she says to me, 'Just keep swallerin'.' So I did, but by the time we got to Trenton, I'd swallered so much my mouth was drier'n a hickory chip. Well, we had lunch, and in jig time we'd taken off again, and we was droppin' down in Boston. Except for missing my usual quota of cigars, I never felt more comfortable nor safe in my life. And then, just as I was goin' down the steps from the plane, I turned around to tip my hat to the pretty stewardess, and cussed if I didn't stub my toe on the gang plank, and turn my ankle."

These cold January mornings we've noticed that Charlie Joseph has a pair of eel spears lashed to the roof of his car as he drives by our house. Charlie is one of the last of the exponents of the manly art of eel fishing as practiced hereabouts. We found a few moments recently to chat with Charlie as he rested in Norm Lee's between trips in pursuit of the wily apodes Pameta. "Been a good season for eelin' so far this winter," opined Charlie. "Cold enough to make strong ice on the eel ponds so's you can walk right out to good fishin' spots. Equipment? All's you need is a sharp axe, and some warm clothing, and a long handled spear, and a good bit of patience. Some days you'll stand out on the ice with a bitter cold wind blowing around your ears, making your hands go numb and blue with cold—and you'll prod that spear up and down in the mud and you won't catch enough shoestrings to feed a female cat."

We reflected on Charlie's picturesque term for an immature eel—shoestring—and then we casually mentioned that we'd read about the life of an eel somewhere. Hatched in the Sargasso Sea, we pointed out, and then the baby eels head for the North American continent and fresh water streams; sometimes in their adolescent state they change from a flounder-shaped fry to a skinny, worm-like fish called an elver, and eventually they reach the mature form of an eel. By this time, we recalled from our readings, the boys had departed from the girls, swimming off for their future rendezvous in the ocean depths—later the ladies made a more leisurely journey to the aforesaid meeting place. Occasionally, we observed, a female would apparently lose the migrating instinct, and remaining behind in some inland body of water, would grow to a tremendous size: four- and five-foot eels are not considered uncommon.

"That accounts for the size of the big whopper I caught in the winter of 1917," exclaimed Charlie. "It was my birthday, and I wanted to give my guests (there were 26 of 'em) eel in vinho d'Alhos as a main course at the party. Tried to buy some all over, but no luck, so I hitched up the family Democrat wagon, and threw in a spear and a double bit axe, and drove over to the Mill Pond, off Depot Road. Well sir, I walked out on the ice beyond the muskrat houses, and chopped a hole about three feet across, dropped my spear through, and started probin'. About the fourth jab, I felt something lodge between the tines, and I slow and careful-like pulled up on the shaft—almost broke my back, but finally the head of an eel, about as big as a water bucket, broke water. Try as hard as I was able, I couldn't drag that beast over the edge of the hole. So I ran back to the wagon, and strung a rope from the rear axle to the spear handle, whistled at the horse, and between the two of us we managed to drag the monster out on the ice. Twenty feet, seven and one half inches long, he was, and about as big around as a nail keg, amidships. I remember we cut off about a yard from the nape of the neck, had enough eel to feed my guests to capacity. It stayed cold that winter, so I just left the rest of the carcass out back of the barn, where it froze stiff as a log. Every time we wanted eel, why I'd take my crosscut saw and go out and hack off a couple of feet."

Attention! All city dwellers, summer folks, colonists, and off-Capers. Of almost equal importance as the forthcoming nuptials of Grace Kelly and Prince Rainier is the weather we're having here today on the outer Cape. Even before you awoke, this morning, there was an effect of benzedrine in the air—a faint stirring in the blood stream, an activity of the corpuscles, a sense of well-being that came from the ingredients being blended by old Mother Nature into the recipe for the day's weather. It was of a quality that made a man eat a mite more of breakfast, one eye cocked out on the meadow, drinking in at the same time the morning scene. In the grass plot under the locusts, magically green these past few days, a half-dozen rheumy-eyed robins, heads perked in an attitude of listening for the angle worm in the turf underfoot. The sudden squawl of a bluejay, and the rattling claxon call of a flicker, perched on a dead stump on the hillside. Forsythia and lilac buds swollen almost to bursting, and daffodils in full bloom, and the tiny, furled nobs that will be blossoms appearing on the beachplum bushes. Spare your olfactory buds the blight of that first cigarette, folks, and step out with us to savor the morning air. Smell that mingling of spring odors in the southwest breeze! Just a mite of the salt marsh at low tide, and a smidgin of newly-ploughed earth and the faintest whiff of warm sun on pine needles. A fine day, city folks, wish you were here.

Big news of the week is the change of gas pumps at Norm Lee's Pamet Service Center, formerly Snowie's Station. Without mentioning brand names, we can state that the big orange scalloped bivalve has been replaced by a five-pointed star.

We were just commencing to hoist monuments into place at the South Truro Cemetery yesterday when Charlie Joseph hove into view. Jack Edwards, from Duarte Motors, was handling the winch controls, and Henry Carlson, the funeral director from Wellfleet, was supervising, and we were acting as general laborer. The heavy rope sling fastened to the marker was groaning under the strain, and the work was progressing satisfactorily. Charlie, we note, was barefoot, and he seemed to enjoy the sensation of walking through the close-cropped bunch grass. He dropped a few words of advice as the stone slid into place on its base, and then, clucking his tongue, he allowed as how he'd lift them stones barehanded, if he was twenty years younger. And, in thinking back over the years, we realized that Charlie's statement was more than an idle boast. Charlie has always been a powerful man—barrel chested, with bulging biceps, and a broad back, and the frame of a simian.

"Yes sir," said Charlie, "back when I was in the Coast Guard, in World War I, I raised a bull calf up on the family farm. He was a frisky cuss, so every morning when I went out to feed him, I'd kind of fool around with him a bit. Put a headlock on him, and pushed him back against the barn wall by his horns, and then I'd get under his belly and hoist him up in the air. I'd usually end up by throwing him several feet into a pile of hay. Well sir, you never saw an animal grow as fast as that critter did. Must have put on two-three pounds a day. And every day, of course, I'd keep up my exercise with him and I think he kind of liked it, especially when I'd lift him on my shoulder and throw him across the barn floor. Finally I was transferred up to Cahoon's Hollow Station, and several months went by without me seein' the bull at all. Then, just before Christmas, I got leave so I come home.

"Next morning, bright and early I put on my old clothes and went out in the barn. You could have knocked me over with a steering-oar when I saw that bull. He'd grown about three times his former size, his eyes was bloodshot, his horns was needle-sharp, his tail was straight out and he was pawin' the floor. First off I thought he was ugly, but then I realized he wanted to play, so I took off my jacket, and pressed a headlock onto him, and then I grabbed him by the horns, and backed him up against the grain chest, and finally I stooped down and braced my shoulders under his belly and slowly lifted him up off the floor. Then I took a deep breath and threw that beast across the floor into a pile of straw. We butchered the poor cuss a week later. Dressed, he weighed 1,850 pounds. Lord knows what his live weight was." On the way home in our truck, later in the afternoon, our No. 2 son, Terry, who had heard the story, said to us, "Gosh, I'd like to have seen Charlie throw the bull, wouldn't you?"

"We both did, son, we both did," we replied.

Come now the time for apologies to Mother Nature for our snide remarks anent the weather a few short weeks ago. We said many nasty, carping things about the tardiness of warm weather's arrival, and the persistent east wind, and the excess of rainfall. We griped about gray overcast, and damp fogs, and a belated, crippling frost. We're willing to retract all our unkind words if only weather like the present keeps up. Take today, for instance, one of many such this past fortnight. Or better still, let's start with the typical sunset of the night before, the true prognosticator for next day's weather: the sun, a blood-red ball, setting in a faint tracing of clouds painting the bay a glorious crimson. This time of year old sol seems to hesitate a mite at the northern end of his run, reluctant to resume his southern travels. The breeze will die away to a still, stark calm, and in the interlude of a pleasant twilight the muted calls of the birds fill the valley. Comes morning with a mild steady breeze from the southwest, a bit of cloud cover earlier, dissipating as the heat of the sun strengthens, tantalizing, satisfying smell of warm earth, and pitch pine, and asphalt blacktop. Busy hum of traffic on the highway and the byroads.

The perennial visitors to town hall, with their perennial questions: "Isn't this building used as a church any more?" Sudden swirls of dust from the roadsides as a car rushes by; glimpse of fragile, beautiful pale wild roses on the meadow; the sudden fragrance of honeysuckle in bloom, and the brassy call of the cock pheasant in the uplands. It's summer, and it's good to be alive.

Well sir, seems good to tally off the faithful colonists as they wend their ways back to Pamet from the big city jungles. Seen about town: artist Edward Hopper and his charming and beauteous wife, here for the season at their cottage where the Hogsbacks meets the bay. Genial, jovial Ev "Esso" Cooper arrived last weekend, just in time to help umpire the Sunday softball game (Old Timers, 5-4). Ev hopes to be here in Truro until the frost strikes this fall. We had a chance to gander at George Kelley's new addition on his ultra-modern home on Tom's Hill (Ed Whiting Co., Wellfleet, builders). Got there shortly after one of the neighborhood children had jumped through a huge plate-glass window, thinking the frame enclosed only Pamet atmosphere; fortunately the lad was not seriously hurt.

After a hectic session with brush and wrench, those two salty barnacles,

Francis "Brud" Mooney and Peter Morris announce that their charter boat is ready to take out fishing parties. Presently moored in Pamet Harbor, the doughty cruiser will be moved to Wellfleet, we understand, ready to invade the domicile of the wily striper and bluefish and tuna.

Another installment of the O'Caghan guided tour of Pamet: we should feel delinquent in our duties as a scribe if we were to leave the Highlands without delving a mite deeper into the maritime history of the area. Probably no words can paint the story of the grim majesty of the Atlantic as seen from the cliffs of the Highland, nor the terrible accompanying tragedies of the storms, better than those of the late I. M. Small, and we herewith take the liberty of quoting from Mr. Small's "Shipwrecks on Cape Cod." Loss of the Ship Peruvian: Over the North Atlantic on the night of the 26th of December 1873 swept a gale and storm so fierce and wild that even the dwellers on the coast were surprised. With almost hurricane force the wind-driven sea rushed mountainous waves towards the outlying sand bar and hurled themselves with a terrific roar on the sands of the beach.

Many weeks before from the smooth waters of the harbor of Calcutta the American ship Peruvian had passed out into the deep sea and with a blue sky and favoring breeze, had spread her white sails and headed for home on her long voyage. Beneath her decks was stored a valuable cargo of sugar and block tin; Boston washer destination. The ship was in command of Capt. Charles H. Vannah, and she carried a crew of 24 men. With such a bright departure they were anticipating a quick and safe voyage. All had gone well with ship and crew until this fateful December morning. All day long the snow had fallen thick and fast, driven over the deck of the ship and through her rigging by the ever increasing gale. Riotous waves lifted the big ship to their crests, only to plunge her, the next moment, into the depths of the deep hollows as they tore madly away into the approaching darkness.

Capt. Vannah had been unable for 24 hours to obtain an observation, but he knew that his ship was approaching the coast of Cape Cod. Hoping every moment that some slight abatement in the storm might give him a chance to pick up some outlying beacon or the glimmer of some friendly lighthouse, he kept the ship's head to the north with all the sail upon the spars that they could stand without breaking. Higher and higher ran the seas, wilder and more terrific blew the gale, often across the ship's decks swirled huge waves, while all about them the dark skies lowered and the angry waters washed when suddenly, just before midnight, with a terrible plunge and an awful crash, the ship struck the sand bars of the dreaded Peaked Hill Shoals, nearly a mile from shore. Utter con-fusion reigned on the ship.

Up to that time only an occasional sea had swept her decks; now waves in torrents constantly swept her and pounded unceasingly her breaking decks. Boats, deck fittings, and everything movable was swept away in the darkness and the turbulent sea, her crew driven to the rigging found there only a temporary place of escape. Soon came a mountain-like wave; it thundered over the doomed ship, tearing away all of her masts and portions of her deck, hurling the entire ship's crew into this mass of thrashing wreckage and churning sea, and their last sad cries were hushed in the waters that covered them.

With the first glimmer of daylight men hurried to the outer beach, believing that some terrible disaster had occurred, and they found the shore for miles covered with portions of the cargo and many broken timbers of the lost ship; but owing to the distance from shore to where the ship went down, only three bodies were ever recovered, and those after many days of washing about in the surf.

That blue water, so quiet now, breaking with such gentle ripples on the shore, does not give you the impression that in a few hours with a change of wind, it could be lashed into a fury, and with towering foam-capped waves, dash upon the beach with the roar of a Niagara.

The weather? Glorious, exhilarating, invigorating. There are vitamins in the air, this morning, and if you don't believe it, take a walk with me out to the edge of the hill west of town hall. Feel that warm sun on your back? Take a deep breath now, as we pass the gate into Bishop Acres, and tune your ear to the bird hassle going on down in the pine grove. Sounds like baby starlings, but our approach has stirred up a sentinel crow from his perch on the highest scrub pine, and now the flock of glossy black birds breaks from cover. The hog cranberry patch is waxy and green, the poverty grass is fresh washed by the recent rain, the turf under foot is spongy and moist, and there's a smell of growing things about. To west'ard a long streamer of mackerel sky, and the horizon blends the bay and the sky with the faintest haze. Dead low tide in the river, sable sand bars showing, and beyond the spidery trestle the faded red scow perches on the edge of Gull Island.

Apropos of nothing, Bud Fisher, the Old Coast Guarder, tells of meeting a southern "surfie" in the old days, and they got to talking about shoes. Said the rebel, "Well sir, my foot measures a tight eight, and I could squeeze into a nine, but size ten and a half feels so good that I wear a thirteen."

And so to a continuation of our junket about town. Let's leave, with considerable regret, picturesque and historical Highland Light, and wend our way back inland: t'wouldn't be fitting to pass Walter Horton's cottage on the left without waving hello, if we can catch him in one of his rare moments of leisure. Walter is a big, raw-boned Easthamer, "smart," as the Cape Codders say, meaning, of course, he's a prodigious worker. Walter is a man of many parts, landscape gardener, butcher, handyman, and raconteur extraordinary.

One day Walter was sitting on his front porch, gazing out across the harbor to where the sandy hook of Wood End could be seen in the late afternoon sun. A pair of be-sunglassed and be-shorted females happened by, probably guests of the hotel across the street, and observing Walter's steady gaze to west'ard, they queried him as to what he was looking at. Walter leered briefly at their bare legs and growled, "Just wonderin' if them dern tugboats is comin' back to finish their job." What job? the girls wanted to know. "Well, you see thet curved point of land out there? Half a dozen big tugs pulled it around like that to let a big ocean liner go by, headin' fer Boston, and they're supposed to straighten it out, tonight."

Down a sharp dip we go, and around the corner on Highland Road, and here on our right is the Lodge, a gauntly beautiful square sea-captain's house, once used to house the help from the Highland House, now owned by Lenore Stephens, and in process of being restored. Across the street is the rambling, elled Cape Codder of Prof. LeRoy Cook, of Dartmouth College. The Cook house could well be the oldest house in Truro, according to historian Shebnah Rich and other reliable sources.

Onion skin, carbon paper, set the margins, adjust the double-space, fill the friendly briar and kindle up. Hoist the halyards on the venetian blinds, let in the bright, reflected light of a beautiful late July day. Fight off the temptation to daydream a mite, listen to the mellow pealing of the chimes as they strike the quarter-to-ten pattern, succumb momentarily to the hypnotic effect of the sounds of the countryside: drone of a power mower in the valley below, measured ticking of the Seth Thomas on the office wall, faint call of a chipping sparrow in the beachplum thicket. First hesitant, soaring rasp of a cicada on the hillside, scrape of shovels on the blacktop of Castle Road (town gang at work abreast Todd's house). Comes the pleasant smell of summer on the southwest breeze through our open window; a blending of bleached grass and pine and salt meadow, and we succumb to the urge for a stroll out on the hilltop. Early morning ground mist has cleared, but a pleasing blue smoke-haze clings to the horizon, swathing the Hogsbacks of South Truro, spilling into the valley of the Pamet. The hills are a study in greens, pale, waxy, and blue-green, and the drab of the scrub pines. By the roadsides, delicate queen anne's lace in full blossom, and heavy budded old maid's pinks.

For the first time in years we went pond fishing yesterday evening, found the junket peaceful and satisfying as ever despite a scarcity of sizable perch. Tepid, indigo water, and lily pads lifting in the breeze, and the heady fragrance of wild honeysuckle on the narrow sand shores, and the clear call of the pond birds added up to an interlude of therapy for jaded nerves.

Truro folks are enjoying the fruit of the upland blueberry crop these days, and stained molars and satisfied expressions attest to the tasty quality of sundry pies and cakes and stewed sauces. Personally, we like the swamp berries a mite better: tarter and juicier, we claim, and certainly easier picking, growing, as they do, at a comfortable, stand-up height, albeit the picker risks the danger of stepping on a blacksnake on occasion, or the fire of a poison ivy attack.

We're working on cemetery lots these days, and the task is more enjoyable this time of year since the pre-Memorial Day pressure is not on us. Then, too, there are more visitors to chat with in the burying grounds, and it's satisfying to chop down the newly-sprouted beachplum growth.

In the first Sunday morning softball game of the season we've missed, the Old Timers defeated the Youngsters last Sabbath, 6-1. Bill Aiken, who had misplaced his glasses, was unable to fill his customary position at shortstop, but pitched creditably, so we understand, for the Youngsters.

Another opportunity for summer folks to buy the finest dishes from Pamet kitchens will be the food sale in Truro Center, August 18, benefit of the Sacred Heart Altar Guild. They're still talking about the Magee spaghetti sauce and the Grindle fudge which went on sale last month.

Tax bills, from Abel, Sydney J. et ux (Margaret E.) to Young, Franklin M., go out this week to an impatient public. We used to have a Zaslow, Meyer, on the lists but since he sold his Beach Point lots, there hasn't been a Z taxpayer on the books. Biggest tax on the list: Massachusetts Institute of Technology, for their South Truro installation, $2,297.86. Phew. Average tax for homeowner with old Cape Codder, all improvements, and several acres of land, about $115.00. Total of the 1956 real estate warrant (rate $38 per thousand) is $110,118,50; and although two taxpayers jumped the gun and paid their bills before they were in the mail, first person to show up at our office with a mailed bill for payment was, as usual, Mrs. Lena Briggs, of Castle Road.

We stand on the threshold of November, month of elections and, among other things, shipwrecks and gales in the old days of the Lifesaving Service. You are reminded of the tremendous power of the sea when you step out these early mornings, and hear the muted roar of the surf on the backside;

when a sudden easterly breeze brings the measured beat of the waves with clearer intensity, and the chill, dank, briny breath reaches with tenuous purpose up-valley. November wrecks? Yes indeed, dating back at least as far as colonial times. Take, for instance, the wreck of the British man-of-war Somerset. On November 2, 1778, this fine ship went to her doom on the Peaked Hill Bars, two miles east of the Race Point Lighthouse.

The Somerset was one of a fleet of British warships which had been throwing shot and shell at Bunker Hill and terrorizing Boston and the surrounding coast towns for many weeks. She often anchored in Provincetown Harbor to provision and harass local shipping (at this period, the town records of Truro show that the selectmen were obliged to issue a non-fraternizing order to the citizens of Pamet, forbidding association and trade with the Redcoats) and a few days before this November day on which she was lost, she left the shelter of the sandspit for the purpose of intercepting some French merchant ships which were due in Boston. On the second day of the cruise, while attempting to reenter the harbor, she encountered thick weather and a northeast gale; losing her bearings she stranded on Peaked Hill Bars, and everything movable was speedily swept from her decks. She carried a list of 500 officers and men, more than 200 of whom were washed into the sea and drowned when the ship stranded.

Next day the ship was beaten over the bars by the giant waves and she was forced near enough to the beach to allow rescue of the remainder of the ship's company. Capt. Hallett of Yarmouth and Col. Doane of Wellfleet with a detachment of militia came down the Cape to the wreck, put Capt. Aurey of the Somerset under arrest, and marched them all up the Cape to Boston, where they were imprisoned.

For more than a hundred years the old ship lay buried in the sands of the beach, then the ever-moving sands and the currents of the ocean tore away the bars and exposed the timbers and rust-covered cannon of the once proud ship; but it was not for long that the remains of the hull lay exposed. Relic hunters carried away many of the old timbers as souvenirs, then the relentless sea drove back the sands and completely covered ship and guns. That was more than 75 years ago, and since that day no part of the old man-o'-war has shown on the surface.

Well sir, if you'd glanced out on the Pamet Valley this morning you'd never have known that the war drums were sounding again in Europe and the Near East. There was a heavy, Dresden china frost carpeting the rolling countryside, and a swirling, pearl gray ground fog blanketed the Narrow Land. Nary a breeze stirring, and the thermometer at 32 degrees, and an almost tangible stillness blanketing the village. At breakfast time (it's an hour later, now, since standard time) the persistent thermal currents from the ocean and a warm sun commenced to dissipate the ground mist, and the outline of the hills to northward began to break through the ghostly cover. Dank smell of decaying vegetation and the salt tang of the Atlantic is subtly present, a proper blend of condiments for the day. Comes the first stir of traffic on the valley road, and Pamet folks set out for the chores of the day.

Our thoughts go to the yarn told us last summer by Bud Fisher, retired Coast Guarder.

The central character of Bud's story is Al Paine; the time, the mid-twenties; the location, Cahoon's Hollow Coast Guard Station. Al was generally considered to be the finest mess cook in the district. But let's have Bud tell the story in his own words.

"Yes sir, Al certainly could prepare the finest vittles you ever tasted. Beans on Wednesday and Saturday night, with a big slab of lean pork, browned to perfection with molasses, and flavored with powdered mustard and a whole onion or two, and slow-baked in the galley coal stove. Hot biscuits, lighter'n milkweed seed, and coffee about the color and consistency of tobacco juice. Why, Al could blend a clam chowder on Fridays—smelled so appetizin' when it was cookin' that the men couldn't shave they was droolin' so. And weekends, when we had chicken, or turkey, old Al would make a stuffin' from stale bread and eggs, and oysters and seasonin' that would cause tears to appear in the eyes of a crew member who had to take his twenty-four hour liberty.

"You'd naturally assume that such a valuable man would be relieved of all other duties around the station, but not so. Cook Paine was required to keep his galley clean, do his share of chores in the bunk room, wash the dishes, plan his meals a week or so in advance, and take the dog-watch patrol on the beach (a minor assignment which called for slogging through the soft sand some three miles to the half-way house, where the stations checks would be exchanged with the watch from the adjoining patrol).

"Well sir," Bud continues, "orders finally come through to Cahoon's Hollow that a relief cook would have to be broken in. Al had complained about the drudgery of the galley and, as youngest man at the station, I got the assignment. So for several weeks I stood at Al's elbow from early morning to late at night, watching every move he made. But somehow, I couldn't get his delicate touch, try as I might. The oyster stew would curdle, and the potatoes would boil dry, and the bread would split in the oven in need of more salt, and the omelet would fall flatter'n a policeman's foot.

"Finally Al says to me, 'Fisher, I'm goin' to teach you to make a good apple pie if it's the last thing I do. Here's my mother's very own recipe.

Now you fetch out the materials from the buttery, and I'll start you off—then I'm goin' on the south dogwatch, and when I get back you'd better have some good apple pies ready for supper or you'll sleep in the barn with the horse tonight.'

"So I sifted out the flour, and measured the shortenin' and pared a bucketful of Baldwin apples, and dumped in the sugar and the spices, and made my crust and rolled 'er out thin, and put all the ingredients together, under Al's eyes. Al guided my hand as I cut the vents in the top crusts, and he checked the oven temperature and set the drafts in the galley range.

"Finally he slipped on the time clock, and started off on his patrol. As for me, I finished the supper dishes, and swept the galley floor, and answered the phone a couple of times, all the while keepin' a close watch on the oven indicator and the clock on the wall. And then, just as I was sittin' down to read the latest copy of the Police Gazette, comes a knock on the screen door, and there was a pair of pretty summer girls, askin' to be shown around the station. I only intended to be gone a few minutes, but first thing I knew, they had me showin' 'em how to steer the surfboat.

"Then I sent them some messages on the wigwag, semaphore flags, and I explained how the Lyle gun worked, and the breeches buoy. We looked at old Tom, the station horse, and then we climbed the bluff near the watchhouse so's I could point out the wreckage of the Castagna, down-beach. I remember I was just tellin' 'em about my part in the rescue when I happened to look along the path, and there was Al, hot-footin' it back from his patrol. Course, that reminded me of my pies in the oven, and I ran for the galley. Got there just as Al plowed up from the south'ard, and we both made a dash for the stove, which was sendin' up clouds of black smoke. I pulled out the cremated pies, and Al stood there lookin' at me, livid with rage. 'Next time I send a dam' fool,' he yelled, 'I'll go myself.'

"My blankets smelled of horse for a month afterwards."

Anatomy of a winter night; wind sharp and biting out of the northwest, smoke colored clouds massed in the sky, moving aside, grudgingly, to let the pale, flame-orange sun shine through at sunset. A brief moment when the shadows of the denuded birch and the alder on the meadow stand clear-etched on the carpet of drab turf and cattails, then twilight. In the western sky, a thin, crescent moon, holding within its frame, like a jeweler's setting, the dark shadowed mass of the shadowed satellite. A cluster of pale, brilliant stars appears in the needlework of blue-black bowl, and the outline of the hills blends into night. There's a scattering of traffic on the road as the nimrods come out of the woods, and Pamet folks wend their way homeward after the day's chores. Friendly lights blink on in neighboring kitchens. Day is done.

NINETEEN FIFTY-SEVEN

1957

We're disturbed by the horrible suspicion that our constant comments on the weather somehow cause this perversity of the elements. Perhaps if we omitted our opening squibs, conditions, weatherwise, would improve. But being a creature of habit, we feel obligated to report and let the temperature and the precipitation fall where they may. Here's our synopis, then, for this second day of April, as seen through the jaundiced eye of a reporter who has just passed his third decade, and finds himself, as neighbor Roger Burhoe once put it, in the old age of youth.

Up betimes, and to our chores. . . . Glancing, as we squirt the scented shaving lather at our scowling countenance, out of doors at the valley of the Pamet, finding it still in winter dress of drab cattail and dun meadow grass. Overhead a murky, leaden sky, heavy with rain, and a squawl making up to westward darkening the backdrop of the locust grove. Fortified against the day's work by a modest breakfast, we pause on the slip of our lawn to admire the faint new tinge of green in the grass, and to listen to the clear syllables of a redwing blackbird practicing his phonics in Kelley's garden patch. "Kwon-gar-eee—" he sings, and a good morning to him, too. And the promise of the morning is fulfilled as the day runs its course, the rain reaching a downpour at noontime which tapers off with a changing wind by mid-afternoon. But the fog and the overcast clear too late to show the sunset, and all in all, it has been a day without much of merit.

If we had a name like Albion Freeman Rich, of South Wellfleet, we'd never allow it to be shortened to Bud, as he's called; and if we could spin a yarn as Albion can, we'd spin more of 'em. Albion is that burly, bristly-haired feller who lives up on the Wellfleet-Eastham line, just across from the entrance to the former Austin ornithological station. Ex-marine, caretaker for the late Dr. Austin, and a cranberry grower by avocation, Al now works for the South Truro Lincoln Lab site as a handy maintenance man. We got to talking with Al the other day, and the conversation turned to birds and bird banding, a subject about which we're abysmally ignorant. We'd always been intrigued by the multi-syllabled sign identifying the

Austin property, and we welcomed the chance to glean some information from Bud anent our feathered friends and the treatment they got at the station.

"Why banding is what we did mostly up there," said Bud, as he set fire to a big brown cigar. "Used to see some 103 varieties of migratory birds, waterfowl, land birds, predators—everything from the common chicadee (he doesn't migrate, however) to rare birds like the Arctic owls. We had several different kinds of traps; some big contraptions were set out on the bay to catch ducks, and geese, and so forth. An then we had land traps for the shore birds, and we even had traps in the little pond on Dr. Austin's property. Object was to trace the migrations of the birds, and we'd do this by examining and recording the bands on the birds—if they had 'em—or by placing our own recorded bands on unbanded fellers. The whole project was under the supervision of the Bureau of Wildlife in Washington, and they coordinated the work of all banding stations."

We interjected the thought that banding must be a rather ticklish task, involving a mite of manual dexterity. "Yes, it is," allowed Bud. "Have to be quick with your hands." We stole a glance at Bud's huge, hamlike fists. "Matter of fact," Bud continued, "for years Dr. Austin had offered a prize to the fastest bander on the station and for years, Gertie Benner had walked off with the prize. She was fast as lightning, and I made up my mind one year I was going to beat her; but every day, when we totted up the score, she'd win handily.

"Finally I had a lucky break. Come to work one day in December, I did, and I noticed we'd had one of them sudden, intense freezes that had frozen a quick skim of ice on every pond in the neighborhood. As I drove into the Austin property, derned if I didn't see the duck pond packed full of waterfowl; looked just like pepper grains on a clam chowder. I expected 'em to fly when I got close, but they never budged despite all the flapping of their wings. Then I realized they was all frozen into the ice. Now about half a body's time, when he's bandin' is taken up in tryin' to corner the birds in the traps, so I suddenly realized this was my chance to beat Gertie's bandin' record. I quick fetched out the pungo and a sharp ice pick and my bandin' kit, and made for the pond. All's I had to do was chop out a piece of ice about a yard square, flip it upside down, birds and all, and slip the bands onto the protrudin' legs of the ducks, and the geese, and the terns, and what all. Then I tossed the whole business up on shore, where the early morning sun soon thawed the birds loose, and off they flew. . . . The former record had been 250 bands per hour but that morning I clamped 600-odd of the aluminum strips on the shanks of the squawking feathered creatures.

Time I had cleaned out the pond I was so sick of the sight of feathers I never wanted to see another bird."

"What did you get for a prize for this Herculean task?" we queried Bud. "A refrigerator, perhaps, or a fishing rod?"

"No, that's the ironical part of it," rejoined Bud. "Come Christmas, I got a big package from Dr. Austin. Opened it up, I did, and there was a handsome, stuffed pheasant."

And perhaps we're looking at today's weather through the optimistically prejudiced eye of a new grandfather, but we find it good, nevertheless. The grandfather bit? Well sir, our oldest child, Patricia Pirnie, gave birth to a six-pound girl at Cape Cod Hospital on February 22, and this is in the family tradition on the distaff side, since Pat herself was born on FDR's birthday. (Our own natal date, strangely enough, is April 1. That explains a lot, sez Snowie.) So the little bundle of joy has been named Erin Lee Pirnie, and her nocturnal complaints at feeding time have inspired us to dub her Erine Go Blaah. And Jimmy Moynahan will never forgive us for the impious reflection on the sacred motto of the Emerald Isle. Although it was Squire Jim who remarked to us, when the stork was crossing the Cape Cod Canal, that we'd soon be married to a grandmother.

In any event, 'tis a friendly, foggy, warm day, and the fog lies down on the hilltops, pinned in place by the cloud cover overhead. Nary a bit of breeze, and the valley is a study in drab browns, except for the pale straw patch of Bloomberg's upper parcel and the fringe of bottle green scrub pines on the ridges.

In the lighter vein, town meetin' quotes of which there were deplorably too few this year. Snowie of Castle Road, when the hassle over disposition of the Dog Account to the Library account (to be or not to be refunded in toto) arose: "Mr. Moderator, it is my observation that although the library may not be going to the dogs, the dogs are sure coming to the library."

The most abject apologies we could utter wouldn't make up for the insults we've cast about high tides flooding the basement of the new home of our good friend Snowie of Castle Road—but we would like to remedy a mite of the damage we've done by offering a few words of praise for the incomparable view to be had from his living room window, overlooking the broad salt Pamet. We dropped by the other afternoon and sat with Snowie, for all the world like two characters out of Erskine Caldwell, just agazin'. In wordless admiration we watched the sun setting over the bay, the play of colors on drab marsh and ice-filled creek, the squabbling of native birds—grosbeaks, and starlings, and chicadees—in Snowie's feeder. "Purty," we murmured, as we got up to leave. "Yep, purty," was Snowie's reply.

Deer Town Father:

I take my trusty pen in hand to compose a short note tew you, seein's how I ain't laid eyes on your svelt figger for several weeks now. I even left some cawfee fer yew on a couple uv Sunday mornins in the usual place, but it wasn't touched when I got back from church, so I presume you ain't bin down to Castle Road lately.

Me and my child bride, Norma, are enjoyin' married life real swell. First off, she kinda objected to my dawgs ridin' in the car with us, but we (me an' the dogs) kind uv flattered her along until now Jeff (he's the youngest dawg) has permishun to ride, and by next week I'm hopin' ter git clearance papers for Lassie, and Norma'll probly hev ter ride in the back seat.

Hear tell as how you tried tew take ol' Snowie's place umpirin' at the softball game last Sunday. Don't see how yew can possibly do a good job without yew hev a good supply uv "Optic Organizer." Thet's the stuff I used to carry in the thermos bottle, remember. It is true that the game you officiated went twelve innin's—and that the young fellers won it behind the brilliant pitchin' uv Jackie Marshall.

While I think of it, here's my secret recipe fer the moustache lotion you wuz askin fer. You complained thet your cookie duster wuz sparce, and ratty lookin' an' orange, whereas yer hair is kinda brown. Well T. F., you take equal parts uv udder balm, skunk's grease, and lampblack, mix 'em up together, and rub in well nights before you hit the hay, and you'll see a big improvement in yer moustache.

By the way, hev we got space fer a yarn? Here goes anyhow. Couple Sundays ago I wuz up to Ballston Beach catin' fer bass when a feller started flyin' a kite from the foot of the bank. My how thet kite could sail. Higher'n higher it went, till pretty soon he wuz complainin' his string wuz almost gone. Well, the breeze was freshnin' from the southwest, and I hated to see him have to haul in the kite, and besides the fish wasn't bitin', so I suggested he let me tie my fishin' line on the end of his kite string and let me reel her out as far's we could go. So we did, and I had a great time lettin' it out, and settin' the star drag, and whippin' the pole up and down to make the kite dive and climb.

Farther and farther she went, out over the ocean, till finally alls we could make out was a tiny speck; seemed miles away. Got to the end of the spool, I did, and by now the kite was so awkward to handle that I had to keep both hands on the gear. I yelled over my shoulder to the other fellow to reach in my fishin' kit (I had it slung over my shoulder) and splice on another line, so's we could play it out by hand. So he did, and after a bit I began to play out the new line, hand over hand. The kite was out of sight, now, over the horizon, and still I played out the line, flying her by feel.

And then, I began to hear some people titterin' in back of me on the beach, and at the same time I began to feel a draft across my shoulder and chest. I looked down, and what do you suppose had happened? Well, I'd been wearing my old knitted jersey from high school days—it was brown with gold letters knitted right into it that read "Wellfleet High School—Southeastern Massachusetts Basketball Champions 1928." And this kite flyin' feller had mistakenly gotten hold uv a loose piece uv yarn up by the shoulder, and he'd tied it on the kite string, and all that was left of my jersey was the lower half of the numerals 1928.

Yours fer beter colyums, Snowie

We looked in vain for the message in the personal ads which would have granted us our year's sabbatical leave from columnar duties, and so, after a brief vacation, we pick up our faithful Royal again, and chronicle the happenings of our town. If we had expected a deluge of protests from avid readers of our deathless prose, we were properly disillusioned. Three people stopped us on the street to ask how they could apply for our job. A nice lady told us we had done the right thing, since our column was beginning to look a mite strained, and, although we camped beside our telephone for hours on end, we got nary a call from our editors. Sic transit gloria mundi.

Well sir, despite our sudden return to earth, we find it a very pleasant earth, here on the Narrow Land, this gloriously beautiful day in late April. The wind has been southwest all day—the Cape's friendliest breeze, and the sky has been swept to a clean, cloudless blue, and it's shirtsleeve warm. Magically the grass has grown, and the juicy pears will blossom before the weekend, and the buds on the scrub oak and the rumcherries are ready to burst. There's a smell of sunbathed, fertile soil in the air, and the peewink chorus is strong, and the red wing blackbirds are bold and it's weather to tear a man between loafing and choring, and we're glad to be alive and living in the valley.

We got a phone call from Fred Davis, the mayor of Holsberry Square the other afternoon. "Hello, Pamet Father?" he bellowed in his usual style. "Come over and help me cut up a tuna fish will you?" We concluded that Fred wanted to share a tuna fish sandwich with us, to be washed down by a draft of branch water—but lo! and behold when we arrived at the neat Cape Codder on Old County Road, there was the genial printer carving steaks from a big, 100-pound fish. "Want you to meet two of my associates," shouted Fred. "Chuck Morrissey and Ray Paquin. We each got one of these babies today; they go better'n a hundred pounds apiece. Took a party boat out of Chatham, and got our first strike within an hour. These other two city slickers got real excited, but I horsed my tuna in with little or no commotion. Here, cut yourself off fifty pounds or so." So we did, and then we sat and talked for a spell, and had a taste of Fred's branch water. Look's like the O'Caghans will eat tuna until they sprout dorsal fins, and their blessings on the Mayor.

Folks hereabouts are still buzzing about the phenomenal success being enjoyed by Peter's Hill Restaurant, under the management, this year, of Joan Colebrook. In former years Joan operated intimate eating spots in Wellfleet, both at the bayshore and at the Old Cahoon's Hollow Coast Guard Station. But to return to the Peter's Hill operation: last weekend the swing shift outfit of Daphne Hellman, jazz harpist, Jimmie Stutz, bass fiddle, and Squire James Moynahan, clarinet and sax, entertained a capacity crowd in the airy nightspot. It's a policy of the place to encourage audience participation so it was no surprise when Julius Monk (impressario of Le Ruban Bleu in Gotham), stepped to the piano, and again when the organizer of the Newport Jazz festival (we've been trying to check his name with Jimmie M. but can't reach the Squire by phone) did sparkling things on the ivories. On Sunday night the more timid musicians sat in (Garry Ormsby on the drums, O'Caghan with the valve trombone) and it was more fun than a Democratic rally. We've had the pleasure of doing occasional duty at the refreshment counter, and it seems good to meet many of our old friends on the high stools. Rumor has it that a small Mexican is responsible for the savory and delectable foods emanating from the kitchen, but that we can't vouch for.

Nights like this come, as our late friend Herb Brown used to say, "one to a package—same as pianos." At sunset your gaze was torn between two breathtaking views: crimson, flaming sun dropping behind a tattered curtain of sepia clouds into the turquoise stretches of the bay; ivory disc of the moon rising, other side of the Narrow Land, into a star-studded bowl. The faintest breeze from the southeast, in which you fancied the salt-tang of the ocean, the brief, damp touch of valley dew at dusk. You heard, too, the muted bird call and the distant, sporadic sound of traffic on the highway, and the ever-present insect chorus, pianissimo, largendo, in the evening chill. And, as darkness crept into the valley you watched the lights of your neighbors pinpoint the meadow, and confused them, momentarily, with the fluttering pale moths, and then the chimes of town hall struck the hour. Away, then, with hurricane Carrie, and a pox on Syria, and bury the other disturbing headlines. It's peaceful here in Pamet this glorious September evening.

COTUIT LIBRARY

Add to the list of amusing signs on the Lower Cape. At Lontie Woods snackerie on the main highway near Money Hill: "Ice Cold Ice."

Well sir, it's been a long time since we've had a yarn from your old friend Snowie. Those pleasant coffee breaks on Sunday mornings are apparently a thing of the past, now that Snowie has entered the matrimonial state, and it was by sheer accident we came across the genial onetime petroleum purveyor at a local dairy bar at the season's end. We matched for banana boats (O'Caghan lost, as usual) and as we sat in Snowie's car, spooning into the delicacy, he launched into his story.

"Ever tell you about the time Pop was helpin' Grampa Snow to draw up his will?" We speared a cherry and dipped it into the thick syrup as we shook our head in silent negation.

"Well sir, poor Gramp Snow was on what everybody thought was his death bed—flu, you know, follerin' World War I,—and he had called his sons down to the family homestead to kind of settle up the estate. By common consent, Pop was chosen to jot down Gramp's last wishes— mostly because he seemed able to contain his grief, and then, too, Pop was good at takin' dictation. Well, Pop tiptoed into the darkened room, and said the usual things you say to a sick person, and finally he sat down and wet the tip of his pencil and opened his notebook.

"Then Gramp, he cleared his throat and tugged feebly at his mustache, and gives Pop the order to commence writin'." Snowie paused to carve into the banana foundation of his dairy concoction and gummed into the fruit.

"'First off' said Gramp, 'I want my power launch, the Helen–Anna to go to Isaiah.' 'Lanch,' repeats Pop, 'spelled l-a-n-c-h? But Father, you know Isaiah gets seasick if he sloshes through a mud puddle. I should think you'd leave the boat to Charlie.' 'All right, have it your way, Horace,' acquiesced the patriarch. 'Now that 38-56 buffalo rifle in the back closet. You see that David gets that.' Again Pop cut in. 'David? Why you know David is gun shy, Isaiah's the feller fer the rifle.' Gramp tossed fitfully and plucked at the coverlets, and agreed to Pop's suggestion, and then:

"'The two saddle horses, Nig and Daisy, I want you should have them, Horace. I recollect you always wanted to be a jockey, and now . . .' Pop shook his head and demurred. 'Nothin' I'd like better, father, only that cussed horse dandruff gives me fits, and besides, I've put on a mite of weight; couldn't be a jockey if I wanted to. I'll turn the nags over to Norman.'

"'But I planned on leavnin' the yellow Democrat wagon to Norman,' interposed Gramp. And Pop said, before the old man had finished hardly, 'Best thing to do with that contraption is to burn it up. You know they ain't a Democrat in the whole cussed family, Father.' Well sir, with that old Grampa Snow had had enough. He reared up on his elbow and he snarled, 'Horace, who in tarnation is dyin' in the family, anyway, you or me?'

"And the shock must've done the old gentleman a good deal of help, too, because he recovered and lived another twenty-odd years."

Tuesday evening, midway of October, and a gem of a day it has been. Breeze out of the southwest, lazy, formless clouds in the bowl of the blue, autumn colors still in the foliage, albeit faded somewhat from last week's brilliance. At dusk with the dying of the wind, a formless, miasmic mist forms on the meadows, stirred by the warm air currents rising from the Pamet to dissipate in the scrub pine of the foothills. Overhead, as the last colors of the sunset fade, the stars loom, suddenly, brightly—big dipper to north'ard, a brilliant jewel glistening over the south hills. The kingfisher of Fratus' Corner leaves his perch on the slanting pine, and a pair of black ducks wing their way up-valley, and the distant whine of a car on the highway sounds out in the still air. There's a smell of woodsmoke about, and the distant baying of a beagle over Castle Road way. One by one, the lights of neighbors' cottages light up, and late comers return from their day's chores.

Rumor has it that several of the motels and cottage colonies on Beach Point are planning to add swimming pools to their attractions in order to lure the wary transients to their portals. Gilding the lily, we call it. Here we have the limpid, tepid waters of Cape Cod Bay at their very doorsteps and folks will be encouraged to eschew the natural salt water and plunge into a chlorinated, artificial pool. These are probably arguments in favor of this new move: no problems with the tide, no crabs to nibble at one's toes, no speedboats to zip menacingly by one's head. On the other hand, we claim that the narrow confines of a pool will breed a generation of effete swimmers, limited to short sprints of a few yards. Then too, what's a day at the beach without a handful of sand in one's lunch, or the ineffable tang of a decaying blackfish in the mellow air. Next thing you know, the proprietors of the summer units will be expected to furnish sun lamps if we have a protracted spell of gloomy weather.

We opened sleep-lidded eyes the other evening to glance at our child bride, and were startled out of several year's growth at the sight of a shiny, evil-appearing machine she held in her lap. "Nothing but a new rug hooking frame," she hastened to assure us. "Simple, lightweight, conve-nient. Just lay the burlap on these wire bristles (they look like a miniature yogi's torture bed), tighten up the levers, and hook away." A far cry indeed, from the days when rug frames were made by the man of the house, and we consider the boughten variety a flaunting symbol of woman's fight for independence, somewhat like the driver's license, the ballot, and pre-packaged cake mixtures.

The accent these days is undeniably on the judicial branches of the government, both as regards law enforcement and prosecution. TV is full of Highway Patrols, and Sgt. Saturdays, and sundry lurid courtroom hassles. We admire the techniques used by the minions of the law; the gathering of minute bits of evidence—a dust mote, or a speck of sawdust from the rare lignum vitae tree; copious use of the radio system, punctuated by numerous "ten-fours"; a frightening chase down the pike, sirens screaming, tires burning on the corners, and finally, the culprit brought to bay, usually after a spirited exchange of lead. We must confess, however, that the old-fashioned methods of the law enforcement officers of our day were not without merit.

Take, for instance, old Bill Gill, the deputy sheriff of Wellfleet of a few decades past. Bill will by remembered as a portly, bowlegged, ruddy-faced gent, who kept a notions, newspaper and candy store on the corner where Tony Ferreira, the barber, now plies his trade. They used to say of Bill that when his tobacco stock got low in a certain item, he'd refuse to sell the last plug of Mayo's Dark Chewing Blend, for instance, because he didn't want to run out. Bill was an expert pool player, too, and it took a good man to stoke the ivory spheres across the green cloth of the tables in the back room with Bill. And if you wanted to lay a small wager with him on the outcome of a chucker of Kelley, they say Bill would surreptitiously remove his deputy sheriff's star before he produced his money—kind of a concession to the dignity of his office. For years, Deputy Gill's court business was concerned with the usual routine affairs; service of a writ of attachment, divorce papers, jury list drawings for the neighboring towns. However, with the advent of the horseless carriage, traffic problems began to multiply. Got so that the young bloods of Wellfleet would go a-roarin' through the town in their gas buggies, backfirin' and generally disturbin' the peace and riskin' the lives and safety of the public.

Bill took to sittin' outside of his store, evenin's, where the sidewalk comes close to the traveled way, and with his badge of office displayed in a prominent place on his vest, he'd stare at the cars as they drove by. Most of the fellers took the hint; at least they'd drive careful abreast of Bill's store. But a couple of 'em, Ralphie Berrio and Charlie Taylor by name, why they continued to roar by the corner just like Bill was no more'n a wooden Indian.

Well sir, Deputy Gill sought out the two one evening at the post office, and he warned them that they'd have to cease and desist their reckless driving, or he'd take measures. He especially complained at their use of an exhaust cutout on the big Buick touring car they drove, saying it was loud enough to wake the dead. With a sort of smirk, Charlie and Ralphie half promised they'd behave themselves, and Bill, he went back to his station on the corner. Couldn't have been more'n a half hour later when the sound of a motor marking down hill from the movie hall came to Bill's keen ears. Thoughtfully he edged to the curb, close as he could get to the road, and carefully he rolled his huge cud of Mayo's dark to one side of his lower plate. As the sound of the Buick grew louder, Bill pursed his lips, and ballooned his cheeks like a tuba player. He drew an imaginary sight on Tubman's house, across the way, made some last minute adjustments for windage and elevation and speed of the target. And then, around the corner swept the Berrio Buick, and Bill quick inflated his lungs, took aim, and let go. . . . The deputy said afterwards he'd have scored a double-header if Charlie Taylor hadn't been bent over, seeking the cutout lever. As it was, Ralph took the whole liquid load and Bill was able to close the case without recourse to law or firearms.

We joined with our fellow townsfolk and fellow Cape Codders at the Congregational Church on the hill to pay final respects to our good friend and onetime colleague at town hall, Mr. John R. Dyer, Sr., of the North Pamet. John died suddenly of a heart seizure in the early hours of Sunday morning last.

A letter from our good friend, Police Chief Harold Berrio, of Truro's finest, says in part: "Left Boston at 11 p.m., made my son Dickey sit way up forward, while I took a seat back near the tail; figgered if the thing split in two one of us'd be saved, and the Berrio name would survive. My, how the old eardrums ached as we climbed to flying height. First thing I knew, my fountain pen started to leak, so I fished her out of my pocket, stowed it with my baggage. Then I remembered that someone had warned me it was possible for ammunition to go off at high altitudes, so I unloaded my police revolver and put the bullets in a glass of water. Luckily, I didn't have to use old Betsey all the way to Florida. Got to the hotel in the wee hours of the morning, and tumbled into bed for a well-earned rest. Next day I was meandering around the pool, when I saw a suspicious-looking gent eyeing me and the other guests. I strolled over behind a potted palm where I could keep him under surveillance, and when I noticed a bulge under his left armpit, I quick stepped over and flashed my badge and grabbed him by the elbow. Turned out he was the hotel dick. Tell Ray Enos, my skeleton crew, to keep an eye on things for me."

We got to reminiscing with friend Snowie about Christmas, old and new, deploring the apparent lack of spirit at the Yuletide season. Depends on your point of view, claimed Snowie, and he forthwith quoted a mite of a yarn about his younger days. "Believed in Santa Claus until I was ten years old," mused Snowie. "And on the year I'm tellin' about, my folks had gone out on a Christmas Eve party, leaving me with my dog Spotty, alone in the side bedroom up at the old homestead. Well, sir, long about midnight, I heard a sound out in the livin' room, and I was sure Santa had arrived. I remembered from other holidays how the bare, undecorated room magically sprouted a tree, and ornaments, and stockings and gifts, during the night—so I decided to take a peak. Bounced out of bed, I did, snuck the door open, and peeped out—just in time to see Pop stringin' pop corn around the branches of a purty scrub pine. Then Pop, he saw me: 'GET TERELL BACK TER BED,' he bellowed, and I never believed in Santa Claus after that."

It's true, though, that the true Christmas spirit has left a mark like a fever chart on Pamet. Some years it has been high, others lower'n a mud turtle in January. During the war years, for instance, when folks were worrying about loved ones overseas, and the economy of the times called for gas rationing, and food shortages, and blackouts, everybody would crowd into town hall to see the kids wax delirious over a ten cent gewgaw, and sing themselves hoarse on the old standard carols. Santa had a voice suspiciously like Dode Kimball's in those days, and when a trusting little tyke would snuggle into his lap and list off her Christmas wishes, there'd be many a misty eye in the crowded hall.

Guess we don't need Christmas so much these days; presents have to be bigger and more gaudy, and music comes from a high-fi tape (spares your larynx, you see), and the kids get up to the big city department stores to see old St. Nick, or maybe they're enlightened at an earlier age. Somewhere in the inflationary spiral, we've lost a lot of values, spiritual as well as financial, and we, for one, would like to experience once more that warm feeling that Pamet folks shared a decade or so ago.

Remember the night, we reminded Snowie, that we stole up to the library with the Community Club recording machine and the Christmas records? This would have been about the time the spirit started to go down. We unraveled the electric cords, and placed the amplifiers outside in the cold, moonlit air, and huddled over the turntable as we dropped on the first selection—might have been "Hark, the Herald Angels Sing." Snowie dropped the tone arm, and the strains of the beautiful carol boomed across the square and up-valley to the snug cottages of Truro. Across the street the lights blazed merrily in the backroom of the liquor emporium, where a group of the boys were playing bid whist. Nary a soul in the light of the street lamp. We went through our entire collection, and, just as we were packing up to leave, the card game broke up and some anonymous man shouted up to us, "What're you fellers tryin' to do—wake everybody up?"

And so we wish a holy and a merry Christmas to all our friends and readers, near and far. May the holiday season be an oft-repeated joyous occasion for them.

NINETEEN FIFTY-EIGHT

1958

So it's New Year's Day, 1958, and we find ourselves in a retrospective mood: to view the vital statistics with the cautionary remark that they may not as yet be complete (delayed return of certificates from hospitals, etc); we find twenty births listed for the town. Of these, twelve are the children of Air Force personnel. First baby to be recorded by us was Alexander Nyers, Jr., and the last, so far for the year, is Dianne McQuaid. This was the year we became a grandfather, when Erin Lee Pirnie arrived at Cape Cod Hospital on February 22; and the most exciting birth of the period occurred when Mrs. John Canavarri, here with her husband for a brief visit on June 11, found the stork waiting for her at South Truro, despite the fact that their appointment was for a later date at their Tolland, Conn., home.

Marriages are off for 1957 from the previous year's total. To us, there's a striking reminder of our own approaching old age when we tally four of our former pupils among the couples. Most notable tying-of-the-knot probably is that of Norma Scaffard and Horace H. Snow, Jr., Pamet's most eligible bachelor. Deaths? As always, too many. And to fulfill the prophesy of the past, the young may die (Margaret Sears Mayo, of Pilgrim Heights) and little Mark Wade, who died by accident just before his fourth birthday. And the old must—to name a few of our neighbors who sleep in the quiet burying grounds of Truro—Georgianna Sawyer, Margaret Thornley, Joe Morris, Joe Peters, Sr., Bill L'Engle, Charles Russell, and John R. Dyer, Sr.

At first glance, you'd think it would require only a few colors on your palette to paint today's scene. A blending of grays for the sky overhead, a squirt of white for the unsullied country snow, some bottle green for the pitch pines, burnt umber for the tree boles. But the more you study the countryside, the more colors you see: a smoke blue where the ground haze rises before the screen of the distant conifers, a dash of ocre tracing the underside of the massed cloudbank to west'ard. Some red in the growing tips of the rum-cherry thicket and warm sable to duplicate the color of the sand patches in the hog cranberry moors. There'll be emerald green in the bay, too, soon's the sun brightens a mite more, and you'd best save a patch of azure for the lightening sky. And, if the task of putting the whole scene on canvas seems too big a challenge, just call Snowie of Castle Road, and he'll show up instanter, laden with his artist's tools, and do the job for you.

The thrill of Bermuda shorts is palling on Joe Gardner, Castle Road's man about town, or perhaps it's the burning shame occasioned by the new song "Short Shorts" (the lyrics, praise be, are not known to us), but in any event Joe is shopping for a new style in trousers. A mild rebuke herewith to Bob and Lora Bumps of Castle Road for the new sign they've placed on their premises: Apple Valley. We'd like to remind them that the section off Bridge Road is most famous for its Endicott Pear tree, fetched over in the Mayflower, so tradition says, and still living in the pot hole below the Bumps' cottage.

Well sir, we've been having high course tides this past week, and Pamet folks have been heading for the beaches in pursuit of the wily sea clam. Most of the natives have been content to explore the golden strands of the bay side, but a few of the hardier souls, among them Arthur Joseph, have gone to east'ard, braving the surf of the Atlantic. So it was that Pamet's fire chief piled into his car, a powerful, four-wheel drive affair and drove up to Ballston Beach, and thence to points north. "Good pickin's, too," quotes Arthur. "The extry high tides and the heavy surf had washed out dozens of huge sea clams, and all I has to do was stop every so often and scoop 'em into the car. Up past Dyer's Holler I went, and almost to Long Nook. Turned around on the hard packed sand, and made a return trip, drivin' real close to the water's edge. Just about had the back of my car loaded, I did, when all of a sudden I felt the wheels sink into a soft spot, smack on the surf line."

Arthur goes on to say how he tried every trick he knew to extricate the mired buggy; let some air out of the tires, threw burlap bags under the wheels for traction, pried under the axles with a plank—but all to no avail. Matter of fact, the car was sinking deeper with every try, and the tide was beginning to rise so that the waves were washing at the frame of the chassis. To top it all off, the sun had set by this time, and it was commencing to get dark. In a last, desperate attempt, Arthur tore open the door of the car, and unloaded those sea clams just as fast as he could toss them in the sand. "I know't is hard to believe," Arthur continues, "but fast as I'd drop them sea clams on the beach, they'd run out their hard, muscular feet, and work their way right under the Jeep.

"First thing I knew, the car began to lift up a mite, and then I knew what they were doing. For some strange reason, them sea clams was crawling right under the tires of the car. Soon's I realized this, I jumped in, started up the motor, slammed her into four-wheel drive, and backed up onto hard ground." We marveled with Arthur at the lucky turn of events. "Bet you went right back and covered 'em over with your rake so's the gulls wouldn't get 'em, didn't you?" we queried. Seemed to us that was the least neighbor Joseph could do as a measure of gratitude for the bivalves which had supplied him traction in his hour of need. Arthur chose not to answer us—at least not directly. "I like clam pie best," was his rejoinder, "but fritters and chowder go well, too."

It all started with a nice little compliment brought home to us by our good bride, recently. Annie had met the brother of our all-time favorite teacher, Miss Silva, (fifth through eighth grades, Wilder School) and the lady had sent word she liked our column. No offense intended, Miss Silva, to your fine husband of lo! these many decades, but to us you'll always be the unattached young schoolmarm from Wellfleet, and we'd like to reminisce with you a bit this evening. Perhaps we could dust off a few memories, and share a laugh or two.

Do you remember the old building as it looked on the September day when your brother Willie dropped you off at the path that led in from the state road? You had to wend your way through several clumps of thorny beachplum bushes, passing close by the big, tandem privy. (That was the year the school committee had voted to build an attached toilet on the west side of the main building, and the picturesque outbuilding was marked for razing.)

You had made arrangements to board over at Willie Hopkins place on Castle Road, and you were to see your folks only on week- ends, and you must have felt a slight twinge of homesickness as you stood there surveying the bleak, slab-sided building. Painted a kind of egg yolk yellow, it was, with green on the heavy box trim. You had to shin up a low concrete wall on your way to the coatroom, an ell which served for the storage of coal and wood as well as a common entrance to the two big rooms, known as the Big Part and the Little Part. Little Part accommodated grades one to four. Big Part had the students (the town reports in those days used to refer to them, hopefully, as scholars) of grades five through eight.

Several of the neighboring boys and girls would have been on hand to greet their new teacher. The Kanes, from up on the hill, and Ernie Snow, and the Ormsby brothers, and a few others who had walked to school. (Bob Morris would be late this first day. Barn chores would have detained him, and when he sidled in, during opening exercise, the pleasant smell of cow and horse would be with him.) You probably made a quick survey of your room: windows on three sides, west, south and east, excellent for admitting light, but also friendly to the wintry blasts a few months hence; the eternal buff paint on the walls, fly-blown and smoke darkened; rough wainscoting and windows and doors a utilitarian gray. The floor would be freshly oiled, and the big, potbellied iron stove would have its only coat of blacking for the year, and the desks would be arranged in geometric precision.

Against the south wall, a battered, walnut Estey knee organ, later to wheeze out its melodies as Miss Patterson, the busty, temperamental music teacher pumped at the carpeted pedals. But Offenbach would be in the room as the shrill reeds gave us his baccarole, and Schubert and Mendelssohn and Greig and McDowell were to visit with us in the year to come. (Miss Patterson is gone now, Miss Sylva, playing music we are sure, for a more appreciative audience.)

Your own desk occupied a place of vantage abreast the stove; on it, the big silver hand bell used to summon the kids from recess, and noon hour. (Remember how the noon hours used to lengthen when Mr. Fogwell, the dapper superintendent of schools, dropped in to pore over the records with the pretty new schoolmarm?) There was a limbér rattan on your desk, too, and a dog-eared Bible, and a collection of Nick Carter detective yarns for the indispensable light touch in literature, and "Cricket On The Heath" and "Tale of Two Cities" and Muzzey's "U. S. History" and assorted spellers and arithmetic texts.

And geography and history books, of course (they call them social studies, nowadays) and a big globe that used to creak when you spun it on its axis. Above your desk, on the wall, was a huge display card from a spice company, with dozens of exotic condiments and barks and herbs, and all along the north wall were the blackboards, soon to be covered with square root symbols, and words phonetically subdivided, and sentences that read: John hit + dog—the—big brown.

There was a flurry as the bus arrived, disgorging its cargo of Pamet youth; boys in corduroy knickers that whistled when they ran for the Hollow, across Depot Road (a never-ending baseball game was played there, and you were expected to umpire, and keep score, and occasionally fill a vacant position). The girls had new cotton dresses, and sensible ribbed cotton stockings, and long braids that smelled faintly of tar soap (best thing in the world to prevent, you know, those unmentionable things that the school nurse, Helen Sheridan, used to search for).

And lunch time—will you ever forget it? Wilder School became a sort of international delicatessen when the hands of the shiny nickel alarm clock scissored up to twelve. The kids would dash out to the rusty, long handled pump, and perform their hasty ablutions, and grasp their dinner baskets, and take seats beside their special beaux. There'd be the heady aroma of cold linguica, and the sulphurous fumes of hard-boiled eggs, and steamy fragrance of clam chowder or beef stew from a thermos bottle.

One question, if we may. If you had it all to do over again, Miss Silva, would you climb that narrow, winding path through the beachplum thicket to Wilder School?

Confusion reigns at our house these days as son Mike prepares his soul, his body, and his luggage for the forthcoming Boy Scout Camporee (May 23, 24, 25) up-Cape way. All we can do to keep the little monster from practicing his bugle calls for reveille some mornings at a time when a self-respecting sparrow wouldn't be out of bed.

Gentle reminder to delinquent doggies: only seventy-one of you shaggy rascals have purchased licenses so far this year. Our records indicate that there were many, many more canines in Pamet last year. Please remind your owners to purchase the nice, shiny brass tags that make you legal, or Mr. Gonsalves, the bad dog officer, will clap you in durance vile.

We got to talking with Bud Rich, the burly, genial handyman at the MIT site in South Truro the other day, and the conversation got around to the picturesque and unusual qualities of the native speech here on the lower Cape. "Disappearin' rapidly, even up in Eastham," bemoaned Bud, referring to the lost idiom, "and it's a shame we can't find someone to list some of those quaint constructions." We nodded our agreement as Bud continued his exposition. "Now you take Easthamers; if I was asked to give the most outstanding peculiarity of Eastham speech, I'd put the rolled dipthong head of the list. You know, the way they say 'naow' for now and 'caow' for cow." "And down in Truro," we interjected, "the corresponding speech figure would be the way the old timers used to pronounce 'coat' or 'boat.' Ed Snow, for instance (the good Lord rest his soul) used to broaden the vowel so's it came out 'coa(r)t'; take the r away, and you have a phonetic spelling of the word."

Ed had many more unusual constructions, too. In addition to differences in pronounciation, Ed would dredge back in the past and come up with words that sometimes required translation. For instance: a 'gump' according to our old friend, was a wedge. "Go fetch the gump," he'd order his son, Ernie, "so's I can cleft this here spile." And Ernie would fetch the wedge, and Ed would pound it into the section of driftwood piling, and she'd split. To Ed, sedge grass was always "sage" and nothing we could do, even a trip to Webster's dictionary, could dissuade Ed from using the word in describing the reed-like grass which grows in the salt Pamet. Those bony, scaly fish that came up the creek early every spring were ellwys, by gosh, no matter if they was called alewives in the encyclopedia. Turnip greens, and sweetcorn, and string beans were always served by the "mess"—a rather flexible term which for us had the connotation of more than a genteel sufficiency. You were fed a mess of corn at the tail of the season, for instance, when the ears were commencing to dry up, and there was a question of waste. No one could utter a double negative in mixed company with more impunity than Ed Snow. If he took issue with you, his mustache would bristle, and he'd shout, "Tain't nuther."

Ed's speech is not to be compared with the professional, studied, so-called New England accent so much favored on radio and TV. With this old timer, the constructions were genuine, and probably had basis in some early Yankee tradition. According to Ed, you went to the dee-po to see the train come in; sent your kids to the school-ouse (drop the aspirate h, elide the two words), took your city friends over to high-land to see the cliffs (equal accent on both syllables) and perhaps noted a heffah (heifer, female calf) on the way. Homeward bound, you'd stop for a bottle of "tonic" despite the fact no medicinal claims had ever been made for the carbonated liquid, and you'd be attacked by "mites" as you drove through Long Nook (we call 'em gnats today). Safely arrived at the barn, you'd unhitch the horse, lead him out of the sharves (shafts), inspect the buckle on the britchin' (breeching), and slip into a jumpa (denim jacket) so's you wouldn't pick up the smell of the stable on your good clothes. Ed used to drop some s's, too. It was upstair, and downstair, with Ed and the possessive pronouns were you'n, her'n, and sometimes his'n.

Larry Wright, mine host of the Blacksmith Shop, tells the petite yarn about Al Rose and Larry's mother to prove that our New England habit of dropping our r's can lead to actual communication barriers in the conversational arts. Seems Aloysius, then a young lad, met Mrs. Wright over in Long Nook one day (she was visiting Larry—lived on the West Coast) and Al excitedly reported to her that he'd seen several Ammy cazz. After three attempts to establish what Al was talking about, Mother Wright gave up, later relayed her conversation to Larry. Larry finally figured out that Aloysius had been referring to the trucks of a military convoy (the war was on at the time) and he translated for his mom: Army cars was the mysterious phrase.

And when the day comes when any future moderator at our town meetin's eschews the use of the authentic and expressive "Aye" pronounced "I" for an affirmative vote, we'll consider that an era of effeteness, of cowardly submission to current usage has been reached. We'll condemn his action by sending him a "billet" (note) telling him he "don't amount to Hannah Cook," and Ed Snow will smile in his grave.

★ ★ ★

We got to talking with Snowie at the Carleton party the other afternoon. We were noodling at the piano, and Snowie was humming a few bars from "Chanson Triste" when a charming, lithe female walked by and we both caught a portion of her conversation. "C'est un homme charmant, avec ses cheveux gris," quoth she in rapid, native French. She was looking, of course, directly at Snowie, as he leaned over the battered Baldwin. And instead of accepting the remark as a compliment, Horace bristled. "No one's going to call me a gray horse," he charged, and it was all we could do to explain that the lady had been actually referring to his gray thatch. And that brought up a yarn, which Snowie spun for us against a background of clinking glasses and assorted small talk.

"That's not the first time I've got involved over a foreign language—and French, at that. You remember, of course, that I worked at old Eben Paine's store for several years when I went to high school," Snowie began, as we played the opening bars of "The Last Time I Saw Paris" (in F-sharp) as background music. "First off, I just delivered orders for Eben in his horse drawn buggy. Covered the territory from Corn Hill to Long Nook to Ballston to South Truro. Then I commenced to take orders over the telephone, and fill 'em, and finally I graduated to waitin' on people in the dry grocery department."

The word dry must have reminded Snowie that his glass was empty, for he excused himself and strolled over to the refreshment section, while we modulated into "Cocktails for Two." We'd progressed to the bridge of the song when our narrator returned. "Third summer of my employment, Mr. Paine decided to try me out at the very top rung of the ladder," said Snowie. "He fitted me to a white apron, and a straw hat and a pair of straw wristers, and set me to work in the meat department. First I did the simple chores: made the corned beef, and salted the pork, and unpacked the meat shipments from Boston. Then, gradually, he taught me to cut chops, and section a side of a steer, and slice a tenderloin."

The memory of the hard labor in Eben's butcher shop apparently called for another trip to the bar. We took advantage of the interruption to massage the black keys in a few bars of "Smoke Gets in Your Eyes." "Never forget the day this society lady showed up at the store. Mr. Paine was out back, pumpin' kerosene, so I had to wait on her myself. I gave the butcher knife a final touch on the sharpenin' steel, and asked if I could be of service. This woman was a real summer complaint. Nouveau riche, you could tell right off, because she tried to order in French. 'Young man,' she said, 'do you have any saucisson?' I could see she was glancing at the cold meat display, so I yanked out a yard or so of Portuguese linguica, and wrapped it up quick as a flash. Then she asked for 'côtelette de mouton,' and I took a chance and said 'how many?' and when she answered with a number, I guessed she wanted some chops, and I got through that item."

Fortunately, the lady then remembered she required some vegetables, so Snowie says he shunted her off to the main store, where Mary Fratus filled that part of her order. We complimented Snowie on his handling of what could have been a rather difficult situation. "But that's not the whole story," Snowie interrupted us, as he excused himself, while we rendered "A Pretty Girl is Like a Melody" for Mrs. Cushman, who was leaning over our piano. "Back comes the lady, in a moment or so," continued our narrator, "and she says, 'Have you any cervelles?' Well, this was one thing I couldn't bluff, so I up and told her I didn't know what she was talking about. 'Brain—brains, young man. Don't you have any brains?' she barked at me. And then I told her off.

"'Lady,' I says, 'you're lookin' at the winner of the Washington-Franklin history medal, Wellfleet High School 1928.'"

You'd look pale and washed out, too, if you'd been out all night. And that's how the waning moon appears this cool, breezy October morning, as it rides out its course over the western sky, where the pale blue bowl blends with the brittle indigo of the bay. We saw it rise, eightish of last evening, into the eastern cleft of the valley, pale orange, swathed in the mist of the creek, looming large against the clustered, distant stars. The wind was strong from the northwest then, but sometime during the night it swung around to a southerly quarter, and stirred the chill night air so that no frost could settle in the valley, and we were pleased to cast an appreciative eye at salvia, and salmon dahlias and even a pair of burgeoning geraniums in our backyard.

And all day the breeze has been pressing in from the bay, marshalling a legion of white caps that batter themselves against the stone jetties of Beach Point; and windblasted plumes of sand rise from the dunes of Pilgrim Lake, and an endless procession of purposeful cottonwhite clouds makes its way across the Narrow Land.

Today, if your business took you to Provincetown, you switched over onto old Route 6, to avoid sand-blasting your car on the new highway; and you felt the buffeting of the wind in the open stretches between the cottages of The Point, and, where the road runs close by the breakwater abaft Snail road, the spray of the wind-torn waves streaked your windshield. From our classroom windows we watched the force of the sou'wester as it funneled up Winslow St., flattening the foliage on the tossing trees of Monument Hill, whipping the red pennant of the storm signal. When Frankie Aresta, the genial janitor came into our room after school armed with his cleaning tools, he shook his head and opined as how the "traps'll catch hell in this weather."

Local notes: lights on at Dr. Bloomberg's across the valley, and Fr. Dave Weden down to close up his Pamet Road summer cottage the weekend. It's a baby girl for our niece (she the former Roberta Kane) and her fine husband, Leon Remington of Boston. Pop Snow has his full crew at work on Fred Davis' studio off Holsbery Road, hopes to have 'er closed in by cold weather. Here's how the Evening Practical Arts classes shape up for the coming year: upholstery and slip covers will commence Monday, October 26, 1:30 p.m. at the town hall, and on Tuesday, the 27th, rug hooking, same place, at 12:30 p.m. For the North Truro contingent, a hooking class on Friday, the 30th, Village Mall, 12:30 p.m. . . .

Our good wife fetched home some apples from the store today. We opened the fancy cellophane bag and bit into a juicy Mac, waiting for the muse to visit us as we composed our column. Things have come to a pretty pass, we thought, when a feller can't find any native grown apples in Truro. Time was when almost every home owner had a small orchard; Baldwins, and Macs, and Gravestines, and Winter Kings and you didn't have to search too far to locate a neighbor who had quinces, and the annual Farm Bureau Fair at town hall always had displays of native grown pears, and peaches, and we recall that Mr. Manuel Corey even used to produce black walnuts at his Edgewood Farm.

Now there was an orchard—small, but well-tended, the Corey plot was located in a sun-washed, sheltered basin south of the big barn. There, in geometric order, Mr. Corey had planted dozens of trees, comprising almost every variety of fruit that would grow in this climate. Folks used to wonder at neighbor Corey's success in pomology. The prosperous farmer-Town Clerk admitted his fine orchard was based on "one-third hen manure, one-third hard work, one-third luck."

It used to be a pleasant experience to drop by the Corey place in early fall when the crop was being picked. On the north side of the house, near the kitchen door, there used to be a big concrete platform, and on this Mr. Corey would pile his apples so's they'd get a touch of frost. Such a smell of blended fruity odors as would titillate the nostrils of a wooden Indian—and woe to anyone caught filching one of the handpicked beauties. Mr. Corey had a stock of windfalls and seconds for giving away.

We've heard tell that old Mr. Joe Peters, Sr., of North Truro, had added his considerable talent to the success of the Corey orchard. Joe, of course, was a master of the art of tree grafting; and early in the spring, so they say, Joe would select choice scions from Mr. Corey's healthy young orchard stock, and graft 'em onto carefully chosen hosts. Arthur "Plady" Francis, who used to assist Joe on some occasions, remembers that his boss was wont to use genuine beeswax to seal the cuts in the bark, wrapping the joints with red flannel from long drawers. "There'd be enough bright red patches in an orchard after me an' Joe got through graftin'," claims Plady, "to set a Guernsey bull wild."

Each year we promise ourself we'll save a list of notes, alphabetically or chronologically filed, of the highlights of the previous twelvemonth—and each year the press of business or just plain lack of system keeps us from the chore. How easy it would be to compose this, the final column of the year, if we had such a file. A for athletics, we'd say: Little League activities, the first formal recreation program in the town of Truro, with Leo Miller as first director, the annual swimming program under Red Cross sponsorship, and the weekly teenage dances at town hall. B for business: generally good, despite foul summer weather, wettest season in years. Transfer of owner-ship of the local Texaco Station, new proprietor Joe Schoonejongen.

We could slip building in here too: largest structure erected in 1958 the Depot Road Cadorette house, now abuilding; smallest, probably Harry Twite's duplex on Collins Road extension. F for fishing, of course—angling good in the Pamet, where the brownies and brookies provided sport in the cold spring months, the salt water bass season so-so, and commercial fishing the best year in many for the North Truro trappers, and may they have more of the same.

Now the memory becomes a kaleidoscope, and we take the liberty of reporting in the order in which the pictures appear. Vital statistics, for instance—to date, 21 births reported, of which four are native, the balance Air Force and transient personnel. Marriages, of the seven licenses issued from this office, five of our town folks are the principals: Beverly Williams—Archie Morrison, Jack Carleton—Connie Janssen, Peter Morris—Carolyn Wood, John Adams—Amy Williams, and Norman Rose—Delores Mooney.

On the shores of the mighty Pamet rose the cottage of neighbor Snowie, one time purveyor of petrol, wit, bon vivant, artist and raconteur; and despite many snide remarks in this column anent high tides and shellfish, the home still stands, and we hope to dive into the limpid waters of the crick from its front doorstep come next summer.

Death touched the town in many fashions: to the old, they say, death must come, and so it was with our good friends John Francis of the North Village and with Chief John Williams of Beach Point, both of whom had served out their three score and ten. But to George Drysdale of Whitmanville, death came too young in life; George left two beautiful young children, and the Drysdale homestead looks sad and deserted these days.

And so it goes. A short year, certainly—since we passed our fourth decade they seem to have taken a handful of days from each year and placed a corresponding number of steps in the old familiar staircases. We've put on a bit around the middle, taken a mite off the top; and old friends seem somehow grayer at the temples, and they repeat themselves when they spin a yarn, and they seem to want to reminisce when we get together nowadays. And every spring, when we go to the cemeteries to cut the lots, there are newly chiseled names on the stones, and we miss an old face at the post office when we go to fetch the mail. Then, of course, old friends seem to mean more, and we make the silent promise to visit a mite more often this year.

NINETEEN FIFTY-NINE

1959

Sunday, by all the rules, should be a quiet, restful day, pleasant to experience, and easy to chronicle. Not so yesterday, as witness the notes of our journal. Up betimes, and fortified against the morning chill by a hearty breakfast of eggs fresh from neighbor Dick Magee's farm, to early Mass, there to follow the services and study our fellow parishioners. Little Paul Hoeffel, the altar boy, caught in the rays of the sun as it streamed through the stained glass windows, looking as angelic as a body could imagine; a group of Air Force boys, bearing the stamp of the military despite their sporty civilian dress; the shapely bald pate of neighbor Joe Nunes of the North Village (hope our cranial structure will be as handsome when we lose our hair). Virginia Souza and her two handsome sons (the younger falling asleep on her shoulder—seems only yesterday Virginia herself was as tiny); the infectious ripple of throat clearing, originating with Charlie Joseph in the back pew. After church, the friendly exchange of greetings on the parking lot—men folks digging for their cigarettes (didn't we read somewhere that smoking was allowed in the early cathedrals?), the minor rush of business at Joe Schoonejongen's, as folks stopped by for their Sunday papers.

Thence to South Truro, where No. 2 son, Terry had an appointment with the chickens of Dick Magee's Oasis; and while he gathers the eggs and spreads the grain, we attack a long-postponed project in the colonel's workshop, fabricating a colonial fireside bench for our good wife. And the colonel himself, jaunty in a Tyrolean hat, supervises us as we use the power tools, advising caution lest we damage our piano-playing digits in the buzz saw. The bench roughed out, we repaired to our own cellar, there to worry away at the sweet-smelling pine with sun-dry abrasives. (Wonder if a body could make his own sandpaper, here in this land of the dunes?) Whenever we work with wood, we recall with many fond sentiments the late Hakon Olsen, cabinet maker par excellence, whose eye was so accurate he could detect the minute differences in the borders of the picture cards of any deck.

And our reveries are interrupted by the frantic cries of our two youngest heirs, who burst into the basement with the electrifying news that Dolce, our springer pup, has fallen through the thin ice of the creek abreast our house. So we seize a coil of rope and sprint for the Pamet, floundering through the alder clumps, stirring up clouds of cattail seedlets, stumbling over meadow grass tufts, urged on the while by the piteous wails of our poor dog as he claws at the jagged ice. Breathless and trembling, we arrive on the bank, and shouting words of encouragement we toss our rope to Dolce, who nuzzles the line hopefully, stares at us with panic-filled eyes.

And then Mike, our No. 3 son, gingerly steps out on the ice, lowers himself belly first on the flexing, cracking skim, and dry-swims toward our pet. Scarcely ten feet off shore, the ice gives away with a sickening crunch, and Mike is plunged into the cold, black Pamet. Words of advice from the neighborhood kids on the bank, yowls from Dolce, confused orders from O'Caghan. Meanwhile Mike proceeds to break his way through the ice, and eventually he grasps his dog with one hand, seizes the rope with the other, and we haul both ashore, a shivering, dripping pair. We recall that other dogs have been lost in the Pamet, under similar circumstances. Tony Duarte found his whole family of scotties in a spring hole in early fishing season (he'd thought them to be stolen) and the Joseph's samoyede fell through the ice and drowned some years back. Well sir, excitement enough for one day, say we.

We got to talking with Col. Dick Magee down at the Oasis, his Truro farm the other day. We were telling him about the new horn we're playing in the Orleans Band—a euphonium (actually a baritone horn with double bell, so's you get not only the traditional mellow tone of the baritone, but the sharp blare of a trombone).

Col. Dick thought the horn's name sounded somewhat like a contagious disease. "And it has five valves," we went on, "first three for regular playing in concert b-flat open tone scale, octave lower'n a trumpet. Fourth valve takes the place of a combination of the first three—too complicated to explain the tone equivalents—and the fifth valve bypasses the air column through the aforementioned trombone bell—makes 'er sound like a wounded moose." The colonel found our description sufficiently amusing; suggested perhaps we should take out a plumber's license if we intended to make the baritone our life study. In addition, our brief dissertation in brass, as it were, evoked a memory from the colonel—a slight smile played about his lips, a twinkle came to his eye, and we recognized the syndrome of a yarn a-borning.

"Ever tell you about the time I played bugle in the Mexican Situation?"

queried our host. We admitted as how that pleasure had not yet been granted to us. "Back in 1916-1917, that would be," continued the colonel. "Time of the Pancho Villa atrocities south of the border. Expropriations of American oil interests, anti-religious demonstrations, raids across the Rio Grande; so finally Uncle Sam decided to send some men to keep an eye on things down there." At this point our narrator rose from his chair and threaded a tape on the stereophonic machine, and soon the persuasive, Latin-American rhythm of "Cucaracha" and sundry other Mexican songs filled the pleasant Magee living room. We found the background melodies altogether fitting.

"Well sir, I was only sixteen at the time, but, being big for my age I decided to bluff my way into the armed forces. They were organizing and reactivating the famous Charlestown [Magee makes it a three syllable word—Charl-ess-town—as do all true Irishmen] Militia, under my good friend Col. Murphy, so I went over to see him of a Saturday night."

But try as hard as he could, Col. Murphy was unable to cut the red tape of the enlistment procedure to accept young Magee. "Finally, however, we got word from Washington that waivers of age would be granted if the applicant showed some special skill, such as radio operator, or cook, or musician. And within ten minutes I had a shiny bugle clutched in my hot fist and had signed my enlistment papers," says Magee. "Couldn't blow a note, of course, nor read one, but I figgered by the time we reached the theatre of operations, I'd have picked up sufficient skill to pass as a bugler."

It was a glorious moment indeed when Richard Aloysius Magee, musician 3rd, marched down Bunker Hill St. with his outfit, just back of the officers and the colors, the July sun reflecting on brass of button and horn, relatives and friends lining the sidewalk. "But the glamour wore off a mite," continues our host, "when we climbed aboard the train at North Station. Dusty, hot day coaches, with sleeping accommodations harder'n a Hogsbacker's heart, and poor food, and warm, stale water, and crowded conditions.

"At long last we arrived at our encampment across the border and things began to look up. They separated the men from the boys, then, and for once I was glad to be considered a youth—because while we musicians trilled away at bugle calls, the foot soldiers had to everlastingly drill in the hot sun, and tote rifles, and dig trenches, and slog away at military problems. Only fly in the ointment was the jealousy among the musicians—feller I'd planned to have as instructor turned against me, and I just couldn't learn the calls by myself. The notes looked like fly specks on the staff, and when I tried for the high ones, my lip would crack."

This precarious condition obtained, according to the colonel, until one day when a shavetail major, anxious to impress a visiting general of his efficiency, pulled a surprise maneuver that called for participation of every soul in camp. "Five in the morning, it was," reminisces Magee. "To the staccato call of the bugle the troops rolled out, sentries were extra-posted, the cavalry unit galloped off into the dawn, artillery was rolled into place, communications were set up, calls went out for advance, retreat, counter attack; you never heard such a confusion of sound. Pretty soon they had all the other buglers busy triple-tonguing the various calls, and finally they ran out of buglers, and the major sent over for me to add to the cacophony. I sprinted up, gave him a quick salute, and took his order. 'Blow Cavalry Charge,' he bellowed at me. And I quick put the bugle to my lips and let out a string of notes that I happened to remember from previous lessons.

Suddenly the mock fighting stopped, the horsemen dismounted, the artillery unit started to disassemble their cannon, and the observers pulled in their telescopes. And then that major turned on me, vicious-like, and snarled, 'Magee, you fool, you just gave Church Call.'"

Pamet kitchens are delightfully redolent of the odor of sea clams cooking in a variety of dishes these days. Last week saw one of the best series of tides, and a consequent high yield of the bivalve delicacies, in recent years. We got to thinking, as we were opening our catch at the kitchen sink, that we should pass on the recipe for sea clam fritters given us many years ago by Mrs. Caroline Fisher, longtime resident of South Truro, generally conceded to be one of the finest cooks in town. This message is, of course, intended for brothers of the skillet, and the language will be so couched; and, since it very often happens that the SPISCULA SOLIDISSIMA is delivered to the man of the house alive, squirting, and in the shell, perhaps it would not be amiss to preface our recipe with a brief course in shucking.

First of all, select a spot near a supply of running water, cover the neighboring area with newspapers (sea clams eject more water than a volunteer fire department when they're being de-shelled), and, extremely important, seize the family cat by the scruff of the neck and lock him in a sound proof closet. Cats behave in the presence of freshly opened clams in a manner analagous to the worst human alcoholic; unless confined, they'll snatch the still squirming mollusk from your hand—and their cries are so pitiable you really should put them out of earshot.

Well sir, then you grasp your sea clam with your left hand, narrow, or snout end pointing to your right, hinge of shell farthest away from you. Select a stiff, 6-inch blade knife, insert the point abaft the poor critters snout, or siphon, push until you feel the for'ard adductor muscle part under the keen steel, then draw the blade smartly towards you, around the rim of the clam, ending up by severing the stern adductor muscle. After you've lifted off the top shell, you'll have a chance to study the anatomy of the animal, and next time you'll put an angle on your blade that will remove less of the muscle, making clean cuts on the muscles. Now you scoop your blade under the palpitating flesh, freeing the other end of the muscle tissue, and PLOP! the entire soft body of the clam will drop out of the shell.

Well sir, now you deftly cut away all the brownish, thin gill structure and, pinching the bag or stomach firmly between thumb and forefinger, you squeeze out the entire gastro-intestinal system. Lastly, you must strip the thin, black membrane that will remind you of weatherstripping from the rim of the clam, douse him in water to remove any stray grains of sand, and toss him into the food chopper.

Now for the recipe: for each cup of finely chopped clams, add a golden Magee egg, lightly whipped with just enough tap water to thin; scant teaspoon of baking powder for the same cup of clams, and just enough table flour to make a gluey batter. Toss in a smidgin of black pepper, and, having lubricated a big, black iron spider with a chunk of salt pork tried out so's she commences to smoke a mite, you drop your batter in and fry golden brown on both sides. Then you tuck a napkin under your chin, serve the fritters with a dab of butter and season to taste. A pox on you if you desecrate this heavenly dish with catsup or other strong condiments. Have some member of your family stand by with a stop watch, tell 'em to ring a bell at the end of twenty minutes or the consumption of 18 fritters, whichever comes first.

Then you stop eating, release the family cat from his closet, and study the tide calendar for the next sea clam tide.

Inevitably, as come the Mayflowers, high school junior proms, the muted roar of Sumner Horton's tractor plowing gardens, the dismantling of living room stoves, and the brewing of sulfur and molasses, so comes the urge for the first natatorial adventure of the season to the youth of Cape Cod. Except for the considerable physic-fortitude involved, the business of taking that first swim today is much less involved than it was in our time. First place, the parents don't seem to regard a pre-season dip with as much disapproval as did our mothers and fathers. Swimming before July 1 brought frowns, and a plunge before June was absolutely forbidden. Seems you couldn't take that first dip before you went barefoot, and that date usually coincided with closing of school and full leafage of the locust trees. Then too, transportation today makes a visit to any swimming spot a cinch. In our time, you did it on foot. You'd stealthily make your way with a group of hardy youths up Collins Road to Truro Great Pond for the earliest dip (ponds were supposed to be milk warm in March) and a mite later you'd try the bay, after a long hike to the Depot, or Corn Hill. And finally, when the fog rolled back from the shore a few weeks later, you'd brave the surf at Ballston Beach or Dyer's Hollow.

In those days we used to have a long lunch period at the old Wilder School—a full hour for meandering the neighboring countryside—and as soon as the weather got warm, the temptation of the first swim would appear in the schoolyard in the form of sundry dares hurled by the boys at each other. We didn't use the word "chicken" in those days, but there were adequate synonyms, and finally, on a pleasant, warm spring day, the young lads would tuck their lunch boxes under their arms, and slip down Depot Road, and across the old Town Pound parcel, and down to the shore by Naylor Hatch's landing (you had to keep an eye peeled for Naylor—he was the fleetest-footed truant officer in Barnstable County) and thence to Marshall's Cove. A clump of scrub pines on the river bank made good shelter for your clothes, and if the tide was high, you had only to take a few cautious steps on your winter-tender soles on the wiry salt meadow grass before you felt the first sudden shock of the icy water. At low tide you'd have to plod through the standing pools and the mud holes, and finally, on the bank just abreast Monroe's Landing you'd find sufficient water to take the agonizing initial plunge. Last one in, of course, was a "rotten egg," or a "cow's tail," or some such. Fortunately, the creek was always so frigid that your swim was a short one, and there'd just be time to dash ashore, dry off in the sun, bolt down your sandwiches, don your clothes (remember how uncomfortable they felt, adhering to the briny drops on your hide?) and trot back to the gaunt, yellow building on the hill.

Well sir, folks on their way across Wilder's Dyke could see the kids, naked as jayhawks, frolicking on the river bank, and invariably there'd be a message sent to school, informing the teacher of our truancy, lunacy, and indecent exposure. So, when we got back to the old Wilder, a grim pedagogue would be awaiting us, and the cross examination would begin. If memory serves, the conversation could have gone like this: Mr. Joe Peters would be the suspicious teacher, Bob Morris, an accomplished storyteller, would be spokesman for the boys.

Mr. Peters: Boys, where have you been?

Bob: We just had a game of hares and hounds, Mr. Peters. Took some paper scraps from the waste basket, we did, and left a trail up by Holway's, and back of Mr. Corey's, and . . .

Mr. Peters: Must have done a good deal of perspiring Robert. You're all wringing wet.

Bob: Yes, sir. And then we headed down back of the town dump, and up Deerfield Road, and back of Marshall's . . .

Mr. Peters: But you just came up Depot Road, Robert, and your hair is all plastered down, and there's mud on your sneakers. Looks to me as though you've been swimming.

Bob: In April, Mr. Peters? Oh no, sir, we finally followed the trail down by the shore, of course, and picked up a bit of mud on our shoes, but it's too cold to go swimmin' yet.

Mr. Peters: Well, suppose we talk it over after school, boys. Maybe we can find out who those youngsters were that Eben Paine saw from the Dyke, about fifteen minutes ago.

And he always found out, too. And even if the rattan switch was brought into play, next year the first spell of warm weather would call for a repeat performance, and we guess that's the way it has to be, come spring.

Ernie Snow was down the weekend, here for the sad task of cleaning out the last of his personal effects from the old Snow homestead on the corner, which will shortly be conveyed to the town for razing in preparation for clearing of the land for a local park. Ernie gave us a whole passel of photographs and mounted pictures which we will display on our office wall to serve as a link with the past. Yellowing chromos of the Cobb Library (bare grounds, gaunt stucco walls—you can almost smell the fresh paint and the freshly graded earth) and Pamet Garage (now Mary Howard's store— with boss Ernie and his helper/mechanic Mike Howard braced against the gas pumps, holding socket wrenches in their grimy hands. We note that standard petrol, in those days, sold for 16¢ per gallon, by the way) and group pictures of the doughty fire department, be-booted, be-capped, and rubber-coated, perched on the glossy new Brockway fire trucks.

Got to talking with Joe Gardner last evening at the Little League baseball practice, and Joe became so engrossed in our conversation that he followed us over to the cemetery by the church, where we had chores to do. You all know Joe, of course. Genial, friendly sort of fellow who spent a good deal of his time around Norm Lee's Texaco Station. Sixtyish, tall, lean, his craggy features are Florida tanned, and he wears heavy, horn-rimmed glasses which give him a professional mien. Joe is wearing faded blue denim outfits these days, but, come warm weather, he'll blossom out in Bermuda shorts that would put a parakeet to shame. Joe is a native son, of course, kin to the illustrious Paine clan on the distaff side, and related to the Snows, and the Dyers, and sundry other early Pamet families. Matter of fact, it was Joe's greatgrandfather who donated the church plot on the hill to the Congregational Society in 1827, and he's also a direct descendant of the Gross family. Surely you've seen the pictures of the famed Gross Sisters in your travels around the Lower Cape? But neighbor Gardner, although he is properly proud of his antecedents, is not content to rest on laurels previously earned. You see, Joe, directly after he had graduated from Wilder School hied off to the big city to make his own way in the world. We didn't get this whole yarn from Joe in one piece last night (the nip in the air at dusk drove us from the hilltop before Joe could complete his autobiography) but we'll draw on memory to fill in the gaps.

"Yes, Terry," (Joe was addressing our No. 2 son, while we gassed and checked the power mowers preparatory to attacking the grass in the Congregational Cemetery). "I'm what you might call a self-made man. Sort of a Horatio Alger. Went up to Boston my first year out of school, bunked in with some of my relatives. Tried everywhere to get a job, but jobs were scarce—we were havin' a mite of a slump, just before World War I. Most Cape boys used to head for the market in those days—they were at home around poultry, and eggs, and vegetables because of their home training—but I couldn't find a thing there, despite the fact I had connections through a distant cousin, Art Cobb, a native of South Truro. From there I started hunting in the South End, and finally landed a job with Beggs and Cobb (old Elisha W. Cobb from the Hogsbacks was a partner in the firm). Started right in at the bottom, I did, working in the tannery in Winchester, working with chemicals, and hides, and tanning materials. Began as an ordinary laborer, and gradually worked up to a foreman's job, and eventually became a full-fledged inspector."

Terry wanted to know what the duties and special qualities of an inspector were. "Well sir," Joe continued, overjoyed at the chance to expound on his beloved trade, "I had to learn to recognize all the qualities of leather. All sorts of hides, where they came from, quality of the leather, type of tanning best suited for processing, wearing qualities, and so forth. For example, those shoes you're wearing are grade 2B cowhide," here Joe glanced closely at Terry's footwear in the approaching dusk, "tanned with Spencer's Solution, soles oak-tanned. Finished shoe should retail for about $8.95."

Terry was properly impressed, but requiring further proof of Joe's expertness, he reached in our truck and fetched out his baseball glove. "This leather? Fine quality cowhide, grade 2A, I should say," opined Joe. "Oil-tanned, from the hindquarter of a Wisconsin Jersey cow, looks like; critter would've been about three years old when slaughtered. A few tick scars right here, but nothing serious. Lacing is rawhide, also oil-tanned, and the lining is what we call kip, in the trade. Keep plenty of neatsfoot oil on it, and it should last you for years."

Only article of leather we had on our person was our size 42 belt, so we pulled it from our trousers, handed it to Joe for his inspection. He looked it over carefully, then: "This'n almost stumped me. Got it now, though. Belly strippin' from a Brahman bull, lined with calf. Cured by Fehling's process, so's it won't stretch, although it seems to have conformed to your girth right well."

Terry believes that man, we can tell by the open expression on his face, but as far as Joe Gardner's dissertation on leather is concerned, the only true word he spoke, in our opinion, was when he referred to the male of the cow family.

This is a day of several lasts. It's the last day, for instance, that we'll peck away at our column in the commercial room of Wellfleet High School, with Miss Richardson chiding us: "Last minute before the deadline, eh?" And this Wednesday, June 17, 1959, marks our last lunch, prepared, as always, with loving care by Gloria Delory and her fine kitchen gals. This, too, is the last full day session of Wellfleet High School. Exams will be finished tomorrow and supplies will occupy the final hours. And we'd like to take this occasion to thank all our colleagues at WCS for the years of happy association with them.

To Dick Cochran, then, our principal—to Elizabeth Hooker, and to Ed O'Brien, and to Martha Porch and to Carolyn Richardson, fellow workers all in the Temple of Learning, hail and farewell. To Ed Bolton, the art man, and Frank James, the music man, and to Dulce Ryder, the singing lady, and to Hardy Atwood, that prince among janitors, au 'voir. And to the kids, too: sorry we won't be together at Orleans, next year; we'll follow your doings in the papers and via the famous teacher's grapevine—and remember, if we had to use the yardstick occasionally to remind you of the rule for changing fractions to decimals (divide the TOP number by the BOTTOM number) it hurt us more than it did you.

Speaking of exams. We're using the Coops this year, as usual, at Wellfleet. And this morning, two cute little seventh grade girls were talking over yesterday's science test. Said pretty Judy Belanger, "Wonder what the answer to that question about diesel engines was?" Replied pretty Marsha Richey, "I checked with Mr. O'Brien, and he said the answer was 'sparkplugs.' But I got it right: I guessed number four— four always turns out right if you guess it."

We were busily proving our payroll yesterday at town hall when in walked neighbor Snowie, grinning from ear to ear, cuddling something in the bulge of his shirtfront. "What'cha got there?" we queried the Sultan of Slade's Landing. "Pet crow," replied Snowie, "I've eaten crow many a time;

never had the opportunity to tame one before." Snowie went on to say as how we'd ought to have a pet crow for our office—claimed it would give some inspiration, much as did that raven for Edgar Allen Poe. At this point the bird stuck his head out from his hiding place, fixed us with a cold, blue eye, and seized our extended forefinger with his powerful beak. We withdrew our bleeding index with a mild imprecation for our attacker. "All's he did was gum you a mite," Snowie half apologized.

We could see the Castle Road man was looking for some publicity for self and bird, so we took out our notepad, commenced to take some notes. It appears Frankie Davis discovered the nest over South Truro way, took out several baby birds, gave one to Snowie, and Snowie named it Crowlet Geoff, Jr., in honor of the Snow mongrel dog. "Built a nice, rustic cage for him down to the house," chortled Snowie, "feed him a handful of cracked corn twice a day, and sometimes a worm or two. And I'm teaching him how to talk—he's had three lessons so far, and you wouldn't believe—say hello to the man, Geoff, Jr."

"Lorks," said the crow. "See? What'd I tell you. Plain as day, he said it." And before we could finish our interview with Geoff, Jr., Snowie had toted him out into the main hall, where the state auditors are working, and the crow went through his routine again. Thence to Lucille Medders' office and, "Say hello to cousin Lucy, Geoff, Jr." coaxed Snowie. "Lorks-s-s," said Geoff, Jr. Last thing we heard from the happy pair was a brief exchange as Snowie got into his car. "What say we drop by the package store and get some pretzels for your supper, Geoff, Jr.?"

"Lorks," said the crow.

Getting so the wind direction doesn't mean a thing in prognosticating the weather. Time was when a breeze out of the nor'west meant clear, cool, dry spells, but this onetime reliable aid to the forecaster has lost its validity. Today, for instance, the gilded weathercock atop town hall has been pointing to the headlands of Manomet across the bay, but, in place of blue skies and crisp weather, we're swathed in a lowering cloud of gray, part mist, with wisps of fog and occasional rain spatters. Several times the sun has attempted to burn through, but on each occasion the caul of the cloud cover has won the struggle. Smells cling close to the ground today. The sick-sweet odor of privet blossom, and the spice of bayberry, and the acrid tang of pitch pine. And there's a blossom for you in a wide variety of shades; delicate Queen Ann's lace in purest white, and old maid's pinks, and heliotrope wild trumpets on the meadow, and palest lavender of the milkweed.

In other summers the wildflower pattern would be scattered on a background of drought-seared poverty grass and wilted meadow tufts—not so this July. Lush and green are Pamet lawns, and the busy sound of the power mower sounds over the landscape in the after supper hours. When it isn't raining there's the promise of rain in the high humidity. We haven't, for instance, had salt for weeks in any satisfying quantity from our clogged shakers—and when we try to slit open our mail at town hall, the letter opener shreds reluctantly through the limp envelopes. But folks will not be dissuaded by the unkind season—Chief Berrio of Truro's finest says the beaches are crowded, and traffic is bumper-to-bumper on the highway, and last night, for one of the rare times this season, Beach Point "No Vacancy" signs were a-burgeoning.

Report of the Committee to Raise a Beard for Truro's 250th Birthday: most luxuriant beard to date—Dickey Steele. New members of the week—Wes Garran and Charlie Holway and Russ Holway of the North Village. Pledges, Thompson Holway and Al Tinker. Thanks to our good friend Arthur Ryan of Castle Road, we are in receipt of a plate depicting beard styles with proper nomenclature listed, and we shall display the pictures at our office so that members of the club may choose a hirsute decoration that not only harmonizes with facial contours, but possesses historical significance. Dickey Steele, for instance, had been growing a Newgate Fringe, but one glance at the handsome variation calling for the addition of a mustache, and Dickey switched to a chin puff Newgate. (Both these varieties are named for the famous London prison.)

Al Tinker has promised to sprout a Dundreary, and Charlie Holway, we understand, will blossom out in a spaded Shenandoah. Our own combination doesn't appear to be a standard style, so we've dubbed it the Hogsbacker. The Committee welcomes all men aboard, so that we may fittingly celebrate Pamet's two and a half centuries of incorporation.

Midafternoon, and the heat lies like a coverlet on the valley. The sun is brass-bright, and a faint blue haze clings to the distant Hogsbacks hills. There'll be tourists along, at sundry times during the afternoon, to poke their heads in at town hall door with the perennial questions: What church is this? (T'ain't a church at all, lady, we'll reply in our best native dialect, she's a town hall—built around 1840—and all public buildin's of that era have this characteristic appearance.) How many people dead over in that pretty little cemetery across the hill? (All of 'em, so far's we know, ma'am.) Where is Truro Center? (Keep a civil tongue in your head, sir—we Truro folk pride ourselves on the lack of concentration of population, rather than an overcrowded business center.)

And so it goes. In the next office Lucy Medders, the beauteous clerk to the selectmen, will issue shellfish permits, and some New Yorker will check the recipe for clam chowder with Lucy, and Lucy'll snap out, "We don't put catsup in our clam chowder on Cape Cod." There'll be the usual amateur photographers up here, too, sunburned men with dark glasses and expensive cameras and tripods and light meters and such. They'll pose their kids on the fire escape, or perch 'em, like barn swallows, on the ancient pipe fence, and two of the brats will tumble into Lucy's pretty geraniums, and somebody'll catch what for. There'll be a feller in to check the tides, and a pair of ladies will attempt to buy our antique schoolmaster's desk, and someone will undoubtedly inquire about the syngagogue. (This one takes a mite of explaining—Rabbi Touro founded the first synagogue in Westerly, R. I., and there's still an understandable confusion over the names.) Oh well, all in a day's work, we suppose.

We've been so busy adjusting to our new school position and mailing out our tax bills, and fetching our pup, April, over to Dr. Killian's place in Provincetown for an operation, that we've quite lost touch with local news. All's we can say is that the town is dead—Joe Schoonejongen and Mary Joseph at the post office both aver that Truro closed up with an unprecedented suddenness this year—and we can testify that the friendly lights in the valley are missing these evenings. Only visitors to be seen are the hardy bass fishermen—and if the yarns we hear are true (stripers galore in the bay, stripers seen as far up-creek in the Pamet as Snowie's Landing) those anglers will be suitably rewarded for their persistence.

Wonder what the roadside jelly stands are going to do about next year's supply of beachplum jelly? It just occured to us that if every snowy beachplum blossom that graced the gnarled bushes this spring had matured into ripened fruit, we'd have had a bumper crop. But somewhere along the growing season the heavy fogs and the drenching rain and the sudden, parching dry spells of late August combined to blight the wild fruit. Doubt if there are a dozen bushels of beachplums in the entire town.

We recall some years back when weather conditions conspired to produce an excellent crop of beachplums. We'd had our eye on a fine, shapely bushful just abreast of the Congregational Church, slowed our car every morning as we drove up the hill to our work, to inspect it. We were waiting of course, for the fruit to be exactly ripe enough for the kettle but, unbeknown to us, our bush was also being studied by Norm Snow. And so it was that one fine morning as we drove up with our pickin' bucket, there stood neighbor Snow, stripping our coveted bush. We made snide remarks, of course, and plucked a quart or two of plums that Norm couldn't reach, and secretly we hoped that our Castle Road friend would trip and spill his berries in the thicket. Norm, however, was quite casual about the whole thing. "Got to get up before breakfast to beat me, boy," he said. And then he blew a cloud of rank cigar smoke our way, and let a beachplum branch snap back in our face, and strode away.

Got to talking with our good friend Art Cobb the other day, and the conversation turned, as it inevitably does whenever we meet Art, to the halcyon days of South Truro. "Ever tell you about Mike Bryne?" roared Art. We had, of course; we'd heard the story about Mike's standing watch over a carload of grain down at the South Truro freight siding to protect it from the dishonest Wellfleeters. Mike had, unfortunately, fallen asleep in the wee hours, and some practical joker had blasted a shotgun in close proximity to Mike's ear that like to lost him his eardrum. But we took a chance that Art wouldn't repeat himself and shook our head in negation.

"Well, it ain't only Mike I'll tell you about, cause Eph Myrick is in the story, too," boomed Art. "Eph, you see, was a mite tetched, but harmless and everybody down to South Truro used to play jokes on him. They'd send him on fool errands, like fetchin' the key for the church stove, or borryin' a pair of two-foot post holes from a neighbor. Eph never did get mad, though, and there was folks around the Hogsbacks said old Eph wasn't near so thick as he made out to be. They pointed out that every time Eph did one of them fool's errands, why by the time the laughter died down, Eph gen'rally wound up with a plug of tobacco or a slug of rum or some other present for his trouble."

We interrupted Art to inquire if Eph wasn't, in fact, a brother of John Myrick—he of mouse tea fame—who used to live where Jim Moynahan now hangs his shingle. Indeed he was, according to Art. "They both come a runnin' home one day after hearin' a fire and brimstone sermon at the South Truro Methodist Church," Art related, "scared of the punishment, they was, and when they both tried to crowd through the kitchen door at the same time they tore it right off'n the hinges."

We'd distracted our story teller, so we tactfully steered him back to frere Eph. "Oh, yes," continued Art. "Well sir, we never had a real blacksmith shop over in South Truro, but Mike Bryne, he'd do a mite of smithin' on a small forge he had, out back of his house. Pretty good at it too. He could weld a wagon rim, or turn down a stove poker, or sometimes even shoe a horse. And one day, when Mike was beatin' out a dip-net rim before the admirin' glances of several loafers, along comes Eph Myrick. Well, someone sent Eph in to see if the hens had laid any square eggs—he went, too, and then Jug Rich made Eph move over a step, claimed Eph was a standin' on a family of angle worms. Meantime Mike had pumped the bellows until he had a good hot fire, and he poked the dip-net rim right in the middle of the coals, and when he fetched 'er out he held it front of Eph's face for a spell. "How hot you suppose that iron is Eph?" he says. And Eph just grinned and shook his head.

Mike pounded away until the piece got cold, and then he shoved 'er back in the forge, and got 'er cherry red again, and again he fetched the iron out. And this time old Eph looks at the glowin' iron and he says, "Mr. Bryne, you give me a dollar and I'll put my tongue to it." Art paused here to explain that the loafers never would have let Eph burn himself, but they were anxious to see how Eph would handle the situation. So they shouted at Mike to go through with the joke, and Mike reached in his pocket and pulled out a shiny silver dollar. "Well sir, Eph walked over and took the dollar out of Mike's hand, touched his tongue to it, and slipped it in his pocket and run off. Perfect example of not watchin' your pronouns, as old Mary Stocker, my school teacher, used to say," concluded Art.

Biggest social event in many a moon in Truro was the wedding, last Saturday morning, in the North Village, of Prudy Joseph, daughter of Mr. and Mrs. Stuart Joseph of "The Moorlands," and Richard M. Berrio, son of Truro chief of police, Harold, and Lillian M. Berrio. We stayed for the reception, of course, just happened to bring along our valve trombone, and shortly we were joined by Squire Jim Moynahan and Bobby Dutra, and last, but not least, by Vin Gannon, he of the hot trumpet. Vin looked dignified in a knobby herringbone suit, and toted a heavy Dublin style briar pipe (he teaches modern Irish literature at Bridgewater State Teachers' College) but his professional garb detracted not a whit from his brasswork. We had a fine time; surrounded by beautiful women, sated with delightful food, sore of lip, and carrying in our ears the memory of Ed Connolly's glorious baritone voice (Ed sang at the nuptial mass) we found ourself wishing for a wedding every month, at least.

The recently shocking revelations of skulduggery in the TV quiz shows of the past few years brings to mind the time some years ago when the members of the Truro Ambulance Association worked a booth at the Wellfleet Town Fair. This would be several decades ago, before the very worthwhile ambulance service was taken over by the lower three Cape towns under the present corporation organization. Col. Dick Magee, original donor of the ambulance, had dipped deeply into his pocket for running expenses of the vehicle, the drivers had, to a large extent, donated their services, but at this point a considerable operating deficit had built up and the informal board of directors decided to take advantage of the forthcoming town fair in neighboring Wellfleet to replenish the treasury.

The fair was Wellfleet's attempt to raise funds for the restoration of what is now the town office building. Among those most actively interested in the affair were Charlie Frazier and Jack Hall and Frank Shay. The locus: Wellfleet's American Legion Hall and the adjoining parking space, and the theme, a real, old-fashioned country fair, featuring livestock shows, vegetable displays, cooking wares. But the closest to a midway would be nightly block dancing on the uneven surface of the town road abaft Nickerson Lumber Co. So the Truro men dreamed up the idea of setting up a booth near Legion Hall, in which would be operated a STEW-pendous, COLL-ossal, ELEC-trifying MOUSE RACE. The booth itself was pre-fabricated, as we recall, in Truro by Carl Benson. Joe Peters, who drove the ambulance in those days, was commissioned to pick up several white mice in a Boston pet shop (some gent in Provincetown had the decency to dive into shallow water so that Joe was required to dash up to the Hub City the weekend before the fair), and Carl's brother, Jack, who had had consider-able experience in the carnival game, was consulted as to the detailed setup of the game.

And so, when the lights glared on at the Wellfleet Town Fair that first hot August night, folks were stirred by the raucous barking of Col. Dick Magee at the "Mouse Marathon." Here's the way the pitch worked. An active, restless mouse was selected from the stable by operator Ernie Snow, placed under a glass bowl in the center of the brightly-lighted booth. Around the bowl was built a large concentric circle of plywood, through which had been bored, at six-inch intervals, holes just large enough to allow the mouse to slip through. Each hole was numbered, and a corresponding number was given to a bet board, built counter-fashion above this tiny arena, so that the bettor would select what he thought was the lucky hole, place his money on the bet board, then lean over as Ernie snatched away the glass bowl, and shout words of encouragement at the bewildered mouse.

If the little beast popped into the hole on which you had placed your wager, the Truro Ambulance Association paid handsome odds of five-to-one. As an added attraction for those not of sporting blood, Col. Magee had several beauteous ladies dressed in bogus nurse's uniforms selling certificates of membership in the TAA to all who would part with a dollar. (We daresay scores of those certificates are gathering dust in Cape attics even today. We always had a hunch folks bought 'em as a kind of insurance against a trip in the gleaming white vehicle.)

The obvious ending for a yarn like this would be a gambit wherein Ernie smeared a daub of limberger cheese on a mouse-hole, as it were; one on which no bets had been placed by the patrons of the game. And we'd like to report that such was the case, since all the profits went to an exceedingly good cause. Not so, however. It wasn't until a few months ago we got the story from Ernie.

He admitted, when we got to reminiscing about the famous Mouse Marathon, that he had in a very subtle fashion rigged the game. "Nothing very dishonest," claimed Ernie. "If you'll recall, I always closed the bets while there was still one hole open for the house. Then, I'd select a female mouse from the stable, point her directly opposite the "house hole," and, when I'd let 'er go, with typical female obversity, she'd turn around, slip through the opening that didn't have to pay off." We pondered that one for a while. "But how in tarnation," we asked, "did you ever manage to tell the females from the males—they all looked alike to us." Ernie sniffed. "Any feller can't tell the difference between a male and a female mouse under them bright lights shouldn't try to operate a game."

Wish we'd had our faithful Royal with us, bound home from Province-town this afternoon. We'd have stopped on the saddle of the hill just south of Pilgrim Lake, and we'd have tried to capture the beauty of the countryside and the late afternoon sky and the stretch of the bay and the landlocked splendor of the lake below. Perhaps somewhere in our type-writer ribbon there'd have been adjectives to describe the clouds—long, furrowed cirrus formations of pearl gray washed in sepia and laced with the pale lemon gold of the westering sun.

And if we'd opened the car windows perhaps we could have told how the wind from the bay was fresh, and odorless and cool—and as hurried and purposeful as the tossing waters of the harbor it had so recently brushed. We'd have had time, too, to report on the tossing of the stubby, drab pine trees, and the pliant, arching tufts of straw-hued poverty grass; there'd have been a squib, too, about the dried, windblown weed that rolled erratically across the brim of the blacktop and disappeared over the moors to east-ard—and a bit about the sun-gilded gulls that soared in the breeze above Moon Pond meadow. Perhaps we'd have reported on the sparse traffic—mostly red-garbed deer hunters hurrying from one fruitless loca-tion to another as the afternoon shortened—and our closing phrases, quite logically, would have to do with the superb stretch of the Cape-tip town behind us, forming a crescent of tiny, jeweled doll houses on the rim of the harbor.

But we hadn't our machine, and the memory of the afternoon is fleeting, the magic moment gone. And so, instead, we must find our inspiration in the after-supper atmosphere of the O'Caghan menage; distractions of the TV (how many good men have died in a blaze of gunfire since 6 p.m.), and the domestic sounds of dishes being put away (our No. 3 son, Mike, must have a marked deck of cards—he's cut low in the dishwashing chore every evening for a week), and the deep-throated bark of our dog, April, in the front yard, and the gurgling of an air bubble in the hot water pipes, and the faint whisper of the dying west wind in our eaves. The weather man allowed, tonight, as how today had the shortest afternoon of the year; and we claim that's why there was so much beauty packed into the few short hours.

NINETEEN SIXTIES

1960's

NINETEEN SIXTY

1960

This morning, from our breakfast table we could see the huddled, dull black juncos in our backyard, hassling with the starlings and the jays over some bread crusts and a tasty tidbit we'd concocted of bacon fat and birdseed. And as we shaved, we peered myopically at the view through the bathroom window, the stretch of our lawn, still faintly green under the gray-boled locusts. Winter-bare shrubbery standing sentinel duty by the post-and-rail fence, the drab, straw-hued cattail patch, and the inky loop of the creek below the northern hill range. A fine day it is, we remarked to ourself, as we slipped on our spectacles, and slapped a bit of shaving lotion on our jowls; and the sand dunes of East Harbor will be a pretty sight this morning.

Local notes: In our mail, a copy of E. J. Kahn's latest book, "The Big Drink—The Story of Coca Cola" which we appreciate no end; the tome couldn't, however, have arrived at a less opportune time, since we're on a diet, and Jack's descriptive passages have us fair drooling to be at a cool coke. Thankee, neighbor Kahn.

The chill, harsh breath of reality touched us recently when a pretty young thing bounced into our room at school and informed us she was in search of a prop for the senior play, "Charlie's Aunt." "We need a pocket watch, Mr. O'Caghan; you *do* carry one, don't you?" After we'd made our indignant denial we gave ourself a quick once-over to see if we'd worn our spats to school, by mistake.

In our mail, a most interesting letter from neighbor Mary Freeman of Wellfleet—the missive was conceived, we gather, at "Topside," Mary's neat, attractive Wellfleet home, written in transit, and postmarked Hyannis. In it, Mary chats about many things—of spring, and ground moles, and pet crows, and church, but her offhand remarks anent the feather duster struck a spark on our otherwise serene surface. "Seems I recall the days when we used a turkey feather duster—long handled, to distribute the dust and make us sneeze! Your generation probably can't remember them," says Mary.

Indeed we do recall the venerable turkey feather duster, Neighbor Freeman. At the risk of dating ourself into our fourth decade, we'd like to claim long acquaintance with that household hand tool. You probably don't remember, Mary, that we were once, some years ago, janitor of the old Wilder School in Truro center. And the janitor's gear, in those days, consisted of a chipped hatchet (to worry your way through the slab pine when kindling was needed), a short handled shovel (to bail out the coal, of course, and to remove ashes from the base of the two pot-bellied stoves), a stiff, worn stub of a broom and the aforementioned turkey feather duster.

The ritual of chores at the school house went something like this, as we recall. Soon's the last bus had loaded with kids, we'd descend on the gaunt, ochre-shingled building and prepare to close 'er up for the night. Latch the window sashes, empty the waste baskets into the stoves, trim the fire, gently shake the ashes, and load up with fresh coal for the evening. (Sometimes we'd close off the chimney damper a mite too soon, while coal gas was still generating in the bowels of the rusty stove. And a bit later the fumes would explode with a sizeable force that would lift the covers or blow the firepot door open.)

Then we'd seize the worn corn broom and commence to sweep—usually in the Big Part, as the room containing the upper four grades was known, and usually along the west wall. (Sometimes, though, the wind would be strong out of the east, and then you'd begin your sweeping on the wind'ard side, so's the dust would blow ahead of you.) Up one aisle and down the other, making sure the point of the broom probed out the sand hidden under the hardware of the desks and seats. You'd have to allow a few minutes to play a tune or two on the battered Estey knee organ as you passed 'midships of the back wall, and finally you'd have moved all your dirt down front, and there you'd scoop it up with the dust pan, and toss it in the waste basket.

The final chore was a lightning whisk with the turkey duster, and we must agree, Mary, that our passes with the tool did little more than displace the dust from one spot, allow it to settle in another. Well sir, it was years after we left our janitorial duties at Wilder School before we again saw a feather duster in actual use. Then, when we assumed our offices at town hall, we noted that Frankie Rose (gone these many years to his final rest) used to belabor the furniture and fixtures of this old building with a moth-eaten feather dust chaser. A real pleasure, it was, to see little Frank swishing his way along a dust-covered settee, or beating at the faded curtain on the stage.

And Frank had his battered, worn broom, too, and thereby hangs a small tale. We recall one day that Frankie came into our office with the news that he'd discovered a dead rat in one of the town hall cisterns (this was, of course, long before the days of running water at the hall) and would we come out and help him fish the critter out because folks were goin' to use that water for washin' dishes, come Farm Bureau supper. So we went out with the good janitor and held on to his belt while he probed the surface of the cistern water with the faithful town hall broom, and gave him a pat of praise as he carefully fished out the decaying rat on his broom, much as a baker slips bread out of the oven. Couldn't have been more'n a fortnight later we were in the kitchen of town hall when the ladies were preparing the gala Farm Bureau supper; and a huge fire was roaring in the black iron range, and several of the women folk were finishing off pies in the oven. And Mrs. Manuel Corey wanted to try her apple pie to see if it was done, so she snatched a straw from the broom standing in the corner, and in the traditional manner of all good cooks, plunged it into the steaming crust. Oh well, takes ten thousand germs, they say, to kill a Cape Codder.

We get so depressed at the sight of our own little annual weed patch that every so often we feel moved to pay a visit on Werner Lieb, our neighbor across the Pamet, for restoration of our faith in growing things. And so this morning, with soil still in our fingernails and the memory of wilted bush roses still in our heart, we climbed onto our blue scooter and putted around the headwaters of the river and drove into the Lieb estate. The Liebs were up and about, of course, and both were gracious and charming, as always, and we were invited on the grand tour by the retired horticulturist.

So many beautiful things to see, and to smell, and to feel. Border plants in unusual varieties: English daisies with petals no longer'n a baby's eyelashes—and portulaca in shades we hadn't dreamed of; pansies in plain blossoms (Mr. Lieb said one of his old customers in White Plains would never buy standard pansies because the figure on the petals reminded her of a Bolshevik); petunias with a fragrance you couldn't forget, and tuberous begonias that are evidently in a race to see whether those glorious, big blossoms can outgrow the shade of their foliage. We stopped by the Lieb rose garden and Mr. Lieb reminded us that last time we'd been by, he'd been stuffing hundreds of pounds of newspapers in the ground to make a mulch bed. "See what the *New York Times* has done for my roses?"

Some of the Lieb plants have proven so succulent for the neighboring fauna that Mr. Lieb has been obliged to install wire screen caps over them and along the same scheme of protection we noted the ripening apples on the bank below the house each wore a plastic bag to discourage birds and insects. And we saw a special moss-grass that Mr. Lieb had developed to fill the ugly cracks between the new bricks on his back terrace—and we saw giant amaryllis bulbs resting from their blossoming efforts, and currant bushes that yield three pounds of delicious fruit each, and we ogled a fruit tree that had once been a gnarled, wild apple whip, now grafted with dozens of choice hybrid scions, the cicatrix of each joint perfectly healed.

In the vegetable garden we sampled baby carrots and (shame on us) failed to identify a huge, green pod as the fava—our acquaintance with that big bean has been limited to the dry seed which has to be parboiled and pickled, and used to chase lager beer, preferably at Portuguese weddings. Well sir, we had just about reached the point where our own ignorance of things green and growing was overcoming us when Mr. Lieb told us a mite of a yarn that made us feel better.

Seems during World War II, what with gas rationing and the austerity of the times, the Lieb greenhouses in suburban White Plains suffered from loss of business, so Mr. Lieb expanded into the poultry business, theorizing that if folks came out from the city for food, they'd certainly buy flowers and plants. The plan worked. And Mr. Lieb's foreman, a European with a good sense of humor, decided one day to mix some peewee eggs in with the large market size eggs. "Along came one of our city customers," says Mr. Lieb, "and when she caught sight of those tiny eggs lying in the basket with the extra large size she remarked, 'Oh, what a shame you didn't let these grow some more.'"

We need rain, was our thought, as we partook of a modest breakfast of poached eggs upon English muffins. You can see it in the dust green of the scrub pines and the set of the locust foliage and the parched, straw-hued patches in the bunch grass. And the creek is a piddling, chocolate brown stream with mud-bordered banks and shallows where ancient snags, long covered by the waters of the Pamet, now lie exposed between the lush green cattails. Somewhere out on the meadow a quail gave his call—today it was "more wet" not bob white, and in response came the soaring, metallic song of the cicada. April, our German shepard pup, came listlessly at our whistle, her flanks still wet from a recent dip in some nearby ditch, and an early risen tourist churned down South Pamet Road, a thin plume of dust rising from his outboard wheel as his tires met the dry of the roadside.

Folks hereabouts are marking their calendars so's they won't forget the big box supper and spelling bee, benefit on the SPCC, that will be held at Truro Central School on Thursday, August 18. Janet Tenney, chairman of the affair, has rounded up a formidable array of talent for the bee, and they will be confronted by a list of most-mispelled words furnished by several of the country's leading publishing houses. We hear tell the list reposes in a safe deposit vault in a local bank, and the seals will not be broken until the night of the contest. Valuable prizes for the winners as well as lucky ticket holders at the box supper have been donated by the merchants of Pamet and generous colonists.

It had occurred to us that the mechanics of a box supper might well have proved a mystery to many of our summer visitors (the last box supper we can recall was run by the Community Club some fifteen years ago here in Truro) so we asked Horace "Pop" Snow to drop by town hall and let us query him. Pop obliged, and while he puffed furiously at a big black cigar, we scratched out some notes. "Box suppers were big affairs when I was a young feller. Ran 'em for the benefit of the church as often as once a month. Best way I know of to get acquainted with a girl—and you can darn soon tell what kind of a cook she is, too. Now here's how you work it. Every woman has to fetch a double lunch in a box to the affair. And since the feller that bids highest gets that box and shares the lunch with her, it's advisable for her to put some kind of subtle indentifying mark on the box so's her boyfriend can tell it apart from the others."

We asked Pop to clarify his last remark. "Well sir, I remember one box supper we had up t' the Methodist Church vestry some years back," he reminisced. "I was sweet on Winnie Ryder at the time, and just before the auctioning began—old Sam Narsty Paine was the auctioneer—Winnie told me to look sharp at the boxes, and I'd get a hint. Sure enough, one of the boxes had four aces from a deck of cards slipped in among the fancy ribbon bows, and I knew cussed right well that four aces wins, so it had to be Winnie's lunch. But some of the other fellers surmised I was after that particular box, so they kept forcing up the bid until finally I had to go to four dollars and a half before Sam knocked it down to me. And durned if it didn't turn out the box I bought had been wrapped up by Winny Hopkins. There was a jar of pickled water melon rind in there I had to eat—made me burp for two days afterward, and Winnie Ryder didn't speak to me for a month. She'd had a toy buggy whip on her box lunch—stood for Ryder, of course." We clucked our tongue in sympathy, and Pop blew a huge cloud of cigar smoke our way and strode out of our office.

The acrid fumes of Pop's stogy had hardly cleared from the room when in came Col. Dick Magee, perturbed no end because our town chimes up aloft in town hall were striking the wrong time due to yesterday's six-hour

electric power interruption. "Let's go topside and reset the mechanism," said the colonel. So upstairs we went—and when we had reached the narrow, rickety ladder that leads to the attic he stepped aside and motioned for us to precede him. For a brief moment we were flattered into thinking that Dick planned to let us have first tinker at the complicated machinery—not so. "I wanted you to test the ladder," he puffed as we rolled up our sleeves and surveyed the gears and sprockets.

So we stood by while the genial ex-engineer seized an oil can and commenced to lubricate the pulleys and cables. "Reminds me of the good old days when I worked for the original Boston Elevated Railway," he mused. "Of course this voltage is puny—only one-ten—as compared with the hot stuff we used to handle on the El." The resetting dial spun under his hands and the huge bells up above responded with a melodious clanging. "I remember one occasion when a report came into our office that there was a bad short circuit on the third rail just beyond Thompson Square, in Charlestown. Seems a workman had dropped a crowbar on the tracks and the whole division, from Everett to Forest Hills was crippled. So the superintendent sent me out to remedy the situation—they didn't want to throw the master switch—afraid that the darkness would cause a serious panic among the rush-hour patrons. So I had to think of a quick solution."

Here the colonel paused to tap a mercury switch of the clock mechanism while we wondered just what we would have done in a like situation. "When I arrived on the platform at Thompson Square with my tool kit, I could just barely make out the cause of the trouble; about fifty yards down the track I could see the shower of sparks and the white-hot crowbar. It would be suicide, I realized, to walk any closer to the short circuit—every piece of metal was alive with high voltage—and that's when I thanked my lucky stars I'd been a pitcher on the Charlestown sandlot league team." The chimes were now approaching the correct time, and the colonel was peering at his wristwatch for the final accurate setting.

"So I reached into my tool kit, seized a heavy monkey wrench and taking careful aim I reared back and threw the tool, with all my might, straight at that crowbar. Out into the blackness it flew, and CRACK it hit the bar and knocked it over onto the wooden ties, breaking the connection. Five minutes later the trains began to roll and service was resumed."

The Magee yarn had suddenly aroused in us a realization of the safety hazards that surrounded us in the unfinished room of the venerable town hall. Pointing to an exposed overhead copper wire, we queried the colonel as to its danger. "Not enough juice in that to tickle a flea," he reassured us. "But how about this pile of trash?" we asked, nudging the paper scraps with our toe. Out jumped a mouse, and up the rafters he scuttled. Pausing momentarily on a beam, the tiny animal then dashed across the bare conductor, stiffened, and dropped at our feet. "Guess the poor mouse must have had a weak heart," said Col. Magee, as the chimes rang out four o'clock on the full Westminster program. And we climbed down the ladder, gladdened by the knowledge that Truro was once more in time with the world.

Twenty-five years ago this morning we awoke to the rumble of thunder and the fitful flash of forked lightning, and the first big drops of a downpour that was to drench the countryside and briefly paralyze traffic on the outer Cape. We remember the damage wrought by the storm: granite posts of the Pleasant View Cemetery in Wellfleet shattered by the lightning, numerous tree limbs torn asunder, washouts and flash floods. And if it seems odd we should recall this one of many summer tempests, perhaps we should explain that this was our wedding day.

We imagine our sister-in-law, Mary Dickey, will remember the day, too—the poor girl fainted dead away when one particularly loud clap of thunder echoed over the roof of the ivy-covered church in Wellfleet. And Father Dennis Spykers should recall, also; he had to raise his voice above the noises of the storm to hear the mutual pledges of the bridal couple. And so, Mr. Editor, if our column seems a mite disjointed and brief today, please forgive us; our thoughts are on the past and those happy, eventful twenty-five years of married life. We feel strangely humble and completely grateful and very much in love with our good wife, Anne, as we look back with much satisfaction to the milestones of our life—a pleasant home, a fine family, good health, interesting work to do, and a host of loyal friends. What man could ask for more? But enough of the whimsy.

As we jounced across the High Head crossing the other day on our blue scooter we noted the heavy equipment of the New Haven Railroad straddling the tracks on Beach Point—a diesel locomotive followed by a flat car containing a powerful winch hauling two openend gondolas. The crewmen were hauling the spikes from the fishplates, hoisting the loosened rails onto the cars, leaving behind a scattered roadbed of splintered crossties.

Thus ends the era of the iron horse for the Lower Cape; and we'll wager that the cessation of service is arousing less emotion than did the extension of the Old Colony line from its then terminus at Wellfleet to Provincetown circa 1870. Despite the day's heat we spent some time this afternoon in research of our town records trying to follow the thread of history that brought the railroad through our town in the burgeoning post-Civil War days. And a difficult task it proved to be; the organizers of the railroad company changed their corporate title several times during the negotiations with the Truro committee. Cape Cod Railroad Company, Old Colony and Newport, Old Colony and New Haven are some of the references that appear in the musty records. And with typical perverseness, Pamet voters at one town meetin' would authorize their town treasurer to purchase stock in the railroad, then negate their action at a subsequent voting session.

There were bitter contests over the relocation of long used private roads when the railroad engineers, in the interest of public safety, attempted to eliminate grade crossings. What to do about bridging Pamet Harbor? (The ship channel was already filling with sand, but folks still objected to a further slowing of the tidewaters of the river.) The question of land titles became acute when Beach Point was reached. East Harbor, once navigable by sizeable vessels, had become a landlocked body of water; the channel had been first bridged, then dyked, by order of the county commissioners, so that a considerable area of man-made land marked the area of the Truro-Provincetown line.

There were sundry claims to this narrow spit of land now become valuable—by the Proprietors of Eastern Harbor, so-called, by various individuals who had cut salt hay along the marshes, and by purchasers of tax deeds. On one section of the Point, the town was requested to "deed, in its corporate capacity the Town lands at Beach Point" to the railroad. Now it appears that many of the complications that beset the Old Colony in the 1870's will come to life with the abandonment of the right-of-way.

Well sir, we considered it particularly fitting that the salvage crew in charge of ripping up the rails of the New Haven roadbed should have chosen Labor Day to work on that section of the track from Corn Hill to the site of the former Truro depot. We presume the men got double time for the holiday, and more power to 'em. But from the sentimental point of view, we submit that there's a touch of melancholy about this end-of-the-summer holiday that lent itself rather well to the nostalgic chore of deleting the last traces of the steel ribbons that once played such a vital part in the economy of the Lower Cape.

Later in the day, as dusk was filling the valley, we drove our kids over to see the denuded roadbed. The rails had all been carted off, and the rusted spikes and the fishplates lay in roughly spaced piles, and from the dyke up south 'ard near Eagle's Neck two tiny plumes of smoke from the cutters torch rose from a patch of dried weeds. History in reverse, we'd seen, and it left us a mite sad.

Kind of looks as though the sun, this late September afternoon, is subscribing to the old philosophy—if you can't lick 'em, join 'em. There've been times, during the day, when the point of transparency, and streaks of palest blue appeared in the overcast and it warmed considerably; but the persistent easterly breeze kept sweeping in the overcast, so that, on occasion, the mist gathered on the utility lines in big, lazy droplets, and the horizon closed in, and the grass patches turned silver, and the blacktop glistened in moisture.

All to the tune, of course, of the muffled booming of the foghorn downshore at Highland, and the mewing of the creekbound seagulls, invisible in the fog of the salt Pamet and the soughing of the breeze through the scrub pine. The cricket chorus is at slow tempo, even muted—and the call of the jay on the hillside lacks the shrewish quality it holds on a clear day. Even the Cobb chimes at town hall have a restful, subdued sound as they tell the quarter hours, and the sporadic hum of traffic on the state highway seems slowed. Weather breeder—clearin'-up spell—Indian summer ahead? Who can tell?

Most folks about town are still adding up the damages of the recent hurricane, but we submit that the storm was not without some minor benefits. Among those we would like to list is the gradual appearance, in many Pamet yards, of piles of firewood which otherwise would not be burgeoning had not Donna made her appearance on the Narrow Land. We've noted neatly tiered locust at Peggy Day's, and at Dr. Paul Todd's, and at Artie Joseph's, and even in our own backyard there's a clutch of the good hardwood drying out for winter use in our fireplace. The sound of the power saw can be heard daily in Pamet, and folks are debating the relative merits of the chain saw versus the reciprocating blade saw. Faster, say the proponents of the chain. Safer point out the blade people.

But the other day when we attempted to engage Norm Snow in a discussion of the matter, Norm had but scant praise for either machine. He puffed furiously on his cigar, hitched up his trousers as he always does when he's about to spin a yarn, and commenced to belittle the effete woodcutting tools of the present generation.

"Smelly gas burners—all of 'em," snorted Norm. "Never can tell when they're goin' to conk out, and then how much wood you goin' to cut?" We attempted to quote some figures indicating that an anemic female can section half a dozen cords of hardwood per day with a twenty-one pound chainsaw. "Pshaw and fiddlesticks," interrupted Norm. "Ever tell you about the time we held the woodcuttin' contest down at father's place? Winter of 1910, that'd be. When we had so much snow the train got stuck down t' North Truro for four days in a cut back of Louis Young's that was so deep all's you could see was the stack above the drift. Colder'n a whale's tail. And work was scarce, too, so father put all his gang to cuttin' up a whole parcel of spars he'd collected from several shipwrecks along the backshore. Spruce, they were, some of 'em as big as three, four feet in diameter. Well sir, it never fails: you put a gang of men to work on a monotonous project, and they inevitably make a contest out of the chore. So pretty soon the fellers had paired off, and they got to racin' to see who could make the cuts through them huge masts the quickest. After two-three days we'd separated the boys from the men, and it boiled down to two teams. Henry Hanson and Barteeze Souza versus Archie Holden, and," here Norm made a modest pause and exhaled a cloud of blue cigar smoke, "me."

Norm went on to explain that, according to all standards, Henry and Barteeze should have won with ridiculous ease. Henry was a giant of a man, strong as a bull, sound of wind, while Barteeze had the endurance of a Maxwell automobile. We nodded at Norm's assortment of metaphors. "But poor Archie Holden was a gnome of a feller—weighed about ninety pounds soaking wet, and every time I gave a yank on the two-man cross cut saw, there was considerable danger I'd pull him right onto the saw cerf." So Norm had to resort to strategy. "Biggest advantage Henry and Barteeze had was their skill at sharpening their saw. Barteeze would take his blade home at night, and everlastin'ly put the rasp to it until it was keener'n a razor. It practically went through that hard spruce by itself. Looked for sure as though we hadn't a chance at the prize—a jug of homemade applejack donated by John Rogers."

And then Norm got his inspiration. Since no specifications had been listed as to type of saw to be used, Norm decided to fetch out of the tool shed a huge, rusty ice saw—eight feet long, it was, with teeth big as those of a rhinoceros. Spent the night before the contest honing the edges, did Norm, and fashioning a helper's handle for little Archie Holden. "We beat 'em with plenty to spare," reminisces Norm. "That refurbished ice saw chewed them spars like a Jersey bull eatin' clover. Matter of fact, every half hour I'd signal Archie to drop his end of the saw and fetch me a sandwich, to keep up my strength—and still I'd keep ahead of our opponents. Frightens me to think what I could have done if I had both my arms."

★ ★ ★

Down at Col. Dick Magee's the other evening we got to talking with the colonel's dinner guest, the beauteous Alice (Mrs. John) Starr of Wellfleet; that nice lady had many memories of her late father, Thede Williamson, who was engineer of the Cape train for decades. Thede was of South Truro stock, and on occasion as a young man, he'd be invited to weekend at his kinfolk's place on the Hogsbacks. "Dad used to say," said Alice, "that in those days folks always had those tall, elegant four-posters in the upstairs guest room and his grandparents further heightened the beds by placing several red bricks under the legs. Seems you got more fresh air from the tiny bedroom windows that way. In any event, Dad said that after a hearty meal of baked beans and ham and Johnny cake and Indian puddin', when bedtime came he'd have to start a sprint out in the hall, head of the stairs, so's he could make a flying leap into the four-poster."

There's Rich blood in the Williamson family, according to Mrs. Starr, and two of her dad's distant cousins, Oren and Nehemiah Rich, are the central characters of a yarn her dad used to tell. "Seems Oren and Nehemiah took the train over to Wellfleet one Saturday," Alice is quoting her father, "and Nehemiah, who was known as Jug Rich, for obvious reasons, plied his traveling companion with ardent spirits, and the two decided to hire a rig at Holbrook's livery and drive over to Bound Brook and pick some beach plums. So they rented a spavined nag and a Democrat wagon, tucked the jug under the seat, and off they jogged down Main Street and across the Herring Brook, and finally up onto Bound Brook Island.

"They kept nipping and discussing the important events of the day, and finally they found a patch of beach plums and they hopped out of the carriage. Loosened the harness fastenin's a mite, they did, so's the horse would be comfortable, and set to pickin'. Come dusk, and the line of the jug had descended just as the sun had; and Oren and Nehemiah staggered back to where they'd left their rig; but only the carriage was to be seen—the Holbrook horse had long gone. Said Oren to Nehemiah, "What d'you make of this?" Said Nehemiah to Oren, "Well cousin, either we've lost a hoss, or we've found a wagon."

So here's the tentative schedule for adult education and evening practical arts courses for the winter. Furniture upholstering, Monday afternoons, town hall; rughooking, Tuesday afternoons, also town hall; conversational French and conversational Portuguese classes will be organized within two weeks, sessions to be on Tuesday nights at Truro Central School. Registrations are still being accepted for all classes.

Speaking of these cultural pursuits, we broached the subject of conversational French to neighbor Snowie of Slade's Landing on a recent visit. We had repaired to the Snow cellar, and as we admired Snowie's latest artistic creation—a delicate sand-and-seashell moulage—we suggested Snowie and his bride should sign up for the course. "I can't speak for Norma, of course, but I have grave misgivings about French. It's the cussed idioms that get me into trouble. Ever tell you about the time I got fouled up tryin' to use my French on a pretty girl in New York?"

We left off admiring one of Snowie's partially hammered steel drums and made negative signs. So Horace filled us in on his background in this beautiful but subtle language. Three years of secondary courses at dear old Wellfleet High, two more at St. John's Prep, and then: "A few years later I met this lovely French girl from upstate New York. She invited me to her house for a weekend, so I borrowed the family Essex and drove up there. My, what a big estate those folks had; I almost got lost in the driveway. Finally I parked the old Essex in back of a big privet hedge, and plodded through the formal garden, and at last I found the family group on a kind of patio."

Snowie says he was anxious to impress the girl's father, so he exchanged formal greetings in French. Things went swimmingly. And then old Pop LeCompte said something about the celerity of Snowie's trip from Cape Cod, and Snowie fumbled for a reply. "Only dern expression I could remember for a rapid journey ended in the phrase 'avec le ventre au terre.' So I used it, only to hear all the LeComptes giggle fit to die. Pretty soon the old man asked me if I'd had difficulty in gettin' into the grounds. I said 'oui-oui' and then I pointed towards the privet hedge and said, 'J'ai mis pied a terre ici.' Hysterics from the family, and the old lady snidely remarked, 'Ou, donc, est votre cheval?'"

It wasn't until weeks later, when Snowie had a chance to refer to his book of French idioms, that he discovered his first faux pas in reference to the speed of his journey could be best translated 'with my belly dragging on the ground.' His second reply to Le Compte, pere, indicated he had just dismounted, hence his hosts inquiry as to the whereabouts of Snowie's horse.

We were afforded one bright spot in an otherwise cheerless afternoon at Provincetown the other day. Sitting in our VW, we were, watching the Orange and Black JV football team going down to defeat at the hands of the Falmouth booters. The weather was chill and damp, and we were looking forward with scant pleasure to an evening of correcting math papers, and our sinuses were throbbing. Along came Mr. Alton Ramey to join us in our car, and to tell us how he'd just returned from a short visit to his native Maine. "Called on my Uncle Hiram at his home in Lubec," said the owner of Kalmar Village, "and he'll be taking his cast off in a week or so." We clucked solicitously and inquired as to the nature of Uncle H's injury.

"Well sir," explained Mr. Ramey, "seems Hi was planning to take the ferry at Lubec awhile back. Arrived at the ferry slip just as the cussed thing was about ten feet from the dock. Nothing daunted, Uncle Hi broke into a sprint, dug his toes into the slip stringer, and everlastingly leaped across the stretch of open water. Made it, too, he did, but in landing, he fractured an ankle, and bashed his head against the deck house, rendering himself unconscious. When he came to in the doctor's office old Doc Frisbee said to him: "Hi, I bet if you'd known that ferry was dockin' instead of pullin' out, you wouldn't have made that jump."

Uncle Hi, we take it, is a modern day, down-East counterpart of Truro's own Sol Hall, who used to live in the cottage now owned by Cleve Woodward, down Depot Road way. They tell many a yarn about Sol's misadventures; about the time Sol, as tree warden for the town, shinnied up into a big silver oak down by Ike Freeman's house, intending to saw off a decaying limb that threatened the safety of the public. But, being left-handed, Sol found it more convenient to sit outboard of the cut, and he ended up by sawing himself clear of the trunk. Perhaps that severe shaking up would account for Mr. Hall's next contretemps, for less'n a week later, when Sol's privy blew over in a nor'east gale, he decided to take advantage of its horizontal position to give it a much needed reshingling. But lo and behold, when the neighbors helped Sol to hoist the privy back on its foundation, they found that the unfortunate man had shingled the building so's the butts were facing skyward.

Years later Sol went up to Boston to visit with a niece and the young lady took him to a concert at the Upham's Corner auditorium. The concert was long and boring, so Sol quickly kicked off his shoes, and in the half-darkness of the hall, took a short snooze. Folks kept squeezing in and out of Sol's row, and in the confusion the Truro man's shoes were irretrievably lost. Sol had to ride to his niece's home on the streetcars in his stocking feet. We submit that these human frailties are what keep the memory of a man alive over the years.

Local notes: Deer season finds, it seems to us, fewer than usual of nimrods in the woods, and only one local hunter we've heard of has had success; that would be our nephew and namesake, Tommy Kane, who shot a doe in Long Nook. Pop Snow and company doing well on Dr.

Bloomberg's garage and kitchen addition on the north bank of the Pamet, and Sgt. Earl Bishop's new cottage atop Town Hall Hill nearly finished. Charlie Snow, Pamet's able road boss, tells us his crew has started construction of the final stretch of the Chapter 90 road that will link Collins Road, south of the MIT site, with the state highway near the Wellfleet line. We wondered, with some concern, if there would be danger in the woods for Charlie's faithful crew, it being deer season and all. "Ain't none of us look like deer," Charlie explained our fears away, "and besides, what with the chain saw sputterin' and Dickie Steele a'jabberin', the hunters will sure hear us a mile away."

To the hunter who shot my beautiful German shepherd dog, April, in the woods near Dr. Paul Powers' yesterday, Saturday the tenth day of December, an open letter.

Dear Nimrod:

Perhaps you are one of those men in red who purchased your license from me this year. Lord knows, I made it easy for you to pin the red plastic permit on your manly chest. As has been my usual custom, I maintained a 24-hour vigil at my office and my house for the issuance of licenses for the convenience of the sportsmen. Or perhaps you subscribed to the theory that all German police dogs, so-called, are born game drivers. After all, are not all Jews either capitalist or Communist, are not all Irishmen crooked politicians, are not all Swedes square-head ignoramuses, are not all colored people unfit for our own benighted offspring to associate with? Or perhaps you decided, it being the last day of the open season on deer, to shoot at anything that moved. I am told that you blasted an innocent bluejay into eternity within a few feet of where you killed April.

Let me fill you in on the background of the fine animal you have wantonly slaughtered. April was the daughter of Col. Dick Magee's Oscar, out of Gigi—born on town meeting day, 1959. My No. 2 son, Terry, was working for the colonel that winter, and on my birthday, April 1 (this is where her name came from) Terry fetched his little pup home to us. She was, from the beginning, a fine dog. I remember how easy she was to housebreak and how her ears used to flop (they were big—we used to call her mule-ears, to tease her) and how she had a taste for bicycle seats—she must have chewed up at least four—but they weren't your bicycle seats, so you couldn't have held that against her. We forgave her, because when we scolded her, she'd look at us with those big brown eyes, and nuzzle against our knee, and ask for forgiveness.

And another thing, Mr. Hunter—April had a penchant for being let out at night. Lord forgive us, I used to grumble when she scratched at the kitchen door in the wee hours—but I'd crawl out of bed and give her a little scratch in that secret place behind her ear that only I knew, and send her out to do battle with a skunk in the garbage hole (that's the only animal, to my knowledge, that April ever hunted) and a bit later I'd have to get up and let her in again.

And that's where I made my mistake on Saturday morning. Half drugged with sleep, I slipped out of bed and let her out just as the sun was breaking over the hills to east'ard. She squatted for a moment on the back porch, sniffing at the mysterious smells of the morning, and I slipped back to bed. They tell me she went on her daily trip with Baskie, the blue tick hound of the Ormsby's. Baskie came back; April didn't.

Let me tell you how your well-aimed shot affected our little circle, Mr. Hunter. Snowie gave April a decent burial, after Bob Morris had directed him to the scene of what we call the murder. Our own land will be henceforth posted against hunting of all animals. And the issuance of all licenses for fishing and hunting will henceforth be limited to our office hours. A pitiful stipulation, we admit, to trade for the loving gaze and the full-hearted love of a true friend.

Yours very truly,
Thomas A. Kane

NINETEEN SIXTY-ONE

1961

We were patiently sanding a huge pulley block in our cellar workshop last Saturday afternoon shortly after two o'clock when the lights blinked several times, and finally went out. It had been snowing heavily since the wee hours of the morning, with the wind strong out of the northeast (we'd taken in our coat-of-arms sign at mid-morning to save it from the buffeting of the gale) and the heavy, damp white stuff had made a new cover for the soiled, hard drifts of the previous storm. The path to the family woodpile had filled rapidly, and the cedar trees on our lawn had suddenly grown tufts of snow on each branch that soon became a solid coverlet, and the utility wires on the poles at the roadside below grew fat, white rolls of insulation that weighted down the spans so they almost touched the roofs of the few passing cars.

We'd done our best to prepare for the storm: dragged in frost-crusted oak wood to feed the fireplace, and drawn off water into every available container, and filled and trimmed the kerosene lamps, and gathered the household candles into one pile. By mid-afternoon our venerable Cape Cod house was shaking in the blast of the gale, our TV antenna howling banshee-fashion, a loose blind rattling on its hinges. We noted that the passing of the town snow plow on its duly appointed rounds came less frequently, and visibility worsened so that the northern range of hills across river, then the loop of the Pamet below Dr. Bloomberg's, then the stretch of cattail patch, and finally the road itself disappeared.

Big wet flakes of snow flung by our kitchen windows, and cold drafts commenced to force their way by the outer doors as the heat left the baseboard units. Then the long winter night: rationing of water and light, and swapping places in the warmer seats before the fireplace, melting snow from the big drift by the kitchen door to wash the dishes, tuning in the tiny battery radio for news of the outside world, closing off the farther bedrooms, marshalling foul weather gear by the porch entrance. Thence to a bed unheated by the faithful electric blanket in a room suddenly become shadowy and mysterious in the guttering flame of the candle. Fitful sleep, interrupted many times by the howl of the wind in the chimney and the creaking of the house beams, and then, to arise on Sunday morning to a scene of unparalleled, albeit cruel, beauty of the countryside.

We were talking with Joe Duarte one day last week anent the cold weather. Had a multitude of complaints, we did, about the frigidity. We pointed out as how folks couldn't work at outdoor jobs, and we mentioned the high cost of heating our house, and the way our poor car groaned in the morning because of the congealed lubricants in its innards. "But I remember the old days when we used to pray for cold weather like this," Joe interrupted. "That would be back in the twenties, when we used to cut ice down at the pond in North Truro. Come a real frigid snap and my father would haunt the ice pond, measuring the skim every day until, with luck, the stuff would be thick enough to cut. Then he'd send out the word for every able-bodied man in town to help us harvest the ice."

We recalled the ancient, rickety, double ice house that used to be located on the shore of the pond. Later it was to be converted to a studio, but before owner Jerry Farnsworth ever got the opportunity to set up an easel in the remodeled building, it caught fire and burned to the ground.

"My uncle John Silva would hitch a horse to the marker—actually nothing but a pair of handles with a sharp, long knife like a skate blade that scored the ice—and scratch a checkerboard pattern on the surface of the ice. Uncle John had a good eye, too; he'd set his first course by the steeple of the Christian Union Church and thereafter you could lay a carpenter's square on the intersection of the lines, and they'd be a true ninety degrees.

"And then the cutters would follow along, pumpin' up and down on those big, sharp ice saws, tracin' Uncle John's marks. Then the polers would hook on to the cut pieces with their long-handled pikes, poling them into the clear channel of open water, guiding them to the foot of the chutes, whereby Uncle Tony "Crusoe" Silva would drop a hook in back of each slab. My dad would have another horse harnessed to a whiffletree, pulling through a pulley on a long line that hoisted the block of ice up the chute and into the house. Come end of the afternoon, when you were loading the last of the ice through the doorway up in the peak of the building, you'd kind of hold your breath as the ice block teetered through the opening at the top of the chute."

We'd always heard that natural ice sometimes had dirt or other foreign matter in it; we queried Joe on the subject. "Why yes, on occasion you would find a bit of straw, or a cattail, or a few vertebrae from some unfortunate animal in our natural ice. But I always felt those things added a bit of character to—let's say a glass of lemonade. And if the straw was long enough, you could drink through it."

But the biggest news item of the week for us, is by far the weekend visit to Truro of Dr. Sam Phillips and his Nina, because they fetched with them a beautiful, 12-week-old German shepard female pup—and they called us up on Friday night, and we went across the river to visit them, and there was our new dog. She's black and tan (just like our beloved April) and she has black toenails and a dew claw, and a strong, jet black tail with a tiny, star-shaped tassle at its very end. And we love our pup very much, and we'll never be able to thank Dr. Sam and Nina enough for their gift. Our house hasn't been so happy nor our lives so fulfilled since last December.

Everywhere you travel about town there are nice things to be seen. This afternoon, for instance, on our way to town hall, we stopped by that flat, open mesa atop Storm Hill, abaft Cemetery Road, and we clambered up the bank to where the site of Truro's last windmill can still be traced by the faint indentations in the earth. (Old Manuel House—lived where Al Paine now lives—was the miller.) Spaniard, so they tell, name probably corrupted or changed in the translation. In any event, we remarked the circular tracks of the ancient wheel that used to head the mill into the wind, and ran an admiring glance over the carpet of hog cranberry vine, bursting with pale pink, sweet-smelling blossoms. Nectar laden bees buzzed on the waxy vines, and the smell of freshly-cut grass came to us from the Congregational Cemetery, where No. 2 son, Terry was at work, and the sight of the valley below was most gratifying.

Thence to our desk, where we caught up with some correspondence, and then to join our laboring son. A yank on the starting cord, and the rotary mower roars into life, and we commence the pleasant, weaving trip through the Congregational burial ground. Full of high resolve to cut in parallel lines, we are soon distracted by interesting spots in God's half acre. Over there to east'ard, the unmarked mounds of the graves of sailors whose bodies washed ashore on the ocean beaches.

Truro, like many of the Cape towns, thus made provisions for a final resting place for the unknown mariners who perished in the ocean gales. We've always considered this to be a civic project not unlike the Tomb of the Unknown Soldier. Here the lichen-splotched obelisk bearing the names of those Pamet men and boys lost in the memorable Gale of 1841. Certainly we should be permitted a brief detour and while we're circling the ornate, wrought-iron fence that girdles the marble monument, we'll turn to say hello to neighbor Frank Laurie, who sleeps nearby.

From here it's just a short way through the blue-tasseled bunch grass to the graves of Naylor Hatch—he used to be our milkman, many years ago,

and we'd like to catch him up on the news. And next to Naylor are Mr. and
Miz Manuel Corey. Perhaps Mr. Corey would like to talk shop a mite; he,
too was Town Clerk for many years in Truro. Perhaps he'd like to know
the tax rate, and the vital record statistics for the year. We can't forget John
Dyer, either. He's out there by the north gate, and he'll want to know if
we're still happy with his uncle John Rich's house, which we bought at his
suggestion some years ago. And we'll visit, too, with Rosalie Kramer, and
Eben Paine, (remember how he used to fill a paper bag with candy and
present it to you when you paid the family grocery bill?) and the members
of the Rose clan, Uncle Frank and Aunt Annie, and Frankie, onetime town
hall janitor, and by the time we've finished, the path of our mower through
the grass will be the pattern of a crazy quilt, and son Terry will glare at us
in disgust for our lack of system.

Mrs. Hazel Williams of the North Pamet called us recently to tell as how
she'd received a phone call from kin of hers, Mrs. Lowell Williams, South
Wellfleet colonist. The whole Williams family was thrilled no end at the
news of astronaut Allan Sheperd's successful flight; and rightly so for Dr.
Ralph Parker, another of the kinfolk, had delivered the hero of the
stratosphere, "launched Allan into space" is the way the good doctor put it
some years ago here in New England.

And speaking of doctors, the other weekend we got to talking with Mrs.
Bell, widow of the late beloved Dr. C. J. Bell of Wellfleet, at the local food
mart. (Our good bride was searching the aisles for specials in the green
stamp weekly steeplechase. All's we can say is thank fortune they don't
often have chocolate-covered ants or rattlesnake hocks as double-stamp
items.) Well sir, as we were saying, we met up with Miz Bell and we got to
talking about things past and present. Our travels took us from the
delicatessen items to the chicken barbecue, past the lobster tank and the
hamburg display, up cereals and crackers, back to garden items (rosebushes
special this week) and our conversation was as erratic as our route with the
shopping baskets. First off, Miz Bell wanted to tell us how she'd recently
attended a GOP women's meeting at the Provincetown Inn, how the
handsome new carpeting on the floor had filled her with static electricity so
sparks were fair shooting from her finger tips, and she dassn't approach her
friends. Being afflicted with a similar faculty for storing up voltage, we
clucked sympathetically.

We approached the fish counter, and Miz Bell stared thoughtfully at the
soulful eyes of a smoked kipper. "And I'm not only a human condenser,"
she added, "I have a capacity for extrasensory communication. At least I

used to, when the doctor was alive." Our curiosity was piqued so we followed the good woman over to dairy products, watched her select a wedge of coon cheese. "Yes indeed, the doctor and I could often communicate by mental telepathy, and a good thing it was, what with the lack of telephones in the old days." She went on to remind us that Ed Snow, who had one of the few phones in Truro, used to take the doctor's Pamet calls, and when emergencies arose, why Ed would fetch out an American flag and hang'er on the front of the house; Dr. Bell would see the flag on his way down Corey's Hill, and stop by Ed's to pick up the message.

But on many occasions, the doctor would already have passed this communication center; like the time he'd been dispatched by Ed Snow to the hinterlands of South Truro, way beyond the stretches of the telephone lines, to make a professional call on old Burleigh Cobb, the Hogsback postmaster. "Doctor had thought it would be a routine house call, so he drove his Sears, Roebuck special directly to Mr. Cobb's. But along about 11:30 or so, just before noon, while Eph Hill was selling me a quart of clams, I got what I can only describe as a message from the doctor. 'Send down the forceps, send down the forceps,' it seemed to say." So the good woman trotted into the doctor's office, and selected the proper instruments, and put them into the doctor's bag, and returned to where Ephie was waiting to be paid for his clams. "Eph," said Miz Bell, "please fetch these down with you on the noon train. Get off at South Truro and deliver 'em to Dr. Bell at Burleigh Cobb's." Eph took the bag and shuffled off to the depot. But no sooner had the old feller left the house than Miz Bell was struck by a horrible doubt—supposing the doctor had actually asked for obstetric forceps? "Well, it was too late to do anything about it, and I had to trust my own intuition," said the doctor's wife. "And when Dr. Bell came home that evening, I asked him how he'd fared with his patient. 'First rate,' replied the doctor. 'And thanks for the instruments. Biggest molar I ever pulled in my life. Funny thing, though—while I was workin' on Burleigh, his cow gave birth to a fine heifer calf. Thought for a while I'd have to assist at that, too.' "

How difficult it is to report the death of a good friend and neighbor. How delicate the balance between sincerity and sentimentality at a time like this. But let's begin at the beginning. Last evening, 6:30 or so, when we came home from the cemeteries with son Mike, our good bride met us at the door with the shocking news that Arthur S. Joseph, our good friend for these many years, had died of a heart attack within the hour. We use Arthur's middle initial to avoid confusion with the name of his son, Arthur F. There was a time when you'd have said Big Arthur, as opposed to Little Arthur—but Little Arthur has outgrown his dad, and the adjective no longer serves its original purpose.

And you could, of course, make reference to Old Arthur and Young Arthur, but somehow our friend never did seem old to us despite the fact that he could carry on a sprightly conversation with folks from eight to eighty. Arthur Joseph was many things to us. Employer: we worked for Arthur before we reached our majority, driving the old spray rig around town trying to eliminate the gypsy moth caterpillars. Advisor: we remember Arthur's words of advice when we were first elected Town Clerk and treasurer. ("You ever need money in a hurry—don't borrow it from the town—borrow it from ME. I may not have it, but I'll get it for you.") Landlord: we lived the first idyllically happy years of our married life in Arthur's cottage up the road a piece, and if the rent was hard to come by, Arthur'd be the last person in the world to remind us of our deliquency. Raconteur: Lord knows the number of times we've quoted neighbor Joseph in our column—and every yarn we ever used served the better to reveal Arthur's own innate qualities of humility and charity, and gentle humor.

But to get back to our own little family group when the news of Arthur's death reached us: Mike was shocked. He told us that Arthur had, less than an hour before his death, offered Mike a ride up to the cemetery to join our No. 2 son Terry, who was busy at his mowing task. And Arthur drove by the Catholic Cemetery and he said, "Look's real good, Mike, same as it does every year and I want to thank all the Kane's for what they've done." And somehow supper was a solemn interlude for us, and all last evening and all day today we've been thinking about Arthur Joseph. Expecting to see him come bouncing down the road in his Jeep, forefinger crooked over the steering wheel in his usual gesture of greeting. Ave atque vale, old friend. May the Caretaker of good caretakers welcome you.

And now that we're in a nostalgic mood, why not a few excerpts from the immortal prose of the late I.M. Small, the sage of the North Village. We have some of Mr. Small's yellowed clippings in the vault. Join us while we browse into the past. Nov. 7, '89: "There seems to be a growing disposition on the part of many people that there is room to doubt the efficiency of the Civil Service in the affairs of a Republican government . . . if we are to adopt and strictly adhere to the principle involved, why should we not extend it to . . . the President of the United States? If Grover Cleveland or Benjamin Harrison faithfully, conscientiously and acceptably perform the duties of Chief Magistrate of the nation, why not retain them in office which their four years experience would seem to have qualified them to fill better than a new and untried man?

. . . "The question is often asked, 'How old is the old windmill? [standing near Highland Light].' This mill was built in the Spring of 1790, and next April will be its 100th anniversary. The timbers of which it is constructed are of white oak and were cut in this town. All the timbers are hewn, and though for many years were exposed to the elements, are still sound with the exception of the sills. These mills were formerly prominent and picturesque objects on all parts of the Cape, but their days of usefulness ended long ago. They are among the many illustrations we see every day of the progression of the world. The march is steadily and always forward."

Small on the franchies: "Well, the great Australian ballot system has been tried (1889) and, I was about to say, found wanting. But the results so far have been fairly satisfactory. In our precinct everything worked smoothly and without any apparent loss of time. Now and then a voter seemed to have become rattled, as in the case of the man who marked for three governors, making an X for the first three names on the ticket, and stopping there. Perhaps he thought if we had three governors at one time we would not need any other officers."

Small humor: "We have often thought it strange that women almost invariably scream and make a break for the nearest chair at the sight of a mouse. It is a mystery no longer. It is plainly evident that the female portion of humanity are the natural and selected victims of the mouse family. Shortly after midnight recently, Mr. B. was awakened by his wife shouting, 'I've got a mouse, get a light quick.' When the light was produced the lady was discovered grasping the falls of her black hair with both hands, while just below her ear dangled the tail of a more plucky than discreet mouse. His temerity cost him his life, and the lady is considering the advisability of sleeping in a wire mask."

Mr. Small on the new generation: "What is the matter with the rising generation? Where is all that desire for literary entertainment which used to find expression in lyceums, concerts, social clubs, etc.? Once we used to think our winter life a blank without two or three lyceums in working order. Where are they now? Are the young people who are growing up less intelligent or less ambitious than formerly? We do not believe this to be the cause of the decadence of the lyceum. But if we looked behind the scenes we would find one great reason for this change in the gradual narrowing of the social lines. Country towns are imbibing more and more the conditions of the cities. We are becoming communities of individuals rather than communities of societies, and distrust is the corner stone . . ."

Mr. Small on the fishing industry: "Reports from Capt. Chase, now fishing for mackerel at Cape Town, coast of Africa, declare that the fish there are the identical mackerel of our New England waters; that the fish are plentiful and easily taken. It is said one consignment is already on the way home and all those interested are awaiting their arrival with considerable interest. We understand fish barrels are not obtained there and fish are shipped in wine casks. That being the case, if a portion of that liquid was left in the barrel perhaps a new and improved quality of fish might be the result by the time of their arrival in this country. We do not hear of any alarming exodus of our fishermen towards Africa, but we do wish Capt. Chase an abundant success. He deserves it . . ."

Mr. Small on the balance sheet of the town of Truro: "The financial standing of our town at the end of the year shows a very favorable condition . . . We submit a financial statement of the town's progression since 1886: Dec. 1886, town debt, $1,724.74. Tax rate per thousand, $20.00. Dec. 31, 1887, town debt, 286.05. Tax rate per thousand, $20.00. Dec. 31, 1888, town debt, NOTHING. Balance in treasury, $227.87, tax rate, $16.20 per thousand . . . Dec. 31, 1889, balance in treasury, $808.06. Tax rate per thousand, $14.50 . . . We do not need or want a further surplus, we believe it to be better policy to lower the rate of taxation than to trouble ourselves about an insignificant debt . . ."

A frequent visitor to our office these days has been Miss Bobbie Nichols, a young lady from Falmouth, Mass., who has become interested in genealogy through a study of the Dyer family tree. Ordinarily, folks wait until they're well along in years before they start browsing through the vital records; not so with Bobbie. This girl has the most phenomenal memory we've ever seen at work. And in the course of her Dyer genealogy, she has, perforce, crossed the family lines of just about every other early Pamet name in the books (over five thousand names in her binder at last count, and she has yet to research the vitals of neighboring towns and nearby states). So if any of our readers wish to link their lines with the original colonists, we suggest they contact our Bobbie.

We imagine the Sears, Roebuck catalogue is being worked over these days as beleaguered parents do some mail order shopping for their kids in the few days remaining before school opens. And if there are complaints that little bodies have grown, and waistlines have expanded, and shoe sizes have lengthened, consider our recent conversation with friend Snowie, the Laird of Slade's Landing. We were sitting with that genial feller on the banks of the Pamet one evening recently, listening to the happy voices of a score or so of kids from Arnold Slade's cottage on the hill, and Snowie got to reminiscing. "Remember how uncomfortable your shoes used to feel, when you tried to squeeze 'em on, first day of school?" We nodded our agreement with a little grimace of pain at the memory.

"Course, we'd been all summer long without shoes and our feet would have callouses quarter of an inch thick on the soles, and our toes would be splayed like a bunch of bananas from gripping the loose sand all season." We asked Snowie if he'd ever had difficulties with tar sticking to his feet, when they oiled the roads in the summer. "Yer dern tootin' I did. My Ma used to inspect my feet every night, and before I went to bed I'd get the soles swabbed with kerosene, full strength, until every last speck of that sticky black stuff had been rinsed clean." There was a pause in the conversation while Snowie went to fetch us a fresh cup of coffee. When he returned, he had the smug look that bespoke a yarn.

"Ever stub your toe while you were goin' barefoot?" he queried us. We had, of course, but we knew instinctively that any pedal injury we might have sustained would pale by comparison with Snowie's experiences.

"I recall the time I was sent out to fetch the cows home for Grampa Snow, up to the north pasture, that big stretch of range that used to run from the barn clean to Bill's Hill, over Long Nook way. T'wasn't really my turn, and I was madder 'n a wet hen because I had a date with a girl up at the evening mail; so every few steps I'd mutter to myself and fetch a kick at something in the road—a piece of stick, or a rotten apple, or some such. Got up by the water tanks on the hill and a swarm of mosquitoes attacked me, makin' me all the madder. Then a pair of skunks headed me off by the old try-works on the edge of Gramp's garden, and I had to take a detour that used up about ten minutes. Grabbed a handful of juicy pears to soothe my temper, and the cussed things were sour and while I was pickin' 'em, I noticed I was standing knee deep in a patch of poison ivy. Time I found the cows, I was just about at the boilin' point and derned if two of the cows wasn't missin', so I had to go way down to Phil Ryder's Dyke to scour 'em out of a water hole. Stepped in a mudhole, myself, and sank clear to my hips." We sipped our coffee and commiserated with this latter day Job of Pamet.

"Finally I got all the cows bunched together, and flicked a silver oak switch at 'em, and headed 'em for the barn. Coming along by the cemetery I spied a big, silver-gray puffball in the dust by the side of the road, so I swung back my foot and everlastin'ly fetched a kick at it: POW. Only thing was, it warn't no puffball, it was a fieldstone about as big as a football. Good Lord I like to broke every bone in my foot. My big toe swelled up size of a summer cucumber, and the pain was somethin' fearful. Had to wear a bedroom slipper to school for two months." We allowed as how Snowie must have learned a lesson from his painful experience. "Sure did: never fetch a kick at anything when dusk is coming on," said Snowie as he thoughtfully massaged a large and rather misshapen digit.

Much doing on the weekend: at the final, bang-up softball game of the season, the Pamet Indians scalped the Wellfleet Clamdiggers 1-0 behind the brilliant pitching of Lee Remington; and it was Remington's home run that won the game. Peggy Day's spacious grounds were jammed with scores of people attending Gilbert Selde's Labor Day farewell party, and the Dr. Sam Phillips go-cart had a workout by sundry lucky young house guests, and the beauteous Maxine Lowry (she's the social secretary to Sec. of Interior Udall) dropped in for a brief visit with Col. and Mrs. Dick Magee. The most deliriously happy young lady we know of is Janey Hoeffel, daughter of Dr. and Mrs. Gerald Hoeffel, who left this week for a year's study at the American University in Athens, Greece. And Bob Bumps has started work on a new house for Ralph Woodward at the corner of Depot Road and Holsbery Road.

There's very real significance to the blind, boarded windows of the summer cottages along Beach Point this late September day. There's a message, too, to be read from the thin, haze overcast that thickens as the day grows older, in the smurred, streaky cirrus formation to west'ard, and the furrowed, somber gray clouds forming where the horizon meets the ocean. The fitful, easterly breeze, laden with the brine smell of the backshore, and the mutter of the surf in the distance, and the aimless, errant flight of the mackerel gulls adds information to the syndrome of the approaching storm.

This noon we peered out from the teachers' room at school and found the harbor strangely empty of boats, and the headlands of Truro etched clearly against the last patch of sickly blue sky; and the noon siren sounded oddly muffled in the heavy air that blanketed the town.

On the trip home from Provincetown we remarked the dunes, sable, shadowless, capped with ragged swatches of bleached beach grass, and the leaden stretch of Pilgrim Lake stirred to the breeze and lapped at the rip rap on the bank below the highway. We paused for a mite outside town hall, studying the gilded weather cock atop the venerable building as he peered boldly up-valley toward the ocean, and we listened to the cricket chorus in the grass, and cast a passing glance at the beachplum copse on the edge of the hill (leaves are turning a mite red), and pleasured in the sight of a clump of goldenrod across the parking space.

Thence to our chores, posting tax money and answering a letter or two, and finally, as the chimes rang the quarter hour after five, to our own home. To find, as we reached our old Cape Codder, that friend Snowie was stuck in the sand at Ballston Beach, so we loaded our sons into the truck, and armed with rope and planks, we hied off to the rescue, only to find neighbor Tony Duarte in the act of towing out the feckless Squire of Slade's Landing. So we headed about and proceeded to Pamet Harbor. Much action there: trap fishermen securing their boats and scows, and pleasure boat owners hauling their craft out on trailers. We noted Joe Flanagan's boat on the beach, and, on advice of No. 3 son, Mike, we unbuttoned the outboard motor and fetched 'er back to Joe's place on Depot Road, stopping en route at Fred Davis', where we took down his coat-of-arms sign and tucked it safely in the barn. And now it's evening, and the wireless is laden with dire reports of the forthcoming hurricane, and our good wife is filling every available container in the house with water, and we await the storm. If preparations for the unwelcome visitor, Esther, could have a lighter side, we witnessed one such today. Glancing out of our classroom window at mid-afternoon, we espied custodian Mickey Bollas daintily snipping the blossoms from the zinnias and the petunias, and after he had gathered a sizable bouquet, fetching it over to Insley Caton's house next door. "Couldn't bear to see 'em all beat up by the storm," Mickey explained to us later in the day.

Truro has received nation-wide publicity in the November issue of the Journal of the American Insurance, a copy of which found its way to our desk through the courtesy of Mr. Frederick J. Keilholz, editor of the trade magazine. Featuring a print of the Corn Hill plaque, the article says in part, "But for a cache of insurance [we forgive the advertising plug] staked out by provident Indians, the Pilgrims might have perished or been even more decimated before that first Thanksgiving 340 years ago. Corn stored by the Indians among the Cape Cod dunes near Truro was found and relished by the famished Pilgrims foraging under the direction of their appointed military leader, Miles Standish. Nearby, in what is now Provincetown, Massachusetts, the Pilgrims made their first landing on American soil November 11, 1620. There, too, they suffered the first cruelties of the new and strange land. While the Mayflower remained anchored offshore, Standish and his men scouted the Cape Cod coast for five weeks seeking the most favorable site for the new settlement.

"The subsequent landing at Plymouth was made December 26. Amid the suffering and uncertainty of those first days and weeks, the cache of food in Corn Hill must, indeed, have been manna from heaven to the Pilgrims.

Later in his account of Plymouth Plantation, Governor William Bradford, who had succeeded the deceased John Carver, described the Cape as a hideous and desolate wilderness, full of wild beasts and men. Truro itself was settled about 1700, and was established as a town in 1709. Fishing and whaling became principal sources of income. Had mutual property and casualty insurance been in vogue then as it is now, Truro might have surpassed the peak it reached in 1850. At that time it had a fleet of more than 100 vessels. However, marine disasters, with property losses and business failures, doomed the fishing and whaling industry."

Much noise of hammering and other tasks at town hall this afternoon as the folks of the upholstering class labor under the direction of Miss Dorothy Crowell. Every evening after the ladies leave their burlap and tacks we're tempted to look through the pieces of furniture for old coins or other valuables—so far we haven't found the time. Would-be nimrods have been dropping by our house recently for hunting licenses, and on Saturday last, just as a pair of Provincetown men knocked at our door, a big, gaudy-plumed cock pheasant strutted up from the meadow, crossed our lawn in almost nonchalant manner, and disappeared into the woods. Fair had the hunters drooling, he did.

Speaking of hunting, we feel that the story of Phat Francis' capture of a deer, bare-handed and afoot (Phat, that is, not the deer) should be preserved for posterity. It happened many years ago, when Phat was proprietor of the Square Deal Store and Garage, located in Truro Center, about where Peggy Day's hillside garden is now located. Deer season, it was, and the hunters were putting on a big drive on the General Fields, north of the village. Under pressure of the drive, a halfgrown buck became separated from the herd, and somehow crashed his way through the scrub behind Dr. Lupien's and paused for breath in Phyllis Given's front yard.

"I was pumpin' gas for a customer at my station, across the street," is the way Phat recounts the story, "and my dog, Mammy, came out from under the store, whining and wrinkling her nose in the direction of the house across the way. First off, I paid her no mind." Phat says he polished the windshield for his customers, and checked the tires for air, and made change. Mammy kept making strange noises in her throat; so finally, as the car drove away, Phat threw a casual glance in the direction of Given's house.

"My years of service in the Coast Guard and the Navy had sharpened my eyesight," continues the rotund Hogsbacker, "because I could make out, behind the thick cover of the privet hedge, the outline of a deer. Quick as a cat, I tiptoed across the road, climbed the bank, and peered through the hedge. Sure enough, there in the enclosure formed by the two ells of the house, was a spike-horn buck, nostrils distended, ears atuned to the slightest noise in the afternoon air."

Phat dropped into the crouch that had made him famous as a tackle in the old Hyannis Normal School football team. Motioning his dog, Mammy, into silence, he slowly slipped through the opening in the hedge, dug his toes into the ground, and, "I threw a flying tackle at the beast as pretty as ever I'd executed at HNS. But he saw me coming at the last minute and sidestepped me so I ended up in the privet hedge. Before he could find the opening in the thick shrubbery, I bounced back, and tackled him again. This time my outstretched hands touched, then went around his neck, and down we crashed, me on top of the buck."

In response to Phat's bellowing, folks down at the store soon came to his aid—old Joe Francis, Phat's father, fetched up a butcher knife and dispatched the unfortunate animal, while Phat hastened off on two important errands. "First, being a law-abiding citizen, I trotted over to Mr. Corey's office (he was Town Clerk at the time) and bought a huntin' license. Mr. Corey allowed as how I only had a few hours to get my deer, it being Saturday, the last day of deer season, and I told him I felt real lucky. Then I called the newspaper reporter and had him come over to Truro for his scoop. Made all the papers, we did, and the Francis family had fresh venison for several weeks. Even Mammy, who had put me on the trail of the buck, got a feed of shinbones." The deer meat, we hasten to report, must have contained some hormones or other chemical agents of fertility, for Mammy shortly gave birth to a litter of nineteen assorted puppies, further justifying her name. Thus was established the dynasty of Phat's dogs, about which reams have been written—but that's another story.

Stopped by Col. Dick Magee's last Sunday afternoon for our weekly visit, and lingered a mite after the other guests had departed. The Sunday paper lay on the table before us, its news content well digested, its ads thoroughly perused, its crossword puzzle neatly filled in. Some obscure item on the pages had evidently caught the colonel's eye, evoking a memory of the past, for he commenced to reminisce on the salad days of his career as public relations man for a big automobile firm in Boston. We assumed the attitude of attentive listening as Dick filled our coffee cup and lighted a fresh cigarette. "Ever tell you about the time I played nursemaid to a hippopotamus?" he asked. We shook our head.

"Well sir, that would be about 1923 or so, shortly after I'd been mustered out of the Army Air Force, and had taken a fling at flying the mail, and had been out in Hollywood, working in motion picture productions; but that's another yarn. Anyway, back I came to Boston, where I took a position as public relations man for Alvin T. Fuller, then New England's largest Packard dealer. Wonderful car in those days, quality merchandise, especially the big twin six special. The Twin could pass everything on the road but a gasoline pump."

We reached down and scratched the colonel's big police dog, Oscar, in the secret spot behind his ear that makes him whine with pleasure. A log fell into the embers of the fireplace with a sudden shower of sparks. "So we decided to dream up some sort of a publicity stunt to promote sales for the Twin. The people of Boston, as you may know, hold their Franklin Park Zoo close to their heart and anything that will benefit the zoo gets the greatest publicity in the Hub press. So I suggested to Mr. Fuller that he buy, and donate to Franklin Park Zoo, some kind of animal with appeal. As a tie-in for Packard sales, I further suggested that we make delivery in one of the new Twin Sixes (they made trucks, too, in those days). Mr. Fuller liked my idea so we contacted the Philadelphia Zoo, and they sold us a half-grown hippopotamus, name of Happy—and Magee got the job of fetching the hippo up to Boston.

"The papers went wild. Every inch of our trip was to be covered by reporters, and a big celebration was planned to meet Happy when he arrived in the beantown." The colonel pointed at our empty cup and we nodded our assent to more coffee.

"Well sir, the journey to Philly was uneventful; so was the loading of Happy into the Packard; so was the first leg of the return trip. Then we hit the first link of the old Boston Post Road, this side of New York. It was a hot day, and when I glanced in the rear view mirror I noticed Happy was perspiring a pink liquid. Stopped at the nearest phone booth, and called the curator at Franklin Park, and he told me that Happy would have to be drenched with cold water every time he got dry. So I spend every cent I had in my pocket, calling sundry fire departments through Connecticut and Rhode Island and Southeastern Massachusetts, making appointments for them to meet me with equipment hooked up to their hydrants so's we could give Happy periodical showers."

Again the Magee coffee pot passed over our empty cup.

"By gosh, I had the pleasure of meeting more'n a dozen fire chiefs along the Post Road. Happy was squirted by every brand of apparatus in the books: American LaFrances, and Maxims, and Seagraves, an Arehns-Foxes, and even a horse drawn steamer, in Westerly, R. I. I tell you, I was some relieved when we backed the Packard up to the hippo tank at Franklin Park Zoo and dumped that critter in the drink." Colonel Magee studied the grounds at the bottom of our cup. "And until this day, I've never seen another such dry animal except you, in the decades that have passed."

Just finished reading "By the Seat of My Pants" an extremely interesting story of pioneer days of aviation by Dean C. Smith. We were reviewing it for John Worthington in our office at close of the day, and John was transported into his own memories of early flying experiences. John got to reminiscing about the post World War I period of his adventures in the Mexican oil fields. "I was probably the hottest flying buff in North America," said John, wryly. "I had the pleasure of knowing many of the men Smith wrote about in his book: Balchen, and June, and Spaatz. Learned to fly a Hisso Jenny in an hour and a half; even bought two of those old crates after the war for a hundred dollars apiece. But back to Mexico. . . ."

John went on to tell how the oil companies were having difficulties delivering payrolls to their crews. The Mexican bandits, it appeared, were intercepting the payroll messengers with discouraging frequency. At one point, the desperate company officials even attempted to wrap the currency in liquid-proof containers and pump them through the oil lines; but news of this subterfuge somehow leaked out, and the bandits cut the lines and appropriated the cash.

"Finally it was decided to fly the payrolls in using surplus aircraft from the war. And from this humble beginning the Mexican branch of Pan American Airlines started. But the feller I started to tell you about," John continued, "was a daring flyer name of Joe Glass. He's now senior commodore for Pan Am, probably the oldest active pilot in the airlines." According to John, the oil companies desperately needed a large supply of nitroglycerin for seismograph field work. "You know how sensitive nitro is," explained John, "a mild burp from a female mouse will set the stuff off. The railroads, of course, refused to transport it, and since roads were non-existent in that part of Mexico, trucking was out of the question, so the infant Mexican Airline was given the contract. The airline offered a bonus of one hundred dollars a trip—six quarts of nitro packed in the front cockpit of a wartime Jenny—and the only man who would accept the job was Joe Glass."

Joe, it appeared, made several uneventful flights, delivering the nitro to the oil fields, then, "Glass decided he'd ask the company to supply him with a parachute, just in case he had to bail out over the rough terrain of Mexico. They sent to the States and got him one of the new-fangled contraptions on consignment. Next flight in, Joe was several hours overdue, so the camp foreman and I flew up to see what had happened to him." Several miles up the coast, according to John, they espied the Glass-flown Jenny, limping just above the dense forest, so they escorted him in—at a safe distance, of course—and followed him to the crude hangar to learn what had caused the delay. "Joe explained to us his oil line had sprung a leak, spraying his goggles and windshield with hot oil. He'd landed his plane on a rocky beach along the coast, repaired the oil line gasket with a patch improvised from a piece of his shirt tail, coaxed the sluggish Jenny back into the air, and since he was short of gas, had brushed the treetops all the way back to his destination and had landed his cargo of nitro. When the airline boss found out the risks Joe had taken, he sent the parachute back to the United States, figuring that a chute would be precious little use to a daredevil like Glass."

NINETEEN SIXTY-TWO

1962

We used to think that the evening distractions of radio and TV were well-nigh impossible to overcome. That would be back in the days of the western . . . and the sound effects of those hell-for-leather epics were always pure poison to our literary efforts. We like to think that the poor columns we've written had their origin in the crack and the ricochet of rifle fire, the creak of dusty leather—chaps against stirrups, the hollow clop of horses' hooves in some wild box canyon, the clink of bar glasses against a bottle of red-eye, the muffled boom of dynamite in the innards of the Wells-Fargo strong-box, the distant howl of a coyote on the south range. But bad as was the horse opera, a new and more virulent TV show has darkened our picture tube and is proving to be a much more serious distraction than the western ever was.

We wish, therefore, to raise our voice in protest against the underwater show: the frogman, skindiver program with all its variations, wherein the steady, gurgling sound of the underwater exhaust accompanies every scene. You're familiar with the format, of course. The scene opens with the frogman hero slipping into his underwater gear. We'd require the services of two valets to don the suit, but Don Deepwater gets into his unaided while he gives a resume of the plot in his deep rich baritone. "I had just thirty-eight minutes to find the wreck of the Poobah and recover the box that contained Mark XXIII, the secret electronic device belonging to our government, but coveted by a foreign power." SPLASH, glup-a-glup-a-glup-a-glup. "A fleeting shadow in the pale green water told me that a deadly hammer-head shark was stalking me, and the wound I had sustained in the brawl at Casa Blanca was bleeding and attracting the huge killer, glup-a-glup-a-glup. And then at last I saw the hulk of the Poobah. But at that very instant two skindivers, armed with spearguns, appear out of the gloom, glup-a-glup . . . a-gleep-a-gleep-a-gloop-a-gloop-a-gloop." But you get the picture. Has a feller gasping so for breath just to watch the thing that we'll likely develop chest structures like the Andes Indians within a generation.

★ ★ ★

As the years pass, it seems we have more frequent occasions to pay our final respects to old and good friends. This week we say goodbye to Col. Dick Magee of the Oasis, fellow Irishman (he'd call himself a turkey, or perhaps a harp), genial host, raconteur par excellence, gourmet, friend. In these latter months, when Dick was ailing, we'd drop by his South Truro home of a Sunday afternoon. Marie Stephens and Snowie and Norma would be there, and we'd sit around the big dining table and talk or do crossword puzzles as the logs crackled in the fireplace. And sometimes the conversation would pall, and we'd steal a glance at our sick friend, and then, "You're looking better this week, Dick," or "Feller your age should peel off a little weight anyway." We'd try to say the things we knew he wanted to hear. And Dick would talk about a spring vacation, or a bit of a rest just as soon as Nell could be left alone for a spell. And so the colonel's long awaited rest has finally come. We wonder if Oscar, the big German shepherd was there to welcome the stranger who called for his master that cold January Sabbath. In any event, thanks for the memories, Col. Dick. Ave atque vale, old friend.

During the recent school vacation our good friend Bobbie Nichols, the teenage genealogist from Falmouth, was working in our office when Squire Johnnie Dyer dropped by. Bobbie, starry-eyed as she worked on the Dyer family tree, queried John anent some distant ancestor. "Let's see," said John, scratching his head as he delved into his mental notes. "You must mean Aunt Hatty Dyer. Oh yes, I remember her. Called up before a Justice of the Peace, she was, for dispersing spiritous liquors to the Indians. And on another occasion she was reprimanded for using strong language on the Sabbath. But the biggest trouble she ever got into was . . ."

"Please, Mr. Dyer, I don't want to hear any more," interrupted Bobbie. The poor girl just can't stand being disillusioned.

"Had all sorts of Dyers in our line ever since the first Dr. William," explained John. "Sea captains, and merchants, and farmers, and public officials, and mechanics, and tradesmen. Branches of the clan in Maine, and Massachusetts, and just about every state in the union." Bobby pointed out her present and as yet incomplete Dyer genealogy contains well over 20,000 names—and she's just beginning to comb the Provincetown vital records. So don't say you haven't Dyer blood in your veins until you've studied the Nichols-Dyer genealogy.

Not without a trace of humor was our first day back at school, following the winter vacation. There's a small section of our front blackboard we usually reserve for the names of pupils we intend to keep after school. Each week when the slate has been washed clean, we chalk a new title for the list. In our quest for originality we've used such headings as "Guest List," "Vacancy," "S.P.C.C," "Teacher's Pets." And just as we were about to give up and settle for Detention or some such, an unknown hand neatly lettered the following caption on our blackboard: "KANE'S HUNDRED." The TV influence, no doubt.

Brother Charlie Snow is a resourceful man. Take, for instance, the time Charlie was commissioned to gold leaf the bronze plaque of the Cobb Memorial Library. 1912 that would have been. "Kind of a rush job, had to meet the deadline for the dedication, one of the biggest affairs we'd ever had in Truro. Elisha W. Cobb, the philanthropist who had given the funds to build the library, was to be there, and hundreds of guests from all over the Cape." But alas, as Charlie points out, just when he'd set up his staging at the new building derned if a dry nor'easter didn't set in that blew for most a week. What to do? Every time Charlie climbed his step ladder and gingerly opened a book of gold leaf and drew his camel's hair brush through his hair to build up a charge of static electricity to magnetize the bristles, why the cussed wind would float the expensive gold leaf away. "Must've been ten dollars worth of gold leaf plastered on nearby beachplum bushes." Charlie was desperate. He was even debating the value of unbolting the heavy plaque from the wall of the library and fetching 'er inside for the application of the gold leaf, when suddenly he had an inspiration. "Happened to be down at Billy May's photography studio one afternoon with all the other members of the clan having a family portrait done, and after Billy had posed us, and he ducked under that big, black cloth to squint through the sighter, I let out a whoop and everlastin'ly scooted back to Truro."

And then Charlie assembled a pile of light strapping, and got himself several yards of canvas, and built a snug little shelter, like a cocoon, smack against the library wall, covering the bronze plaque. "Crawled inside with my kit," says Charlie, "and closed the hatch after me. Then I lighted up a lantern, and spread my sizing all over the letters and the numerals, waited for it to get tacky, opened my gold leaf, and applied it, easy as pie. Timed it just right, too. By the time I had finished A.D., 1912 the air was just about exhausted inside my shelter, what with the kerosene lantern and the cigar smoke, and I was commencin' to get dizzy. Yessir, my gold leaf's been up there on that sign for fifty years, and I'm proud of it."

★ ★ ★

It's worth the loss of sleep these mornings as the days lengthen and the countryside shows the syndrome of the vernal season. Take today, for instance: the early flood of pale gold sunlight limning the pines of the eastern hills, the delicate tracery of the locusts sketched on the wallpaper of our bedroom, the bird chorus in fine voice in our back yard, shrill jays and bold starlings, and a cherry red-wing blackbird sending up his kwongaree from the alder copse in the meadow below. Feller'd have to be as insensitive as a chopping block to lie abed on such a day. So we arise and dress, and perform our matutinal ablutions, admiring the weather between sundry minor household chores. Set the control hand on our handsome new barometer (Dr. Sam Phillips advised us, when he presented us with the instrument last weekend, that this was a magic barometer—set the hand for the weather you want, said he, and she'll get it for you) and peek out the front door. Front door is actually the back door on our Cape Codder. Faces South, you see, as do all authentic Truro front doors, with complete disregard for road layouts, natural topography or neighboring houses.

Well sir, there we espied a bush-tailed gray squirrel, raiding the last smidgin of feed from a bird tray, and a quartet of fat, beady-eyed quail huddled under the lilac bush. Thence to our kitchen to start the coffee pot, glancing, the while, at the thermometer on the back porch. 38 reads the thin red line, but with this bright sun she's bound to climb. Comes the insistent scratching of our pom, Mokie, from the door of his back apartment, and we free him, and follow his dancing steps outside for a brief survey of the lawn: daffodils in their circular bed swollen, ready to blossom, the sweep of grass' new green, wet with last evening's light frost. The loop of the fresh Pamet sparkling in the morning light.

So what matter the dry easterly breeze that will spring up to chill the afternoon, or the suspicious smur that will blanket the horizon as the sun sets tonight! There's much merit in the day. The peewink chorus will be strong tonight, and perhaps there'll be the twilight honking of geese flying to south'ard, and the neighborhood kids will be playing scrub in the old garden patch across the road.

We dropped by Snowie's house the other day. Norma, his child bride, was away at a Reddy Kilowatt convention, and Snowie was lonesome. After we'd cheered him up a mite, we dared to advance a plan which had been hiding in the back of our mind for quite a spell. We worked up to it gradually—that's the way you have to approach Snowie otherwise he's liable to veto new ideas. So we allowed, casually, as how we were getting bored with our placid existence. Same old schedule every day: up betimes, to our chores at the Temple of Learning then a stint at our desk at town hall, thence to chase a lawn mower across the same old green grass, and later perhaps a session at our faithful Royal, composing deathless prose. Jades the heck out of a feller, we complained. We hanker to do something daring, unusual. "Sounds as though you plan to go back bartendin'," interrupted Snowie. Not so, we denied. What we really had in mind was a short trip of exploration—say the Pamet River. Been years, we pointed out, since we'd boated the limpid waters of the fresh Pamet and if only we could locate a light craft, say a canoe, why we'd . . .

"Say no more, O'Caghan," shouted Snowie, his eyes alight with enthusiasm. "I'll be your manager, organize the whole cussed expedition. We'll borry a canoe, sure enough, provision her for the trip right here at Snow's Landing, tote her up to the headwaters of the Pamet in your truck, and commence our junket at, say, Dode Kimball's, or even farther if we can find enough water."

"Kind of a poor man's Pilgrim exploration," we joined in. "But what'll we take for supplies?" Snowie quick produced a pad and pencil, started to list materials. "Let's see. We'll need your typewriter, of course, and plenty of onion skin, and sandwiches and something cool to drink. And a camera, and a sketch pad for me, to pictorially record the wonders of the creek. Did I mention something cool to drink? Oh yes, we'll want a copy of Shebnah Rich's "History of Truro" to help locate landmarks, and plenty of cigarettes to smoke away the gnat flies, if there are any around, and we might's well take along some fishing gear in case we sight a lunker trout. First-aid kit, and sunburn lotion and something cool to drink, of course." He scribbled madly on his pad. We thought perhaps we could arrange the loan of a tape recorder; be fine to get the call of a bull frog or a nesting black duck on tape.

"Yup," assented Snowie, "and an eel spear—you know the crick has oodles of summer eels—and a basket to fetch some water cress in, and a quahaug rake to explore the mudholes of the salt creek, after we've made the portage at Wilder's Dyke. And let's not forget something cool to drink."

So our good bride is dusting off the pith helmet from the side chamber, up attic, and come the right combination of tide, weather and energy, we propose to undertake the Pamet expedition within a fortnight. Our terminus will be Depot Beach, where Fred Barshie Sylvia and Billy Joseph will be waiting with our truck to fetch us back to our respective wives. "And I hope they have something cooling to drink," adds Snowie.

At this writing neighbor Tony Duarte must be settled in his new bay-front cottage at North Truro. Over the weekend we saw Tony and a sizable crew of men moving furniture and sundries from the original homestead on South Pamet Road. The former Duarte property will serve as headquarters for officials of the National Seashore Commission Historical area.

Dropped by the bloodmobile at Provincetown after school this afternoon to make our donation, found VFW Hall a beehive of activity. We were met at the door by Johnnie Grace, one of the organizers of the project, who allowed as how we'd be able to accommodate an inch-and-a-half pipe in our arteries. We shuddered at the thought. Stepped up to the first table, we did, to where one of the high school lassies commenced to fill in our card. "Age?" she queried. We mumbled something unintelligible. "Date of birth?" she was firmer this time. "Promise not to tell a soul," we entreated, "April 1, 1916." We've always felt no teacher should admit to more than thirty-nine years—old age of youth, as it were. So on we went to the second station, where that nice Mrs. Moon dredged a clinical thermometer from its alcohol bath and aimed it at our mouth. "Let's take a look at that bulb," we demurred. "That's no oral thermometer." "You're not in school now, young man," she snapped at us, then, "under the tongue and let's feel your pulse." She jotted some figures on our card.

She gave us a healthy push to Station 3, where Miz Reis, crisp, efficient in her white nurse's uniform, pointed us to a chair. We tried to butter her up with nostalgic reference to our days together on the Lower Cape Ambulance. "Remember the time we took that feller to . . . " "Sorry, no time for chitchat," interrupted the R.N. "How much do you weigh?" We whispered the figure at her. "Ever have jaundice, epilepsy, anorexia?" She fired a long list of diseases at us. We replied in the negative in each instance. On went the blood pressure machine (they have a new type cuff, self-adhering, something like interlocking cockle-burs, and when Miz Reis ripped the gadget off our arm it sounded as though she had stripped our very hide away). We shuddered, then relaxed as she tenderly held our hand, but only for a moment. With one lightning jab she ran a kingsize scalpel into our ring finger, squeezed a quantity of blood into a tiny pipette, dropped the precious stuff into a vile-looking blue chemical.

"H'mmm," she said, then, "move along, please." We slid into a chair next to the local restaurateur, "Mac" MacFarlane. A Gray Lady came out from behind a curtain, handed us each a paper cup of water, advised us, with a grim smile, it was our turn next. We gave a tiny, devil-may-care wave to Jimmy Cordeiro, who followed us, and proceeded into the bed area. A brisk, efficient nurse, red-haired, wearing startling harlequin glasses made us comfortable. "And what is your line of work," she inquired mechanically. She doesn't really care—we grumbled to ourself—won't even listen when we tell her. She's supposed to put you to ease. "Work for a sporting-goods house," we murmured, "make second bases out of quadruple amputees." "Mmmm—that's nice. Make a tight fist," said she. And we did, and a few minutes later we were being conducted to the lunch station, where we partook of black coffee and orange juice, and gossiped a mite with Mssrs. Cordeiro, MacFarlane and Grace. The figures scrawled on our paper napkin indicated we were to leave at four-ten; and though the company was pleasant and the snacks tasty, we reluctantly slipped into our coat and hied off to Truro. Looks of the crowd, Johnnie Grace and his committee will meet their quota today.

Big news in the valley this week is the arrival of the E. J. Kahn clan for the summer. We're hard put to report all that's happened, or is going to happen, to the Kahns. To begin with, Jack and his beauteous bride, Ginny, and at least two of the boys had parts in a play written by E.J. for the occasion of Jack's twenty-fifth graduation reunion at Harvard last week. Ginny was still hoarse and in half-voice when we talked to her. And Jack said the Harvard arrangements committee couldn't have been nicer. "They even made arrangements to board our dog, Barge, while we were partying." Arrived at the summer home on South Pamet, Jack promptly launched a weekly paper for youngest son, Tony. We had the pleasure of scanning the first mimeographed sheet—it will be called Park Here—and found it fine. Seems all the old grads were celebrating get-togethers; Martin Robbins was in New Haven, marking the (did we hear correctly) 25th reunion anniversary of his Yale class.

Much business at town hall these days in the vending of shellfish permits. Judging by sales to date as compared with last year's figures, we hazard the guess that close to 1,500 licenses will have issued from the selectmen's sanctum come Labor Day. All we can hope is that the entire body of license holders should not take it into their heads to visit the clam flats at one time. In any event, Lord pity the poor bivalve. On occasion, when Lucy Medders is busy at her adding machine, we assume the responsibility of selling the licenses. A typical transaction goes like this. "Staying in Truro? Familiar with the regulations? Here's a card with all the rules and here's a ring. What for? Why that's to measure your clams and quahaugs. Lay 'em on that ring, lengthwise, and if they slip through, they're under two inches—got to put 'em back. Cherrystone? Well, we don't identify 'em by market names, we call 'em quahaugs. Quoting from Pratt's History of Eastham, which you see here on the desk, 'The quahaug is a round and thick shellfish. It does not bury itself in the sand, and is taken with an iron rake. It is but little inferior to the oyster. It is cooked in various ways: roasted, boiled, fried, or made into soups and pies. About half an inch of the inside shell is of a purple color. This the Indians broke off and converted into beads, which they called black money; it was double the value of wampum. The sea clam is found on the flats at low water. Before the Indians learned of the English use of the hoe, they hilled their corn with these shells, for which use they were adapted by their size. The small clam is found in much greater abundance; they bury themselves in the sand, from four to eighteen inches deep. The Indians were very fond of them, and being unacquainted with salt, they made use of them and their liquor to season their ansaump and boiled corn . . .' "

This little discourse is accompanied by display of the various shells. "And where do you pick these clams?" "No, no, lady," we hasten to correct the eager customer. "You dig clams, or scratch 'em, or rake 'em, or even roodle 'em but you never PICK them." And then we point out the Pamet Harbor area on the big wall map, and trace the roads from town hall down to the shore. We accept the tourist dollar and wish 'em well. Then, just about the time we're back, ears deep in our cash book, the door will open, the summer boarder will return. "Forgot to ask you, any chance of findin' Little Necks down there?"

We'd met Peggy Malcolm down street the other day, and she reminded us that the town chimes were out of kilter. Seemed to be a delay, she pointed out, between the ringing of the Westminster's quarter hour program and the gonging of the hour and half-hour. We promised her we'd have a try at fixing the mechanism; and come that gloomy, wet Monday afternoon of last week, we sat at our desk, debating whether to attack the chore. Of a sudden the Boston Irish accents of the late Col. Dick Magee spoke into our ear. "Come on, O'Caghan," said the voice. "Get up there and titillate those chimes. You ought to be ashamed of yourself." So we climbed up to the second story, and shinned the frail, trembling ladder through the trapdoor to the unfinished room overhead where the striking mechanism is located.

"Wait for me, O'Caghan," said Dick, "I'm out of puff." So we paused for a mite while he lighted a cigarette, and then we commenced to peer at the complex of motors and gears and levers and wires and switches. "One thing, she's as dry as a chip," said Dick. We reached for the oil feeder. Empty! "Who's gonna pay for the oil?" we queried into space. "Dig down,

O'Caghan," said the voice. So we painfully crawled down the ladder and climbed onto our blue scooter and drove off to buy the oil.

Back at town hall, we commenced lubricating the machine. "Don't forget those pulleys overhead," advised Dick. "And while you're about it, might's well climb up to the belfry and squirt the final screws and the hammers." We considered open rebellion; decided, in deference to our old friend, against it. Up we climbed, eyeing the narrow square of the hatchway overhead, making mental comparison with the length and breadth of our own posterior. "If you get stuck I'll come up and yank on your legs," said the colonel. So we wriggled through, and, by dint of much squirming and stretching, we managed to anoint most of the dry pulleys and hammers. The return trip was uneventful except for one breathless moment when we were buttoning down the overhead hatch and our foot slipped a mite. We had our free hand hooked over a beam, and in it we clutched the oil feeder. The sudden slip caused us to give a hearty squeeze on the pump handle of the oil can, and a stream of heavy oil shot straight at our left ear.

Col. Dick was waiting for us. "Been looking at this mechanism," he said. We heard him rub a cigarette out on the floor. "Better drop this gadget back one place on the disk. That'll shorten up the time between the Westminster chime and the hourly toll. And certainly you've noticed that the hour bell rings OK on the program, but not when she's supposed to ring the hour and the half-hour?" We grunted our assent. "Trouble is, this big cog wheel and the lever it's supposed to contact—they've both got so worn that they don't meet properly; they'll have to be replaced." We ran a finger over the two surfaces under discussion. Sure enough—the metal casting had worn down most noticeably. "Get your hand out of there, O'Caghan," warned the colonel. "Time for the hour to strike." We did, just in time. A second or so later and we might well never have played the piccolo again, we reflected.

We promised Dick we'd dig into the files and contact the feller from Vermont who services the striking device. "Don't forget, O'Caghan and keep an eye on the machinery, here. I'd invite you over to the farm for a cup of coffee, but I have a different address these days." We stood at the top of the ladder as he clambered down. "Au 'voir et bonne chance," we said, waving through the trapdoor opening.

"Nice to have metten up with ya!" said the colonel, and he pulled at the peak of his jaunty Air Force cap and went down the stairs. We heard the short, deep-throated bark of Oscar, the big German shepherd, the slam of a car door, the sudden jazzing of a motor, then silence.

★ ★ ★

Well sir, our long awaited junket down Pamet River finally took place last Saturday. We'd been trying to borrow a canoe for several weeks, to no avail. Finally, in casual conversation with Dr. Manuel Furer, our neighbor on South Pamet, we learned that the good doctor had a plastic sailfish hull he'd be glad to loan us for the trek. We immediately con-

tacted our partner-in-adventure, Snowie. Told him of our good fortune. "Bully for you, O'Caghan," he chirped over the phone, "although I had just about clinched a deal with Joe Wiley—he has a canoe that will be available next week. Meet you at the Landing at 2 p.m." We reflected that inasmuch as the sailfish was white in color, it would more nearly approximate the appearance of a true birch bark canoe, anyway. At quarter to the hour we were pounding at Snowie's door, and sharply at two we were loading our gear into Snowie's truck—mosquito repellant, dipnet, water jug, fishing pole, paddles—and ten minutes later we were grinding to a stop at the Cresap Moore place, on Aunt Sal's Lane. (The Moores are friends of Dr. Furer, and the Furer craft was temporarily stored up-river.)

We introduced ourselves to Mr. Moore and his beauteous wife. "We've come for the sailfish—today is the day we make the trip from Ballston Beach to Pamet Harbor." So in went the long, slim white hull, and over to Ballston parking space we churned. The boat slipped into the stagnant, muddy waters of the outermost pool of the Pamet easy as could be. And then we loaded all our gear aboard. "Toss you to see who takes the stern paddle," said Snowie. And he won the toss, so we cautiously slid up into the bow position, steadied the tiny craft while Snowie clambered into the stern and shoved off.

"Know where you're going?" we queried our helmsman. A grunt and a nod from Snowie and, seconds later, the grating of our keel on the sandy bottom of the south end of the pool. "Must've picked the wrong end," growled Snowie, somewhat superfluously. So around we spun, and several paddle strokes later, crunch . . . ch . . . ch, we grounded on the north end of the tiny pondlet. "Whyn't we head 'er down that fire ditch, headin' directly west," we murmured sarcastically. And we did, by gosh, and found the ditch just exactly wide enough to accomodate our craft. Granted, we hadn't room to paddle, and we were obliged to seize the cattails and the poison ivy on the banks, but in due time we glided out into the big, limpid expanse of the widened crick below Thatcher's big hill.

First stop. Snowie picks several beautiful pond lilies, almost capsizing the boat as he leans over and plucks the stems. Then a blast on Snowie's conch whistle, and all hands pick up paddles and get underway. Past Kimball's Landing, and around the serpentine channel below the Joseph homestead. In the shallow, muddy river, big, underwater fields of algae-like water plants and schools of tiny minnows. Here a turtle pops his head from among the lily pads, and on the bushlined banks at eye-level, a startled mourning dove whirs from its nest. "Hoter'n a Hottentot's breath," groans Snowie between pulls on his paddle as he points out the freshly-severed cattails floating on the water abaft Dr. Bloomberg's. "Muskrats did that. They're makin' houses for the winter—sign of a cold season approaching."

We absorbed this bit of weather prognostication with due respect. "Mind keepin' this craft approximately mid-channel?" we requested. "It would break a snake's back to follow our wake." As though the word snake had been magic, we suddenly espied a slim, black water snake wriggling, periscope-like, through the water, watched him glide up the bank and disappear. On we paddled; past Dyer's Range (white birches growing almost to the water's edge) past Hector's Bridge (you can still see the rotted stumps of the pilings in the crick), past Fratus' Corner (there's a fresh-running spring here that attracts the trout—a brownie big's a quart bottle broke the surface as we passed) and finally to the culvert. Out we climbed, legs cramped from our crosslegged position in the tiny sailfish and up the bank we dragged the boat, and along South Pamet on the lengthy portage to the salt crick. "Wish I had a camera to record this," grinned Joe Schoonejongen, as he watched us slide our boat into the rock basin. And we'll continue the chronicling of this junket next week, if we can find our water-soaked notes.

At the Aiken-Andrews wedding last Saturday we ran through the whole gamut of emotions. Misty-eyed at the church, we were, what with the fine organ music, and the simple but impressive ceremony: Rev. Dick Aiken's voice and the beauteous bride and her maids, and the handsome ushers. And later, as we gorged at the reception atop Flagstaff Hill we sandwiched in conversation between trips to the hors d'oeuvre tables. Said hello to Cathy and Bill Sanford, and to the Osbornes, and to the Dr. Weperts, and to a nice couple we'd met last summer, name of Joyce. The latter gentleman told us he'd recently visited the land of his ancestors (and ours) and thereby hung a tale. "Tiny little village in County Galway," is the way Mr. Joyce put it. "I was having a taste in a local pub and got into conversation with an old tad. 'And what might your name be?' asked the Irishman. 'Joyce,' says I. 'Bloody Englishman!' sneers the tad." And Mr. Joyce was forced to admit the truth of the accusation. "My ancestors actually did migrate to Ireland, from England, some 700 years ago. But the Irish keep good records." We commiserated with Mr. Joyce for the cold reception he'd received on the ould sod. Pointed out that we, too, despite forty years, man and boy, in Pamet, are still considered an outsider.

DELETE REST OF TF COLUMN, INSERT FOLLOWING BY SNOWIE . . . ED.

Deer Mr. Editor: My gorge is still risin' after reedin' that sheep dip by Town Father about our trip together down the Pamet River last week. To put it mildly, TF plays with the trooth. Here's what reely happened, on my word as a Cape Cod gentleman. First off, the reeson we had trubble findin' the proper channel out of the mud hole that marked the beginning of junket at Ballston Beach was because O'Caghan was sittin' in the bow. And he's so broad across the stern that yers trooly just couldn't see around him. And when we went down that first fire ditch, it wasn't the gunwales of the sailfish that wuz scrapin' the sides of the bank, it was O'Caghan's spread. And we wouldn't have scraped on any snags er shallows at all if he hadn't weighed the poor boat down so's her nose was practically under water. And when he sez I couldn't navigate middle of the channels, let me point out that paddlin' with him on the bow of the boat was like pushin' a bicycle with an elephant sittin' on the handle bars.

Ever' so often he'd lean over to grab at a pond lily or a cow slip or a marsh mallow, and the cussed craft would teeter fit to make a body seasick. And that bit about the snake—I still think he made that yarn up so's he could inveigle some snake bite remedy out of me—but nothin' doin'. So let me tell you what really happened after we portaged the sailfish across Wilder Dyke and put her in the wattr by Joe Schoonejongen's.

"Let me take the stern paddle," whined O'Caghan, "or I won't continue the trip." So Mr. Ed., against my better judgment, I swapped places with him. And almost as soon's you can say Obadiah Brown, we were in trouble. The extra weight in the stern caused us to lose steerage way, and our boat started down the crick leavin' a wake like to break a snake's back. Every fifty feet I'd have to scream over my shoulder at him, and then I'd pole the boat off'n the bank.

Didn't have time, hardly, to look at the beautiful countryside we were passin'. Dr. Brigg's locust grove, and Naylor Hatch's Dyke, and the inlet that looks up at Eva Gray's and Al Paine's place, and Monroe's Landin', and the neat cottages perched up on Marshall's Bluff. One time I spied a big school of perch abaft of Savage's Point, below Slade's Studio, but I dassn't watch 'em swimming because O'Caghan was paddlin' away in the stern, and it was all's I could do to keep the nose from the sedge grass. We came up on a nest of marsh hawks at one spot, and I'd of had a good look at them, too, but he chose that time to pick up the whistle and let out a blast—showin' off, he was, for a goodlookin' girl who was sun bathin'.

Finally I got so mad I decided to teach O'Caghan a lesson. To put him off'n his guard, I commenced to reminisce about my early experiences on the river. Told him about the time I almost drowned my late, sainted grandmother when I got the family pungo hung up on a pilin' (John Thomas, Lord bless him, saved us from a watery grave) and then I gave him a brief outline of the installation of an eel fyke. Time we made the turn leadin' down to Sladeville where the river broadens, I had him soothed into a false state of security. And suddenly, just as he took a big sweep with his paddle, I slipped off the bow of the boat, into the limpid waters of the crick. The suddenly lightened bow shot into the air, the stern went under water, and O'Caghan was plunged into the Pamet. Came up spouting like a whale, he did, and I almost drowned for laughin'.

Some five minutes later we pushed our craft ashore at my landin' and after we had brought all our effects ashore we commenced to dry out. O'Caghan was taken with a fit of shiverin', so I brewed him a cup of strong coffee and then he opened his wallet and took out his belongings to dry. Two crumpled dollar bills, a recipe for shish kebab, picture of his family, registration for one blue motor scooter, two stubs of tickets for the Melody Tent, pledge card of the non-smoking society of Barnstable County, one cork pad for a spit valve trombone, membership slip for the town Democratic Committee. And we never did finish the trip to Pamet Harbor.

We'd trade about three days for one yesterday. And of the twenty-four hours that made up Tuesday, we'd choose the magic hours of dawn to witness and to chronicle. We awoke at our accustomed quarter after five to feed and dispatch our No. 1 son, Ran, on his milk route—and having delivered him to the sub depot in the North village, we drove back by way of Truro Depot Road. A mist, thicker'n pea soup, lay in thin blankets over the Pamet Valley, and the sky shaded from purple-gray to gold, reading from west to east. Tooling the VW down Freeman's Hill to the Depot was a trip into cotton batting; and the dank, salt smell of the flats at low tide came chill through the open window, and the strident scream of the gulls rose to answer the noise of our motor.

At first we could see only the familiar, closer things—the outline of the clam warden's shack, and the gaudy yellow trash container, edge of the bank, and the stones marking the abutment of the railroad trestle. Vaguely, through the mist, the tracing of a beached dingy, a patch of sedge grass standing wet-footed in the ebbing crick, a garish sign giving advice to takers of shellfish. Even as we studied these landmarks, the sun rose, just above the fog blanket, and of a sudden we could see the slim, white masts of the sailboats abaft the yacht club, clear-etched above the ghostly hulls and the fog turned to sepia and then to milk white, and finally to gold, and carried on its changing background curtain the nimbus of objects outlined by the sun. It was eerie to get out of our car and mark the rainbow outline of our own reflection on the fog-bank. Then a slight breeze commenced to stir the flag on the neighboring building, and the mist formed in wavering ranks, and marched out to the bay, and in jig time it was full day. Gone, just like the summer folks, we reflected.

It seems only yesterday when the voters with D after their names could be counted on the fingers of both hands. We overheard Pop Snow telling the election officers that he remembered the time when there wasn't but three Democrats in this precinct: Tony Rose, and Willie Hopkins, and Will's father, Reuben. And when we had made our final tallies, we bade the chief good night, and locked the voting materials in the vault, and hied off to our snug home; there we became intrigued by the TV election coverage, and derned if it wasn't close onto three before we went to bed.

Thence to the Temple of Learning this day, and to administer term tests, and to correct those already given; and after our pedagogical duties we took the VW back to Truro only to learn, as we enter our office at town hall, that word has come from Boston that all election materials must be impounded and kept under surveillance pending a probable recount of votes. Chief Berrio had received the news by police radio. He looked grim as he relayed the message to us. "Make sure those ballots are secure in the vault," he warned us as he examined his service revolver and took a stand near the heavy steel door. We explained as how we'd filed all the voting parapher-nalia in the original wooden ballot boxes, tucked 'em neatly in a far corner of the big concrete box. "They're safe as a church," we asserted.

Five minutes later we decided to fetch out some election pencils that had been tossed into the boxes with the ballots—no sense in sharpening new pencils we reasoned with true Truro penury. So we slipped by the chief, reached into the pine box and, "Get out of the box," growled the man in blue. And we did, quickly and shamefacedly. We left town hall at 5 p.m., clanking the heavy vault door behind us. Harold stood by to watch us twirl the dial, and then he fastened a big seal, improvised from scotch tape, across the crack of the door and scrawled his initials, HMB, across the seal. "I'll be back at frequent intervals during the night to check on the vault," said Harold. "And I'll be here to see you open it tomorrow during your office hours."

At eight-thirty this evening comes the strident jangle of our telephone, and over the wire comes the anxious voice of Al Bettencourt, one of Pamet's election officers. "Hate to bother you, O'Caghan, but I can't seem to find my lower plate anywhere around the house. I remember taking 'em out during the voting at town hall yesterday and putting 'em on the table near the ballot shipping box, you know, the pine one. In the excitement of the counting, I forgot all about my dentures. Did you see that plate anywhere?" We explained to Al how the election materials had been locked up tighter'n a drum, how Harold was watching them with an eagle eye. Al begged us to get permission from the chief to search the box. "I'm invited out to a steak dinner tomorrow night," he explained, "and I need them choppers worse way." We phoned up the man with the gold badge. "I don't care if he dropped his bifocals and a picture of his late mother in the box," roared the chief. "No human hand enters it until we get word from Kevin H. White either to recount the ballots or otherwise break the surveillance." A fitting testimonial, we submit, to the incorruptibility of Truro's police force. Especially when you consider that both Al and Harold have the big red D's after their names. But, as the chief pointed out, this situation transcends party lines.

Comes news to our desk today of the death at his Truro home of David L. Snow, long time selectman of Pamet and local contractor. Dave was the last of the famed triumvirate of Snow-Dyer-Hart, having served nearly thirty years in his town posts. A man of outstanding integrity and ability, Dave was known for his economy of speech and, to us, at least, for his dry Yankee humor. Many's the night we sat with Dave in town hall, on registration of voter sessions, when hardly a score of words would pass between us; yet we felt we had communicated with the old man of Truro politics most sufficiently. We recall, too, the time Irving Horton was belaboring the ancient typewriter at the hall in one of his first chores as a freshman selectman. Dave watched Irv's poke and find technique for a mite, then slyly observed, "Hadn't you better fetch in a bucket of water, Irv?" Irving reached for a capital P. "What fer?" "Well, you're poundin' that typewriter so everlastin'ly fast she's gettin' hot. Bucket of water might cool 'er off."

Dave did the remodeling on our old Cape house when we bought it back in '44. The evidence of his honest, good work will be here for us to see as long as the building stands—and never did a body get so much value for his money as we did. We worked for Dave, too, in the years after the war; painting mostly, and here we'd like to add our testimony to that of dozens of other Snow helpers who'll tell you Dave was about the fastest painter in the county. Not the neatest mind you, but the fastest. Take the way Dave painted blinds; Dave always wore a pair of paint-stiffened canvas gloves used a worn, short-bristled brush. He'd stuff some Mayo's dark plug into his battered corncob pipe, seize a blind, toss it on a pair of carpenter's horses, dip his brush in the paint, draw it with a lightning stroke down the slats. This motion would leave a smidgin of paint on each slat. Then Dave would work his way back up the blind, spreading the paint into each corner, a quick swipe down each side rail, same for the crossrails, and Dave would flip the blind over on t'other side, where he'd repeat the process. The sound of his brush rippling along the blind slats was like a burst of machine gun fire.

It was Dave Snow who built the vault at town hall, too. Along about 1943 the state began to heckle the town of Truro to install a safe depository for its valuable records and its money. John Dyer drew the plans and David Snow was awarded the contract for the big concrete box. We watched every phase of the construction, from the removal of the ancient floor timbers to the pouring of the sand cushion atop the vault to the installation of the heavy steel door. We remember the day when Dave was floating the cement of the inside floor. He had hit upon a novel method of rigging a staging from which to work. Planks almost exactly the width of the inside of the vault had been jammed against the side walls with wedges driven from underneath—then the mortar had been poured, and Dave had crawled inside the vault on his planks, commenced to smooth the mix with his trowel. All went well until Dave reached the inner-most plank; suddenly the wedge came loose, the plank dropped into the soft mix, and Dave expressed his feelings in no uncertain terms. Then, too, we recall the day we had the heartbreaking chore of delivering a message from the Secretary of the Army to the Cleve Woodwards notifying them of the death of their son Cleve, Jr. We stopped by Dave's house, and he offered to drive over with us. "Seems as though two friends could do better with a message like this," he said in his quiet way. And it was Dave's firm handshake and his sincere words that comforted Cleve in his great loss. Ave atque vale, old friend.

★ ★ ★

We read a rather spirited defense on Cape business people in a local paper the other day. The tenor of the article was to the effect that your Cape storekeeper is a nice feller, really much maligned. We offer the following neither in confirmation nor rebuttal of the theory; it's just a yarn.

Our good friends and neighbors, the Fred Meiers, once ran a small restaurant in Truro Square, in a building (long since razed) that abutted on the property of Manuel Marshall, rented, in those days, by Johnny Fratus. The menu featured home cooking and a specialty of the house was fresh chicken, served in various ways—salad, soup, roast, you name it.

The homey touch was further fostered by Miz Meier herself, who would appear from her kitchen when the tourists entered, attired in dust-cap and apron. She once told us about her dealings with a party, and here are her words, near as we can recall. "So these city folks came in and sat down, and looked at the menu—asked me if the chicken was really fresh, and I said yes, and they ordered chicken salad, and I went out in the kitchen, looked in my ice box and found I was plumb out of chicken. So I quick sent the kitchen boy over to Eben Paine's for a canned chicken, and when he came back I had him everlastin'ly pump some water from the squeaky old pitcher pump to cover the sound of me opening the can of chicken.

"Then I sent him out to throw the breakfast table scraps to Johnnie Fratus' chickens in the yard just back of the store; then I made up the salads, and served them to my people. They looked kind of odd when I set out their food. After they'd eaten, I took their check. One of them said to me, 'Lady—you don't kill those chickens to order, do you?' I smiled and shook my head no. 'Then how come,' he said, 'we heard that almighty squawking from out back just when you were getting our salads ready?'" Mizz Meier said she expected to be queried anent the freshness of the hotdogs when Eben Paine's hog got noisy later on in the season. She never did, though.

Seems good to hear the brave, sure beat of the town chimes. They were repaired last week by the I. T. Verdin Company of Pittsfield, Vermont, and the library trustees have also had work done on the clock at Cobb Library. As so often happens with things mechanical, the three clock faces at Cobb have been unsychronized for many months. Last time we drove by the library, the clock men had removed one of the big, translucent glass dials, and the tower gave the appearance of a sightless eye. We could see right into the tiny cubicle, and the sight of the geared clock motors reminded us of the times we'd climbed the steep roof with Col. Dick Magee to work on the clock. "One hand for the job and one for yourself," Dick used to advise, as we cautiously crept up the shingled incline. The latch of the tower door would invariably be rusted, and we'd have to burgle our way through, belly up, over the doorsill, and cautiously straighten up among the shafts and gears. "Watch out for live wires," the Colonel would puff and then he'd peer at his wrist watch and call out the time as we delicately turned the dials to set the hands. Sometimes, on a gray, sunless day, we could barely see through the translucent faces, and we'd have to set the hands more or less by guesswork; if the difference in time was too great, (we'd find after we'd descended to the ground) we'd have to go aloft again and make a final adjustment. On one occasion Dick espied a dead mouse in the corner of the tower and was moved to remark with true Irish wit, "No wonder the thing's out of kilter—the poor engineer's dead."

Reports filtered into town hall after the weekend that a car had plowed across the island at Betsey Holsbury Square on Depot Road, narrowly missed the granite marker, broke off a road direction sign, rolled up the bank abaft Leaycock's place. Couldn't have been damaged too severely, for the vehicle had left the scene without reporting to the local gendarmes. Chief Berrio of Truro's finest, appraised of the incident, drove over in the black and white cruiser. We spoke to him later about the crime. "Not much to go on," admitted the chief. "No tire tracks, no paint nor chrome at the scene and, of course, no eye witnesses as we know of. Only thing we did find was a zucchini and two half ripe tomatoes. So on my record I'm putting a paraphrase of the famous French Surete, 'Cherchez le vegetarian.' " We quick slipped the raw carrot we'd been about to eat into our desk drawer.

NINETEEN SIXTY-THREE

1 9 6 3

And now that the old year has run its course, we'd like to write our own summary of local news events that made the headlines in 1962. It's always good to see a new business enterprise sprout in Pamet. Such was the case with the establishment of Win Farwell's donut shop, which was built on Joe Duarte's new fill on the banks of the salt crick, site of the old package store, more or less. Win had started his shop on a modest basis, on Joe Schoonejongen's land the previous year, but 1962 saw the building moved across the dyke, enlarged, and generally refurbished. "We had a good year with our hand-cuts, sandwiches and coffee," says Win.

Neil Pirnie, Truro's newly appointed shellfish warden and dump custodian, made the news with his policy of living with the clams, as it were. Neil has a tiny shack on the shores of Pamet Harbor, from which he closely supervises his fellow man in pursuit of the wily bivalve. Last we knew, Neil was still sleeping on the premises, but we'll bet a two-inch clam ring he gave up last night, when the thermometer dropped to minus two. "Big event of the year for me down at the shore was the big tide of last October," said Neil, when we called him. "Washed out my bulkhead, it did, and seeped through the floor of my shack so's I was ankle deep in cold water when I hopped out of bed early one morning." (The same tide we recall, had our good friend Snowie and his bride Norma marooned on their premises at Snow's Landing, and they say the pitiful cries of quahaugs drowning in the Snow cellar was something fearful to hear.)

Mary Joseph's retirement as postmaster of Truro after decades of faithful service to her fellow townspeople was observed in a town-wide celebration at Truro Central School that found many of us misty-eyed as Mary received gifts and words of well-deserved praise from the committee in charge. Departed citizens, of course, to be recorded in the vital statistics of Truro for 1962: Col. Dick Magee and his lady, Nellie Cobb Magee (how we miss our Sunday afternoon junkets to Cobb Farm). The young—Lou Steele, and the old—Arthur L. Cobb, both of the North Village; and neighbor Lucy Kelley, and Manuel Dutra, and our long time selectman and friend David L.

Snow, to name some of the too-long list. Marriage of the year would be that of Bill Aiken and Janey Andrews, although legal technicalities of residence required that the actual ceremony be performed in Provincetown; at least the reception for the charming couple was held in our town.

From a personal point of view, we shall have to vote for the Snow-O'Caghan junket down the Pamet River as a worthy news item for 1962. There are still those of our readers who insist that the trip was but a figment of our imagination—a bit of journalistic license, in the fashion of the Al Bettencourt false teeth in the ballot box yarn. Not so! For the doubters, now's a good time, when the banks of the crick are frozen solid, to follow the course of those intrepid explorers, locate for yourselves the sundry indentifying objects left by S and O'C to mark their progress.

Meantime, a very happy and prosperous New Year to one and all. May the sand in your steamed clams be scarce, as Dick Magee used to say, Lord rest his soul.

Up betimes, so's we could be of help to our good wife, who is ill of virus, and to the refrigerator, there to unwrap a king-size package of bread dough and to prepare flippers for the four hungry male O'Caghans. And whilst the pure white dough rises and the fat smokes ever so slightly in the skillet, we cast a jaundiced eye on the weather in the valley. Nary a sign of sun, and won't be, we wager, this whole afternoon. A light, steady breeze out of the nor'east, and a persistent drizzle that smears the kitchen windows, and drips from the gutters on a soggy sod and puddles where the frost-impregnated ground can absorb no more moisture. The locusts and the scrub pine toss fitfully in the wind, and a dank, mysterious fog commences to form on Dyer's Range and down-valley toward Wilder's Dyke.

When we open the door to Mokie, the family pom, the smell of the ocean rushes to meet us; and the distant murmur of the surf pulses in the morning air. A damp, bedraggled jay perches on the post and rail fence, and a trio of starlings is worrying at the compost under the forsythia bush. There's slush on the blacktop, the remnants of last night's quiet, brief storm, and the thin red line of the thermometer reads 41, and the Phillips barometer is low and dropping almost perceptibly.

But by midafternoon, as we finish the dinner dishes, the first break in the clouds comes with the freshening west wind—skim ice is forming on the puddles, and there's a new, different sound to the rushing air as it meets the oak copse on the ridge between our house and Morris'. Thin, pale shaft of sunlight focuses briefly on the empty, staring windows of Dr. Bloomberg's house across river, and a scattering of seagulls form ranks in the fresh crick, make flight plans that take them out to the bay in sweeping purposeful flight.

Well sir, we've been actively engaged in politics for more years than we like to own, and this is without exception the most unpleasant local campaign we've ever witnessed. We're referring, of course to the current complex race for the combined offices of selectman, assessor of taxes, and board of public welfare, and the unprecedented rash of rumors that has been circulating about town as the campaign enters its final phases. Far as we're concerned, we hardly dast go any place but church, lest we be drawn into some political donnybrook. Stop at the paper store, we do, and send one of the kids in for the daily. Steam on the windows and the sight of men gesticulating and shouting in each other's ears tells only too plainly that a hassle is in progress. Any place where more'n two people can congregate is a potential debating site and the debating we've heard this season is a mite too strong for our blood. Guess we're getting old. There are, of course, folks who enjoy the bitter exchanges of the campaign—but then, as the late John Adams used to say, "Allus has to be someone to clean privies."

So we've taken a page from the book of our good friend, Jim Moynahan, the Squire of Pump Log Point, way over South Truro way. Jim has been a firm disciple of homeopathic medicine for these many years. "Treat likes with likes," says Jim—Jim intones the philosophy in Latin. "You have a case of poison ivy? Then induce an artificial rash, and you defeat the irritation of the noxious weed. Got a cold and a temperature? Take one of those mysterious homeopathic drugs that produces a counter fever, and you've got it licked." And that's what we're trying to do anent the political rumor situation.

Every time we hear a rumor about a political candidate, we cast about in our mind until we find something real nice about the same candidate. Here's how it works. Take a dark, nasty rumor about Johnnie Worthington; why in tarnation folks should want to pick on poor John at this stage of the game, when he's stepping out of office, is more'n we know. Click! We turn on the machinery of our memory. Why wasn't it only a few years back that John, together with Ferdinand Davis and George Glover deeded to the town that beautiful tract of shorefront property known as Gull Island? They had purchased it from private interests some years previously, held it (against many tempting offers from would-be developers) until town meeting action authorized its purchase—at a price, incidentally, that scarcely covered the expenses of the trio. Seemed at the time, that townsfolk just couldn't conceive of any citizen doing business with Truro on a nonprofit basis—many viewed the whole transaction with suspicion, although today it's quite evident we're all glad that John and his friends put public spirit ahead of profit.

The rumor: the selectmen are alleged to have approached one of the candidates for selectmen, attempted to persuade him to withdraw his name in favor of "their man." We scan the screen of our memory for some typical example of honest behavior on the part of our colleagues. How about the time Irv Horton came into our office, took a stamp from our roll, and dropped three cents into the petty cash tray. "This'n is for my private correspondence," explained Irving. And we know that medieval tortures couldn't elicit from either Mssrs. Dyer or Horton their chosen candidate for the forthcoming election. A pox on the rumor.

The Civil Service Classification rumors: the situation is too complex and bitter to explain in the short space allotted to this column. But we join with our thinking townspeople in deploring the irreparable damage being done to our police department and the alienation of friendships of long standing. Suffice it to say we count ourself a friend to all the principles involved—and since the gold badge looms brightest, we try the Moynahan method on Chief Berrio. Lord, how many times has it been we've donated blood on the table next to Harold? Red Cross blood donor sessions, or blood for a neighbor, it was all the same to the chief. If we should need 60 ccs of type O tomorrow, we'd call Harold first thing. He'd be there quicker'n you could say Obadiah Brown.

And so it goes; the mysterious conversation overheard in the grocery store anent the proposed removal of a trusted Pamet public servant. The local "sea-lawyer" interpretations of the recently enacted conflict-of-interest law and the 70-year compulsory retirement law, as it applies to candidates for the office of selectman. Care for some of our homeopathic pink pills for pale people, folks? Or would you rather be a privy cleaner? Meantime, absentee ballot applications continue to be processed at town hall, and the familiar brown manila envelopes of the ballots themselves continue to arrive at each mail. Looks like the heaviest vote in years.

We got to thinking as we drove from choral practice in Wellfleet tonight, how often we used to see, in the pond area abaft Paradise Valley, the shadowy figure of George Richardson, or one of his house guests, say Ralph Baker, or George's brother-in-law, a feller name of Clark. George has been dead these many years, but on a black night like this, when the west wind is moaning down the valley and your car headlights sweep the roadside where the tall pines come up to meet the blacktop near Round

Pond, why somehow you expect to see one of those old acquaintances raising a hand in the time-honored gesture of the hitchhiker.

When we first knew George Richardson, he. lived in a badly dilapidated cottage in the valley beyond Ryder's Pond. On rare occasions we'd find ourself in Paradise Valley, painting bug's nests for the tree warden, or spraying gypsy moth caterpillars in the springtime, then we'd halloo outside George's door until we detected signs of life, and we'd visit a mite with him. Rumor had it that George was a college graduate, that he'd moved to the Cape and become a hermit because of unrequited love, that he lived on a diet of roots and animals (muskrats were supposed to be staple on the Richardson diet) and that he had uncanny skill as an angler, a nimrod, and as an axeman. Sometime in the early thirties, George's house caught on fire in some mysterious fashion and burned to the ground (the fire engines had difficulty in plowing through the snow choked roads of the back woods) but George was uninjured; shortly afterward he gathered up his pitifully scant belongings and moved to a shack on the shores of Great Pond, where he was to live for many years. It was during this period we got to know the old hermit rather intimately. Emboldened by our friendship, we broached the usual questions to George. Had he a college education, as we'd always heard? Not so.

"Born and brought up in Cambridge," is the way George explained the fallacy, "and as a young man I made my living selling Encyclopedia Brittanica to the college students at Harvard. Read a good deal, I did, from my own sample set and of course I dressed Harvard fashion too. But that's as close as I ever came to a college sheepskin."

How about the broken heart yarn, we wanted to know. "If my heart was ever broken, I never felt it. Matter of fact, I married young in life, sired two children, a son who is now a lawyer up-city way, and a daughter who is an R.N. in the greater Boston area. Moved down to the Cape because my family had been colonists for years, and I liked the spot. My wife and kids preferred to live in the city. It's as simple as that."

As for George's diet, he ate store food when he had the money— hamburger and fried eggs and canned beans—but when the larder was bare, George enjoyed roast raccoon and muskrat, and water cress from the ponds, and a dandelion salad, and sauteed mushrooms, all from nature's bounty.

"Darn tasty, too," he'd explain, and we had no reason to disbelieve him. Winter time, you'd often see George settin' out fish traps through the ice at Ryder's Pond and although we never heard him claim to be any great shakes with a gun, we knew he could hone an axe to razor-like keenness. Why then did he dislike the task of cutting wood to such an extent that he'd drag long, dead oak trees into the living room of his Paradise Valley home and stuff the butt ends into the ancient cook stove, feeding the trunk into the fire as it burned away. The practice made for clouds of acrid, eye-watering smoke in the house; it's quite possible that George burned down his own home in this fashion. We used to cough and gag when we visited the old recluse. "You must have a tech of a cold," he'd say as we wiped our streaming eyes.

It's been almost a month since the passing of George P. "Dode" Kimball, our good friend and neighbor across the river on North Pamet. Just occurred to us how much we're going to miss Dode from the local scene—for even in retirement, Dode was a forceful and picturesque person, in speech and action. First time we ever met Dode Kimball we were tending bar at the Blacksmith Shop, and as we turned from the back bar to pour a libation for a customer, we espied a heavyset ruddy-complexioned man, big-jowled and completely bald. "I'm Kimball," he bellowed. "Goin' to live in that old blank-blank Coast Guard Station up at Ballston Beach. What the blank-blank is your blank-blank name?" Profanity poured from him like water; strangely, it seemed to offend no one of the select clientele of the Blacksmith Shop. Part of the man's personality, it was—and long's we knew him, we expected to hear, and we always did hear, the most lurid of language.

Dode always did things on the grand scale. Take, for instance, the get acquainted barbecue that Dode threw for his Truro friends and neighbors; started out by having built a huge barbecue pit, complete with electric spit. And the Kimball basement was given over to the food service—salads, and sweet corn, and side dishes and desserts too numerous to list. A monstrous, golden brown pig roasting on the spit, and dozens of people milling around the bar, waiting for the host to announce the service of the meal. We recall how it started to rain along about mid-afternoon, how Dode matched the rumbling of the thunder with his profanity; how we all crowded into the garage-basement and ate to the point of gluttony. One of the most successful parties of the decade.

We made the mistake, that afternoon, of boasting a mite about our man-sized appetite (we could put away a goodly share of vittles in those days). Well sir, Dode overheard us; promptly invited us to breakfast with him at a later date. When we arrived on the morning in question ("You're late, man," was Dode's greeting, "G——D——it all, I bin up for hours.") our portly host had the grill of his restaurant-size range smoking hot—and he promptly proceeded to fry slab bacon and double-yoke turkey eggs in quantity sufficient to feed a basketball team. We ate until the viands ran out our ears; and when we could stuff no more, Dode grudgingly allowed as how we had a fair appetite. "But I could eat four times that blank-blank breakfast when I was your age."

He'd done much more than eat when he was our age, too. On one occasion we heard him enumerating the highlights of his career. "Used to be one blank-blank fast runner. Got cups for records I set in the blank-blank hundred yard dash. Then I got into the entertainment business. Ever hear of 'Kimball's Starlight Acres?' First blank-blank outdoor dance floor in New England. Had all the big bands booked there, at one time or another, Mal Hallett, and Paul Whiteman and the Dorsey Brothers. Never saw a band leader buy a blank-blank drink in my life. Cheapest bunch of blank-blanks you can imagine. Later on I opened a small roadside stand near my home in Nashua, New Hampshire. Specialized in homemade ice cream. Blank-blank ice cream was so good that business increased to the point where we had to build on. Pretty soon we had a full-sized restaurant in operation. Got to serving so many turkey dinners that we put in our own turkey ranch and that's what developed into Kimball's Green Ridge Turkey Farm and Restaurant."

We got to talking with Dode one day anent the trials of the small business entrepreneur. "But it had its good points, too," mused Dode. "I remember right after prohibition went into effect, when I had my ice cream business. We were allowed to keep a certain amount of alcoholic flavoring extracts for the ice cream—and I had gallons of pure Jamaica rum on hand that I used in my blank-blank tutti fruity ice cream. They call it frozen puddin' today. Well sir, the rum was supposed to be in a bonded storage area, and I was supposed to sign it out in small quantities as I needed it for makin' the ice-cream. But every once in a while we'd throw a party at the house and I'd go down to the bonded warehouse and draw out a gallon of the stuff. I remember once I went there—third time in a month—and the inspector at the warehouse said to me, 'Kimball, that ice cream of yours must be some strong.' And I said to him, 'Why, blank-blank your blank-blank eyes, that tutti fruity is about as strong as your blank-blank curiosity.' "

In late years, Dode got himself a dog—a big, brindle female boxer named Sonya. The two were inseparable. Sometimes, we'd see Dode driving down to the mail in his blue Caddie, and Sonya would be seated proudly on the front seat with her master, while Grace, the lovely and charming Mrs. Kimball, would be occupying the back seat. "Sonya don't like to be crowded," Dode would leer, with a sidelong glance at his bride. We used to tease Dode about the remarkable similarity between Sonya and her master. "She looks just like you, Dode," we'd say as we rubbed the dogs heavy jowls. "You're blank-blank right. She's a beautiful dog," he'd bellow.

So it's ave atque vale to George P. "Dode" Kimball, Squire of Little America, bon vivant, raconteur par excellence, dog lover, good host, and fine neighbor. May his tutti fruity be as strong as his conversation.

Comes a call from our No. 1 son, Paul Randolph, a senior at the University of Mass. one night recently, telling as how he'd made the Dean's list, and as how he'd popped the question to his girl, Maureen Riley, of Arlington, Vermont. They'll be married March 23, and it's a happy parent we are to make the announcement.

In our mail, a nice note from Howard A. Lincoln, of South Yarmouth, in which he points out to us that the task of fitting a new handle to an axe is called "hanging" an axe. Mea culpa, kind reader Lincoln. Our trouble is we were born a few years too late to have owned the true Cape Cod idiom as our own, but early enough so's we vaguely recall the picturesque language of such native Truro folk as Ed Snow, and John Grozier and John Adams, and Naylor Hatch. We deplore the passing of the patois of the Narrow Land, and if we had time we'd gather up the figures of speech that once graced the conversation of these men and preserve 'em for posterity. We should have added, Mr. Lincoln, in our squib about the new axe handle, that we'd made her tight in the axe head with a gump fashioned from cherry wood—you'd certainly have recognized the Cape word for wedge (pronounced wage, of course).

And speaking of that vowel "e" remember how the old timers always called that reedy grass that grows in salt tidal waters sage grass? The dictionary identifies it as sedge grass. Ed Snow always called his coat his "cut"; not quite the way our faithful Royal spells it. Phonetically Ed's pronounciation was as though you said court without the r. Naylor Hatch, another native, we remember for his culinary vocabulary. Naylor liked his victuals and except in mixed company he'd call that authentic salt cod dish by its true name, Cape Cod S—of a B—. This too, in the days before a president of the United States had given his blessing to the strong phrase.

John Adams was master of the simile and the metaphor. "You don't amount to Hannah Cook," he'd scowl in disapproval. Whoever in tarnation Hannah Cook was we never learned—but the very inflection of the name as John mouthed it established Hannah as a valid standard of inferiority. After a particular lean farming season, John was wont to complain, "We'll all eat wind sauce and air puddin' this winter." John Grozier used to "cally"— calculate— when he made a prognostication concerning the weather. Who's to carry on the dying vocabulary of the horse and buggy era? Would our kids know what a trace is? Or hames straps? Or britchin' (breeching)?

Would they accuse us of political leanings if we insisted on riding in a Democrat wagon? Would they dash for the botany reference book if we mentioned a whiffletree? But we digress. Mr. Lincoln goes on to say we shouldn't have bored out the old handle—a few hours in the range oven would shrink the wood so's it would slip right out. Correct, Mr. Lincoln—but we were in a hurry. And on one occasion, many years ago, we burned out a handle from an axe in the fire box of the faithful Glenwood—took the temper out of the metal, we did, so's the blade never would hold an edge thereafter. Nice of you to write us, Mr. Lincoln.

We've eaten out of doors, and we've slept in the open, and we've imbibed, on occasion, under the vast vault of the sky—but this is the first time, man and boy, that we've been so drawn by the beauty of the day we felt moved to compose our immortal prose without the four walls of our dwelling. Got the first smidgin of inspiration, we did, as we drove to church over in Wellfleet. Despite our haste, we noted the jewel-like qualities of the ponds in their setting of bottle-green pine and emerald oak, the lush, natural shrubbery of Herring Brook Valley, and the cool shade of Wellfleet's big elms. We drove by the softball field to watch the teams warm up for their weekly go and there, too, we were charmed by the blue, cloudless sky, and the steady sou'west breeze that made wavelets in the poverty grass beyond the outfield, and the perimeter view with its ever-changing panorama: the white marble stones of the Methodist Cemetery to the east, and the pine ridge to the south, punctuated by the spires of the Congregational Church and town hall and the friendly screenery of the woods that completed the boundaries of the field.

Thence to our own home on the South Pamet, there to seek out the sheltered back yard, where the big locust shaded us from the hot sun. So we fetched out our faithful Royal and commenced to peck out our column, the while listening to the bird chorus—jays and flickers and a cheery bob white—and enjoying the scent of garden heliotrope and sweet William and meadow grass and decaying locust blossoms that lay like soiled snow on the close-cropped grass. Traffic is sporadic on our road; cars driving by in clusters as church lets out up on the hill and the faint, wind-distorted pealing of the chimes comes on the quarter hour. A thin wispy cirrus cloud slowly moves across the sky, and we almost doze in the warm rays of the sun. Glorious day here in Pamet, city folks—wish you were here.

Snowie has been needling us to make another exploratory trip in one of Pamet's lesser known waterways, this time the Little Pamet. Folks with historical bent will recall that this stream was inspected by the Pilgrim fathers on their original trips of exploration in 1620, and historians will agree that, had the Pilgrims found what they considered to be sufficient water supply, they might well have settled in Truro. Well sir water, or no, we plan to re-explore the Little Pamet from source to delta within the month with our doughty friend, Horace H. Snow, Jr. There are details to be worked out. Is the plastic sailfish of Dr. Manuel Furer still available for scientific purposes? Can the portages across the unnavigable loops of the stream be made on foot (rumor has it that water snakes as long as a buggy whip haunt the Little Pamet) and who wants a slithering, slimy (we slipped in the word to arouse snake lovers, like Bill Elliott, Jr.) snake crawling up a trouser leg. How about the big crossing of Phil Ryder's Dyke? Will Chief Berrio supply police protection for a pair of dauntless explorers as they drag their craft over the blacktop? There are other hazards, too, acres of poison ivy, waiting to caress the bare biceps of Snowie and O'Caghan with noxious tendrils, snapping turtles the size of washtubs, blackducks jealously guarding their nests, and snags in the hollow channel that could disembowel the frail Furer sailfish.

But a snap of the fingers to all these perils. The Little Pamet will be conquered.

Working on tax bills this morning (better the day, better the deed) at town hall, we engaged in idle chatter with Chief Berrio, of Truro's finest, who had dropped by to bring his police log up to date. "How's crime?" we queried the chief. "Quiet—and that's the way we want it. Oh, someone tossed a rock through Joe Schoonejongen's window last week and there's the usual rash of late summer beach parties to keep an eye on." "How about the case of the delinquent dachshund?" we wanted to know. "Tell me what you know, and I'll see how close you come to the facts of the matter," replied the chief, as he drew a worn notebook from his pocket. "Way we heard it," we began, "is that this ornery dachshund was loose on the sands of Ballston Beach, in violation of the town by-laws. Call went out to the police department, and it was answered by Officer Belisle, who handles the beach detail." We went on to say how the brave cop had approached the snarling beast, and despite a bite in the region of his gastrocnemius muscle, had managed to subdue the dog, which he carted off to Provincetown, where Don Westover of the Animal Rescue League took over. "But hardly had the dachshund been placed in durance vile," we continued, "when the telephone commenced ringing. No less a person that Attorney Ozzie Ball on the wire—seems Ozzie was representing the owner of the dog, one Fred Gwynn—and could Gwynn have his dog returned, and would there be any court action?"

Harold interrupted us at this point. "Better let me finish the story; I know the facts. The name Gwynn meant nothing to Officer Belisle but when Ozzie explained that Gwynn is actually Francis Muldoon, of the well-known TV show Car 54, we decided to extend professional courtesy and drop the charges. Besides, the dog didn't actually bite Don, he sort of gummed his leg."

Speaking of Pamet's men in blue, we'd like to devote a paragraph or two to Fred Sylvia, special cop assigned to church duty and extraordinary events such as the recent Kimball auction and this afternoon's baptism party at Janet Tenney's place. Fred is the prototype of the tough cop: tight-lipped, steely-eyed, sparing of speech and smile. But underneath the blue shirt and the Sam Brown belt beats a heart of gold—and thereby hangs a tale.

Fred helps us out with our grass cutting on Saturdays, and our most recent mowing job was up at Snow Cemetery where we were attacking the knee-high grass on a clutch of lots that aren't in perpetual care, but which we wanted to do so's the beautiful burying ground would look more soignee, as they say in French. So we gassed and oiled the mowers, and went our separate ways and except for chance meetings back at the truck when we serviced the machines, we didn't see Fred again until noontime. We loaded the mowers, and wiped the sweat from our brows, and climbed into the truck. "Ever see a quail perch in a tree?" asked Fred. We allowed as how we never had. "Well look over in that locust and you'll see a mother quail."

We looked and we saw. We wanted to know what she was doing in this unquail-like posture. "She's the reason why I didn't do a clean job of cuttin' that Whitman lot," said Fred, mystifying us no end. We started the engine and let in the clutch. "I was day-dreamin' and pushin' the mower through the tall grass over yonder when all of a sudden this quail flew up right under my nose. I looked down and saw only inches from the mower, a nest hidden in the grass with ten eggs in it. The mother had dislodged one of the eggs so I rolled it back to the nest." We're glad to know that Freddie shares the same warm feeling that caused—was it General Grant—to detour his men when his line of march crossed the locus of a bird's nest. And this morning on our way to church we drove into the Snow Cemetery, peeked cautiously at the aforementioned nest; sure enough, the mother bird was setting on her eggs, her feathers making a perfect camouflage in the dry grass.

For one brief, zany moment this morning as we walked by Fratus' Bend, we had the almost uncontrollable urge to take off our shoes and socks and plow barefoot through the wind-rowed, golden pine needles at the roadside. It's that kind of day. Summer-like, shirt sleeve warm with a lazy, faint breeze out of the sou'west, just enough to stir the last, lemon-yellow clinging leaves of the locusts. Overhead, the sky is a blend of gossamer haze and pale azure, with nary a cloud to be seen. And the countryside smells of decayed leaves and matted, dew-dampened grass.

So we walked to church this morning—or attempted to. Hardly had we reached neighbor George Morris' driveway when Jackie Kelley hove to in his battered VW bus and raised inquiring eyebrows. We signaled him on, shouting as how we were getting a mite of exercise. He drove off, shaking his head in disbelief. Came then Mrs. Arthur Silva, and she, too, stops beside us and grinds down the window of her car. "Something wrong with your car?" she queries. Again we politely refuse a lift. Then comes the incident of the temptation to wade through the pine needles and then we cross the road, and remark how low the crick is. A newly formed islet with grass sprouting from its surface has appeared midway of the tiny basin near the culvert. And the stain of the watermark shows a foot or so above the present level, and the cattail banks loom high out of the water. In a tiny whirlpool among the tufts of meadow grass a broken alder twig circles in the current, amid the dust-like layer of cat-o-nine tail seed, and a big, bold bluejay flashes among the low growing swamp alder, and a clutch of wild ducks fly in a tight wedge formation up-valley, and the sporadic sound of traffic comes from the highway.

We got to thinking as how we hadn't had a meal of seaclams for some time, and by the time Mass was over, we'd about made up our mind to go forth in pursuit of the wily bivalve. At ten we were on the beach at Pond Village, booted, bundled, armed with rake and seaclam net bag, accompanied by our good friend Neil Pirnie. But the tide was still too high; nary a bar showed above the tiny wavelets, and the only other living things we saw were some slate gray gulls who waded casually at the water's edge. So we philosophized a mite with Neil, waiting for the waters to ebb. And then we got to reminiscing, as we gazed at the big, brick-faced engine room of the freezer. Neil had worked at the cold storage in recent years, but he's familiar with the Worthington-diesel era of Pond Village. Our own memory goes back to the days of Gabe Elder and Bert Ingraham and steam power so we rather smugly dominated the conversation.

We knew Mr. Elder but slightly but Mr. Ingraham, despite the difference in our ages, was one of our acquaintances. Our mutual interest was music; this would be back in 1932, perhaps, when we were learning to play the tuba under the able tutelage of Tom Nassi, of Orleans and we'd been invited to join Hayes Small's Highland Orchestra. Our introduction to this musical ensemble came about as a result of our friendship with Hayes' son, Willard, who was a classmate in high school. And so it came about that one Friday after school we rode over to North Truro in the school bus, toting our big silver-plated bass horn, and disembarked at the Highland House. Spent the shank end of the afternoon exploring the area we did, played a chucker of golf on the deserted course, bowled a string or two on the ancient single alley across Highland Road, made a rapid tour of the cattle barns. (Hayes was to suffer a disastrous fire in the horse barn that very winter.) If memory serves, we paid a visit to another of the Small clan, Uncle Isaac Morton, affectionately known to his fellow townsfolk as Mort in his Marine Observatory Station out on the bluff, north of the lighthouse. (Mort was then in the twilight of a career that had seen him spotting ocean vessels for the Boston Board of Trade for many decades. He remembered the tragic sinking of the steamer Portland and the ship Jason, among many other marine disasters.)

But we digress. Come supper time and we returned to the Small domicile, there to scrub up at the kitchen sink while Willard's mother, Mrs. Katherine Small, dished out the hearty, country fare: vegetables from the Small garden, and pork from a recently butchered pig, and rich milk from the Small dairy. And as a pleasant background, we had small talk from the patriarch of the Small clan, E. Hayes, who was then campaigning for the office of representative to the general court from the second Barnstable district (he won, in a tight contest, and his victory caused him to resign his position as Truro's moderator.) Hayes was a colorful wielder of the gavel, too.

Just time enough after the evening meal for us to sneak a quick cigarette before the other members of the Highland Orchestra commenced to arrive. Ralph Tinkham and Joe Francis, first and second trumpeter, respectively. They were engaged in a heated discussion anent the relative quality of the Vega and the King trumpet. The argument never was resolved, because Ina Snow arrived about that time, and the two gallant brass men went out to help her fetch in her cello. Ina unswathed the big, handsome instrument and propped it up near a steam radiator; she explained it played better when it was warm.

And then Thede Nickerson drove up in his Buick, remarking as how he'd almost missed the rehearsal; feller had been late making an appointment at Thede's monument shop in Provincetown. "Don't know as I'll be too quick on the valves of this old trombone," said Thede as he slipped the green flannel wrapper from his shining brass horn. "Been chipping away at a stone all day, and I must have hit my knuckles a dozen times." Came Emma Smith then, and she sat down at the well-kept Small piano to run through a few measures of "Let Me Call You Sweetheart," a waltz just off the presses. Son Ernie Small joined in for the last few bars. Ernie played a C-melody saxophone, and he could read directly from the sheet music. And then Hayes set up his drums, and gave a quick roll or two on the snare, and the music was passed out, and just as we started to tune to the piano A, in came Bert Ingraham.

As Bert tenderly took his violin from the case, he explained his tardiness. "Traps loaded with fish today, butterfish, and whiting, and mackerel. We just finished cleanin' up for the day." And then Bert perched a pair of steel-rimmed spectacles on his nose, and slipped a clean white hankerchief under his chin, and resined his bow vigorously, and gave the strings a final, delicate tuning, and, "Let's warm up with number 6, Happiness Schottische. Here's the beat." And his big foot smartly rapped out the tempo, and we took it up at four. They say Mr. Ingraham was a hard taskmaster at the freezer. Expected a generous day's work for a day's pay; no differential for night shifts, no overtime pay, of course, and if a feller took too much fish home to feed his family, why he soon heard about it. Be that as it may, we found Bert Ingraham a fine concertmaster. We've an idea he and Hayes Small are doing drum and violin duets somewhere in the Valhalla of retired engineers and politicians.

NINETEEN SIXTY-FOUR

1964

Lights on at the Keezer place, over on Hatch Road. One day last week we received a mail piece from a Boston distributor from whom we purchase lawnmowers in season. The flyer described a deal on snow throwers, and contained a neatly lettered placard which advised "PRAY FOR SNOW." We scotch-taped the card to our office door at town hall, sat back to await the reaction of folks who visited our place of business. The state road crew, and the town gang, as we might well have known, beamed approvingly, and asked if we had any special prayer we were using. "That check from the town came in mighty handy for Christmas," said Ray Joseph, who plows Pamet by-roads. "Hope you don't really mean that," sniffed Irv Wheeler. "I've had a shovel in my hand for days—the white stuff sure blows around down on Beach Point." And Isaiah Snow, with true Snow humor, peered at our little sign and turned to us with the query, "Which one?"

Great family, these Snows, and that's why we write about 'em so often. It's been a long time since we've heard a good yarn about old C.W., patriarch of the clan, but yesterday, between games of cribbage with one of the scions of the Snow tree, Horace Jr., we heard the following story. We'd just eked out a win over Snowie and he'd reached for the cards with the usual remark. "Loser deals." For want of something better to reply we twitted him with, "Guess we sort of tied you up that time, eh?"

Snowie popped the pegs back in the starting holes, gave the deck a quick riffle, flipped out the hands, and, "Ever tell you about the time my grandfather and his brother George saw the immortal Houdini on the stage in Boston?" We answered in the negative as we discarded a nine and a king in Snowie's crib. "Gave you dead mens' cards," we muttered. We cut for our friend, and he turned up a jack. Pegged his two points, did Snowie, and as we played out the hand he began his story.

"Well sir, I got the yarn from my late Uncle Norman, so I know its gospel truth. Seems the Boston Post was running ads that Harry Houdini, the great escape artist, would appear for two weeks in the Old Howard—in those days a vaudeville house rather than a burlesque palace, as we remember it. As usual, the world-famed performer was offering a big prize to any man who could bind him up in such fashion that he couldn't get free within a given time limit. (Fifteen two-four-six, and a pair is eight.) It so happened that my grand uncle George was home for a brief visit (he was a sea-going captain) and the two brothers decided to make the trip to Boston, do some shopping, combine business with pleasure, and take a crack at the Houdini reward offer." We totted up a dozen holes, added two extra for muggins when Snowie forgot to take his full count.

"So the brothers Snow took the early train up to Boston; bought a round trip ticket each from Ike Freeman, the station master, and along about noon they arrived at the South Station. Norman says they had oyster stew and fried clams and apple pie at the South Station restaurant (don't all Cape Codders have seafood when they go to the city?) and afterward they took a cab to Washington St., where they bought some clothes in the big department stores, and sometime later they were comfortably seated in the Old Howard just as the curtain rose on the first vaudeville act. Uncle George managed to grab an usher by the sleeve and send a message to the management that two Truro, Cape Cod men were in the audience—that they figgered they could tie Mr. Houdini up tighter'n a bull's eyelid in a sandstorm. And in jig time the usher reappeared and conducted them back stage." Sixteen—without a fifteen—and the pegs dropped into place.

"Norman used to say the two brothers strode out onto the stage as though they'd been actors all their lives. Bowed to the audience, they did, and shook hands with the Great Houdini, and when he gave the signal that he was ready, they pounced on him with two coils of rope as though he were a dory loose in a nor'east gale. By a prearranged plan, Uncle George was to use knots he'd learned on shipboard, while Grandfather Charles was to depend on farmer's hitches. So they went to work with gusto. In quick succession George whipped a clove hitch and a bowline around the bulging Houdini chest, while Charles threw a series of square knots and a plowman's lock knot around the great man's lower limbs. In rapid succession came timber hitches, fishermen's knots, and a special hitch Uncle George had learned from the local trappers called a Portuguese tuna strangler. Charles gave the coup de grace with a combination diamond-hitch and a monkey's fist.

"They say poor Houdini looked like a Christmas turkey when the two Pamet men finally stepped back and nodded at each other in satisfaction." "What was the outcome of this affair?" we wanted to know, as we rounded third street and headed for home. "Well sir, the stage attendants popped Houdini into a trunk, which they locked, and dropped the trunk into a big tank of water, and while the manager stood by and counted off the time, derned if the trunk didn't pop open and out jumped Houdini. The Snow brothers always claimed they should have searched the escape artist first. They knew sure as shootin' he had a sharp knife and some keys hidden somewhere on his body. But they got the ropes they'd tied him up with as a souvenir of the show—and that brand new manila was cut in several places clean's a whistle."

"Whistle over that," we crowed, as we pegged sixteen to win the game.

Selectmen's clerk, Lucy Boyd, entrusted us with stencils of the 1964 warrant which we'll have run off on the school duplicating machine tomorrow. She didn't say we could peek at 'em, and she didn't say we couldn't—so we peeked. Among the interesting matters for disposition at the February session will be: a request for $50 to pay for the installation of state assessment system, $2,400 for the purchase of 3 tail-gate sand spreaders. (Will the town invite Jim Moynahan to take the first ride on the sand trucks to play appropriate tail-gate jazz on his venerable Albert system clarinet? Move over, Jim, and we'll join you, unless it's bitter cold, with our valve trombone.) The rowdyism by-law, so-called, will be voted on, but moneywise, as the Madison Avenue hucksters say, the big item will be a request for $19,000 for a new fire engine and $2,050 for a new police cruiser. (Does our memory serve us correctly when we write that Truro's first two, count 'em—TWO fire trucks cost this municipality $3,000?)

This would be in the early thirties, following a bad fire which burned Mary Fratus' house to the ground. This conflagration, coupled with the great forest fire of 1927, moved the good voters to give their stamp of approval for the purchase of two Brockway pumpers. Thus both villages of the town were covered, the firemen of the rival crews each having a shiny engine to drive. Underpowered and overloaded were the poor Brockways. Dave Snow was moved to say they couldn't pull a woodtick off'n a sick hound, and John Worthington, we recall, had to call on all his engineering experience when he installed vacuum pumps on the intake hoses so's the trucks could draft water in later years when the centrifugal plates became worn. But the Brockways did their job for a decade or so, until they were replaced by later model apparatus.

Mention of the fire department of this town invariably brings up the name of the late Col. Dick Magee, generally conceded to be the father of that organization. In the pre-Magee days here in Truro, fire fighting had been a matter of men, shovels, brooms, pump cans, and perspiration. But when the handsome, be-moustached Irishman appeared in Pamet, he brought with him the enthusiasm of a true spark. He begged, borrowed, would have stolen, if necessary, equipment from his fellow fire chiefs in the Greater Boston area. Many's the trip we made to Boston in one of Magee's farm trucks to fetch home nozzles, and plaster hooks, and gas masks, and fire alarm cable and boxes, and couplings and hard hats, and sundries too numerous to mention. Under Magee the department burgeoned. A fire alarm system was installed, volunteer labor, of course, from the North Village clear over to the chief's place, Cobb Farm, beyond the Hogsbacks. Too bad the wire couldn't have been buried underground; it might well have been in operation today. But the overhead wires had a way of breaking on windy nights, and a safety feature of the system would cause the sirens to blast off in each fire house to notify the firemen of an open circuit. Got so's a feller had to jump out of bed at night and shut off the whistles a mite too often and when Col. Dick went away to war after Pearl Harbor, the fire alarm went the way of all faulty systems.

Dick even bought his own fire engine. First off he had an ancient White chemical, pre-1920, it was, with right-hand drive, and a cone belt clutch, and an outboard gear shift that would challenge the skill of a Sterling Moss to manipulate. The White refused to start for a fire one winter day, so the colonel traded her for a rebuilt Maxim of a much later vintage. One of the memorable moments of our young life was the day we first drove this juggernaut. We'd been working at Cobb Farm and our chores were interrupted by the clang of the code box in the basement of the barn. Quicker'n you can say Obadiah Brown we dashed for the engine stall, sprang into the high seat, kicked at the starter, thrilled as the big Waukesha engine roared into life.

By the time we had made the second of the several backs and fills required to jockey the engine out of the garage, the chief himself had appeared on the scene, resplendent in glossy rubber boots, white raincoat and white helmet. "North Truro dump," he bellowed at us above the roar of the exhaust. "Give 'er the gun!" Little matter that the puny blaze had been extinguished before we reached the scene; hadn't we double-clutched the rig on Perry's Hill and thundered through Truro Square before the admiring gazes of our fellow townsfolk? Hadn't we stomped on the siren button and yanked on the leather thong of the bell as we passed the Central School? And when we arrived at the now-extinguished fire, hadn't we jotted down the names of the firemen for the chief? A heady wine, this.

Many years afterward, long after Col. Magee had given up his position as head of the Truro fire department, we chanced to drop by Anderson's junk yard in Wellfleet for some minor items of salvage. "Take a look down back," said Andy, wagging a thumb over his shoulder. So we picked our way through the rusting bones of the ancient cars and the battered water tanks and the tangled chicken wire. And there, in a weed-grown corner we spied the faithful Maxim. With a cautious glance over our shoulder we climbed up to the mildewed seat, and seized the big steering wheel and kicked at the clutch, and made the classic motions of the double clutch backshift. We'd like to think that scrap prices never rose to the point where Andy got ambitious enough to cut up our old friend. Better she should rust her days away on Cape Cod soil.

Local notes: John Dyer, Jr., informs us he has given the old family barn to the National Seashore Park folks. The latter had been looking for an authentic Cape Cod barn; found 'em scarcer'n hen's teeth. "And we'd just about made up our minds to tear our barn down, it was so rickety. When the Park people approached us, Ma and I had a real search of our consciences—hated the thought of making a gift when the Democrats are in office, but then we figured the building wouldn't last more'n a year or so. So we signed the papers, and they're commencin' to take 'er down, board by board, and I hear tell they'll move it to the Evelyn Higgins property, which will be a historically restored area."

We got to thinking about the disappearance of barns in Pamet. In our day a barn was an indispensable outbuilding for the local folks. Many, of course, have been converted into attractive cottages (the Keezer barn, for instance, which didn't, as a matter of fact, start its career as a barn, but as the old South Truro School House). But most barns, we're sorry to say, ended up in kindling piles or just plain rotted away. Ed Snow's huge barn (gosh, how pleasant it used to smell, of horses, and cows, and hay) located where Tony Duarte's insurance office now stands, was flaked sometime in the early thirties, used, in part, to build the cottage where Tony honeymooned on South Pamet. John Gray's barn became a studio when Cleve Woodward bought the property. On our own premises, the big John H. Rich barn had already gone into such disrepair we were forced to raze the building. Always promised we'd use the wide pine boards for some worthwhile purpose, but just never got around to it.

The Corey barn and C. W. Snow's barn were of a comparatively modern vintage—probably had been built on the site of former like edifices, but they were big, soundly built affairs with modern conveniences such as manure pits and electric lights. They served for the storage of hay (remember the hoisting rig the C. W. barn had down on Castle Road?) and they were living quarters for the work horses and the carriage horses and the cows, and they provided basement facilities for the family pigs. Too, the big, weather-tight doors could be closed so's the menfolk could do chores under cover in foul weather, and there were usually adjoining carriage sheds and harness rooms. (Wonder if we'd recognize the tangy odor of harness oil, these days.) The hay loft made a fine place to play hide and seek on gloomy winter afternoons, and it's a wonder more barns didn't catch fire, when you consider all the young fry who learned to smoke in those venerable old buildings. A sprig of early-flowering arbutus, then, to Squire Dyer and his mother, Ruth, for their generosity to the Park.

Shades of our Hibernian ancestors: somewhere in our personality there's an Irish quality that makes us respond to minor incidents—and the weather—so our mood fluctuates like a fever chart. Take this morning, for instance. Up betimes, we were, the while glancing out the bedroom window, where the south view, through the shading locusts, showed a golden sun washing the countryside. We smiled as we dressed but when we peered from the bathroom at the meadow, we saw a clinging, damp mist over the winding crick and the cattail patch, and we opined as how it would be another day of sub-normal temperatures. Down goes our mood-graph. Brisk ablutions, and a quick shave with one of Warren Wilson's new stainless steel blades, and we run a hand over cheeks as "smooth as a schoolmarm's knee," as the late John R. Dyer used to quote the simile used by his long-dead father, John B. And our mood improves. Reach for the toothpaste, to find a nearly new tube cruelly strangled about the neck. "Drat those boys—if we've told 'em once, we've told 'em a hundred times to start squeezing the toothpaste from the bottom-danged if we won't have our bride buy tooth powder from hereon." Down the mood.

But the refrigerator yields two big, brown eggs, and we're reminded of Frank Joseph's fresh eggs of a decade or more ago, and as the water boils for their bath, we cheer up a mite. A glance at the thermometer reveals that the thin, red line is in the mid-fifties and the stirring of the alder bush out on the meadow is less frantic than yesterday, so the nor'west wind has abated a mite, and up goes our quotient of cheer.

Breakfast over, we make our morning rounds of the estate. The huge clustered blossoms of the hydrangea are fading, and we note where red mites are feeding on the ground juniper, and there's a withered leaf on our prize rhododendron, and a wisp of a cloud suddenly darkens the sun; down we go. The west garden, however, is a perkerupper. Tuberous begonias in a riot of blossom, and hardy phlox delicately lavender, and asters so pretty we have to back up a step or two to admire them, and we catch our heel in the wicket of Geof's croquet set, and like to fall down. Down, too, our spirits. Then comes the faint buzz of bees clustered on the globe thistle, and a sudden smell of warm sunlight wafting up from the meadow nook bringing the nostalgic odor of freshly cut grass (Geof must have done his softball field last evening). Up.

We shall long remember this year 1964 as one of firsts for O'Caghan. First trip to the hospital for us, with first anesthetic and first surgery; first pair of bi-focals, when Dr. Max Berman found that the lenses that enable us to see well at a distance gave us only a blurred vision close-to, and we're still trying to get used to the cussed specs. And then just last week we came home from work one afternoon to find a handsome, trim electrical organ in our living room. Quicker'n you can say Obadiah Brown we dragged out the bench, kicked off our shoes, flipped the switch, titillated the stops and the draw bars and caressed the keys. Give us a month to learn the registrations, as the book calls the controls, and we'll have more fun than a red weasel in a chickenyard.

Don't get us wrong, but we'd like to raise a feeble voice in protest against the new house being erected, here and there in Truro. Not that we object to the lines nor the style in general, but we deplore the lack of a good, old-fashioned attic, unfinished, of course. You could find such delightful things in an attic, especially if you bought an old Cape Codder, as we did. We well recall the first time we prowled under the eaves of the old John Rich house, just before we signed the papers for the purchase. The things we found!

A box full of old spectacle frames, for instance, octagonal, some of them were, and half-lenses (they've come back into fashion, these latter; Jim Moynahan has a pair of reading glasses he uses when reading music for his ancient, but efficient Albert system clarinet). And we found molds for making bullets, and tubs full of decaying trawl lines, and a moth-eaten swallow tail coat, and a pair of shoe-lasts, and an abrasive stone for polishing silver ware, and a collection of yellowed newspapers recounting the assassination of President McKinley. But all the gems we found in the house that was to be our own pale into insignificance when we compare them with the treasures we found in the attic of the house that our folks bought back in the mid-twenties. The old Dahl house, that would be, located on Corey Hill, just above the post office.

Mrs. Dahl had been, for some years, proprietor of an ice cream parlor down in the Square and, after she'd closed shop, she fetched the left over furnishings up to her house. In the unfinished attic we found all the so-called ice cream furniture—chairs and tables made of heavy gauge wire, in fancy twists, with walnut tops. And there was an Edison phonograph with a sizable collection of cylinder records and the fancy, big horn that was supposed to magnify the sound to a suitable volume. And in connection with Mrs. Dahl's traffic in tobacco, a tobacco plug-cutter, for those folks who had money enough only for a portion of a plug of Mayo's Dark.

Probably the most intriguing bit of memorabilia we located was a cigar trimmer. Nickel-plated, it was, with a sizable storage compartment in its base, and a platform above where you'd insert the blind end of your stogie to be neatly nipped off.

Many's the happy hour we spent in the gloom of the attic, showing our school cronies how the cigar-cutter worked. Put your finger in the tiny hole of the machine, press a lever, and neat's a whistle, the epidermis of your digit would be shaved away. The trick was to press just hard enough to allow the razor keen blade to remove the outer layer of your hide, without drawing blood. We calculate that there was enough epidermis stored in the base of the cigar clipper to recover several dozen human beings, time we had finished with our experimenting in the O'Caghan attic.

We recall, some years later, discussing this bit of apparatus with Charlie Snow, Truro's most avid cigar smoker. Did he remember the machine, we wanted to know. Indeed he did. "All the stores had 'em in the old days," said Charlie. "But most cigar smokers preferred to bite off the end of a cigar. More satisfying. And if you found you had difficulty in gettin' a good draw from a 7-20-4 or a Blackstone," added Charlie, "they used to say all's you had to do was put a mustard plaster on the back of your neck; that would draw about anything."

One day last week, as we were entering the Temple of Learning in Provincetown, we noted that the door of room four was ajar, so we stepped in to say good morning to our colleague, Paul Boire, teacher of science and math in the Junior High. "SHHHHH," he shushed us, as he slipped a cigar into our breast pocket. We raised inquiring eyebrows at his generosity. "The guppies have had babies, here in the fish tank," he explained. And then he tiptoed over to the aquarium, and we followed, also on tiptoe, and there, sure enough, in the breeding tray of the tank we espied a pair of mother fish, proudly piloting two tiny schools of baby guppies through the limpid water. "Proudest moment of my life," exclaimed Paul. "But the cigar?" we queried him. "Well, I had 'em to pass out after the election, but my man lost, so this makes a good excuse for giving them away."

It is with a deep, personal sense of loss that we add out thoughts to those of the staff of the *Provincetown Advocate* and to those of his many friends afar and abroad of Paul G. Lambert, our longtime editor. It was Paul who first encouraged us to work up a column for his fine weekly, and our ambition, over the years, has been to attain, in some small degree, that touch with the written word that always characterized his writing. We shall miss Paul and his good-natured banter, his tongue-in-cheek criticisms of the reportorial field. Ave atque vale, old friend.

Been snowing since sometime in the wee, dark hours of the night, it has; and when first we awoke just at the first gray of dawn, we took the pale ghostly shade of the country-side to be a heavy fog, because the house was warm, despite a lowered thermostat. And then, to our sleep-dulled eyes it seemed as though there might be a heavy frost in the valley, or perhaps the shank end of a moonlight night. Not so—in the pale rays of the porch light we saw big, feathery snowflakes drifting down through the still air and we remarked how the ground was covered, and the blacktop of the town road, too, had its blanket, and the locust trees and the post and rail fence and the evergreens all had their frosting of the white stuff.

After breakfast we again inspected the spread of the front lawn, there to see a flock of fat, dumpy quail foraging for food in tall grass between our house and Morris' and a squirrel scampered up a locust tree, frightened by the yipping of our pup, Mokey, and the snow powdered down from the gray limbs as he ascended in almost liquid motion. So down Depot Road we go, it being a mite early for church, noting a pair of rabbits by Miz' Holly's place, peering at us from the shelter of a rambler rose. And we saw as how the new Cadorette place on Mill Pond Road is rapidly a-building, and when we got to the parking place at Pamet Harbor we saw a dozen or so ducks in the open water of the basin. And the clamflats were most beautiful in their cover of white, and the leaden waters of the salt crick flowing under the pilings of the railroad trestle served only to accent the scene. Beautiful day, withal, and we wish you were here, city folks.

Among the nice presents we got for Christmas, a huge cribbage board, with pegs as big as the late Frank Joseph's thumb. And so we sat at our kitchen table like a spider awaiting a fly on the holiday morning, peering out at the driveway, looking for the familiar sight of Snowie. He showed up mid-morning. We casually mentioned as how we'd like to christen our new board. Just happened to have the deck of cards handy, and a fresh pot of coffee on the stove, and our new bi-focals perched on our nose. Make it two out of three, we suggested, and we'd be finished by the time our child bride arrived home from late Mass to start the vegetables. Snowie allowed as how he'd be pleased to give us a lesson at the ancient game of fifteen-two.

We stationed No. 4 son, Geof, behind Snowie's chair to kind of check his counting (Snowie has a habit of tossing his hand into the discard pile before we can verify his score) and the game began. At the very outset we noted that our opponent was holding the big cards, so we determined to play a pegging game. Trapped him into taking pairs so's we could get three-for six, and managed to lure him into seven and eight runs that gave us final advantages. In this fashion we eked out narrow victories the first two games, but then we softened and agreed to give him one last chance to recoup his losses (one house rule provides that a lurch, or skunk game counts double, so it would be possible for Snowie to tie the score).

Good thing we had Geof on hand to act as referee, too, because our opponent tried every trick in the book to beat us. He'd start to play a card, and when we pounced on his play with a double or a run, he'd withdraw the pasteboard and assert he'd changed his mind. But virtue prevailed and we pegged out on the final hand. "I'll never play on that king-sized monster again," he vowed. "And I protest your spy hanging over my shoulder; he makes me nervous," he shouted as he slammed out the door.

That afternoon swollen with our earlier victory, we challenged son Mike's girlfriend, the beauteous Carol Souza from Provincetown, to a chucker of crib. Tried all the same techniques we'd adopted in the morning, but that slip of a girl trounced us three straight. As we sulked off to lick our wounds, she beamed at us, "But you see, my uncle Joe Fageegy Francis taught me how to play."

NINETEEN SIXTY-FIVE

1 9 6 5

Took all morning for the weather to make up its mind, this Sunday of late February. First off, we had overcast skies and a light, fitful breeze out of the southwest, and a barometer reading that seemed to drop, ever so slightly. And then the breeze freshened and the sky was swept clear, and the sun shone bright and warm in the valley. The pattern repeated itself several times during the morning, and finally just before noon, she cleared and she's been clear ever since. After lunch we offered to hang some washing on the line for our child bride, and the sheltered back yard was most pleasant, the sod was soft under foot, and the very last of the soiled snow drifts were shrinking away in the sun, and the birds were carrying on in great fashion in the cedar tree on the hillside. The smell of clean laundry bleaching on the line reminded us of spring, and we closed our eyes for a spell, and projected our thoughts a few weeks into the future.

Some years back, a conflagration occurred in the barn Eben Paine used to rent from the Marshall's, down next to his store abaft the old state highway in the square. We remember the barn as a ramshackle, weatherbeaten building, with a sagging ridgepole and bare spots on the sidewalks where the shingles had come loose. Close by the road, it was, just above Eben's kerosene shed, about where Peggy Day's prize dahlias grow nowadays. If memory serves, Mr. Paine had no facilities for keeping his horse over at his own place, on Castle Road; the horse was indispensable for the delivery of groceries, and the unused portion of the Marshall barn provided comfortable and convenient quarters for the spavined equine. Many's the time we drove around the grocery route with Eben Paine.

A tall, lean, ruddy-complexioned man was Eben, with snowwhite hair, and a generous, snow-white moustache. Permission granted for the junket to say, Ballston Beach, we'd follow the old gentleman up from the store, sniffing the while at the pungent aroma of kerosene and molasses and vinegar that wafted from the open door of the adjoining shed that made up the Paine complex, and sniffing with a mite less satisfaction at the heady barn-smell that came from the Marshall shed. We'd help Mr. Paine harness the black horse, toss the worn leather straps over the bony back of the patient critter, watch admiringly as Eben wrestled the bit into the beast's mouth, stand by as he tightened the buckles, and gave a reassuring pat on the horse's rump as Eben backed 'er into the shafts of the Democrat wagon. Then down to the town pump (located a mite west'ard of the store) where the mare would fortify herself against the long trip up Head-O-Pamet with huge drafts of cool water from the big granite trough (don't let 'er have too much, boy, she'll get logey), and thence to the wooden platform of the store, where we'd load the groceries aboard. On one such occasion, we'd just about made the halfway mark of the Pamet loop, about up to Joe Atwood's place, when word came via Mr. Atwood's telephone that the Marshall barn, back in the square, was afire. Eben quick turned the carriage around and whipped the surprised horse into her fastest gait, a sort of shambling trot—and back we rocked to the center of town.

As luck would have it, Mrs. Ethel Burhoe, who clerked for Eben in those days, had spied a wisp of smoke curling from the open door of the building, and she'd hollered out to the sizable crowd of folks who were waiting in the square for the noon mail to arrive. It chanced, too, that Charlie Snow and his town road crew were passing through the square on their way to dinner, and all hands headed for the fire, armed with shovels, and brooms, and buckets of water from the town pump. Almost before you could say Obadiah Brown, the smoldering hay in the loft was put out colder'n a mackerel. Mr. Paine thanked all hands and invited them to stop by the store for a cold bottle of soda pop, and while they were quaffing the Moxie, Mr. Snow and Eben reconstructed the probable anatomy of the sudden conflagration.

Eben remembered he'd had some hay delivered the day before by old Nelson Dyer, from up Wellfleet way. The hay had seemed rather damp at the time, he remembered, probably because Nelson had been caught, middle of his hay makin', by a series of early summer showers and hadn't been able to dry'er out thoroughly. And then the hot sun, beating down on the roof of the barn, had warmed up the hay loft, and there wasn't enough circulation of air through the packed area to carry off the heat, and. . . . "That is," said Mr. Paine to us, "unless some careless youngsters was smokin' in there. You smoke boy?" We shook our heads in horror at the thought—tobacco hadn't touched our lips since the time we got sick on a Postmaster cigar, months before, we assured him. So the barn was saved, and so was the big, vicious red pig that Mr. Paine was raising in the sty under the building. In fact, Eben afterwards claimed that pig produced the best pork ever to come out of the Paine pork barrel. "I figger maybe that pig got a good sniff of the smoke from the fire in the barn; gave kind of a faint, delicate smokey taste to the meat," is the way he accounted for it.

The fishermen, this opening day of the 1965 trout season, especially appreciated the weather. And as a bit of a bonus, fishin' was better than ever it has been in the past. The banks of our Pamet were lined with ardent anglers from the dark hours of the morning until dusk closed in—and the fishin' was good. Warren Alexander, from Provincetown, appears to be high liner, with a sixteen inch, two pound plus beauty, taken in the very gurgle of the culvert. And our own two sons, Ranny and Geof, did right well with a clutch of fish which they dangled under our nose while we were still abed (they'd gone off to their respective favorite spots, Ranny to Gull Pond, Geof to Great Pond in the wee hours of the morning) while we were still pounding our pillow. Of course, Dad had the grisly chore of cleaning the finny delicacies when the lads made their second sortie to the limpid waters of the fresh crick, where Ran took a fish that almost equaled the Alexander beauty.

A riot of birdsong fills the neighborhood—and rabbits are commuting across our lawn, bug-eyed as you look at 'em front view, white powder puff dancing in the air as they scamper for the protection of the high grass. Mokey, the family pup, sniffs the air and makes a fair imitation of a point, and we follow his gaze and see a fat, sly woodchuck peering at us from behind the blasted apple tree abaft the fallow garden site. It's a glorious day, folks, one we'd rate B-plus in our mark book if it happened to be a school day. We defy any one to drive down Depot Road without emitting an Oh or an Ah at the sight of the two beautiful apple trees in full blossom, one at Wenneman's pink house, the other in Miz' Dalton's front yard. We've gone out of our way several times lately just to ogle them. Wind is light, steady, and a mite south of east, to judge by the stirring of the shrubbery—and it smells of the ocean, too; and there's a thin veil of cloud cover to west'ard, and the rising sun has the clear, pale look that foretells a cool day. Every shadbush in the valley is in flower—delicate, almost spectral—and the beachplum in sheltered spots shows its profuse blossoms, and the oak trees across the river are in full tassel.

We recall the Memorial Days of the thirties with much fondness and nostalgia. True, old Mr. Parker, father of Miz' Hayes Small, was too old to appear at town hall, but as last surviving Civil War veteran he'd sent his greetings to the audience. And Hayes Small, then a representative to the general court, was to orate most eloquently from the tiny stage, and one of the high school kids would render Lincoln's Gettysburg Address during the morning program. The Wellfleet Town Band would be there, (Tony Dennis, of Provincetown, was the director) to play Nearer, My God To Thee, and other appropriate sacred music. And then the ceremonies at the hall would end, and Henry Hanson, commander of the combined Truro-Wellfleet Legion Post, would snap out his orders, and the building would be emptied.

Every single school kid in town would join in the line of march, and there'd be gold star mothers in a shiny, black hack, and all the veterans of World War I in their tight-fitting uniforms. And then the drums would roll off for the first march, and down Town Hall Road we'd go. The kids would wave their flags in time to the music, and the shuffle of all those feet on the blacktop, and the barking of Henry at the head of the line, and the color guard with the beautiful big flags flying in the breeze; a fine sight it was. Nice parade route, too—all down hill, from the town hall chuck to the square. The band always appreciated the easy march, and consequently they played almost continuously; round the Catholic Church corner we'd tramp, and by Tom Gray's house, and past Dave Snow's curve, and finally, down under the shady locusts of Dr. Lupien's, and then into William Gray Square, where a big crowd of townsfolk would be waiting.

One last selection from the band—probably Stars and Stripes Forever—and then the decoration of the memorial plaque, and a ragged volley from the firing squad. (Remember the embarrassed look on Joe Curley's face as he fumbled with the stubborn bolt of the old Springfield rifle?) Taps, then, played by a member of the band standing stiffly at attention in his trim uniform, and then the reply, muted and ghostlike, coming from up back of the abandoned barn on the hill. On one occasion, we recall, Tony Dennis chided Joe Francis (who played the echo on that occasion) for taking so long in replying. "One of Phat Francis' dogs was up there—darn cuss kept tryin' to get at my ice cream cone—I finally had to give it to him."

All winter long we'd been promising our French III class we'd some day fetch our friend Snowie to school for a visit; but our plans always seemed to go awry, until the kids began to express disbelief in any such person. "He's a figment of your imagination—something you use as a filler in your column," said Richard Russe. "Il n'existe point," added Cathy Santos in her best French. So it must have been somewhat of a surprise to pretty Judy Lane when we popped into Felton's excellent Cottage Restaurant on opening night accompanied by our good bride and the Snowies.

We hadn't a chance to introduce Judy to Horace, but now we can say, editorially, Yes, Judy, there is a Snowie. Scion of a Truro family (Nicholas Snow was the first to bring the name to this country), Snowie was born and brought up right here on the Pamet. Attended local schools, where he excelled in sports (first base on the SE Mass championship Wellfleet High School team in the mid-twenties). Later was accepted at St. John's College at Annapolis, Md.; was obligated to leave school when the Depression touched the family purse. Snowie then struck out on his own: sold insurance in the Hartford, Conn., area, clerked in a drugstore chain in New York, finally returned to his native town in the mid-thirties and went into business with his dad in the local Shell Station.

Any one who ever filled up at Snowie's pumps will testify it was the most unusual and interesting spot in the county. Service with a smile was the Snowie motto—and service he gave: everything from baby sitting while mother ran up to the post office, to relaying phone messages, to de-ticking the family dog. From patching the kids swimming tubes (for free), handing out recipes for clam chowder, Snowie had enough of the human weaknesses to make him seem real.

In the period just before the war, Snowie met a pretty Irish gal at the station one day, and he married her, and subsequently their apartment upstairs rang to the wails of a tiny little baby whom they christened Kenneth. But it would require a good sized book to chronicle the aspects of this man of many parts. Suffice it to say, Judy, that there is a Snowie and as long as people have screens to be repaired, and shutters to be painted, and bricks to be laid, and food to be eaten and convivality to be shared—why there'll always be a Snowie.

We'd visited Pamet Harbor several times last week, shortly after the workmen had commenced to couple the big discharge pipes that will be used in the harbor dredging job. And one fine breezy afternoon we managed to pose a few questions to Capt. Scott, prime contractor on this long-awaited project. When, we wanted to know, would the dredge itself show up on the job? The captain, a prematurely white-haired, blue-eyed feller of lean wiry build allowed as how he was sorry to inform us that there'd been a change in plans. "We're assembling our discharge line here in Pamet Harbor," he explained in cultured tones most unbecoming to a dredge captain, "but then we're going to tow the whole assembly over to Provincetown, where we have a short—two weeks perhaps—job. You'll agree it would be very difficult to do this work in the narrow confines of the shore down there; and if we waited to do the Provincetown job in the fall, we'd find ourselves on the open shore in hurricane season. So as soon as we complete the Provincetown job, back we come to Truro."

He added that the Pamet Harbor project would probably take four to six weeks of pumping. So we tried not to show our disappointment as we watched Capt. Scott's crew jockeying the big pipes around with their truck crane (it's actually a converted torpedo carrier) and drop them, complete with their steel float tanks, into the waters of the harbor. But, we philosophized as we checked the outboard-powered dingy towing the pipes out into midstream, we've waited years for the Pamet Harbor job—a few more weeks won't hurt us too much.

So we saw the dredge that's going to do our harbor job anchored by the town wharf at Provincetown when we went over to Beachcombers last evening, and, sure enough, down at the Depot this morning we noted that the pipeline the contractor had assembled on the clam flat area had been towed away—but there were sundry left-over sections and flotation tanks piled by the old railroad right of way, a promise, as it were, that the dredge would soon be back.

So its a toss-up as to whether they'll by playing ball at Snow's Field this morning—one minute the weather is black as Teet Newcomb's derby hat, another the sun tries to peek through. And the sound of traffic on the highway across the hills is pulsing, steady, indicating enough volume so good Chief Berrio, who had been in his office doing paper work (two accidents in town yesterday) reluctantly cut off his conversation with us, piled into the new cruiser and hied off to traffic duty. "I'll be the happiest man in the county, come Labor Day," he sighed.

At the risk of attracting an errant summer visitor to the venerable building, we're composing our weekly prose with the doors wide open; momentarily we expect to see a car drive up, see be-shorted, camera-armed folks climb out, hear their muttered, "this must be a church—but what's with the typewriter?" and answer the perennial questions in our best, most unctuous Town Father style. "No Marm, this here's the town hall . . . Never WAS a church, but it was, at various times, a shoe factory, and a factory for the making of Panama hats—built around 1840 or so—although the town of Truro was settled in the last decade of the seventeenth century, incorporated in 1709.

"That map on the wall? Why that's Graham's map of 1833—shows the extremity of the Cape at that time—notice how the landlocked body of water we now call Pilgrim Lake was once an open harbor? Truro Synagogue? Sorry, sir, that's a misnomer. What you have in mind is the first synagogue built in the United States, at Newport, R. I., by one Rabbi

Touro. Similarly in the two names causes the confusion. Populated? Native, year round, something over 1050, give or take a few—but we estimate summer brings us a five-fold increase. No, the winters aren't too bad here. Lots of wind, but actually we enjoy a maritime climate; temperature usually reads eight/ten degrees higher here in cold weather than it does in Boston, directly across the bay.

"Center of town? Well there really isn't much of a center: fillin' station, general store, post office, liquor store, doughnut shop where they make handcut doughnuts, library, fire station—that's about it. You're welcome. Drive carefully, the traffic's heavy today."

But no visitors arrived. Only the relaxing gossip of the birds in the pine copse below the hill to be heard—and the faint whine of cars on the highway, and just now, the mellow pealing of the bell at the Congregational Church summoning the faithful to worship. And the wind is sou'west, light and fitful, and the clouds keep thinning and massing up, and a blue fog-mist clings to the distant hills, and we dassen't say more about the sun than to predict if she does come out, it'll be hotter'n we want it to be.

Made our usual afternoon trip down to the harbor this sunset-time, found the sand piled against the parking lot bleaching in the sun. Noted the discharge line again aimed at Gull Island, with the dredge Seapuit resting in the basin against her chores of the morrow. We hear tell the town fathers will request the Division of Waterways to alter the dredging contract so's the Seapuit will suck sand only to the mouth of the channel, then complete her job next spring, after the winter storms have had their fling at the sand bars that block the entrance. Meantime, Capt. Scott proposes to truck his dredge over the road to Chatham, for his next job. It appears he dassent tow the craft around the tip of the Cape, since she's far from sea-worthy. All the sidewalk engineers at Pamet Harbor are standing by to see how the Seapuit will be dismantled for the journey over the road.

It's always pleasing to hear the reminiscences of an older person on the subject of such an important project as the dredging of Pamet Harbor and yesterday we quizzed our friend Snowie on the subject. "Yessir, I was ten years old at the time they did the first dredging job down here—that would be in nineteen-twenty—and I remember goin' aboard the dredge for an occasional meal. Wonderful food, as I recall. Big dredge did the job—hydraulic, she was, able to suck prob'ly five times what this little cuss is doin'. The crew, on the off-shift, used to live up to the house formerly owned by my late Uncle Norman on Castle Road. Never forget the day they broke through the channel bar into the open bay; all hands got intoxicated, and they had turkey aboard the dredge.

"And shortly afterwards the Iris, suspected of being a bootlegger, came into the harbor, and she grounded out on the shore, and she was about the biggest craft ever to use the basin. And some time later my late grandfather, C. W. Snow, who had disapproved of the layout of the channel, took a gang of men down to Pamet Harbor one moonlight night and had 'em dig through the isthmus that separated Pamet River from the South crick. Shortly afterwards the two streams blended, and the channel filled up, and the whole area lost its value as a harbor." Snowie swears the original channel was dredged to a depth of thirteen feet at low water, although the figure seems a mite big to us, remembering, as we do, the occasion when one of the Glass boys drowned in the channel in the mid-twenties. If memory serves, Seraphine Rego, then a surfman at Pamet River Coast Guard Station, reported the water, when he had recovered the body, at somewhat less depth.

And like most Pamet folks, we've changed our whole way of life since the dredge Seapuit started the Pamet Basin job. Time was when we'd close up shop at town hall, late of the afternoon, and head straight for home and family. Oh, once in a while we'd drop by Snowie's place for a quick chucker of cribbage, and, on occasion, we'd visit with Squire Fred Davis over on Holsbery Square. But for weeks, now, we find the VW heading almost of its own accord, down Depot Road way every afternoon. And once there, we find the regulars—Fred Sylvia and Donald Silva, and Donnie Noons, and Frankie Davis, and Isaiah Snow, and his brother Charlie (Pop would be there, too, except for his cracked ribs—but he's healin'—be back in circulation shortly) and many, many others. "Pumpin' like all get-out," Charlie Snow will say, if the dredge is spouting her usual stream of dirty discharge water on the spit of Gull Island. But, at the first unusual cough of the big twin diesels, every man at the parking lot rail tensed. Uneasy glances are exchanged, not a word is spoken until the even bark of the exhaust resumes. On occasion the engines will swing the dredge too far on a cutting sweep, and as the Seapuit moves ever so slowly beyond the point of maximum operation, all hands will commence to grumble. "He's takin' her over too far—she'll blow that discharge line sure'n shadbush." And like as not, WHOOSH, with a sudden, chilling roar, the big rubber connector will blow loose, there'll be scurrying of the crew on deck, the battered outboard skiff will fetch a man out to the separated pipeline, and Frankie Davis will cluck, "I knew dern well he was about three degrees too far south'ard." But yesterday when we dropped by for our daily inspection, only a few strays at the parking lot—the Seapuit pumping mightily on what they call the dogleg of the channel, and the boss man, Capt. Scott, set comfortable in his truck, munching on a sandwich and listening to the baseball game on his car radio. We. wish him well, despite his ruptured pipelines.

★ ★ ★

Gone is the fall foliage, except for a handful of faded, limp leaves on the locusts, and raggy, drab brown leaves on the scrub oak, and faded, dying embers on the huckleberry patches on the hillsides. Only show of color in our view is the young maple on the front lawn, which is shedding its big, yellow floaters from the top down, so's the top branches show bare and stark, like umbrella ribs. And the smell of fallen leaves is strong when the sun warms the nook between our place and Kelley's—almost a ferment, it is—and yesterday, while we were hanging the storm windows, we heard the sudden, brassy call of a cock pheasant in the alder copse; but his alarm was brief and shrill. He knew that hunting season is on.

It is with mixed emotions we view the town this weekend of Halloween. Perhaps it is because folks were baffled about the exact night for the observance of the spooky holiday—we had tiny callers at our door last evening and again tonight, and the grownups had their party as early as Friday night last. In any event, we're thankful to be able to report that vandalism and dangerous pranks haven't—up to this writing—been in evidence. True, there was a sad-looking dummy hanging from the library flagpole this morning, but that's the only sign of Halloween activity we've seen. Nary a soaped window, nary an up-ended privy (where in heck would you find one, nowadays?), nary a greased door step. Over in Wellfleet, it's reported, there was considerable nocturnal activity—property damage, trees cut down and laid across public ways, if our information is correct.

We got to talking with Snowie on the subject when he dropped by our house after his Sunday stint at the fire tower today. "Seems to me we hit a sort of happy medium back in the good old days when we went out of a Halloween night," he opined. "Lots of good, clean fun, but very little destruction or spite work." We nodded our agreement. "And it was kind of a neighborly affair, too. None of the kids had cars in those days, and we were perforce limited to the area we could cover afoot.

"But there were always a few people that seemed to make good victims for Halloween pranks. Down Castle Road, I remember, we used to pick on Willie "Beachgrass" Hopkins, partly because he used to get real angry, partly because the pretty lady schoolteacher used to board at his place, and it was a chance to strike back at the authority she represented. One night my cousin Clayton and me, and Georgie Paine snuck over to Willie's and smeared his back door step with axle grease and rigged up a tick-tack on his parlor window. We hid in the lilac bush front of the house, and commenced to vibrate the tick-tack against the window pane with a piece of string, and pretty soon the back door opened with a bang, and Willie came charging out. He slipped on that grease and catapulted halfway across the driveway. Didn't hurt him any, though; Willie was a wiry cuss."

We learned only recently that yesterday marked the final day of our friend Snowie's work at the fire tower in South Wellfleet; and ever since, we've been disturbed by vague fears for our own safety. After all, the drought is still with us, and it would make us feel much more secure if we knew that Snowie still held forth atop his tower of steel, binoculars glued to his keen eyes, nostrils a-twitch for the first faint odor of smoke, guardian of the woodlands and the good folk of this Narrow Land. We called him to tell him how we felt. "Nice of you to put so much faith in me, O'Caghan, and I must say as how it's well-deserved. Ain't been a fire big enough to fill a teacup in this whole area that I haven't spotted since I've been on the job. But the boss-man says close 'er down, so last night was my last trip down the steel stairs of the South Wellfleet tower."

We asked him if he'd had any interesting experiences on the job. Indeed he had. "They range all the way from the ridiculous to the sublime," he said, shaking his silver-white mane. "Like, for instance, the time I closed up shop at six, sharp, grabbed all my belongings: lunch-box, and extra jacket, and water-jug and the binoculars that belong to the state (they require you to carry 'em home with you at night because they're too valuable to be left in the tower). And I dropped down through the trapdoor and let 'er down over my head, and gingerly fished out the key and locked the door behind me, and derned if I didn't drop the cussed thing—fell all the way to the ground, it did, and spent half an hour lookin' for it, but to no avail."

Snowie went on to say he finally drove home, and called up the boss warden, who lives up-Cape a bit. "And he told me that I'd better dern well get up there next morning and find a way to enter the tower, if I had to cut a hole in the floor with a saber saw." In preparation, Snowie, bright and early next day, fetched his black dog, George, up to South Wellfleet in his car; once there, he paused to give desperate, final instructions to the canine: "Key—key—key——" he said to George, clearly, distinctly, and George promptly sat down and commenced to dig at a flea behind his left ear. "No—no, George," Snowie said and, pointing to the grass patch under the tower, "Sick—sickem—sickem—" and George extended his big, pink tongue and licked everything within reach, Snowie's outstretched hand included. "Why you dumb animal, I oughta ship you back to Phat Francis where you came from," shouted Snowie, and he raised his lunch-box in a fit of anger and flung it in the direction of the tower. George, quicker'n you could say Obadiah Brown, dashed after the box, and Snowie, of course, dashed after George. They arrived in a dead heat, and in the subsequent struggle, the sandwiches spilled over the ground, and derned if Snowie didn't lay his hand right on the missing key.

Tote out the portable typewriter, set 'er up on the kitchen table, make a sandwich of onionskin and carbon paper, fetch out a block of scrap paper and a sharp pencil, assume the expression of the reporter hard at work on a Sunday morning: pursed lips and squinted eyes, and furrowed brow. All bespeaking inner turmoil as we attempt to gather notes for our weekly column. But the muse will not be wooed—so we open the kitchen door (in direct contradiction to the order of our good bride, who points out that errant drafts are wont to sneak in through the combination door. "Working for the oil-men, are you?" she usually adds). But mother has gone to late Mass, so we pull on the inner knob with a devil-may-care-flourish, and pause for a bit to examine the valley.

This morning, we find, a feller is well-advised to add a bit of love to his description, for the sky is gray and threatening. You have the feeling you're looking at the under side of a big pan of gray biscuits, spread from horizon to horizon. And there's not enough breeze to stir those clouds, just a mite of a breeze that touches the dried seed-pods on the locust, setting 'em in slightest motion. Grass is still green, to be sure but the hydrangea foliage has turned that leathery, funereal sepia-almost-black that bears witness to the recent hard frosts.

Against the drab background of the cattails and the meadow grass, the clump of redberry below Bill Bloomberg's glows like dull red coals above the slate-gray of the loop of the fresh crick. And there's a windrow of fallen maple leaves still marking the base of our post and rail fence, brown and withered, and the patches of brown on the hillside of Dyer's Range almost balance the spread of the bottle-green scrub pine. Temperature in the mid-forties, but it feels colder. Our Phillips barometer reads 29.8 and it refused to budge a whisker when we tapped it with a gentle forefinger. Nary a sign of life on the meadow—usually there's a big, white-tailed hawk soaring the air currents above the river—and not even a car has driven up our road in the past hour to disturb the quiet of this Sabbath.

It's been a long time since we've raised our voice in protest to something. We're not referring to big issues, like local politics, or dress codes for school students, or beach stickers. We aim much lower. Our complaint is lodged against the over-worked word, the cliché, the tired idiom. Some years ago it was the adjective fantastic—the word was used so frequently it lost its true meaning. So and so has a fantastic appetite—a beautiful sunset would be fantastic—and, of course, the performance of any given automobile would be fantastic. Next came the suffix, wise. The expression was supposed to have originated with the hucksters of Madison Avenue, but it received almost immediate acceptance by the man in the street. "Price-wise it's fantastic," you'd hear a salesman croon. Or, "Voice–wise a Mario Lanza he ain't." The latest overworked adjective in our vocabulary is the word knowledgeable. We've heard it applied to dumb animals, individuals with an IQ of 67, even to geniuses. Our dictionary defines the word as "possessing knowledge or understanding" but present usuage has given a positive quality to the adjective that far exceeds the true definition. If you're on the dull side of the IQ spectrum, for instance, it should be explained in just what area you're knowledgeable—and why—otherwise, somebody'll assume you're bright.

The clan O'Caghan got to talking this afternoon at the dinner table about architects and their work. It all started when our good bride mentioned that Our Lady of Lourdes Church in Wellfleet was crowded every Sunday. "Getting too small, it is, for the congregation. They'll have to build a new church before long." This brought the observation from No. 4 son, Geof, that he'd read where some prominent churchmen were objecting to elaborate physical plants for churches—cost too much, detracted from the audience attention to the preacher. We took the opportunity to spin a bit of a yarn anent the subject. "First architect ever did a job in Truro of any consequence," we commenced as we sliced some more roast beef, "was George Clements, from up Yarmouth way. He had drawn the plans for the remodeling of the old Pamet River Coast Guard station—which Alfred and Lily Marx had converted into a beautiful home—and when the town voted, in the mid-thirties, to build a fire station in Truro Square, the supervision of the project went to Mr. Clements. . . ."

"Pass the cauliflower, please," said No. 3 son, Mike. "Nowadays," we continued, unflustered by the interruption, "we think in big figures; probably cost us as much to shingle the fire station as it did to build the whole cussed thing back in the old days—but no matter. Total contract, as we recall, was $1,500. Charlie Joseph and Manuel Dutra won the contract, and shortly after town meetin' the job began. The site—directly across from Cobb Library, as you know—had been nothing but salt meadow, under water at every high tide. But volunteer firemen had carted hundreds of tons of sand down from Arthur Joseph's sand pit, abreast the Catholic church on the hill, and the locus, theoretically, was ready for the building." "Condiments over here, please." Mike had taken advantage of a brief pause in our conversation while we split a baked potato, preparatory to burying a pat of butter in its innards. "Charlie and Manuel had bored down through the soft fill and had planted some long cedar posts that, in theory, reached hard-pan, below the mud in the salt march. Down went the heavy sills, hard pine, four-by-six, spiked to the pilings; up went the corner posts, and the studs, and the plates; roof rafters and sheathing, and shingles and trim, and brick work—" "Dessert?" this in a sotto voce from No. 2 son, Terry.

"But when it came to installing the front doors, Charlie and Manuel ran into difficulties. Clements had designed the building to resemble, as closely as possible, a Cape Cod cottage; the front of the building had two multipaned windows framed into shingled panels which were intended to flip overhead, on big pivoted hinges, at a finger's touch. But to locate the center of gravity for the heavy doors required more titillating than the adjustment of a railroad watch. First time the doors were tried, light-weight John Lucas was snatched off his feet and near catapulted over the roof. And when the fulcrum point of the hinge had been relocated, it required the combined strength of Charlie, and Manuel, and Henry Hanson to pry the door open. At long last, however, the doors were balanced, the fire apparatus and the ambulance were duly installed in their new quarters, and the building was informally accepted by the building committee.

"But in the ensuing months, insidious forces were at work under the building. The sand slowly settled, sills sank into the mud, raw, unsightly gaps began to appear in the knotty pine finish of the interior, and the famous Clements door began to jam. On more than one occasion, it was necessary to start up the fire engine, when a call came into the station, put the truck into first, nudge her gently against the big door, and use the power of the Brockway truck to open the door."

"So what's that got to do with architects?" queried Mike as he poured himself a glass of milk.

And it's ashamed we are to admit that, up until yesterday we hadn't a smidgin of Christmas spirit. A year ago this time, we had sat in for carols at the Universalist Church in Provincetown, throwing our cracked bass at the trompe d'oeil plastered walls of the venerable building while Paul Nossiter's girl angels from Sea Pines School blended their own alto and soprano tones. And we got the spirit. And yesterday noon, as we were saying, comes a card from Nanna Moynahan, one hundred two years of age, from her present home in Long Island, and the picture of that grand lady, and the memory of her Irish wit and her strength, and her loyalty of a sudden made us feel warm all over. May the good Lord hold you, Nanna, in the palm of his hand.

NINETEEN SIXTY-SIX

1 9 6 6

Except for our own South Pamet Road, where the exposure is northern, the errant snowflakes of yesterday and today have made little impression. But here, of course, we're in the lea of the range that guards the valley, and the sun can't reach into the shaded areas, so we're usually the last spot in town to say good-bye to the winter frost. Speaking of snowflakes, we've seen every variety of the white stuff since yesterday morning: tiny round hard pellets when the wind was nor'west and the temperature was in the low twenties; and then a shift of wind to the east'ard brought the true, crystal flakes in from the ocean. And this morning, with the wind again blowing in from the bay, those big, lacy fellers that seem so reluctant to land on the white expanse of the countryside. The sun is bright, albeit there are a few maverick clouds to blank out its light every so often and the temperature is a comfortable twenty-six, and the Phillips barometer is on the rise.

Out of doors there's a clean, sterile feeling to the air, and the birds are in fine voice. At breakfast time we heard a pair of jays scolding the juncos in the backyard and all in all its a fine day, surpassed only by last Thursday, the memory of which is still with us. We single out that portion of the day when we drove in to school at Provincetown betimes, when the sun peeked through a morning cloud cover to focus on the ramparts of High Head and the dunes eastard of Pilgrim Lake. What would have been only a beautiful morning became breathtakingly so when a sudden puff of wind raised the loose snow on the lake's surface so that, for a brief moment, a churning, fog-white mass swept over the ice, masking the sight of the eastern sand hills. Then, as suddenly as it had arrived, the squall abated, and the sable dunes came clear to view, each clump of beach grass etched against its background, and the crescent stretch of Provincetown clamored for attention from the left window of our faithful VW.

Our new pup, Le Duc, is in the one ear up, one ear down stage. We've managed to extend his night's sleep to somewhere in the neighborhood of five a.m., at which time the poor feller gets so lonesome we just have to bail out of bed, remove the barrier that restrains him to the kitchen area, and brew him a pan of warm milk. Then we have a long conversation, punctuated by a bit of ear-scratching on our part, a mite of gnawing of our slipper laces on his. And then the family cat, Punc, appears on the scene and gets chased behind the refrigerator, and so begins our day.

A bit of conversation with Snowie led to a discussion of eels: their preparation for the frying pan beginning obviously, with the skinning. We agreed with Snowie that the late George S. Williams was about as fast and neat at skinnin' an eel as any person we'd ever known. We can see George now, cigarette dangling from his lower lip, neatly clad in denim overalls and jumper bleached almost white from constant scrubbings. George would dip one big paw into the bag and fetch out a squirming, slimy eel. "Catch him right behind the ears," he'd advise—although we never did manage to locate the eel's aural appendages—and then George would take a fresh grip with his other hand, this time using a pad of burlap to make sure of his grip on the poor eel's head. With his sharp knife, he'd neatly make a cut around the throat, slit it down just a mite in a southerly direction, then he'd snap the vertebra clean, and peel down the skin like you'd peel a banana. "Nothin' to it," he'd observe, as the white-meated, denuded critter wound itself around his wrist in its death agonies. Once in a while the skin would tear, or George's grip would slip and the eel's head would come loose, and the audience would utter an almost inaudible gasp of disappointment. "Must be gosh-derned Republican—they're slippery, you know," is the way this bedrock Democrat would explain the mishap.

Snowie was moved to add that one of the fine touches that makes an eel a delicacy is its tendency to indulge in reflex motion long after it has been skinned, and beheaded, and even cut up into bite size portions. "I've seen a healthy winter eel still squirmin' when it had been in deep fat long enough to turn it golden brown. Adds something to the flavor, it does, like sensing the squirm of a freshly opened quahaug on your tongue." Thank fortune its a few hours until lunch.

Biggest tides in a coon's age—the figure of speech is based on the four-legged mammal—have washed at the shores of the Narrow Land this past week. Over in Provincetown the water was bubbling up through the catch basins along Commercial Street, and here in Pamet we have it on no less an authority than friend Snowie of Castle Road that just yesterday the tide rose chock to the back door of his home at Slade's Landing. Washed out a portion of Snowie's retaining wall, it did, and fair had him boxed in his own dwelling for an hour or so at full flood. "I got up during the night to see if the nocturnal tide would be higher, but, except for some good-sized waves due to the high wind, it was a rather disappointing anti-climax," he reported.

And then we got to reminiscing (this was after church this morning) about big tides we'd known. Like the one that washed out Naylor Hatch's dyke, between Peggy Malcolm's property and the old town pound, off Depot Road. Or the memorable tide of 1910, or thereabouts, which made spaghetti of the railroad tracks south of Truro Depot. They still tell how Capt. Joe Francis, father to Anthony Phat Francis, realizing that the noon train faced disaster on her down-Cape trip, seized a pair of red drawers from the family clothes line and signaled the locomotive to a stop just above Grove's Crossing. Grateful New Haven Railroad officials rewarded Capt. Francis with a lifetime family pass on their line.

Yesterday, as we were working on some last minute material for the town report—cemetery trust funds, as a matter of fact—in comes Sergeant Don Belisle, of Truro's finest, to pass the time of day. Don was perturbed, and we didn't blame him after he'd shown us the clipping from a New England tabloid which vilified the minions of the law. "Tell the Fuzz nothing but your name if arrested," advised this article. "Cops are against the average citizen—they'll frame you in any way they can."

We offered our sincerest sympathies to Don. "This can only apply to the big cities," we soothed. "We can't imagine a citizen of this community using such language in reference to Pamet's men in blue." Don appeared to be momentarily pacified. "Your words make me feel better," he said. "But in this article they claimed that big city cops accept graft, fix tickets, use sections of rubber hose to extract the truth from suspects. . . ." We clucked our tongue in sympathy. "Not so here, Don. We know of not one member of the police department who'd use any such tactics to win a case in court." But the problem of enforcing law in the old days wasn't so simple. We're reminded of the roaring twenties; roaring they may have been for the big cities, but here in Truro, the problem of local law enforcement was based on the sale of alcoholic beverages, disturbing the peace, motor vehicle infractions, and an occasional case of wife-beating.

Old Joe Atwood, duly elected constable of the town, was the only peace officer in Truro. Joe used to pin on his badge, when called to duty, and fetch out his double-barreled shotgun, and tuck a fresh cud of chewing tobacco in his cheek, and hie off to the scene of the crime. They still tell of the time that Joe was required to serve an eviction notice on Anthony R. Phat Francis, postmaster of Truro, who was about to be deposed from his position, and whose lease, according to rumor, had expired. If memory serves, Phat was moonlighting in those days, working for Lane Construction Company on the new state highway going through Truro. In any event, Constable Atwood tucked the legal writ in his pocket, hied off to Long Nook where Phat was keeping the time sheets for Lane Company.

Discreet inquiry yielded the information that Phat was ensconced on the roof of a tar paper shack at the Lane sand pit. So Joe trudged over to the building and shouted up to the wanted man. "Come down, Francis, I have a paper to serve on you." "If you want me, come up and get me," was the Francis reply. So Joe propped his shotgun against the side of the building, and seized the rails of the ladder, and clumb up. But no sooner had his head appeared over the roof of the building then Phat aimed a kick at the old law officer, to such telling effect that Joe was knocked to the ground. Extra minions of the law were summoned, Phat was seized and carried off to jail, and in subsequent court action justice was served. But for some years thereafter, the office of constable almost went begging for candidates.

Nowadays, of course, as we pointed out to Don, we've enough men wearing the blue of Pamet's finest to apprehend a dozen Phat Francises. In place of the unwieldly shotgun that Joe Atwood used to carry, each member of the department sports a compact Colt .38 and a billy club, and a lever-type gadget that clamps around a criminal's wrist that, when his captor gives it a twist, will pulverize radius and ulna of the recalcitrant prisoner. Then, too, in the police supply closet, we've seen such exotic gadgets as tear gas guns, and sawed off shotguns, and riot sticks, and truncheons, and other unmentionables. "Never mind the newspaper article," we consoled Don. "Everybody loves the fuzz here in Truro."

Our dream, as we recall it this Sabbath morning, was about dieting. We were seated at the skipper's table at the Beachcombers Club, knife and fork clutched in our hot fists, napkin tucked under our chin, awaiting the first course of a heroic meal. Hovering over the big black range was none other than Howard Mitchum, tasting the savory soups and sauces, piercing a roast with the touch of a master chef. A hot fire blazing on the hearth, puffs of steam escaping from the kettles, mouth-watering odors permeating the club room, the pleasant clink of glasses blending with the swish of the tide under the pilings of the building foundation and a snatch of song, deep male voices accompanied by the twang of a guitar.

Comes genial, white-haired Snowie, bearing seared rib of beef, swimming in rich gravy; but as we reach for the dish, he snatches it away. "First we serve the skipper you pernicious, hungry nipper." And he scales the plate down-table to a leering Carl Black. Out of the crowd steps Charlie Schmidt, a platter of oysters Rockefeller in his ham-like fists. Our fork had time only to graze the crisp, grated-cheese-spinach covering of a bivalve when he snatched it away. "You'll not set a tusk, suh, in this fine mollusk." And so it went. The Malicoats, pere et fils, slipped hot, garlic-buttered Portuguese bread and slabs of golden cheddar cheese under our nose, and Eddie Euler gave us a smart rap on the wrist when we managed to get a grip on a chicken drumstick that protruded from a small mountain of sauteed mushrooms. He then deposited it before a smug, chuckling Bruce McKain.

And we'd have been sitting there yet, drooling, suffering, if Jim Forsberg hadn't reached out and tapped at the sacred brass bell that summons order out of chaos at the Beachcomber's. Of a sudden, the dream faded, all except for the harsh jangle of the bell. And then we felt a sharp elbow in our ribs, and the voice of our good wife grated in our ear. "Get up and answer the phone, before the whole house wakes up." So we rolled out of bed, and fumbled the instrument from its stand. "This is Ahl up to the plahnt," came the unmistakable Orleans twang of dispatcher Al Ducharme from Frank Joy's office. "Mind callin' Terry? We got a bit of a storm a-goin'." So we roused our No. 2 son, and packed him a thermos of coffee and a snack, and sent him out into the pre-dawn blackness to plow snow.

In the rays of the porch light, we saw the swirling, wind-driven flakes of a wet sou'easter settling on the rather considerable cover of white stuff. The thermometer stood even at the thirty line, and the marks of Terry's prints in the snow showed packed and mushy. We opined to ourself as how this'd turn to rain soon's dawn arrived (started to drizzle, it did, a mite later—after eight o'clock Mass, to be exact) and then we peered at the Phillips barometer, and tapped the glass, and noted how the hand dropped, just a whisker. And then we padded back to the kitchen and laid hand to the refrig handle, thoughts of our dream still passing through our mind.

And then a little voice spoke to us: "Don't forget, O'Caghan, you're going to lose weight—remember what the clothing salesman up in Hyannis told you when you tried to squeeze into that suit? Notice how the captain's chair sort of snugs up to your derriere? And how the faithful VW settles to port when you get behind the wheel? So settled for a meagre breakfast of black coffee, and a soft-boiled egg, and one of Dr. Hiebert's diet pills."

No. 4 son, Geof, was glued to the TV screen this afternoon when Snowie dropped by to challenge all comers to a game of scrabble. One of those nature tour programs had Geof's attention—the featured creature was the American bald eagle—and no sooner had Snowie spied the huge bird than he launched into a yarn. "You won't believe this, but. . . ." he began, as he slipped out of his great-coat. "Once when I was just a kid, prob'ly in my early teens, word reached my grandfather Snow that a big whale had come ashore up in South Wellfleet on the bay side. Grandfather was the only man in the county who had the facilities for extracting the oil from whales or blackfish, so he sent me and Uncle Isaiah up to fetch the carcass home."

There was a brief pause as Snowie and our child bride pawed through the inverted letter blanks to see who got first turn. We took advantage of the maneuver to fetch out the dictionary. Snowie is wont to attempt unheard of words, so the Webster is called in as arbiter constantly. "Drove up to about where the Dill family used to live, we did, and then we took a side road down to the shore, and Uncle Ide and I set to work on that huge critter, carving off slabs of blubber with the razor-sharp tools, loading 'em into the big double wagon. When we'd filled 'er chuck to the tailgate, we fetched out some grain for the hosses, and broke out our own lunches—high noon it was—and soon's we'd finished off the last of the cold baked bean sandwiches, we clumb up onto the seat and started back to Truro.

"It was warm, and the cargo smelled a mite in the sun, but the wind was blowin' toward us, so it wasn't too bad. Couple of hours later we were just drivin' along the top of Town Hall Hill past my grandfather's garden, headin' for the try-works, when all of a sudden I saw a monstrous, white-headed bird, wing spread must have been close to six feet, runnin' across the plowed land for a take-off." "Did you stand up in the wagon and salute, and whistle a few bars of the 'Star Spangled Banner?' we sneered. "I knew you wouldn't believe me—all's you have to do is pick up the phone and call Uncle Isaiah, and ask him to verify my story," screamed Snowie.

We refused to make the call, of course; best way we know of to torture this feller is to leave things hanging, something like dropping one shoe on the floor to heckle the person downstairs, or playing an unresolved seventh chord on the piano when you know a music lover is listening. We'll never know if Snowie actually did see an eagle that day in the distant past, or if perchance it was a giant crow with dandruff.

Another Sunday of blessed rain. Wind out of the sou'east, light and steady, and the rain comes in fine, small droplets that soak the green turf, and gather in puddles on the shining blacktop of the town road. Too, the rain is putting its magic touch on growing things: the reluctant buds of juicy pear seem ready to burst, and the choke cherry is likewise burgeoning, and the shapely maple on our front lawn shows the first fuzzy display of spring tassel on every whip-like branch.

On our way to town hall this morning, after eight o'clock Mass, we admired, through the rain-streaked glass of our faithful VW, the carpet of hog cranberry in the little saddle across from Hester Burn Callander's place—about where the old windmill used to be—and the bottle-green patch was dotted with tiny pink blossoms.

Usually, at this time of year, with the sun high in the sky, it takes an easterly wind to chill the air; not so yesterday. All day long the wind came from out of the northwest, a true cold Canadian air mass, as the meteorologists say—and a feller had to keep his jacket on for outdoor chores. We spent the day cleaning our cellar, carting off some things (reluctantly, we admit) to the town dump, moving such priceless things as a worn out lawn mower and half-empty paint cans and discarded furniture from one spot in the basement to another.

And then we moved our locus of operations outdoors and raked down the steep bank of the locust grove, making piles of brush and broken boards and bull briar so's we could burn it all come the rain. But today is the Sabbath, and Mother's Day to boot, so we'll have to forego the pleasure.

Much adult fun at the Beachcomber's last evening, where friend Snowie cooked the meal of beans and franks and salad. Never, in our opinion, did the plebeian kidney bean nor the lowly frankfurter, nor the ordinary table onion taste better. Perhaps it was due to the breathtaking view from the dining room window of the clubroom; mayhap, too, the appetite was sharpened by the titivating odor of fresh Portuguese bread warming in the oven, perhaps the brilliant conversation spiced the food. All's we know was that every bite tasted fine. Johnnie Alexander finally wheedled from Snowie the information that some of the more exotic ingredients in the green salad were fiddle fern, cattail roots, and Pamet dandelion. After the repast we joined several other members in an exciting game of darts, latest recreation at the club; haven't had such excitement since a horsefly got under the collar of Ezra Hopkin's nag, Sam, many years ago when we were driving down to fetch back the afternoon express. We lost a dime during the evening's play.

We were beset this morning by a brief, bitter-sweet moment of nostalgia, accounted for in part when we met some old friends yesterday, by the realization of our accumulation of years, but most of all by the day itself. And a typical Pamet summer day it is. A sou'west breeze sweeps the countryside; the sky is July blue, a bit hazy, with nary a cloud to blemish the view from horizon to horizon and the burned grass is straw-colored, and the locusts are unreal in their dress of palest green, and the scrub pine and the oaks and the alder and the rumcherry blend their greens in a most pleasing pattern of color.

But we found the scene reminiscent of a time some decades in the past. A scrawny, be-spectacled lad walking to the church on the hill, sporting a new cap purchased a few days ago at Matheson's dry goods store in Provincetown, walking into early Mass and popping into a pew, burning with adolescent embarrassment as John Gray, he of the beefsteak face, usher in those days, tapped us lightly on the shoulder and whispered, "Take off your hat, son." Titters of amusement from our neighbors, the Gray kids, and the Cabrals, and the Josephs and the Mooneys. The agony of sitting still while Father Dennis, in his faint Dutch accent, harangued the small congregation, the buzzing of a greenhead fly in the open window, and the ineffable smell of the hot sun on pitch pine and the tang of the salt marsh below the valley. The hypnotic effect of the guttering candle flames, the clang of the heavy brass altar bell at the climax of the Mass, the shuffle of feet and the muffled thud of the kneelers being pushed out of the way as the good father intoned the final prayers.

Then out into the hot July day, and the pause at the foot of the steps while the kids took off their shoes and stockings and felt the blessed relief of bare feet on the hot asphalt. Off with the suitcoat, too, and off with the choking necktie, and the casual exchange of gossip as we paced off down the highway with the other kids. At Dave Snow's Corner, pause while two of the Gray kids—that would be the Tooch Gray kids, Hattie and Daddy—played a simple game of snapping old maids pink blossoms. At the bottom of the hill, we stopped to throw sticks at Eben Paine's big, red pig in the basement apartment he occupied under Eben's shed. And a bit further along, all hands groped in their pockets for a coin to buy a gill of Turner Center ice cream at Austin Rose's store, end of Wilder's Dyke.

Eva Gray, the genial clerk behind the counter, allowed as how there'd be Eskimo pies in stock next week. And that's as far as our day dreaming took us this morning, because Father Evans arrives at church, beckons us into the vestry and briefs us on our duties as lector for the day. But after Mass, as we climbed into our faithful VW, we found ourself reaching for our shoelaces, and the feel of hot tar under foot glazed our eyes for one brief moment even as Johnnie Perry, the special cop on traffic duty, waved us out of the parking space. It's a glorious day, folks—wish you were all here to enjoy it with us.

Last Wednesday was a sad day for the O'Caghans. We stood at our kitchen door with an arm slipped around the rather generous waist of our child bride as the big yellow school bus rolled slowly by our door. And we remarked to her, "First time in twenty-odd years that we haven't sent a kid off to school on the bus." And then we both sniveled and wiped away a tear or two, and sat down to breakfast.

Big day for shellfish lovers when the town fathers opened the flats

Saturday. Ideal weather and a timely tide found several dozens of folks in pursuit of the soft-shell steamer on the bars of Pamet Harbor. We were working at town hall in the morning, catching up on our homework, and Selectman Vin Benson was likewise employed, and in came a trio of city folks in search of a license. After Vin had signed the permit with his usual flourish, up spoke the leader of the party. "What's a good time to go after these here now littlenecks?" "They're not littlenecks, they're steamer clams," explained the Town Father. "And when's the best time to pick 'em," persisted the city feller. "You don't pick 'em, you dig them," sighed Vin. He added, "And you'd better dig 'em at low tide, unless you plan to dive for them."

We tackled a job we'd been promising our good wife we'd do for lo, these many months this morning. Changed our clothes after Mass and trudged determinedly down cellar, where we surveyed the chaos of lumber scraps, and old clothing, and lawnmower parts, and plumbing material, and assorted paint cans, and hand tools, and flower pots, and scraps of wire, and fishing gear, and rubber boots, etc.

So slowly but surely, we worked our way across the floor, sorting out stuff that could be salvaged, toting the rest to our VW truck to make up a load for the dump. And what memories in the assortment of things we handled! Here a pair of snowshoes given us some years ago by the late Donald Pirnie. ("One of these days we'll have a big snow storm and you'll have to get to town hall for an election, or a wedding license, or some such," he advised us.) There a ship's adze—traded a bucket of sea clams for that, too—let's see, could it have been Howie Dickey's of Wellfleet? We sharpened it once, but when the chore was done, we had nothing that required adzing—if that's a permissible verb.

Roller skates, basketballs and a football in a limp state of deflation. Ice skates: could these have been the ones No. 3 son, Mike, was wearing that bitter cold afternoon when our dog, Dolce, broke through the ice out there to find the poor springer trapped in a narrow open pool, unable to clamber up on the jagged ice that surrounded him? How Mike slipped off his coat, grabbed the end of the coil of rope we carried, and plunged in after the dog? A proud father O'Caghan followed his son up off the meadow that day, to wrap boy and dog in a big blanket before the roaring fireplace.

Here's the chassis of the very first rotary power mower we ever owned. For years we'd hacked at the bunch grass in the cemeteries when the Memorial Day cutting was due, and slow and agonizing work it was. And then, one day we saw advertised in the Sears catalogue this new, magic, work-saving machine, guaranteed to cut grass of almost any height. So we stopped in Boston next trip we made with the ambulance, and fetched home the machine in back of the big white vehicle, and from the first time we used it we blessed it most sincerely. How's a feller going to throw away a relic like that?

Here's a pair of window sash originally installed in our house when Dave Snow did the remodeling 'way back in '42. We can remember Dave hanging the sash weights, tying each with a bowline. "That'll hold long's you live," he smiled at us around the stem of his big corn cob pipe. But we've since replaced the nine over six sash in the kitchen with a big multi-pane window, so's mother can look down in the meadow while she washes the dishes. So back in a corner go the windows. How could a feller throw them away?

Back in the days when we used to drive the Lower Cape ambulance, we'd slip behind the wheel of the big white Caddie at a moment's notice, any hour of the day or night, and hie off to Boston, or Fall River, or Providence, quicker'n you could say Obadiah Brown. But since we've retired from that job, we've become a real home body. It's been more moons than we can remember since we've spent more'n a day away from our bed and board, so if we dwell a mite on our weekend trip to Westfield, Mass., there to visit No. 1 son, Ranny, and his bride, Maureen, and their two kids, Mark and Meredith, we hope you'll forgive the personal quality of our remarks.

"Throw a clean shirt and some underwear and socks and your razor and toothbrush in a bag, and wait for me in the car; I won't be a minute," instructed our wife. Three quarters of an hour later as we were dozing over some dreamy music on the car wireless, the door opened, and in jumped Duke, the black police dog. "He's going to board at the vet's in Eastham, while we're away," explained Anne. "And I'm a few minutes late because I had to write instructions to the boys about what to cook, and I had to see all the lights were off, and the thermostat set, and the TV unplugged in case of a thunder storm, and I put out some food and water for the cat—"

We put on our best, frozen smile, and muttered HMMMMM and backed the car out onto South Pamet Road. With a misty eye and lump in our throat we handed over Duke's leash to Dr. Schneider, and then, under the expert tutelage of the DeGroot girl we married some decades ago, we tooled the faithful VW along Route 128 to the Mass. Turnpike, and headed 'er into the sun. Shank end of the afternoon we arrived at our destination, smooched our way through the branches of the younger O'Caghan clan, went for a short walk while our school teacher son followed three football games on two wireless and the TV set. Back at the supper table Ranny asked us how we liked the winter home.

We allowed as how we'd always had a warm spot for Westfield, ever since the late John Dyer told us this town was the buggy whip capital of the world. "And our first bicycle was a Columbia, son. Notice as how they're still made right here in Westfield." Our good bride noted that she'd seen a big sign on a complex just down the road a piece that identified the place as the home of Stanley Home Products. In turn we pointed out that the boiler in our cellar was an H. B. Smith product, and Ran added that the Kellogg Brush Company was hardly a stone's throw from his house. "They make a fine hair brush, Dad. Better buy one and use it while you still have a few sprigs."

His snide remark made us stiffen, and we decided to put him in his place, but quick. "Easy enough to point out the big things about a town," we sniffed. "But how about the small items? Did you notice, for instance, that the squirrels around here—most of 'em—are neither red nor gray? They're almost black. Funniest critters we ever saw. And how about the front door steps on the houses; have you observed that they have castiron stringers, with plank treads and risers bolted to 'em? You didn't eh? Probably because of the big foundry business in the area."

And on Saturday we toured the countryside, and Ranny pointed out all the good trout streams he could find, and we clucked our tongue over the still-low reservoirs and the visible pollution in the Westfield River, and chuckled as our good bride braced her feet and emitted little screams as we rode down precipitous mountain roads. "My ears are cracking," she complained. "Too much smoking," we leered. And we ate too much, and the strange bed had us tossing half the night, and it seemed we hardly got there before we were saying, "Good-bye—see you all Thanksgiving." And never did the jeweled tracery of the Sagamore Bridge look more beautiful in the November twilight to a pair of Pamet travelers.

NINETEEN SIXTY-SEVEN

1967

We feel we've finally become somewhat of a local character when a letter addressed to "O'Caghan, Town Father" finds its way into our post office box here in Pamet with no questions asked. The letter in question is a nice note from one Dick Frizzell, Eastern Specialty Products, Inc., Boston, and North Eastham, who was nice enough to invite us to a forthcoming meeting of the Mass. Chapter of American Theater Organ Enthusiasts. Thankee, sir. Wish we could make it.

Nature has turned on the charm this weekend, as though to atone for the unbelievably horrible weather of the week past. The wind has gone around to sou'west, and the barometer is high and steady, and the temperature on our back porch reads a mild sixty-four. The sky is bland blue, hardly a wisp of cloud to be seen, and the countryside, in the bright afternoon sun, is breathtakingly beautiful. Recent rains have flooded the fresh crick so it overruns its banks all the way down to the culvert, and the grass in our valley will never be greener. Shadbush blossoms somehow have withstood the near-hurricane force winds and the driving rains of Wednesday and Thursday last, and today they are joined with rumcherry in delicate sheets of white on the fresh meadow, and on Dyer's Range, and in the nook between our place and Kelley's, and just about everywhere you look in Pamet. And the last of the daffodils add their bit of gold to the scene, and Japanese quince is in full bloom, but the lilacs haven't a prayer of blossoming before Memorial Day—things are at least a fortnight tardy on the growing season.

And we've heard more birds this spring than we can recall in many a year. This morning, as we were putting the coffee on to brew, our neighborhood was a riot of song. And as we stepped out on the porch to inspect the rising sun (almost in line with Mary Gray's house—'twon't go much farther north this season) we saw a tiny, ruby-throated hummingbird inspecting our child bride's bleeding heart in the perennial bed. Most welcome, too, was the absence of the dank, ocean smell that's been in the air this past week, and with the subtle odor of the land breeze we found ourself listening for the

234

boom of the foghorn from the Highlands, and when we didn't hear it we muttered a bit of a good riddance. And the locusts haven't leafed out yet, so we can still see portions of the valley that'd ordinarily be screened from view come this late of May, and what we see is good. Wish you were here, city folks.

We spent a pleasant hour with Uncle Tony King and his sister Carrie Williams (kinfolk to our child bride) yesterday afternoon. Uncle Tony is a retired contractor, born here in the Pamet Valley, who spent most of his adult life in Rockport, Mass. A man of good memory and subtle humor, he got to talking about his childhood in Truro.

"They talk about the kids nowadays bein' discipline problems as though all precedin' generations were angels. Well, they weren't. Least-wise, not my generation." We settled back in our chair to make some mental notes as Uncle Tony launched into a yarn.

"Nowadays, the kids concentrate on Halloween to raise the devil. In my day, we used to play most of our pranks on May Day. Guess it was because warm weather was comin' on, and the sap was stirrin' in the trees, and in young folks, too. This was long before May Day was celebrated as the birthday of the Russian revolution. In any event, I remember one May Day, we fellers—George Hatch, and the Joseph brothers, and I can't recall the others—why, we went up to the Congregational Church. It so happened that May Day fell on a Sunday that year and we noticed that they were having a sunset service in the church.

"Folks in those days used to stable their horses in a big, open shed just below the hill, between the church and town hall. We could hear the singin' from the buildin', and the music made a fine cover-up for our nefarious activities. Quicker'n you could say Obadiah Brown, we unhitched every cussed horse from his rig, and swapped 'em around—must have been three dozen of 'em. And when those folks came out of church—it was dark by then—why, they found strange nags between the shafts of every wagon. The mix-up was so bad that several families had to wait till the next day, when they drove down to Manuel Marshall's blacksmith shop, and asked him to help sort out the livestock. Manuel knew everybody's horse like he knew the palm of his hand." We clucked our tongue. "You don't look like such a hellraiser," we demurred, as we appraised Uncle Tony's pink cheeks, frank expression, honest eyes.

Yesterday morning we packed up our artist's brush and paint, and hied off to the salt crick, where we painted new numerals on son Terry's boat, which we beached at Snowie's Landing. As we traced the block letters and

swatted gnat flies and patiently bore up under the snide remarks of John
Jordan and Snowie (where's your tan, O'Caghan?) we noted that the
neighborhood was filling up with strange cars. Then we recalled that the
auction of C. Arnold Slade's personal effects was to take place up at the
homestead. Several folks asked us if we proposed to attend the affair and
make bids on the furniture or the canvases. We begged off, claiming a
dislike of crowds. Actually we opined that the auction smacked of a Roman
holiday. Without going near the place, we could picture stout ladies in
sunglasses overspreading canvas chairs, munching the caterer's sandwiches
and snuffing out cigarette butts on the once proud Slade lawn.

We never hope to accumulate many worldly goods, but if fortune should
shine on us, we propose to follow the example of the Egyptian Pharoahs
and take our precious belongings with us. We're going to drag our
hammond organ out on the back lawn, and surround it with our bride's
handbraided rugs, and heap on our French books and our mortar and pestle
and the wooden coffee mill, and our imported English steel carving tools
and set 'em all afire. There'll be no auctioneer's gavel pounding on our
acres, if we can help it.

And what a fine Sunday afternoon of late July is this'n. Warm: temperature in the mid-seventies, wind strong and steady out of the sou'west
making the locust toss, twisting the foliage of the maple tree so the obverse
shows in duller green contrast. There's a blue haze in the sky, and a light,
wispy veil on the hills across the valley. And the smell of growing things is
in the air, and we're glad we cut our own lawn this morning because the
ineffable odor of the clippings comes to us through the open windows.
Honeysuckle is in full blow, and the ivy geranium on our porch adds its
dash of color to the house, and, except for a touch of mildew on some of our
ramblers and our shrubbery due to the recent damp weather, the bushes
look lush as ever we've seen 'em. The cigar-shaped seed cases of the cattails
are turning brown, and rumcherries have reached full size, waiting for the
sun to give them their characteristic red color, and the marshmallows up by
Bound Brook Island are in flower. Sedge grass in the salt crick is
burgeoning, making cover for the unsightly drift of winter and the bare
peat banks, and the fallow garden sites in our neighborhood have produced
goodly crops of hay, but there's no one these days to cut 'em, alas.

Never have we seen the local business spots busier—Joe Schoonie's, and
the post office, and Mary Howard's, and Win's hand-cut Doughnut Shop,
and Charlie West's Mobil Station, and the local liquor emporium of Joe
Duarte. The call of the cash register is in the land, and all we need is good

weather from here 'till Labor Day to make up for a rather slow start.

We got to thinking yesterday, after we'd been pushing our lawn mower for several hours, about the soft drinks of yesteryear. It's possible, of course, that memory favors those sweet, vari-flavored, carbonated concoctions; and we've heard tell that there are more taste buds sensitive to sweets in a child's mouth than in a grown-up's. But we maintain that the tonics—and we use the New England word purposely in preference to the rather sterile soda favored these days—the tonics, we repeat, had more variety, back in the halcyon days of our youth.

Remember what a thrill it used to be to slide back the wooden cover of Charlie Joseph's tonic cooler on a hot summer afternoon. You'd just come from swimmin' at the Depot, and the salt water had given you a terrific thirst, and the tar road under foot had cooked your bare feet, but the thin dime in your tattered, faded dungarees would buy a thick, man-sized candy bar and a bottle of pop. So you'd push aside the shaved ice (the Duarte brothers, Tony and Joe, had just made their afternoon delivery) and the assorted colors of the tonic caps would stare up at you. Ginger ale, golden, heavily-bodied, guaranteed to raise burps that'd tickle your nostrils and bring tears to the eye, a far cry from the tasteless, insipid stuff we buy today. And sarsaparilla, slightly medicinal, herb-like (Snowie always claimed his grandmother Snow could brew a similar tonic from local sassafras root), and birch beer, colorless, but zesty and full bodied, and an attraction in that era of prohibition because it contained the magic word beer. And lemon and lime, and grape, and cream soda, and the original cola.

And just about the time you'd forgotten the old favorite, Moxie, derned if the handsome young feller mounted on the white horse that was affixed to the gleaming Rolls-Royce chassis wouldn't drive slowly through town, and there'd be a run on that bitter, health-giving drink. And a few days later, when Ralph "PeeWee" Ormsby would beat all the boys his age in an underwater swim at Slade's Landing, the fellers would say as they shook their heads in admiration, "PeeWee's been drinkin' his Moxie." Gone, gone, the tonics of yesteryear. Gone with the giant, crisp pilot crackers that used to ooze peanut butter through the pinholes into your grubby hand, gone with the Oh Boy bubble gum, each piece big as a blind slat, capable of producing a bubble the size of your head. Gone with the coffee, fresh ground in Eben Paine's big mill with it's counter-weighted wheels so heavy they'd continue to spin long after the last bean had passed through the grinder, gone with the Post Master cigar two-for-a-nickel (C. Arnold Slade's favorite smoke), gone with the long rows of bulk cookies (finish off the pound with a dime's worth of Fig Newtons, Mr. Paine). But we become maudlin.

★ ★ ★

"Next time I stop in at my favorite Chinese restaurant in Boston," sighed Snowie the other day, "I'm going to look at their calendar—this must be the year of the earwig." Which is Snowie's rather obtuse but nonetheless picturesque way of saying that the Narrow Land is infested with that insect. It's the damp weather, of course. July, says the weatherman (as if we Cape Codders didn't know it) has been a record breaker for overcast days. And in this seventh month of the year, when the countryside usually looks like dry cereal and the cicada raises his metallic voice in the heat of mid-morning, things never looked greener. Ponds are up to their normal level, possibly a mite higher and on one of our motorcycle trips to Wellfleet last week, we noted that the roadside spring beyond Coles Neck Woods, just beyond the turnoff to the Wellfleet dump on Old County Road was flowing over the blacktop, something we hadn't noticed for years.

Speaking of dumps, Luke Wilson and Charlie Flato were at town hall the other day on other business, and both raised their voices in indignant protest over the sign that identifies the entrance to our own Truro dump. "Disposal Area indeed," sniffed Luke. "What's the matter with good old fashioned four letter words?" We hastened to explain that the town hall gang makes all our signs these days and the newly purchased sign machine is such fun to use, according to Supt. Joe Noons, Jr., that they lean to polysyllable words whenever possible. Matter of fact, John Perry who used to call himself keeper of the dump, now wants to be referred to as the custodian—of the town disposal area, of course.

We hear much enthusiastic response and promises of support for the newly-incorporated Truro Historical Society these day. Folks are saying they'll glean their attics for items of historical significance and help in other concrete ways, and we've made up our mind we'll donate to the THS our valued copy of Enoch Pratt's History of Eastham, Wellfleet and Orleans, published in Yarmouth, Mass., in 1844. Among the early law you'll soon be able to peruse from this yellowed tome are the following, as enacted by the freemen of our parent town:

1685. The Court passed a law to inflict corporal punishment on all persons who resided in the towns of this government who denied the scriptures. Also, that no minister in any town, should leave his congregation till complaint was made to a magistrate, and that magistrates should compel the congregation to do their duty. . . . This law made to enforce the comfortable support of those who labored in the work of the ministry. The Town voted that all the horses belonging to the inhabitants should be marked on the fore shoulder with the letter E, to distinguish them from those which belonged to inhabitants of the other towns, they having a different mark. It is also voted that all persons who should stand out of the meeting-house during the time of divine service should be set in the stocks . . . The Court at Plymouth shall hold three sessions each year, for the trial of cases civil and criminal, composed of the Governor and at least three magistrates, while the selectmen shall try all cases under forty shillings . . . from which appeals are allowed.

1667. The town voted that every housekeeper shall kill twelve blackbirds or three crows, which do great damage to the corn.

1680. Complaint was made that the Indians did great damage to the town's commons by cutting pine knots (for the purpose of making tar) and other timber. The town ordered that no Indian shall cut pine knots, or wood or timber, on the said commons.

1694. The settlement of Truro was commenced by emigrants of this town. Stephen Hopkins, supposed to be the son of Stephen Hopkins who came to Plymouth in the Mayflower, married Mary Myrick, 1667. He was one of the party who traveled into the interior around Pamet River, now Truro, to view the land, and endeavour to discover the inhabitants. Whilst wandering in the woods, they observed a sapling bent down to the earth, and some acorns strewed underneath. Stephen Hopkins said it was a deep trap. Mr. William Bradford, afterward Governor, stepping too near, it gave a sudden jerk up, and caught him by the leg.

This is a season of farewells—not only to the summer folks who are off to their city homes, but in our own household, to No. 4 son, Geof, who is starting his sophomore year at Nichols College, and to No. 3 son, Mike, who this week swaps his Hood milk uniform for Navy blues. Mike has been accepted for dental technician training on the West Coast. And it seems only yesterday we were worrying about bedrooms for our kids, and quiet corners for them to study. This winter we'll be rattling around in this big house of ours. And who's going to beat out boogie-woogie on the Hammond while we're trying to compose our deathless prose, and whose going to mess up our workbench down in the cellar and keep us abreast of the trials and tribulations of the Boston Red Sox? For a while at least, no more toothpaste tubes strangled heartlessly around the neck, and no trail of soiled socks leading to the bathroom, and the gas tank of the VW won't be always near empty; but our heart will be just that. So we'll transfer our affection to big Duke, the black police dog, and rub his ears and tell him how we miss the kids, and we'll pray that the holidays will bring Geoff home and that Mike's two years in the Navy will speed by.

We got to thinking, as we slipped a new blade into our safety razor this morning, about some of the barbers who've practiced on the lower Cape and about things tonsorial in general. Seems a shame that Truro can't support a good barber these days; time was when each of the villages had a barber chair. Louis Gariepy, mild, quiet man with the strong accent of his native Canada still in his speech wielded brush and razor down at North Truro, while Charles Myrick, a city feller from up Chelsea way, held forth in his combination notions store-barber shop in Truro Square. Charlie Mike, as he was known to the local trade, was a grizzled talkative feller of deliberate motion; wore steel framed spectacles that perched down on his nose, and walked about his shop with a plodding, heavy step. Come night, after the evening mail had been assorted, Mike would shoo the loafers away from the well-whittled bench out by the back door, and then he'd stuff the day's receipts into a paper sack, and lock up the tiny building, and trudge off down Castle Road to his home near Snowville.

Charlie Mike had learned his trade in Boston. Good man with a pair of hand clippers, was Mike, albeit those cussed things used to nip at the sensitive hairs back of your neck; and if you jumped a mite in the ancient cast iron chair, Mike would lay a heavy hand on your shoulder and blow the loose hair off'n your neck with a breath that was redolent of the odor of onions, garlic, or fish. You could always tell if Mike considered you on the threshhold of manhood, for during your haircutting session he'd peer through his bifocals, tweak the end of your nose a bit, and ever so gingerly snip the hairs away from port and starboard nares. The tiny back room shop boasted a fly-blown mirror on the wall, and the aforementioned antique chair, and a tiny shelf on the wall with the tools of Mike's trade—clippers, combs; a fancy cylindrical brush used in subduing the pompador style haircut, several bottles of slickum and bayrum. On the wall, a gray, sour-smelling towel, and, on an adjoining peg, a big drop cloth in fancy gingham pattern. We remember the ritual of the late summer haircut at Mike's place. Walk up to the sagging screen door of the shop and fetch a polite holler for Mike to step in from the store. Like as not, he'd be serving up some ice cream to a customer, but in due time he'd come shuffling into the pleasant gloom of the shop. Meanwhile, you'd slipped into the chair and then Mike would shoo a fly away with his towel, perform brief ablutions at the rusty iron sink, dry his hands, and reach for his barber tools.

"Not too much off the top—and part her wet, kind of high, left side," we'd suggest. But our suggestion would fall on deaf ears. "This is the way I always cut hair back in Chelsea," Mike would point out. And Chelsea style we'd get, regardless of carnial contour, current style or personal preference. The only exception Mike would make would be when a youngster asked for a baldy sour. Then Mike would fetch out his biggest pair of hand clippers and shear the poor feller bald as a cueball in shorter time than it would take to say Obadiah Brown.

They say Mike's moment of glory came the day Elisha W. Cobb arrived in Truro for the dedication of the brand new, E. W. Cobb Memorial Library. As we mentioned before, Mr. Cobb was a local boy who had made good in the leather business up Boston way, and he had donated the library and its locus to his fellow townspeo-

ple. 1912, it was, and a hot summer day. Truro square crowded with humanity from all over the lower Cape—free music by the Provincetown Town Band, free ice cream from Charlie Mike's store, free oratory from a selected list of guest speakers. Mr. Cobb arrived promptly at ten, climbed out of his chauffeur driven Stearns-Knight touring car, glanced approvingly at the new building on the hill, then ran an exploring hand over his chin. "Guess I'll have a shave," he said to Charlie Mike, more a question than a request.

So Mike dusted off the chair, and broke out a new, fresh towel, and stropped his best straight razor until it was keen as a schoolmarm's glance, and then he dropped the chair back so's it was almost horizontal, and he lathered up Mr. Cobb real fine, and adjusted his bifocals, and commenced to scrape away at the Cobb beard. Quarter of an hour later, Mike wiped away the last of the lather, anointed the Cobb face with liberal splashes of bay rum, adjusted Mr. Cobb's big, four-in-hand tie, and whisked away the dust from the Cobb morning coat. Coin of the realm passed hands as Mr. Cobb gave himself one final inspection in the fly-specked mirror, and ran his hand over a glass-smooth chin.

"Fine job, Mr. Myrick. There's a chair waiting for you in Boston City Club any time you want to work there. Only thing is, you ought to know that barbers in the city these days don't stick their finger inside your mouth to stretch the skin around the corner of your lip—they ask you to run your tongue out yourself. Seems to be a mite more sanitary, don't you know." And off went Mr. Cobb in his Stearns-Knight, waving in friendly fashion to all the Truro folks.

NINETEEN SIXTY-EIGHT

1968

A mid-afternoon sun is pouring through the nine-over-six sash on our settin' room windows, and its rays pass through an assortment of our wife's precious bottles, giving a rather bizarre effect to the reflected light on the wall next to our Hammond organ. Pale acqua wash of the Buffalo Lithia water jug, bold amber of the Skilton, Forte Co., pickle jar, cobalt blue of the Jos. T. Brown Pharmacist vial—she'll have our windows so crowded, soon's warm weather arrives and she can go a-bottling again, that we'll be hard put to see out to the meadow. If we asked her to take out a long-handled rake and scratch through a tangle of roots and sod, and break her nails clawing up dirty old bottles, she'd have us in Second District Court before you could say Obadiah Brown, on charges of cruel and abusive treatment.

But the weather, as we started to say, is cold. And breezy-northwest, something in the nature of a branch-tosser, is the wind. And the temperature has reached a reluctant twenty-four above, and there she stays. Barometer is twenty-nine point five and falling a mite since morning. It's that time of year when a feller sees the sun high in the sky rising earlier and setting later each day and he expects warmer weather. Here we are, two months past the shortest day of the year, deep in the grip of winter; yet two months before the shortest day of the year—say October 20—we'd yet to feel a real cold day.

But perhaps we can explain it all away by saying Truro hasn't yet had its town meetin'; after next week we can look for a break in the weather. And the ground is rock-hard with frost underfoot, and there's a faint dusting of snow on our bank of the fresh crick. Out on the state highway this morning the bright sunshine reflected on the salt crystals left in the sand scattered by the road gang after a recent snowfall, and a million diamonds winked at us on our way to church. The sound of a car going up South Pamet was so alien to our ears we got up from our typewriter just now to view the phenomenon. And conscious of noises for the moment, we heard a jay squalling out on the meadow, and wonder of wonders, a plane roaring overhead, chasing the scattered clouds out towards the ocean. Wish you were here, city folks.

Coming back from church in Wellfleet this morning we were trying to ease our bride's nerves with inconsequential chatter (she'd taken the pledge against cigarette smoking some twenty-four hours earlier, and despite our offer to join her in abstinence from tobacco, we could sense her tenseness). "Biggest yellow perch I ever caught in my life came out of the east side of Great Pond there—measured something like 12 inches in length," we mentioned. Pause. "The one Geof caught three years ago could've eaten yours for bait," she snapped. We fished out a sour ball and pressed it into her reluctant hand. "Try this—lemon flavor'll make you forget the cussed cig–" An elbow in the ribs reminded us we weren't to mention the horrid name.

Down the north side of Great Hill we churned in the faithful VW, then abreast of Prince Valley Road we pointed out the cottage where Archie and Millie Holden used to live. "Remember how Archie used to swallow his cud once in a while, like a cow? He'd toss a handful of table salt down his craw to bring up the tobacc–" Another elbow in the ribs. Our good wife slides out the ash tray, eyes a particularly long, clean cigarette butt, then firmly dumps the container in the travel trash bag. "Don't forget this goes in the trash barrel when we get home."

We're atop Corey's Hill now, Truro village before us, town hall and the Congregational Church twin sentinels on the opposite hill range, the houses of Castle Road snugged in their nests of scrub pine and locust. "Look at that chimney over there," we advise, as we brake the car for our turn. "Someone's got a nice fireplace blaze. You can see the smo–" Again elbow meets ribs. Tires of the VW hiss in the sand of the ramp as we head briefly due east, and we find ourself staring with pardonable pride at our own fresh Pamet.

Truro town dump is the richer, these days, by well nigh a dozen old cars, carted to the locus by a local contractor from the Francis property in South Truro. Thus disappears from the area the informal collection of rolling stock gathered up over the years by Pamet's own Anthony R. Phat Francis. And the sight of these old vehicles—rusted to a scabrous brown, proud chrome radiator shells long since corroded away, headlamps reduced to sightless sockets—the sight of those brave old cars lying in the dump brought back a flood of memories.

We first knew Anthony Francis as the postmaster of Pamet, and later the proprietor of the Square Deal Store up the road just a piece from the square. Phat had been, from his early teens, an automobile buff. "And it wasn't because I was too lazy to walk, either," Phat was wont to say. "I just loved machinery, is all, and I wanted to get from one place to another fast as I could." And in getting from that locus to another locus, Anthony had acquired—and worn out—an unbelievable number of cars. They graced the back yard of his leased property below Manuel Marshall's place, and many's the local kid who learned to shift through the speeds of a transmission by making dry runs behind the wheel of one of Phat's cars. In those days cars had several patterns for the three-speed shift, a far cry from the standard shift range of the pre-automatic transmission era. The Buick, for instance, was the exact opposite of the standard shift. First was where high would be found in the standard, second corresponded to reverse, and high could be found at the standard first gear.

The Dodge, too, had a mongrel shift, and the Reo. And the Stutz? Why for goodness sake, the Stutz was a right-hand drive to begin with, and the gear shift was outboard of the operator, with a slot-and-tang lock arrangement that required more than a smidgin of skill to manipulate, although to tell the truth, Elizabeth Freeman, a lady school teacher from Wellfleet, could handle a Bear Cat like an expert. But we digress. In Phat's yard, as we started to say, lay the bones of many an ancient vehicle, sort of an elephant's graveyard, as it were. We recall some of them vividly: a Nash touring, formerly owned by a Mr. Paine, of Long Nook; a Jordan sport sedan, handsome car, a decade ahead of its day in style and performance, but given, alas, to burning out clutches.

An Autocar truck, cab-over style with a pancake engine so tiny you'd swear she couldn't pull a wood-tick off'n your neck. But she was geared low, as Phat used to explain, and if you weren't in a hurry, she'd get you there, and a decent load, too. And there was a Maxwell in one corner of the lot, and a Studebaker, and a Dort, and an Ajax (illegitimate brother to the Nash Phat used to explain). But Phat's old stand-by, the car he used for delivering telegrams about town and dashing off to Wellfleet or Provincetown on errands was a Model T Ford. But no ordinary T was this. She was underslung so she clung to the road like a panther and she had a distributor in place of the standard timer, and rumor had it she had a special gear ratio in the rear end that made her unbelievably fast. But the Ford had her weaknesses, too. Her front end, despite a set of Sears, Roebuck tension springs installed by her owner to eliminate the wobble of radius rod and pitman arm, her front end, we report, was loose; and her radiator leaked like a sieve. Ah, memories.

The sun is willing, but the sky, worse luck, is uncooperative this Sunday morning of mid-March. To be sure, the pale golden orb finds an occasional hole in the clouds to peek through, but it's more cloudy than clear. Warm though, a hard-to-believe sixty-two degrees on our back porch, and at eleven o'clock the thin red line is still climbing. Wind is from back of the hill to the south'ard of our house, so we can't tell whether she's exactly sou'west or sou'east, but if memory serves we noted 'er to be a bit of a bay breeze when we checked it down at Snowie's this morning. And the barometer's a notch or two over thirty, falling ever so slightly. Soft and damp the turf underfoot, and the stubborn, deep-buried frost patches are yielding up their moisture in tricklets on the blacktop of our side roads. There are a quantity of frost-heaves, too, on the highways, so's local drivers slow up a mite lest they bounce their innards out on the bumps.

And last week's torrential rain built up such a huge pond at the spot just below our house abreast Louise Fratus' place, that Joe Noons fetched his town road gang to the locus. Dug up the drain pipe under the road, they did, and found it plugged solid with willow roots. When the tangled mess had been cleared away and the pipe replaced, the area was dry as a square dancer's throat. We commend the highway crew on their good work. But about the weather—did we say we'd heard much loud bird song this morning? Kind of a spring sound to the call of sparrow and chicadee, in our opinion, perhaps a prediction of things soon to come rather than a contemporary report of the vernal equinox, only a few days away.

Yesterday afternoon we allowed ourself to be dragged from the comfort of our fireside chair by the blandishments of our good wife. "Put the book down," she wheedled, "and turn off the radio and take a walk with me up back near Baldy Hill. Do you good to get some fresh air in those lungs." "First off, you'll have to promise there'll be no foraging for old bottles in the woods," we hedged. She agreed, so we slipped on a warm jacket, whistled up Duke, the big black police dog, and out we all went. Like Lot's wife of the Old Testament, our bride turned around before we'd even left the back yard. "Shame, how our house turns its best cheek, as it were, towards the puckerbrush, where nobody can see it." We allowed as how it was a shame—but we reminded her that all authentic Cape Cod houses were built with their front sides facing south, and let the roads and highways come where they will. "That way, you always got a good dose of sunlight in the original parlor and the master bedroom y'see."

"But the kitchen, where the poor housewife spends most of her time, is located on the dark, cold side of the house," complained our bride. "Maybe that's why most of the original houses had kitchen ells built on them." We cast one last glance at our home, and avoiding Duke's playful, mad rush at our shins, we paced off up the rather steep grade. Reached the first wood road that runs along our southern boundary towards Howard's place, we did, and turned east, heading for Baldy Hill. "There's the spot nephew Tommy Kane almost de-brained himself when he ran his sled into a pine tree," we puffed, as we pointed out a narrow, precipitous path through the pines. "And right ahead of us, you're reminded that there's a complex of road intersections that'll lead you to either the Meldahl-Young place or up to the state highway right abreast of Tom Hopkins' driveway, or over what we used to call Whiffletree Hill to the town dump, or down through Meier's Swamp to South Pamet, or up Lee Falk's driveway to Baldy Hill, kind of a poorman's Place D'Etoile."

But she wasn't listening; her attention had been captured by the glimmer of sunlight on a shard of glass half buried in the pine needles. And as for Duke, he was sniffing deeply at the rabbit run, and our geography lesson had been wasted. However, any pedagogue worth his salt doesn't give up easily, so we drew a deep breath and started off on another tack. "Right about here is where the big forest fire of 1927 burned when the southwest wind blew it across the old state road and chock to the ocean, back of Wells cottage. Lasted three days, it did, blackened hundreds of acres but fortunately only consumed one house, a summer cottage that had just been built by Ray Freeman, located about where the state highway garage is now." A clink of glass behind us, and we turned to find our child bride toeing a fractured Sloan's Liniment, circa 1890.

So we shared our reminiscences with Duke. "See that big tree overhanging the road there?" Duke pointed his moist nose at the pine in question. "Well sir, there used to be a big hornet's nest dangling from a lower branch that was most fascinating to observe, what with the hornets buzzing in and out of a tiny hole in the bottom. Many's the time we'd ridden up here with Waldo Brown in the truck wagon after a load of hay that was waitin' for us down in a tiny meadow just below the hill there. And one day Waldo couldn't resist the temptation any longer, so he reared back with a rock and let 'er go at the nest. Quicker'n you could say Obadiah Brown, the air was black with angry insects, and we had to whip the horse to a gallop.

"Are you listening, Mother?" "Hmmmmm?" she answered. "Would you mind running back and fetching my scratcher? I've just unearthed a Cheseborough and a Moses Atwood."

In the midst of our chores yesterday (we were cleaning the yard) we heard, through the thin, low-lying fog, the strident honking of a flock of geese, increasing in volume as the birds flew in from the south, reaching such a peak directly overhead as to cause our dogs, Mokey and Duke, to perk up their ears and circle the lilac bush, barking at the mysterious call of the invisible birds overhead. Kind of a sound that made us want to call out to neighbors George Morris and Jackie Kelley to find out if they, too, had heard the measured honking. But we settled by querying our child bride as she came out to drape some laundry on the clothesline. "Yes, I heard 'em," she sighed. "Before you know it, it'll be Fourth of July, and then Labor Day, and . . ." As if we needed reminding of the fleetness of this life—what with our birthday approaching within the fortnight.

Wellfleet, we submit, is regressing to the hoss, if not to the hoss and buggy days. We don't need to read the Wellfleet Town Report to learn of the equine population of our neighbor town. All's we have to do is drive up there of an afternoon and exert just a mite of peripheral vision. Before you can say Obadiah Brown, you'll espy a horse—big or little, brown or black, carrying some pink-cheeked youngster on its back or peacefully browsing in a pasture; dobbin is everywhere about the village. We hear tell the horse has become a sort of status symbol in Wellfleet—better your child should own a horse than have her coming-out party at Al Graham's waterfront complex.

And, as in France, where the farmer's importance in the community is judged by the size of his manure pile, the shellfish town is giving considerable weight to a man's social standing, using the "dressin" (a genteel Truro word) in his barnyard as a yardstick. Wellfleet, as it were, has gone off the shell standard—gone the days when a man used to point with pride to the mountain of oyster or scallop shells near his shuckin' shed, while a couple dozen herring gulls mewed their approval from the ridgepole on his house. Why, they've even got those fancy, streamlined horse trailers up there to fetch their animals back and forth to the auction rooms up-city way. A far cry from the good old days when a man figgered if you couldn't drive your animal home from the jockey's—another good old Truro name for a horse-trader—why the hoss wasn't worth owning.

Much activity at the town dump these days, and we note that what some folks throw away, others seem to gather up and fetch home. The other evening, for instance, we watched Duncan Young tossing a truckload of pecky-wormwood driftwood among the empty cans and broken furniture of bay four of the disposal area. And no sooner had he left than a well-dressed man who had deposited a meagre sack of garbage for the gulls to claw over—why this feller pulled out several rotten beams and hauled 'em back of the shed for salvaging. Freddie Sylvia tells us a man can make a few dollars just standing by with hammer and wrench to separate brass and copper from the appliances tossed away.

This is one of those mornings we have trouble getting going on our weekly prose offering. So up comes Dukey, the big German shepherd, to offer us his velvet-soft ear to rub as we fetch out typewriter and onionskin. "I'll help you with your column," he says, as we thread the paper into the faithful Royal and sit there, guessing at his thoughts. "Gray out of doors, as you can see without moving a muscle and it's been raining; flagstone on the back porch is slick and cold to the touch—and it should be. After all, the temperature must be down to forty-two, forty-four. Wind is out of the east. And mixed in with the smell of Mooney's new lab and Freeman Dodge's big red setter and Jack Kelley's dachshund, I can smell the brisk, salty tang of the ocean. If the windows were open a crack, you could hear the muffled roar of the ocean, too—stronger than usual, what with the past several days of an onshore breeze. Heard a cock pheasant a few moments ago, out on the fresh meadow. He seemed to be complaining about the fishermen who are strung along the banks of the crick, in search of the wily trout."

We were visiting the handsome frame Wellfleet school building yesterday afternoon, and we glanced around at the grounds. The well-trimmed lawn with that huge oak tree, good Lord, had it grown that much since we taught here? The steep grade of the blacktop road, where cars of the teachers and the school bus used to skid to a stop on snowy mornings. We owned the first VW among the staff, and the morning we churned up past all the other vehicles represented a minor satisfaction we still recall with a smile. The clump of pines to the north'ard of the school, where the kids used to sneak for a smoke during lunch hour. And the little clearing where we used to set up a plank and dissect animal carcasses as part of our biology program. No lab in the school, you see, and the classroom was too close to the cafeteria for the privacy we needed for carving away at dead rats and such.

Yes sir, we had an agreement with the late Col. Magee to pick up all the rats he could poison at his chicken farm over in South Truro. And every time someone brought in a fox carcass to town hall for the three dollar bounty we paid, we'd wrap the furry feller in a newspaper and tuck him away in as cool a place as we could find, and tote him to school next day. Sometimes the specimens would be in an advanced state of decay, and on those occasions the outdoor lab seemed particularly appropriate.

Never forget the weekend we had spent at Walter Horton's butcher shop in North Truro, pawing through his offal cans in search of choice specimens. Choice items of the lot were two cow heads which Walter had neatly severed from their owners' bodies with one skillful blow of his butcher knife. We wrapped the heads in newspaper, tossed them into the back seat of our car, and bright and early Monday morning, we toted them down to our homeroom. A basement room had once been used for home economics, hence it still had a sink connected behind the teacher's desk. Got a piece of burlap from the custodian, Cliff DeLory, we did, and propped the two heads in the sink, and covered 'em over neatly with the burlap. Shortly afterwards the kids commenced to straggle in, while we did our morning chores—checked the register, filled in a few blocks of our lesson plan book, sorted out our dissecting tools. As each kid entered there'd be a sidelong, curious glance at the shrouded objects in the sink. But Wellfleet kids are notoriously polite and not given to asking questions, so we weren't queried about the mysterious lumps under the burlap.

First bell rang, and we stepped out in the corridor to check against any last-minute arrivals. As we did so, one of the young ladies in the first row (could it have been Ned Lombard's daughter, or perhaps Carol Daisy? Derned if we remember) she quick tiptoed up to the sink, seized the corner of the shroud, and pulled it aside. There, side by side, were the two bovine heads, bloodshot eyes popping from their sockets, rubbery nostrils dilated, tongues hanging from the open jaws. Several of the girls liked to swooned, and there was a collective gasp from the entire room.

It wasn't until Alfred Pickard, class expert at dissection, started to work on the heads that the tension eased a mite. "Grab them horns there," said Alfred to his assistant, "while I saw the top of the cranium off." And saw he did, neatly and expertly, with a hack-saw he'd borrowed from custodian DeLory. "Now we'll take out the brain," said Pick, and quick as a wink, he did just that. "And I'm ready to bet," he continued as he lay the organ on a board, "it's about as big as any in this group."

Well sir, our head's still buzzing from the excitement of the wedding of our No. 3 son, Mike, and Carol Souza of Provincetown. To begin with, we couldn't have had more beautiful weather if we'd paid a million dollars for it. One of those glorious June days, warm and bright and sparkling—and the guests all togged out in summer finery, and the bride and the groom, even if we do say so, handsome and manly. And Addie Gregory making beautiful music on the church organ, and Diane Brown from South Wellfleet sharing her glorious voice with us as she brought tears to folks' eyes with Gounod's Ave Maria, and César Franck's Panis Angelicus. Then off to Provincetown Inn and much fun and dancing and good food and good conversation. Lord, we're glad these affairs don't come along too often—we couldn't stand the excitement.

And we got to thinking, during the ceremony, of Mike when he was a little tyke: the summer afternoon when we were all swimming down at the railroad trestle—he couldn't have been three at the time—and the other kids were jumping off the bridge, so out he toddles to the splintery plank platform and jumps trustingly into the swiftly running current. Jackie Kelly helped us fish him out and tow him ashore, and derned if he didn't want to do the same thing all over again. And the time John Joseph was building the dormer on the south roof of our house and we both noticed the extension ladder vibrating against the gutter and up comes Mike, fetching a handful of nails to us. And the time we bought the new bike for Mike when he took over the paper route from an older brother; we hid the machine in the attic, but derned if Mike didn't stumble across it. He was nice enough, though, to feign real surprise when we rolled it under the Christmas tree. And watching Mike and his brother playing Little League ball at Snow's Field, and teaching him to drive the old Model A Ford, and the time he broke through the ice and saved our poor springer pup, Dolce, from drowning out there in the fresh crick, and the man talks we used to have when we were cutting cemetery lots together. And his Junior Prom and his first date, and the fun we had playing duos together on the battered upright piano. And proudly watching Mike playing the sousaphone in the Cape Music festival, and seeing him in his Navy uniform, climbing aboard the plane with a trace of mist in his eyes as he kissed his Mom good-bye.

And now he's a man, a husband and we hope some day he'll be a father—we know he'll make a good one. In the beautiful words of the marriage ceremony, may peace dwell always in your hearts and in your home; may you have true friends to stand by you, both in joy and in sorrow; may you be ready with help and consolation for all those who come to you in need; and may the blessings promised to the compassionate descend in abundance on your house.

It's always interesting to learn what other folks think about our beloved Pamet, so when Jimmy Matello, genial custodian of the Temple of Learning engaged us in conversation during lunch break the other day in school, we subtly sounded him out on the subject. Seems Jimmy had been assigned the job of driving the kids from the Veteran's Elementary School over to John Perry's Hillside Farm for a first hand look at the chickens and the livestock. "Had to stop at Beach Point and get my passport validated," teased Jimmy, "and I had to promise the customs inspector I wouldn't steal any shellfish or berries, or other edibles. So we got to the farm about nine o'clock and the kids piled out of the bus, and the Perrys took 'em around the premises. They saw the chickens laying eggs, and they watched Miz Perry sorting the eggs and packing 'em in cases, and then Mr. Perry turned on the automatic feeders, and finally they watched the hired man plucking fowl on a machine. Ingenious gadget it was, with rubber fingers on a drum, turned by a motor, so's it stripped them feathers, already scalded loose, clean as you could do it by hand.

"Then the kids went outside, and Mr. Perry gave 'em some carrots to feed his saddle hoss, but pretty soon the hoss got tired of the vegetables, so I offered him one of Ruth Wilson's fresh baked corn muffins, straight out of the Provincetown High School kitchen, and that nag devoured it instantly. Just another point to prove our food here at school is excellent." We agreed, of course; we had found PHS vittles superior long before they had received the stamp of approval from the Perry horse. And how, we wanted to know, did Jim find the other sections of Truro he'd driven through on the memorable morning. Corn Hill, for instance, which he'd seen from nearby Perry Farm. "So it's a hill," said Jim. "With cottages on it, and seagulls flying over it, sand, and beachgrass, and pucker brush, and lots of wind, probably."

How about the Pamet Valley—watering spot of North America, far's we're concerned—salt and fresh crick, and beautiful hill ranges both north and south, and neat, authentic Cape Cod cottages snuggling against the pine-covered slopes.

"Oh, I've been up your way on occasion—had my visa stamped for the extra territory. Just about get the car in high gear going up one road when you're heading back where you came from. Never did get a look at the ocean—where is it anyway? And I didn't see a fire plug, or a street light, or a sidewalk, or any other sign of civilization up there." We turned the other cheek. Long Nook Valley? Just another dry crick bed, according to Jim. How about the Highlands, known in Colonial days as Tashmuit, the very cradle of civilization in our town? Just a watered-down lighthouse and a golf course, sneered our janitor friend. But we had touched on an area that aroused his curiosity. "I am a bit curious about that big stone tower over there in the woods," admitted Jim, cautiously. "Brief me on it."

"Well sir," we explained. "That tower came from the old Fitchburg Railroad Station originally located on the site of the present North Station. When the old Fitchburg and Boston Railroad went out of business, the complex containing a big auditorium and two handsome stone towers was torn down. One of our Truro summer residents, feller name of H. M. Aldrich, stockholder in the company, asked if he could buy one of the towers. It appears he had a sentimental interest in the structure because Jenny Lind, the famous Swedish Nightingale, had sung her final American concert from the tower and Mr. Aldrich, so rumor has it, had carried the torch for her. The tower did pass into his hands for a token sum, and he arranged to have it dismantled, stone by stone, and freighted down to this beautiful, wild parcel of land he owned, located southeast of Highland Light. By gosh, down she came, on the old New Haven flatcars, and F. A. Days, contractors from Provincetown, carted the stones over to the Highland locus, and the Days' masons painstakingly put her together again, stone by stone.

"For some years thereafter, a feller could visit the site, and at one time you could climb the inside staircase and view the countryside from the top platform. And then the scrub oak encroached on the tower, and the staircases collapsed, and finally, the Air Force took over the area, and now it's off limits to the public. But Truro folks still insist that on certain moonlight nights, when the wind is just right, they can hear the soaring, beautiful soprano tones of a woman's voice coming from the direction of the Aldrich Tower."

We hear tell Pat and Oakey Souza have purchased the old post office building here in Truro center from Helen Richmond. Rumor has it they're going to raze the Civil War vintage edifice, grade the site, and build a tasteful, modest complex that will house some businesses and Uncle Sam's mail-dispensing agency. There'll be more than one moist eye in town as the dozers tear at the venerable structure—but common sense dictates that the old Wilder building has long outlived its usefulness. We suppose that all the old memorabilia have long gone from the former school: the tarnished brass clapper hand bells that used to summon the kids in from recess and lunch; the display board of exotic spices from every corner of the globe; wrought iron double desk frames (remember when Dave Snow sawed them in half at the request of the school committee? Seems they had come to the conclusion that the students did better at their studies if they sat solo).

Is it possible there'd still be a few of those hardwood block outfits up in the attic that were used to teach fractions? Or perhaps one of those long-snouted inkwell fillers? We'd be eternally grateful if Oakey could locate and donate to this dedicated pedadogue Bernice Francis' leather strap, the one with the holes that could raise lumps on a feller's palm the size of thick bites, or the rusty dipper that used to hang on a nail by the squeaky iron pump, or even one of the hand-forged spikes that we used to hang our coats on in the cloakroom. Keep your eyes peeled, Oakey.

Thirty-six degrees, reads the thin red line of the thermometer outside the selectmen's office window at town hall, but it feels warmer. Whether it's because we're well fortified against the chill by our usual breakfast of eggs en coquille and hot, strong coffee or whether we've subconsciously compared our own weather with what we saw briefly on TV this morning for the rest of the country, we don't know, but as we said before it feels warmer. We awoke several times last night to hear rain dripping from the gutters outside the bedroom window, to the accompaniment of the wind wailing through the denuded locusts and along the eaves of the house. Blue Monday, we'd like to call it, but it's not blue; rather it's a dull, lifeless gray, with a precipitation that's half mist, half rain scudding in from the ocean, and a lowering gray cover that masks the top of Dyer's range across the fresh crick.

And when we dashed out to our car with some of our town books tucked under our rain coat, the fine, driving rain sought out our exposed neck, and clouded our spectacles so's we could hardly navigate to the faithful VW in the parking lot. And just before we slammed the door behind us we paused for a mite and heard the muted thunder of the surf on the back side, and the dull call of the foghorn down at Highland. Nary a car did we pass on the way to town hall. Joe Schoonie's store complex empty as a discarded rubber boot, the salt Pamet at low tide, with bared brown sedge flats and scattered debris from the recent flood tides. Cobb Library in its coat of new gray paint staring with sightless eyes to south'ard, the empty windows attempting to focus in on the stump of the flag pole, crippled by the big blow of last month.

Lots of our friends and neighbors are down with the so-called Asian flu, and we got to talking about the matter with Wellfleet's Doctor Sid Callis at the annual meeting of the Lower Cape Ambulance officers at Provincetown the other night. Dr. Callis opined as how there could be a question about the infectious agent. There's always a bit of the good old fashioned virus around, and folks are apt to identify it as Asian or Hong Kong flu; sounds a bit more romantic and dangerous. He favors a later date for the arrival of the true bug—say January or February. We agreed it would probably be the latter month; it will probably time its arrival to coincide with the annual town meetin' of Truro.

Which reminds us—and we don't propose to be Gertie Gloom this Monday morning—of the so-called smallpox burial plots here in Truro. From the time we were knee high to a grasshopper, we've heard about the smallpox graves hereabouts. Old Ed Snow used to speak about them frequently. "There's one of 'em down to nor'ard, beyond Highland near East Harbor," he used to say. And then he'd squint, remembering, and, "One clear over t'other end of town, near the Wellfleet-Truro line, up near the Driver property. And there's a single grave twixt the South Truro

Cemetery and the old Snake House—now Waldo Frank's place—and then there's a whole family buried just beyond the Powers' place, on a little hill overlooking the Snake House crick off'n Holsbery Road. Every last one of 'em died of smallpox, and folks was afeared the bugs'd spread, so they buried the bodies away from all the homes and even the regular buryin' grounds."

The rules of good journalism say a feller should dig into the vital records of the town and find out what caused the deaths of these good people. But every time we've perused the old books, we've found such entries as general debility, inflammation of the bowel, old age, catarrh, and so forth. We're tempted to believe that there must be some other reason for these isolated internments. Fact is, some years ago we got to talking with our good friend, the late Arthur Cobb, and he told us of at least one case when common cussedness, compounded by economy on the part of one old Cape Codder, was the reason for a burial outside the usually accepted God's Half Acre.

"Well sir, this feller Cobb, he named all his children—boys, that it—names that began with an O. There was Onesimus, and Oren, and Obed, to name just a few. Came an epidemic of some sort one winter that carried away several of the Cobb children. And the old man, rather than buy himself a lot in the Pine Grove Cemetery, why he up an buried them kids right in his own backyard. Nobody said a thing, it being none of their business, but shortly after pore Miz Cobb, the mother began to suffer from fits of depression. Said she couldn't stand the sight of them little mounds in the back yard. So finally Cobb, he disinterred the bodies and had 'em put in the South Truro Cemetery." We can't vouch for the facts of Art's story, but we do know that one of the burial plots in South Truro is a Cobb lot, and that several of the small stones on the plot read—Oren, Onesimus, Obed.

But enow of gloom and pessimism. To all our good friends and readers near and afar, we wish a very Merry Christmas and a Happy and Prosperous New Year.

NINETEEN SIXTY-NINE

1969

Yesterday's storm cleared with all the classic weather phenomena that should have given us weather colder'n a whale's tail. Wind shifted around from southeast to northwest, barometer climbed about as quick as you could say Obadiah Brown from a twenty-nine reading to mid-glass; and the sun set with that pale, brittle yellow that foretells real cold. But not so this last Sabbath of the year 1968. Wind's been westerly all day long, and the barometer has inched up a mite more, and the sky, for the most part, has been clear. But the turf underfoot has softened from its rock-frost hardness of mid-week, and a feller'd dast leave the top button of his jacket open against the breeze, and at supper time, when we peered at the back porch thermometer, the thin red line stood at thirty six and seemed reluctant to drop any lower. Oh, no doubt, she'll freeze tonight, when the valley cools and the evening wind dies away.

A get-well wave to Pop Snow, a wish for his continued improvement, which son Snowie assures us is happening down on Castle Road. And to Lloyd and Elsie Rose, stricken by the bug at their home up in the pond section, short sniffles and gosh dang it, is everybody ill this week? A get-well wink to Norma Snow, who has been laid up the weekend, too. We were about to commiserate with Hester Burn Callander, who we understood had sustained a serious injury while skiing up-country during the holidays. But just an hour or so ago we waved to her in her car passing our home here in the valley so we have to assume she's mended. Edgar W. Francis II stopped by our office at town hall the other day to pick up a birth certificate for himself, and informed us that his son, Edgar W. Francis III is now the proud father of a son, Edgar W. Francis IV, born recently here on the Cape. How long does this Roman numeral business go on?

What with all this newspaper coverage of the student infiltration and seizure of college nerve centers up-city way, we can't help comparing the situation with events that used to occur at our own Wilder Grammar School

255

here in Truro. Granted, the roles of students and administration were switched in the local affair, but there's enough similarity between the two to bear retelling.

Ordinarily, the school day at Wilder Grammar was one of monotonous routine and precise scheduling. Nine o'clock, exactly, and Miss Nellie Silva, teacher of the Big Part—grades four through eight—would step out on the concrete platform, raise her arm, and give a couple dozen shakes of the hand bell. Kids would come galloping in from all directions, snatch a last drink from the pump, toss their coats on the hooks of the cloakroom, rush to their assigned seats. Miss Silva would make a final inspection for stragglers in the cloakroom and entries, then she'd set down her big hand bell and give a tinkle on the tiny push bell of her desk, and the room'd become silent as a church.

Nine-five, attendance: Herbert Rose—HERE—Clarence Cabral—HERE—Robert Morris—PRESENT—(snickers, and a glare from Miss Silva for the departure from form). Nine-eight, a reading from the Holy Scriptures, usually one of the psalms. Nine-ten, Lord's Prayer (awkward break as the Catholics dropped off just before the "for thine is the kingdom." Nine-twelve, a chapter from some lurid paperback dime novel, probably Nick Carter's latest detective story. Nine-twenty, tinkle of the desk bell, arithmetic for the 8th grade and while the other grades lined up their text books for the coming periods, the eighth graders would lapse into the drill on fraction-decimal equivalents. "One eighth equals twelve and a half per cent."

And that's the way school went, almost every single day.

The passing of Anthony R. Phat Francis, colorful Truro figure for many decades, brings many memories to mind. Phat presiding behind the service window of the Truro Post Office, a huge cigar clamped in his jaws. Phat dispensing gasoline, groceries and wisdom at his Truro Center "Square Deal Store." Phat delivering telegrams around town in his stripped down Model T Ford. Phat in the era of his dog-raising period. Sheriff's raids on his premises in the square, yielding up scores of yelping canines to be carted off to the SPCA kennels, and as often, released to their belligerent owner. Phat quoting Massachusetts law on the floor of town hall—sometimes right, sometimes wrong. Phat gathering up constituents for support at the polls, when his name would appear in several contests.

The stories about Anthony R. Francis are legion—and of all we've heard, the one we like best is the yarn that tells how Phat, one warm summer evening, took a group of friends in his Model T Ford to the movies in

Wellfleet. After the show, the modified T, her truck body jammed with passengers, roared off to Truro, but not before Phat had replenished her leaky radiator from a gallon jug he kept for that purpose next to the driver's seat. First passengers to be discharged were the Adams brothers, Sid and Bill, so Phat tooled the Ford down their driveway. But something, possibly a sudden ground fog or excessive speed or a momentary distraction, caused Phat to lose control of the car, and off the road she went, rolling over at the base of a steep sand bank abaft the Adam's house. In the ensuing confusion, the cork of Phat's water jug was dislodged, and the luke-warm fluid poured out on the driver's thigh. A sharp scream rent the night as Phat begged, "Get a doctor, someone. I'm bleeding to death." Ave atque vale, Phat, old friend.

Stopped in to say hello to Snowie and Norma a few days ago, found they have a new house guest. Pop Snow has decided to bunk in with them until spring, and the transition from his house on the hill to the cottage on Snow's Landing was accomplished with commendable speed and dispatch. "Fetched my clothes and my cribbage board with me, and the cat will take up residence here soon's Horace Jr. can catch the critter. I'll miss the traffic on Castle Road, but there's a lot to look at down here on the river." And then he challenged us to a game of cribbage and we got the living bejeebers beat out of us as he laced us three straight. Matter of fact, we just missed a lurch on the last chucker by a couple of holes. But the bitterness of defeat was somewhat softened by Pop's running fire of conversation as we cut and dealt and pegged our way around the board.

"Kind of sad," we mused, "that there's such a paucity of finned creatures in the crick these days." Pop glanced out at the surging water—tide was coming in—and nodded in agreement, as he cut himself a jack for the deckhead. "Yessir, 'tis a shame. Back a few years [Pop's definition of "few" usually runs up to five decades or so] we used to fish this here river just about all the year round. Winter time we'd set out eel fykes; and when cold weather really arrived, we'd seine for frost fish, or billfish; and with warm weather, why we'd spear flounders right out there on the river bottom— feller could pick up fifty, maybe seventy-five or a hundred dollars hard cash for a few weeks part-time work. Came in mighty handy back in those days when we had no such dern thing as unemployment compensation."

We saved a pair of nines and a pair of tens, hoping for either an eight or a jack to complete a doublerun. Pop concealed a grin as a trey turned up for the cut. "Eelin' took lots of time and a considerable amount of gear," the silver-haired gent explained as he slapped down his cards—fifteen-twoing us mercilessly. "We used to get old twine from the traps, and set up our fykes at the good spots on the crick—couldn't block off more'n half the channel of the river, you see—and we'd drive stakes down in a V-shaped business so's the apex of the V would empty into the trap. Say, take a look at this hand and see if they ain't twenty-four points; my eyes ain't so good as they used to be." We confirmed Pop's count, then took our own puny five count.

"And then we'd draw the trap each day, and one year, so's we could get the best dern price, we decided to hold 'em for Christmas, so we carted all them cussed eels up to Black Pond, and stored 'em in carts. Leave an eel in salt water when it gets real cold, and they'll die every time. I know, cause my father lost a whole cart full of eels once that way—leastwise, he would have, but when he noticed they was losing their pepper, he quick hauled 'em up to the barn and put all hands to work skinnin' 'em for shipment." We riffled the cards desperately, got up and walked around our chair to change our luck.

"Now on big years, when all hands had a good season with eels, that'd be Naylor Hatch, and my father, and Tony Rogers, and maybe Frank Joseph over t' Corn Hill—why we'd get in touch with a broker in New York, and then we'd notify the freight agent, and he'd have a special freight car put on the sidin' down here to the depot. We'd cart our eels down there, iced, twenty-five pounds to the box and we'd ship 'em alive to the city. With luck, they'd bring a good price. Lord, that cussed sun ain't been out for two weeks, but she's shining in my eyes right now so I can't see the cards. Is that a twenty count?" Twenty it is—sun or no sun. And we gave up on beating Pop.

We drank deeply from the cup of victory at Snowie's yesterday afternoon, where we had gone to seek revenge for our ignominious defeat at the hands of Horace, Sr. in a cribbage contest the week before. Shellacked Pop first, we did, and then we took on Junior and beat him two out of three; and just as we were reaching for our coat and hat, who should come in but Uncle Isaiah. So we beat him, too, and if it hadn't been we had promised our good bride we'd be home early for supper, we'd have taken the whole dern clan on in repeat games. If any single factor besides skill added to our victory yesterday, it was simply that we remembered to wear our bifocals, so's we could see the cards real plain and peg properly. Then, too, we insisted on a seat facing east, so's the sun wouldn't blind us as it set over the salt crick. We're looking forward to next Saturday's grudge match.

And it's been clean-up time in our town. Makes a feller dizzy to count the loads of trash and brush going to the dump these days; and often you can catch the faint odor of burning brush in the evening air as folks burn off the fallow garden patch or touch fire to the puckerbush patch. There are swollen growth tips on the bushes as should be swollen this time of year—lilacs in the south yard, and juicy pear at the meadow's edge, and forsythia by the post and rail fence. And an evening or two ago, just as dusk was falling, we saw a flock of quail crossing the road at Fratus' Bend, beady-eyed in the glare of our car lights, their tiny legs a blur of motion as they sought out the bramble thicket beyond the fence of the town road. In the still, sun-flooded moments before dusk, if a feller has the patience to stand out on the north path, he can hear the bold, brassy crow of the cock pheasant in the alder next the cattail patch, and it's pleasant to hear an honest, vernal sound, as true an index of spring as the lengthening day and the smell of damp earth in the warm sun. Wish you were here, city folks, to enjoy it with us.

And our child bride, we're proud to report, recently won first prize for the most valuable and interesting ink bottle displayed at the May monthly meeting of the Cape Cod Bottle Collector's Club. She describes it as a cobalt umbrella—and by gosh she dug it up herself (but hot needles under her fingernails wouldn't elicit from her the location of her find).

On the night she drove up to Brewster to show off her ink bottle, we begged off—our sinuses were plaguing us—so we had to get the story from her secondhand. We had retired early, our sinusitis had mysteriously cleared up soon's she had left the house, and just as we were in the climax of a dream in which we were clobbering every window-cluttering Remington's Bitter and Moses Atwood octagonal, and Skilton-Foote pickle flask with a baseball bat, derned if we weren't shaken into consciousness by our bride.

"And I won first prize," she was screaming in our ear. "Two dollars—but it's not the money, its the honor of the thing." We agreed, seeing as how it probably cost two bucks to drive the car up-Cape and back. And then she continued. "Stay awake now. They had amber and white bottles, and those fancy ones with a sort of snorkel on 'em to dip your pen into; but my umbrella type was positively the best. And when I think how close I came to fracturing it with the clam rake when I was claming through that dump—"

What dump, we wanted to know. After all, a good wife should share her most precious secrets with her spouse. But the question went unanswered. "Next I'm going to pursue the wily glass insulator of telephone and power lines. They're getting very scarce. And you have to specialize in your collecting nowadays. And after that, maybe I'll get into the Barnstable brick bag—"

★ ★ ★

No. 4 son, Geof, has been wanting a garden for many years, so this year he laboriously turned over the sod of the fallow site by hand. A tiny little patch, hardly big enough to accommodate a dozen tomato plants and a few hills of cucumbers. And Geof looked at the package of hybrid corn rather wistfully, and observed he'd like to pop in a few hills if he had room. We pointed out that corn not only takes up lots of space, but it's fair game for the local birds. They'll scratch it out of the ground before you can say Obadiah Brown.

"Must be some way to stop 'em from raiding your seed," growled Geof. And we allowed as how there were several old tried and true methods. Ed Snow use to dip his seed in creosote. You should see the reaction from some hungry old crow when he bit into one of those seeds. And Manuel Corey used to build a most realistic scarecrow when he planted that area down at Fratus' Bend next to his strawberry patch. Why coming home from the evening mail as dusk was filling the valley, a feller'd dern near jump out of his skin if he took the short cut across the Bend and nudged up against Mr. Corey's scarecrow in the darkness. Old C. W. Snow used to build a bird-blind up on the hill, where the kids play ball nowadays and he'd lie in wait behind the blind and blast away at the blackbirds and starlings and crows when they came to raid his garden. He'd string up the carcasses, too, as a sort of warning to the other birds, but it never seemed to do much good. And the crows would always send out a sentinel to spy on the old feller, and then all the feathered thieves would fly way down to the far end of the field, out of range of the shotgun.

Mr. Joe Peters, senior, had probably the most effective way of fooling the birds who were after his corn seed. After he had planted each hill, he'd extend his fingers, claw fashion, and punch a cluster of holes in the ground. His theory, y'see, was that the birds would fly down, and seeing the holes in the ground, they'd reason that some enterprising bird had already been there and had taken the corn.

The stirring foliage of the locust filters the bright sunshine so that interesting shadow patterns form in our kitchen, momentarily dulling the blush of the ripening tomatoes on the window sill, blending the filtered shades of lavender of our bride's whiskey sampler flask and the pale blue of the Skilton-Foote pickle bottle and the aqua of the Atwood's Bitters. Out of doors the emerald green of the lawn is restful to the eye, and a plump, rusty-breasted robin has his ear cocked to the sound of some subterranean worm in his tunnel.

One brief errand took us to town hall this morning, and on the way we gave our usual approving Sunday morning nod to the flowering pampas grass at Snow Park and to the lemon-yellow seed pods on the ailanthus trees on Peggy Day's property bordering William Gray Square. And Stu Joseph's basset hound looks limp and dead in the grass at the corner of Bridge Road, so much we stopped our car and gave him a whistle. Derned if he didn't open his heavy-lidded eyes and raise his head a mite, and then he slumped back to sleep. Don't know as we blame him, it being so warm and comfortable in the straw-hued poverty grass next to the pines. On the return trip we admired the trim flight of a trio of black ducks heading oceanward up the fresh crick, and we slowed the car at Fratus' Bend to allow a chipmunk to shift his tail into high gear and sprint across the road.

Lucky we had the forethought to hold off finishing our new coat of arms signboard. This past week, Monday, Sept. 22, a new five-pointed star was added to the devices of the O'Caghan shield. We're referring to the birth of Heather Anne, daughter of our No. 4 son, Geoffrey Daniel and his wife, Carol Days, at Cape Cod Hospital—weighed in at 7 lbs. 10 oz., did the little tyke, and both baby and mother are doing fine. On our grandparental visit to the hospital we saw our good wife unerringly pick her grandchild out of the whole clutch of tiny bundles of humanity in the baby ward, long before we could read the pink card of identity on the bassinet. And later we talked to fellow pedagogue Paul Seeley, also a patient at CCH (surgery on a damaged metacarpal) and, as we ticked off our grandchildren, eight to date, with another soon to be greeted (probably before this column gets into print) we suddenly slumped a mite from our usual ramrod posture and studied our graying thatch in Paul's hospital mirror. "Never mind, O'Caghan," comforted Paul. "You'll be retiring one of these days."

The telephone rang at our house at three in the morning, just a few days later, and the darkness of the bedroom and the insistence of the bell momentarily confused us. For one brief moment we were twenty years back in time, and the call meant a trip in the ambulance. "Hope it's not a car accident," we muttered to ourself, as we slipped into our trousers. It wasn't, of course—wasn't an ambulance trip at all; other hands, younger and steadier than ours, take care of such things nowadays. But it was a call from No. 3 son, Mike, announcing with pardonable pride that he was a father. His wife, Carol (Souza) Kane, had presented him with a daughter, who'll be named Anne Elizabeth, at the Naval Hospital in Little Creek, Virginia. Weighed in at 6 pounds, ten ounces, did Anne, a fine healthy infant, and according to her father, a beautiful one. So the score to date: nine grandchildren, two boys, seven girls. Enough males to carry on the family name, it's true, but how about a few more grandsons as insurance runs, fellows?

In this era of the generation gap, when it's hard for us old timers to adjust to the tastes and the mores of the younger set (mod haircuts, bell-bottom trousers, mini-skirts, maxi-skirts, over-amplified abortion of guitar and drum they call music) it is indeed a pleasure to hear a sincere compliment paid to our kids. Such was the case last week when a busload of Provincetown High School teenagers hied of to Natick for a Shakespearean festival. The manager of Howard Johnson's was kind enough to send a note to our school informing the administration that he found our students ladies and gentlemen. Kudos and a serving of scully-jo all around.

In the same vein, it's fine to note that Halloween here on the Lower Cape was lacking in vicious vandalism and other excesses. In our own neighborhood, we dare say, there wasn't even a soaped window. And despite the fact we kept our big dog, Duke, stoppered up in the house, only a handful of kids dropped by to sample our treats. Collins Dickinson and Paul Oliveira, being the only two unmasked visitors, were the only youngsters we recognized.

A far cry from our day, and, we're ashamed to admit a vast improvement. The kids on Halloween night would gather in groups and set out on foot. Some of the pranks would be repeated each year: you could make book.

For instance, there'd be a big bread box or two hanging from the halyards of the flagpole at Cobb Library. And several of Phat Francis' abandoned cars would find their way from his auto graveyard back of the Square Deal Store down into William Gray Square. (Poor Mrs. Francis, Phat's mother, always fell for the diversionary tactics of the kids. Two or three would keep her busy at the penny candy counter while their buddies would be pushing the cars down hill just a broom-handle length from the front of the building.) Uncle John Rich's pump would have a thick lather of gummy axle grease smeared from spout to handle, and the post office building often had a gunny sack jammed down the back chimney, effectively choking off the draft of the stove below. It was about this time of year that Mr. Manuel Corey, orchardist par excellence, would have his fall crop curing on the cement platform at the north entrance of his house. And if luck held, the Amos and Andy program on the Corey radio would have that good man glued to his headset, and the muffled sounds of footsteps in the backyard would go unnoticed. MacIntosh and Baldwin never tasted so good in the years since, and somehow, the filching didn't seem theft on Halloween night.

But the climax of the evening came when someone would suggest the overturning of a privy or two. The ground rules were complicated, but flexible; you didn't, for instance, lay hands on the property of a widow, or of old folks who'd have difficulty restoring this indispensable outbuilding to its proper position. And the privy of an unoccupied house was about as sporting as shooting fish in a barrel. And, of course, church privys or those located on the property of sick persons were off limits. A story they always used to tell when privy-turning time came that holiday evening involved men of the previous generation, among them Leonard Gray and his brother Tom, and some others whose names we can't recall. Seems they swooped down on Myrtie Jordan's place in the dark of night, and just as they were raising the neat, square building to the critical point of center of balance, a feeble voice came from within the structure.

The project was abandoned immediately, of course, and it was later learned that a guest of Myrtie's, an overly modest city feller, had made his nocturnal trip without the usual lantern the natives always used to tote at night. In any event, Myrtle made sure the affair could never be repeated. Within a week the Jordan privy was jacked up against the woodshed and spiked to the larger building, and there she sets to this day.

Phone rang at our house the other evening and when we picked up the hook, came the friendly voice of Snowie over the wire. "We're going up to Kenny's wedding over the weekend, O'Caghan; could you stop by a couple of times while we're gone and feed the cats?" We gave our assent, of course, and extended our best to Kenny. In due time, we tooled the faithful VW to the vacant home of our friend on the banks of the salt crick.

How silent the house without the booming voice from the living room welcoming us: "Come in and set a spell." The vacant chair in the corner facing the TV. The pile of unread books on the wire-spool table. The huge ashtray shining, sterile, and nary a whiff of cigarette smoke in the room.

And so after we'd opened a can of cat food for Buggsy and the gray tiger female, we paused for a moment by the big picture window and got to thinking about the things we've done over the years with this likeable old reprobate. Remember how Snowie used to send his Packard roadster across Wilder's Dyke (empty except for his dog, Penny). And how we'd slip a package from the shelves of Duarte's liquor emporium on the front seat and turn the big machine around and head 'er back, in low gear, to the beaming proprietor of the Shell Station?

And the Halloween parties at town hall, where we used to dream up the most horrendous shadowramas we could think of to scare the bejeebers out of the poor kids? On one such occasion, poor little Punchy Prada got so frightened his mother had to take him home before he could join the apple bobbing at the shank end of the evening. And the trip we made to Benson Wild Animal Farm in Snowie's post-war caddie limousine with a carload of neighborhood kids. Left Pamet, we did, with near a bushel of sandwiches; those youngsters must have cleaned it out before we'd reached the canal. And our own son No. 2, Terry, was coming down with measles and we didn't realize it and within the fortnight—but you can guess the rest.

Christmas carols in the square; gosh, how a crew of willing men could drag an organ up those steep stairs and string yards of wire for the fancy bulbs with little fanfare and chip in to buy material for the decorating, too.

It was Snowie who first introduced us to Chinese mustard at a quiet little restaurant in Boston's Chinatown. We like to choked as we stuffed a steaming eggroll dripping with the stuff down our gullet. And the canoe trips we've made down the Pamet, with portages over the dyke and perils of water snakes and giant mosquitoes. And we've buried each other's dogs, victims both, of an assassin bullet—but enow the whimsey. We're thinking if Snowie retires and moves away, as he's threatening to do, we'll have to do the same.

NINETEEN SEVENTIES

1970's

NINETEEN SEVENTY

1970

As the morning gives way to noontime, a gradual freshening of the wind until the sound of the nor'easter penetrates the double-sashed windows of our house. As the wind quickens the fog dissipates, swept overland to the bay, and a flock of gulls flies purposefully down towards the salt crick. Rain during the change of weather, too, enough to streak the window panes and to wash our soiled car. Also to swell the trapped puddles on Wilder's Dyke and at Allie Paine's Corner on Castle Road, where we drove before church to gossip a mite with friend Snowie.

Something missing along the way. Then we recall that Stu Joseph's mournful, flop-eared basset hound has gone to dog heaven. That's why he's not standing by the roadside, inspecting us and our car as we drive by. May the faithful canine find meat-covered bones by the bushel. And may his days be pleasant, endless periods of cat-chasing, free of any tick or flea.

Snowie, unfortunately, had little of interest to offer, but the Pamet abreast his house was a thing of winter beauty. At flood tide, the ice floes were jammed edge to edge from the north bank to the south. In the few tiny spaces of open water were the water fowl of the neighborhood, including those formerly owned by the late Courtney Allen. What manner of radar do these birds have that enables them to plunge down to the river bottom in search of some winter tidbit and surface minutes later, a score of yards further downstream, to find the same open pool?

And later, at eleven o'clock Mass at Wellfleet, we offered our condolences to Paul Lussier on the church steps. "No golf for you today," we clucked. "Haven't been out for so long I won't know the difference between my putter and my mashie-niblick," moaned the genial banker.

In our mail, a nice letter from Johnnie Marshall, Truro native and treasurer of J. L. Marshall and Sons Construction Co. of Pawtucket, R. I. After we'd run an appreciative finger over the embossed letterhead, we got down to the substance of the missive. "Just a note to let you know that I recently visited with Father Dennis, who was pastor in Truro and Wellfleet almost from the time I was a child.

"Father Dennis would enjoy receiving a little news now and then from the folks in Truro. He is 87 years of age, still likes to smoke El Producto 'Bouquets' and he still talks a great deal about his wonderful friends and the wonderful days he spent in Truro and neighboring towns."

A reminder: most of our early beloved priests were known by their given names only. Please don't forget that Father Dennis' full name is Rev. Dennis J. Spykers.

We're reminded by Johnnie's letter of the good cleric's earlier days here in Pamet and our own associations with the genial man of the cloth. Father Dennis it was who taught us the art of serving Mass, from the lighting of the altar candles to the lengthy Latin responses to the proper handling of the censor. My, how the strong incense used to irritate our tender nostrils. The ancient Church Latin we found particularly difficult, especially after we'd had a taste of the so-called classical Latin in high school. We found that the diphthongs were pronounced differently, that the letter C was hard not soft, that the V was always pronounced as W, that many other consonants and vowels were completely different from the language of Caesar.

"But church Latin derives from the language spoken by the common people in everyday conversation," Father Dennis said. "That's why the vowels are different and the consonants are softened up a bit. They call it the vulgate or vulgar language." We must have looked shocked at Father Dennis' explanation for he hastened to explain that the word vulgar in this sense simply meant common—man in the street—as opposed to highly cultured. So we memorized the confiteor and all the other prayers by heart, but our high school Latin suffered considerably in the doing.

We almost learned to drive a car under Father Dennis' direction. His automobile was a pre-owned buick Victoria whose chief claim to fame was its ability to crawl along in the wake of the hearse in funeral corteges at a snail's pace, but in high gear. But we hadn't yet attained our sixteenth birthday, so we weren't allowed to actually touch the wheel. Good thing we didn't, in a way, because the buick had a mongrel shift in those days that would have required much time to unlearn.

Later, when we were taking a course in public speaking at Boston University under the direction of a grand old spinster name of Agnes Knox Black, Father Dennis called us one day on the phone and asked us to drop by the rectory with a book—any book—that would help him get rid of some of the annoying Dutch accent in his speech. As would any crass freshman, we proceeded to launch into a discussion of the mechanics of speech. We demonstrated the position of tongue and lips in the fricative and the labiodentals.

"Never mind all the fancy names, young man," said Father Dennis as he emptied his blackened corncob pipe in the ashtray. "Let's see if you can teach me how to pronounce the th combination." So we opened our book to the anatomical chart showing the various positions of the mouth parts and then we slowly pronounced the accompanying pattern sentences. "This thin theory theoretically," or "Thumping themselves on the thorax, they. . . ."

Make a long story short, we spent the whole afternoon with the good priest, but by supper time the poor man was still pronouncing the words with much display of his handsome gold incisor, "Dis tirty-tird tread-tumper tinks tuh trows of trolling."

Father Dennis is living at the Catholic Memorial Home, 2446 Highland Ave., Fall River, Mass.

Earlier this morning, we hied off as usual to friend Snowie's on the banks of the salt crick. The current was beginning to move the big blocks of crystal white ice from their mooring spots on the bank down to the bay. Our host was perched at the living room window with his binoculars glued to bloodshot eyes, examining what he claimed was a trio of black ducks engaged in mutual rescue work in the swirling black waters abreast Cat Island.

"By gosh," he exclaimed as we tried to focus in on the action with our naked eye, "one of them poor birds is stuck in the ice and the other two are pecking away at the ice—and now he's free!" But by the time we'd wrenched the glasses away from Snowie and located the birds, all's we saw was a threesome of coots haggling over what looked like a half-opened mussel.

That's the way it usually is at Snowie's house. Miracles take place just before the guest arrives: an otter braving the tide, a bald eagle with eight-foot wingspread perched on the pines of Castle Point or a mammoth striper leaping out of the sedge grass. Look sharp and you'll still see the rings he left. Should have been here just a whisker earlier. And that's the way we feel about the city folks. You should have been here today to enjoy it with us.

Just as we got to our office at town hall one afternoon last week, neighbor Joe Peters from Ryder's Pond section of town was leaving the building. We exchanged the usual pedagogical greetings appropriate to the afternoon—It's Friday, Thank God—and Joe went on his way.

We got to thinking about Joe and his days in the profession, especially those halcyon years at the old Wilder Grammar school. The building houses our post office these days (although we hear tell Uncle Sam is accepting bids for a new PO, and about time). It's slightly changed from its original structure, but

we can remember the venerable old place as though it were yesterday.

Used to be an ell east end of the building which housed the coal room and the two cloakrooms. The thing we most recall about this section of the old Wilder was the smells. The smell of split pine drying out in the coal room. The choking odor of coal dust when the coal supply got low in the bin and the janitor had to rummage around in the loose stuff to fill the battered coal hods for the two big potbellied stoves of the schoolrooms.

A veritable smorgasbord of smells from the cloakrooms, where the kids used to stash their lunches as the school bus ungorged its load of humanity each morning. The spicy tang of linguica nestled in its homemade bread wrapper. The rich, heady odor of fruits from Truro trees. The distinctive smell of gingerbread or spice cookies. And then the smell of the clothing hastily hung on the wrought iron pegs on the matchboard sidewalls—sheepskin coats moistened by melted snow, heavy outerboots redolent of the barnyard and hand-knit wool caps or gloves sending off the olfactory clue of association with the family cow.

Then the schoolroom itself. Buckling beaverboard walls painted the traditional industrial buff yellow, fly-specked and occasionally dappled, up there beyond the reach of the janitor's broom, by a dried spit-ball. On the north wall, the dusty blackboard and the cardboard case containing the spice samples from all over the world, courtesy of Slade Company. (Many's the unsuspecting kid inveigled into chewing on fiery peppercorn stolen from that display case.)

Here, next to the teacher's desk (of low silhouette so's the teacher had an uninterrupted view of the classroom), the rusty iron stove sprouting its plume of smoke pipe that ran overhead, suspended by wires, to its thimble in the wall. On certain occasions, when the wind caused a backdraft in the chimney and the lower controls were fixed just right, coal gas would build up in the stove. After several faint rumblings, like reverse peristalsis, the cussed thing would blow up with a horrendous roar.

Here, too, the shallow closet that held the school supplies. Paper and pencils and blotters and bib pens. (Remember how we used to lick the end of those pen points to remove the film of oil so's the ink would adhere to the steel, and how the kids used to vie for the privilege of filling the desk ink wells from the shapely, long-nozzled copper pourer?)

Over there on the west wall, a pair of settees where kids engaged in special projects were allowed to sit, away from the less imaginative students. (Here it was that O'Caghan and Meier set up a homemade Punch and Judy show one gloomy afternoon and almost caught the school afire with the smoky, kerosene lamp that flared up just as the alligator was about to devour Punch.)

Along the back wall, the ancient, wheezy Estey knee organ, belabored on Wednesday mornings by Mrs. Josephine Patterson, the vocal music teacher from Provincetown. (We still have in some secret hiding place a notebook of music appreciation we composed under the Patterson tutelage and if memory stirs when we hear the cradle song from Berceuse or Finlandia, or Anitra's Dance, we're sure we'd find the opening measures sketched in our yellow notebook.)

To be sure, we have opening exercises today at our Temple of Learning, but they're sterile affairs as compared with the action-filled moments at Wilder School after the morning bell rang. No Lord's Prayer these days, of course. Nor any reading from the Scriptures. But back in those pleasant years, we got a good dose of each, followed by a half chapter from Nick Carter's latest detective adventures or Tom Swift's impossible inventions.

Mr. Joe Peters, we got into this profession too late. We envy you, sir.

Town hall last week was the scene of much confusion as Pamet canines were delivered to the scene for administration of rabies shots in accordance with the recently enacted state law. "Tell all your doggie friends they can thank a Republican governor for this," we hissed into Duke our police dog's ear as we let him drag us into the venerable building. That was the last opportunity we had to spread propaganda for the mother party. Dr. Schneider in his starched white vet's smock stood ready at his post to administer the vaccine with an assortment of deadly-looking needles. Above the clamor of barks, yelps, whines, and the anxious commands of sundry owners, we answered the question of the harrassed girl at the desk.

Name? "Duke," we replied. "No-no," interrupted Marion Oliveira, who seemed to be acting in some supervisory capacity, "not the dog's name—

yours." By that time Dr. Schneider had asked us Duke's weight, and even as Duke strained at the leash to get the olfactory identification of a frizzle-haired mongrel in some youngster's arms, the needle went home. So did we, soon's we could drag our pet from the hall. And just as we were loading Duke into the car, derned if we didn't observe the good vet and his helper, and poor Ralph Houser and Hayden Tyler, all teaming up to administer shots to Tyler's dogs, who had apparently refused to budge from their owner's car in the parking lot. Hasn't been so much excitement at the mairie, as they say in French, since the Lord Mayor of Truro, Cornwall, England visited us after World War II.

This week on the Lower Cape witnessed the passing of an era with the death of Sheldon Osborne "Ozzie" Ball. The colorful Provincetown resident was a man of many parts—lawyer, landlord, musician, real estate and insurance agent, bon vivant and raconteur, among others. Whenever we feel moved to boast that we came to the Cape at an early age, we are properly put in our place by the memory of hearing Ozzie once telling a patron of the Blacksmith Shop that he, Ozzie, had come to Truro before he was born—subtle reference to the fact that his mother had arrived in Pamet in what the folks of our Victorian era used to refer to as a delicate condition.

But there was never anything delicate about Ozzie. Master of the bon mot, Ozzie was known to bring humor even to the hallowed confines of the courtroom. Consider the time he was waiting to try a case at Provincetown and on the docket before him was the late Truro dog-lover, Anthony R. Phat Francis, defending himself against a charge of possessing unlicensed canines. At one point in the hearing, when the action slowed a mite, Ozzie pointed to Phat's grease-stained, paper shopping sack which contained the Truro man's notes and legal references, and probably his lunch.

"That must be the well-known *in the bag*," quipped Ozzie.

The incident we will always associate with Ozzie dates back to our days in Wellfleet High School. Ozzie was dating one of the young teachers at that institution, and we were at an age when it seemed smart to heckle the poor lady pedagogues. And Ozzie met us one day after school, and with his big, easy smile he advised us, "You ought to behave in school and study hard, and some day you can go to law school as I am, right now. And besides, if you act up with my lady friend any more, I'll beat the bejabers out of you." Good advice, old friend. Ave atque vale.

We keep asking ourself if the weatherman meant what he said in yesterday's prognostication over the wireless: shifting winds and clear, dry, delightful August weather.

As we sit down to our faithful Royal and poke at our sagging eye glasses we claw at damp, blotter-like paper from a sticky elbow, and try to sort out the notes for our column from a sticky brain. To open the doors of town hall wide is only to admit more of the damp morning air, and perchance an early rising tourist who's looking for a beach sticker. (Sorry sir, they're not being sold here this year; or, if the tags on the car indicate he's from La Belle Province, "On ne vend pas les permits de plage ici cette annee.") But a change of air we must have, and as we hook back the weighty portal, we can hear the muffled sound of traffic on the highway to east'ard and by gosh, that's all we can hear this morning. In short, if a peaceful, humid morning is what you want, join us in Pamet this day.

Comes word to town that Warrant Officer Robert F. Washington, U.S. Army, formerly stationed at North Truro Air Force Station, has been awarded the Air Medal, for having distinguished himself by "Meritorious achievement, while participating in sustained aerial flight, in support of combat ground forces in the Republic of Vietnam. He actively participated in more than 25 aerial missions over hostile territory . . ." We salute him, and wish him Godspeed and an early, safe return to his wife and family here in Truro.

On our way home from up-Cape last Sunday with our child bride, we stopped for a bit of refreshment at a roadside stand. Hardly had we delivered the solo ice cream cone to her when up drives Dr. Gordon Lupien, our good friend and neighbor for lo these many years. Appears he and his beauteous wife, Lottie, were on their way back to the city driving two separate cars, because of much impedimenta left over at the season's end. After we'd made the usual small talk, Dr. Gordon allowed as how he was a mite tired. "Lottie had me cleaning out the cellar and the side chambers," he explained. "And I must have lugged a truckload of trash to the dump—old papers and boxes and bottles."

Sounds of strangling from our good wife. "B-B-B-bottles?" she gasped. "Old bottles? What section of the dump did you . . . ?" And almost before we could make a civil adieu to the Lupiens, the VW was careening down the highway, and minutes later we were studying the heaped trash and garbage of Truro's disposal area. "I'd guess it must have been about there," said our determined wife, pointing to an area where hungry seagulls were worrying at the refuse. And almost before you could say Obadiah Brown, we were picking our way through the offal, fighting off green head flies, worrying about giant rats underfoot, until finally we got to the spot indicated by her outstretched finger. Our clawing efforts yielded three Slade's mustard jars, one pale green Skilton Foote pickle, slightly cracked, unfortunately, and a milk glass miniature cover for a mason style preserve jar. Greater love hath no husband than that he probe the town dump for his wife.

We've had the pleasure, on many mornings this summer past to arrive at sparrow burp, as they say in Truro when an early hour is spoken of, in time to catch Donnie Horton's dad, Irving, helping to open up shop. "I can't insult Pop by offering to pay him," sighs Donnie on such occasions, "but I really should give him a lube job on the house. He's a real worker, whether he's counting cash, or pumping gas for an early customer, or stocking the shelves, or just plain sweeping the office floor." We'd noticed that Horton, pere, excelled in all these chores, but the thing we'd mark him in our markbook for is his skill in delivering the rental bicycles to their proper display area on the grass plot out front of the station. We like to bugged our eyes clear out of our head the first morning we saw Irving straddle one machine and seize the handle bars of two other bikes in his calloused paws, and then, by guppy, give a kick at the foot pedals of the bike he was riding, and ride it, no hands, smack across the parking area, guiding the other two-wheelers just as a Jersey cow would guide her twin calves. We used that figure of speech when we complimented Irv, and he liked the simile.

"Aw shucks, I guess I'm just a farm boy at heart," he shrugged. "I miss farmin', and livestock, and poultry and the early to bed, early to rise routine we always had when I was a kid, down at Perry's farm. Never feel more comfortable than when I have a hoe in my hand, choppin' weeds in the hot sun. My cottage business is fine—I like to meet people and offer 'em a service—but I druther be peddlin' milk to their kitchen doors, like I used to do in the good old days when we had our dairy up to Highland." Good Lord, we'd almost forgotten that era in Irv's life.

"Yessir, up at three o'clock, milk the cows, pasteurize and bottle the milk, load my truck, eat a quick breakfast, deliver both wholesale and retail, solicit new customers, collect the accounts, and if I got through early, I always felt I should help with chores around the farm." We seemed to recall that Irving had, during those halcyon days on the milk truck, taught himself a trick that made him the envy of every milkman on the outer Cape: the gimmick of picking up six empty milk bottles in one hand. Could he still do it, we wondered? Indeed he could, vowed Irv. Matter of fact, he'd do it for us right now, except for the fact that real glass milk bottles were scarce as hen's teeth. We heard him grumbling as he strode over to his car, climbed in and slammed the door. "Gee-hup!" he hollered as he turned on the ignition switch.

NINETEEN SEVENTY-ONE

1971

If the weatherman gave us all the ingredients for a perfect winter day and told us to put 'em together, we're sure we'd come up with a January Sabbath just like this. Of wind, a smidgin from the southwest, light and steady, abating a mite after lunch so it's nearly flat calm at the shank end of the afternoon. Set the thermometer somewhere in the mid-30's, so folks will know it's January, and focus a warm sun on the countryside to start a January thaw. Take the half-foot or so of fresh white snow that covers the Truro hills and season well with animal tracks: rabbit and fox and field mouse and even the domestic trail of dogs and cats. Frost the east side of each tree bole with the same white stuff, and watch the delicate icing tumble to the ground as the afternoon sun brings its warmth to bear. Drape some icicles on the south side of the house, and set 'em to dripping in ragged tempo as they shrink magically. Fasten a pair of mackerel gulls to the clear bowl of the blue sky to nor'ard, and set a pair of chicadees to chattering in the cedar tree on the south slope, and spray the whole area with that clear, cold magic stuff that makes you think of fresh laundry. Keep the barometer high and the traffic sparse and kick out a log or two from the snowcovered woodpile for a blaze on the hearth tonight, it'll be cold and still and clear, judging by the present weather picture.

Young feller who hasn't yet given his name to us dropped by town hall the other day to inform us he thought he had located the site of the original Pamet Harbor Light House, a project he'd been working on for several months past.

"I walked out on the railroad right of way, southerly from the Corn Hill crossing, and there on a small promontory of land jutting out from the track site, I found traces of old, broken masonry," he whispered to us in conspiratorial tones. We hated to disillusion the poor man, but before he got too involved in this erroneous research, we determined to tell him the story of the late Anthony R. Phat Francis, and his dogs, and his cottage at Corn Hill basin, and the final, tragic fate of that building.

Back in 1933, we pointed out, the U.S. Government decided to honor its obligations to the veterans of World War I by paying advance bonuses, the reason for the prematurity in payment being a desire to prime the economic pump, since this was in the middle of the Great Depression.

Among the Truro men who collected rather sizable amounts of money on this occasion was the aforementioned Phat Francis. And Phat, in accordance with the intent of the Government, promptly put his money to work.

He purchased from farmer Joe Cabral of the Whitmanville section, a lot of land located at the edge of the Corn Hill basin. Then he contacted the New Haven Railroad and bought the long abandoned Corn Hill freight house, and had the building moved over his newly built corduroy-seaweed road to the Cabral site, and placed on a concrete foundation already poured there by an Uncle of Anthony DeLuze.

From then on the Francis cottage remodeling job took on the appearance of a true WPA job. Men came, and worked, and departed. A pump was driven in the cellar by willing hands, but the water that poured from its spout proved too brackish and salty for human consumption.

Dry wall sheathing was installed and new doors and windows were hung in place, and in due time the cottage was ready for the finishing touches. Phat himself took charge of the decor. Matter of fact, after he'd chosen the paint, a combination of restroom yellow and bilious blue, if memory serves, he even deigned to slap on some of the mixture himself, although Mike Howard, who worked there at the time, vows that Phat would paint only a horizontal band in each room that extended from a couple of feet above the floor to the top of the window frames.

The explanation? Phat's rather generous girth prevented him from stooping too low or reaching too high—so the top and bottom strips were left to various underlings. But we digress.

In time the cottage was finished—finished, that is, by Phat's standards. No electricity, no lights, no bathroom, no potable water, but shelter, nonetheless. Perhaps not for man, but certainly for beast. Because at this point, Phat's pack of German shepherd dogs had grown to the extent that they were no longer comfortable in their basement apartment under the Francis general store up in William Gray Square. So Phat transported all the canines, in small groups, to his new cottage on the shores of Pamet Harbor, and there, we'd like to say, they lived happily ever after. Not so.

Soon the animals began to tire of their solitary kennel. On occasion, they'd escape from the cottage and travel around the countryside, scaring the bejeebers out of folks, and sometimes, it was claimed, raiding a poultry yard. In any event, complaints reached officials at the town, county, and even the state level. And eventually, a raid was pulled on Hope cottage, as the tiny building was now affectionately known, and the dogs were scooped up by the minions of the law. In the confusion of the attack, someone either accidentally or with malice aforethought set fire to the building, and almost before you could say Obadiah Brown, the structure burned to the ground.

We like to think our stint behind a lawnmower today was somewhat therapeutic. Lord knows we needed a mite of sedative after our evening as MC at the annual Junior Prom the night before. Not that we danced, or stayed out late partying, or found it embarrassing to stand before the mike, introducing the kids in the line of march. What shook us up, and it's only correct to use the modern idiom in this connection, was the music and the musicians.

We arrived at venerable Provincetown town hall, according to plan—eightish—checked in with class advisor Paul Warner of the Provincetown High School faculty, pinned on our white carnation, ran over the program for the evening. And then we cast an eye on the activities shaping up on the stage—that stage where such famous bands as Guy McNelly and Doc Eisenburg, and Mal Hallett and Larry Funk had played for proms in the past.

Big bands—name bands, bands you'd hear on all the national radio services—every man resplendent in tuxedo, gal vocalist breathtakingly beautiful in her evening gown, dim lights and soft music, and couples, by gosh, holding hands and dancing cheek to cheek. The waltz contest, and . . . BANGGG, CRASH—rimshots—twang of bass guitar—scream of an injured sea lion—can that really be a trombone? Out on the stage bounces a huge black man—Afro hairdo—granny specs, ankle length mumu—bare feet—spotlight on the drummer—a study in basic black-black dungarees and black tee-shirt, barefoot, too.

The psychedelic light picks out other members of the band, similarly clad, each attacking his instrument, guitar, sax, electric piano, as though he had a personal grudge to settle with it. The entire dissonance is gathered up in mikes and fed through several amplifiers, each the size of a restaurant frig, and fired at the audience.

By the time grand march time arrived, we thought we had developed a sort of boilermaker's deafness. Not so; the huge leader coaxed even more volume from his men as they rocked through selections from "Hair." Our right tympanum ruptured, so we turned it in the direction of the nearest speaker.

Moments later the march ended, and while the judges were still debating final choice of a queen for the affair, the band lapsed into a slow-beat, acid number identified by Tiny as being a ballad. The kids on the floor below started dancing. Partners separated by at least a dory length—expressions of glazed boredom on every face—semaphore motions of arms, feet picking out a pattern on the floor that reminded us of volunteer firemen stamping out grass fires.

Shades of Guy Lombardo: Stardust, where is thy four-four beat? The last words we recall Tiny uttering were addressed to beauteous Ida Souza, as she received her crown from last year's first lady. "Right on, Queenie, right on." And that's when we broke down the back stairs and headed for Pamet.

It's cemetery grass cutting time, and a few evenings ago, when the dusk was getting so shadowy we dassent use our power tools any longer, and the mosquitoes were beginning to swarm over our head at the Congregational Cemetery, we paused by the burial plot of Manuel Corey, long-time town clerk of Truro. As  we bent down to snip at a weed that was encroaching on the clump of beautiful blue hydrangea that graces the monument, we heard, "Hello, Mr. Town Clerk—how goes Truro?"

Those melodious bass tones could belong to none other than our predecessor in office, so we decided to shop-talk a mite. "Fair to middlin', Mr. Corey," we replied. "Started off the year with something over $160,000 in certificates of deposit in the bank, but it looks as though we'll have to cash a portion of 'em in, to give us operatin' cash until taxes start to come in. Tax rate? Looks like—now don't let this shock you, in your time it was lessee, maybe $16 per thousand—looks like about $60 this year. How come? Well sir, school costs are up. And we've joined a new vocational regional technical school district. We'll be sending kids up to Brewster to learn to be carpenters, and bricklayers, and mechanics, and such. All costs money, you know. And the fire department is expanding its equipment—costs over $20,000 for a fire engine these days. Remember when we bought two Brockway trucks for was it $3,000?

Police department is growing, too. Two special cars on the road all the time. They call 'em cruisers. Six full time men on duty, and now we're forming an auxiliary squad of 15 (jokingly referred to as the Mod Squad) to handle riots and such. Riots? of course there could be riots. Consider the protests all over the country—college campuses and city administration buildings. No, no, none at town hall as yet. They're mostly protesting against the Vietnam War.

And there's a movement underway called Woman's Liberation, Mr. Corey. What do they want to be liberated from? Derned if we know, exactly—seems they want to hold down the same jobs as men, for the same pay, and they've been burning their—ahem—underwear. No, no, not their corsets, Mr. Corey—think a bit more to nor'ard—in protest. Young folks all over the country living together in what they call communes growing all their own foods. Bet they'll never produce such strawberries as you used to, down at Fratus' Bend. And they're smoking a hemp weed that has almost the same effect as alcohol, and they're taking dope to escape from the troubled conditions of the day, and they hate the generation represented by their parents. Call it the Establishment, they do. Wouldn't do to omit telling you about the pollution problem. Seems the air is saturated with poisons; can't even burn the town dump any more. And there's poison in almost everything we eat, caused by sprays and other insecticides that have gotten into the food chain. Why, there's even mercury in the lakes and rivers and oceans—swordfish is full of it."

"Hold on there, boy," boomed the Corey voice. "Say no more. It's a sacrilege to mention such things in this restful spot. Swat those mosquitoes away and go home. See you next year. Hope it's improved by then."

The angel of death has touched within the circle of those very dear to us three times within the past fortnight. The variety of his choice brings home to us the old saying the old must die; the young may.

For on July 16 our youngest grandchild, Jennifer Ann Kane, was found dead in her crib by her parents, our beloved No. 1 son, Paul Randolph, and his lovely wife and our beloved daughter-in-law, Maureen (Riley). There must be a reason in the eternal plan—we're still searching for it. And perhaps this is the proper time to thank God for the health and happiness he has granted to the members of our clan to date—so many tragedies could have happened to such a prolific family.

And last evening we learned of the death of Jean C. Pirnie, neighbor, friend, fellow teacher, a lady of much wit, intelligence, and strength. She had lived a full life and we know that the tragedies she had experienced and the suffering she had undergone will be offset by classrooms of beaming, bright kids ready, willing and able to conjugate irregular Latin verbs.

And finally, a few words about Snowie—it somehow seems pompous and affected to refer to him as Horace H. Snow Jr., his legal name.

For this past year we've tried to report Snowie's progress following his serious, radical surgery for cancer. We hope we hadn't been overly optimistic when we quoted incidents that indicated Snowie was conquering the dread disease. Somehow we thought all the evidence of recurrence of the malady could be dispelled by prayerful, hopeful thinking.

Not so—and the dreadful, debilitating sickness depressed us so we dreaded, on the one hand, dropping in to see our very best friend, while at the same time, we knew our absence from Slade's Landing would affect him, also. Our memories of Snowie—and we share these with myriad friends of this handsome, personable Truro institution (is this too impersonal a noun to use when we speak of Snowie?) are innumerable. We had known the man since the mid-thirties and now would be as good a time as any to quote Snowie anent his way of life.

"If I had it to do all over again, it would be just the same for me—a good cigarette to drag on, a glass of whiskey splits to nurse on, the love of a good woman, the friendship of many."

And so we try to compose a setting for Snowie in eternity. May you have, dear friend, limitless quantities of Shell gasoline to sell to the summer folks. (Remember when you identified the mysterious chemical, TCP in Shell gas as Tom Cat Piddle?) For you were, first and foremost, a good salesman, because you loved people, and they loved you—as witness the horde of good folks who attended your memorial service at the Congregational Church last Friday.

May you have dogs—plural, please note—two mongrel, flea-bitten dogs for you to de-tick and pat and yell at when they snarl at your friends who call on you in the Great Beyond. And whisky splits: a bottomless container of the same. None of your fancy imported brands.

But, as you once advertised in the *Provincetown Advocate* in rebuttal to a statement we'd made about you in our column, "I drink plain rotwhiskey and branch water."

You'll need a pair of binoculars up there, too, Snowie, so you can watch the birds, and the gals, and growing things, and the incoming tide of the salt crick, and the glorious sunsets of our Narrow Land. And a cribbage board, and a partner to play this best of two-handed card games with.

And don't forget the scrabble contests, Snowie—dammit, we still think you used to cheat a mite with those mysterious three letter words you needed to fill in a block that yielded triple scores. Ave atque vale, old friend. Save a place for us.

★ ★ ★

We got to thinking, as we turned on the valve of our auxiliary water system down in the garden (our child bride had threatened to divorce us if we overtaxed our domestic well as the drought increased its stranglehold on the Narrow Land this summer) about water, and water systems hereabouts. Generally speaking, water is not difficult to locate nor to fetch out of the ground here in Truro. There are a few spots, notably down at the Highlands of North Truro, where the deep clay veins make driving a well difficult, but elsewhere, a copious supply can be had for the driving, in wells varying from a mere ten feet or so (as was the case in our lowland garden) to systems of 150 or more on high ground such as town hall or Red Sand Hill.

Our dissertation is not concerned, however, with buried pipe, but with that aspect of the water system which can be seen above ground. We consider it mildly deplorable that there are no longer any dug wells in town. They were picturesque affairs indeed, with their fieldstone and brick curbings, their neatly framed houses, and their sturdy pulleys and ropes. If memory serves, the old Mailziner house on North Pamet sported an excellent dug well, and Willie Rose had a similar supply in his back yard in Long Nook. The Rose kids used to complain that lizards and salamanders would occasionally hitch a free ride up in the water bucket, but we never heard of the Long Nook folks catching any exotic diseases from their well.

You'd have to give second place for eye-appeal to the good old Red Jacket pumps, with their long, graceful handles, and their curved spouts. Somehow the Red Jacket always seemed to have a characteristic squeak analogous to the hollow, metallic sound of a Model A Ford exhaust system. You had to be sparing of lubricants, lest the water come out oil-tainted, and, being exposed to the weather, even such long-lasting stuff as axle grease soon wore off the bearing spots. In a day when school boys used to boast of reception on their crystal radio sets, they used to compare the efficiency of their family Red Jacket pumps. It was a matter of no little pride to have a pump which could fill a twelve quart bucket in, say, 30 strokes.

The presence of a windmill in one's backyard was a sure sign of affluence. The summer colonists had them, of course, and such wealthy natives as C.W. Snow, and the Head-O-Pamet Josephs, and Frank Joseph, and Manuel Corey. Like the mournful sound of a train whistle, the labored groan of a windmill caught in the brisk northwest wind is a never-to-be-forgotten country tune. In theory, when the wind reached a given velocity unsafe for the operation of the machine, the tail of the mill was supposed to shift around, swing the fan broadside to the breeze, and cut off the motion of the blades, but more often, the mill would continue to pump insanely, overflowing the tank, usually located on some nearby hill to take advantages of the law of gravity in giving pressure, of a sort, to house and barn. Came later the gasoline engined pump. Remember the time the safety valve failed on the late Dr. Ryman's pump on Tom's Hill? By guppy, the one-lung Hercules engine crammed 'er so full of water the tank blew up and shot through the roof of his cottage. Looked, as some witnesses said, like a Chinese sky-rocket.

But Pop Snow used to say the best, quietest, most efficient pump ever made was the hot-air pump. "All you needed was a ten inch Stillson and a screwdriver to service 'em. How'd it work? Well sir, it had a fire box below where you built firewood, coal, anything that'd burn. The hot air went into a compression chamber, forced the pistons back and forth, and, with a simple system of valves, pumped the water. Too bad they don't have them hot-air pumps nowadays, just think of all the water they could pump with the election speeches they'll have next November."

In this connection, we're reminded of the Horace Snows—pere et fils—back in the days when they operated the Shell petroleum emporium here on Wilder's Dyke in Truro. Snowie used to tell the story of the day he was busy at his station, putting water in a car battery perhaps, and Pop, catching his breath between jobs—he was opening cottages for folks he served as caretaker—was standing on the platform of the station. Sally Carleton and Ray Sweeney, among others, were witnesses to what follows. Up drives a big, shiny car, with a number plate bearing symbols indicating that the vehicle was that of an important personage up at the State House. Out steps a portly, important-looking man who was smoking a cigar; not a workingman's White Owl, like Pop's, but a green-flecked stogie obviously of Cuban vintage. Addressing himself to Pop, he inquired, "Can you tell me where Mr. Arthur Joseph lives?" Pop had deduced by now that Mr. Big was an official of the Insect Control Board, or some such, since Arthur was at that time Truro's tree warden; two things just seemed to go together. "Yup," replied Pop, continuing to pull on his cigar. An awkward silence followed and finally the man asked, "Well, where does he live?" "Up that road a piece—say a mile or so—little mite of a cottage perched up on a hill, right side of the road," said Pop, gesturing with his stogie. The VIP thanked Pop, drove off up-valley. Said Sally Carleton to Pop, "But Pop, didn't we just see Arthur Joseph on his way to Provincetown?" Pop blew a huge cloud of blue smoke, nodded in agreement. "Then why didn't you tell the man so?" "Young lady," replied Pop, "he didn't ask where Arthur Joseph was—he asked where he lived."

★ ★ ★

We've heard several applicants at town hall inquire whether softshell clams—steamers—can be taken, and the answer is no, not at present. They're in too short supply. But speaking of the Mya arenaria so much coveted by just about every one, we're reminded of the days when clam digging was permitted, on the Corn Hill flats and up the salt crick as far as Monroe's Landing, on a commercial basis. This would be back in the days of the Great Depression, when any means of making a dollar was most welcome. As one who spent many a day of agony at the task, we feel qualified to conjure up the memory of a session on the clam flats.

Here's how it went. Height of tide, of course, determined the time of our arrival at the river, and it usually seemed we had to be there at some pre-dawn hour when the darkness seemed unfriendly and the soft sand dragged at our rubber boots as we toted our baskets to the river's edge. There'd be a concerted tugging of boot tops and a sizzle of cigarettes being tossed into the limpid water, and then the muffled splashing as the diggers picked their way to the clam area. Most of the boys belonged to the school of dry diggers, but we preferred to scratch away in midstream, where the flowing water, elbow deep, cleared away the sand and mud, leaving the clams neatly washed and ready to be scooped into our basket. There were advantages to this method, as pointed out above, but, on the other side of the scale, consider the poison ivy pollen that used to float down stream in season, infecting the digger's arms, raising blisters big as a half dollar. Then, too, the entire job had to be done in a stooped position (your dry land digger could drop to knees, as though in prayer) and back muscles would be fair paralyzed at the end of a three hour session.

Each day, as the tide started to come in, there'd be a good-natured race between the top diggers to see who could top off his three bushels first. The winner was usually Stanley McAnistan, a wiry, small Irishman who used an unusual one-handed hook motion on his clam hoe, while with his other hand he'd claw out the wily bivalves in a lightning motion. The discovery of a thickly infested spot was a secret to be more closely guarded than a woman's age. Ed Snow, we recall, had an uncanny ability for picking out the productive bars, and we usually detailed a man to trail the old fellow, and we'd crowd in on him if he found a good bed, ignoring his yells of protest.

The acid test of every clamdigger came on those still, hot mornings when not a breath of air stirred among the sedge banks. The smell of mud would be rank, and suddenly a cloud of gnats would descend on the working men.

Hundreds of the tiny pests would hover over your stooped body, crawling into ears, eyes, mouths. And nothing would drive them away, be it clouds of cigarette smoke, waving of hands, or cursing. Much later, we'd be finished with our day's quota. The clams would be given a final washing in their lathe-constructed containers, and all hands would form a chain gang to lug the dripping washers up on the beach. Jake Smith would dash back to the flats to dig an extra half bucket of steamers for his girlfriend (he claimed she never got her fill of them) while the rest of us swore we'd never taste another clam again—steamed, fried, in fritters, or scalloped in ambrosia of the pink honeysuckle from the fresh crick of the upper Pamet.

And the price? A princely three dollars a barrel, such a barrel as you'll not see these days. A barrel consisting of three bushels, heaped so's you couldn't get another clam on it to save your soul. Rumor had it at that time that the wholesaler used to stop his truck up the road a piece and scoop off all those toppings and make himself several extra bushels. Could be. All's we hope is he has been sentenced by the Head Clam Digger to dig clams in mud up to his hips, surrounded by a cloud of angry gnats, with poison ivy pollen caressing his bare forearms, for a century or so—if that's the truth.

Our good wife, in one of her rare concessions to our taste, deigned to slip a bottle of Moxie into the shopping basket at the supermart yesterday afternoon. We hadn't seen the delicious, bitter-sweet soft drink around the stores for years, and we'd long since regretfully considered that Moxie had gone the way of so many things of our youth—like Piedmont cigarettes, and Postmaster (2 for a nickel) cigars, and Brown's Beach jackets, and the Pierce-Arrow automobile and the Iver Johnson bicycle, and Cloverine Salve, and the Alladin kerosene lamp, and chloride of lime for malodorous privies, and home-refined skunk grease, and native-stuffed chourico, that fiery, spice-laden blood-pudding stuffed into pigs' intestines and eaten with much relish by the Portuguese and all their friends.

But we digress. Back to Moxie, that dark, refreshing brew of our youth. By guppy, next to pure spring water itself, there was nothing in this world to satisfy a summer thirst like Moxie. Something about the medicinal, herb-like bitterness of the stuff put it in a class by itself—far beyond the over-sweet pap they used to bottle under such names as birch beer and lemon–lime and cream soda.

And if the subtle health messages of the hucksters couldn't sell Moxie, the annual summer appearance of the Moxie Man did, clad in a trim, immaculate jockey outfit and riding a huge, papier mache white horse mounted on a Rolls Royce chassis. Why he'd sell Moxie to even the late John B. Dyer, Truro's most ardent prohibitionist, who wouldn't allow ginger ale in his home because of the connotation of the name.

In the twenties, by guppy, they used to say of a feller with lots of spunk that he had Moxie—so highly was the drink regarded. As, for instance, the day Bob "Dudsey" Meier was accidentally beaned by a fist-sized rock while playing a hotly contested game of duck on the rock at Wilder School. Tottered and slumped to his knees for a bit, did Dudsey, but almost before you could say Obadiah Brown he was back on his feet, bloody but unbowed. Moxie.

NINETEEN SEVENTY-TWO

1972

A day of incomparable beauty here in Pamet. Consider the following: sun, bright and warm to flood the valley and bring out the intense blue of the vast sky. Of wind, nary a whisper. Earlier we'd followed the high air currents by watching the motion of a few errant clouds, and read 'em a shade north of west. But now the clouds have been swept out oceanward, and not even the outermost branches of the trees are in motion, so we'll call it flat calm. There's still a thin veil of snow covering ground and buildings from last night's quiet storm, but in the warmth of the day—four degrees above freezing on our north porch—the white stuff is melting rapidly. Our house eaves are dripping in erratic pattern, and puddles are forming in the low spots of our lawn, where underground frost keeps the moisture from seeping down into the turf. A feller'd best take the fresh, pure morning air in small drafts and squint his eyes a mite to limit the ocular intake of the beauties of this last Sabbath in February. If there is a smell outdoors today, it's the odor that comes in with fresh washed laundry from the line. In all, a glorious day.

We must be getting old. Every so often we'll meet up with a neighbor, and we'll get to reminiscing about things we recall vividly from our youth, and we'll say, "Remember the winter the steamer Robert E. Lee went ashore up off Manomet, and the beach was loaded with marshmallows and pie filling, and water soaked Oh Boy bubble gum, and every dern school kid in town chewed so much of the stuff he suffered from the carminative effect, and the school room suffered from the . . ." and like as not we're met by a blank stare.

Take one day last week when we got to talking with Fire Chief Ray Joseph at town hall. "Fire department never does any burning off nowadays, does it Ray?" we deplored. "Remember when they used to torch the fresh Pamet, so's to get rid of wood ticks and mosquitoes and other insects?" A sympathetic cluck of the tongue from Ray. "Long before my time. You must think you're talking to my late beloved dad," was his reply. And we suppose he was right. But that's not to say we can't reminisce a mite for our own pleasure. This'd be say around the late 20's. Cape Cod Mosquito Control was just about getting under way at that time, and in addition to ditching the meadows and soaking the breeding spots of the pesky insect with sundry deadly oils, the CCMC had an idea that a roaring blaze that'd clean out all the dead cattails and meadow grass and low growing pucker brush would be no end beneficial to the general cause of eradicating the pests.

So, along about this time of year Charlie Joseph, then assistant forest warden for the town, would get the authorization from the county seat to enlist a group of men to do the job. And on a suitable morning, when the grass was tinder dry and a gentle zephyr was blowing in from the east'ard, all hands would gather down at Charlie's store and pile into his truck and aim for the headwaters of the crick at Ballston Beach.

Last minute instructions from Charlie: "Don't, under any circumstances, let 'er get away from you. Pay particular attention to the side meadows that lead up to private owners like John Dyer, and Peter "Shook" Morris and John Rich's place, and Fratus' Bend." And then all hands were issued shovels and brooms and burlap bags to be soaked in the limpid waters of the river and applied to any errant blaze, and then Charlie distributed some kerosene cans to several underlings, and they poured the stuff on the tinder dry brush bordering the town road, and touched matches to appropriate spots, and whoof—off she went. Quicker'n you could say Obadiah Brown the entire meadow, from bank to bank, was an inferno of blazing grass and brush—sparks flying high in the air to lose themselves in a pall of black smoke, the roar of burning material and the false draft caused by the blaze drowning out the excited, muffled cries of the firemen. Wild-eyed animals scurrying ahead of the fire—frantic rabbits and a red fox, and, abreast the Farwell place, a dun-colored doe and her fawn, streaking for the uplands. On any other occasion the breeze would have remained light as milkweed silk all the day long. Not so on burning day. Almost invariably the wind would pick up minutes after the blaze had been set, and from then on there'd be a frantic rush of men, in response to an urgent beating on an empty bucket or the hysterical hollering of a splinter group, to an area of danger. And mostly, the fire would be contained at the last moment, although we do recall one time when a dory, property of the Fratus family, if memory serves, was cremated instanter, and a year or so later Ed Snow's privy was slightly scorched. We can't honestly say if the mosquitoes, in those memorable years, were fewer in number—but it certainly was fun.

★ ★ ★

Signs of spring. Cars bearing athletic-looking young folks, with surf boards protruding from open windows, forsythia in almost-full blossom (we're a week behind the upper Cape towns, as usual). The song of the Rototiller worrying away at the damp, cool soil at Pamet gardens, ululating call of the mourning dove from some nearby hillside, tiny purple flowerets of Johnny jump-up in the grass. Motorcycles buzzing along the by-ways (Ray Dundas' oldest lad taking the other nine kids one at a time on his new bike). George Junior Morris tooling his brand new Honda into the town dump, where he insists we take a spin. Richard Perry on his way to Artie Joseph's sand pit, where the police take target practice, also mounted on a new cycle, and looking as though he'd enjoy chasing a criminal through the back woods, and so it goes. Temperature this glorious spring day is trying to sneak by the 70 mark, and the breeze is out of the southwest, and the sun is mental bright, and there's a delightful smell of spring in the air. Fresh crick mud, and green grass bruised by the rake of neat neighbors cleaning their lawns and clothes lines laden with household goods airing in the breeze. Flickers singing, and cock pheasants boldly crowing out there on the meadow. Spring, at long last, is here. Give April a D in your mark book, fellow pedagogue, and join us in hoping May will make it all up.

We're in the area of the dump, so why not skip over the hill to east'ard where a clump of lilac and a slight depression of an ancient cellar hole in the ground mark the locus of the homestead of Jonathan Lee, one of Truro's most famous mooncussers.

It will be recalled that the mooncussers patrolled the ocean beaches between the standard watches of the official government Life Savers, with the thought in mind that vessels in trouble, if they couldn't be rescued, should at least have the attentions of a group of men to remove valuable cargo. They got their unusual name from the fact that they hated the earth's satellite, since a bright orb made for safe navigation along the back shore. But in the dark of the moon, many's the vessel that would lose her bearings, especially if her skipper were steering by dead reckoning, and on those occasions the craft just could possibly go aground, and the mooncussers would swarm around her like hornets.

On certain overcast nights, rumor has it, the men would build fires on the beach, and a vessel coming up the coast would mistake the conflagrations for a friendly beacon, and the ship would wear in too close, and soon the treacherous bars would lay hold on her keel, and she'd be hard aground. Cape Codders have a saying that when you butcher a pig, you use everything but the squeal; in stripping a vessel, the mooncussers had the same philosophy. Every cussed thing that could be pried loose would find its way to some local storage spot.

Well sir, after a goodly number of vessels had been lured ashore in this fashion, the insurance underwriters cautioned all captains to pay no heed to lights on the backshore of Cape Cod, especially off'n Truro, and business for the mooncussers began to drop off. Looked as though they'd run out of vessels, soon, but it was Jot Lee who came up with a solution to the problem. Jot, it seems, had an old cow long past her prime. He was about to dispatch her with a wood maul one day and convert her into cow burgers and other related dishes, when he happened to glance at her hooves. He noted the splayed pedal extremities were extraordinarily broad—almost like a camel's—and this started a chain of thought in the crafty old feller's mind. Camel, sand—sand, beach—beach, backshore. . . .

So that evening he quietly made out to the barn, fastened a rope to the cow's halter, and led her, by back roads, over the dunes to the ocean. There he tied a pair of coal-oil lanterns to her horns, one green, one red, gave her a hearty slap on the rump, and headed her off to nor'ard. Jot said afterward the old critter waddling over the sand, must've looked, from a distance just like a coasting vessel complete with riding lights. And she must have looked realistic to the skipper of a packet offshore a few hours later, for he headed straight for the riding lights of what he afterwards claimed bore a remarkable resemblance to the Elijah Mayo out of South Truro.

The old cow's success, though, turned out to be her undoing. Jot worked her in the soft sand ten nights in a row, and though she brought in a lumber schooner on her final try, the effort of plowing through the soft sand proved too strenuous, and she expired at the surf's edge off Brush Holler. Before Jot could drag her off the beach, the captain of the schooner landed in a dory, and filed a full report with the insurance agent. And that was the end of Jot's scheme. Jot gave her a respectable burial, though, marked her grave, down near the sickle pear tree with a piece of the taffrail from the lumber schooner.

Ave atque vale, dear Jim Moynahan, our friend of lo! these many years. The genial Irishman died in Milton, on the holiday morning, and graveside services will be held at South Truro Cemetery as soon as his widow, Ethel, makes the final arrangements.

We first met Jim at town hall, shortly after WW II, when the gaunt, friendly guy and his beauteous bride, Ethel, were looking for some property on Cape Cod. We're happy in the knowledge that we were instrumental in locating a fine old Cape Codder for them over beyond the Hogsbacks.

We knew and loved Jim as a fine father, a good husband, a man of considerable expertise with the Model A Ford, a scholar of most refreshing ability in such things as languages (French, Italian, Japanese). And Jim was a musician of good repute all over the Narrow Land, and from New York to the Berkshires. We'll never forget the first time we saw Jim wet the reed of his ancient, battered, $3 Albert system clarinet and wail into the opening bars of "When the Saints" at some local jam session. Jim used to ride the ambulance with us when we were dog-tired, encouraged us when we were down in the dumps following a hard session at school, cheered us with a funny story when we were exhausted with the task of wheelbarrowing the sand out of our cellar-to-be—the memories are endless. May the Director of the biggest Dixieland Band of them all have a first seat for you in the woodwind section, Jim Moynahan.

Yesterday morning—six thirty it was—vagrant air currents and other acoustic conditions combined to bring to us, at our South Pamet house, the sound of the Truro police rousing the sleepers in the rest area a half-mile away at Red Sand Hill. "Rise and shine, folks," came the mellow voice of the man in blue through the electric bull horn in the cruiser. "This is Officer Perry of the Truro Police Department. We hope you have enjoyed your night's rest courtesy of the town of Truro. Now we request that you wake up and move along to enjoy the delights of the lower Cape. Please do not use the rest area for toilet facilities. We are going to turn on some martial music so that you can join us in morning calisthenics. Have a good day folks!"

And with that the strains of "American Patrol" crashed out in the morning air, and we could envision sleepy-eyed tourists, piling out of their cars up there on the state highway. As we went down cellar to fetch out our sea-clam rake so's we could hie off in pursuit of the wily bivalve, we paused at the end of the sidewalk and did several kneebends in time with the music.

Things are pleasant here at the big white building that the summer visitors so often identify as a church. Take last Friday, for instance. We were sitting at our desk, posting taxes, when the strains of "When the Saints Come Marching In" titillated our tympani. "What station do you have the radio turned to?" we queried Tessie Silva, the office gal next door. "WRKO, same as usual, and I've got the Rolling Stones doing a vocal now, turned down real low, so's not to bother certain people in the building," she sniffed.

So we arose from our desk and cocked an ear out the front door. We caught sight of a group of people in the parking lot of the Congregational Church, grouped around a small black combo—tuba, guitar, trombone, and a couple of instruments we couldn't make out—and they were giving out with some of the most delightful dixieland we've heard since poor Jim Moynahan put his horn away for keeps. "Funeral over there," explained Chief Harold Berrio of Truro's finest, who had just appeared on the scene. "Some artist feller from Provincetown, I hear tell." And then Tessie and Alberta Fields, stirred by feminine curiosity, left us to watch the store while they plodded down the sandy path that crosses Bridge Road for a better look at the proceedings. Came back a quarter hour later, they did, puffing with the exertion, shaking sand from their shoes, delighted with the whole ceremony. "And a young feller sang 'You'll Never Walk Alone' at the end of the affair," said Tessie. "And the poor man blowing the tuba stepped into a hole in the road and fell down—didn't miss a note, though," concluded Alberta. Sounds like a fine way to say good-bye to one's friend.

Other local notes: Cobb Library is getting a new roof with Pilgrim gray shingles this time, being expertly installed by neighbor Dave Colburn of Provincetown. And Tony Kolz dropped by our office at town hall yesterday to inform us he's taking up permanent residence in our fair town. And Jack Noons' bulldozers have finished the contract for spreading clay and otherwise grading off the base of the local dump (don't they call it disposal area in refined parlance?) and the lower deck looks like a football field. Seems a shame to dump garbage and trash on it. Gordon Russell, owner of the former Holway property up on the highway was kind enough to drop by our office a few days ago and present us with a clutch of red clay bricks, neatly embossed KANE (they're manufactured near his home town in Connecticut) and the handsome units will be used in the hearth of son Terry's new home now abuilding on Depot Road. In our mail, that perennial letter bearing on the return address space the legend "Superintendent of Schools, Provincetown, Mass" to remind us of our imminent return to pedagogical duties. Where has the summer gone?

And wasn't it about this time of year, a few decades ago here in Truro, that the annual Farm Bureau fair and supper used to be held at town hall? How long has it been since we elected a director to that venerable association? Is there a possibility the Farm Bureau could be revived? Seems to us it would be better to gather together to admire the fruits of toil and the bounty of Mother Nature rather than to rake each other to the bone over matters political or the condition of the town dump . . . but we digress.

In our day, Mr. James Rand served the town as director of the Farm Bureau, and his efforts were nobly crowned when, late in the summer, the harvest supper would be held at town hall. And we recall, the affair took place on a Saturday, and from early morning folks would start arriving at the building in the family conveyance of their choice—mostly Model T Fords among the automobiles—with a goodly number of Democrat wagons drawn by the family nag, groomed to a T for this occasion.

The venerable structure would soon be crammed with the product of the summer's work. Downstairs in the lobby there'd be caged fowl-hens and roosters, ducks, geese, turkeys, and an occasional Guinea hen all waiting to be judged for finest of show. Upstairs the ladies would display their fancy work, and hooked rugs, and flower displays, preserves, baked goods, while across the hall, in the men's department, lay the fruits and vegetables, and the eggs, proud offerings of Truro farmers. Joe Cabral, if we remember correctly, always raised the biggest watermelon, Manuel Corey invariably had the best plate of apples, and Alec Francis, the most monstrous hubbard squash. When it came time to judge the ladies' entries, Mr. Rand and his committee seemed to take more time and certainly more samples of the delicious fare than seemed necessary. When the blue cards denoting first prize had been properly placed, it would be late afternoon, and the line of impatient would-be diners would already be forming outside the dining room door. Among the guests you'd note the Ray Freeman family from Wellfleet, and Thede Nickerson and Si Young from Provincetown, and just about everybody from Truro and North Truro.

Supper would be a masterpiece of the culinary art. The ladies, flushed from the heat of the kitchen, would be bustling about the groaning trestle tables, refilling platters with pink sliced ham, and dumping more savory yellow-eye beans into the giant bowls, and pouring endless streams of boiling coffee, and forcing second helpings of salads and desserts on all hands.

The Herculean repast over, everybody'd shove back the chairs, and willing hands would clear away the upstairs gallery and the settees would be dragged out, and then there'd be a battle of music. A vocal exercise in which the men would attempt to drown out the ladies in matched songs; from the Golden Book of Songs the gals would trill away on "Spanish Cavalier," while the gentlemen would bellow away at "Soloman Levi." And later, for sentiment only, the kids would request the old standards: "Old Black Joe" or "Juanita." Come to think of it, many of the old chestnuts would be barred today, because they cast slurs on minority or ethnic groups. But back to the party.

Then, thrill of thrills, we youngsters would gawk as Hayes Small and his Highland Orchestra took the stage and tuned up. Hayes at drums, Ralph Tinkham and Joe Francis trumpets, Bert Ingraham and Clarence Snow, violins, Ina Snow, cello, Thede Nickerson, trombone, and Emma Smith, piano. Down through the hatch in the dance floor would go the settees to make room for dancing, and soon the strains of the Schottisch and the Portland Fancy and Gallop would fill the hall. Wouldn't it be nice to do over again—just the same?

Raindrops are making free-form patterns on the puddles of the blacktop outside our office window, falling so slowly we can count 'em. By our best estimate, four per square foot in the time it takes to say Obadiah Brown. And the wind is so light you can hardly call it a breeze. And it's from the southwest. Any warmer and it would be uncomfortably so. The slightest exertion raises beads of perspiration on a feller's upper lip. We saw 'em on Al Bettencourt's clean-shaven face at church this morning even as he sorted out change, a modern day money lender in the Temple. And at church, too, we became enamoured of Cathy (Silvia) Anderskow's three charming and beautiful toddlers. Learned a mite later that the Anderskows have three older kids, all, according to sister Mary Louise, just as pulchritudinous. But we digress.

The overcast is a mixture of low-lying cloud cover and clinging fog, and we can hear the muffled bass tones of the foghorn down at the Highlands. You could safely bet your last nickel that traffic will be thick as blackstrap molasses on the highway this afternoon, that there'll be car accidents of varying degrees of seriousness, that the wise Pamet native will stay at home and find some household chores to do. We propose to mow the rear lawn and if the mosquitoes will let us, yank up those bush bean plants that have yielded their final mess for the tribe O'Caghan. We might even de-tick the family dog and snip off a few glads for our child bride. Her disposition suffers on a gloomy, warm day like this, and some colorful flowers might cheer her up a bit.

We were propped up against the fender of our faithful VW in the parking lot outside the supermart yesterday, eyeing the passersby in our typical non-lecherous fashion when our child bride broke into our reveries with the usual cart full of groceries to be loaded into the car. Chicken again, we grumbled to ourself, eat much more of this stuff and we'll be breaking out in pinfeathers. Why in tarnation won't that wife of ours buy Moxie for a soft drink, fine, semi-bitter, herb flavor to the stuff. And cider—why this watery, pale substitute for good old fashioned apple juice. Got a darn good mind to trot up to Edgewood Farm this evening—belongs to the Schmidt-Young families now—and see if they don't still have the old cider press stowed away in some dark corner—and there must be an apple tree with a few bushels of spotted MacIntosh ready for pressing. And as the VW tooled out of the parking space, we got to reminiscing about the good old days, when, in response to the call from the farm on the hill that Francis Mooney, the genial, gray-maned caretaker, was ready to entertain a small group of friends at a pressing, and we'd gather, on a beautiful fall afternoon, at the Sheldon Dick Barn to attend to the chore.

The choicest of the crop had previously been disposed of, and the remaining Macs and Baldwins and Fall Greenings, windfalls, or worm drilled, or slightly bruised, would be stacked in a huge pile near the ancient wooden ciderpress. We'd fall to with great gusto, washing the fruit, then shoveling it into the hopper to the grinder, where, with satisfying crushing noises and much spattering of juice, the apples would be sliced to uniform size by the keen knives of the machine.

These slices were then transferred to the oak tubs, and the heavy handles would be inserted in the wooden screws to press down on the pulpy juicy mass. At this point we'd strain the pale golden cider as it ran from the wooden trough, and pour 'er off into glass jugs. There'd be sundry rest periods, during the golden afternoon, when we'd heatedly discuss the merits of the college football teams of the nation or politics, or the proper method of taking the wily sea clam in his lair. When fatigue made our hands lag at the press windlass, there'd be a trip to the darkest corner of the cellar, where a venerable charred oak keg would yield a bit of "poteen" as Mooney used to call it, heady, invigorating nectar made of this same cider, matured over the months, brewed with a secret method involving raisins, and potato yeast, and a strange bubbling action that allowed the gasses to escape through a water trap. And we were just about to empty a tubful of mashed pulp into the nearby trash can when the sobering voice of our child bride interrupted our daydreams.

"I asked you what flavor ice cream you'd like here at the roadside stand and you said 'poteen.' Never heard of it."

NINETEEN SEVENTY-THREE

1973

We made our usual brief junket down Pamet Harbor way this morning, and as we rolled down Ike Freeman's Hill and out onto the parking space by Pamet Harbor we got to thinking of the old railroad station that used to grace this spot. Gaunt, slab-sided, painted the standard mustard-ochre of the New Haven system, the building inside

presented a most intriguing appearance, with its fly specked walls, and its big, bold clock, ticking off the time in inexorable measure and the potbellied stove with its soft coal fire to give an unforgettable aroma to the waiting room. And often, while you were listening to the clack of the telegraph in Mr. Freeman's tiny cubicle behind the ticket window, you'd hear the distant, melancholy wail of the freight whistle from up to south'ard, beyond Grove's Crossing.

We recall one time questioning the station master, Harry Marlin, about the mysterious whistle code of the railroad. Harry was a wizened, wiry feller who had come from his native Brewster— Punkhorn way to be exact—by way of much bumping, thanks to his longevity, to Truro, where he found the work satisfying, and the natives friendly. He was aware the nearby basin of Pamet Harbor teemed with soft-shelled steamer clams and since there were long periods between trains when an ambitious man could slip down at low tide and dig a few washers of the delicacies, and ship 'em off to Boston for a good price, why Harry found the Truro location most enticing.

But we digress. On the occasion of which we speak, we were down at the Depot, watching a rusty freight locomotive clanking busily on the main line, shoving cars about in what to us appeared to be utter confusion. There was a switchman on the siding, yanking levers this way and that, and the rest of the crew was engaging in hand signaling and waving flags, and what interested us most, that cussed locomotive kept tooting its whistle in a senseless pattern. We noted that Harry was unoccupied at the moment, so we sauntered over to query him anent the strange noises.

Here Harry took a searching look at the clamflats, where the tide was fast ebbing. At this point, the engineer gave three short blasts on the whistle and Harry, anticipating our question, volunteered, "That means, back 'er up, slow." A glance at his big gold pocket watch, another squint at the tide. From the meadow at Mill Pond a heifer calf owned by neighbor John Gray now clambered up the cinder bank and stood curiously staring at the panting locomotive. The whistle emitted several short, angry shrieks as the engineer leaned out the cab window. The frightened heifer dashed back to the pasture and Harry observed, drily, "That means look aout, caow." Another glance at the basin, another brief consultation with his watch, just as the engineer pulled his cord for three shorts and a long. "How about that one. Harry?" we asked. "Well sonny, that means I got just about time to dig a washer of clams before the noon train." And off he went, and so far as we know, that's just what he did.

We did a double take a few days ago as we drove up by the Truro post office, glanced over our shoulder, and noted we could see clean over to Depot Road. The rather sizable sand hill that used to occupy the spot had been bulldozed away, leaving the venerable old building perched up on a knoll, exposed to all the elements. We got to thinking about those golden years, so long ago, when we attended the then Wilder Grammar School, later to serve as the local dispensary of the U.S. mail. And we saw in our mind the rank weeds that used to surround the building during the summer, soon to be trampled by restless feet when school opened, and inkberry growing along the fence, from which we used to strip the soft purple berries to make a vile, dye-like liquid that fermented in the inkwells. The rusty, squeaking pump on the concrete platform outside the coatroom door would be ready to yield its usual supply of crystal clear, ice cold water, soon's Dave Snow had put in a new set of leathers. Remember how, when a buddy who could be trusted pumped the handle you'd cup a grimy hand under the spout and slup up the cool liquid? And if he couldn't, he'd give the handle a quick fillip or two, and the resultant flood of water would run down your neck line chuck to your belly button.

And when the kids gathered there, on the first day of school, there'd be prodigious stories of adventure of the summer just passed. Bob Morris had gone to the Kickapoo Indian Show at North Truro and had seen a beauteous lady sawn in half. He'd even bought a bottle of the marvelous tonic, endorsed by several folks in the audience, on the basis of previous experience. But the stuff turned out to be nothing but a potent diuretic. Ralph Ormsby had worked on his Uncle Frank Joseph's farm all summer long. Pitched a mountain of hay, and hoed his way through the gardens, the equivalent of a line from here to the Canal, he'd betcha. The Cabral boys (they're resting up there in God's Acre on the hill, now) had helped fight the big brush fire atop Peter's Hill in the North Village, and they'd heard the popping of bottles in the flames as the fire reached the secret cache of liquor stored by John Lucas, the friendly neighborhood bootlegger.

Rusty Taylor, the state boy from Long Nook had gone to Boston, seen his first big league baseball game. He was fair itching to show the boys how to pitch an inside curve. And Manuel Perry boasted that he now owned a one-tube Crosley pup radio, better'n any crystal set in town, guaranteed to bring in WLS, the Sears, Roebuck station out in Chicago. Duds Meier had learned how to drive a car—only 12 years old, was Dud, and the task of depressing the heavy duty clutch on his dad's ancient Locomobile touring car gave him cramps in the gastrocnemius muscles. And to be shared in common—those memories of the German gliders at Corn Hill—they'd established some sort of record riding the warm air currents that rose over the cliffs of the bay shore. Forbidden by international treaty following WW I to fly power craft, they were—poor Germans were a broken race—they'd never go to war again, you could bet your Iver Johnson bicycle on that.

We lived only a stone's throw from the slab-sided, venerable old building, so it was unnecessary for us to fetch a cold lunch to school. But, in the perverse manner of all kids, we often struggled to forego the pleasures of a hot home-cooked meal in order to join the other students in toting a couple of sandwiches to be devoured with our schoolmates. And sometimes we had the opportunity of trading our viands with children from other ethnic or social backgrounds. We can see it all now, the black hands of the battered alarm clock on Mr. Peters' desk scissoring up on the noon hour. Restless shuffling of feet, an occasional furtive rumble from an empty stomach, a surreptitious stowing away of books and pencils. Then, the smart tinkly of the bell as Mr. Peters banged down with his palm on the button, and the general hectic rush for the coat room.

There in the friendly gloom of the gray painted anteroom would be the lunches packed in brown paper bags or homemade wooden boxes. (Willie Rose's kids had boxes made of mahogany from some vessel shipwrecked on the backshore, with real brass hinges. Or for those kids from families of means, boughten, shiny metal boxes from Sears, Roebuck.) Invariably, Mr. Peters' voice would cut through the babel of conversation with a stern, "Wash your hands, everybody." The memory of all those tiny microbes described in the hygiene class would aid in herding the kids in a mad scramble to the back platform, where, as one of the older boys primed the pump and levered away at the rusty handle, the rest of the kids would work the thin sliver of soap through grubby hands, rinse briefly under the ice-cold stream of water, then dash back to the building.

No delicatessen ever titillated the olfactory nerves more delightfully than did the classroom of Wilder Grammar School as the wax-paper wrappings were torn from sundry sandwiches and thermos bottles were uncorked and locally grown fruits were peeled. Over in the corner the Cabral brothers would be preparing to devour huge Vienna style loaves of home-baked bread, stuffed with Linguica and green peppers. Robert Duds Meier in the next row would be studying a mason jar filled with pickled pigs feet. Down near the red hot potbellied stove, a pork chop in Robert Gray's eager hands was giving off the unmistakable aroma of flowers of garlic from its long bath in vinho d'Alhos. And Herbie Rose was preparing a huge hamburger pattie for its searing over the hot coals. Side dishes of mustard pickles, and watermelon rind, and slabs of pie and cake, and cold Indian pudding would appear on the desks, and shiny MacIntosh apples would be polished on the questionable areas of a trouser seat. And there'd be huge, brown specked bananas, and heroic sized jugs of milk from Pamet's own cows, unpasteurized, unhomogenized.

We recall in particular the noon we managed to trade a prosaic corn beef sandwich to Wilfred Cabral for a brown, stuffed bulkie from his dinner pail. A quick peek inside revealed a thick leaf of lettuce, and a mysterious black sausage of uncommon aroma. We took one huge bite, and just as the flavor reached our taste buds, Wilfred was kind enough to warn us.

"That's homemade chourico, you know—and Ma went kind of heavy on the red pepper this time."

We've always considered that bit of advice to be the understatement of the boy's life. And, many glasses of water later, when the tears had cleared from our eyes and the fire from our alimentary tract had faded and gone, we made a vow never to eat chourico, that delectable Portuguese sausage, again.

Smell of chicken baking in the kitchen evokes memories of early days when we worked for Mrs. Sarah Yates, poultry Ms. of an earlier era here in Pamet. Sarah was a mild-spoken, deliberate lady, widder of a Methodist minister who eked out her existence based on her church pension by raising a few chickens at her property on Castle Road. We worked for Miz Yates on occasion, and that's how we temporarily at least, lost our taste for the bird. Saturday morning butchering was the cause of it all; Miz Yates favored a technique that involved stabbing the poor birds—you held 'em by the head as their trussed feet kicked against their thongs—with a thin, sharp knife that was supposed to penetrate their brain structure. Properly done, the stabbing would cause the bird to relax its muscles so's the skin tension would relax, allowing you to pluck the birds easy as pie. Dry-plucking it was called, and the resultant bird was supposed to look so appetizing, as compared with your ordinary scalded carcass, that it brought a premium price. But we hated every minute of the task, the blood-letting and the agonized squawks of the trussed birds, the reproachful glances of the rigid, red-combed roosters as they were dragged from crates to meet the sticking knife. And, over all, the smell of hot blood, and the itching from the pesky hen lice.

We had always considered our experiences in Miz Yates' cellar sufficiently grizzly until we heard Anthony Marshall tell of his good aunt "Bobeena" Marshall, so nicknamed because of her pronounciation of the word bobbin, an item she had occasion to mention because she had worked for years in the cotton mills of New Bedford. A huge, semi-invalided woman, she spent her days supervising the activities of several state wards from her kitchen on Depot Road. Mostly she sat in her cushioned chair, issuing orders all day long to the household underlings, doing what chores she was able to do while seated.

Anthony's life had been a guarded one until the day he entered Aunt Bobeena's kitchen to be greeted with a sharp command, "Tharling. Aunt Bobeena want you to . . ." and here she launched into a detailed account of work projects for nephew Anthony. (Seems the state boys were otherwise occupied.) It involved scattering a few handfuls of corn on the henhouse floor, pegging the door shut (providing the birds had been lured into the building), selecting a plump, healthy looking bird from the flock, and fetchin' it into the house to Aunt Bobeena. Anthony, of course realized the bird was eventually to find its way into the pot, and while he did not relish the idea of being a part to the crime, he planned to be absent from the actual butchering, God willing and his reflexes sufficiently speedy.

Shortly he had captured his bird, and with trembling hands, he toted the squawking bird into the Marshall kitchen, to be greeted with words of praise from Aunt Bobeena.

"Tharling. T'ank a you. Nice chickeeng." Here she took the hen from Anthony's hands, and before the astounded boy could move from the spot, she skillfully wrung the bird's neck, drew a razor-sharp knife across its throat, and plunged it into a dish which lay in her lap. "And to this day," says Anthony, "nearest I can come to eating chicken is a fried egg."

Stories, especially cocktail party stories, usually go in pairs, we've observed, so we'll start 'er off with the yarn told us many years ago by Horace Pop Snow, anent Samuel Paine. "Lived over Long Nook way, did Sam. And not, by any means to be confused with the other Sam Paine who earned the nickname Sam Narsty, because he never took time to blow his nose, and the poor feller had catarrh somethin' awful. But this Sam, Samuel C., was an apothecary. Kept shop in the former post office building that Mrs. Clarence Day had moved up from the square to her prop'ty on the hill. Had all his drugs and patent medicines and other notions in the ell of the house, and since it was one of the few places of business in the village, why the young fellers used to hang around there evenin's, while they were waiting for the mail. Always a-playin' jokes on poor old Samuel, they was.

"I remember one evenin' me and Willie Hopkins and Will Honey were in the shop, seein' how long we could take to buy a couple plugs of Mayo's Dark tobacco and I spied the big ball of wrapping string Sam'l had down to the other end of the counter. The string was in one of them old-fashioned cast-iron cages, with the bight end stickin' out of a hole. So while Samuel was cuttin' a dime's worth of tobacco from the plug with his big, fancy plug cutter, I quick pulled on the string and tied 'er tight to Willie Hopkins' coat tail. Willie paid for his tobacco, turned on his heel and went out the door, and started runnin' full speed across Wilder's Dyke. Poor old Samuel heard the string rattling in the holder, and he tried to grab it, or cut it off with his pen-knife but his eyesight was so poor he couldn't get it, and time he finally chopped 'er off with his knife, the string was almost all gone."

We had hardly chuckled our way through the punch line when Anthony Marshall came up with his sequel. "Poor old man certainly was handicapped. Got deaf in his old age, and his eyesight, as you pointed out, was poor, and over the years he had neglected his filing and labeling system, so that all his medicines were either piled willy-nilly on the shelves, or stowed away in wooden drawers, with nary a tag on 'em. My dad, John Marshall, senior, used to tell how Mr. Paine would fill a prescription or an order for a patent medicine in later years. 'Ipecac?' he'd repeat the customer's order. 'What's that label say on that drawer up there? Oh, no label on 'er, eh? Let's see now.'

"And old Samuel would open half a dozen or so drawers, and wet his thumb, and dab the moistened digit into each drawer, tasting the substance that clung to his thumb. 'That tastes about right,' he'd allow, after several samplings. 'But Ipecac and Smith's Udder Ease Powders are somewhat similar so you better try a small dose of this first. If you don't go numb and your lips don't pucker up, you have the right stuff.' "

Anatomy of a summer storm. Sunday morning and we awaken with the odd feeling it should be sunrise, but there's no sun to be seen gilding the eastern range.

Peculiar, oppressive stillness to the air, and only the most hardy birds are trying out their voices: a clutch of sparrows, and a sentinel crow, far up on the hillside, and a catbird giving out with his own feline call this morning. The house grows darker as the clouds thicken. Comes the distant rumble of thunder, evoking a complaining whine from our dog, Duke, as he returns to the back porch, his patrol of the property unfinished. The still morning air commences to stir, soughing through the locust branches, and the first big droplets of rain patter on the shrubbery and the house eaves gather up the wet stuff and release it in irregular gouts from the edge of the shingle courses. Through the open window comes the sudden nostalgic smell of honeysuckle blossom, and the tang of fresh cut grass. The kitchen window panes streak and blur, and the view across valley to Dyer's Hills damps out, and we reluctantly switch on the lights and set the coffee on to brew. A quick prayer that the rain won't be heavy enough to convert our swamp garden into a rice paddy as it did in the recent torrential downpours, a glance at the clock to see if the ancient adage "rain before seven, clear before eleven" can be invoked this morning. Not so; the hands of the clock scissor up onto eight hours. Lord, if only we could choose the spots for the rain to fall. Upland territory could use a shower every day, but only the mosquito, looking for flooded ditches to hatch her larvae, could use the wet stuff in the lowlands.

Receipt of our Coleraine postcard this morning evoked memories of a yarn once told us by the late Sherwood Bud Fisher who, in our mind, will always represent the old Coast Guard Surfmen: the prototype of that hardy breed who manned the stations along the back shore for so many years. Here's Bud's story.

"I remember the time the vessel Montrose went aground about half a mile south of the Orleans station. Old Capt. Nickerson was in charge of rescue operations; fourth of March, it was, temperature down to about four above zero, wind a howlin' and a huge sea breakin' over the bows of the craft. We dragged our beach apparatus to the scene, and Capt Nick managed to lob a shot from the Lyle gun over the top riggin' of the

Montrose. But just as the vessel's crew commenced to make fast and haul in the heavy line for the breeches buoy, a huge sea struck the craft, and she broke in two. Five men were left stranded on the bow section, and they all drowned. But two men managed to cling to the stern, which drifted ashore, and we threw them a handline and hauled them out of the boilin' surf.

"One thing about that wreck. It taught me to respect the Lyle gun to such an extent I began a thorough study of the equipment. Never saw a Lyle gun? Well sir, the Lyle gun is a small brass cannon, especially made for the Coast Guard, used to fire a shot attached to a line over the riggin' of a ship in distress offshore. The crew of the vessel in turn hauls up the heavy line, fastens it to the highest spot in the riggin', and rigs a pulley to haul a canvas bosun's chair back and forth on the trolley arrangement, transporting the crew.

"My own idea was that we were a mite skimpy with the black powder propellant. I figured if you put a good load in the barrel the shot would run truer, and carry farther, come high wind or whatever. So the first day I had a chance to supervise beach drill, I rammed an extra measure of black powder into the barrel, and gave the order to fire, at the drill post—WHAMMO. After the smoke died away, I saw that the explosion had burned the end of the faking line clean off. I quick spliced the line to the firing iron, and next time, using the same heavy charge, I took the precaution of soaking the line in a bucket of salt water to see if it would protect 'er from searing away—but this time, she simply sheared clean off. Too much propellant, apparently. Made another splice, I did, and finally admitted, in my own mind, that old Capt. Nick and the other experts in the field knew what they were talking about when they made up the powder charges for the gun.

But I wasn't out of the woods yet. When Capt. Nick came back from liberty, he called for a quick practice with the Lyle gun. Ran an expert eye over the equipment, he did, and when he got to the faking line and the firing iron, he bellowed out, 'Someone's bent a new splice on this line.' And then he put on his reading glasses and looked a mite closer. 'And it's a Wellfleet oysterman's splice by guppy. But it's whipped Nantucket style and the whole thing has been set down with Mayos' Dark plug chewin' tobacco. Fisher, come into the office. I want to talk with you.'"

Gadzooks, what with this energy crisis, local petrol stations (Provincetown) running out of gasoline, five per cent reduction of electric current effective this week, folks picking the dump for every last scrap of wood to toss into their fireplaces or wood-burning stoves, the president's emergency message anent the situation to be telecast this evening, we got to thinking about warm houses, warm beds. And therein can be found a passel of memories on the part of this aging citizen.

We recall those folks in our day who had, perforce, to sleep in cold bedrooms—no central heating in our Cape houses in those days. Windows open a crack to the bitter nor'west breeze to dispel tuberculosis bacilli from the atmosphere and so dern cold it'd freeze liquid at the bedside (Carrie Adams used to say she had to chip her upper plate out of the water tumbler many a winter morning). Certainly if you are a native Truroite of our vintage, you remember the nightly ritual of hitting the sack. When the first cold snap struck, the big, shiny gas burner (as they called solid fuel stoves in those days for some mysterious reason) in the living room was stoked into the red glow of life at bedtime. The method of retiring changed as inevitably as the seasons. By tacit agreement, you'd be allowed to slip out of your clothes and don your nightgown, or pajamas in the lea of the stove. You'd rotate slowly in the heat, like a barbecued chicken, absorbing the energy particles, and finally goaded by an insistent parent, you'd grasp the small kerosene lamp, fling open the living room door, and dash off to the bedroom. The lamp would smoke and flare dangerously in your shivering grip, but finally you'd pop 'er on the bed table, and dive into the ice-cold coverlets. You'd huddle into a compact ball, and pull the quilts over your head, so the warmth of your own breath would be imprisoned with you.

As the winter progressed and the weather got colder, various mechanical aids were brought into service. The faithful hot water bottle, for instance; an excellent bed-warmer indeed, but not without its shortcomings. The cussed thing would leak, at the most inappropriate times, sometimes because the rubber wore out, sometimes because of a razor sharp, unmanicured toenail. Then, too, if you weren't careful to press out the bubble of hot air after you'd filled it to allow a mite of space for expansion, the hot water bottle had a tendency to expand like a poisoned pup, and occasionally she'd rupture right in your bed.

For them as distrusted the rubber bag, there were various substitutes. Roger Burhoe, from over Long Nook way, we recall used to favor a soapstone: a huge, square block of grayish material that he'd pop into the oven of the kitchen range an hour or so before he'd be ready to retire. You couldn't help admiring Roger's dexterity as he juggled the smoking soapstone into a red flannel bag and expressed it gingerly to his bedroom. But there were occasions when Rog'd get involved with an exciting episode of the then radio thriller, Dr. Fu Manchu, and the stone would get super-heated, and he'd like to burn himself out of his own bed as a result. Lacking a soapstone, you could even make use of the lowly red clay brick, or any substance that would hold the heat.

We once heard the story of the late Sam "Narsty" Paine of Long Nook, who had neither soapstone nor clay brick available. So in his capacity as caretaker for the Methodist Cemetery, he came across a fragment of slate tombstone that had crumbled into sections, due to the elements. He fetched home the piece of slate, and het 'er up on the top of his parlor gas burner, and took 'er to bed with him, wrapped up in a leg he'd cut off his last year's winter pajamas. But he'd overheated the bed-warmer, and in his sleep, he had pressed the calloused soles of his feet firmly against the slate. The next morning, as he hobbled out of bed, he asked his wife to examine his tortured pedal extremities. "Redder'n the eyeballs of a ruttin' bull," she informed him. "And hold on, Samuel—put your feet together—I can read just as plain as day, 'Gone, but not forgotten . . .'"

NINETEEN SEVENTY-FOUR

1974

Last time we looked, the thermometer on the back porch read twenty four degrees, and we'll wager she hasn't gone up a notch in the last hour. Mostly because the sky is overcast so there's nary a bit of warmth from the hidden sun, and in part because the wind is still out of the northwest, a quarter generally conceded to produce breezes cold as a banker's heart. Partly, too, because there's that layer of snow on the ground from yesterday's storm—a layer say, knee-deep to a tomcat—powdery, and even-spread as a frosting on one of Rene Boespflug's cakes, and as yet unsullied by dirt from man afoot or in automobile. The valley, where it lacks the snow cover, is a study in grays and browns, of locust tree bole and branch, and alder clump and tattered cattails and pimpernel grass and rumcherry switches nodding in the cold wind above their white blanket. And the countryside is quiet. We'd almost welcome the querulous squall of a blue jay this morning, or the grind of gears as a truck down on the highway double-clutched for Corey's Hill. Time to fetch some kindling up from the cellar and build a fire to dispel the gloom and the chill of this February Sabbath morning. Wish you were here to share it with us, city folks.

Not without a bit of humor, these hectic days before town meetin' and election. Proof? Consider the visit we had from Dick Kelsey, Chatham photographer a few days back. Dick had been commissioned to take some aerial views of Pamet Harbor, and of Ballston Beach, and of the Highland Golf Course, and the south section of Beach Point for the town fathers. Came the pealing of our phone at town hall and, "Like to drop off some pictures for your perusal. If I fly over Snow Field during the noon hour, could you be waiting over there to pick 'em up?" We said yes, of course, and a bit later when the tiny blue and white monoplane buzzed town hall, we quick slipped on our coat and whipped over to Snow Field.

First pass, Kelsey dropped an empty milk carton to judge the wind drift and direction, then with a graceful swoop, he idled over on a southwesterly course and popped a package from the open door of his plane that landed practically in our outstretched arms. We waved a thank you to him, and prepared to hie off to town hall in our car, but the errand had apparently not yet been completed. Back swooped the plane, this time barely clearing the pine trees of the Snow Field perimeter, and a be-goggled head poked out of the cabin as the engine dropped again to idle. "Should have stayed right in your car, Mate. I could have popped 'er right through the window for you!"

Another light note came from acting Chief of Police Win Farwell, told in the crisp, TV style so popular with the cops and robbers series: "Awakened at 6:18 by a strange sound outside bedroom window of my home on South Pamet Road. Reached for service pistol under pillow, realized I had left it on Sam Browne's belt hanging on back of chair. (Pistol under pillow invariably promotes headache.) Rubbed sleep from my eyes, pulled on uniform trousers (shoved both feet into same leg on first attempt) seized revolver in right fist, walkie-talkie radio in left, cocked gun and flicked on radio simultaneously. Wiped steam from window pane, scanned area from left to right. Sinister-looking clump of daffodils peeking through pine needles, rumcherry bush sheltering insolent bluejay, garbage can blown over by recent winds, and—gadzooks—two huge black and white ruminants browsing on bunch of chives by kitchen door. Dash for telephone. Call Mooney ranch down the road a piece. Advise owner George Mooney to stand by corral gate to head off animals. Finish dressing instanter, climb into police cruiser, give long blast on federal tweeter-whoofer siren, pair of steers leave premises at full gallop, still munching on chives. Burn rubber in driveway, proceed at high speed pursuit down South Pamet Road. Mooney brothers waiting to detour steers into pasture. Gate slams behind animals. Ten four. Over and out."

Animals, by gosh, have often been the bane of Truro's finest, in proof of which this yarn, told us many years ago by Pamet's chief emeritus, Harold Berrio. It all started when Harold's police radio flashed a report of an attempted mugging on Head of the Meadow Road. So Harold made arrangements to meet the young couple who had originated the complaint, at a designated area, where he queried them in great detail anent their frightening experience. Seems the pair had driven into a secluded wood road to "do some kaloopin" as the chief expressed it. Just as they got to the hand-holding stage, they heard the sound of air escaping from a rear tire. Boy, disgusted, gets out with flashlight to repair tire, girl sticks head out of window, gazing dreamily into the pitch black night. Comes the dainty measured sound of footsteps on the pine needles, a warm, grassy breath, the smacking sound of pursed lips, the nuzzle of warm flesh.

"So, naturally, thinking it was her boyfriend, the gal puckers up and smooches," explained the minion of the law. "And right in the middle of the kiss, she heard the sound of her boyfriend, other side of the car, wrenching off them lug bolts. Realizing she was being smooched by some strange masher, she let out a scream. The smoocher wrenched himself free, with a sound like a toilet plunger being ripped loose, and whoever he was went crashing off into the woods."

Well sir, Harold snapped his book shut as the kids finished their story, and he vaulted into the cruiser, and drove back, siren wailing, lights flashing, to the scene of the encounter. Grabbed his bug light and played it on the ground, determined to exhaust every clue before he called on the resources of the County Identification Agent. He played the beam of the light here and there, and finally, there on the soft sand, he found the unmistakable prints of a donkey.

"Follered those prints in a general northwesterly direction for almost two miles and derned if they didn't lead right up to the Governor Prence Motel. And derned if there wasn't a cussed donkey, mooching a head of lettuce from the produce truck parked near the delivery door. But when I yelled at him, he slipped away into the night, and last I saw of him he was navigating for home, down Pond Road way."

The South Pamet Kanes shamefully proud this day at news from son Mike, calling from San Diego to tell his mother he'd made Dental Technician 1st in Uncle Sam's Navy—this at a time when ratings are most slow in being awarded, especially in this specialized field. Perhaps, when Mike arrives in July with his lovely wife Carol and their two kids for a month's leave, he'll be able to work up a partial plate for his dad. Seaclam shells will be just fine.

Folks around town are waiting for the initial reports from Pamet Harbor, where Truro's first lady harbor person is supervising boat traffic on the ramp and in the basin, and generally keeping an eye on things maritime. We made the mistake of referring to the lady by her given name, since that's what was printed on her appointment certificate—Carole Rey—and few of her friends knew whom we were referring to. "Oh, you mean C. Rey," they corrected us. Perhaps we should drop by the basin some day soon and catch Harbor Person Rey when she's not too busy and fill her in on the historical and special and physical background of this interesting area. "Back in the twenties," we'll begin, "this area used to be called the Depot. The New Haven Railroad tracks and the tiny complex of buildings—the cattle-loading platform and the freight house and the passenger station— dominated the scene. Across the spur siding was a big coal bin, from which Ike Freeman, the station agent, used to fetch soft coal for the potbellied stove in the depot and it seems there was always a boxcar on the siding, ready to unload or take on some freight.

"Then, as now, the Depot was a popular bathing beach. Feller could go down there at low tide and dig himself a bucket of clams, and soon's the tide was high enough, he could go for a swim. Dive off the trestle if he'd a mind to. (Remember how the kids used to stand trembling on the outboard platforms that held the water barrels while the three o'clock passenger train rumbled across the bridge, breathing steam and sparks just inches from their bare hides?) And then you could hitch a ride up town with Ezra Hopkins, the mail man, in his ancient Model T Ford beach wagon, or if he had a full load, you might climb up on the Democrat wagon beside Roger Burhoe, and help him hand out the still-warm bread from the city bakery to customers along the road. Sell a dozen or so loaves before you got to your destination, Eben Paine's Store.

"But the harbor itself was entirely different in those days. The main crick used to flow out through an opening down Corn Hill way. Trap boats, we recall, could chug in there for moorings at half tide, the water was that deep. And Gull Island was connected with what is now Depot Beach by a narrow isthmus that had been banked with neat cubes of brown peat cut from the river bed when the original channel was dug, some years before. So there were actually two separate entrances from the foreshore: the aforementioned Pamet River, and the channel, so-called, which began at the present, jettied entrance, ran due east to a rather sizable basin that still exists, abaft the yacht club. On the shore of the basin, about where the boat ramp is now located, there used to be the bones of a beached sloop—you could just make out her name IRIS on her weathered counter—and rumor had it she'd been engaged in the rum-running trade, had sprung a leak, and had been abandoned on the shore of the newly dredged basin.

"In any event, the IRIS lay there for years, her water-filled hold swarming with crabs and minnows, eels skulking about the barnacled keel at high water. 'Don't go near the channel,' our parents used to warn us, every time we set out for the Depot." And that's part of what we'll tell C. Rey about the Depot and her new job.

So the wind, at long last, has swung around to the sou'west, and today, the final day of June, is bringing all the bonuses that come with that happy breeze. Temperature's up in the mid-eighties, and there's a haze in the sky that makes things take on a mite of a bluish cast, and the smell of summer is in the air. Blacktop baking in the sun, and sundry grasses and pollens, and fresh meadow mud, all add their aromas to the sultry afternoon. Hum of traffic comes to our ears from down on the highway, and a plane drones overhead, and earlier there'd been much whoofing and tweeting of police sirens and fire sirens and, for all we know, of ambulances and rescue squad trucks; but the doors of the fire station when we drove by, were buttoned down, and we hazard the guess the fire must have been of the false alarm variety. Along the roadsides the rumcherries (seems only yesterday we were reporting them in blossom) are hard, green pellets building up to the ripening stage. Queen Anne's lace in first blossom, nodding gravely to its neighbor plants; old maids pinks and goldenrod still filling out. And the birds are in song this afternoon, mourning doves mournfully gossiping on the hillside, and a leather-lunged quail telling everybody he's Bob by name, and white in color.

Drove by the home of the late Arthur Cobb on Pond Road down in the North Village the other day. Darn near stopped in for a bit of gossip and maybe a yarn until we remembered that poor old Art has long been sleeping in God's Little Acre on the hill. But we did recall a visit we paid to Art many years ago. Raining that day, it was, probably late in the fall of the year and something about the weather, sudden spray of raindrops on the multi-pane kitchen window, driving scud of mist and droplets on the narrow pond across the street, prompted Art to delve back in memory to his days in the old Life Saving Service.

"Weather like this, up to the back side, the feller on patrol had to figger pretty close on tides and wind," boomed Cobbie, as he settled into his favorite captain's chair and scraped the dottle from his blackened briar. "Sometimes the tide'd be running right up to the bank, and you'd have to decide, instanter, whether you'd take the alternate route top of the dunes where the wind'd like to blow you half a mile inshore or stick to the beach, pick the right time to gallop between the waves, and make your patrol along the shore. Quite a gamble." Cobbie was paring Mayo's Dark plug into the briar, and now he paused long enough to kindle the tobacco aflame.

"I remember the time I had the south patrol from Highland on the midnight watch. Drivin' rain, something like this, wind off to the east'ard—say a mite north of east—the night blacker'n the inside of an undertaker's derby. Lord, how I hated to leave the warmth. Finally I got up my courage, and gulped down one last cup of Ida Hatch's bitter black coffee to fortify myself against the elements, put on my foul weather gear, and grabbed the door knob.

"'Ain't you going to take a lantern?' asked Hiram Rich as he sort of checked me over. And I replied right smart, 'No. Lanterns is for old ladies and smooth-cheeked boys, Hiram.' And with that, I slammed the door behind me, and buried my head down in my collar, and trudged off down shore."

We gathered there must have been bad blood between the two surfies, Cobb and Rich and then we recalled an earlier yarn told us by Cobbie, in which he had hoaxed Hiram into blowing into a bogus lung-pressure tester. The cussed thing had sprayed lampblack into poor Hiram's eyes, and he had sworn to—but we digress.

"Well sir, about half an hour later I come up to the claybanks near Long Nook, and from the sound of the surf a'pounding at the foot of the rise, I judged I'd either have to detour up to the top of the bank, or sprint along the beach between the waves." So Cobbie listened for the breakers, until he caught the rhythm of their breaking, and he waited until their strength waned a bit—counted 'em in a series of seven, did Cobbie—and then he took a deep breath and dug his rubber boots into the sand, and off he galloped, skirting the very edge of the lower bank.

"Then, by guppy, just as I was almost across, I stumbled over something that brought me a-sprawling arse over tea kettle. Soft it was to the touch, and hairy, and as I ran my hands slowly over it, I could feel a big pair of lips, and some teeth, and a pair of eyes, squinted hard shut, and my left hand picked out a big, bony spine. 'Good Lord,' I said to myself, 'this feller must have been a circus giant. He'd go a good six hundred pounds.'" But the Cobb hands continued to explore, and soon discovered at the end of the spinal column a stout, hairy, tail. "Then it come to me; realized right away I was astraddle of a critter from some cattle boat. Quite often the cattle would die at sea, and the crew would dump 'em overboard."

By this time the cycle of seven waves had been completed, and the surf was mounting higher on the strand, and Cobbie had just time to clamber to his feet and dash for safety, else he'd have been drenched by the surf; might even have been washed off his feet.

The rest of his patrol passed uneventfully. Made it in proper time to the half-way house, did Cobbie, and paused for a moment to pass the time of day with Manuel Corey, the surfman from Pamet River. Cobbie's story of the huge animal on the beach evoked only the slightest interest from Corey. Manuel had stumbled across things on the beach as would turn a feller's hair white; and then the two men buttoned on their foul weather gear and headed back to their respective stations.

"Started carryin' a lantern after that. Gov'ment regulations, anyways. And no sense breakin' a leg because you can't see where you're going."

Disillusioned no end, we were, to learn from John Worthington when he stopped by our office at town hall the other day, that one of our childhood legends was without basis in fact. We're referring to the romantic yarns that used to explain the presence of the rotting hulk of the old sloop Iris in the original basin of Pamet Harbor. We had been told, and so reported, that the vessel had been engaged in the rum running traffic, that she had slipped into Pamet Harbor to avoid seizure by the Coast Guard, her cargo of strong spirits had been lugged ashore and hidden in a nearby cache and when it came time to disembark, the owners of the Iris found that the channel had shoaled so the deep-keeled craft couldn't navigate back to deep water.

Not so, said John. The Iris, in fact, had been high liner of the Provincetown fishing fleet, and her skipper, Captain Mayo, had determined to give her a decent burial, as it were, in the tiny landlocked inlet of Truro Harbor. Wish we'd been out cutting cemetery lots when John came by.

Remember how the late Horace Pop Snow used to tell how he'd lost the first joint of his right index finger? The Snow brothers, David and Charlie and Norman and Horace (Isaiah was too young, else he'd have been there too) had been assigned chores on a rainy day. Fall of the year, it was, and first thing on the docket was cleaning and topping turnips in the barn. And like most boring chores, turnip topping had to turn into a contest to make it barely tolerable to the energetic young fry. Feller who topped the biggest quantity of the root delicacies would be dubbed champion for the week. "And they everlastin'ly went at it," to quote Horace.

"But I'd spent a good while sharpening my knife—heavy, long-bladed affair, almost big as one of them South American machetes and the keen aidge gave me just a whisker of an advantage. That is, until I took my eyes from my work, and raised the blade in that chopping motion, and brought 'er down to where the turnip crown should have been—only my finger was in the way. Chopped off that joint cleaner'n old Doc Bell could have done it with his scalpel." Pop says he almost lost his taste for turnips as a result of his injury. "Especially when they came out with a special pink hybrid from Burpee Company."

You wouldn't have given a McGovern campaign button for the chances of a good day if you'd arisen at sparrow burp this morning and studied the weather as did we. To our myopic eyes the countryside was most gloomy. Thick overcast, barely stirred by a light sou'west breeze, low barometer, temperature in the 70 degree area. Salt clogged in the shaker, Sunday go-to-church clothes limp to the touch; it even seemed to us the egg water took a mite longer to boil, due to the heavy atmospheric conditions. Lord, we reflected as we scraped the stubble from our chin, if only we could wring the dampness from the air and distribute it evenly over our parched lawn. And the fresh crick we noted as we made our brief pre-Mass junket about town, is as low in its banks as we've seen it. Border of dark brown and marking the area between the cattail roots and the limpid waters of the Pamet. Shrubbery needs a good hosing, and the vegetable garden wants a drink, too.

But even as we change to cooler clothes, comes the sun, hot and sultry between the wind-driven clouds, and the traffic picks up as folks wend their way to the ocean beaches, and the sudden, rasping metallic call of the hot weather bug fills the valley. Not too bad a day after all.

Ordinarily no Gertie Gloom we, but we got to thinking as we studied the calendar today that its only a few weeks till the opening of school. And like most retired pedagogues we feel the urgent nagging feeling of preparing for the opening session that's not for us. And our memory goes back even further, to the old days when Wilder School served as the Temple of Learning for this section of the town.

Naylor Hatch would have been the janitor then: a thin, wiry man who doubled as truant officer (we can vouch for the reputation Naylor had of being able to outrun the fleetest kid in town). Naylor chewed the biggest cud of tobacco in Truro, he could out eat any man in Pamet at the church bean suppers, and he possessed a vocal range that enabled him to sing any part from first tenor to deepest bass. But we digress.

In connection with his janitorial duties at Wilder, Naylor usually commenced to spruce up the building a few weeks before classes commenced. He'd sandwich these chores between his regular work on his farm. First of all, he'd sweep the floors clean with the worn stub of a broom found in the wood room, and then he'd swab the splintered, hard pine boards with a foul-smelling liquid that sometimes, long after school opened, would weep from the wood pores. Result: the kids would slip and slide in hair-raising fashion. The blackboards would get a coat or two of black asphaltum and turps—the slate blackboard had not yet been installed—and on alternate years the desk tops would receive a layer of varnish. Over the years, the varnish had built up to a considerable thickness, and sundry designs such as initialed hearts and naughty legends had been perpetuated under the amber cover.

The venerable potbellied stove would sport a fresh once-a-year polish, and Naylor would worry away at the spider webs and the dust of the summer with a big, ragged turkey feather duster. The coat rooms would receive similar treatment, as would the back room, where the wood and coal were stored. If the pungent, split pine supply was low, Tony Rose, from up towards the Wellfleet line, would be notified, and he'd drive down in his brass-radiatored Model T Ford with a quarter cord of wood. (Tony, in those years, was one of three registered Democrats in the town of Truro. But to our uneducated eye, he looked just like other folks.) Like as not, the Red Jacket pump near the Big Part door would have dried out her leathers during the summer season for want of use, so Charlie Snow would come up to overhaul the rods and the lower cylinder.

And the schoolyard would be a tangle of old maids pinks and inkberry and beach plum and rumcherry and poor man's grass, but Naylor knew that the scuffing, busy feet of the school kids would soon wear paths in the jungle. And there were incidental chores, too; a pane of glass to be set, or a desk to be refastened to the floor, flagpole halyards to be replaced, a new plank in the wooden step, nails for the sagging board fence.

Having put the main building in good order, Naylor would then direct his attention to the big, duplex, co-ed privy. Beachplum bushes thrived mightily around the building, and Naylor was obliged to hack out the paths with the axe from the wood room. And having made the building accessible, the janitor would thin a strong batch of sylpho-naphthol and belabor the interior walls with the solution. And then he'd go over to Eben Paine's and buy half a dozen cans of chloride of lime and dump them into the privy vault. It would be many weeks before the choking, chemical odor of the chlorinated lime would abate so's a feller could visit with his friends in the little house. Wonder if you can still buy that stuff in the local grocery stores?

Childhood friend and school mate Robert Gray, until recently resident of Truro, died last week at the Cape Cod Hospital. We'll always remember Robert as the champion duck on the rock player at the old Wilder Grammar School (he was so tiny he could weave his way through the other players without being tagged), as a rival newspaper boy who used to challenge us on his Ranger bicycle (we used to push a heavy, cumbersome Iver Johnson bike in those days), as a fellow altar boy (poor Robert always had trouble finding the candle wick with his taper), as a friend and neighbor, always ready to explore the hills for a productive blueberry patch or beachplum thicket. We used to send Robert out on the thin ice at Arrowsmith's Swamp to see if the first skim would support us for winter skating and we'll miss the friendly little man. Ave atque vale, old friend.

We got to browsing through the law books at town hall one day recently when the question of the so-called Blue Laws was raised in connection with the issuance of licenses for Sunday businesses. The title of the ancient, leather bound volume: "Perpetual Laws of the Commonwealth of Massachusetts; from the Commencement of the Constitution in October, 1780, to the Last Wednesday in May, 1789." Blew the dust from the ancient tome, we did, and opened to the index: Academy, Andover, we read, then American, Leicester, Alewives in the County of Barnstable; Bastard Children, Murder of; Cursing and Swearing; Derby-School; Engines; Fire; Flax-Seed and Gun-Powder, Storage of; Indians of Mashpee; Lime Casks, size of; Peddlers and Petty Chapmen; Pot and Pearl Ashes; Rogues and Tythingmen in the Tavern Act; and a host of others. Finally we found what we were looking for and turned to page 198 of the venerable law book. "An Act for Making More Effectual the Provisions for the Observation of the Lord's Day." By George, best we make a copy of this on the duplicator and rush 'er in to the police office.

"Whereas the observance of the Lord's Day is highly promotive of the welfare of the community by affording necessary seasons for relaxation from labor and the cares of business; for moral reflexions and conversations on the duties of life, and the frequent errors of human conduct, for publick and private worship of the Maker, Governor and Judge of the World, and for the acts of charity which support and adorn a Christian society . . . be it therefore enacted, That no person or person whatsoever shall keep open his shop, warehouse, or workhouse, nor shall upon land or water do any manner of labor, business, or work, nor be present at any concert of music, dancing, or any publick diversion, show, or entertainment, nor use any sport, game, play, or recreation on the Lord's Day (works of necessity and charity only excepted) upon penalty not exceeding twenty shillings. That no person shall recreate, disport, or unnecessarily walk and loiter, or assemble themselves in the streets, lanes, wharves, highways, common fields, pastures or orchards of any town on the said day, of penalty of the sum of five shillings."

It occurred to us perhaps we could study the entire body of this statute during the winter, so that next summer, when the problem of the Nudie Beach again raises its ugly head, we would have the tools to cure the situation.

Until then we'll fight it in our own way. Tooling up South Pamet Road on our white Yamaha motorcycle, we'll stand tall in our stirrups and shout at the pedestrians headed for the back shore, "Repent! Stay away from Nudie Beach. Clothes make the man—and the woman."

NINETEEN SEVENTY-FIVE

1975

Much cawing of crows in the valley as we stepped out to get the morning paper, and frost to bejewel every blade of grass, every bearberry leaf, every winterbared shrub in the valley. And today, January 6, 1975, we picked a panful of prime Brussel sprouts from our garden, and scooped aside the warm blanket of seaweed to tug a mess of carrots from the soil.

One of the side effects of nice weather like this is the yarns folks get to spinning about the good old fashioned winters they've known in their youth. We remember how Pop Snow used to reminisce about the cold, snow-filled winters of his youth. Thermometer hardly ever went above freezing from, say, Thanksgiving until spring peeper time, usually about first week of March. And when brother Isaiah Snow, seeking more space for burial plots in the family-owned Snow Cemetery, razed the ancient brick and granite tomb on the hillside, Pop was full of dire predictions.

"These here mild winters are bound to give over to the old-fashioned kind," he growled. "Then the ground will be hard with frost—three feet deep—and where in tarnation you going to store a body, now that tomb is gone?" Kids of our generation had always considered those old tombs to be more decorative than for any practical purpose. Not so, Pop would hasten to correct us. He could recall dozens of time when the local gravedigger had found the soil rock-hard with frost—had fetched a couple of saw horses to the tomb, and had bridged 'em with the casket of some departed neighbor. "Winter of '98 old Sam Narsty Paine stored a body up t' the Congregational tomb—can't give you his name cause it would be sort of disrespectful to the dead—and when finally the frost came out of the ground next spring, and they went up to do the buryin', derned if this feller's beard hadn't kept a-growing', sprouted right through the lid of the coffin." Far be it from us to challenge Pop and his stories.

Got to talking with our nephew, Tommy Kane, yesterday; learned that he is preparing to butcher his second pig of the winter. Save any money by raising the animals? we wanted to know. Not really. Even without charging for one's time feeding and cleaning up the animals' living quarters, the cost of a pound of home grown pork figures out to something over $1.25 per pound. "But it's prime meat," asserted our namesake. "Lean, and flavorsome, pork chops big as a first baseman's mitt. Hams that'll fill a bushel basket," and he went on to enumerate, with typical Kane hyperbole, the virtues of the home-grown porker. And when he'd finished, we checked his list against the pork products we used to obtain from that favorite farm animal back in our day—and found many missing.

"How about hog's head cheese?" we inquired. "Lord a'mighty, Miz' Burhoe used to trim every last scrap from the pig's head, including those big, hairy ears and she'd dice 'em up the size of bread croutons, and cook them all together with certain chosen bones and tendons loaded with natural gelatin. And then she'd turn the stuff into fancy wooden molds and press it out, fit for the gods! Tongue? You didn't save the tongue? Tongue boiled in spices—bay leaf and whole cloves and allspice—and skinned while it's still hot and served up with a boiled early rose potato? Boy, you haven't eaten. And pig's feet . . . Clean 'em with a tooth brush, we used to—so they were pink as a baby's behind—stewed with homemade sauerkraut, daubed with homemade mustard, the hot English dry powder mixed with white vinegar—make the tears come to your eyes just to look at it.

"And we haven't even gotten inside the carcass yet. How about the organ meats, as they so delicately put it these days. Stew made with lungs and sweetbreads and fresh turnip. Or liver and kidney pie? But the real crime of omission, boy, is your failure to make the chef d'oeuvre—Portuguese morcela. Blood pudding, if you want it in plain English, but actually, there's nothing plain about this gourmet dish. You start by catching the pig's blood in a wooden bowl, stirring it well with table salt so's it won't coagulate. And then you add to this generous portions of leaf lard, fresh from the pig, and sliced onion, and garlic, and saffron, and cumin seed, and when the stuff assumes the color and consistency of fresh crick mud, you stuff it into casings you've previously prepared by rinsing out the pig's intestines with lemon juice, tie 'em up with stout string, and simmer a few days while those morcelas age for flavoring. Almost lunch time, Tom. Come to have a bite with us?"

"No thanks, Unc—I'm not hungry."

Shank end of our ride this morning took us over the Hogsbacks, along Old Country Road, past the site of the old South Truro Methodist church burial ground beyond the bearberry and scrub pine to east'ard; and finally to the driveway leading in to Cobb Farm or the Oasis, as it was known back in the days when the late Richard A. Magee managed the extensive property for his wife, Nell. In the blink of an eye, we got on our mental train and rode back through the years to that period of the outbreak of World War II, Sunday morning, December 7, 1941 when news of the sneak attack on Pearl Harbor by the Japanese reached Truro.

The knot of men gathered at the fire station discussing in shocked, unbelieving tones this tragic event, making their plan to help the country in some capacity, wondering who would be called to wear the uniform, expressing concern over an attack by some foreign power on this exposed peninsula we call Cape Cod. In due time the young, able-bodied were called to wear the uniform, and some of the older folks moved to the industrial cities to work in war plants; the rest of us stayed at home, doing the civilian jobs we had to do, gathering up scrap metal for the metal drives, riding bicycles to work when the scant three gallons of gasoline per week were not sufficient to operate our automobiles, planting gardens to supplement food budgets reduced by the ration system. Too, there were those who felt the need of wearing a uniform and bearing arms on the local scene and when the civil defense units were organized, many donned the forest greens outfits, and drilled in the local fire stations, sort of a poor man's local Green Beret unit. And over on the Hogsbacks of South Truro, on a high knoll where the Cobb Farm property line meets the town road, the town fathers had installed a tiny cubicle to house the Truro civil aircraft watch.

The late Fred Benson was chief warden and as soon as the building had been erected and utility wires had been connected, Fred set about drafting his crew. Long before the days of women's lib we're proud to say that Fred accepted ladies on an equal basis with men. He wouldn't go quite so far as to schedule some defenseless female on a night watch with a lecherous male plane spotter, but the duty roster, in all other respects was coed, in a manner of speaking.

The tiny, stuffy building was heated by a kerosene stove that would asphyxiate a bull elephant quicker'n you could say Obadiah Brown if you didn't keep a window open. The alternative, of course, was pneumonia by reason of the bitter drafts of air that invaded the place when winter gales came whumping in across the Hogsbacks. But then, you were expected to keep an ear turned, in the black nights, to the sound of enemy aircraft. (The handbook on the premises gave certain clues to the throbbing exhausts of the Fokke-Wolfe, and by day you were expected to identify, at one quick glance, the silhouette of a plane traveling at nearly the speed of sound and tell whether she was friend or foe.) No matter that the Air Force had installed a sophisticated electronic station up off Collins Road manned by highly trained experts—the Truro sky watchers continued their volunteer work without complaint.

Well sir, our watch was perforce a graveyard shift—we worked at the local liquor emporium in those days—and our partner was the late Herb Brown. Herb was, among other things, the slowest moving mortal on Cape Cod, a characteristic that in no way hindered his skill as a plane watcher. But he was unemployed at the time, and since he could sleep all day long, he was as alert as a hoot-owl for the night shift. Herb was also an inveterate card player, and the first night we worked together Herb showed up with a cribbage board and a deck of dog-eared, greasy cards. The rest of the story should be quite obvious. No sooner had we checked in for our watch in the tiny cubicle, when Herb would break out his board and cards, leer at us across the table and say, "Your first deal. You lost last night, remember? This makes 387 games for me, and. . . ." And that's why we heard the tiny voice as we drove down by the Oasis driveway this morning. "Fifteen two, fifteen four, and four is eight. And I'm out. Lurch for you, double points. Deal 'em up." It was ten years after the War before we again got up enough courage to play a game of crib.

Made our usual weekend junket to the town dump a mite late this Sunday afternoon, and after we'd joined with custodian Neil Pirnie in a wailing session over the Red Sox loss in World Series Game number two we made a brief tour of inspection around the disposal area. Gathered up an armful of dry shingles for the night's kindling in our fireplace, explained the operation of an electric mangle to keeper Pirnie, he being too young to have seen this appliance at work. (Mrs. Elsie Borgarello had one of these, years ago. She could do flat work on it about as fast as the sheets and pillowcases could be pulled from the clothesbasket. And to see her slip a man's dress shirt behind that roller and draw it out looking just as though it had come from the laundry was a work of art, no less.) And about that time we drifted over to the dumping area proper, where a battered Ford van was parked, its occupants obviously studying the seagulls as they soared overhead or glided down to snatch up some goodie from the garbage. "Come over here and meet cousin Neal Small." It was the cheerful voice of Edwina Wright, one of our very favorite pedagogues and a friend of long standing. So we did. Swapped a few yarns with Mr. Small, and tried to sell him a copy of the Bicentennial Shebnah Rich History of Truro (he already has two copies, thank you) and learned that the transplanted native son had actually been recording the sounds of the dump. We stuck our head inside the cab as Edwina pressed the tape recorder button. In cultured tones came the Small voice, "And now we present 'Seagull Symphony' (don't choke on that ham fat, you crazy tern, you). Listen especially for the adult voices in the background. Note the deep, rich tones (keep those folks from dumping for a minute, will you, Mr. Pirnie? They'll disturb this segment)." And so it went. Proving, as we've always contended, that you meet the nicest people at the dump.

Reception has been poor on our little office radio this week— something about the humidity in the atmosphere has affected the fluorescent lights over our desk and in the vault so's they transmit a crackling, sputtering sound to the faithful Emerson, and we are constantly obliged to flick the light switches, sit in the darkness when a crucial play comes up during the ball games. Couldn't help recalling, one recent afternoon, as we thumbed the dial to blank out a particular offensive blast of rock an' roll, the old time radio sets of the early twenties. All's you needed in those days was a crude blueprint, several yards of copper wire, and empty cardboard salt box, a selector switch, and a crystal—and you were in business.

Memory dims, unfortunately, but we recall the tedious task of winding the wire around the salt carton, making loops at certain critical points—a drop of solder here, the placing of the headphone jack, the delicate titivating of the cat's whisker on the crystal—then the dramatic, satisfying feeling that came over you when the first reedy sound of music or the faint, wavering tones of a human voice sputtered through the headphones.

The kids at Wilder School would check mornings to see if Long Nook had picked up Big Brother during last evening's fog—and arguments over reception were not to be settled until the day when the radio stations would finally send out verification certificates. (Herbie Rose used to display a dogeared, soiled card proving he'd tuned in KDKA, Pittsburgh, on a Crosley single tube Pup. But the purists of the crystal set school belittled Herbie, said he'd gone out of the league with his new-fangled battery set.)

Came the day, however, when the crystal sets were relegated to the attic, and tube sets took over. Power for these early boxes was supplied by batteries; and they ranged in size from the tiny C-battery, so-called, to the common, household dry-cell, to the big, square B-battery, to the storage battery. (Lots of folks used to slip the battery out of the family car, splice 'er into the maze of wiring behind the radio. If reception proved uncommonly good of an evening, chances were good the car battery would be dead in the morning, and the Model T would require a push to start.)

One of the minor benefits of the battery-radio era would be the arousal of interest in the study of chemistry. We remember, for instance, that Mike Howard, a schoolmate at Wellfleet High, discovered that tired dry-cell batteries could be rejuvenated by having a mite of acid (household vinegar would do the trick, too, though not as well) into their innards. And while Mike was working on this experiment, he accidentally discovered that silver from a dime could be transferred, by electrolysis, to a garden variety penny and at dusk of a Truro day, a nearsighted store-keeper might accept the coin of lesser value for a ten-cent piece—but that's another yarn.

What we started to say was that there finally came a day when the demand for a radio dealer in Truro became apparent. Folks were beginning to graduate into the tube sets in large numbers—every rooftop boasted a long and sometimes complicated antenna system, and claims were being made of reception from as far away as Cleveland, Ohio. Thus it was that Mr. Anthony R. Francis, one of Truro's leading businessmen (Phat operated the Square Deal Store in Truro Square) took on the franchise for several leading brands of radios. If memory serves, you could order, through Phat, the Majestic, and the Fried-Eisemann, and the Atwater-Kent. Phat, however, was partial to the Super Het (he always insisted that markup played no part in his preference—it was a matter of workmanship and performance).

Well sir, the Square Deal Radio Shop began to move sets almost as soon as the first ads appeared in the Provincetown Advocate. Mr. Francis being a man of substantial girth and no longer in the flower of youth, he refused to climb any roofs or otherwise engage in arduous labor—if you had an antenna and a ground, he'd deliver the set to your house and hook'er up. If she worked to your satisfaction, you accepted delivery, and paid your money.

"And mostly, they'd buy," Phat would reminisce. "Once in a while I'd have to check over the wiring hookup, run a bit of salt paper over a tarnished connection, or even step out back and pour a bucket of salt water around the ground rod—best way in the world to spruce up a weak ground. But when I turned the switch of a shiny, new Super-Het and the tubes lighted up, and the sound of the Washington noon time signals commenced to come in, loud and clear through the speaker—why, the sale was made." We remember querying Phat anent the alleged frailty of the early sets. We'd heard the stamping of a female mouse in the same room would rupture the filaments of the early tubes. "Not so; and let me tell you a story to prove my point," rejoined Phat. "I mind the time I was goin' to deliver a Super-Het to Mr. Manuel Corey, then Town Clerk of Truro. Slipped 'er out of the carton, and brushed off the excelsior, I did, and seized 'er in my arms and headed for the front steps of my store. Got about halfway down when I slipped on a banana peel some summer boarder had dropped there, tumbled flat on my stern, with a crash that loosened the small change in my pocket, dislodged my upper plate, and ruined my $1 Ingersoll timepiece. The radio looked to be whole, however, so I toted it over to Mr. Corey's, hooked 'er up, and derned if we didn't tune in Louisville, Kentucky, at two in the afternoon."

Most sad, it was, to gather with friends of Dr. Charles E. Hutchings at the North burying ground to witness the graveside services for this good friend last Friday. Charlie had been our confidant and advisor for many years. In the days when he practiced here in Truro, we called on him professionally on several occasions. It was Charlie who pierced daughter Pat's ears when she reached the age appropriate for that fashion. Charlie, too, who stitched up son Terry's toe when this No. 2 son put his foot under the blade of a power mower. And we still admire, each morning when we shave, the neat sutures the good doctor introduced into our own face when we tried to exit from an automobile via the windshield.

The last time we talked with Charlie he was preparing for retirement as school physician for the city of New Bedford. We made mutual plans to do some gardening, and to beachcomb together, and to pore over the musty records at town hall in research of the Hutchings family tree. All of which proves that the best laid plans of mice and men. . . . So it's ave atque vale, dear friend. May you find peace taking those temperatures in the place where good doctors finally retire. We forgive you for the hoax you perpetrated on us so many years ago, when you played a recording of the spring peepers over the phone to us, and we recorded the earliest arrival of the hyla ever to be witnessed in Truro. Our sympathies to Charlie's wife, Irene, and all his children and family.

Got to thinking, as we pecked out the addends of a column of figures for our tax collector's deposit at the office the other day, about sundry machines we've admired and used over the years.

When we first took the oath of office, some 33 years ago, we remember how David L. Snow, then chairman of the board of selectmen, took us into the tiny, shabby office we were to occupy for some three decades. Handed us the key to the office door, did Dave, and, after swearing us to the utmost secrecy, he handed us the combination to the cabinet safe, written on a slip of paper. "Don't let this get into anybody's hands except your wife's," he cautioned us. "Best you memorize it and then burn it." We did just that.

"Now this," Dave continued, pointing to a battered, dusty Victor adding machine, "is for the use of both offices—selectmen's and yours. Full-bank adder, as you can see, like they use in the banks. Always have a full picture of the numbers you're punching into the machine before you pull the crank.

Never make a mistake, that way. Sometimes she sticks after you've punched the keys down. In that case all's you have to do is," and here Dave suited the words to a graphic example, "is to lift the whole cussed thing in the air, and let 'er drop on the desk. She'll clear up instanter."

And there were many instances, over the years, when we had to follow Dave's instructions. "No sense in throwing the tape away after you've done your work," the old fellow counseled us. "Dern stuff's expensive. We selectmen always save the stuff—and rewrap it on the spool, blank side foremost. That way you can use it twice." We did that, too.

As time went on, and we got to the point we had to compute the interest on taxes on overdue accounts, we used to glance with envy at the shiny Monroe calculator in the selectmen's office. At tax-making time, after the cherry sheet had been received by the assessors, and they were busy multiplying the valuation of each piece of property by the rate per thousand, we used to watch John Dyer, expert on the Monroe, entering the amounts on the keyboard, then flipping the carriage by means of the ornate handle, and finally cranking the machine to obtain the final tax figure.

"Nellie Cobb Magee—one hundred and twenty six dollars and fifty cents," he'd intone then. "Better let me check that again. Seems like an awful high tax for just 36 acres of land and a few buildings."

And so, when we were alone in the office, we'd occasionally sneak into the selectmen's office and try to work out an interest problem on the Monroe. Principal times rate, six percent, in those days, times time, to the nearest month, backdated to the previous October first. But, the truth to tell, we always took longer with the machine than by the old-fashioned pencil and paper method.

Our ancient Victor full-bank adder finally gave up the ghost. Happened at the end of the year, when we were trying to reconcile our bank statement. Balance of the town account had reached something over a hundred thousand dollars, for the first time in history. We realize now that the poor machine probably found the huge balance too big to handle. In any event, we summoned up our courage and mentioned to the selectmen we'd like to buy an electric adding machine, a ten-key model. After we'd represented every argument we could muster in favor of the new gadget, we waited for their approval. "I suppose you're right," allowed Burt Hart, then chairman of the board. "And she prob'ly won't burn too much electricity. But don't throw the old machine away. You might have to use 'er if the juice fails."

Mr. and Mrs. Ernie Deming in town for a few days, guests at the Weeden home on South Pamet. It's always easy to get involved in an interesting gab-fest with personable Ernie, and on Friday last at town hall the conversation quickly passed from the amenities stage to the nostalgia and the remember-when stage.

Started when we asked Ernie if his young son still was engaged in the art of hang gliding. Indeed he was. "The lad finds the dunes along the backshore excellent for the sport. Last summer—this is a little known fact hereabouts—a hang glider established some sort of local record. Remained aloft for over two and a half hours, riding the thermal currents of the cliffs just north of Long Nook. Most of the time he was hovering so close to the edge of the dunes his friends were able to pass him cigarettes and a can of beer just by reaching out over the ridge."

What a perfect time to tell Ernie about the German gliders who came to Corn Hill in the late twenties. Wait until the poor guy stops to light up a cigarette, and then, "Yessir, we can recall the summer of '27. You'll remember that Germany, in accordance with the Treaty of Versailles, was forbidden to have any powered aircraft. But in order to train men for some possible future air force, the art of gliding was promoted by the German government. And an American merchant, J.C. Penney, sponsored a gliding school here in Truro. It was located on Corn Hill, then owned by the L.D. Baker estate."

The big garage was converted into a hangar for storage of the gliders, and several cottages in the Corn Hill complex were turned over to the glider crews for housing facilities. Gadzooks, what a glamorous group of men. In typical Teutonic style, the Germans were divided into leaders and followers; the officers wore monocles, and carried swagger sticks, and sported highly polished leather puttees, and their uniforms were always spotless and creased—sharp enough to cut the very beachgrass that grew on the areas that served as their landing patches. The crewmen, blue-eyed, blonde, handsome giants, would click their heels and salute at the slightest excuse, and the entire group soon made inroads into the cocktail party set and swept every available female from the local dating lists.

What a pleasure to watch those glider crews in action. Orders barked in guttural tongue, salutes snapped off at each phase of the operation. Back would roll the big doors of the L.D. Baker garagehanger. In would trot the ground crew. Out the slim, stream-lined glider, borne on the shoulders of the men. All hands standing at attention, waiting for the officer of the day to make his appearance from the nearby barracks.

At long last, the debonair flyer comes striding through the sand, pulling on a cigarette cocked at the angle later to be made famous by FDR (and in an ivory holder, for gosh sakes). The staccato barking of commands as the captain slips into the tiny cockpit, anchor man grasping the tail of the glider and setting his heels firmly into the sand to hold the plane against the tension of the big rubber cable that is now being run out by the other members of the crew, as they strain with all their might.

Visualize a sling shot, if you will, and place the glider in the pouch of the sling, and string your men along the lines where the rubber is fastened to the Y of the slingshot and there you have it. And when the tension becomes so great that the crew members are unable to drag the line out any further, and the poor anchor man can feel his heels slipping through the sand, out from the cockpit of the plane comes a leather-gauntleted hand, a quick bark of command, and—Whoooooom—the tail man releases his grip, and the plane shoots into the air. And on days when the sou'west wind held steady, that glider used to soar on the thermal currents all the way from Corn Hill chock down to Cale Knowles' Crossing, back and forth, back and forth. Established some sort of record, if memory serves.

But the next year the Germans changed their base of operations to the Marconi Site area of South Wellfleet. Lord knows how many broken hearts they left behind them here in Truro.

George and Alix Beiers' Mediterranee Restaurant we discovered, on the occasion of our 39th wedding anniversary, is a place where a gourmet could easily become a gourmand. The atmosphere of the grand old eating place is restful, the decor pleasing to the eye, the service impeccable, and the food—ah, Snowie, dear friend, you should have been there. The boeuf tenderloin was of that superb quality that used to make you loiter through a meal with your eyes closed, a supreme compliment we paid the chef in your memory. French bread so crusty we felt embarrassed at the noise we made chewing it. Ordinary boiled potatoes raised to sainthood with a sprinkle of parsley and seasoned butter. A pressed duck pâté reclining upon a leaf of cosy lettuce. Tie the whole together with a vintage red wine, top off with fresh strawberries big as golf balls, write fini to the meal with a cup of delicious coffee. In about a week we're going to drop the hint to our child bride to fetch down our Gourmet Cook Book and try a few recipes in the Mediterranee style.

NINETEEN SEVENTY-SIX

1976

Is there a word for a class reunion which has only one surviving member attending the function? Such is the affair that neighbor Flora Peters, of the North Village, attended at Hyannis last week, when she drove up to register on the grounds of the former Hyannis Normal School. Stir of excitement at town hall last week as the art students and the municipal family realized it was the ninety-second birthday of the grand lady of the palette. May your canvas stay taut and your colors blend well for a long time to come, Flora.

It's satisfying, in a nostalgic sort of way, to note that the windmill is making a bit of a comeback here in Truro. Way up at the Wellfleet line, Flora's grandnephew, Larry Peters, has had a brand new windmill, factory boughten, as they used to say in Truro, installed on the homestead property. We've been invited to attend the official turning on of the Peters mill, and we've dusted off the enameled dipper that once graced the hand pump at Wilder School so's we can ladle up a cold drink from Larry's tap.

The installation of a windmill in the old days presented several problems. If you lived on a hill, where the fan could take advantage of every breeze that blew, it was fine for providing the needed energy to pump scads of water. But the higher the hill the deeper the well and in that era, pounding down a deep well was extremely expensive. Then, too, the long hardwood rods had a tendency to snap off when they weakened with age, and the bottom cylinder and valve system were costly and subject to malfunction. However, the selfsame hill that gave these problems had a positive value, too, for you could install your supply tank atop the friendly elevation, and take advantage of gravity to supply pressure for the entire water system at lower elevation. So the ideal situation would probably be the one that existed at the George Joseph property back when we rented from fire chief Arthur Joseph—call it the early forties. Arthur's windmill, a rusted, rickety Champion, if memory serves as we give the brand name, was located about halfway up the steep hill that could block off the prevailing westerly breezes; the mill tower was just tall enough so's the fan poked above the crest of the hill. And the supply line ran underground up this self-same hill to a grove of pines, where a pair of huge cement cisterns had been plastered into the ground. The mill was allowed to run constantly and if the wind blew for several days on end, the surplus water would simply flow by the wooden covers of the tanks, and gully its way down the hillside. This would happen quite frequently. But then, when a spell of calm weather arrived, the cussed mill would groan to a stop, and the law of supply and demand would catch up with the cisterns. As customer closest to the top of the hill, we'd be, obviously, the first to notice the drop in water pressure. We'd ring up Arthur on the crank telephone.

"Water's down, Arthur," we'd say. "Special town meetin' tonight, and we'd like to take a bath so's we'll smell sweet." And Arthur would chuckle and then he'd walk over to the barn, where he'd flip a switch to turn on the auxiliary electric pump. Before you could say Obadiah Brown the big Myers bulldog would have rammed a fresh supply of water up to the tanks, and the crisis would be over.

The network of pipes supplying the Joseph complex had been installed years before. Most of the lines had been galvanized pipe, and something in the chemical makeup of the water in the area led to the formation of a thick lining of sediment in the pipes. As a consequence, the water pressure would sometimes be weaker'n a constipated kitten—the simile is Arthur's—even though the tanks on the hill were near full. This would call for some hydraulic engineering on Arthur's part. He'd round up a crew of workers and scout out the loop of pipe that had developed the arteriosclerotic condition, and cut out the offending section. But quite often he'd replace the galvanized with more of the same, and the remedy would be short-lived.

We'd been living in Arthur's cottage for a couple of years when he dropped by one day and asked if we'd like to help clean out the cisterns. Folks down at the homestead had been complaining about the taste of the water, and it was possible some pine needles had fallen into the tanks; besides, this was a chore that needed doin' every couple years in any event. So we fell in step with Arthur, helping him tote the long-handled scrub brush and the buckets of lime he proposed to wash down the interior of the tanks with, and shortly we were watching our landlord prying loose the battered wooden cover of tank number one.

"Drained this one dry yesterday," explained Arthur. "We'll scrape off the loose scale, and scrub her down with that brush, and then we'll slap that lime on the walls. She'll be sweeter than a honey-bee's heel time we're through." And with that, he gave a last tug at the hatch, and up it came in his hands.

We both peered down into the gloomy interior of the tank and then, as our eyes got used to the darkness, derned if we couldn't make out the vague outlines of a pair of skeletons, still partly clad in tissue and fur, paws up on the bottom of the tank.

"Gadzooks," we retched. "And we've been drinking out of that cistern for Lord knows how long." "Look at it this way, boy," Arthur comforted us. "Could be you've been getting all your water from the other tank. Besides, you ever hear of dilution? Dozens of cities dump their waste in the Mississippi River but there's so much cussed water flowin' the poor bugs are diluted away to practically nothing."

"William R. Hopkins" reads the neatly chiseled letters on the white marble stone in the Methodist Cemetery on the hilltop. Willie Reuben, to fill out the middle name; but more properly Willie Beachgrass, to differentiate him from a clutch of Will Hopkins who were contemporaries.

"How'd he ever get the name of Willie Beachgrass?" we once asked Ed Snow, a knowledgeable man and a close enough neighbor to Will to answer our question.

"Beachgrass?" Ed grinned. "Why Willie, he got that name because he used to take the good lookin' young school teachers that boarded at his mother's place on Castle Road out for walks to the beach. Walked through the beachgrass, they did."

Willie's peripatetic adventures with the schoolmarms aside, we remember the man as a tall, almost cadaverous feller with the biggest Adam's apple we'd ever seen. Folks used to say Will was so skinny because he'd been handling the elements that went into paint all his life. "About a red nose whisker away from lead poisonin' is Willie," is the way Ed Snow used to describe Will's precarious state. But Willie lived to a ripe old age, lead and turps and Japan drier notwithstanding, and his final days as janitor at Truro Central School were, we're sure, moderately satisfying—even though they couldn't compare with his career as a young carriage painter.

"My, my, that Will Hopkins was certainly a fine carriage painter," is the way Pop Snow used to praise his neighbor. "Went up to Boston to learn his trade, did Will and after some years, when his folks was gettin' along in years, he decided to come back and go to work on the lower Cape. Set up shop in Wellfleet, did Will, up at Holbrook's barn. Old Mart Holbrook rented Will a big stall in one corner of the building, and Will fixed 'er up proper. He had a big canvas that hung from the loft overhead, to separate the area from the barn proper and he ran a hose into the stall so's he could wet the area down to settle all the dust. He had a batt'ry of lights wired up to Mart Holbrook's generator so the place was brighter'n a new nickel, and of course he had the best tools and materials money could buy: badger brushes and camel hair stripers and imported German pumice stone, and chamois pads. And he bought the best varnish that Sears, Roebuck sold, and the finest of spirits, and of red lead for metal running gear on the carriages. And when Will was workin' on a job, he wouldn't let a soul into the shop, for fear they'd stir up the dust, and it'd settle on the surface of the paint or varnish. They tell about the time old Sam Paine, the keeper of the hearse down at Long Nook, drove up to Wellfleet and fastened the nag to the hitching-rail at Holbrook's barn. Climbed down from the hearse and walked over to Will's paint shop and said to the Truro man:

"'How much to paint the hearse? Two coats of flat black on all woodwork. Scrape and sand all the metal work, prime with red lead, and apply two coats of black enamel. Two coats of spar varnish over all, rubbed down between coats with rottenstone. Magenta stripes on the wheel hubs and on the whiffletree and the shafts. Might's well tell you, Will, the town appropriation for this job was eight dollars. And oh yes, Will, how about them pineapples atop the body—think they'd look good gold leafed? Kind of gussy 'er up a mite, don't you think?'

"And Willie stuffed his pipe with tobacco and set 'er afire and said, 'Better go back and tell the selectmen to gussy up the appropriation a mite. I wouldn't paint that hearse for eight dollars if I was goin' to have the next ride in it.'"

We've been cutting our cemeteries for the second time of the growing season, and although the grass on the treeless, shadeless stretches has been burned to a crisp, there are still those pesky yellow flowering weeds and plantains and such that need to be shaved away. And under the locust trees and in the shady lea spots, there's sufficient grass to make for satisfying cutting. Mower blades have to be extra sharp to shear away the dried, limp stuff, and we have occasion to adjourn often to our cellar where we grind 'em down on our emery wheel. We got to thinking the other day as we ran our thumb over the bright edge of a blade, testing its keenness, about the time we got involved in a contract with old John Adams who lived down below our house in Hell Holler. But let's begin at the beginning.

In those days our family used to take milk from the local farmers. From Mr. Manuel Corey, for the most part, because that's where we'd first bought milk but when Mr. Corey's cows went dry, we'd shift over to Mr. Naylor Hatch, and when the Hatch cows ceased production, we'd buy milk from John Adams. On one such occasion, we were loafing around the Adams barnyard when we caught sight of a handsome canvas body top. It so happened we were at the age when most boys like to sleep in a tent; but tents were beyond our financial abilities, and the old ice-wagon body looked like an ideal substitute for the factory-made item. We'd, by gosh, tack some screening material over the driver's end, rig up a screen door for the stern to keep the mosquitoes out, pop a single cot inside. Simple, inexpensive, and good for the health. We'd sleep out doors until the snow fell a foot deep on the ground.

We walked over to where Mr. Adams was milking the last cow of the herd. Would he consider selling that old wagon top out there in the yard? "I been lookin' for a body to fit 'er. Make a fine wagon to sell my vegetables out of when I go peddlin' in Provincetown. All's I'd have to do is paint over them words 'CRAWLEY ICE CO.' and I'm in business." But the old gentleman must have seen the disappointment in our face, because a moment later, as he finished stripping the cow and rose from the three-legged stool, "But I might consider sellin'—how much you willin' to pay?" Chagrin. Embarrassment. We explained as how we hadn't any money. "How about workin' it out? Pay you twenty five cents an hour. You pay me $3.00 for the wagon top. I'll even cart 'er up to your house—free."

Elated, we struck flesh with the grizzled old farmer and agreed to show up, bright and early next day, to start working off our debt. Well sir, the following day dawned with a promise of being the hottest dern day of the summer. Huge ball of sun in a cloudless sky, nary a bit of a breeze, cicada's brassy, soaring song rising in the still air. And off we went to the Adams farm. Got there just as old John was coming out of the barn, arms loaded down with mowing machine blades.

"First chore of the day," he grinned, "is sharpenin' up these here blades." And he led the way to the big grindstone next the woodpile. Gadzooks; to this day we can remember every detail of that torture machine. Heavy blue plank frame on which was mounted a huge circular grindstone, its axle extended into the form of a forged crank waiting for willing hands to turn it. Suspended over the stone, a rusty tin can with a pin hole in its bottom, so's a tiny trickle of water could be directed to the face of the stone, adding to its cutting qualities. This, we said to ourself, is going to be a tough job but the thought of the snug canvas sleeping apartment sustained us.

Meanwhile, Mr. Adams had straddled the framework of the apparatus, and, seizing one of the blades in his big fists, he pulled the peg of the watering can, nodded to us to begin our rotating, and bore down on the wheel. Hours later, soaked with sweat, our spine tortured with cricks, blisters big as pullet eggs on both hands, dehydrated and half blind from the intense sun, we groaned with relief as John gave a final fillip to the last mowing machine blade. "Whyn't you use a power grinding wheel, like the other farmers use?" we had the temerity to inquire.

"Dern things'll take the temper out of the steel. Make too much noise. Give off sparks that could start a fire. And dern it all, boy, it's lonesome, sharpenin' all by yourself. Didn't you enjoy the mornin'?"

If mid-morning can be said to be 10:30 am, we'll use the term to say that at this hour the temperature stands at that perfect reading sought by professional air-conditioning companies: 68 degrees. Had we been well-trained in meteorology, we'd have been able to predict the sudden shift of wind to the northeast; the weather symptoms were all to be read when we awoke, betimes, this morning. A blood-red sun rising through a layer of cruller-shaped clouds, colored lead-gray; a dipping barometer, a sudden clinging fog that finally dissipated by the time the Paul Revere bell commenced to ring at the Congregational Church a bit ago; and finally, the shift of the newly-restored clipper ship atop Cobb Library at the aforementioned hour. There's a strong smell of salt ocean in the air. And the sound of the surf on the backside filters down-valley, providing background sound effects for the lighter music of the bird chorus in our neighborhood—the lilting, provocative whistle of a cardinal greeting a glorious July Sabbath. The repetitive promise of a bob-white quail predicting more-wet and the querulous squall of a jay complaining of bird affairs to which we are not privy. But last night's sudden showers, accompanied by the rumble of distant thunder and the dramatic flashes of lightning in the distance, have refreshed growing things and settled the dust of the roadsides, and rinsed the blossoms of the wild roses fringing the meadow's edge. In all, a fine birthday for our nation.

Speaking of this Fourth of July and the fashion in which we used to celebrate it some years ago, we got to thinking as we heard the sound of a salute to the holiday emanating from Town Hall Hill earlier on, in the form of a half-dozen firecrackers being set off by some hardy soul in defiance of the laws of the Commonwealth, of the good old time when explosives were not verboten.

Remember the good old-fashioned torpedo? An onion-shaped, tissue-wrapped object, filled with gravel, in which were secreted a half-dozen king-sized gunpowder caps, each one containing enough black powder to supply an explosion equal to a modest- sized hand grenade when you tossed one against a solid object. Sensitive to pressure, were those torpedoes, and many's the Truro kid suffered a lacerated palm when he squeezed a torpedo in his bare fist. And the firecrackers came in all sizes, from the lady fingers, dainty, spaghetti-sized explosives braided together, waiting for the application of a glowing punk stick so they could provide the rapid-fire effect of a gatling gun when you touched 'em off. If you craved a bigger explosion, you could buy from Mary Howard's temporary stand a package of salutes: two-inch, three-inch, and up to six-inch monsters, guaranteed to blast your hand off at the wrist if you weren't careful enough to toss the red paper-wrapped cylinder away as soon as the fuse started to sputter. And, when dusk fell on the holidays, you dug into your brown paper bag and fetched out the nocturnal variety of your fire works. Sparklers, that looked for all the world like the welder's rods of today. Many's the grass fire was ignited by a sparkler tossed into the dry grass of Pamet. Roman candles, that spewed forth balls of fire into the atmosphere. Sky-rockets, varying in size from slim, inch in diameter affairs to powerful gadgets the size of a man's wrist that required a launching tube fabricated from a section of pipe buried in the ground.

The big hill back of Ed Snow's barn was a favorite site for the setting-off of fireworks. And when the store bought products ran out, the local boys were sometimes required to finish off the evening by dragging barrels of tar to the hilltop and adding some worn out automobile tires and kindling a huge bonfire.

We remember the time Ernie Snow discovered, somewhere in the recesses of his dad's barn, a big can of calcium carbide, a relic of the days when automobiles used the chemical to generate gas to light the lamps of their vehicles. Ernie was then a student at Wellfleet High School. He had gleaned enough knowledge from his chemistry course to know that the gray, lumpy stuff would explode under the proper conditions.

"Make a good, homemade explosion for the Fourth," he said to his friends. And before you could say Obadiah Brown, we had set to work constructing a piece of apparatus to use the chemical. Someone located a ten-quart milk can, complete with a solid, wooden bung. Could it have been Robert "Duds" Meier who made the wooden framework to hold the can? In any event, we recall the first trial of our home-made cannon. Ernie measuring the active ingredient into the milk can adding a smidgin of water: watching the stuff ferment, inhaling the acrid, pungent gas that poured from the narrow neck, pounding the wooden bung solidly into the can, waiting for the pressure to build, then touching a kitchen match to the tiny touch-hole previously punched into the bottom of the container. POOOOOW. The bung rocketed into the air, and hammered into the partition of the cow stall at the rear of the barn. Old Daisy, the golden Guernsey who was quietly munching her grain, preparatory to the evening milking, like to broke out of her stall from fright. Ernie's father, old Ed Snow, claimed she fell off on her milk for a month afterward.

Well sir, that evening, after the usual Roman candles and the sky rockets and the big salutes and the bonfire had been touched off on Atwood's Hill, there was a brief pause in the festivities. The sparklers died down, and folks started to wend their respective ways home. And then Ernie, accompanied by his cronies, climbed up the hill, and set up his improvised cannon on the cribbing. Dumped the remains of the calcium carbide in the milk can, did Ernie, and added a good dodger of water, and pounded the bung firmly in the opening, waited a few moments, and fetched a match from his pocket. "We'll point her to the east'ard," he ordered. "Wind's from the sou'west, and the bung will travel farther, y'see." And with that he scratched the match on the seat of his overalls and applied it to the touch hole. WHOOOOOOOOM. The milk can recoiled like a French howitzer, the bung ripped through the air. Came the tinkling of glass from below the hill: the projectile had taken out one of Ezra Hopkins' window panes.

Seconds later the irate farmer came storming across the blacktop. Ernie lamely explained how the accident had occurred: learned about the gas in chemistry at high school, hadn't realized how powerful it was, never dreamed it would fire that heavy bung across the street. Sorry, Mr. Hopkins. "Sorrys don't count," shouted Ezra. "Be over t' my place early in the morning. You can work out the price of that pane of glass!"

Its been so long since we've touched the keys of our faithful Royal to compose a column we know our copy will be loaded with mistakes: typographical, grammatical, and in the field of punctuation. Please forgive. And to that host of friends who were kind enough to remember us in their prayers, with cards and notes, and with beautiful plants and gifts of fruit during our recent sojourn at Cape Cod Hospital, our heartfelt thanks.

One of our pleasant assignments early in July was a trip to radio station WPLM in Plymouth, where we were honored to be invited to present a short Bicentennial greeting via tape, for broadcast over the Fourth of July weekend, to the British Isles. Here's an excerpt from the letter of acknowledgment from our Mother city of Truro, Cornwall, England received at town hall during our recent sick leave.

"The members of the Truro City Council, the citizens of Truro, and I, were very warmed to receive the Radio Broadcast expressing good wishes from your township of Truro to the City of Truro on 5th July 1976, in connection with the USA Bicentennial celebration. On behalf of the City Council and the citizens of Truro, I have the honour to reciprocate those good wishes, and to express the hope that your township and all those who live there will prosper in the years to come. I sincerely hope that with the passage of time, the informal link of friendship which exists between the

City and your township may be strengthened.

"Yours sincerely, Eve Coombe, for the Mayor of Truro."

We are reminded of the last time our town of Truro had a connection with Truro, England. This would have to be some 20 years ago, and if some of the details have dimmed in our memory, blame it on old age. In any event, the Lord Mayor of Truro, England was touring portions of the United States, and in response to an invitation from our own Truro, he had managed to squeeze in a flying visit to Pamet. The list of guests assembled at our tiny town hall represented a fair cross-section of the local population. Many of the names native to the British Isles: Snow, Dyer, Rich, Hopkins must have struck a familiar chord in his Lordship's ears. In addition, though, there was a second generation Italian named Bisceglia, then instrumental director for the outer Cape towns, who had been requested to appear at the gala affair with a brass group picked from his student musicians. Their names were strong on the Portuguese end of the spectrum: Sousa, Silva, Ferreira. And the Town Clerk was there, too, sampling the cookies and the punch and the tea: a hybrid, name of Kane.

Well sir, sharp on the hour of two of the afternoon up drives the Mayor's party, and out steps his honor, dressed in the full regalia of his office. Scarlet breeches and jacket, velvet headpiece shaped like a wrinkled mushroom, the rather portly gentleman wore a huge chain around his neck from which dangled his gold seals of office. Tiny Worthington, the only native-born Britisher in town, stepped forward to welcome the mayor, and an honor guard conducted him up the narrow stairs to the strains of "God Save the Queen" rendered by the brass octet under the able baton of Mr. Bisceglia. A reception line formed in front of the tiny town hall stage, and the townspeople were introduced to the Lord Mayor. More appropriate music from the brass group, a genteel raid on the refreshment table, and then an exchange of gifts. From Cape Cod Truro, a copy of the latest town report, a hand illuminated copy of the seal of the town (could it have been one of the late Ed Wilson's masterpieces?), jars of beach plum jelly from Dr. Madeleine Winslow, herself a true Englishwoman in spirit if not in citizenship.

The Lord Mayor, in turn, presented us with a handsome directory of his Truro, together with a large tin of Cornish gingerbreads, which we promptly delivered to the town vault for safekeeping. Brief, dignified, warm is the way we'd describe the occasion.

And there's a sequel, of sorts. The following year the voters of Truro generously appropriated a sum of money to install central heating in town hall. And after the contractor had tightened up the last steam pipe and the electrician had wired up the thermostat, the town fathers stood around for a bit and Mr. Selectman John Worthington suggested as how we should have a brief ceremony, perhaps a ribbon-cutting at the cellar door, or a formal twisting of the main fuel valve. It was then we remembered the Cornish Gingerbreads and before you could say Obadiah Brown, we had fetched 'em out of the vault, and all hands munched on the spicy disks as John threw on the master switch. Delicious.

A high barometer and a sweeping northwest wind and such other magic ingredients as the weather man has put together this morning have produced a day of such pristine clarity you can see—literally for miles— such things as the rough outline of the hill ranges, and the cobalt sweep of the harbor with tiny whitecaps clear to the horizon, and the shingle courses of houses across the valley. Makes the pre-autumn colors stand out, to ; the sere, drab foliage of the willow tree at Snow Park, and a sport maple gone orange in Arrowsmith's Swamp, and sepia tasseled pampas grass by the roadside. Nary a cloud in the sky. Temperature in the low sixties—barely shirtsleeve weather—but fine for outdoor chores. And a sudden dry quality to the air that makes the doors shut for the first time in months without binding in their frames, and the salt to flow freely from the shaker, and laundry to come in from the line crisp and fresh. Goldenrod a rich, scattered treasure by the roadsides, and Michaelmas daisies, as Laura Johnson refers to those lavender-petaled, gold-centered flowers, in full blow. Granted, the fishermen have a legitimate complaint this morning—it's too windy to leave the shelter of Pamet Harbor in search of the wily blue or striper—but for the rest of us landlubbers, it's a glorious fall day.

Every time we finish up a session at our woodpile, and feel the temptation to assume a smug attitude of having accomplished a good bit of work, our thoughts turn to those stalwart sawyers and splitters and choppers of an earlier day, and we give a wry smile of self deprecation and hush up instanter. Not that we don't have the tools to work with nowadays—hand tools, that is. We'd rate the modern thin-steel Swedish buck-saw blade head and shoulders over those thick, coarse-toothed blades we used to worry through a log with in the old days. Inexpensive, too, these Swedish cutters and when they lose their set or become dulled, why you throw them away and buy a new one.

Any man worth his salt back in the twenties was expected to cut and saw and cleft enough wood to supply his own uses—at least two stoves—every year. Walter Horton, when he lived in Eastham as a young lad, used to step out in the barn every evening after supper and, by the feeble light of a kerosene lantern, work up a cord of wood. "Pitch pine, that is—oak, er maple er locust prob'ly a mite less. Father had an idea the exercise was good for your digestion, and it kept us boys from havin' after supper arguments."

It's always a risky business to list the men who stand out in memory as top woodsmen, you're liable to omit some worthy axeman, but the names of Henry Hanson, and Archie Holden, and Wilfred Grozier, and Charlie Francis certainly come to mind. And don't forget Tony Rose, who lived up on the shores of Ryder's Pond, on the Wellfleet line, where, even in those days of sparse timber, there were considerable stands of pine and hardwoods. Tony was a man of less than average size, but wiry, as Ed Snow used to say, as an Ivers and Pond piano. Wore big horned rimmed glasses and a drooping, salt and pepper moustache, and—we can see 'em even now as we close our eyes—heavy brown canvas work shoes. Among his many wood customers, Tony used to supply the Wilder Grammar School building under contract with the school committee. And along about the first week of school the janitor would send word to Tony that the wood room in the east ell of the building was running low of split pine, and would Tony please deliver the usual amount at first convenience. And back at his farm, Tony would plan his work so's he could cease and desist from the ordinary chores and the perpetual sawing of logs to allow time enough to make a run to Wilder School. He'd work up a final pile of green pine, that is, he'd drive his ancient Model T Ford up on its power transfer jack, and using the 18 horses under the hood, he'd hook up his belt driven buzz-saw and hack through a couple of cords of the pungent, resinous wood.

And then he'd uncouple the Ford, and drive 'er over to the seasoned pine, and everlastingly load the poor Model T until her springs rode on the axles and the tiny four cylinder engine threatened to quit. And, calling his handsome big collie up on the passenger seat beside him, he'd hie off for Truro.

We kids would be waiting for Tony, and as the old gentleman maneuvered the Ford across the soft sand of the schoolyard to a spot close to the woodroom ell, we'd encourage the roaring motor and the chattering transmission bands, and sometimes we'd brace against the brass radiator shell and push with all our might until the tail gate was snugged up against the concrete wall. Then all hands would form an endless line, piling the sticky wooden slabs in each other's arms, trotting up the steps to the woodroom, dumping our cargo in place. Almost before you could say Obadiah Brown the chore would be done. Thanks from Tony and his dog. And off he'd go, the Model T fairly flying through the sand, and up Corey's Hill to southard. The school would smell delightfully of fresh pine for weeks afterward.

★ ★ ★

Over at Cobb Farm, some few decades ago, after Col. Dick Magee had returned from the wars, he decided to install a few hives of bees on the premises. Our readers will recall that, during the fifties, word had leaked down from upper New England that a time-honored home remedy consisting of honey and vinegar—honeygar—was being used in Vermont and New Hampshire and Maine, to build up resistance to colds in folks, and to cure such a variety of illnesses as rheumatism, arthritis, pulmonary disorders, upset stomachs, cardio-vascular ailments, you name it.

"So I've decided to raise bees," explained Col. Magee. "Might even revive some of the old Baldwin apple trees on the farm, make my own cider, let 'er sour, and produce enough vinegar to brew up honeygar for the entire town. We'll be the healthiest community on Cape Cod."

So the good colonel did indeed put in some bees; Italian stingless, he called them. But at the same time, Col. Magee had a pack of German shepherd dogs on the premises, and the dogs used to take great delight in harassing the bees, and the bees, in turn, forgot that they were stingless. And on more than one occasion visitors to the farm were attacked and stung. Eventually, Ralph Houser, the colonel's general handyman, got orders to phase out the bees, and they disappeared from the area. Now this is only conjecture, but it seems reasonable to assume that the swarm of bees that suddenly appeared at Bessie Brewer Poor's place, a mile or so north of Cobb Farm, might just have originated at the latter site. In any event, Bessie showed up at the local Shell Station one morning, and shared her problems with Pop Snow, then proprietor of the petrol emporium. "Know anything about getting rid of bees?" she queried the old Yankee. "We've been hearing the derndest, most mysterious noises in the walls of our house over on Grove's Crossing. And we've finally come to the conclusion that we have a swarm of bees in the sidechamber, east side of the house. We can see them coming out of a small hole in the box finish, and at night we can hear the humming of what seems to be thousands of insects, all through the house."

Pop snickered, drew a big draft on his White Owl cigar, and allowed, "Why, Miz Poor, I'll come down to your place tomorrow morning, soon's sparrow burp, and I'll fetch my extension ladder with me, and I'll light up one of my cigars, and climb up the ladder, find the home in the house finish and blow a few clouds of smoke down inside. And before you can say Obadiah Brown, I'll put them bees to sleep, open up the trim with my saber saw, take out the bees."

Sure enough, next morning Pop did as he had planned. But the bees apparently weren't privy to his formula. Instead of blanking out as Pop blew the acrid cigar smoke into their abode, they in fact, became belligerent—streamed out of the hole in the box finish, buzzing like all get out, and attacked poor Pop, who had all he could do to shinny down the ladder and escape in his battered red Chevy truck.

"Should've smoked an R.G. Sullivan. Them White Owls are too mild."

And on Thursday last, at brief ceremonies on Town Hall Hill, we joined with Chief Lepore of Truro's finest and Francis Silva, chief dispatcher, in dedicating the new Bicentennial flagpole. The flag we raised on the halyards was one presented to the town in memory of the late Jim Moynahan, longtime Pamet colonist, jazz musician par excellence, raconteur, scholar, journalist, fine family man, and friend to many here on the lower Cape. We could almost hear the wailing, foot-stamping sound of Jim's ancient clarinet as we hoisted the flag aloft. Ave atque vale, old friend.

NINETEEN SEVENTY-SEVEN

1977

By guppy, if this isn't a true January thaw, we'll settle for it until a more clement change in the weather comes along. After the frigid days we've had, near gale-force nor'west winds and dusting of snow, we're thankful for the bright sunshine, and the reading of the thin, red line—exactly 32 on our back porch thermometer—and the high reading of the barometer, and the intense, clear blue of the sky. Earlier this morning we drove down to Pamet Harbor and saw the skim ice clinging to the shoreline looking for all the world like the issue of a cataract, floating over the sandbars. We saw a clutch of gulls riding the air currents at the base of Corn Hill, and admired the sere cattail carpet being combed by the wind; and later, in our own backyard we heard the creaking of dry limbs on dead locust trees, and felt the bite of the cold air on our fingers as we pinned the laundry to the clothesline for our child bride. We felt the crunch of the snow underfoot, and smelled the clean, pure air, and listened to a trio of bluejays quarreling in the cedar tree. And then, before we sat down to the faithful Royal, we glanced through the first of the seed catalogs that arrived in the holiday mail.

Town hall employees had their annual Christmas party this year upstairs in the tiny auditorium. The selectmen and their wives attended, and the Town Clerk and her husband, as well as Joey Noons, Truro's superintendent of streets, and several of his men. Foreman Russ Holway and his able assistant Abbie Tinkham didn't enjoy the occasion as much as they might have—they kept glancing out the windows to see if there were any signs of snow in the air. But there was a holiday feeling in the room, and much good food, and an innocent punch, and an exchange of gifts, and a tiny, decorated pitch pine tree which we forgot to bring upstairs.

"What's that trapdoor's purpose in the floor over there?" asked Mr. Selectman Sam Levy, as he reached for a slab of cheesecake with strawberry topping.

Gadzooks, makes us feel old when we realize we're the only person in the town hall family who remembers such oddments in the venerable building.

338

"Why that trapdoor?" we mumbled around a crusty Italian pastry, courtesy of Mrs. Louis Ciampa, "once served a practical purpose here. Years ago, all's we had for seating arrangements was a bunch of long bulky settees. Couldn't carry them up the stairs, y'see, because the angle of the corner was too short and those settees were used downstairs, at suppers and other functions, and upstairs, for the meetings. So they used to pop open that trapdoor and pass them by hand either up, or down, depending on the circumstances."

"You're pulling my leg," Sam smiled around a tuna fish sandwich. "Not so," we demurred. "And you see that handsome maroon velour stage curtain on the stage," we gestured with a free hand—our other hand was occupied with a sliver of fruit cake. "The town appropriated $400 to buy that back in the forties over the objections of thrifty minded Mollie Horton, who offered to take the original tattered oilcloth curtain home and patch it up on her sewing machine. (In all fairness, it should be reported she was making a little joke.) And when they took out the handmade windlass that used to hoist the original curtain, we all realized that C. W. Snow, who had turned out the drum and forged the crank at his shop down on Castle Road, was a true mechanic in his time."

"And how about that little trapdoor overhead?" queried Sam, as he gummed a portion of coconut cake. "Why that?" we replied. Our good wife had restrained us from reaching for the chip-dip combination, and our diction was clearer. "Last time we can recall using that was at a Halloween party, when our dear friend Snowie hid up there, and released a crepe paper bat that slid down a wire right into a jammed audience of kids at the climax of a horror program. We had realistic sound effects, and Police Chief Harold Berrio came dashing up the stairs with his revolver drawn, ready to apprehend the villain of a skit we were presenting, and the kids like to went into hysterics, and Punchy Prada, may the good Lord forgive us, wet his pants and had to be taken out of the hall by his mother. Fun. See that back room over there?" We pointed out one of the tiny anterooms adjoining the stage. "That's where they used to count votes, at town and state elections. In those days, we were allowed to take out ballots in blocks of fifties, during the voting periods. And when the tellers knocked off counting to get a cup of coffee or or have a smoke, they sometimes would be approached by an anxious candidate for office. 'How'm I doing?' he'd query the teller. But the election official knew it was against the law to divulge any results before the final tally was in. So he'd have to speak in cryptic fashion. He'd say something like, 'Your brother-in-law voted yet?' And the candidate would take the hint, and scoot off to pick up some added support."

* * *

Our child bride is mending at Cape Cod Hospital, where she was taken last Monday following a fall on the ice which fractured her hip. We miss her about the house.

A follow-up on the windmill item reported last summer, re the Larry Peters project up at the Truro-Wellfleet line. It will be recalled that Larry, inspired by memories of his youth when the creaking of a windmill represented pleasant memories, had Paul Daley, of the well drilling business, install a system on his property near Ryder's Pond. Larry didn't cotton to the idea of installing an unsightly tank tower on the premises, so he had Paul connect a pressure tank at ground level. However, the mill pumped water at such high pressure that the welds in the improvised tank ruptured, and a new factory-built tank will shortly be installed, Ah, the power of that moving air.

We dropped by the funeral home in Wellfleet this afternoon to pay our last respects to Elizabeth Freeman, teacher par excellence, successful realtor in the area, benefactor to many. As a callow freshman at Wellfleet High School many years ago, we first experienced the benefits of Miss Freeman's pedagogical talents. We can see her now wheeling that big gray Stutz touring car up Main Street to the gaunt, dilapidated frame building on the hill overlooking Wellfleet harbor, tossing aside her morning cigarette (how the Wellfleet burghers used to frown at Miss Freeman's chain smoking) striding into her tiny office to organize things for the school day.

The lady could teach any subject in the curriculum: math, social studies, French (spoken, it's true, in a flat New England accent, but grammatically correct), English. English was her forte. She could teach a moron to diagram a compound-complex sentence, or to identify the parts of speech with ease and enjoyment. In history class, she could make dull events and dates come alive. The incidents leading up to World War I, for instance, had more meaning for us after we learned she had lost a brother in the ill-fated Lusitania.

Miss Freeman with her spirited defense of woman's suffrage was years ahead of her time in the women's lib movement. And she felt obligated to carry her teaching well beyond the ordinary classroom requirements. When graduation time came each June, she'd meet with the members of the tiny senior class and teach them manners and protocol. How to introduce classmates to visiting dignitaries in the reception line. Remember the time she was directing the boys in the art of shaking hands? "NO, no," she corrected Bruce MacAfee, a North Truro lad with hands as big as a smoked shoulder. "The ladies will be wearing rings, and if you squeeze their fingers like that, you'll cut them to ribbons." Or to the girls, on the business of eating a sandwich at intermission time of the gala reception at the Big Chief dance hall. "Don't gobble them, girls—nibble, daintily."

The poor woman had no singing voice, but when Mrs. Josephine Patterson, the vocal music teacher lined the kids up and sat down to the piano, Miss Freeman would pace back and forth and coax heavenly music from the most ungifted monotones. She could coach basketball when the occasion arose, or stoke the ancient coal furnace at WHS when the janitor was sick. But most of all, she was a warm, sincere, human being. May you have none but A students in your classes up there, dear friend. Ave atque vale.

Add to these the memories of the late George Leyden, dedicated, beloved principal of Provincetown High School for many years, and our good friend and boss when we taught there. We recalled the time George paced into one of our morning classes, to find the kids a mite restless. There'd been a major victory the night before for the PHS basketball team, advancing the orange and black five to the playoffs of the Tech Tourney, and the win had the youngsters fair buzzing. Mr. Leyden slowly strode across the room to take a position with his back to the window, so the morning sun would be shining in the kids' eyes—a modified third degree police technique. Heavy clearing of the throat, a pucker of the lips, a set frown on the brow, a steady stare from those piercing Irish gray eyes. One by one the kids stopped their whispering, shuffled their feet uneasily under the desks, dropped their eyes to their textbooks. Now to hold them at attention for a mite, without uttering a word.

It was at this point we noticed that the big fuel oil tank truck outside in the driveway had completed its unloading. The driver was now climbing up into the cab, and in seconds the powerful diesel engine would roar into life. We'd seen it fired up many times and this particular engine was started by some sort of explosive device that went off with the decibels of a Howitzer. The last kid was just succumbing to the hypnotic Leyden stare when—BANGGGG—the diesel starter exploded. Poor George like to jumped out of his suit. The spell, for a moment, was broken but nary a student dared to crack the faintest smile. A final clearing of the throat, the heavy pacing across the classroom, the door shuts, and every pent up breath in the room escaped, audibly. We turned to the blackboard and started chalking up a quad-ratio equation for the kids to factor, more to cover up our own emotions than in the interests of abstract math.

On another occasion we were translating Cyrano de Bergerac with our blue ribbon French class, and again the big Irishman paid us a visit. His eyes moistened a bit as we put into English the poignant, dying words of Cyrano in the nunnery and at that moment an outburst of noise came from the adjoining room, which was connected to our room by a door. Quietly Mr. Leyden heaved to his feet, quietly he tiptoed up the aisle, placing his huge hand on the doorknob, prepared to yank the door open and surprise the culprits on the other side who were evidently taking advantage of a substitute teacher. But Mr. Leyden was not aware of the fact that some kid, as a prank, had loosened the set screw of the doorknob, and when he tightened his grip and gave a tremendous pull, the darn knob came off in his hand. Frantically we placed a finger to our lips and tried to signal the seniors to refrain from showing any emotion. As well attempt to stop the flow of the tide. Giggles from the girls—Cathy Santos and Judy Lane—guffaws from Eddie Veara and Steve DeRiggs, and if we fail to list the other members of the class, blame it on the failing memory of an aging pedagogue. And Mr. Leyden? Just for a moment he lost his poise, and then he, too, burst into laughter. Bless the man, may he rest well in the Big Temple of Learning. Ave atque vale, old friend.

It's unfortunate the religious and the lay calendar couldn't coincide this year, because 1977 happens to be the fiftieth anniversary of the famous Truro forest fire. In 1927, Palm Sunday fell on the 19th of April—Patriot's Day in Suffolk County, Massachusetts—but we hasten to assert that anyone who was living in Truro on the occasion of this huge conflagration would remember the fire, calendar variations notwithstanding.

The whole business began innocently enough, on that peaceful Sunday morning, with a minor grass fire down Prince Valley way, on the property of the summer colonist named Capron. At the time, rumor had it that the Caprons had spent the weekend at their cottage, and, upon their departure early of that Sunday morning, they had emptied some hot wood ashes from the kitchen stove in the back yard.

When the ensuing blaze was noted by neighbor Burleigh Cobb, the South Truro postmaster, the local fire department was notified, and the flames were extinguished. But later in the day—probably midafternoon—Burleigh again called in an alarm from South Truro and before you could say Obadiah Brown, the skies to southard of Truro were blackened by a huge column of smoke emanating from flames that fed on hog cranberry and scrub pine and oak. Charlie Joseph, forest warden at the time, summoned his doughty fire fighters by phone and direct contact, and all hands roared off to the Prince Valley area, only to find that the blaze had worked its way into the thick wooded section of the valley, and was now inaccessible to the puny shovels and brooms of the smoke eaters.

We remember vividly, standing with a group of townspeople at the foot of Red Sand Hill at midafternoon, watching the holocaust roaring up Prince Valley on the wings of a southwest wind, blasting at Ray Freeman's newly constructed summer cottage with the force of a huge blowtorch, then soaring across the state highway in a shower of burning embers. By midnight of that first day—Sunday—the fire had reached almost to Ballston Beach, skirting the properties along the south side of the Pamet River, threatening the residences of the Fred Meiers and the Farwells, up the road a piece.

Warden Joseph had sent in a call to E. Hayes Small of North Truro, and Hayes had dispatched his big farm tractor to the scene. The tractor was put to work plowing several furrows between the Meier property and the raging fire—this tactic, plus the efforts of the firemen in tossing shovels full of earth on the smoldering roof of the Meier house, saved the dwelling.

Meanwhile, up at Great Pond, a group of men using a portable gasoline pump delivered to the scene by the county, had set up a station to smother the flames in that area. But the pitch pines, ignited by the roaring blaze, absorbed the puny stream from the county pump, and eventually forced the volunteers into the limpid waters of the pond. On Monday the wind abated, temporarily, and several tongues from the main fire worked their way along the ocean front south of Ballston Beach and, at the other end of the conflagration, into the spur valleys of South Truro. The bell of the South Truro Methodist Church was used to summon help to that area. Henry Hanson and his crew used a bottle of turpentine to prime a pitcher pump at a vacant cottage in that village to fetch in a supply of water that eventually saved the building. Wellfleet, by now threatened with the blaze, sent in men to help combat the fire, and Provincetown dispatched its ancient copper-tanked chemical pumper, affectionately dubbed the camel, to aid their Truro confreres.

It was Mother Nature, however, who finally came to the aid of Charlie Joseph and his beleaguered firefighters. The wind shifted on the third day, and the blaze did an about face, and headed directly back for Prince Valley. By mid-afternoon of that Tuesday, the flames found nothing further to feed on, and, in the swale back of the old Joseph Cobb property in Prince Valley, the biggest, most extensive forest fire in the history of Truro came to an end. We'll never see another conflagration to match it.

We made a mental note, as we saw a car pull into the post office area to use the pay phone, that this was the only motor vehicle we'd seen in our travels (state highway excepted), and the paucity of folks at this once busy spot got us to reminiscing. Why, back in our day, this time of year, the evening mail would just be coming in, and Truro Square would be teeming with humanity. Cars would be neatly parked front of the post office, nosed up to the lane left open for the mail carrier. David Snow's big black Hudson sedan and his brother Horace's box-like Essex, and brother Charlie's Peerless touring car. The earliest of the season's colonists would be there, too—the Abbey sisters in their dad's Hupmobile, and Amy Washburn behind the wheel of the family Nash, and Cal Stevens' two daughters secure behind the dash of a fancy Maxwell. Beauteous gals all, and if we've neglected to list more names, forgive us, ladies.

You might say the period before the arrival of the mail corresponded, in its time, to the cocktail hour of today. Eben Paine's store was open for business, with Lucy Fratus and Eben himself behind the counter, dispensing groceries and general merchandise. And across the square, Charlie Myrick's confectionery was competing for trade with Austin Rose's tiny, lamp-lit ice cream parlor. And the tantalizing smell of frankfurts browning on the charcoal grille at the tiny stand perched on the edge of the path leading to the post office (part of the Meier complex, it was) would set a body's mouth to watering, even though he'd just left the supper table at home. Grownups discussing business and politics in little knots among the parked cars, and kids nibbling on ice cream cones or dashing across the road to engage in a game of hide and seek back of Cobb Library. June bugs beating senselessly at the screen doors of the stores, and voracious mosquitoes coming in clouds from the fresh meadow back of Ed Snow's house.

Dave Snow would pull his big pocket watch from his pocket, and peer at it and allow, "Mite late tonight, ain't it?" (referring to the evening train, of course). "Or is my watch fast?" But no sooner had he tucked the turnip away when, from over the other end of the Wilder's Dyke, you'd hear the rattle and the backfire of Ezra Hopkins' Model T Ford as Ezra jammed the gas down on the quadrant for the final run down the Depot Road grade and across Wilder's. Mary Joseph the postmaster (by guppy, Mary insisted we use the masculine form long before the days of women's lib) would slam the doors of the office wicket, and the crowd would mill toward the tiny office lobby, forming a queue. Ezra would turn the Model T station wagon in a cramped turn, and with much chattering of the transmission back 'er into the slot reserved for him. And then willing hands would seize the bulky gray canvas mail bags and drag them up the dusty path and shove them back into the sorting area, and Mary would attack the letters and the parcels as though each piece of mail rated with the Armistice documents in importance and need for immediate delivery. In due time the chore would be finished, and Mary would unhook the wicket shutters and slam 'em back, and at that signal folks as had lock boxes would clean them out, while the general public stepped up to the window and queried Mary with the usual, "Anything for Mather, or Olsen, or Scott? Might as well give me Benson's, too they couldn't make it to town tonight."

And if you were lucky there'd be a special delivery letter to run out to some distant section of town. Mary'd pay eight cents for the chore. . . . But the dream is broken.

There goes a car up to the Blacksmith Shop. No Studebaker touring car this; rather one of Detroit's faceless look-alikes. A mongrel dog sniffs at the fence post at the corner of the old post office lot, vacant these many years. Comes the acrid smell of processed charcoal from an outdoor grille. And we head for home, followed by a single anemic mosquito.

We got to thinking, as we watched a pair of cyclists pumping their way up our road this morning, about the contrasts in bicycles—present day versus the days of our youth. We mean to take nothing from the sleek, expensive machines of the current era. Exotic ten speed affairs, with derailleurs calculated to enable a body to climb the steepest grades with ease, or those standard English three-speeders with a complicated rear hub that contains more gears than the chime mechanism at town hall. And they're about as heavy as a bucket of sand, are these modern bikes with their lug-welded frames and saddles the size of a mature banana, and tires about the size of a spring eel.

Not so in our day. We can recall the famous marques of the twenties and thirties. Each mail order house had its own private brand. Sears, Roebuck, and Montgomery Ward, and Spiegel, and Charles Williams, each with its own unique characteristics and its color schemes. And remember the Ranger? A khaki brown, single tooth sprocket bike with a double bar frame that included a tool case. That cussed Ranger must have weighed as much as a small piano. The Columbia, then as now, was a fine bike. The girl's model had a small sprocket mounted forward that gave a mechanical advantage for the weaker sex. They had to pedal faster than their male counterparts, but the ladies could climb our steep hills with much more ease than the boy's model. Nowadays, when a cyclist has a flat tire, he drops his bike off at a local garage, and the mechanic makes the necessary repairs. But back in our day, every bike owner had at hand a tool kit that included patches, and shredded rubber bands, and a bottle of shellac to glue the tire back onto the rim after he had plugged the puncture. You could also buy a tube of gooey material called Never Leak, which you squeezed into the valve of your leaking tire; the stuff was supposed to find the nail hole or whatever, and ooze out until it found the hardening effect of the atmosphere, and permanently seal the leak. It seldom worked as advertised.

We learned to ride a bike on a makeshift frame with loose, bearingless wheels. When traffic was light on the state highway next our house, we used to push and straddle the thing and shove off down the hill heading for Truro Square, praying that there'd be no cars crossing our path, since we had nary a brake on the machine. Many's the time we bounced into Ed Snow's barn, draggin' our feet vainly on the blacktop, ending up against the partition of the cow stall. Once we had mastered the business of balancing the rickety home assembled bike, we graduated to more sophisticated bicycles. On one occasion we recall, we borrowed a bike from one of the Deluze kids. The bike had no coaster brake, and you were expected to stop the thing by back pedaling on the sprocket. But on our first trip down from David Snow's hill into Truro Square, we managed to get the cuff of our overalls tangled in the chain, and by the time we got to Eben Paine's store, we were effectively stripped of our overalls. We had to walk home partially covered by several sheets of newspaper.

When the Cape started to become popular as a summer resort and traffic on the state highway burgeoned—this'd be in the early thirties—folks started to agitate for a police department. Not a full time, uniformed force, you understand, but a warm body or two in uniform to direct traffic at the busy intersections of the squares in Truro and North Truro from, say July first to Labor Day. Money was appropriated at the annual town meeting and in due course two men were hired for the jobs. The Truro honcho was Thede Parker, retired from the Everett Police Department. Thede was a portly, ruddy-complexioned man with rimless glasses and a friendly personality, who seemed to enjoy his work directing traffic in front of Cobb Library. He was wont to hold up long lines of cars coming down Corey's Hill when a shapely young thing wanted to cross the square from Eben Paine's store to Charlie Myrick's ice cream parlor, and he'd hook his thumbs in his Sam Brown belt and glare at any motorist who dared inch his car up to the cross walk while the lady was sashaying across.

Odd how certain details stick in one's memory. The uniforms of Truro's finest in that era were of an odd shade of olive drab khaki. We remember one time when Rupert Whitcomb, summer colonist who taught Romance languages in Norwich University during the winter, approached Thede Parker outside the post office. "Nice uniform, officer," he said. Thede beamed and nodded his thanks. "Know what they call that color in French?" continued Whitcomb. Thede shook his head. "Why, it's called merde d'oie." We could hardly wait for Cobb Library to open that afternoon so we could look up the word in a French dictionary. Gadzooks . . . goose dung.

We got to thinking about the task of buttoning up our house against cold weather as we watched the portents of winter weather ahead the other day: a brisk nor'west wind whipping white caps up in the bay, furry brown caterpillars hurrying to some unknown destination across the blacktop, gray squirrels flowing up a tree bole, their cheeks loaded with a choice acorn. First decent weekend, we'll fetch out the storm windows and check the gaskets and give 'em a coat of paint if needed, and fasten them in place. Then we'll take inventory of the woodpile, chuckling a mite as we recall how the late Capt. John Harrington Rich, who once owned this property, loaded some of his hardwood logs with gunpowder, so's to teach the feller who was purloining the old Yankee's winter fuel a good lesson. Within days, the news spread around town that a man down South Truro way had a horrendous explosion in his kitchen that blew his stove chock through the wall of the ell.

Back in the days when we used to drive the Lower Cape Ambulance, it often happened—or so it seemed—that folks became seriously ill during the holiday season. Certainly we remember that the ambulance was usually busy at that time. Many accident cases were due to increased traffic, as well as the usual medical trips.

It was a few days before Christmas, as we recall. We had been to one of the Boston hospitals delivering a terminally ill patient to his treatment center. So serious was his condition that his relatives, who had accompanied him on the trip, decided to stay in the city nearby, so we were obliged to make the long trip home in the Caddie alone. The weather was foul. It was a cold, windy day with sleet forming on the windshield and making the roads treacherous. The coffee and doughnuts we stowed away at the restaurant on the Southern Artery were lead in our stomach, traffic was heavy and every red light seemed against us. As we progressed down the South Shore the sleet turned to snow, heavy and sticky, making the driving even more hazardous.

It seemed hours before we got to Plymouth, and even there, the gay Christmas decorations on the storefronts and the red-faced shoppers huddling into their coat collars against the cold and the snow did little to dispel our deep mental gloom. We stopped for the traffic light abaft Jordan

Hardware Store, ground down the car window for a breath of fresh air, heard the chimes from some neighboring church ringing out the mid-afternoon hour and nodded to a blue-clad policeman standing on the sidewalk.

And then came a blast of a horn from across the intersecting street, from the line of oncoming traffic. We peered through the snow and recognized the big maroon Packard limousine belonging to Dick Magee, our Truro friend and neighbor, who was apparently city bound for the holidays.

The lights changed and the Packard glided up beside our ambulance. Through the open windows came a quick exchange: "Keep driving back about a half mile," advised the beaming fire chief/gentleman farmer. "And I'll turn around and follow you to that roadside stand where they sell Christmas wreaths and such. I have a surprise for you and the town of Truro."

So we did just that. We pulled into the big garden shop, and before you could say Obadiah Brown, the Magee Packard pulled in behind us and out stepped the dapper Magee, all togged out in his city clothes—melton overcoat with plush collar and homburg hat. It made us smile in spite of ourselves.

"Give us the biggest tree on the lot," he shouted to the proprietor. The man pawed through his stock and selected the most beautiful Christmas tree ever we'd seen in our life. He shook her free of snow and stood her up on the butt end and loosened the branches.

"We'll take it," said Dick. He paid the man. Then we turned to him and said, "How in tarnation are we going to get this giant in the ambulance?"

"Got your prepositions wrong, O'Caghan," said Dick. "We'll get it on the ambulance." And by guppy, that's what we did. We scrounged some strong cord from the shopowner, then we lashed that Christmas tree to the roof of the white Lower Cape Ambulance. The butt end stuck out over the cab by several feet, and the limber graceful tip extended past the rear bumper by as many more. Any conscientious cop along the road could have ticketed us for unsafe driving conditions. But it was, you see, Christmas, and all we got were beams of approval from the bluecoats on the way home, down-Cape.

NINETEEN SEVENTY-EIGHT

1978

We bailed out of bed in the wee hours this morning, aroused by one of our infrequent attacks of insomnia. We brewed ourself a cup of hot chocolate, whispered a few words to Shebnah the Shih Tzu pup when he emerged from his sheepskin-lined nest behind the refrigerator, and then we opened the kitchen door and listened to the night. We heard the first faint stirring of the nor'west wind through the bare locust branches; the hum of a nocturnal automobile heading north on the state highway; and just as we were about to drain our cup and return to bed we heard the faint, treble piping of a hyla-spring peeper-pinkle-tink—call it what you will.

By any name he's a welcome harbinger of spring. The sound came from down Fratus' Bend way, if we could trust our ears. Then we went to bed, to arise betimes and find the wind freshening and the sky to eastard red and angry from the rising sun.

We had our first personal contact with the conservation/ecology /resource movement when three men appeared at our office one day last week. We knew one of 'em—short, vibrant enthusiastic Dick Lazarus of Brewster. He'd seen us about a computer program for our office on a previous occasion. And the other two lads looked strangely familiar, and rightly so. They turned out to be older siblings of our own Ollie Durell, member of Truro's Beach Commission and charpentier par excellence, as they say in French.

"No, I'm no longer in computers," said Dick in response to our raised eyebrow. "I'm in the energy conserving program, together with these gentlemen. We specialize in. . . ."

But before he could finish, Durell No. One took over: "Hear that wind howling along the building outside?" he asked. "That wind should be harnessed. It could supply enough electricity to heat this town hall and light 'er up like a Christmas tree, and. . . ."

Durell No. Two interrupted his brother: "I hope you don't let the janitor burn the paper I see in the wastebaskets," he said. "Should be recycled, of course. And the beautiful shrubbery you have outside. . . ."

We glanced out the corner of our eye and espied a gorgeous crimson azalea just about to burst into flower. "No reason why you couldn't interplant 'em with vegetables," he said. "It'd be a practical use for the soil. Huge Russian sunflowers would produce seed for the birds next winter, and. . . ."

Back to Durell One. "We'd be glad to handprint some posters while we're here, advising folks not to flush the johns except once a day," he said. "Save five gallons of water, more or less, on each flushing."

"I notice you have some seedlings growing on your window sill," said Durell Two. We looked at the puny peppers and Egyptian onions, and nodded assent. "Certainly you must have a passive energy solarium-greenhouse at home?" he asked.

"Not yet," we admitted. "But we have a couple dozen brand new double-glazed sash, and we'd always planned to get some plants and. . . ."

"House face the south, like all these old Cape Codders?" queried Durell Two. Right on.

"Plenty of open space so's the sun can reach the house walls?" he asked. Correct. "Then here's how you build the thing."

And with that, he seized a pencil from our desk, and sketched out a greenhouse before you could say Obadiah Brown.

"No charge," he said. "Just send me a dozen tomatoes from your first winter batch."

Dick Lazarus finally managed to interject a few words. "As I was saying at the outset, we specialize in indoor. . . ." Here he fished for the proper word. "Privies?" he asked. "No, latrines?" Hardly. "Commodes? A bit old-fashioned, but it'll do until folks get used to using the Swedish trade name.

"Talk about energy saving! No water, no electricity, no expensive plumbing to install or maintain. They are stylish, too. And despite rumors to the contrary, you can install one of our commodes in your living room, completely assured there'll be no odor." (Why in tarnation a feller'd want to install his terlet in his living room we couldn't fathom.)

"By year's end, given the average family, you'll have about a bushel of perfect compost for your garden, and. . . ."

"Next!" shouted Mr. Selectman Sam Levy from the adjoining office, and our trio gathered up their sales material and moved along. "Hello, gentlemen," said Dick Lazarus. "I'm no longer in computers, I'm in energy. How does the town of Truro feel about waterless, indoor. . . ."

Looks like a good summer for local business folk. Joe Schoonie has refurbished his laundromat, new machines gleaming through the open doors of the establishment, and his riverbank complex lists an expanded restaurant and a sporting goods shop. Across Wilder's Dyke, Betty Gay Associates have taken over the former Mary Howard store, dispensing fresh fish and gourmet foods, delicatessen items and sports gear. We last week sampled some floundered filets from the Minnow Trap and found them delicious. The Blacksmith Shop is being readied for opening at the end of the month. We wish all our local merchants a fine season. Oops, we almost forgot to mention Paul Souza's Bayberry Gardens in its Long Nook location, originally Norm Rose's laundromat. They have a fine stock of plants, shrubbery, seeds, fertilizers and cordial and efficient service from the entire Souza family. May their cash register ring loud and clear. It couldn't happen to nicer folks.

Al "Oakie" Souza welcomes this good weather. "We'll be able to finish shingling my roof," he said. Al is referring to the Wilder School building, where he operates his real estate appraising business.

By the time we had returned to our desk, we had placed him: Waldo Brown, by guppy, grandson of Ezra Hopkins and boyhood chum, albeit some years older than we. He had taught us how to milk a cow, how to harness a horse, how to smoke tobacco, and how to pitch hay onto a hay rick among many other things.

He moved to Provincetown after his grandfather died, lived with his stepfather, Seraphine Steele, finished high school in Provincetown, joined the Coast Guard and served well and faithfully in that outfit. He retired a few years back; now lives in Falmouth, patriarch of a sizable clan. As we pressed the book into Waldo's hand, we roared out our recognition, which took the wind right out of his sails, by gosh. And then we ran off to a clutch of remember-whens, punctuated by denials by Waldo and clucks of disapproval from his attractive wife.

"We never dast wear our best clothes around the barn when you were milking the cows, Waldo," we said. "Else you'd aim a stream of milk at us and holler, 'Open your mouth and catch it, or I'll make believe I'm a fireman, puttin' out a big blaze.'"

Waldo gave a feeble grin. He said, "Now I'm interested in researching the Hopkins family. I'm as far back as my great-grandfather, and . . ."

"And remember the time," we interrupted, "you let us drive the hayrig back from that little meadow back of the Fratus homestead, near Manuel Corey's place? We should have known better, because you always were kind of mean about giving up the reins. But no sooner had you slipped them to us, you jumped down off that big load of hay, and we lost sight of you instanter. Next we knew, we could hear stones zipping by our head.

Turns out you were trying to target in on the big wasp's nest that hung from a pine tree limb right over the road, about a foot or so from our head. Lucky thing you missed, or we'd have been attacked by those nasty buzzers."

"Tch Tch," said Miz Brown. "And he claims our grandchildren get their bad behavior from my side of the family."

"Or the time you had a grudge against Ernie Snow," we said. "And you got a group of us kids to help you string a wire across the road at Fratus' Bend. And when poor Ernie came jigging up the road on his new Ranger bicycle, headed for Joseph's farm with two cans of milk strung on the handlebars, why you yanked the wire up out of the sand so's it came even with his Adam's apple, like to cut the poor guy's head off."

"Ahrumph. . . . Should be fairly easy," said Waldo, disregarding our anecdote completely, "to trace the Hopkins family clear back to Giles of the Mayflower."

"Surely you recall," we said, "the time we younger kids were begging you to let us take a few drags on one of your cigarettes: Piedmonts, if memory serves. And you claimed you were fresh out of tailor-mades, but you'd roll us some corn silk specials. And this'd be about the year Lane Construction Company was putting the new highway through Truro. They were using oakum to caulk the joints in the drainpipes, and you substituted oakum for corn silk, and we dern near choked to death with the first puffs."

"You'll have to excuse me for now, old friend," said Waldo, kind of red-faced. "I'll just take this book out into the next room and . . . we can chat again, sometime. . . ."

Fine with us, Waldo. Then we'll be able to remind you of the time you loosened the dory plug in Harry McAnistan's clam dory down at Pamet Harbor, and when poor Harry had loaded his craft with washers of steamers and settled down in the midships thwart and commenced to haul away for the landing, why. . . .

The sun is setting, blood-red, into the cobalt blue bay, and the breeze which has been out of the northeast, light and steady, has abated to a flat calm. There's a mild flurry of traffic on the side roads, reflecting the homeward-bound cars on the main highway. A trio of gulls are flying down valley to the bay, their slate-gray bodies brushed by the rays of the setting sun. And from the hillside to southard, there's the querulous squall of a sentry crow, and from down Castle Road way, the faint baying of a hound dog.

We note with amazement that you can still buy the handsome, nickel-plated Aladdin lamp. Mantle Aladdins were commonly used in stores and public buildings. One of the local stores which boasted these efficient lamps was Anthony R. Phat Francis' Square Deal general store in Truro Center.

The business of preparing for the dark hours of night at the Square Deal was almost a ritual. Phat's mother, a tiny, wiry Portuguese lady, would carefully remove the chimneys and give 'em a quick polish on her apron, while son Anthony would fill the reservoirs with kerosene, and delicately adjust the valves. He'd titillate the feed handle to just the right position, pump the pressure up to the correct level, and then he'd scratch a wooden match on his shoe sole and gently apply the flame to the mantle.

"Got to be careful with these dern mantles," he'd caution us bystanders. "Female mouse could rupture 'em with a half burp. And they're expensive."

Once the flame had turned into the intense, white-hot light on the mantle, Phat would carefully pick up the Aladdin and put 'er in place in the big front shop window. But here his lighting plans would vary, most mysteriously, from night to night. Most evenings, he'd place a lamp in each window. But on other occasions, after a muttered conference in Portuguese with his mother, Phat would put a lamp in one window only, leaving the other window blank and dark. Sometimes he'd illuminate the right, sometimes the left. And on rare occasions, he'd pop two lamps in one window, be it port or starboard.

No amount of questioning could elicit from Phat the reason for his erratic patterns of lighting the storefront. "You ask too many question, boy," he'd brush us off. "Now run down and get the store mail, and I'll give you a candy bar."

It wasn't until years later, after Prohibition had been repealed, that someone got the truth out of Phat. Seems our local entrepreneur had connections with the rumrunners. He'd be notified when a convoy of liquor was on its way down-Cape. And it was his job to scout the local highways, to see if the state police or the county fuzz were lurking about. If he saw anything suspicious, he was required to display his lamps in the store windows in a prearranged system. When the liquor trucks hove over Corey Hill to southard, they could see the blinking lights of Phat's store far below, and they'd adjust their route accordingly. Sometimes by going around Pamet Loop, sometimes by detouring down Castle Road, sometimes, even, by jamming on the brakes and reversing their route. And that's why we still have a soft spot in our heart for the good old Aladdin lamp.

NINETEEN SEVENTY-NINE

1979

Suzanne Nielsen, the beauteous redhead who works next office to us at town hall as general expeditor for the selectmen, stopped by our desk one day last week at the shank end of the day. She fidgeted a mite, groped for words, and finally said, "Would you think there was something seriously wrong with me if I told you I heard music in the wee hours of the morning and heard voices?"

We stand in loco parentis for Sue, who comes from far away Michigan. So we felt obligated to put her mind at ease. "Lessee now, Sue. You're living in Wellfleet, in that cottage just next to the Candle Factory. Hmm. Ah yes. Clear as a bell, once you know the story of the old Wellfleet Band.

"Back in the early thirties several members of the John R. McKay American Legion Post decided that their organization should have a rebirth. Included in their plans for the legion post was the formation of a military band. And to this end they sent word out to any and all interested musicians on the Lower Cape. From Wellfleet High School they drafted, among others whose names we can't recall, Ned Lombard, Sonny Berrio, Clayton Gilliatt and Clayton Bishop.

"From the grownups they enlisted Wilfred Rogers and Truro's Joe Curley Francis. And we had the pleasure of joining the group with our Wellfleet High School B-flat tuba.

"From over Provincetown way we were joined by Alphonse Wager, Jack Edwards and the Ramos family, including old man Joe, the blacksmith on baritone, and his two sons, Joe and George, on saxophone and trumpet. From the North village came Joe Francis. And before you could say Obadiah Brown the Wellfleet Legion Band was up to full strength, balanced well in all sections, equipped with good instruments and a complete library.

"Oops, almost forgot the most important person in the band. That'd be the late Tony Dennis, a bandy-legged, bespectacled little man with a twinkle in his eye and rhythm in his heart. Drove the Texaco tank truck out of Provincetown daytimes, did Tony, and on rehearsal evenings he'd show up in Wellfleet to take over the band. He had a shiny brass trumpet under one arm, ready to play a difficult passage for one of his players. He held a baton in the other arm for beating out the time for march, overture, or concert waltz. 'Give us a roll-off,' he'd command drummer Mannie Gaspie, veteran of the original Provincetown Band.

"The horns would blare for the introduction and you could hear Jack Edwards on his sousaphone thundering out the down beat as Joe Curley Francis followed with the afterbeat on the peckhorn. The wailing clarinets would thread through the melody of the trumpets with a shrill obbligato. A clang of cymbals, a slur of the trombones and, on occasion, a shout from Tony to catch the attention of his men whose eyes, for the most part, were glued to their music."

But Suzy's eyes are drifting toward the Seth Thomas clock on the wall and we know she's not following our yarn.

"Oh, last but not least, our rehearsal hall was the Boy Scout building, donated to the town of Wellfleet by philanthropist Mary K. Lawrence, located just about where your house is. Probably some sort of poltergeist, a hanger-on from the Wellfleet Band days, still frequents the premises."

Sue demurred. "But the voice, a shrill, male voice, penetrating through the sound of a march. It sounds like P on the trio, P on the trio," she blushed.

"Why, that has to be good old Tony Dennis admonishing the band to play the trio 'piano,' meaning softly in Italian. He always used a kind of musical shorthand when he directed the band."

It's a hot, sultry July day, not yet 10 o'clock of the morning and already the thin red line of our back porch thermometer is approaching 80 degrees. We don't need to study the panel of instruments in our living room to tell the humidity. The limp shirt we took from the closet and the blotter-like consistency of the Sunday paper tell us it must be in the 90 percent range. Not to mention the beads of perspiration that form on our upper lip and refuse to evaporate, notwithstanding a brisk sou'west breeze that fills the valley.

The sun is brassy and hot. And the thin cloud cover that filled the sky yesterday has dissipated. Last evening the fireflies fluttered about our shrubbery and a whippoorwill tried for a local record with his string of ululating, monotonous calls. We expect to hear the soaring, sassy call of the cicada at any moment this morning.

Was it our imagination or did we really feel a slight tug on the handlebars of our white Yamaha as we tooled the bike down Depot Road on our way from church this morning just as we got abreast the Marshall driveway two hills removed from the Wilder building?

We'd have liked to putt up the sandy road and find old Mary Marshall, matron of the clan, at the black iron range in her summer kitchen stuffing fresh sweet corn into a huge kettle, preparing her vegetables for sale to the summer folks.

Big, handsome woman was Mary Marshall. Behind her back we called her Mary Big Feet, for obvious reasons. She had a powerful voice, a beautiful gold cap on her front upstairs incisor, huge, ornate earrings in her ears and the musical lilt of her native Azorean language in her speech. Mary used to eschew the wheelbarrow or the market basket or the horse and team when she wanted to fetch heavy weights about the farm.

She'd gather up driftwood from the salt crick, bind it together with a piece of cordline, toss it on her head, and balance the load. And then, with her hands crossed over her ample bosom, she'd pace off barefoot up the steep grade of the river bank, marking her progress with snatches of song from her native islands.

She could fill a huge kettle with blueberries or cranberries or bayberries and center it on her cowlick and walk it home with nary a slip. But back to the summer kitchen. The purpose of the kettle of steamed corn was to supply the customers with free samples of the delicious vegetable. Buy a couple dozen ears and Mary would invite you to sit down in the wooden swing outside the kitchen door and partake of a huge steaming ear, swathed in butter and sprinkled with salt.

And before she stuffed the corn in a secondhand paper sack, she'd offer you a chilled, peeled cucumber to be eaten like a banana. Or perhaps an early astrakhan apple, blush red. And as long as there was room in your bag she'd add nubbly summer squash and top it all with crisp chard or a bunch of carrots or beets. If business was slow you'd get a free lesson in Portuguese. "You speak Portuguese, rapaz? No? We start now. Bom dia. That mean good day, hello. Como está? How are you? A deos. Go with God, good-bye," she'd say.

Then you'd wipe off your chin, dribble a few coins into her big calloused palm and head off down the driveway saying goodbye to the cows cropping grass along the fence line and offering your apple core to the sway-backed nag drinking at the water trough in the barnyard. If you were lucky you'd meet Mary's son, Plady, just coming into the farm.

He was a tiny, gnome-like feller, so-called because he was bald as a billiard ball. He had a fine arrangement with his employer up-city way. He'd work all winter and take off several weeks in the summer so he could help out with chores on the Marshall farm.

If he were in the mood, Plady'd launch into a yarn based on his earlier experiences as a merchant seaman. The familiar plot would involve a fracas on board a coastal freighter, a gigantic chief engineer who had threatened Plady and ending with Plady seizing a monkey wrench and repelling the brute. Plady's punchline was, "And he never crossed me again." And then would come the strident soprano voice of Mary across the hill, "Arthur?" Mary never used the Portuguese nickname for her son.

She would continue, "Arthur, come turn-a the windmill on. Agua. She's getting low in the tank." Memories, memories.

There's hardly a spot along the state highway that doesn't ring a bell in our memory, as we were reminded when a bosky chipmunk crossed the road in front of our car abaft Aunt Mary's Lodge as we tooled the faithful Datsun to church this morning. Turn back the calendar a trio of decades, give us back our robins egg blue Model A Ford, pile our No. 1 son, Randy, into the narrow front seat, whistle our liver-and-white springer spaniel Dolce (Marge Snow, gifted soprano and serious student of the Italian lyric had suggested the name for our dog when he was just a pup) aboard the jaunty car and hie off up the highway on a Sunday morning to scavenge a load of wood trimmings left by the contractors when they had graded and cleared the area up by the town line.

Pull in at the cutoff and unload our cargo including teenager, tools of the trade, buck saw and axe while our beautiful springer immediately sets off in pursuit of imaginary and perhaps real rabbits, foxes, woodchucks and chipmunks. And so we set to work, gathering up the dead oak and the pine, sawing it into lengths to fit the tiny deck astern of our Ford and finally, the Model A loaded to the scuppers, we packed the tools aboard and whistled for Dolce who had, meantime, crossed the highway in search of some elusive game.

But even as the poor dog sprinted back through a pine thicket, up the highway from Provincetown comes a speeding automobile. Despite all our efforts to stop Dolce from crossing the blacktop, and despite a valiant effort on the part of the driver to bring the big automobile to a stop, dog and car meet in the center of the road. We rushed out with Randy to pick up our unconscious Dolce, who was bleeding from the nose, eyes glazed and limp. We wept as we loaded him into the Ford, accepted the apologies of the driver of the car (one of the Roderick brothers of Provincetown) and fetched the poor dog home.

All night long we tended our pet, applying cold compresses to his fevered head, dribbling diluted aspirin solution down his throat, holding him in our arms and, we're not ashamed to admit it, praying for his recovery. Come morning, by guppy, good old Dolce staggered to the door and indicated in no uncertain terms he wanted out. We still recall the bush he visited that morning with much affection, since it marked the certain indication of Dolce's recovery.

For the rest of his life, we forgave Dolce anything untoward in his behavior, chalking it up to his earlier accident. A puddle on the kitchen floor? Remember the poor dog's accident, we'd remind our bride as we fetched out sponge and bucket.

He actually nipped the feathers out of the family rooster? Tsk tsk tsk. Must be a delayed result of the time he took that crack on the head from Capt. Roderick's car up by Aunt Mary's Lodge. Even the time he chased a bird out on the meadow and fell through the skim ice and son Mike had to swim through the frigid water to rescue the liver-and-white pet, we all forgave him.

"Somebody must have made a trade off when we prayed for him, the time he was hit by the car. Don't hold it against poor old Dolce," was always our excuse.

A veiled threat hangs over the Narrow Land on the wings of the thin caul of cloud cover spreading a light sou'west breeze. The barometer is about midway of the quadrant, budging not a smidgin. The thin red line of our back porch thermometer stands at 26 degrees, a notch higher than it was at breakfast time.

On our morning walk with Shebnah we noted shards of ice building out from the chocolate brown banks of the fresh crick. But the main channel is open water. Lead-blue berries clustered on the bull-briar by the roadside added feeble color to the countryside. And the faithful bottle green scrub pine, the straw hued cattail patch and the gray-boled locusts set the pattern of winter colors.

But our lawn is still jewel green and the pyrocantha, the bushy yews and the rhododendrons are alive and well and living in Truro. If nature doesn't supply us with color enough, there'll be Christmas lights strung in the square and on Truro homes before you can say Obadiah Brown.

Got to thinking as we delivered our car to the agency in Hyannis last week for routine servicing, about the contrast in automobile salesmanship today as compared with that of our day. As we looked at the young man attired in comfortable dungarees seated at a desk in one corner of the showroom waiting for a live one, as they used to call the customers, we recalled the automobile purveyors of former years.

Old Man Connolly of Hyannis, Buick distributor, didn't wait for the customer to come to him, but made his usual grand tour of the Lower Cape each year when the new models came out. He'd show up in Truro, driving a shiny, nice-smelling Buick. He'd be dressed in a blue serge suit and he'd have a flower in his lapel and one in the bud vase in the back compartment. He'd pick up Mr. Manuel Corey and Miz Corey, take them out to dinner at Libbey's Restaurant in Wellfleet and soft sell his product.

Or Roy Howes; remember how he'd make a sales pitch for the racy, stylish Lincoln based on the pure comfort of the ride? He'd tuck his client in the lush seats of the vehicle, tool 'er up Highland Road, where the frost heaves were the worst in town, and show how the car would ride like a baby carriage.

Burt Hart, a confirmed Studebaker man, used to say he always found a pack of White Owl panatellas on the seat of the demo when he was taken out for a test drive. And Dave Snow, who would drive nothing but Hudsons until they disappeared from the market, admired the way the Hudson salesman offered to fetch the Snows to church on a Sunday morning. (Miz Snow was the daughter of a Methodist minister.) In later years there was George Williams, whom we'll always associate with the Model A Ford.

As though it were yesterday, we recall the morning George loaded that first of the gear-shift models with local men, Henry Hanson, Tony DeLuze, Earl Eldredge and Al Paine, and roared out of Truro Square heading for South Truro. There he floored the Model A coming down Meeting House Hill and climbed Perry's Hill in high gear. Performance, by guppy.

Those salesmen wouldn't have known what to do with a posh office. They worked out of their cars and their hats. And the prices. We adjusted our bifocals and peered at the computer sheet on one of those alphabetized sports cars on the floor following the n/c items on the list to get to the extras. The deluxe luxury package included two-tone paint, air conditioning, AM/FM radio, electronic analysis panel (to tell you, among other things, if your ashtray needed emptying). The bottom line read $12,400. Good Lord, we bought our home with eight acres of land for a quarter of that amount, just a few decades ago. Across the floor, a Peugeot four-door sedan, with sun roof and all the other extra goodies for, hold onto your hat, $16,200.

The dozing salesman must have heard our gasp of disbelief, for he casually got to his feet, came over and started to list the selling points of the big blue monster. But we were thinking of other cars, other days. To be precise, the Bentley sports car we once saw in Ed Wilson's driveway, trim, beautiful and powerful. And as we were fair drooling over the car, comes Ed to explain the hidden features of the Bentley. "And she's got a built-in toilet under the front passenger seat. Feller could drive from here to California without getting out of the car," Ed said. Play that on your deluxe package, Mr. Salesman.

NINETEEN EIGHTIES

1980's

NINETEEN EIGHTY

1980

Up betimes, this Sabbath between Christmas and New Years, plotting the manner of making points with a clutch of our visiting grandchildren.

How better to do this than to work on the breakfast menu, uncovering the raised bread dough bought at the supermart a few days ago, and fabricating a batch of flippers. Outer wrappers having been already discarded, the kids could draw the conclusion that the dough is handmade and we do little to discourage that idea.

Stretch the plastic dough in hand and fasten it to the ripple surfaced counter board to hold its shape while we note the fat bubbling in the fry pan. Soon as it's hot, we drop the fritter shaped objects in the fat and let 'em fry. Meanwhile we study the fresh meadow to find it little changed from last week. Drab colors of cattail and meadow grass, bared branches of rumcherry and locust form delicate networks against the lead gray background of the fresh Pamet. Searching, golden rays of the rising sun competing with the disc of the moon setting to west'ard.

While the kids fight over bathroom rights we watch those flippers, toss them over with a steel-tined fork and study the shade of gold.

Was it last night close to midnight, while moonlight filled the valley, we heard the raucous crowing of our rooster out in the henhouse? And how stands the thin red line of the thermometer? Forty-four degrees, and rising. Barometer? Midway of the quadrant, but inching up a mite from last night's setting. Wind? Well sir, judging by the swaying of the locust branches, she's—TURN THOSE FLIPPERS, FAT'S SMOKING—from the northwest.

The weather represents a contradiction in terms. Who ever heard of a December day, wind fresh from the nor'west, with a temperature relatively shirtsleeve and a bright sun shining? COME AND GET 'EM, KIDS!

Idly flipping the pages of one of our wife's specialty magazines the other day we ran across an article on early American utensils. And there, prominently displayed among the ceramic ware, was a handsome spittoon. The author of the article was convinced that his readers couldn't identify this item. Wish he'd offered a prize for those as recognized that indispensable utensil of the earlier part of this century, for surely we'd have sat down to typewriter and pecked out the following message:

Sir: The handsome clay object you picture is a spittoon, a container designed to catch tobacco juice liberally diluted with saliva. It was used hereabouts and all over the country up to the early part of this century. Our own familiarity with the spittoon centers around Truro and folks in this famous Cape Cod town who either chewed tobacco, or operated business establishments open to the public. Most of the stores, barber shops, markets, railroad stations, professional offices of lawyers, doctors and dentists were graced with spittoons. And it was considered a minor social grace to possess the skill and accuracy to expectorate a stream of brown liquid, prob'ly Mayo's Dark or Apple, a considerable distance exactly to the maw of the nearby spittoon.

The maw was, of course, not exactly delineated by the diameter of the bowl. The rim of the spittoon was in the shape of a flattened opened cone. If you had accuracy enough to spew a load onto the outer rim of the funnel it would find its way down into the bowels of the bowl. Naturally, where accuracy is a virtue folks could gain a reputation that sometimes approached the boundaries of folklore.

Take Archie Holden, for instance, a tiny, gnomelike man. Worked on the state highway. Always had a cud of tobacco in his cheek. When he'd step into Charlie Mike's barber shop in Truro Square, Mike would say to him, "Want t' spit her out, before you set down?" And Archie would reply, "Not yet, Mike. Still got a lot of flavor left." He'd gum his cud while Mike would set the water to boil on his tiny kerosene stove and strop the straight razor and work up a lather in his soap cup. About halfway through the shave Archie would elbow a signal to Mike and rear up out of the cotton drop cloth. Then Archie would sight in on the battered wooden box, filled with sand half way across the room. (Mike refused to scrub out a spittoon, so he used disposable containers.) Then he'd inhale mightily and let go. Mostly, he hit his target.

A new face at town meeting this year is that of the very attractive gal who is doing counseling and related professional services for the elder citizens of the lower Cape, Elinore Thorkildsen. The Thorkildsens are the new owners of the former Keyes property on the shores of Slough Pond on the Truro-Wellfleet line.

We had met the lady earlier on. Got to talking with her about Professor Keyes, as he was always referred to hereabouts. Had we known him? Indeed. What did he look like? Well sir, open your Muzzey's American History, find the photograph of President Woodrow Wilson and you'd have a very good likeness of the Professor, closecropped white hair, steel-blue eyes, rimless glasses and a mouth with the embouchure of a trumpet player. He always wore a bow tie, tweedy casual clothes and deer-skin gloves, winter and summer. Why? Because he drove a beautiful, Brewster-green, canvas-top roadster, Rolls Royce, of course. One drives a Rolls with driver's gloves, doesn't one?

We got to know Prof. Keyes when we clerked at the original Truro liquor emporium. Wellfleet was dry as a bone in those days and we had many customers from the neighboring town. We once made the mistake of asking him what year his beautiful Rolls Royce was.

"One doesn't identify a Rolls Royce by year," he gently corrected us. "But this model came off the factory line in 1929."

The good professor taught at MIT. During World War II he became involved with the development of an invention connected with photographic equipment. It would be in poor taste to suggest that he made a great deal of money from his laboratory endeavors and if you attempted to prove this assertion by Prof. Keyes' living habits, you'd come a cropper. But he still drove the 1929 Rolls Royce. Matter of fact, several years after we had severed our connections with the Truro liquor emporium, we chanced to meet up with the good professor under the following circumstances.

We had assumed the job of driving the Lower Cape ambulance. Our vehicle was a brand-new 1941 Cadillac with hydromatic transmission, more horses under the hood than E. Hayes Small ever had in his stables, the engine honed to peak performance and an eager driver behind the wheel. We had delivered a patient to one of the Boston hospitals, had mugged up with coffee and doughnuts at our favorite restaurant on the Southern Artery, and, at midmorning we had just braked to a stop at the traffic lights at Hanover Four Corners. This was long before the construction of the new highway system on the South Shore.

Well sir, we idly glanced out the driver's window just as a shiny, Brewster-green, ragtop Rolls Royce glided up beside us. Upon closer inspection we recognized the familiar, cherubic face of Frederick G. Keyes. We nodded. He returned our nod.

This would be a good time to put this fellow in his place, we said to ourself. The customer/clerk relationship no longer exists. All's we have to do is jazz this big V-8 up so's she's tugging at the bit, as it were, with the brakes just nagging to hold 'er back. When that light turns green, we'll everlastingly jam down on the accelerator and pull by old Prof. Keyes as though he were glued to the asphalt. We smiled benignly at Prof. Keyes, even as we noted he had slipped the big Rolls Royce into first gear. He returned our friendly gesture and tromped down lightly on the accelerator. The Rolls hummed. We titivated the gas pedal on the Caddie and felt the transmission bands tighten up against the brakes. Then, the light turned green. WHOOM, Prof. Keyes' expression turned from Woodrow Wilson to that of an Indianapolis 500 driver. Took us several minutes, and a distance well into the old measured mile they used to have in Hanover, before we were able to overhaul and finally pass the green Rolls.

Appearances, we told ourself as we backed the Caddie into the garage that day, can certainly be deceiving.

A squib, if we may, on the subject of billboards, as we remember those much maligned outdoor advertising signs. In addition to the permanent displays of the U.S. Tire company that greeted the traveler as he entered each town on the Cape, there were, in addition, numerous billboards of a more transient variety along the state highway. Transient in the sense that their displays were changed several times each year, in accordance, we suppose, with the bids received from sundry conglomerates of the day, manufactures of cigarettes, and soft drinks, among others.

The gentle art of advertising must have been counseled by experts in the field, for those old billboards were in strategic locations, places where the big signboards were bound to catch the eye, where the man behind the wheel could momentarily take his eyes from the winding road and read the message displayed.

In Truro, for instance, there was a billboard planted on the sharp corner where the Blacksmith Shop Restaurant parking lot is now. Traffic slowed there, for obvious reasons. A feller would have to back shift for the steep hill. He'd have time to read about the virtues of the current coffin nails, as Dave Snow used to term tailor-made cigarettes, Camels, or Lucky Strikes, or Chesterfields. For traffic headed in the opposite direction, southerly, up-Cape, there was another billboard perched at the base of the steep hill on Miz Sherman Grant Rich's property that met the eye of drivers crossing Wilder's Dyke. In addition to its display value, this structure served as a sort of gymnasium apparatus for the local kids. They used to dare each other to walk out on the beams which braced the billboard—no hands allowed, of course—and, if they were lucky enough to attain the top stringer without tumbling down into the briars and brush below, they were expected to balance their way along the dizzying top frame. But we digress.

Up the road apiece, just after you crossed the Truro–Wellfleet line, there was another billboard on the south bank of Herring River, competing, as it were, for the eye of the motorist with the natural beauties of that meandering stream and the meadow below. At Joe King's corner, the Fisk Tire company touted its product; little tyke, pajama clad, with a tire on his shoulder and a guttering candle clutched in his hand, yawning as he headed for bed, giving meaning to the slogan, TIME TO RETIRE. The power of visual suggestion made many a person gawk as he stared at the display.

When it came time to change the displays, a battered panel truck would come down Cape and nose its way along the weed-grown road back of Charlie Joseph's complex on Wilder's Dyke, and two employees of the Donnelly Advertising Company would climb out and start to unload their gear, buckets of paste, and long handled, jointed brushes, and bundles of folded paper. They'd attack the face of the billboard, scraping the faded, loose paper away, and then they'd carefully unfold the new advertising material, arranging it by coded symbols. They'd slap on the paste and gingerly hoist the big sheets aloft on their brushes, and stick the sheets in place. Rub the bubbles out and pound the seams tight, and repeat the process. Gradually the display would take shape. OLD GOLD CIGA- RETTES, TREASURE OF THEM ALL. A pirate treasure chest, half buried in the sand, doubloons showing from the half-opened box, and a healthy, tanned young man drawing, with obvious satisfaction, on an Old Gold.

The overall-clad men would give a final swipe at the billboard, and stand back to admire their work. Then they'd load their gear back into the truck and back out on the main highway, headed for the next job. We Truro folks had a personal interest in that Old Gold ad, for one of our prominent artist-colonists, Edward A. Wilson had designed the display for the tobacco company. We always felt it must have been satisfying to see one's art spread all over the country. In later years we asked Ed how it felt. And did he, perchance, approve of the product from personal use of those mellow, satisfying cigarettes?

"Hell no," was Ed's reply. "I'm a cigar and pipe smoker."

Our granddaughter Andrea is away at camp, and if we thought the chore of writing our weekly column would be easier because of the missing distractions ("Poppa, toast me an English muffin, peanut butter, light brown." Or, "Lace up my roller skates, please!" Or, "Mind if I bring in my pet white chicken to watch you type?"), we're sadly mistaken. We keep thinking of that poor tyke exposed to hairy black spiders, forced to eat plain toast—dark brown, sans peanut butter, probably deprived of her crayons and drawing materials, leading the regimented life of the summer camp. We visualize the group singing to the accompaniment of a battered upright piano—Andrea trills out solos with us at the console of the Hammond organ—and even the swimming, in some turtle-infested pond, must be distasteful to her after her customary visits to the beautiful, unspoiled beaches of Truro. But we digress.

The big bluefish we'll have for lunch today was practically caught to order yesterday afternoon by our longtime friend Dr. Martin Bradford. "Blues are boiling in the water just below our house," he reported by phone at mid-afternoon. "Want one?" And almost before you could say Obadiah Brown, the good surgeon was at our door, with the blue still practically quivering. Thankee, doctor.

We join with many hundreds of lower Cape customers of the First National Stores in deploring the passing of that almost venerable institution in this area. Our good bride reminds us we've been buying our vittles at the FNS for 45 years.

She has much praise for the outfit, quality food, reasonable prices, congenial employees. Our memory of the organization goes back several decades to the time when the chain store originated as a competitor of the Great Atlantic and Pacific Tea Company hereabouts. Early on, it operated under sundry names, O'Keefe, John P. O'Connor among others. We associate the business with ruddy faced Irishmen from up-city way who studied the lower Cape for favorable locations and hired ambitious young men to build up local trade. Take Wellfleet for instance. The A&P, called the red-front because of the fire-engine red they painted their stores, was located in the Gordon Block, so-called, corner of School Street. Presided over by Wilfred Rogers, native son, the red-front had what amounted to a monopoly in the dry grocery business. True, Art Pierce and Horton and Gill still did very well with their independent markets. They stocked fresh meats and fish and other perishables. But when you priced the standard brand or house items, the chain stores could undersell them every time. Bought in carload lots—Wilfred Rogers used to explain—stores from coast to coast. Efficiency in every step of the operation and, of course, cash on the counter.

But the independents extended credit to their customers, and somebody had to pay for that practice. But the A&P monopoly was not to last forever. Turn of the decade, probably 1930—Tio (Uncle, in Portuguese) Rogers, leased the space in his building directly across the street from the A&P to the fledgling outfit O'Keefe Company, that was to become the First National. O'Keefe painted their storefronts a kind of nondescript brown, which rival manager Rogers promptly dubbed Ca-ca brindle, and competition between the two stores instantly burgeoned. And folks took advantage of the rivalry, by comparison shopping.

Scotty Rattray, boss man of the O'Keefe store, a ruddy faced little feller with ill-fitting dentures, would study his price lists and spread, by word of mouth, specials in Uneeda biscuits or Rival canned goods while Wilfred would gloat over specials in A&P house items of soft drinks brewed by the Crowell family in South Wellfleet. And Scotty added another feature, home deliveries of orders by Bob Lombard. The service boosted business from Truro folks, who found the four-mile trip to Wellfleet a mite expensive. A shopping trip to either store would make a body draw comparisons between the two managers. Wilfred with his latest jokes—told even as he snatched your groceries from the shelves and piled them on the counter, and inquired about your relatives in Truro. Or across the street, Scotty Rattray noting your location so's he could send Bob down to deliver your order if your Model T Ford malfunctioned. One thing the two men shared in common: both were expert at mental arithmetic, and for a grocery list with more than a dozen items, they could be compared with the modern computer once you put a pencil in their hands. We can see Wilfred and Scotty now, big brown paper bag in front, checking off the packages on the counter, jotting down the individual prices, then skimming up and down the columns, scribbling the total. We often thought the two men should have been matched in a contest of addition.

Speed and accuracy, of course, the desired ends. But you'd expect Wilfred to throw in the yarn about the traveling salesman kneeling to say his prayers in the farmer's guest bedroom while he added. And Scotty would be required to whistle a passage from some bagpipe tune as his pencil raced up and down the columns. So it's ave atque vale to you—O'Keefe, O'Connor, First National Stores. Hail and farewell.

The passing of Leo Mitchell, for many years resident of Provincetown, local businessman and employee of the Mass. Dept of Public Works (Highway), professional musician, good neighbor and family man, deserves more than a paragraph or two in the local dailies. When we think of Mitch, our memory goes back to the summer of 1934, when Joe Roberts, Provincetown entrepreneur, built the first lower Cape outdoor dance area at the north end of Beach Point, close by the Truro-Provincetown line. In retrospect, the dance platform was an unbeautiful slab of concrete, sur-rounded by a chain-link fence, with a tiny cubicle at one end to enclose the as yet to be selected orchestra. The garish colored light bulbs strung overhead certainly drew the attention of the passersby, but they also lured myriad gnats and greenhead flies and mosquitoes as dusk approached. But at the time, we teenage kids found Roberts open air dance hall a place of magic, tinsel and beauty, and on opening night every ablebodied boy and girl—and many an older dance buff—showed up at Beach Point.

Once, it had rained heavily all day long, but inclement weather had no effect on the size of the crowd, pressed against the gate and the entire spread of the chain link fence. The tiny parking lot was jammed full of cars, and it was with some difficulty that the small squad of taxis bearing the band managed to crowd into the driveway just as the lights went on and the sun sank in the west. Gadzooks, how we ogled those musicians, young, debonair, tuxedo clad, toting their instruments into the cubicle. And Leo "Hod" Mitchell was the handsomest of all. City feller from Chelsea, Mass., he had organized a truly big band—full instrumentation of trumpets, trombones, reeds, and of course, complete percussion—over which Hod himself presided. From cowbell to coconut shell to jazz whistle to tom-toms to snare and brushes and bass drum big around as a family dinner table, Hod could play 'em all—with the precision of a metronome, the artistry of a symphony percussionist.

Mitch, as he was later to be known in lower Cape musical circles, did himself proud that night, and for many nights to follow. Folks came from all over the county to dance to the music of the Mitchell Band. When the open air season ended, Mitch moved into Provincetown, where he played at sundry clubs and halls. We had the pleasure of playing with Mitch in later years, when he sat in on drums for the Provincetown Band, and at the Provincetown Inn, where we jammed with Squire Jim Moynahan and Ira Bates. Always the gentleman, the fine musician, the true friend, was Mitch. We shall miss him. Ave atque vale, Mitch. May the library up There have all the old standards for you to play—Stardust, and Under a Blanket of Blue, and Sunny Side of the Street.

Ah, the games we play at town hall when the weather's hot and the chore of writing dunning notes to delinquent taxpayers palls on us. Up we lurch from our desk, and resolutely we bypass the coffee urn, and finally we arrive at the mini-gallery where the latest works of Truro artists are displayed. This past fortnight the walls of the converted dining room have been graced with three dimensional plaque and shadow box orginals by

Anna Maria Poor, granddaughter of Henry Varnum and Bessie Brewer Poor. They range all the way from simple plaster of Paris rectangular solids to comparatively elaborate transparent plastic cases, with a common theme throughout: bones. From tiny, exquisitely cast human hands—carpals, metacarpals and phalanges—to femurs bridging two slabs of plaster, each bone neatly fractured, giving a sense of separating rather than joining to a set of legs stiffly flexed, cast in an alloy that looks like aluminum. Makes you want to tap the patella, lightly, to test the knee reflex. We find the display strangely disturbing, especially on an overcast day, when shadows play in the corners of the room and the building creaks in a strong wind. Looking for someone to share the eerie feeling, we paused by the tiny cubicle referred to as the confessional by town hall personnel, and asked Florence McGinn, senior citizens' coordinator, if she'd like to study the objects d'art with us.

Florence checked her files, ascertained that we were, indeed, a SC, and joined us. To make our tour interesting, we suggested a game. "Five minutes to study 'em all, Florence. And then you have to make up your mind. If the building caught fire, which one would you fetch out to safety?" Our companion nodded and started the petit tour clockwise, while we worked in the opposite direction. Time. Lady has first choice.

"I choose the plastic box with the gold leaf clothespins standing palisade fashion on the back wall, and the fishing weight hanging down from the net in which the dead bird is imprisoned. I just know, as soon as I got the box outdoors, that bird would open its eyes, and stretch its wings, and FLY AWAY!"

Pretty hard to beat Florence's choice. We had opted for the bent bedsprings with the cigar butts jammed into the coils. Simple. Straightforward. Phat Francis reincarnated. We didn't even tell Florence how we'd voted. So come up to town hall before the exhibit is removed, and play our little game. You might go for the dessicated sand eels suspended from the cast metal tetons, as they say in French, or. . . .

So light was the rain last night and of such short duration that no one we've spoken to this morning heard it fall. But evidence of the showers is on the puddled blacktop of the town road, the dampened flagstones of our back porch and in the smell of rain in the grass and the shrubbery. The air is moisture laden this morning, so droplets still hang on the limber outer branches of the locusts and on the growing tips of the yews and azaleas.

Town hall chimes have struck quarter to 10, and the sun responds to the mid-morning notice by breaking out from behind the cloud cover. The breeze is fresh from the sou'west, the temperature is a balmy 70 degrees and the barometer is inching up on the quadrant. Cricket's song pulses in the undergrowth, punctuated by the querulous squalling of a bluejay on the hillside and a sudden, sporadic run of traffic on our road. Four-wheel drive vehicles a-bristle with fishing rods heading for Ballston Beach.

A few dashes of color relieve the greenness of the meadow—sprays of goldenrod, a trio of scarlet bull briar leaves and a flame red Virginia creeper that climbs the utility poles. In all, it is a beautiful late summer day, this day of equinox. Wish you were here to enjoy it with us, city folks.

Last evening we shared an enjoyable time with fellow townsfolk at the Congregational Church, where the Divertimento String Quartet played delightfully—a celebration marking the successful completion of the rebuilding of the belfry of our venerable meeting house. We felt a strong affinity for the first violin, the only musician in the group who gently tapped his foot as he played, a habit we allow ourself as we blow our valve trombone.

Joe Noons and the men of the highway department are busy these days doing the fall oiling of the town roads. Joe seems a mite tense as he lays out the work. So many factors to be considered, he explains. The weather is all important. A couple of rainy days can throw the whole schedule out of sync.

"We're sandwiched in between Wellfleet and Eastham and the other Lower Cape towns—all of us waiting for the oil trucks to deliver our quota of the stuff, and it all depends on the weather. We have our trucks standing by ready to follow the tanker, spread sand with the mechanical spinners, and it all has to be done before cold weather sets in. Nerve wracking, is what it is."

Tsk, tsk, Joe, set the calendar back a few decades, and reminisce with us about tarring the town roads in the old days. Consider the problems that faced old C.W. Snow, then Pamet's superintendent of streets. Equipment? Let's check the inventory. A tiny road scraper, held together with baling wire and drawn by a pair of horses, used to scuff off the worst of the bumps on the town roads and hopefully fill in the hollows; a supply of sand from local sandpits, strategically placed in sundry spots about town, so's C.W.'s two ancient trucks, a Brockway and a Dodge, could distribute the stuff on short hauls. The sand wasn't screened, and the resulting effect, with sizable stones scattered over the tar, was not unlike puddingstone that jarred vehicular traffic for years after it was spread. At places where it was impractical to cart in sand, jagged scars were inflicted by the side of the roads, and the road men would dig what they needed from the banks, scattering the sand by shovel as they followed the tar truck. The viscous, black tar would form puddles in the depressions of the roads, and they'd require a second visit from the road men, who'd attempt to sop up the surplus tar.

In those days, every kid in town went barefoot from the day school let out until the pealing of the handbell at Wilder Grammar called us all back to classes. Sundays during the summer excepted, of course, when we were required to force our aching feet into our Sears, Roebuck footgear.

Well sir, those tar puddles gave us all problems. End of the day, after we'd finished our foot traffic about town, doing errands at Eben Paine's Store, or fetching the mail from the post office, or picking up the evening milk from Ezra Hopkins' or Ed Snow's, a feller'd come home, ready to read a chapter from Tom Swift or perhaps listen to the latest adventures of Dr. Fu Manchu on the crystal radio set. But he'd be met at the kitchen door by a stern mother, who'd greet him with the admonition: "Don't you dare come in the house without cleaning up those feet!" So you'd fetch out the kerosene can, and yank the potato from the spout and decant a liberal dodger of the acrid fluid into a tomato can, and douse a rag into the kero, and carefully sponge the black tar from the soles of your feet, while instructions came from behind the screen door.

"Be sure you get between your toes! I don't want the sheets soiled."

And then you'd pump up a basin of water from the Indian Red Jacket hand pump, and lather up with Ivory soap, and finally you'd be ready for inspection and hopefully, admission to the living room, where Dr. Fu Manchu would be plotting the takeover of your beloved America. With luck, the cat whisker of the crystal would stay in place on the radio, and you'd manage to stay awake long enough to hear the end of the installment.

And Joe Noons thinks he has problems.

The countryside is greening ever so slightly, thanks to recent light rains. It fell too late for the gardens, of course, although our own plot is producing a spate of tiny green peppers, with white blossoms bursting out on the spindly plants. And although we've had our fill of tomatoes, we mourn the passing of the delicious red fruits. Like most of our fellow tillers of the soil, we druther go without 'em than eat the artificially ripened, tasteless orbs that the supermarts try to foist off on us during the winter months. We ran a finger down along the row of carrots this morning and found 'em stout and sizable. We'll give them a touch of frost to sweeten the flavor. It's time to yank the last of the beets before they get woody and the cabbage is burgeoning in the cool weather. If we search carefully we'll find some broccoli flowerets in the giant plants. The sad smell of decaying vines and fruit permeates the area. It's almost time to strip everything bare, lay down the chicken manure and have at it with the tiller.

Got to thinking as we drove up Corey's Hill on our way to church this morning about Datie Hatch. Our memory was piqued by the sight of Datie's summer kitchen, which, many years ago, was moved from its location close by the Hatch homestead up the road a piece. The Ray Dundas family now occupies it during the summer months. When we first moved to Truro back in the mid-twenties our neighbor across the highway was a tiny, wiry widow well along in years—Datie Hatch. She had buried her husband, a retired lifesaving veteran, Isaiah Hatch, some years earlier. She lived in genteel poverty in the well-kept, snug Cape Codder that had been in the Hatch family for generations. Kept a few chickens, did Datie, and had a tiny garden, and she probably received a meager pension from the government. She managed to keep body and soul together and contributed to the support of her church and to such worthy charities as Red Cross, the Salvation Army and the then infant Cape Cod Hospital. Our sainted mother soon became friendly with Datie. We used to visit her frequently and help with the household chores. We split up kindling, fetched wood from the stack out back, worried away at the ancient, deep-well pump and filled a clutch of water buckets for her, drew kerosene for her lamps, weeded the vegetable garden, spread a layer of paint on the buttery floor and delivered her scant supply of mail. And Datie would reciprocate in kind. Whenever she baked a batch of bread or fried up a mess of seaclam fritters, she'd call us over and deliver them into our eager hands. Those vittles were fit for the gods, no less. Come cold weather the grand old lady would present us with warm mittens or a muffler she'd worked up with her arthritic hands.

Just a skip and a jump from the kitchen of the Hatch house to eastard the path between the trumpet vine and the rambler roses led to a small frame building which served as a storage house and a summer kitchen. The inside walls were unfinished with wide boards which had been taken from some early salt vat located down in the valley. They were crusted with a white excrescence and still smelled of salt water. A section of the building was partitioned off and freshened up with whitewash and it contained a black iron range, a dry sink and some simple kitchen furniture. It was here that Datie used to do her cooking, come warm weather. We first had the functions of the summer kitchen explained to us the day Datie called us over to do a rather unusual chore for her.

"That half-wild cat that has moved into my shed has produced a litter of kittens," she said. "They're out back, under the pine chest of drawers—the one with the Sears, Roebuck catalogs on it. No sense we keep 'em. They'll be running around, killing all the birds they can catch and they'll be more'n half wild."

And then she gave us detailed instructions for getting rid of the tiny, mewling kittens. She had a big bucket of water standing out in the sun ("they won't mind it so much if the water's lukewarm . . ."), a generous-sized sugar sack with a draw string on the top and a piece of soapstone—actually a bedwarmer—just the right size to fit over the sack and slip down into the bucket.

"Now I'll take the mother cat over to the house and give her a saucer of milk and you tuck the kittens into the sack, pop it into the bucket, place the soapstone on top of it and just leave it there until the bubbles stop rising to the top. Then if you'll take the shovel and dig a hole under the trumpet vine good and deep we'll give them a good burial." Datie's sensible explanation of the drowning of the kittens and her generous acceptance of a share of the responsibility when she used the plural pronoun notwithstanding, we had a most difficult time carrying out her instructions. First time around, one of the kittens opened a tiny blue eye as we were tucking it in the sugar sack. The second time they all started mewing. But finally we closed our eyes, gritted our teeth and finished the job. Sometime later we tamped the red sand in place under the trumpet vine, hung the shovel on its peg and walked slowly over to the house. Datie was waiting there with a platter of blueberry pancakes still steaming hot. "Run along home there," she said. "Tell your mother to put plenty of butter and sugar on 'em. And, thank you, young man." To this day we feel the faint pang of sorrow every time we eat blueberry pancakes. And if Ray Dundas should ever invite us into his summer kitchen, we'd have to block our ears with cotton lest we hear those tiny kittens, warm water or no, giving up the ghost.

The thin red line of the back porch thermometer has risen nary a whisker since breakfast time, despite a sun almost free of cloud cover rising over the valley and a breeze from the nor'west light as a field mouse's breath. Twenty-six degrees, barometer high, and creeping up even higher on the quadrant.

Winter colors are spread on the canvas of the countryside. The faded straw of the cattails, bone gray of the locust boles, and drab, bottle green of the scrub pine are relieved here and there by the bold splash of crimson redberries and the sepia spray of poor man's grass and pampas. The fresh crick is low in its banks and the ponds between here and Wellfleet display bands of beach indicating the low water table. We could stand some rain or snow.

Black ducks have settled in for the winter in large flights. Several times of late we've seen them planing over Wilder's Dyke or tracing the serpentine channel of the fresh Pamet as they patrol the countryside. Dusk comes early to the Narrow Land as we move into mid-December. The shortening days serve as background to Christmas lights and plumed woodsmoke from neighborhood chimneys. The traffic is moderately heavy on the highway, indicating that folks are shopping up-Cape. The lonesome baying of Ormsby's hound dog at sunset, the cawing of a sentinel crow on the south hillside and the mellow pealing of the town chimes signal Truro at its best.

We deplore the passing of the delightful custom of ringing church bells for sundry occasions, ranging from christenings to weddings to funerals, not to mention the more ordinary celebration of weekly services and even civic events outside the strict supervision of the church. Remember Truro's 250th birthday a few years back? The bell-ringers assigned to the task of yanking on the rope at the Congregational Church learned when they entered the musty chamber below the belfry that on a previous occasion, Pamet's 300th birthday, an earlier crew had scrawled on the plaster wall: "Charles A. Joseph and John R. Dyer, Jr. rang the bell for two hours, July 4, 1920." The end of world Wars I and II were marked by joyous ringing of church bells here and elsewhere about the country. On more serious occasions the hills of Truro echoed the pealing of the bells. Remember when the great forest fire of 1927 raged over the Hogsbacks of South Truro and exhausted volunteer firemen called for help in that area by tolling the bell of the venerable Methodist Church?

In our own time the faithful of the congregation of the Sacred Heart Church were summoned to Sunday Masses by the clanging bell. Thereby hangs a tale of sorts. We were drafted into service as an altar boy at Sacred Heart by that saintly, yet dour Dutchman, Pastor Dennis Spykers. Already on the roster of altar boys were Herbie Gray, and Bob Meier and Herbie's cousin Robert. There was much rivalry among us for the favored position on the bell side of the altar, where the action was. At the climax of the Mass, it was the duty and privilege of the starboard acolyte to seize the big, leather-headed mallet and bang away at the ornate brass bell. It you misjudged and rapped the bell with the metal ferrule of the beater the resulting crash would startle the worshipers out of their wits. Then Father Dennis would turn around and glare at you, showing his gold tooth to emphasize his displeasure. We coveted the bell position mightily, but being last on the roster, we had a long apprentice to serve. And then poor Herbie Gray sickened, consumption, they used to call the dread disease in those days, and died. A few months later the Meier family moved away to the city and we found ourself second in the hierarchy of the altar boys of Sacred Heart. But Robert Gray was a hard boy to replace. He had seniority. No matter how hard we worked on the duties of the job—we learned every dern word of the Latin responses letter perfect. "Introibo ad altare dei," we'd intone, loud and clear, and "Mea Culpa, mea culpa, mea maxima culpa," all at the proper time. But Bobby Gray still hung on to his job.

We even tried arriving early for Mass. We rode our Iver Johnson bike up the steep hill 10 minutes early, only to find Bob, who lived right next door to the church, standing at the vestry door with the keys in hand waiting to let us in. To make matters worse, the tiny little feller wouldn't even let us ring the bell before Mass. By the time we'd slipped into our cassock and surplice, he'd be trotting up the aisle, heading for the stairs leading to the choir loft. He'd give the bell rope a couple dozen pulls and he'd trot back downstairs. And while we were searching for a match to light the taper so's we could touch off the candles on the altar, derned if Bob wouldn't produce a kitchen match from his pocket and beat us to that task.

In desperation, we decided to outwit him in at least one of the rituals. So we quietly sneaked up the choir loft stairs one morning and shortened up the bell rope with a half hitch so's the frayed manila would be far above the little feller's reach. Fix his wagon? Not on your tintype. Derned if he didn't climb up on the settee nearby and make a flying leap at the bell rope. He looked like Quasimodo at the Cathedral of Notre Dame as he rose and fell with the momentum of the heavy bell overhead. Ah, memories, memories.

NINETEEN EIGHTY-ONE

1981

As beautiful a mid-winter day as ever you'll see on the Narrow Land is this first Sabbath of February. At breakfast time the thin red line of the back porch thermometer was but a decade above the zero point of the scale.

A heavy frost whitened every surface in the valley, the trees, shrubs, the post and rail fence, the bared spots of the town road blacktop and all the outbuildings. We conjectured for one brief moment if Shebnah would be frost coated if we put him outdoors on his leash. So we breakfasted upon two huge brown soft-boiled eggs with English muffins, bundled up in cold weather gear and went for our matutinal perambulation of the neighborhood.

We brought back images to be stored in memory. Joe Rich's brook was still open water, thanks to its brisk current. A quartet of black ducks huddled along the bank, skittering downstream as we invaded their privacy. Their orange landing gear dangled in the water. We hesitated by the culvert just long enough to allow the sun to rise above the eastern pine range. By the time we'd reached Furer's garage gold flooded the valley, outlining the gnarled rumcherry tree with its myriad frost crystals, each a perfect diamond.

Just beyond Ebbert's driveway field mouse tracks in the snow made a configuration of colons separated by a needle-thin line where the tiny creature's trail dragged. Sheb shoved his nose in the snake-like convolutions and sniffed mightily. No air was ever more pure than this. The quiet of the morning is almost tangible. Wish you were here to enjoy it with us, city folks.

TV fare of late seems to have been a mite more boring and of poorer quality than usual. Case in point: the recent opus featuring a house obsessed by a spirit who, judging by the electronic gadgets installed in the premises, must have been a graduate of MIT. Among the cute tricks performed by the gadgetry were a garden hose that unreels, takes aim and wets down a couple of lovers playing post office in the garden, and an ornate sliding iron gate that crushes automobiles trespassing on the premises.

But we digress. Closest thing to a haunted house we can recall here on the lower Cape was the old Tom Hatch place in South Wellfleet: a rather ornate, turn of the century style of architecture with gingerbread finish. Bay window affair it was, located east of the state highway about where Al Rich's fruit stand now stands. Tom had built it for his bride, an Irish immigrant gal, probably on the profits he had made repairing the steeple of the Provincetown Methodist Church following the Portland Gale of '98.

But for some reason he never finished the upstairs living quarters. From the day the Hatch's moved into their new home they occupied a tiny apartment in the cellar of the building. Tom died first. Bridget held on to her living quarters as long as she could. But without a man around the house the property began to deteriorate. Shingles rotted from the roof, the doors sagged on loose hinges, window panes cracked and fell from the sashes.

So Bridget moved down to Wellfleet village, where she finished out her years in genteel poverty. But she never sold her South Wellfleet house. Too many memories of happier years stayed with her, probably. In later years folks began to spread yarns about the gaunt, weathered building. Later automobilists driving down the highway reported seeing mysterious lights in the vacant windows. "Nonsense!" Lawrence Osterbanks, a next door neighbor tried to dispel the rumors. "Nothing but the reflection of their own headlights."

A lady fiction writer summering in Wellfleet wrote a story about the Hatch house in which she had the ghost of a shipwrecked sailor appear in the dusty living room, leaving a puddle of salt water and a scrap of seaweed behind to prove he'd actually been there in person. Well sir, this publicity directed the attention of all the younger crowd to the haunted house. And we Truro kids were tempted to visit the place.

So one night during intermission of the dance at Big Chief Dance Hall several of us piled into Bush Thornley's maroon Chevrolet sedan and roared off up the road, vowing we'd put to rest all these here spook stories about the old Hatch place. It was a windy night, nary a star in the sky. As Bush braked down and yanked the wheel over and the Chevvie bounced up the narrow driveway we could see the house with its gaping doors and windows, surrounded by knee-high weeds and gnarled rumcherry trees. Something that looked like a bat flew out the broken attic window. As Bush cut the ignition, we could hear the grating of a dead limb on a silver oak tree.

"Just keep the lights on, and I'll run through the place top to bottom," directed Ralph Ormsby. He seized his girl by the hand and dragged her up the narrow path. And at that very moment a gust of wind stirred inside the house, and a white object skittered by an open window, appeared briefly in the yawning door and showed up in the adjoining window. Ralph's girl screamed mightly and the couple returned to the car.

"We'll come back next week with a flashlight," explained Ralph. "Feller might fall through the floor and break a leg . . ."

We met Jack Hall, yclept the Laird of Bound Brook Island many years ago by the late Paul G. Lambert, editor of the *Provincetown Advocate*. We had much to talk about at the supermart in Orleans last shopping day. At the fish counter we pawed over the limp looking specimens in their plastic containers, shrouded in Pliofilm. Three butterfish big as the palm of your hand, dollar forty-odd cents. Couple dozen rusty steamer clams, snouts hanging out like dead worms, close to three dollars.

"Jesus wept—and well he might," groaned Jack. "When I owned the boat Pilhasca out of Provincetown we wouldn't have had the gall to offer any one fish like that for free."

We hastened to add our own complaints. Reminded Jack we Truro clammers used to dig steamers down at Pamet Harbor during the Depression years, a barrel per tide per person. Come rain or snow, heat or cold, gnat flies, greenheads, poison ivy pollen floating on the water, depressed market prices, we made every tide.

We left Jack shaking his head, grumbling under his breath only to meet him again at the produce counter. Realizing he left us in a bad mood, Jack apparently decided to boost our spirits a mite. "I like your occasional yarns about old cars," he said as he fingered a bunch of bananas, green in color, golden in price. "Remember the beautiful old Rolls Royce silver ghost I used to drive? Actually, it was made up of two Rolls touring cars I had bought up-city way. I had Earle Rich (what a master mechanic he was) rob parts from one and install 'em on the other until I had one excellent, complete car. The stripped model I towed out back of the barn on Bound Brook Island. We planted flowers on the tonneau and the kids used to sit at the wheel and make believe drive.

"Well sir, one fine summer day my son Darius and I were driving over to Provincetown on business. Over Corey's Hill we came, down past Snowie's Shell Station. There, braced up against the state highway fence on Wilder's Dyke was Anthony R. Phat Francis, his thumb extended, looking for a ride. Now under ordinary circumstances, or in a closed car, I couldn't have brought myself to stop for the man. He had on his usual winter ulster, belted up with a scrap of rope, his tall silk hat, and over his shoulder was his usual burlap bag in which he fetched fish home to his pack of dogs.

"But we were riding in a touring car. There was plenty of room in the back seat for Phat so I braked the Rolls to a stop and Phat shuffled up and climbed aboard. Off we went, past Cobb Library and Eben Paine's store, up David Snow's hill. Finally I dropped the car into high gear when we reached Long Nook. To be polite I tossed a question over my shoulder to my passenger in the back seat. 'How many dogs do you have nowadays, Phat?' 'Sorry, can't hear you back here, Jack,' came the answer. I should have realized Phat was in trouble with the town fathers of Truro over his big family of canines. He wouldn't have given the figures had he been tortured over glowing coals.

"So I changed the subject. Politics? Yessir, Roosevelt was doing a good job. Too bad they hadn't elected Al Smith. But of course no Irish right-hander would ever be president. Legion affairs? Look for Phat in uniform at the Armistice Day parade, come next November." And so it went. Before you could say Obadiah Brown the Rolls was purring along Commercial Street. Jack began to notice when they had reached Bangs and Pearl that folks on the sidewalk were staring at the car and pointing, and bursting out into applause. Aha, the Rolls will get 'em every time, said the proud owner to himself.

But by the time they had tooled into Lopes Square, Jack realized it was more than the silver ghost that was arousing the populace. So he reached out and focused the rear view mirror to pick up the back seat area. Sure enough, there was Phat, doffing his silk hat, waving grandly, and posturing for the sidewalk crowd. "See you on Wilder's Dyke again some time," said Phat as he climbed down from the Rolls. "Enjoyed this no end."

The sun, praise be, is out strong this morning, coaxing a reluctant thermometer up above the freezing mark, where it was stuck all day yesterday. Thirty-six degrees, with the promise of a higher reading in the clear blue sky, and a northwest wind abating slightly.

The motion of the locust trees has lessened from wild tossing to a sort of arhythmic waving. The dried cattails out on the fresh creek bank react in broken measure to the combing of the wind. If there's a cloud in the sky, it's hiding over the horizon. Birdsong wavers with the air currents, bringing accents on the wrong syllables of the redwing blackbird's "Kwongaree." The nostalgic smell of woodsmoke comes in varied doses.

We drove to church in Wellfleet by way of Old County Road and saw nary an automobile in motion the entire five miles of our trip. The bay, from the vantage points of the South Truro Hogsbacks, was a jewel-studded bed of cobalt. Closed homes of the summer colonists stared at the rising sun from the steep hills of the Cobb Farm area. A crow's nest blotted the branch of a big pitch pine near Pamet Point Road. Herring Brook meandered through the sere grass banks below George K. Higgins' driveway. In all, a day of considerable merit, albeit, too cold for our liking. Wish you were here to enjoy it with us, city folks.

Goodies in our mail: a nice note postmarked Truro, Iowa, from a lady named Opal Rankin, which says in part, "We are a small town of 390 population, in the southern part of Iowa, 30 miles south of Des Moines, four miles off Interstate 35, a farming community. The town was laid out in 1881, as Ego. As the story goes a railroad man came through on the train, visited with some of the citizens, and the matter of changing the name of the town came up. He knew of a Truro, Mass. He said it was a nice place, and so the change was made. We don't know the man's name, and all the elder citizens are gone. Could you give us any information on Truro, Cape Cod? We are planning an observance, and could incorporate it in our plans."

We immediately sent off a letter with a brief outline of our town, promised we'd send pertinent material, town reports, photos, soon's we could find the time. Meantime, any of our folks bound for the west coast this summer might plan to drop by and visit our namesake municipality.

It's nice to hear the voice of an old friend over the phone on unexpected occasions, especially that of a person who spent his younger days here in Truro, moved away, as so many have done over the years, and finally came back to the Narrow Land, prompted, no doubt, by sand in his shoes. We're referring to Robert Bush Thornley, for many years a colonist of South Truro, who spent every summer of his formative years in his parents' summer home, the former L.D. Baker place off Fisher Road. His call reached us at town hall last week. The nature of his communication, of all things, chicken manure. Could it still be obtained at Perry's Farm? Indeed it could. So Bush allowed as how he'd drive down from Harwich, where he is enjoying his retirement. One thing led to another, and Bush got to talking about the time he and his young friends primed the pump at . . . but let's begin at the beginning.

"It was one of those unseasonably cool summer days," as Bush tells the story. "Too cold for swimming and besides, the tide was low at Pamet Harbor. So we South Truro lads, Bob Olsen, Vin Benson, Bud Mather and myself, were sitting out back of my house, discussing the event of the day, baseball. Bob was predicting success for the Boston Braves, National

League team of that era. Bud Mather liked the Red Sox. I opted for the New York Yankees, even though I came from New Jersey, since we had no team of our own. Then we started to discuss the relative merits of the then popular cigarettes, Chesterfield versus Lucky Strike, versus Camels, but ended in a draw, since Mather didn't smoke.

"How about the impending attempt to swim the English Channel? Gertrude Ederle, we all agreed, didn't have a chance. Swab her with all the goose grease in the world and she wouldn't have the endurance to breast stroke her way through those cold waters. A pause in the conversation, and of a sudden, Bob happened to glance over to the southeast. The afternoon train had just chugged its way past Fisher Road Crossing, and he shouted.

"'Hey, look over there! Smoke on the horizon!' So we jumped up and headed for the area. Up Fisher Road we ran, down the railroad tracks to southard. There, just beyond the crossing that leads to what is now the spur heading for the Hopper place, we saw a sizable brush fire burgeoning beside the tracks, heading on a northwest wind for the old Nason place. Well sir, we pounced on the flames, trying to stomp out the fire with our feet. No luck. There'd been a dry spell and the grass and brush was like tinder.

"We realized the fire would soon reach the house so we dashed for the building, pried open the kitchen door with a piece of lumber, and got into the kitchen ell. There was the old pitcher pump, big as life. But how to prime her? We opened the cabinets fast as we could. Finally Bud Mather found a jug of maple syrup on a shelf. We popped the cork and poured the sticky stuff down the pump, and as Bob Olsen worried away at the handle, we finally heard the old pump give a gurgling sound. She caught on, and we had our water. We everlastingly pumped on the creaking handle, but by the time we had filled a bucket, we looked out the door. Too late. The grass had already ignited the lower shingle courses, and the fire was racing up the sidewalls.

"We took one last look around the beautiful house. In the parlor, I saw one of those ancient Estey knee organs. So I sat down and pulled the stops, Dispaison, tibia, full tremelo, pumped 'er up, and ran through a quick chorus of 'Nearer My God, to Thee.' After all, that's what they played on the sinking Titanic, and just as the house started to roar in full flame, we dashed out to safety." Stout lads all. We salute our old friends.

Among the correspondence we've not had time to answer is a note from Henry Morgan, who, with his beauteous wife Karen, has deserted the Truro scene for the greener skycrapers of Gotham, where he now works in radio, his first love, and as a consultant in entertainment programming.

We've known the bespectacled, acidic, but basically friendly guy since his pre-WWII days when he used to summer with Ozzie Ball at the old Ballston Beach colony. Always got along well with Henry, perhaps because we were born just hours later than he. We turned out to be the April 1 baby . . . but we digress.

We'd like to spin a bit of a yarn about Henry and about a pair of saddle horses named Tony and Spinner, with lesser characters Pop Snow and his son Snowie completing the scenario. This would be back in the early fifties, off season, perhaps April. Henry had arrived in town in his spiffy new Studebaker convertible to ease his jaded nerves. We met by chance at the Shell gas station. All hands exchanged greetings, and Henry said he'd heard we had a pair of saddle horses down at the Snow stable on Castle Road. Could he perchance do a bit of riding? Indeed he could.

But mind which horses he saddled up. Tony was a gentle, mild-mannered animal, even of gait, obedient to the reins and clearly spoken commands. Spinner, on the other hand, was a mean vicious nag, sway backed and knock-kneed, wall-eyed and extremely jealous of his stable mate. Be best, we advised, if Henry could wait until we had some time off from our chores so's we could join him on the trail. But Henry pointed out he was experienced, he'd handled all sorts of horses in Central Park, so he'd solo. And he was certainly dressed for the occasion in a turtleneck sweater, camel's hair coat, custom fitted breeches, and shiny English boots.

We briefed him on the location of the tack and laid out a route to follow—up Meeting House Road, left at the Methodist Cemetery, across to Tom's Hill.

As Henry gunned the Studie across Wilder's Dyke, Pop puffed on his White Owl cigar and allowed, "Hope he knows what he's doin'. He'll scare the bejeebers out of them hosses with them fancy clothes he's wearin'."

Snowie added his two cents worth. "Henry's one of my best gas customers. If he isn't back in half an hour or so, we better go check on him."

Well sir, the clock at Cobb Library had hardly tolled off the designated thirty minutes when we heard the Morgan car tooling down Castle Road. So all hands went out on the front platform to meet the returning horseman.

"My Lord, look at the poor feller," clucked Pop as Henry climbed out. Look we did. Henry's glasses were awry. A button was missing from the camel's hair jacket. The fancy boots were coated with dust. And the Morgan countenance was flushed and angry. Add a sprig of pine needles in the curly thatch and a slight limp to Henry's usual swagger, then listen to his story of the brief ride.

"Did just what you told me. Saddled up the lean horse, let him out of the barn, climbed up and headed up by the windmill. Hadn't got more than a few hundred yards when I heard the thunder of hooves behind me. Looked around, and here comes that other beast, snorting fire and glaring at me with that wall-eye. Before I could get braced he drew up alongside, reared up with that hind leg, and WHAMMM, kicked poor Tony in the ribs, just missing my leg. I yanked the reins and turned around, and headed back for the barn, with that mad nag following us. Dust and sand flying, overhead branches grazing my head, thought we'd never make it without another attack. But we did. I dismounted fast as I could, led Tony back in his stall, and that goddamn Spinner walked in behind us, gentle as a lamb. He'd kicked the chain right off the eyehooks back of his stall, nudged the stable door open, and followed us. Next time I look for recreation here, I'll go fishing."

Pop had a bit of advice. "No need to do that. But next time you go hossback ridin', you better wear bib overalls. Can't say as I blame the poor hoss, you look so fancy. And that shavin' lotion prob'ly got on his nerves, too."

The name of Fogwell came up recently during a title search at town hall. We dated ourselves by stating we knew the gentleman. We can see him now, Jerome P. Fogwell, to give him his full cognomen. He was superintendent of schools for the Lower Cape district, comprising the towns of Wellfleet, Truro and Provincetown.

A tall, portly man was Mr. Fogwell, with rimless glasses and thinning, premature gray hair. Used to visit the old Wilder School when we were in the sixth grade. When he drove up in his big Buick automobile, the kids knew that the strict schedule of the day would be somewhat modified, for it was the practice of the superintendent to hold private conferences with the two lady teachers in the building, Miss Bunny Francis (recently deceased) and Miss Helen Silva. On those occasions, the familiar clanging of the hand bells, summoning the pupils in from recess and from the noon lunch period, would be delayed by substantial periods of time. We'd take advantage of the situation by extending the games of baseball in the nearby Holler, or traveling farther afield in playing fox and hounds.

Meantime, Mr. Fogwell would be inspecting the physical plant, from the duplex privy set in the beachplum bushes eastard of the building, to the schoolrooms themselves. Rumor had it he spent considerable time going over the school registers with the lady teachers to see if the figures balanced. Bob Morris peeked through the window of the Big Part (grades five through eight) one day, and reported to his schoolmates that Mr. Fogwell seemed to be "settin' awful close to Miz Silva at the desk, and she was blushin' all over." But then it may well have been a mite hot in the poorly ventilated classroom.

Well sir, when the bell finally did ring, and we trooped back into the building, all hands were treated to a lengthy discourse from Mr. Fogwell. Subjects varying from such ordinary things as care of town property—"I notice some of you have been carving your initials on the desks—this will cease forthwith."—to truancy. "Mr. Naylor Hatch, the truant officer, will apprehend any truant and enforce the state law. You will not be absent from school without a valid excuse from your parents."

Then he'd review the general accomplishments of the sundry grades. Arithmetic seemed to be average. The recent spelling bee had indicated superior skill in that area (Gertie Rose had finally gone down on the word pneumonia) and history and geography were adequate. Vocal music, under the direction of Miz Josephine Patterson, rated kudos. The Wilder singing group had done a superb job on "Now the Day is Over" (four part harmony) and penmanship, using the new Palmer Method, was superior. But don't forget to spit on the new nibs before you dipped them in the inkwell. It made the ink flow freely.

Then there'd be a pause as Mr. Fogwell removed his eyeglasses and polished them with his handkerchief. The superintendent was about to depart from routine discussion of school affairs and launch on a discourse of matters scientific, political, or whatever.

This would be the era of expansion in aviation. The Germans were experimenting with a lighter-than-air craft called the dirigible, a cigar-shaped affair filled with helium, and they proposed to set up regularly scheduled flights across the Atlantic. And a young daredevil named Charles A. Lindbergh was readying his monoplane, named the Spirit of St. Louis, to solo, first time in history, from the U.S. to Europe. Mr. Fogwell laid the background of Lindbergh's flight.

"I certainly hope this Lindbergh feller will chart his course well south of the North Pole," he said. "I've just finished reading an article on magnetism and gravity of our planet Earth. And from it I've learned that there's an area, up near the North Pole where the earth loses its pull of gravity. If this young man gets up there, his plane will shoot off into space, and he'll never be heard from again."

The weather belies the calendar this Sabbath morning midway of the month of May. Wind is strong out of the nor'west, almost October-like, driving squadrons of clouds across the sky in purposeful flight towards the ocean. And the floor of our valley reflects the scudding clouds in alternate patterns of sunshine and shadow. When the bright golden orb has its way, the pale blue of the sky overhead is the more intense and pleasing to the eye.

Goldfinches feeding on dandelion thistle in the backyard seem like moving flowers themselves, and the ever-present quails and mourning doves bob about our recently cut grass—in all, a pleasing sight. The recent rains have made the shrubs and the lawn burgeon mightily. Gone are most of the dry patches from last season's drought, and the fresh crick is high in its banks.

One day last week, as Shebnah took us for our walk we noted a ripple in the brook by Furer's. Closer inspection revealed a sizable trout trying to cross the shallow bar separating it from Duck Pondlet. We hope the poor fish finally made it to spawning grounds. The lilacs are approaching full blow, adding their nostalgic, heady smell to the air—beautiful. This morning we delivered our crew to the South Truro Cemetery, and as we were leaving by the west gate, we espied our friend the mockingbird, perched in the cedar tree on one of the Rich lots. So we stopped for a moment to listen to him serenade the countryside with arias from the library of the robin, the quail, the towhee and the catbird, and all his other feathered friends. Wish you were here to enjoy the day with us, city folks.

Our sainted mother had few faults, but we must admit she implanted in our personality several learned fears—the fear of snakes, for instance. "A blacksnake," she warned, "can form a loop by taking its tail in its mouth and chase you all over, and . . ." She never did say what the snake would do after it caught up with some unfortunate sub-teenager.

Had it not been for the counter effect of our peer group, she'd certainly have turned us against the natatorial arts. According to her, if you went swimming within less than an hour of partaking of a meal, you'd certainly get violent muscle cramps and drown instanter. And then, of course, your body'd sink to the bottom and if they couldn't fish it up with a grappling iron, they'd fetch in a cannon, fire it over the surface, and the vibrations of the explosion would coax you up from a watery grave.

Thunderstorms? With the first faint rumbling of thunder in the distance, the poor woman would herd the entire family, including the family dog, Tobey, and the cat—always named, for some mysterious reason, "Whizzer"—into the house. Then she'd close and bolt the doors, yank down the shades, uncouple the antenna lead of the Crosley pup radio, empty the water bucket down the kitchen sink, light a brace of holy candles and have us form a tight knot in the innermost, darkest corner of the house.

We were encouraged to pray, but our efforts would be interrupted by the occasional whimpering of the dogs as a particularly loud clap of thunder shook the house.

Mother was always torn between two choices during a thunderstorm. She dassent take off her eyeglasses because she'd be blind without them and unable to supervise rescue efforts if the lightning actually struck the house. And if she left them on, she knew the metal frames attracted electricity like a lightning rod. To make matters worse, we wore glasses at an early age, so we, too, had to make the decision as to wearing them during a storm.

We had just outgrown some of these secondhand fears when a momentous event took place over in South Truro. It was early in July, and the year was 1929. High tide was early in the afternoon, and we had stuffed down a hearty midday meal and had bicycled off to Slades Landing to join a group of our friends. While we were changing into our bathing suits in the abandoned boat shed, one of our friends came in with a monstrously long blacksnake he'd captured by the roadside. We swallowed our fear and gingerly felt its skin—not sticky and clammy as we'd heard—and when the snake was liberated he did not form the classic hoop position with tail in mouth, but left the area in a perfectly normal fashion. Long before the hour after lunch was up, we had plunged into the swift current of the salt crick, and nary a cramp did we experience.

But about mid-afternoon the God awfulest thunderstorm ever suddenly roared in from the bay. We kids huddled in the boat shed while the thunder boomed and the lightning sent its forked tongues earthward, and finally, when the rain stopped as suddenly as it had started, we dressed and made our way homeward.

That evening we walked over to Naylor Hatch's place for our daily milk supply.

"Hear about the lady killed by lightning over Walter Rich's house this afternoon?" queried Miz Hatch. "She was closing an upstairs window against the rain. Had steel-frame eyeglasses on. Got too near the window, and a bolt of lightning struck her. Killed her instanter. Delia McDonald, she was, kin to Mr. Rich. Tsk, tsk, tsk."

We attended our first rehearsal of the Provincetown Choral Society at St. Mary of the Harbor last week. Director Dave Peters has chosen, among other material, appropriate Christmas music by Buxtehude and Saint-Saëns, and as we adjusted our bifocals and studied the key signatures and the note values, we got to thinking about the yarn once told us by the late Horace "Pop" Snow, a lyric tenor of considerable talent in his youth, who had lost his voice when the hydraulic hoist of a truck body malfunctioned and dropped the consarned thing on Pop's neck. But we digress . . .

"I gorry, I remember the winter I joined the Meth'dist Church quartet," Pop would say. "Isaiah Hatch sang second tenor and I led the group. I sang first tenor and Charlie Newcomb sang baritone, and old Joe Atwood was bass. Joe's sister Mary used to accompany us on the knee organ, and we'd rehearse up to his house. But, come cold weather, poor Mary developed rheumatism in her hands and had to give up playin' for a while, so we did all our singin' a cappella. Easy enough, so long's we had someone to start us off in the right key. But old Ide Hatch, he had a tendency to tighten up—nerves, no doubt—when we had a singin' engagement, and first weddin' we did, why poor Ide started us off at such a high pitch he put me up in the soprano range. I like to ruptured my larynx.

"After the ceremony, we had a meetin' of the group, and we suggested to Ide he'd best send up to Boston and buy a tuning fork. That way, he could get middle C on the fork and adjust for the proper key to match the signature of the hymn, or whatever.

"Well sir, he took our advice and in a few days down comes the tunin' fork by mail. We tried it out at rehearsal—worked fine. All's you did was pound the tines on a solid object, and then you held the stem real steady against a hollow object—Ide used an empty cigar box—and out would come the pure sound of middle C. And Ide would say, 'Now "Jesus Loves Me" is in B flat—that means I lower the pitch one full tone, and that's the foundation note of the triad chord. Do, mi, sol, do!' And off we'd go. Who needed that cussed old Estey knee organ?

"So we entertained at the Truro Forum, and down to the Highland House, and up at town hall for the Sons of Temperance meetin'. Howlin' success (no pun intended) everywhere we went.

"But then we got our first request to sing at a funeral up to the Methodist Church on the hill. Abe Chandler from the North Village, if memory serves. Saturday afternoon, two o'clock, so's all hands could get through the ceremony early enough to do the barn chores. Our quartet all dressed up in bib and tucker, arrived at the church a mite early, so's we could pick out appropriate songs and warm up a mite. Five minutes to the hour—the church comfortably filled—up drives Mr. Hutchings with the hossdrawn town hearse. The pallbearers come a-shuffin' in with the guest of honor. Mr. Tunnicliffe, the minister, waits until the church quiets down, and then he nods to Ide Hatch.

"And Ide fumbles for his tunin' fork, and then he turns to me and he whispers, 'Dern it all—I forgot the cigar box. Think we can hear this gadget without a resonator?'

"'Try it,' I says. And he did. Give it a good rap on the edge of the pulpit and held it aloft, but we all heard different tones, apparently, because when we hummed the openin' chord, 'twas way out of tune.

"Ide stopped us instanter. 'Let's try it again,' he whispered, and then he banged the fork, and before you could say Obadiah Brown, he pressed the stem against the coffin lid, and out comes a perfect middle C.

"Smart man, that Ide Hatch. Could have gone places in the music business."

The early deadline this week for our deathless prose has us sitting down to the faithful Royal at the unusual time of Thursday afternoon. The feeling is akin to making radical changes in our daily habits—as though we were to start our daily shave by scraping away at the left upper lip instead of our Adam's apple, or to scull our morning coffee right handed instead of with our paw sinister, or perhaps to head west instead of east with Shebnah on our matutinal jaunt. But the weather bears chronicling in its usual first paragraph position. For a beautiful winter day it is, bright of sun and nearly breezeless. The ground is soft under foot, and still, by guppy, as green as any emerald. The temperature at mid-afternoon was a pleasant 40 degrees, and the barometer high and holding steady.

Up the road a piece we observed the ditch near Jack Kelley's house showing open water, and limber, almost green sprouts on Jack's cultivated blueberry bushes. Further along, at Isaac Rich's brook, a black and brown bird, the color scheme of a woodcock, skimmed the surface of the bubbling water, fixing us with beady eye as he headed for the main crick. The nice smell of winter was in the air, like fresh laundry. We would hear the sporadic hum of traffic on the highway and saw a lone crow pumping purposefully down valley and interesting cloud patterns in the western sky. Wish you were here to enjoy this day before Christmas with us, city folks.

We have purposely refrained from any discussion of the mysterious killer animal that roams the Truro hills, mostly because we've had no personal contact with the beast, and also because even at town hall, where emergency messages clear through our colleague, Ed Oswalt, accounts and descriptions of the fisher, bobcat, mountain lion, lynx, you name it, have varied beyond belief. It's not that we haven't taken precautions against the animal's depredations. We dusted off the family shotgun and bought some fresh ammunition, mostly buckshot, and checked the flashlights for proper functioning. We reinforced the doors of the chicken house, and built up a pile of wood right smack by the back door so's we can dash out, come nighttime, and fetch fuel for the stove under the glare of the outside light. We shortened Shebnah's chain on the back porch, and listen for his slightest whimper or warning. Of course we're on Ed Oswalt's list for inoculations, furnished through the Truro Board of Health, should we suffer a bite or scratch. And it could happen, because we reactivated our long abandoned outdoor privy, in the interests of energy conservation, of course, and it's a good 20 yards from our house to that tiny building, way out there in the dark. We'll be happy when Ed has the carcass of that animal tacked on the door at town hall.

NINETEEN EIGHTY-TWO

1982

Congratulations to E.J. Kahn III (Terry to Truro folks) and his lovely bride, Rose, on the occasion of the birth of their daughter on December 26. The arrival of a daughter is the first on that side of the family in two generations of Kahns. It is a happy event in itself, but the date, just one day after Terry's mother's birthday (Ginny is a Christmas person) adds much to the blessed event.

Well sir, the holidays are over, Truro's pigslayer has retired to his lair for the time being. Most folks we know are embarking on the new year armed with resolutions of commission or omission. The kids went back to school Monday.

It seems only yesterday we were wending our way down the narrow path from our house to the old Wilder Grammar School to join our schoolmates under similar circumstances. We would huddle in the warm sun, lee side of the building, and swap information about what we had done over the vacation, who had company for Christmas dinner and how we had made out for presents.

When opening exercises were over—salute to the flag, the Lord's Prayer, a selection from the dog-eared Bible on Miss Silva's desk, a half chapter from Nick Carter's latest detective story, and the tally of attendance for the register—why, the heat of the stuffy room would bring out further smells to titillate the nostrils. These included the rich, acid odor of the barnyard from drying work boots (cow ain't bad, Bob Morris used to say, "but you take hoss mixed with a little pig and pheeeeew, the only thing worse is hen!") and coal gas leaking from the feed door as Miss Silva choked down the drafts of the overheated stove. There was a faint chemical whiff from the toilets, newly moved and attached to the west end of the building, and perhaps a hint of Glover's Mange Cure, emanating from some girl's pig tails. (There had been an epidemic of head lice in school just before vacation).

And how could we ever forget the artificial, heady aromas of boys' hair tonic? Every boy of our generation did business at one time or another with the novelty houses that advertised in Popular Mechanics or Boys' Life, selling subscriptions of Clover Leaf Salve to earn a premium such as a single-shot 22 rifle. The ad showed an unidentified animal looming large in the sights, and you were promised you could rid your neighborhood of "varmints." Or you could earn a woolen skater's cap that actually added speed to your efforts on the ice. Everybody, it seemed, won at least a bottle of vile-smelling hair grooming cream called (word of honor) "Slikum." The darn stuff stuck your cowlick down like axle grease. It smelled like artificial violets and clung to your combs and hairbrushes like road tar. Poor Charlie Myrick, our local barber, used to hate Slikum. When you sat in his chair exuding the telltale odor of the stuff, he'd quick splash a good dodger of bay rum on your topknot. "That'll fix'er," he would opine.

There are a couple of developments in the ongoing saga of Truro's "Animalus Oswaltensis." Early last week Frank Frost, next door neighbor to town hall, appeared in our office toting a dummy double-barrel shotgun, fabricated by a relative of Frank's way up in Maine, where he had been visiting.

"My brother-in-law gave me this so's I could go out in search of that goldern pigslayer," said Frank as he displayed the weapon. It was of carved wooden stock, complete with hammers and latch, with two huge barrels fabricated of hard wall plastic pipe. "I bet I could scare him to death with this here piece."

All the office staff nodded in agreement. A few days later the production staff from a city TV outfit showed up at town hall and took over the selectmen's office for an interview with Selectman Ed Oswalt. Ed handled the session with his usual aplomb, playing down the sensationalism, but releasing the pertinent facts of the case.

To add a bit of spice to the interview, someone phoned Frank Frost and asked him to fetch his mock shotgun over to the parking space, where he could attract the attention of the cameraman by gesturing at the pine woods and pointing his weapon. We were disappointed when Frank demurred.

"I'm not photogenic," he explained. "Besides, it wouldn't be smart to cry wolf. It might be there's a real wild animal prowling around Truro."

Those brief hopes we entertained at breakfast time regarding the possibility of a preview of spring have been dispelled, sorry to say. As we brewed our coffee and soft-boiled our eggs, we noted that the thin red line of the porch thermometer read 28 degrees, warmer than it has been at that time of day for more days than we can remember. Nary a breath of air stirred in the valley and a clutch of sepia-bellied clouds sat stalled on the northern horizon. And when we opened the kitchen door to let Shebnah in for his matutinal snack, we could hear the birds in full song—the rasping, metallic call of the starling, the cheery "dee-dee-dee" of the chickadee, the querulous squall of the jay and a mixed chorus of sparrow chirps.

But now at mid-morning the temperature has edged up but a single degree, and the wind is freshening from the nor'east, nippier'n a cornered raccoon, and the clouds are thickening in the sky, grim, gray, and well defined against the bowl of the blue. Gone are the birdsongs, although an assortment of feathered friends visit our feeder, and the barometer is dropping ever so slightly. We look accusingly at the calendar, which assures us this is the last day of February, fetch in some dry wood for the living room stove and watch the laundry flapping in the breeze in the back yard.

Three cars have passed our house as we compose our deathless prose and the chatter of a chain saw up-valley comes to us on the moving ocean wind. Wish you were here to enjoy the day with us city folks.

Pamet folk and other myriad friends of Arthur Silva, our neighbor on South Pamet Road are shocked at the realization of his sudden death in Jordan Hospital, Plymouth, where Arthur was taken following a heart seizure last Thursday. He had been visiting his son, Arthur, Jr. We counted Arthur a friend and we shall miss him. To his wife Turrie and all the children, our sympathies. Ave atque vale.

On the other side of the eternal ledger, comes the announcement of the arrival of a baby boy at Cape Cod Hospital a fortnight ago to Kenneth and Deborah (Santos) Hnis, of the Snow Field area of Truro. Todd Andrew is the little feller's name and he weighed in at seven pounds, one ounce. His proud daddy, Ken, hopes to have the tyke jogging within the year.

To Flora N. Peters, that grande dame of the North Village, congratulations on the occasion of her 98th birthday February 21.

Maddie Miller, our coworker at the Temple of Democracy was sans car the other day, so we gallantly offered to drive her to her parents' home come lunch time. Up South Pamet Road we tooled the faithful Datsun, pointing out spots of interest along the way. Since Maddie's family has lived in the area only a few decades, we thought she would find it interesting that Ezra Hopkins' home stood right on that corner next to the original state highway—a beautiful old Cape Codder, a rambling structure with a rabbit warren of rooms upstairs. It used to be a rooming house in the old days, called the Union House.

In later years it belonged to Dr. Elaine Elmore Dakin, psychiatrist and proprietor of the board house. She had a roomer on her list one hot summer day and she got up early and touched off the kerosene water heater so's her guest could shower before work. The cussed heater flared up, caught the house afire and it burned to the ground, despite valiant efforts by the Truro Fire Department.

And this is Fratus' Bend, a curve in the road to break a blacksnake's back. Mr. Manuel Corey used to have a strawberry patch out there in the meadow with the best dern berries on the entire Cape.

Our own beloved home is on the right. It used to belong to Capt. John Harrington Rich, long-time captain of the Pamet River Life Saving Station. We found relics of some of the shipwrecks he'd worked on. Perhaps Maddie would like to drop by sometime and inspect the spoke from the wheel of the ship Jason or the marlin spike from the barge Coleraine?

Now out there near the meadow—you call it Eugene Kinkead's home—is the house that once belonged to Isaac Rich, common ancestor to the other Riches of the area, white-headed Joe and red-headed Joe. Red-headed Joe lived in what is now Dr. Manuel Furer's place and the old timers will tell you of the tragedy that occurred there when a toddler, a baby girl of the family, stumbled into the open fireplace and suffered such burns that she died.

And so it went. We had the young lady as a captive audience, so we rattled on. Ed Wilson's big spread is on the left. You can still see the level spot where Ed's tennis court was built. The players there would make a select list of the famous people who vacationed onthe Cape in those days, Kenneth MacKenna, Kay Francis, VIPs from the art world, journalists, educators, and, of course, psychiatrists by the dozen.

Over there on the right? The Ebbert place, you call it. But back in our day it belonged to a gruff old feller by the name of Frederick Meier. He, in turn, had bought the place from one George O. Thompson, sometime preacher and stock salesman who practiced architecture part-time. He had remodeled the original Collins home so's it was a nightmare of cupolas, dormers, towers and gingerbread. The Meier family lived with the rococo structure, but when Miss Ebbert bought the place in the thirties, she had it restored to its 1800 condition.

Incidentally, there's an antique automobile buried on the prem-ises, a Pierce Arrow touring car, if memory serves. It was easier for the Meiers to inter it than drag it off to the dump.

The Atkins place is on the left. Jack Kahn of the *New Yorker* loves it and calls it his home these days. Somewhere in the west ell there's a big iron hook screwed in a beam. One of the early Atkins was a butcher and he used to hang his meat carcasses up there and open the windows in cold weather to freeze the meat.

The Mooney-Joseph farm was familiar to Maddie, so we touched but briefly on it. We told her how Arthur Joseph had a thriving milk business there, how one day his prize Guernsey bull attempted to gore the patriarch of the clan, old George Joseph, and how George's son Charlie fashioned a bight from a stout manila line and immobilized the bull by fastening him to an overhead beam.

We were in the Miller driveway by this time and our eyes lighted up in a sort of deja vu. "I gorry, Maddie," we said. "We'll never forget this precise spot. Y'see, during World War II, early in the summer season, probably 1943, someone in one of Ozzie Ball's cottages reported seein' mysterious, intermittent flashes coming from this hilltop. They were plain as the nose on your face, because the entire Cape was under blackout conditions. So the local Civilian Guard was called out and a bunch of citizens joined 'em. Up we snuck to see if we could catch a spy. We all huddled at the bottom of Farwell's hill and Francis Mooney, who had served in the Coast Guard in WW I, decoded the flashes for the motley crew.

"'Near as I can tell,' he whispered, 'It says "Come ashore at once."'' Well sir, before you could say Obadiah Brown, Albert Rose, captain of the Guard, barked out an order, 'Let's go get 'em!'

"With that, all hands gripped their shotguns a mite tighter and we all raced up the driveway. When we got there, we discovered that a transformer lead on the utility pole was shorting out in the damp evening air, and sending off erratic sparks into the night sky."

Our kids presented us with a weather station on the occasion of our recent retirement. The handsome panel has been in operation for almost a month and we've yet to see anything but easterly winds recorded by the blinking red lights of the directional guage. The velocity is averaging about 10 miles an hour. The barometer is low and dropping slightly on the quadrant. The sky is lead-gray, brooding, and saturated with moisture. A few drops of rain spattered on our windshield as we drove home from early Mass in Wellfleet.

It is with sad heart and fond thoughts that we report the death at Cape Cod Hospital this week of our good friend, Harold Berrio of the North Village. Harold was the first appointed police chief of Truro, and served the town ably and with much compassion and understanding for many years. Ave atque vale, dear friend. You will be missed.

Yesterday, to freshen up after a three-hour stint in the Methodist cemetery, we took an outdoor shower. Noting that Shebnah the Shitzuh looked a mite grimy, we yanked the protesting pup under the shower head, lathered the bejeebers out of him and rinsed him off, despite his heroic efforts to avoid the spray. The poor guy looked like a fawn-colored mop with three Smith Brothers cough drops stuck haphazardly in the yarn. Then we tethered Sheb to a nearby locust tree while we tidied up the stall. The chore couldn't have taken us more than five minutes and when we sauntered over to see how he was drying off, we discovered he had dug a hole in the turf and had rolled in the black topsoil so his color had changed to dishrag gray. We were obliged to repeat the canine ablutions and return him to his usual station on the flagstone porch, where he dried off minus a dirt rinse.

Our granddaughter Andrea Mary goes to camp today for a two-week sojourn. She informed us, tartly, that no visitors are allowed and we told her we plan to sneak into the area, with our valve trombone tucked under our arm, to bolster the story that we are going to entertain the kids with a concert.

"They have cops up there, and they'll arrest you," she warned. There was nary a tear in her eye as she dashed out the door laden with spare sneakers, her tattered eight-year-old blanket and the comics section of the Sunday paper. But we did get a hasty smooch.

Our garden, like most others in town, is almost a month behind in its growth. To add to our problems, we have squash bugs and cucumber beetles in abundance and a goodly supply of green caterpillars on our kale, broccoli and cabbages. So we dust and spray, and when we catch sight of those pests at work, we make a wry face, snap 'em up between thumb and forefinger and squeeze them to death.

One morning last week we arrived at the garden early, just in time to see a whole army of slugs slithering back into the tall grass, leaving tattered greenery behind. We found an empty cola can, gathered up several dozen of the repulsive crawlers and fed them to the chickens, who seem to consider them delicacies.

As we dumped the squirming slugs over the fence, we got to thinking about the yarn our dear, late friend, Art Cobb, used to tell about a neighbor of his family's when he lived in South Truro many years ago. That'd be the Joe Rich clan. But they called the father Jug Rich, not only to distinguish him from the other Joseph Riches on the Hogsbacks, but also because this Joe used to do chores in the area, and everywhere he went, he fetched his wheelbarrow along, with a jug of home-fermented wine bouncing on the floorboards.

Jug had a retarded son, whom folks called, obviously, Little Jug. Little Jug was harmless and obedient to his dad. He could do simple chores like pump water for the household needs and the livestock, milk the cow, gather the eggs and buck up wood for the stoves. He could weed the garden, too, if you showed him what plants to leave in the soil. His ma had taught him to wash clothes in the big wooden tub and he could polish the windows with a dollop of kerosene on crumpled newspaper.

Well sir, one summer day Arthur had an errand to do that took him by Jug's house, located toward the end of Lombard's Holler. "Come up by the back door, and there was Big Jug splittin' some kindlin' wood at the choppin' block. Miz Rich was hangin' some laundry on the clothesline," said Arthur. "And to be sociable I asked where Little Jug was. His father said he didn't know but he must be around somewhere. And all of a sudden I heard this everlastin' whoopin' sound, and Little Jug comes out of the swamp below, stompin' through the tall grass and wavin' a big dip net in his hands. I asked Big Jug what in thunder his son was doin'.

"'Why Joseph is catchin' bugs fer the hens, crickets, grasshoppers, greenheads and sometimes butterflies. Hens like 'em. Makes 'em lay like goodun's. And it saves on grain, too.'"

Art Cobb had no objections to the Jug Rich modified diet of insects for those hens. But, he told us in later years, when he worked as foreman in the packing plant of the Pond Village Cold Storage, he used to view with suspicion the habit of some of the hands who took home fish trimmin's and gurry and trash for their hens.

"They told me they was puttin' the stuff in their gardens, but one day Charlie Mott brought me a dozen eggs from his flock. I cracked one open next mornin' fer breakfast, and the smell of fish filled the kitchen. They say he fed so much fish to his hens the poor things grew scales instead of feathers. Tsk tsk tsk."

We stop by Helen Freeman Olsen's place in Wellfleet couple of times a month to have our blood pressure checked and to reminisce about the good old days in Pamet. This morning the conversation turned to some of the picturesque homes and the interesting folks we had both known who lived near the harbor when we were kids.

Helen still has a warm spot in her heart for the brother-sister team of Ephie Hill and Hannah Lewis, and their niece, Nina Rich, whom she used to visit in their old Cape Cod house on the banks of the crick. Poorer than church mice, they were, but they always managed to put a snack on the table for a visitor—a bowl of clam chowder brewed up from soft shellers old Ephie used to dig daily out on the clam flats, or an omelet whipped up from fresh eggs produced on the premises.

Ephie had a serious impediment in his speech. Very few people could understand him well, with his weak consonants and his slurred vowels, and he was stooped in posture to a degree that made him fit exactly to the stub-handled clam hoe he wielded daily.

Aunt Hannah, Helen recalls, used to involve her young visitor in her morning toilette. The old gal would sit in her rocking chair and pull her hair aloft in a tight bun, and it was Helen's job to neatly snip off any remaining hairs that frizzed out at Hannah's neckline.

Meanwhile, poor Nina would be filling nickle notebooks with meaningless hieroglyphics and spooning huge quantities of blanc mange aboard. Nina's IQ was of such a level that even Betsy Holsbery, certainly one of Truro's most dedicated and competent teachers, had no success in teaching her the most basic skills.

The Hill-Lewis home was always neat and clean, and warm with a warmth far beyond the heat that radiated from the black iron kitchen range. In later years, after Hannah died and Nina had to be hospitalized, poor Ephie found it difficult maintaining the old homestead. He searched out an old croney from South Truro, John Myrick, and the two men gathered up their meager belongings and moved to Wellfleet, where they rented a small apartment above one of the several stores on Main Street.

Eph would occasionally take the noon train to Truro, when the tide was right, toodle about in his beloved clambeds, fetch the shellfish back to Wellfleet and sell them to his old customers. This income, together with his old age assistance, gave him a living.

It was John's job to cook the vittles for the pair. He'd gone to sea as a young man, and he cooked aboard the vessels, so his culinary efforts were adequate. But he had a tendency to be frugal. He kept a teapot on the stove, and each day, instead of emptying out the limp grounds, he'd add a smidgin of fresh tea and fill the kettle with fresh water. After some months, Ephie complained that the tea seemed a mite strong, and, over the objections of John, he dumped the teapot out in the cast iron sink. There, among the grounds, was a dead mouse.

"Taw tam foo," Ephie shouted at his roommate. "We bin drinkin' mou tea aw winner."

Thereafter John Myrick made a few concessions in the interests of sanitation. He kept adding new tea leaves to the old grounds, but each day he'd inspect the contents of the teapot. And Ephie, for his part, invested in a wooden mouse trap which they baited with a lump of cheese. Never caught a single mouse.

★ ★ ★

Our last column for the calendar year is written under the following weather conditions. Raw, overcast, with an occasional drizzle of easterly rain. The ocean wind light and fitful, carries the muted sound of surf pounding on the backshore.

Temperature a chilly thirty degrees, but it's the kind of cold that bites at exposed fingertips and makes a feller button up at the neck. You might be able to find enough soiled, packed snow from last week's storm in some sheltered spot in the valley to fashion a handful of snowballs, but otherwise the ground is bare, and amazingly enough, the grass is still green under the locust trees.

Seagulls are in an odd flying formation, riding the wind on their way down-valley—slate gray and white to match the sky. A sassy bluejay punctuates the streak of blue as he brakes to a stop on the post-and-rail fence.

The state highway was almost as bare of traffic as our own South Pamet this morning as we made the petit tour to early Mass. The only signs of life worth reporting are a pair of brown dogs at Money Hill, bedecked in Christmas ribbons, frolicking by the roadside.

The passing of Wilfred Rogers, Sr. at Cape Cod Hospital last week evokes a few lines from one of his lifelong admirers.

We first knew Wilfred when he managed the A & P in the late twenties. What a pleasure it was to drift down to the A & P at lunch hour when we attended Wellfleet High School, and wolf down a satisfying lunch of canned sardines and soda crackers, washed down by a nickel bottle of cream soda, topped off with candy bars the size of a flashlight, at three for a dime. And from our perch on an empty soap case, to observe Wilfred waiting on a customer, snatching dry groceries from the shelves, wrapping his big fingers around the canned vegetables, spearing a piece of pork from the pickle barrel, and, when the order had been heaped on the worn counter, to see him jot down the prices on a brown paper sack, and add the figures quicker'n any adding machine extant at the time.

Wilfred was a man of strong interests and loyalties. He was proud of his Portuguese ancestry, of his church, of the John R. McKay American Legion Post, of the Wellfleet Chapter of the Grange, and, of course, of the Great Atlantic and Pacific Tea Company.

While we were still in high school, the aforementioned legion decided to form a marching band to help with the celebration of local festivities. Members were enrolled from the high school, and from the rapidly disappearing ranks of the original Wellfleet Town Band, of which Bill had been an avid trombone player.

Rehearsals were held at the Boy Scout building, located about where the candle factory now stands, and the small but enthusiastic group, under the baton of the late Tony Dennis of Provincetown, gradually built up a library. We played at sundry parades on the Lower Cape, from Provincetown to Orleans, and what we lacked in quality we made up in volume and spirit.

We recall one Memorial Day when the band had been commissioned to play for the parades and observances in Eastham, Wellfleet, Truro and Provincetown.

Eastham went swimmingly, short line of march, all level, of course, since that town hadn't a hill big enough to hide a female mouse, according to Joe Curley Francis, first alto horn.

Wellfleet was almost as easy. Downhill from Pleasant Hill Cemetery to the center of town, with a brief address by Cyril Downs, Sr. And then came Truro, where we assembled at town hall, ran through the usual Gettysburg Address, remarks by veterans of several wars, including those of Mr. Parker, sole survivor of the Civil War, and some sacred music.

Then we formed ranks in the parking lot and stepped off along Town Hall Road, heading down hill to Truro Square. Tubas and trombones in the front line, of course, and between numbers Wilfred, with whom we marched elbow to elbow, gave us a running commentary.

"Born right here in Truro, I was. Nice town, but a bit slower'n Wellfleet. Old fashioned. No movies. No doctors in town. Only one barber. No chain stores. No social organizations, like the Grange.

"And, by gorry, folks here are still drivin' around with hosses and wagons. You can count the cars in Truro on one hand. Chuckle, chuckle, chuckle."

We protested vigorously, but our argument was foreshortened by the drum major's signal for roll-off. But just as we were finishing a Sousa march, rounding Dave Snow's Corner above Truro Square, Wilfred nudged us with his elbow and we took our eyes from the music to notice a generous pile of horse droppings smack in our path. It's hard to give a nod of thanks when you're making a windy run on a big horn like the tuba. Ave atque vale, good friend. Thank you for the memories.

NINETEEN EIGHTY-THREE

1983

Our sainted father used to promise himself he'd one day retire from the old Boston Elevated Railway, where he presided over the fareboxes as a conductor, move to Cape Cod and raise chickens for the rest of his days. A wild vermiform appendix put an end to his plans in 1922. We often wonder what would have happened to our branch of the clan O'Caghan had penicillin and surgery techniques been a few decades earlier on the medical scene. But we digress.

Our own retirement finds us with much to do. On most days a full agenda. Among our pursuits, the working of wood on a clutch of power and hand tools we've accumulated and installed in our basement. We've fashioned a few signboards for our friends— adaptations of coats-of-arms which are supposed to represent characteristics or occupations of the family.

We've learned to use bandsaw and jigsaw and drill press with reasonable skill. We say this because we can still count five digits on each hand. Our latest project was a candle sconce copied from Handberg's "Shop Drawings of Shaker Furniture." To aid and abet the chore, we referred constantly to neighbor Aldren Watson's "Early American Furniture" (good text) and the result, thanks to a discovery of authentic, aged half-inch pine and a slab of cedar with tiny knothole, turned out quite well.

We plan to attend the birthday party being tendered to neighbor Flora Peters, of the North Village on Valentine's Day at the Christian Union Church. Ninety-nine years young, is this grand lady. An exemplary family person, a fine teacher, alert and active in many local affairs, she is a credit to her church, her community, and her country. God bless, and continued good health, dear friend.

One of the huge willow trees at Peggy Day's place above Wildam Gray Square came down in a recent blow, and the sight of the tangled limbs and monstrous bole lying like some fallen giant got us to thinking about the yarn the late Horace "Pop" Snow used to tell about the prosthesis the Snow clan fabricated for a lady relative who had lost a leg in an industrial accident up city.

"Poor Aunt Til. Arrived here in Truro missing that leg," Snow told. "Couldn't afford an artificial one, so father, he called us boys together one day and allowed as how we ought to make a false leg for her. He'd read up on the subject, and he'd come to the conclusion that willow wood was about as close as you could come to exotic woods they used off-Cape.

"It's light, structurally strong and easy to work with hand tools. Fortunately, down by the landing at what is now Sladeville, there was a big willow with an assortment of limbs of all sizes, and grains, ready to be cut off."

In a division of labor typical of the Snow family, brother Charlie was dispatched to saw off a dozen or so assorted willow limbs and a female member of the family had, in the meantime, obtained approximate measurements of Aunt Tillie's stump and comparative measurements of her remaining lower limb. And when the willow branches were delivered to old C.W. Snow's workshop, the old gentleman sorted out the wood and selected a healthy looking, limber stick.

He sawed it to the approximate length and set it up in his foot-treadle operated lathe, and tooled it down to the dimensions scrawled out on the work plan. Then he carefully cut out a section for the knee joint, and inserted a stout strap hinge, complete with a grease cup for lubrication. In the meantime, Horace was fashioning a foot from a shoemaker's pattern they'd found among C.W.'s collectibles and the foot was connected to the lower leg by a ball and socket joint appropriated from a derelict John Deere mowing machine.

Charlie offered to do a bit of cosmetic work on the limb, wanting to paint the ankle area flesh-colored and dab a mole in place to make it look realistic. "Aunt Til wouldn't show her ankle to a doctor, let alone the general public," said C.W., refusing his son's offer.

And then they appropriated sufficient elastic strips and fasteners from a retired lady's corset to make the adaptor that would attach the prosthesis to Aunt Til's stump. They sent it via the aforementioned lady relative with detailed instructions for fitting, and stood by for information regarding the results.

They were soon available. The limb was comfortable, free moving, quiet in operation and light in weight. But it was a whisper short. Poor Aunt Til was about an inch and a half short on the port side.

"No problem at all" said C.W., and before you could say Obadiah Brown, he had removed the strap hinge at the knee and extended it by putting a gump under each end.

You'd think the matter of the artificial leg was over and done, to the complete satisfaction of all persons concerned. But it was not so.

"We made that leg middle of the winter," is the way Pop tops off the yarn. "And then there came an early spring and one day Aunt Til was changing her dress and she noticed, by guppy, little green sprouts coming out of her wooden leg. She had to carry a pruning knife with her for a month to cut off them shoots."

It was before our time, of course, but Arthur Plady Francis used to tell the story of the shoes he and his brother, Joe (Curley) wore and enjoyed so many years ago. Plady, as his name indicated in Portuguese, was a short, gnomelike man, bald as a billiard ball, and a great spinner of yarns. His brother Joe made up for Plady's alopecia with a full shock of kinky black hair. One of the few things they agreed on was the fact that shoes were precious objects in the Francis household, expensive, and meant to be cared for, reserved for school and church, and to be kept pliable and shiny with lampblack and tallow, and taken to the cobbler when the heels ran over or the taps got thin.

"I remember the time we picked up our shoes at Mr. George Joseph's shop down on the Dyke," is the way Plady used to tell the story. "Paid him off with some fresh aigs, and some cash, and some chores around his shop. Took 'em home under our arms, after admirin' the neat way Tio George had trimmed the leather soles and countersunk the brads.

"And the next Sunday me and Joe got dressed up in our blue serge suits, and stuffed our feet into the shoes—they were a mite stiff from their overhaul—and off we walked to church with my mother. My Lord, by the time we got to Ed Snow's place our feet were streaming, and hurtin' like they were in a vice.

"But goin' across Wilder's Dyke, Joe found somethin' to take our minds off the torture. He'd been taking lessons on the cornet, and he had a good ear for a tune, and he said to me, 'Arthur—you listen real close—I'm goin' to twist my ankle just right, shiftin' my weight, and you'll hear the first few notes of "Onward Christian Soldiers" comin' from my shoes.' Sure enough, right in perfect time and tune, out comes the notes. He ran through the refrain several times, and he had it perfect time we got to Eben Paine's store.

"'Now, Arthur, I been listenin' to your shoes, and by guppy, your right sole is just a third lower'n my right shoe. If you keep in time with me, and balance just right on the ball of your foot, we'll have two part harmony—ready?'"

But by that time the boys had lagged behind considerabley, and the bell at Sacred Heart was clanging to summon the parishioners, and Miz Francis glanced around, and saw her sons draggin' their feet, and before you could say Obadiah Brown, she had dropped back, and seizing each lad by the earlobe she gave a yank and urged them on their way, scolding them the meanwhile in Portuguese.

"But on the way home we continued our shoe music," Plady used to finish his yarn. "And before the summer was over we could do a passable job on 'Sweet Adeline,' and 'Good Night Ladies'."

We're having a mite of trouble with the Randall Thompson "Alleluia," one of the featured numbers of the Provincetown Chorale Society's spring concert, to be held May 1 (if the following paragraphs are taken to be a plug for the concert, so be it). The music is not difficult, and certainly the words are easy. The Latin Alleluia is repeated constantly throughout the piece but the phrasing is what bothers us.

Here's a movendo movement on page 11 where the tempo picks up, and the syllables of the Alleluia are unevenly distributed over a series of eighth notes, and the whole passage is punctuated by sforzandos and stringandos and rallentandos—so at last week's rehearsal we sidled up to the beauteous redhead, Betty Kelley, who directs our group, and mumbled out our problems.

"Why all you have to do is PRACTICE," she bellowed, with complete disregard for the private nature of our conversation. "Carry your music with you and sing in the car or in the parking lot while your wife's shopping—or while you're walking the dog or best of all, in the BATH-ROOM, while you're performing your matutinal ablutions, or whatever."

We slunk back to our seat, red with embarrassment chuck to our cowlick. But next morning we took her advice. We dassent use the bathroom lest we awaken our good wife, but we did tuck our music under our arm and out we went to the old original John Harrington Rich privy, which is still in reasonably good condition, although it has of recent years been converted to a grain storage facility in the chicken yard complex.

Opened the door and brushed aside the heavy, dust-laden cobwebs, and gathered up some empty grain bags and cleared away the port seat. Our privy door lacks the traditional crescent moon aperture, and the tiny glass window hadn't been washed since the Great Truro Forest Fire of 1927, so the light was poor. But we nonetheless opened our music and hummed a scale to see if we could find the opening A. Thompson gave us bass voices a fifth to sing, rather than the usual foundation note of the scale. It's fairly high in our range, and has to be sung PP— barely whispered, yet not falsetto. Wish we had a pitch pipe, but this sounds about right.

Watch the change in time signature from 4-4 to that single effective bar in 2-8 time. Keep the volume down, still PP—AAA-CHOO. A sudden violent sneeze, probably caused by a sniff of dust, of such strength as to bare a section of the adjoining seat, exposing the battleship gray paint that Willie Hopkins, down Castle Roadway, used to formulate for his neighbors—guaranteed to dry overnight, a big selling point of the specialized application involved. But we digress.

Mind the turn of the page. If we dast, we'd write in the note that follows but Betty threatens she'll expel anyone who marks up a score from the chorale. And so it goes; here's a dramatic drop from MP to a dolcimisso, and another 2-8 bar. This passage we know by heart, so our memory drifts back to the good old days, when James B. Rand used to direct the Methodist Church choir, or any other group that was of a mind to raise their voices in song.

The poor man had tendonitis in his directing hand that distorted his fingers so you couldn't really understand his subtle changes. His favorite musical treat was to have the ladies and gents engage in a battle of music. Ladies sang Spanish Cavalier, while the gents roared out Soloman Levi. He'd always declare the contest a draw.

At long last comes our bête noir. Ending with the rallentando and the FF, and we rear back and bellow for all we're worth. Comes a faint tinkling of glass, and we glance aside to observe one of the window panes shattered, and, as though on signal, comes a frantic gobbling and whistling from the turkey pen next door. We hope the audience will be as warm and receptive at the concert. And there's more—when our good bride gathered the eggs that eventful day, she reported the biggest yield of the season. Next session we're going to try for double yolkers.

Our good wife has always been a lady of hobbies—not, you understand, to distract her from the boredom of household chores or a drab husband, but because she likes to keep busy. Early on in our married life she took up, not necessarily in this order, aluminum tray fabricating. (This involved covering the metal with asphaltum, etching a design in place, then exposing the object to a dollop of nitric acid. The finished product was beautiful, but we strongly suspect that those acid fumes were the cause of our thinning hair. But we digress.)

In rapid order came rug braiding (never will forget the time she dragged the baby scales out of the attic, at a time when we had already named what we thought was our final child Geoffrey Sufficient). Turns out she wanted to weigh some wool for purposes of dyeing the stuff.

Then came bottle collecting—had we forced that woman to labor in the woods in ancient kitchen middens in search of bitters flasks, she'd have gotten a divorce instanter. And furniture refinishing (varnish dust in our delicate sinuses be hanged) and other hobbies we've long forgotten. But now the cycle has come full term.

Our bride is quilting. Not the old-fashioned technique, but a business that can be done in one's lap, with a miniature wooden frame to hold the material taut as the tiny pieces held together by thousands of stitches is sandwiched on a backing with synthetic batting for the filler. Our mind went back in time to other evenings as we watched those skilled hands working on a pattern with some exotic title (could it have been Ducks In a Barnyard?).

We recalled the time the ladies in our neighborhood got together for what was probably the last quilting bee in the area. Miz Ethel Burhoe was the hostess. Among the gals invited to the bee were her daughters, Phyllis, Ruth, and Virginia; others we can't recall.

The gals fetched their quilt tops to Ed Snow's house—Miz Burhoe was an in-law, and kept house for Ed. They cleaned out the big south room that had, back at the turn of the century, served as Truro's post office, and they set up a pair of home built wooden quilt frames, to which they sewed the materials on cloth strips provided.

Then, accompanied by a rattle of local gossip, the ladies had at their chore. Stretch the quilt top on the roller provided, tuck in the thick, white cotton batting, align the material of the bottom, and then stab the sandwiched layers with a thick quilting needle, and draw 'er up snug.

Come noontime they had finished four quilts—had delved into local politics, swapped recipes for Indian pudding and quahaug chowder, checked the calendar to compare a last year's wedding with a recent visit from the stork, covered the sick list occasioned by the recent epidemic of Quinsy sore throat. Then they took a half hour out for lunch. They swapped cold baked bean sandwiches and pickled pork chops, and finished off a giant pot of tea. Then back to the afternoon session.

Along about three of that winter afternoon it clouded up, and the room got dark, despite several Aladdin lamps pressed into service by Miz Burhoe. But at long last the final quilt came off the frame. And about that time up spoke Phyllis. "Anybody seen my calico kitty? She was here right beside me all day." Then the ladies heard a faint mewing, and a search of all the baskets was made. Finally Phyllis discovered a small lump in one of the quilts, and they opened 'er up, and there was the kitten. Not an impossible situation when one considers that surgical instruments are sometimes left inside the field of operations. And remember the time one of our local mechanics left a tire iron inside a casing? But that's another yarn.

Got about abreast of the site of the original meetin' house when a memory nagged at us. So we stopped the car and drifted back in time. A hot summer day some few decades ago. We had started the usual round of cutting the grass, aided and abetted by a good friend and summer neighbor, Don Buffington, who lived up South Pamet from our house. It was to be a day of minor happenings. Don, who had a passion for mushrooms, had picked a big paper sack full of innocent-looking fellers that were flourishing in the hog cranberry patches of the burying ground. He planned to have 'em for lunch, but along came Squire Jim Moynahan, in search of blueberries.

He took a look at Don's collection. First mushroom he identified was a deadly mamanit. "Hits the central nervous system," Jim explained. "Paralyze you quicker than snake venom."

Needless to say, we discarded all the mycological specimens instanter. And then, along about mid-morning when we broke for a cold soda, derned if we didn't hear, above the soughing of the warm sou'west wind, a keening, wailing sound of human voices emanating from the tiny hollow due west of the cemetery. Our view of the spot was impeded by scrub pine trees, so we could only hazard guesses as to the identity of the strange sounds.

Chief Harold Berrio of Truro's finest had been called on to investigate the ungodly wailing. Rumor had it that a group of weirdos—political activists or a coven of witches or a club of would-be hog callers—were responsible for the ululating sound waves. We asked Don if he'd dast go over with us and clean up the mystery once and for all.

So over we walked, detouring from the sandy rutted road, pushing through the pitch pines, and there, huddled about the obvious leader of the group, a gaggle of young folks who identified themselves as voice students of Maestro Alberini, the famed opera tenor who summered in Wellfleet with his equally famed wife, Martha Atwood, coloratura soprano. Alberini explained that the tiny hollow, surrounded by trees, air conditioned by the prevailing bay breeze, was a unique spot to practice singing exercises. And with that he turned his attention back to his students.

"Now we'll do a chromatic scale, articulating with the syllables loo-loo-loo." And he set the pitch for them and waved his hand for the tempo, and his two unwanted visitors sheepishly sidled back through the pines. We shared our knowledge of the Hogsback vocal group with Chief Berrio next time we saw him. He seemed satisfied, although he did ask us if we had sniffed any whiff of funny tobacco (them city folks are fond of marijuana) and when we said no, he allowed as how he had no grounds for a complaint.

They were too far away from any homes to be disturbing the peace, and who in tarnation cared if they were trespassin? Nothin' over there but a family of red foxes.

So this afternoon, weather permitting, we plan to drive over to Pine Grove with our music folder—we'll find that tiny punchbowl, and we'll hunker down on the hog cranberries and we'll work on Ching-A-Ring Chaw, the Aaron Copland adaption of an early American folk tune that will be featured in the spring concert of the Provincetown Choral Society on May Day, no less.

Maestro Alberini will be close by—he sleeps under a white marble down in the east corner of the cemetery, and Jimmy Moynahan is buried t'other side of the driveway, but he'll be glad to set the pitch with his ancient Albert system clarinet. Don Buffington is gone, too. He's buried in his native New Jersey, but when summer comes, perhaps he'll join us in a search for some comestible mushrooms where the locust trees shade the damp grass. Ave atque vale, friends.

In best bib and tucker to the wedding of our granddaughter, Jennie Crosman, of Eastham, to James Nagle, of St. Johnsbury, Vermont. The ceremony was held at Our Lady of Lourdes in Wellfleet, where we exchanged vows with our bride so many years ago. But the circumstances were different. Jennie had cold weather true enough; our wedding was marked by the most horrendous thunderstorm in decades. Music for her wedding was furnished by Les Chandler, master of the electronic organ. Beautiful, beautiful. We can recall humming a few bars from the wedding march at our nuptials. But we hope the kids will be as happy as we've been over the years and we're looking forward to dandling our first great-grandchild on our knee.

This morning we are nagged by one of the seven capital sins— envy. It's one of those rare occasions when we covet the powers of Mike Dukakis, governor of the Commonwealth, in his right to declare sundry holidays and other festive occasions.

For, if we had the power, we'd name this Shadbush Week. Or Juicy Pear Week, or Josiah's Pear Week, depending on the common name you assign to the beautiful, ghostly white shrubs that grace the countryside of the Narrow Land.

Never have we seen them more breaktakingly gorgeous in all our years, man and boy, in Truro. Their pure whiteness is accented by the background of still drab swamp growth, sere cattail carpet, and as yet unfurled alder bushes, and lowbush blueberries.

The pale blue May sky overhead, innocent of 'ary a cloud, reflects the strong light of the sun—still well below the zenith, and the shadows are well-limned. The pencil line of shingle courses on a house wall—locust branch shadows engraved on the emerald green turf. Utility lines forming the ledger lines of a music staff on the blacktop of the town road. Lilacs are taking over from the now-fading forsythia, their tight purple blossoms a promise of the full blown beauty to come.

Dandelions gone to seed, attracting the finches that cling to swaying stems, feeding on the tiny fluffy seedlets. The maple trees are half blown—their shadow translucent on the rich warm earth below.

It's been just a year since we formally retired from our town jobs. And every time we're queried by a friend, "How are you enjoying your retirement?" we answer as truthfully as we can, that we're not yet quite used to the unaccustomed leisure.

We miss the routine of arising early, driving the petit tour of Truro, unlocking the town hall door, spinning the dial of the vault, smelling that stale, moldy smell of imprisoned tobacco smoke and ancient leather book bindings.

And in the plain, manila envelope usually reserved for girlie mags, comes a package and a brief note from our good friend Henry Morgan, now residing in Gotham, in which we discover a pattern of a tiny spire, taken from a miniature church-birdhouse Henry bought at a yard sale when he lived here in Truro. Could we duplicate the wooden pyramid, asked Henry? Come hell or high water, poisonous snakes in the cellar, rust on our woodworking machinery, or dust on our bifocals, Henry, you'll have your church spires by the Fourth of July. And may the miniature woodpeckers that attack such objects eat 'em in good health.

Memories of Cobb Farm: Before we add to the list of domesticated animals and fowl that graced Cobb Farm, we should tell about the dogs that Dick Magee installed on the premises. Like most city folks, Dick had an ingrained suspicion of strangers—few in number, to be truthful—who occasionally found their way onto Cobb Farm property. The boot-clad traveler on the bay beach, armed with clam rake and in pursuit of the wily sea clam; the berry picker, in search of blueberries, bayberries, swamp elderberries, whatever; the hunter, accompanied by his rabbit hounds, or skulking over the hogsbacks on the trail of a white tail deer—all had the effect of keeping Magee on his toes. And if a tourist by accident turned in to the narrow driveway leading to the farm from Old Country Road and ended up at Dick's gate, the crusty, red-faced Irishman would come pacing out, and he'd direct a cold stare at the intruder and suggest he point his car back where he came from and get.

Then, one spring, Dick and Nell made the Grand Tour of Europe. Spent a good deal of time in Germany, where Dick got to know several quasi military figures (he had served as an aviator in Rickenbacker's Squadron in World War I) and there he fell in love with a German shepherd pup the Teutons were raising for security training. Shortly after the Magees had returned to Truro, came a crate by express, and in the crate was a half-grown dog which bore the name Eido. Dick spoiled the dog from the very outset. Took a crash course in German so's he could more properly communicate with the animal. Drove him about town in the big maroon Packard limousine, introducing the aloof canine to everybody at the post office. Called Eido up on the seat of the Cobb Farm fire engine when the apparatus rolled to a fire. And of course gave him free run of the farm property.

So, when guests arrived at the farm for dinner, or cocktails, they were greeted at the gate by this huge, slavering dog, with his ears cocked aloft, and his pencil-size fangs exposed, barking loud enough to raise the dead in Pine Grove Cemetery, a half-mile distant. Eido would christen the tires of the visitor's car, retreat to a position inside the gate, where he'd tear up a section of turf with his big claws, keeping up a horrendous yammering the while. And eventually someone would emerge from the house, the security man, or perhaps Ethel Lisenby, the beloved, able cook, or some member of the family—the boss himself, if available. Then the guests would be coaxed from their car and conducted to the patio, while Eido sniffed suspiciously at their ankles.

The original Eido lived for many years, and sired many offspring. And from each succeeding generation, Dick would select the finest male and convey the original name to him. For those who insisted that the Magee dogs had designs on their legs, Dick had a comforting word of advice: "They only bite goddamn Democrats." Being a registered Demmie from the first day we voted, we frequently wore a faded Landon button when we entered the sacred confines of Cobb Farm over the years. Never got nipped once.

★ ★ ★

It's nothing we did, folks. The frown on our good bride's face these days is caused by the fact there aren't any beach plums this year. The dearth of that tart fruit is curtailing her production of beach plum jelly, a hobby akin to our own dallying with vocal and instrumental music. We tried to persuade her to jar up some marmalades and other comfitures, but she insists it'll be beachplum or nothing. And not only are the beachplums absent from the tangled, roadside bushes, rumberries, which blossomed prodigiously, even formed tiny green fruit, never did develop. Juicy pears, in riotous white blossom were in scarce supply this season. We wonder what the old timers did in an off season like this, because all of the above, and other berries as well, elderberry, and checkerberry, and huckleberries and even rosehip and cranberry, were picked, come late summer, and used in various ways.

Truro kitchens smelled of stewing fruits this time of year, pickel pear and quince, and apple preserve, and while the housewives labored over a hot stove, the men folks were surreptitiously laying down a supply of wine for the winter. They'd spirit their supplies down into the round cellar, or tuck 'em away in the woodshed or a corner of the barn, in deference to the prohibitionist code of the day, and when they had a few spare moments, they'd get to work. Wash out and scald the big earthenware crock. Wash the berries, and pick 'em over, discarding stems and rotten fruit. Dump in the berries, and add a generous amount of sugar, and if you wanted to hasten the fermenting process, perhaps a yeast cake purloined from the home supply, cover the crock with a clean scrap of cheesecloth, and put 'er in a dark corner where the temperature was reasonably constant, and leave her be. In a few days the stuff would start to bubble, emitting delightful odors, and the pulp would break up and the liquid would assume a beautiful color. Amber, purple, or red, depending upon the fruit you used. Then came the critical date when you decided the fermenting process had ceased so's you could bottle your product. Critical because if you stoppered it up too soon, the stuff would continue to ferment, generating a tremendous pressure inside the bottles, likely to shatter them at some unpredictable point, and if you let your wine brew too long, the sugar would be converted into alcohol, but the resulting liquid would be sour and flat.

One way to forestall this unhappy result was to sample the liquid with considerable frequency, using a rubber tube to suck up the wine from various levels, tasting it as do tea tasters, cradling the liquid in the hollow of your tongue, rolling it over the taste buds, then swallowing it ever so gently. We never saw a wine sampler expectorate the precious stuff, as do the experts of Tetley tea.

Well sir, one time Anthony Cookie Deluze decided he'd make a batch of dandelion wine. A spring product, y'see, something to fill in the long gap of the summer months while berries were ripening on Pamet vines. There was an excellent crop of the wild yellow flower that year.

Cookie gathered up a generous half bushel of blossoms, together with the milk-laden stems, down at the old Mill Pond Pasture, almost before you could say Obadiah Brown. Fetched them home to the barn, cleaned out a corner next the feed bin, and set up his crock, and placed all the necessary ingredients therein. The barn was sufficiently warmed by the cows so's an ideal temperature was maintained, even though the nights were a mite chilly. The fermenting process went on to his satisfaction. And in ten days or so, the wine seemed ready for bottling. So Cookie invited neighbor Clarence Jakie Smith over to help him run his test. Fetched out a red rubber tube, did Cookie, and gently inserted it into the crock, so's not to disturb the sediment, and drew up a generous mouthful. Tasted it carefully, swallowed, and pronounced it good. Handed the hose to Jake, and nodded for his co-tester to do likewise. Jake did as instructed. Ended up gulping down a huge mouthful of dandelion brew. "Excellent," he exclaimed as he shook his head. "Could we try another?"

"No," said Cookie. "That tube is from my mother's enema outfit. And she's going to use it this afternoon. Got to fetch it back to the house."

We attended our fiftieth class reunion, Provincetown High, class of 1933, last evening. The get-together has left us emotionally drained. Counting the gaps in the class rolls—five of our classmates have died, and several were unable to attend due to ill health. Noting those inescapable signs of old age—the drooping posture, graying looks (if looks there be to gray) the expanded waist lines, the inevitable bifocals, the surreptitious fishing for pills as the meal was served, the fumbling for names and events so important to us all five decades ago, the nagging memory of a song popular at the senior hop, unavoidable statistics, how many marriages, how many kids, how many grandchildren, and, horrors, how many great-grand children? Exchanges of family snapshots. Come see us if you're ever in, are there any members of the faculty of PHS still living? Take care of yourself. We'll try for another in, say five years. Better make that two . . . one.

NINETEEN EIGHTY-FOUR

1984

When we walked Shebnah at breakfast time, we admired the waning moon in the western sky—a huge white wafer eroded on the side away from the rising orb of the sun—we heard the fresh crick, solid in its sheath of ice, groan and crack as subtle temperature changes traveled its shallow channel. As we replenished the bird feeder with sunflower seed and speared a gob of suet on the bole of a locust tree, we used our lateral vision to focus in on a pair of sassy jays in the cedar tree studying their breakfast with beady, hungry eyes. Certainly a morning to start the nose running, to bite at exposed cheeks, to tingle the fingers—but breathtakingly beautiful, nonetheless.

The death notice of Elsie Witherstine in the daily paper touches us deeply. During the years we drove the Lower Cape ambulance, Elsie was on many occasions our attendant nurse on cases ranging from bloody automobile accidents to complicated obstetrics, to suicides, homicides, the whole gamut of cases to be found in a country ambulance service. We loved Elsie, and we still carry the memory of that tiny, wiry lady, administering tender loving care and expert medical help to some unfortunate patient at any time of the day in her cool yet sympathetic manner.

The local doctors loved her, too. Dr. Hiebert and Dr. Cass and Dr. Perry and Dr. Corea. They appreciated her competency and her professionalism, and her genuine human qualities. And of course, she was beloved by the myriad patients she attended over the years, under all circumstances. We could write a sizable book about the trips we made with this remarkable lady.

Unforgettable was the time Elsie worked over an attempted suicide all the way to Hyannis, aspirating fluids and partly digested food from the patient through a plastic airway. Or when Elsie's white uniform was saturated with blood from an auto accident victim—the last words we heard through the sliding window were Elsie's, assuring the dying lady she'd tell her kids she loved them. Or Elsie persuading a close relative that his powers of healing were temporarily missing, that he should allow her to call in a medical doctor to ease the pain of his wife's fractured hip. Elsie making the quick rounds at Cape Cod Hospital to visit patients we'd delivered to that institution. But most of all, Elsie in the confines of the ambulance cab, on the way home from a nasty trip, offering us advice in her sincere, inimitably friendly way. Family problems? Money, or the lack of it? Health? She had many of the answers. God bless, Elsie Witherstine. We are the better for having known you. Ave atque vale, dear friend.

To Flora Peters, grand lady of the North Village, on the occasion of her one hundredth birthday—congratulations, and much happiness to you.

All the other warm bodies in our house having gone off to a flea market somewhere up-Cape, we find the quiet atmosphere at first very relaxing. But Shebnah notifies us with constant visits to the kitchen door, where he sniffs at the jamb, that he'd like a bit of exercise. So we bundle up and hie off up the road with our pup.

Sheb stops at all the usual checkpoints—the quivering aspen marking our east boundary, a gnarled, drooping beach plum bush that points out over the drainage ditch; the cement stanchion indicating the underground phone service to Jack Kelley's house; the pile of fieldstone east side of Jack's driveway; the cement fence post with the blob of hardened sap atop, directly under the balm of gilead tree (one of the few remaining in Truro, so far's we know); discarded beer can at Kinkead's driveway—in our pocket it goes—a nickel saved is a nickel earned, as the old timers used to say, although we used to pick 'em up long before a refund was offered.

And so it goes. Past Mary Gray's house. There she is at the kitchen sink—we blow her a kiss, read her lips as she frowns at us: "Damn fool, I'll tell your wife." And here's Isaac Rich's brook, gurgling through the culvert as it has since earliest times. And remember when old Mr. Quigley had the big red ox, and when he had occasion to cross the road with his yoked beast, summer traffic would grind to a halt as the old man gee-ed and hawed and touched the animal's flanks with a willow switch.

Wilson's driveway on the left—have a good mind to stroll up and visit with Ed for a spell; perhaps he'll ask us to deliver the massive engraving stone he used to mail up to the city where they transferred his inimitable art work to the photo plates—he'll hand us the keys to the sporty gray '35 Ford and warn us to take it easy on Fratus' Corner as he tucks one of those tiny cigars under his neatly clipped moustache.

Roll the memory book back a few decades as we allow Sheb to tug us along Meier's sandy road. Ah, this is the Meier homestead as Edward Hopper painted it, as we saw it when we delivered papers here in the twenties: sagging porch along the north side; a strange, turreted cupola breaking out from the roofline; an awkward bay window to eastard; gingerbread finish and dental work on the shingles; and ornate outbuildings and a clutch of henhouses half hidden in the pines of the south hillside, the latter connected with cat walks.

All this architectural display the work of one George "Gut" Thompson, sometime Methodist preacher, manager of the Ballston Beach colony, self-taught architect (you can still see samples of his work in the Orleans Inn, across from the Stop and Shop Mall in Orleans), broker of stock issues and gold mine enterprises—but there's Miz Meier, warm, motherly person, standing on the porch, waiting for her paper. Just so happens we have a sheaf of political flyers in our paper bag, given us by a feller in a blue business suit down street. He'd slipped us a quarter on the promise we'd distribute 'em to our customers. "John D.W. Bodfish for County Commissioner?" exclaims Miz Meier. "Why I wouldn't vote for him for dog officer. There isn't an honest bone in that man's body." End of scene.

Around the sharp curve and up Atkins Hill. (This cussed Iver Johnson bike needs a dodger of oil on the chain and some grease in the wheel bearings, pumps too hard.) Interesting home, this King place. Kind of sorry to see them leave—they've sold out to Dr. Washburn. They're leaving that huge bird apartment house, though, and maybe they'll give it to their paper boy—even though the purple martins haven't been seen around for years, that house'd look good on a post out near our privy. And in the King kitchen, by gosh, there's a big hook in a ceiling beam, and the old timers used to say that back when the Atkins owned the place, there were certain moonlight nights when, if you quietly snuck down into the kitchen, you'd see something that looked like a body hanging from that hook, but soon's you got close to it—whoosh, it'd disappear.

But that's as far as Sheb wants to travel. Too bad we have to turn around. We're almost up to the Joseph homestead. Remember the afternoon poor Mr. Joseph got gored by his bull, and son Charlie, single-handed, wrestled the huge animal to the ground and slipped a halter around his neck and. . . .

The transition from winter to summer has been, as always on this Narrow Land, rapid and at times traumatic, what with a blistering sun to cook the unwary and sap the energies of those doing outside chores. But we love every minute of each day. We sneer at the woodpile and thumb our nose at the thermostat on the wall, and yesterday afternoon we stretched out on the chaise longue (stet, Mr. Proofreader, this article of outdoor furniture is, indeed, the Long Chair) and leisurely whittled a door button for our daughter Pat's new home, sipped iced coffee, watched the grass grow, and whistled a few bars of "In The Good Old Summer Time."

Somehow people are able to remember specific dates of cold spells easier than they can recall heat waves. Almost every individual of our generation will tell you that the coldest day they can recall was town meetin' February 15, 1943, half-a-gale out of the nor'west, temperature 15 below, all day long, bay frost shading an otherwise cloudless sky, more pipes froze than you could shake a stick at. Barely made a quorum of 36 voters to conduct the business. Adjourned downstairs at the hall because Frank Rose, the janitor, couldn't get 'er warm enough to live in the upstairs auditorium.

But of hot weather, people speak more vaguely. They'll refer to some long, hot summer of the past, within a calendar decade.

Or the summer when we had no rain for weeks on end, and it was so dern hot that when the ice cream arrived from up-city way on the noon train, swathed in insulating blankets, but mushy and half-melted, it would take half the afternoon for the local merchants to pack the stuff in fresh cracked ice and rock salt before it was firm enough to be tamped onto a sugar cone or combined with sundry sauces and nuts to build a college ice at the ice cream parlors.

We're equally vague about the exact date Snowie fried the eggs on his parking lot at the Shell station. It had to be during the early forties, because we remember working in the local liquor emporium at the time. We'd had a solid month of torrid weather, so this must have been last of July.

One day Snowie, as was his custom, cranked up the big, brown, beautiful Packard roadster he owned, and ordered his mongrel pup, Piddle, behind the wheel, put the car in first gear, and steered 'er out on the narrow highway of Wilder's Dyke, headin' north, straddling the crown of the blacktop.

Other traffic, sparse in those days, obligingly detoured to the side of the road, and in jig time the Packard whispered up to our place of business. We patted Piddle on the head, took the note from the horn ring, and read the message: "The usual. And keep in touch. I'm going to fry an egg out by the gas pumps at high noon."

We completed our end of the errand. Tucked a small package on the seat, twisted the wheel so's the Packard headed back to southard, stepped off the running board, and went back to our chores.

About mid-afternoon, we rang up Snowie on the ancient "mag" telephone.

"Went fine as silk," he assured us. "Took just nine minutes to fry a double-yolk brown egg so's the white was solid, the yolk firm as a banker's no.

"Only trouble, when I went in to get my camera to take a picture to satisfy all them doubtin' Thomases, derned if old Piddle didn't come out to the pumps, saw that egg settin' there, and ate 'er up instanter."

The pleasures of having a namesake are sometimes outweighed by the embarrassing moments occasioned by having the same name on the mailbox, the voting list, or the phone directory. A few years back, when our nephew Tommy Kane was one of the most eligible bachelors in town, we frequently were aroused from our bed in the late hours of night by the pealing of the telephone. We'd fumble the instrument to hand and mumble a sleepy, "Hello." And from the other end of the wire would come a sultry, suggestive female voice. "Tom? Like to meet me at the Merry Martini? I'll buy. Got paid today." And we'd gruffly inform the poor gal she got the wrong Tom Kane and hang up instanter. Nowadays Tom, the younger, has settled down. Sticks close to his home, tends to his electrical business, gets his kicks from gardening and from raising chickens and other livestock. The birds and the bees these days have a different connotaton for him, we're sure. And our nocturnal phone calls have changed, too. Several times a month we'll spring from our bed—our days as an ambulance driver give us the drive—as the bell peals, mumble a confused greeting. "Hello, SOS, au secour, every damn light in the house just went out, blue sparks shooting from the transformer outside on the pole, toilet bowl charged with electricity, and our dog's hair is standing on end. Can you come over right away? Oops, wrong number? Can you give me the right one so's I won't have to look it up?"

Why in tarnation that boy didn't take up a normal occupation like— say—the florist business, or undertaking and embalming, we can't say. Sometimes we wish he'd go back to his former way of life.

Up a full hour before the sun climbed over the eastern hill range to find the thin red line hunkering down at the fifty degree line. Nary a whisper of a breeze in the valley. A ground fog clings all about. Barometer up a mite from last night's setting, well over the halfway mark on the quadrant. And so we to our matutinal chores—shower, shave and a good scrub job on our teeth, both natural and those fashioned by our skilled dentist, Michael, son No. 3. Thence to the kitchen, where the false glow of the rising sun illuminates the area so we can dunk a pair of giant turkey eggs in boiling water (delicious, rich, orange-gold yolks, but requiring a jack-hammer to punch through the shells) and to slightly burn our morning toast. Shebnah, that little imp, had slipped from our grasp as we opened the door but by the time we had eaten, his brief jaunt around the neighborhood was over. Apparently there were no other dogs loose for him to socialize with, so he now sat on the porch, looking coy and innocent, ready for a liver flavored hardtack bone.

Off to church. All wipers switched to full speed to squeegee the moisture from sundry glass areas of the faithful Honda. By the time we had put the shady area of South Pamet behind us at the S curve of Fratus' Corner, the sun touched the lee side of our car and we enjoyed the sudden warmth. Traffic nonexistent. There might have been three other vehicles to share the highway with us, south bound, and even Main Street, Wellfleet, almost deserted. And this the next-to-last weekend of the tourist season! The weather of mid-morning holds the promise of being a super delightful day.

We view our sudden relegation to the status of Prumus Maritimus bachelor with mixed emotions. Happens every year about this time when the scattered bushes show the first pink tinge of ripening beach plums, life at Number 3 South Pamet changes drastically for the O'Caghans. Every able-bodied occupant of the premises, resident or guest, is given a pail and instructed to go forth and fill it, the implication being that if you return with an empty bucket, no meal.

In the first flush of the harvest, the mater familiae accompanies the picking party. Her chief job is to wrangle permission to enter private property in search of the wily beachplum. Ordinarily a person of unimpeachable truth, she will, on occasion, display her big blackthorn cane to gain sympathy for her ailing femur and as a last resort she will quote an archaic law from the early colonial statutes that allows those of Indian blood to "search out and take for their sustenance all manner of wilde beasts and fowl and shellfishe and growing things." With her hair tied up in a red bandanna she looks like a Pamet squaw, albeit a beautiful one. But she never actually claims to be of Indian blood, you understand. Our kitchen becomes a busy production line dedicated to conversion of the beautiful fruit to the finished product. Kettles of the berries are gently boiled, than tucked into cheese-cloth lined strainers to drain the juice. Sterilized jars cover all available counter space, and parafin in a limpid pool in a spare saucepan will be poured atop the jelly to seal out any stray bacteria. Sugar? Our home looks like a warehouse. And the hens refuse to eat the discarded pulp and seeds. (We tried to convince our bride she should force the pulp through a screen, get more juice that way. But she told us to tend to our wood carving. You only squeeze the pulp when you're making jam.)

The cheesecloth hanging on the clothesline, faintly stained, gives a sinister air to the premises, as though someone had been trying to remove the evidence of a bloody crime. Because every burner of our range is otherwise occupied, we've been eating sandwiches, with scant elbow room on the crowded kitchen table.

This week the sign goes out under the locust trees by the roadside, and we'll be perched on a beach chair, perusing old copies of Penthouse, giving our sales spiel to prospective customers. Unique flavor. Loaded with vitamin C. A mite expensive? Yes, but consider the labor involved. How'd you like to pinch every stem from those cussed berries. Jars? Gone up considerably since last year. The only consolation to come our way—an egg customer dropped by the other day—espied the fancy baby scale on the kitchen table (our bride uses it to weigh the sugar and the berries) gave us a friendly dig in the ribs and whispered: "You old dog, you. Picked out a name yet?" Gadzooks, we straightened our bent shoulders, paced out in the yard, picked up a flat stone and scaled 'er chuck out to the fresh crick, opened our jacknife and whittled "TK loves ADEG" on the trunk of our Atkins maple.

Live dangerously, we always say.

This morning saw the biggest, fiercest-looking, proudest hawk as ever we've espied, man and boy in our many decades on the Narrow Land. We had a few spare moments before early Mass in Wellfleet, so we drove by way of Old County Road.

Dropping down Perry's Hill we could have been distracted by a scattering of beauteous female joggers heading our way, but nature lover that we are, we cast our eyes heavenward, and, gadzooks, there, swooping down across the road from what used to be known as thousand dollar hill, next the Kahn estate, comes a huge, gray feathered hawk, with white belly and shins, his wings set at full dive, ailerons and tail a-bristle. He disappeared, momentarily, in the pitch pine stand, then rose at full throttle, circled a utility pole once, and came to rest on the very tip of the pole.

His dive apparently yielded no prey but his rigid posture indicated he was still searching for the field mouse or rabbit, whatever, that had eluded him. Had he been in full flight, we'd have had nothing with which to compare his size but eyeing the stretch of his streamlined body as it protruded either side of the tip of that utility pole, he had to be at least 30 inches in length and the fact we were on our way to church should add no end of veracity to this squib.

Mary Morris Dutra (George Dutra's widow, as folks hereabouts refer to her, just in case she'd be confused with other ladies of the same name) died last weekend. She will be missed by a host of friends as well as by her family and close neighbors. Mary's death is a personal loss to Town Father. Many's the time we've called her over the years with a question about a local person, place, or event when we were composing our weekly column. Her answers were always given cheerfully and accurately. A typical query would go as follows: "Mary, the name, if you please, of that little fat man, spoke with a heavy accent, covered the Cape from a Hyannis business location, sold all the grocers hereabouts, specialized in soda pop."

"Why you mean Mr. Panesis. Nice man. Honest as the day is long. Carried many of the stores on credit when money was short. Had his own bottling plant. I miss him."

Or: "Mary, a bit of background on Joe Francis."

"Which one? There were at least three, all living in town when I was a girl. There was Joe Beezarain, so called because he was always predicting rain in his strong Portuguese accent. Sort of a pessimist, but a good man. Hard worker. Then there was Joe Crackapole. So strong that when he pounded down the trap poles with a big maul, he sometimes cracked the pole. And, of course, over South Truro way there was Joe Hawk, or Joe Flores, came from the Island of Flores in the Azores. Take your pick."

God bless Mary Dutra. Ave atque vale . . . and thanks for your help over the years.

A stir of excitement at our house the other evening when granddaughter Andrea came home with a frog she'd captured down Castle Road way. She popped the poor creature into the kitchen sink to check its general vital statistics and it slipped down into the garbage grinder. Fortunately the machine is operated by a hand switch, so all she had to do was fish him out—to the accompaniment of much hysterical screaming—a scared but unimpaired amphibian. Hope he fares as well at school, where Andrea has him on loan to her science class.

We've had a hidden urge for years to indulge ourself with a bit of poetry. And what better time than at Christmas, when deadlines are at variance with the usual dates and the holiday spirit with its forgiveness of human frailties prevails.

So we take our faithful Royal in hand, and with apologies to the author of The Night Before Christmas, whose poem we shamelessly paraphrase, we offer the following:

T'is the Sunday 'fore Christmas, and we rise betimes
To the crow of the rooster, the peal of the chimes.
We perform our ablutions, lather and shave,

Breakfast on eggs en coquille so to brave
The chill of the valley on our daily purview
Of neighboring scenes with Sheb, the Shih Tzu.
Not a creature is stirring, be it man, bird or beast
As the sun climbs the hill ranges off in the east.
There's a breeze from the bay, putting tree limbs in motion
And it combs through the cattails and heads for the ocean.
While Shebnah checks dog news on bushes and posts
We feel, of a sudden, a closeness to ghosts
Gone before us to rest, at the call of their Maker
High up on Gross Hill, in God's Little Acre.
(May their pleasures be varied, and may they partake
Of music, and card games, and angel food cake
Ave atque vale—In peace may they dwell
Save a place for us all, friends, Hail and Farewell.)
Then back to the living. We pause on the bank
Of Issac Rich Brook for a moment to thank
The Lord for our blessings. Fine family, good health,
Food on the table, of true friends a wealth.
Readers who charitably tell us white fibs
When they read our My Pamet, do they true like those squibs?
A trombone to blow with the Lower Cape Band
Cheek by jowl with musician friends best in the land
Memories, too, from the Temple of Learning
Colleagues we loved—an occasional yearning
To stand in French Class, pronouncing a vowel
Or gaining attention by rapping a dowel.
Forty years at town hall—paydays, taxes and notes
Sharing problems with others, recording the votes
That gladdened the hearts of the people elected
Embittered the candidates voters rejected.
Life's ledger we saw as it swung in the balance
With a birth or a death in the big white ambulance.
But now from town hall comes the call of the chimes
And we must be church bound. We turn
As memories fade, for one parting look
At the limpid clear waters of Issac Rich Brook.
Wish you were here, who in big cities dwell,
To enjoy our Pamet—Joyeux Noel.

NINETEEN EIGHTY-FIVE

1985

As is the custom this time of year, folks are wont to sandwich in between best wishes for Happy New Year the usual query. Was Santa Claus good to you this year? The list of gifts stuffed into the stockings of our neighbors—especially the kids—gives us pause as we delved back into memory of the good old days when hard cash was in short supply and Christmas gifts were less pretentious, albeit no less appreciated.

We can recall the first day back at Wilder School after Christmas vacation. The big yellow school bus would disgorge its cargo of screaming, itchy kids at the roadside where the gnarled beach-plum bushes gave scant shelter to the gaunt double privy. They'd push and shove their way up the sandy path to the platform where the rusty iron pump marked the entrance to the cloakroom and the woodroom. Someone would commence to worry away at the heavy iron handle and the mossy dipper would be filled and passed around—more a social gesture than a measure of matutinal thirst.

"I got a Crosby Pup radio," crowed Pulsenia Perry. "Only one tube, but we can bring in WEEI and WNAC and, at night, with the long antenna, we can get stations as far away as KDKA. That's Pittsburgh, Pennsylvania."

(Ghetto Blasters. Is that what they call 'em? Chrome boxes big as a baby's coffin, perched on a kid's shoulder, turned up fit to shatter the eardrums instanter, worth a month's pay in the good old days.)

Ralph Ormsby pointing down to the sagging wood fence where stood in splendor his new Ranger bicycle. "I had almost enough to pay for it myself, so my father made up the difference—but I'll be pine-conin' next week and I can pay him back."

(Trail bikes, motorcycles, multi-terrain vehicles—we'll be hearing them roaring along the back trails, driven by little tykes hardly big enough to peer over the controls.)

There's Bob Morris, proudly swinging a copy of a Louisville Slugger baseball bat. Turned out for him on Charles W. Snow's big wood lathe from a slab of hardwood taken from the barge Coleraine, wrecked off Highland a few years ago. "I furnished the power myself. Stomped on that ol' foot treadle for more'n four hours. I bet I can hit a ball clear over the hill from the diamond in the Holler at Sherm Rich's place."

(Ice skates and hockey equipment and outboard motors and fishing gear and other recreational gear of a value to ransom the hostage crew of an international airline.)

And there's Phillie Burhoe, all togged out in a new wool dress with hair ribbons in her tight braids and a choker at her throat. Same style as her mother has worn for years and years—all the product of that lady's skillful needle.

(We daresay the money spent on Cabbage Patch dolls and their wardrobes here in town would outfit all the girls at Wilder School for at least a decade.)

Robert Gray's father, Tom, had friends connected with the Wellfleet Movie House; and Bobbie was clutching passes good for three shows, no less, at that venerable institution. He was agonizing over his choices. But for sure he intended to view Phantom of the Opera with Lon Chaney. Did he dare hope that Joe Peanut Rogers, the ticket taker, might lose count of Bob's visits and let him in one extra time?

(How boring it must be to have the vast library of TV films with scenes to make an adult gasp available to sub-teenagers at the flick of a switch.)

Mike Howard, resplendent in a tight-fitting skull cap—genuine wool, machine woven, keeps the hair out of your eyes as you zip around the ice on your imported German steel clamp skates. One size fits all shoes. And if you sell two dozen extra jars of Cloverine Salve, you'll earn the bonus package, itching powder to torture your friends; the pillow pooper you tuck under an unsuspecting visitor (no end embarrassing), that leather reeded gadget you slip under your tongue enabling you to throw your voice. Be an overnight ventriloquist!

(Electronic games, synthesizers, aquariums. The list is endless.)

Even Wilder School had a Christmas present one year. The school committee in its generosity had decided, in the interests of pure creature comfort for pupils and teachers of the school, to uproot the ancient privy from its roadside location, move it up to the main building, where it was buttoned on to the west wall. "They'll spoil heck out of them scholars," Ed Snow sneered when he learned to the project. "Next thing you know, they'll want runnin' water—or them new-fangled electric lights."

Join with us in thinking kind thoughts and wishing many happy returns of the day March 31, to Henry Morgan, who will celebrate his 70th birthday in Gotham. Henry had visited Truro (he was one of Ozzie Ball's favorite tenants at Ballston Beach) since pre-WWII days, later built a home here off Holsbery Road, where he lived year round for several years until the siren call of his early love, radio, called him back to the city. To Henry and Karen, much love, best of all good things. We'll toast you in absentia good friend—do as much for us on April Fools Day, which is our birthday.

Poor pickin's at the supermart in Orleans yesterday. Nary a sample lady with her sausage tidbits or exotic ice cream flavors cramped in the slow traffic aisles, so we headed for the cheese counter and quietly speared a few cubes of imported fromage. Feller with a ribbon in his lapel speared us with a chilly stare as we raised the glass dome of the Danish special, unsalted, so we sauntered over to the produce lane, munching as we went, and bent over and rescued a head of lettuce and an artichoke that had fallen to the floor, making sure we caught the eye of the guy with the ribbon as we tucked them back in their niches on the cracked ice.

We felt like telling the company man we often policed the sidewalk for wind-blown papers as we wait for our bride to finish shopping, so there. And if those samples weren't made to be taken, why put them on display?

Practical jokes, in our opinion, should be well-screened. They shouldn't be harmful to the victim, as in the cases of the hot-wired door knob or the slats removed from the bed frame or the work shoes spiked to the floor. They should show some imagination, originality and yet be simple in structure. All of which is our way of saying we met summer colonist Ralph Hartwig of the outer reaches of Tom's Hill at the PO the other day. He allowed as how he had a yarn to tell us. Nostalgic. Humorous. Brief and uncomplicated. Time, the early fifties.

Ralph, whose summer rental at the Tony Duarte cottage on South Pamet was about to run out, discovered he could take an extra fortnight's vacation, due to schedule changes at his home office. He happened to mention this to neighbor Graham Whitelaw, who by coincidence, was vacating his own cottage on the dune south of Ballston Beach that very day. Why didn't Ralph take over the Whitelaw place for the extended vacation? Forget about rent. Good to have the place occupied in the off season. But, there were a few house rules to be observed. Please don't disturb the cliff swallows nesting out there on the dune. If you use the fireplace, check the ashes before you dump 'em. We don't want a fire on the hillside. If that mother fox shows up with her pups, maybe you could feed her your table scraps. And, most importantly, "I'd appreciate if you put out the American flag every day," requested Graham. "And early, y'see, it's a kind of contest between the Whitelaws and Martin Robbins over there on the North dune at Robbins Roost to see who gets his flag on the halyards first every morning. So far this summer, we're ahead of that Kansas cattleman by a substantial number of days. Promise?"

Ralph vowed as how he'd see old glory hoisted aloft every day at sparrow burp, long before Martin had rolled out of bed. First day, Ralph set the alarm clock, bounced out of the sack and trotted for the flagpole, flag under his arm, but a quick sweep of the area revealed that the Robbins flag was already flapping in the breeze. Drat it all.

Next morning Ralph sleepily bailed out an hour earlier, stubbed his toe in the half light, raced out to the flagpole, only to observe through the morning mist that Martin had again beaten him to the chore. And so it went, each morning Ralph would rise a mite earlier, only to find he'd been scooped by the wily rancher. Finally, in desperation, Ralph phoned up the Robbins house.

"How in (bleep) do you manage to beat me to the flag raising every morning? What time do you get up, any way?"

"Why I'll let you in on a secret," boomed Martin. "Fact is, I never take that flag down. That is, except for a few times I let old Graham beat me, to kind of throw him off the track. By the way, how about dropping by for a game of poker tonight?"

Ralph declined with regrets. Figured Martin would be wearing those Western boots and Lord knows how many aces he could tuck away.

The jackstaff on our back porch is too short to display our flag at halfmast, but we did our best by adjusting the halyards to present the ensign down from the peak in memory of our good friend and neighbor, Ken Lash, who died last week in a Boston hospital.

Nationally known as a poet, editor, philosopher, and man of letters, Ken, in the short time we knew him, placed high in our list of acquaintances. We shall miss our occasional visits to his cozy home down the road a piece where stimulating conversation and a lively exchange of ideas prevailed, enhanced by the smell of good cigar smoke and punctuated by the shuffling paws of Ken's dog, the Puli, Abe, crossing the floor. Among other subjects, we were searching for the answer to a mutual enemy, cancer. Ken apparently found his in a hospital bed at MGH. Ave atque vale, good scholar. To quote from an epitaph in the Methodist cemetery: "To live in friends we leave behind is not to die."

In our mail, a nice note from Mary "Mame Tom" Gray, one-time resident of Truro, lately of Wellfleet, but currently living in North Eastham and a mite unhappy with her recent change of habitat. Mary's letter (she's a hale 93 years of age) should be posted on the bulletin boards of every English class on the Lower Cape. Her grammar is flawless, her spelling and punctuation straight A, and her penmanship as steady as a banker's stare, a perfect example of early 20th century Spencerian script. Love that gal, wish we could see her relocated in the town she loves best, Wellfleet.

The sight of Tony Rose's Pond peeking through the thinning foliage to west'ard of the highway on our way home from church this morning provided the inspiration for our weekly yarn.

In truth, this tiny kettle pond is actually Ryder's Pond, but so interesting and picturesque a feller was Uncle Tony Rose, as folks hereabouts used to call him with much affection, that his name became associated with it and gradually we got to calling it by a new name.

Uncle Tony and his wife Aunt Fanny lived in, and loved, the old Freeman place on the pond's shore. He was a spare, wiry man with a big, flowing moustache, twinkling brown eyes. Seemed always to be a bundle of energy. She was the perfect country housewife. Despite the handicap of a missing eye (she wore glasses with a frosted lens), she could cook like a master chef, sew intricate fancy work and join her husband in rough outside chores. An ideal pair. Perhaps because they were childless, the Roses favored pets, the usual felines—to keep company in the house and to control the mouse-rat population in the barns and chicken houses—but always a collie dog. Handsome, sleek, long-nosed, sable and white, intelligent and trained to aid in all the farm chores as well as to offer protection to the property.

The collie could help drive the cows to pasture distant from the pond, and herd 'em home come milking time late afternoon. He could hunt out and destroy any ground hog bold enough to invade Uncle Tony's gardens, repel the sly foxes from the henhouse and meet a suspicious character at the driveway and drive him on his way chuck to Herring River.

One chore performed by his dog that Uncle Tony was particularly proud of was the canine's ability to run errands far from home. He could deliver a note attached to his collar to neighbors a good distance away. To nephew Joe P. Rose, to Frank Williams' place up Pamet Point Road, to Dave Curran's home, despite traffic on the highway and the distractions of beagle hounds that often hunted in Herring River Valley. And one day Uncle Tony was haying, down at the lower medders at Bound Brook, a good two miles from home. Hotter'n Tophet, it was, and coming up on middle of the day, and one of the Driver boys, Charlie, was blueberrying nearby. When he got close enough to speak to the busy farmer he asked, "Where's your dog, Uncle Tony?"

"Why Spot?" replied Uncle Tony. "He's to home, mindin' the place, but he'll be along come noontime, give or take a few minutes, with my lunch. Aunt Fanny will pack it in my lunch pail. Three, four sandwiches, slab of apple pie and a bottle of cold milk and then she'll call Spot and hang the bucket around his neck and tell him, 'Go, Spot. Go, and don't you stop at

Ryder's place to visit with that lady dog or pay any attention to the ducks a-nestin' in the green near Cole's Neck Woods, and hurry right back. We have chores to do. Want you should dig out a woodchuck hole near the swamp garden.'"

Young Driver listened to Uncle Tony's explanation, then glanced at his pocket watch.

"But it's already 10 minutes past noon, and I don't see ary a sign of your dog, far as I can spy."

Uncle Tony looked at him and said sharply: "Of course he ain't due yet. Your watch is on this new-fangled daylight saving time and old Spot, he's a farm dog. Works on standard time. Sun time. And soon's you hear the whistle on the train coming down Cape, you'll see that dog instanter."

And Charlie did, of course.

Shebnah's canine alarm clock was thrown out of whack by a late waning moon under a thin layer of clouds and a sun that rose into a mottled, clearing sky over the eastern hill range. The promise of the first clear day in a solid week of wet, chilly depressing weather had the Shih Tzu pup vaulting up on our bed an hour or so earlier than is his custom.

Jammed his cold wet nose into our exposed ear and whined out a few phrases in his native Chinese, then hopped down and tapped his way to the kitchen door, where he patiently sat until we had donned robe and slippers and fumbled our way to his side. As we nudged an assortment of bones from our path, we clinched his tether in place and hastily took inventory of the local scene.

Breeze still easterly, but more from the south, we judged. An honest, jagged opening rent the cloud cover just above Kelley's chimney. Light enough in the sky to note a splash of red berry across the fresh crick and the still green serpentine twists of Virginia creeper embracing the utility pole.

But mostly it was a study of drab shades: pewter gray of locust trees and camouflage, nondescript browns and sepias of poor man's grass and cattail patch. The smell of ocean hung in the moving air, dank and salty. Above the rush of the air currents, light birdsong, the chipping of sparrows and the distant querulous complaint of a lone bluejay. Back then to the warmth of the kitchen and to familiar chores, measuring the coffee for the brewer that emits those gentle belching sounds, carefully splitting a bagel so's it won't jam in the slots of the toaster, twirling the boiling water in the spider to make a miniature maelstrom that holds the egg white in place for poaching.

Philosophical thought for the day. Waldo Frank's quote of the ancient Hebrew scholars comes to mind. "Each day God makes his earth anew. . . ."

NINETEEN EIGHTY-SIX

1986

Diary of a dedicated lower brass man: last Tuesday night at band practice our respected leader, Bob Brimmer, reminded us all that our next rehearsal would be a joint venture with the Nauset Regional School aggregation. We're frankly trying to woo members for our Lower Cape Concert Band to join the half dozen excellent musicians and fine kids already enrolled with us.

"Beef up those lips," Brimmer advised us. "And if you don't have time to play the horn at least an hour per day, I would advise the cup mouth piece players to take their mouthpieces with them on their daily chores, and practice blowing into 'em. We want to show those kids we can hang with them in a long session."

Well sir, if Bob told us to jump from the Provincetown Monument into a wet sponge, we'd do it. We think that highly of his advice.

Saturday, 8 a.m. Dropped by our brother's house to check on his health, and stepped out on his deck, overlooking Arrowsmith's Swamp. There we saw sundry livestock browsing below. Took our spare mouthpiece from our pocket, warmed 'er up a mite, cupped our hands to make a bit of resistance to the air column, and everlastingly blasted out the long tones from the introduction of Victory at Sea.

Much ado from the animals. Nephew Tommy Kane's sheep stopped grazing and bolted for the shelter. John Rice's black angus steers forsook the baled clover and crowded into the angle of the fence nearest us, bellowing full strength. And a rooster way over at Marshall's farm challenged us to do battle.

We quick put the makeshift bugle away.

10:15 a.m. Hyannis-bound with our child bride. Stopped for a red light at Brackett Road in Eastham. Fish out mouthpiece, Marcato movement from R. Vaughan Williams' Folk Song Suite. Comes interruption from gorilla type truck driver ahead of us. "The bleepin' light's still red and get that bleepin' horn fixed."

We sheepishly stow the mouthpiece away, promising our wife we'll keep it out of sight for the balance of the junket. 12:30 p.m. Arrived at Cape Cod Mall. Order light lunch for wife and self at the Italian specialty quick food place. Counterman-cashier reads total of our check from his tape. We fumble in our pocket for money, fish it out together with, you guessed it, the mouthpiece.

Cashier turns pale and fumbles under counter just as we expose the shiny metal object to full view.

"Phew," he gasps, "that thing looked just like the business end of a .357 magnum. I came within a whisker of ringing up security on the silent alarm."

1:05 p.m. Dab the telltale tomato sauce from our chin and sally forth to Sears, Roebuck, but first to their clean, pleasant restroom. Place is empty. Mirrors gleam like diamonds. A fine place to not only toughen the lip but also to see our reflection in the glass.

Check general posture, facial expression, tuck-in diaphram, and expanded chest cage.

Refer to Arban's method for the trombone: warm up the mouthpiece, pucker up, take deep breath and create echo chamber for outlet with cupped hands. Ideal situation to have a go at Sousa's Stars and Stripes Forever—the bridge where the lower brasses burst in fortissimo, just before the trio. It can be done single tonguing, but most directors play Sousa's marches up tempo, and it behooves a brass man to double tongue the rapidly phrased quarter notes.

Count down. Two measures for nothing and then: tucka-tucka-tucka, tucka, tucka, tucka. Wait for echoing phrase, upper brass, repeat: tucka!

The door of the restroom bursts open, and in comes a uniformed security man. He is red faced and has his hand on the butt of his side arm. He wants to know if we're ill or just disturbing the peace.

We explain about the exercise for our embouchure.

He apparently never heard the word. He starts to take us by the elbow and suggests we accompany him to the security office.

Lucky thing we could make reference to a mutual friend. Call Herman DeSilva, he'll vouch for us. He's in hardware. He is handsome, dark haired, Portuguese descent, red-cheeked, and lives in Provincetown.

The security man took our word. We owe you one Herman.

Big milestone in the life of the O'Caghans. Our 50th wedding anniversary was celebrated on South Pamet Road yesterday. We lost count of our progeny when we had ticked off one daughter, four sons, ten grandchildren (two unable to attend) and two great grandchildren. Add beloved spouses and a few collateral relatives, and you have a houseful.

The outdoor barbecue was, unfortunately, rained out, so we had to fetch in the lobsters, the clams and the corn, and string some banners in sundry rooms about the house.

We shall be forever grateful to our kids for the big bash, and we thank the good Lord for preserving our health to reach the golden anniversary. He has, indeed, been good to this family.

Our house is redolent of the tantalizing, fruity odor of Astrakhan apples—a gift from Larry Peters, who left a sack of the firm, blush red apples at our gatepost, in the fashion of the old days, when folks added a touch of mystery to their charities. It's been near a half century since last we saw August Astrakhans—brought a lump to our throats and we can't make up our mind how to divide them between eatin' out of hand or having our bride put them into a pie. Larry's grandfather, Mr. Joe Peters, Sr., was the farmer nonpareil of Truro in his day, and it's nice to note that the grandson is carrying on the traditions of the old man. Can't help wondering if Larry can graft fruit trees as Joe did. Thanks, Larry.

Holiday deadline has us sitting down to the faithful Royal a day earlier than usual. And the Saturday afternoon is brooding, lugubrious, pewter-gray under a mod'rate cloud cover that lightened at noon, but has now closed in tighter than a banker's fist. Temperature is 44 degrees, but the dampness emanating from the soaked sod underfoot makes it feel a good bit colder. Barometer sulking low on the quadrant, and the tiny red eye of our weather panel says the wind is due north, but so light as to fail to register on the velocity dial. The birds must expect some foul weather. They've well nigh cleaned out the cylindrical feeder of its charge of sunflower seeds. Silent is the countryside, except for the faint muffled rush of surf on the backside. That's all that's left of the violent, fast moving southeaster that like to shed away the Narrow Land middle of the week. Our locust trees have shed enough branches on the property to heat the house for a few days if our wood stove were in operation, and the blacktop of South Pamet Road is littered in several spots with pine needles and washed sand. But Christmas lights shine in neighborhood homes even though the afternoon is only half gone by the clock, and folks at the post office seem cheerful and in the Christmas spirit, and we wish you were here, city folks.

We hinted around to the members of our family in the matter of a Christmas present for the pater familias. We wanted a musical instrument made of wood—no slide, valves, or strings and big and long as our Honda automobile. Give up? Why an alpenhorn, of course. We can see ourself now, standing on the back porch with the stem big as a tree trunk reaching out beyond the cement walk, mammoth bell pointed to east'ard so's the mellow tones will ride the sou'west wind. We just know neighbor Jack Kelley would be so entranced by the unique music he'd join us with a matched baritone horn instanter. Garry Ormsby and Jack Kahn no doubt would fill out the quartet. Unfortunately, looks at this point as though we'll have to settle for one of those new-fangled lazy man electric equipment controls—the kind you plug into the socket and activate by clapping your hands to turn say, the Tellie, on or off.

And a Merry Christmas and a happy, healthy and prosperous New Year to all our readers.

NINETEEN EIGHTY-SEVEN

1987

Folks don't do as much walking nowadays as they did in the old days, and more power to 'em, with their automobiles and their mopeds and their multi-speed bicycles. And even for those who jog about town, we've noticed they practice the art by daylight. And thereby hangs a tale, as our good friend Fred Waterman Davis used to say. It has to do with walking, nocturnal, that is, and with beacons and landmarks, or lack of them, and with a picturesque citizen of the town—a state boy at the Marshall place down on Depot Road, name of Henry Hanson.

Henry was a handsome, blue-eyed, giant of a man, a convivial feller who liked to visit with friends about town, usually in the evening when his long day's work was done. He was not averse to tasting of the grape on occasion, or of stronger ardent spirits when they were available. And this takes us to the winter night in question when Henry, foreboding weather conditions notwithstanding, slipped into his sheepskin coat, assured his foster parents he'd be home at a decent hour, and strode forth from the warm Marshall abode at Holsbery Square, headed for the home of a friend on Castle Road. The evening proved most enjoyable. Henry and his partner Norm Snow defeated their opponents, the brothers Isaiah and Charlie Snow, in a torrid game of bid-whist. Liquid refreshments flowed like water and a light supper of linguica and beans was served up shank end of the evening. The festivities over, Henry thanked his host, slipped into his winter gear, and stepped, just a mite unsteadily, out into the night.

The weather had worsened. Nary a sign of a star, so's it was darker'n the inside of your watch pocket. By the time Henry had turned the corner of the Snow driveway on to Castle Road, it started to snow—thick and heavy and blinding, with a shifting breeze so's you couldn't even tell which way the wind was blowing—Highland Light, off to the nor'east, blanked out by the white stuff. Lights of the homes along Castle Road long since extinguished, after all it was close on to 10 o'clock. But Henry proceeded with cautious step, using a combination of dead reckoning and occasional gropings to locate the board fence by the roadside. In due time he arrived at Wilder's Dyke, passed by Charlie Myrick's barber shop, located the stout toprail of the state highway fence, and crossed the dyke nice as you please. Next, the warm, pungent animal smell of Ed Snow's barn assaulted his nostrils, so he maneuvered slightly to starboard and felt the grade of Depot Road rising under his feet. But once past Wilder School his aids to navigation failed him. Nary a scrap of fence could he locate, no whiff of animal manure reached his olfactory nerves—wind shifting every minute or so—and then, miraculously, he heard the neighborhood windmills.

Each had its own characteristic sound. Lack of grease in their gear cases, worn shafts, the irregular rhythm of a fan with a blade bent or missing, each mill sent out its unique tone, and Henry tuned in like a bat in a cave. The fact that the young Viking had near perfect pitch served him well this dark night. There was John Adams' mill over to southard—long drawn out groans, B-flat, if you had a pitch pipe to compare. Next, the high pitched whine of Uncle Manuel Marshall's machine—octave higher, give or take a mite. Down the saddle of the road between the Marshall properties, then to Henry's left, the grating metallic sound of Henry Holsbery's new Champion mill. But with a shift in the wind, came suddenly the blended notes of Selectman Dick Rich's mill and that of Charlie Aydelotte, way down to west'ard. At least, that's how Henry translated the sound waves. Headed for what he thought was home, and ended up in John Corkey Gray's place, where he borrowed a kerosene lantern and, aided by its feeble light, managed to get to his proper lodgings. Next day he was telling his friend Norm about the previous night's difficulties. "It was Mr. Richard Rich's mill threw me out of kilter," he explained. "He must have greased the cussed thing, because it had a different tone—went from baritone range chuck up to alto."

We love to handle wood. To shape it on the band saw, to whittle away with chisels and gouges, and of course, the old reliable pocket knife. It smells nice when you work it, feels good under your hands, and, with a fair amount of luck, it sometimes turns into a reasonable facsimile of a shorebird, or a decoy duck—pintail preening is a favorite of ours or a half-hull model of some sailing vessel of bygone days.

Abbie Tinkham, custodian of the dump, keeps an alert eye out for scraps of lumber, and it's amazing how we can accumulate a sizable pile of pine, or cedar, sometimes even hardwoods such as mahogany or oak. There are occasions when our good wife visits our studio downstairs. (We eschew the word cellar or basement in describing our worksite, for obvious reasons. You can't, for instance, invite beautiful young gals down into your cellar, for gosh sakes to examine your great blue herons or the half-hull model of the slaver Dos Amigos (c. 1842).) But we disgress.

If Pop Snow were still alive, we'd have a willing, able critic of our hacking. We can recall how he'd classify tyros of the carpenter trade back in the good old days. "Any man with a kit of tools and a pair of bib overalls can get a job carpenterin' nowadays," he used to bemoan. This would be during WWII, when men did indeed get work at Camp Edwards and other military establishments simply because manpower was at an all-time low. "Why some of them fellers makin' well over a dollar per hour ain't worth their salt. I bet they couldn't put a button on a privy door."

The figure of speech intrigued us, and we felt moved, one morning at the Shell Station where Pop was gnawing on the usual White Owl cigar to suggest as how we didn't think the task of fashioning a button for an out house was much of a test of a carpenter's skill. Take a scrap of soft pine, saw 'er off to the proper length—in proportion to the general dimensions of the door—then simply whittle it down in a gentle taper, bore a hole to contain the wood screw that fastens 'er to the frame, sand and paint to match the finish, screw in place, not too snug, not too loose, and presto, the job is done. Not so, according to Pop as he blew a huge cloud of smoke in the general direction of the cage housing Tookie, the pet toucan of the shop. "You have to remember there's two kinds of buttons," he growled. "They's the single type, with the long latch on one side, stub on the other, used for cabinets and small closets. No need for balance here y'see, so a man can screw it up tighter'n a banker's wallet—keep youngsters, especially, from nosin' where they don't belong. But a fancy, double hung button, that's a fixture of another type altogether. I'm talkin' about the buttons we used on woodshed doors and barn doors. Had to be strong, don't y'see, to keep the animals in, once you shut 'em up for the night. You could always tell a man good with tools, by looking around his property—if the fasteners on his outbuildings were shapely and strong, and if they hung in place when they were turned—give him a good mark.

"Now we ain't mentioned the privy button yet. Easy to see it had to meet all the requirements I've listed. After all, a feller needs privacy in this area, and a secure button mounted indoors should provide it. But if the cussed thing was to secure, it could cause some trouble too. Take the time poor old Charlie Hardy—neighbor of ours down Castle Road—sickly and agin'—took his lighted lantern out to the privy one night after supper, stepped inside, and twisted the button in place. Made of ash, from a wagon tongue, it was, big around as your wrist, screwed into the frame with a lag from a shipwreck the size of a railroad spike, hove to so's it took all a man's strength to twist it. Well sir, Hardy had a spell come on real sudden, managed to let out a yell heard all around the neighborhood. But when we got there, we dern well couldn't force that dern door open. We had to chop out a panel, and reach in and twist the button. Saved Hardy, we did, but first thing next morning my brother Charlie removed that cussed latch and replaced it with a soft pine button that a female mouse could open by burping against it. What we lost in privacy we made up in safety, y'see."

Every time we pass the fire tower in South Wellfleet, the sight of the partially razed structure—the entire box-like observation room has been scalped from the framework—had us self-querying whether the Commonwealth intends to tear down the rusty steel landmark completely, or to rebuild the observation room. Our old friend Snowie served briefly as an observer at the tower years ago. He used to regale his friends with stories about the job. Dreary and dull and uneventful, for the most part, but on rare occasions during dry spells, one of the Cape fire towers would, indeed, spot a telltale plume of smoke in some secluded area, and then the radios would crackle out their messages, and the observers would focus in on the potential blaze with their crude maps and indicators, and attempt to triangulate the fire so's the local fire department in the crucial area could search out and destroy the blaze. Snowie remembered one evening, just at dusk (conditions were so dry that spring all hands had to work overtime) when a nervous observer up-Cape—Snowie in his loyalty to the corps, would never say where the call originated—frantically phoned all his co-workers and reported a huge fire out to eastard. More experienced reporters searched the area with their binoculars and discovered the fire was, in fact, the moon rising over the Atlantic.

Blessings on the man who sold us the wood stove a few years back. It kept us reasonably warm during the recent 24-hour blackout due to the snow storm, het up various stews and soups and scorched our bread to a semblance of toasting. Our one regret is that we've remodeled the original privy on the premises into a storage place for chicken grain; the tiny building would have come in handy, but then again, maybe we've forgotten how to use the facility. Our electric blanket was useless as dew-claws on a mongrel dog, but we improvised—found an earthenware jug in the cellar (good thing we don't cart all our treasures to the dump as our child bride so often suggests), filled 'er with hot water, and fetched it to bed. Soles of our feet felt rather tender morning after the big storm, and when we inspected them closely, we discovered part of the legend inscribed on our hide:

Boston on one foot, Molass . . . on the other. Gadzooks, could it be possible our container had once held the product of the ill-fated molasses tank that ruptured in the Hub over a century ago, causing much loss of life and property?

But we digress. Judging by the strength of the wind, the total amount of snow, length of the storm, and height of typical drifts about town, we'd rank the recent storm, on a scale of one to 10, a strong eight. If you're looking for a 10-pointer, take the famous Valentine's Day storm of '41 . . . even considering today's sophisticated snow removal equipment and increased manpower and pre-warning via radio and TV, we still insist that the gale on that occasion, nearly half a century ago, far exceeded this 1987 storm in all areas.

Yesterday (Saturday), we found the afternoon a mite boring. We'd been shopping with our child bride, most of the household chores were done, and it was a bit gloomy down cellar, where we ordinarily do our whittling and we got to thinking. Why a half century ago, under similar circumstances, we'd be heading for Cobb Library, there to while away a few hours. Might even join up with Mike Howard or one of the Ormsby brothers, Donald or Ralph, if they weren't otherwise occupied. Climb the steep brick stairs, shoulder open the heavy ornate door, hang your hat on the hatrack and scrub your feet on the door mat, and, by all means, *lower your voice*. For Cobb Library, due in no small part to the dominating influence of librarian Miz Sarah Yates, required you to be as subdued in volume as you'd be in any European cathedral. Under the watchful eye of the Castle Road lady, a plumpish, gray-haired widder with wire-framed spectacles dressed in sombre black (a surprising contrast to her attire at her Castle Road home, where, as lady poultry farmer, she wore L.L. Bean knickers and canvas tennis shoes), we'd survey the spacious reading room.

No changes; portrait of Elisha W. Cobb, donor of the building, staring down from its place of honor just above the big fireplace. On the mantle below, half model hull of the hermaphrodite brig whaler *Eschol*, built at Magoun and Sleeper shipyard, right here, by golly, at Pamet Harbor, back in the last century. Next in line, a shiny leather helmet, relic of some long forgotten German military outfit of WWI, awarded to the town following a successful liberty bond drive. On your starboard side, separated from the entrance aisle by a fancy railing reminiscent of the altar rail at Sacred Heart Church, up the road a piece, the reading room. Wainscot high bookcases on three walls, labeled according to their contents—the Dewey decimal system not yet in use. Two round oak tables bearing ornate brass student lamps, kerosene, of course, with green shades. Artificial light was used only when the library got so dark on a winter afternoon as to make perusal of the stacked periodicals almost impossible—*Boy's Life* and *Liberty*, and *Popular Mechanics*, and *Collier's* and *Saturday Evening Post*. Much diversion, entertainment, and we daresay even intellectual stimulation came from those reading sessions at Cobb Library. Because when you left, you always had a book under your arm (provided you had no late return fees outstanding, although you could work out your debt at Miz Yates' chicken farm in your spare time).

The kids were particularly intrigued by the classifieds in *Boy's Life*, where sundry so-called joke articles were offered for sale. For a few coins, you could buy a leather gadget you slipped under your tongue, and become an instant ventriloquist. Dern thing never worked for anyone we knew. Itching powder was a mite more successful. If you could maneuver into an intimate position with a friend and slip a pinch of the stuff down his or her collar, the results were most satisfying. We recall that one of the Rose kids from Long Nook—could have been Herbie or Lloyd—sent for a gadget referred to in the ad as a noise-maker. Turned out to be a dried animal bladder with a built-in whistle which you inflated and stuffed under a seat cushion, and the unsuspecting victim sat on the affair. Lloyd planted the squawker in neighbor Mae Atwood's easy chair, she being a bit myopic and a trusting soul. She like to fainted dead away when the bladder did its job. Memories, memories. . . .

Had our first taste of spring watercress the other day, thanks to the generosity of neighbor Patty Morris, who appeared at our door, braving the snarls and frantic barking of our watchdog, Shebnah, to make her presentation. Purely to find out whether Pat has become a true Cape Codder, we asked her where she had plucked the peppery plant. "Over that way," she said as she swept the entire northern horizon with her hand. And that's the way your true Truroite indicates the secret spot where blueberries thrive and wild mushrooms burgeon—vague, but not impolite.

Watercess was always a favorite dish of our good friend Snowie. And when he went in search of the plant, mostly over on the banks of the fresh crick at North Pamet, he often misjudged the depth of the water where the delicacy grew. Or he protested the presence of a fat bullfrog hopping from a cowslip to a patch of cress. "I don't believe those dern frogs are house broken," he'd explain. "They may be using my cress for loos, as the English put it." But eventually he'd gather up a mess that had passed all sanitary inspections, and he'd visit around the neighborhood, giving away the surplus. His favorite dish, as we recall, was a soup much like Portuguese kale soup, with the watercress replacing the usual greenery of the latter delicacy.

And our town road gang, bless 'em, have finally succeeded in unplugging Isaac Rich's brook, the tiny rivulet that runs under the road between Mary Gray's and Dr. Manuel Furer's. All winter long the southern drainage area has been flooded—the culvert under the road unable to draw off the surplus water. Our lads had made several futile attempts to remedy the situation, but finally, one day last week, foreman Mikey Francis came up with the answer. "We tried the usual methods—working a wire snake through the pipe, applying full pressure from the fire engine we borrowed for the occasion. Best we could do was increase the flow by a tiny amount. Got so desperate I asked around the neighborhood (Mike lives in South Wellfleet, where folks have strange hobbies) and found a feller who owns a pair of tame muskrats. Fetched them to work on April Fool's day (better the day, better the deed, I always say) and tucked them into the pool south side of the culvert. They played tag there for a while, and then—they're curious critters, y'know—down they dived, and apparently headed for the entrance of the pipe. Minutes later Dickey Steele, on watch at the other end of the culvert, yelled out, 'Here comes the male now, and he has a big branch in his jaws . . . and now here's the female—she's got one, too.'"

Make a long story short, those two muskrats cleaned out the pipe before you could say Obadiah Brown. Ought to be some way we could reward the animals; wonder if they like dog food Meaty bones, perhaps. But we digress back to the weather. Don't let the occasional call of the peepers fool you, nor the raucous kwongaree of the redwing blackbirds. Tain't really spring yet.

Got to talking with Roger Dias at his home on Pond Road of the North Village yesterday about our days teaching together at the Temple of Learning in Provincetown, about the astronomical prices of real estate on the Narrow Land, the foul weather of recent days, about the approaching Easter holidays. "One thing you can be sure of," Rog asserted, "there'll be the usual rush to the package stores to stock up on spirits ardent. Seems we can't celebrate a holiday without liquor." Roger is a near teetotaler, eschews tobacco in any form, lives on a health diet too complex to review at this point. His remarks anent liquor opened up a flood of memories which we shared with him even though he kept one eye on the TV screen as the Red Sox battled to victory over their opponents.

In the Prohibition Era, we pointed out, liquor was distributed by several local bootleggers, some of whom acted as retailers for the off-Cape big dealers, others who made their own booze, following secret recipes and methods of production. By far the largest of the brew and distill operations was that of the late Joe Cabral, a successful Portuguese farmer who lived in the Whitmanville-area and supplemented his farm income by manufacturing alcoholic products in his huge barn, just abaft the main house, and far enough from the highway so's it was difficult to catch the faint whiff of fermenting mash mixed with the hearty animal odor of horse and cow. John Lucas was a part-time laborer at the Cabral place, and on occasion he'd tell how the operation functioned.

"We had a huge wooden barrel in the cellar of the barn, close by the manure pile. It was my job to gather up everything that had gotten too ripe or partially decayed fruits, vegetables, sometimes grain that had become musty, left over garbage from the house, dump it all into the barrel, together with the same overripe fruit that old Joe would fetch home from his peddling expeditions into Provincetown, add some water from the pump nearby, dump in a sack of sugar and a block of brewer's yeast, and let 'er ferment.

"Every morning I'd go down cellar and stir up the mash with a cut-off dory oar, and on more than one occasion, I'd espy a big barn rat swimming feebly on the surface of the stuff, and I'd put him out of his misery with my oar. Sometimes he'd stay on the surface, and I'd fish him out—but if he sank?" (Here John would give a big expressive shrug of his shoulders.) "And after a spell, the mash would be completely fermented and we'd bail 'er out of the barrel and transfer it to Cabral's still, up on the first floor. Looked like a creation of Rube Goldberg, did that still. A complicated contraption of copper tanks, tubing, boiler pit, condenser, exhaust system. I'd build a hot coal fire under the boiler, dump the mash in by batches, clamp down the seals, and wait for the distillate to evaporate out from the boiler and reach the coils, where a jacket filled with cold water from the Cabral pump would turn the vapors back to liquid that ran down the condenser and landed in the end tank. Most times there'd be a neighbor on hand to test that first run. He'd take a greasy, cracked tumbler from a peg on the wall, hold it patiently under the brass spigot, and wait for the glass to fill, drop by slow drop. Then with a local toast (down the hatch with Joe's first batch) he'd raise the glass of hot, lemon-hued liquor and toss it off. Delicious—smooth—all's we need now is some carmel to give it some color."

The stuff sold for 75 cents per pint, and if you caught the old man in a generous mood, he'd preface the sale by offering you a free swig from the same, finger-printed glass. In all truth, we never knew anyone to succumb from Cabral's booze, nor even to go blind, dead rats and copper oxide from the still notwithstanding.

Neighbor Jackie Kelley hasn't looked so happy since his last camp-out with the Scouts in the middle of one of last winter's most horrendous snowstorms. His joy comes from the fact he's driving a classic MG two-seater he picked up somewhere in his travels. "She's lacking a bonnet, and it'll probably be difficult to find parts for her—but it's more fun driving that car than flying any plane I ever took in the air."

Jack's reference to his flying days recalls the yarn his pal, Peter Morris, used to tell of his first—and only—flight with the now staid postmaster. "Jack had access to an ancient biplane flying out of the old Chatham Airport," is the way Pete tells it. "Made arrangements with me one day to meet him on Fisher Beach, where he'd land the craft and pick me up. Right on time, he was, and he landed the old craft smooth as silk on the rather rough surface." "I'll need some help getting this underpowered crate off the ground again," the pilot advised his anxious passenger-to-be. "So when I gun 'er, you step up to the wing, close to the body, and shove like this." And that's what Peter did. The tiny engine roared full throttle, Jackie body Englished from his seat in the cockpit. Peter braced his feet in the soft sand and everlastingly shoved against the wing. Down the beach taxied the aircraft, bouncing at each hole in the sand, and finally, as a favorable gust of tail wind goosed the underwings, the plane lifted off the ground.

"Hang onto the wind strut," Jackie bellowed over the roar of the engine. "Soon's we've reached a good cruising height, you can haul yourself up and climb into the passenger seat." "How high will that be?" queried Pete, as he stared down at the blurred terrain below. "About 1500 feet, give or take. . . ." The rest of Jack's estimate was lost in the slipstream. "Not for me, old friend," answered Pete, as he released his grip on the strut and plummeted the relatively short distance into the swirling waters of Pamet Harbor Channel, where it splits the jetties. Landed on his feet, just like a cat, in about waist deep water, but suffered not so much as a bruise, and Jackie felt the sudden weight loss, trimmed up his rudder and ailerons to compensate, made a quick turn around Gull Island, and wagged his wings in salute to Pete, who was by then wading ashore, salty, but unbowed.

Should this column get into the hands of anyone from the Yarmouthport area, we'd appreciate any recollections they may have on the following item. The year, 1927, a period when news items via the early battery radio or the local Cape press assailed the senses of a teenage kid most vividly. Not necessarily in chronological order, we can recall: Gertrude Ederle, first woman to swim the English Channel; names like Dempsey, Tunney, Firpo dominating the boxing scene; the famed trial of Sacco and Vanzetti; and, closer to home, the grounding of the Eastern Steamship vessel Robert E. Lee on the shore of Manomet, with an assortment of cargo reaching the Truro shores following its jettisoning by the crew; the scary, three-day forest fire on Patriot's Day that charred hundreds of acres of woodland in Pamet and neighboring Wellfleet; the establishment of the first glider school in the USA, at Corn Hill, sponsored by millionaire department store owner J.C. Penney for a crew of German would-be aviators. (Germany was forbidden by the Treaty of Versailles to operate engine-powered planes.) Then the tragic loss of the US submarine S-4 when it was struck by the Coast Guard cutter Paulding on a trial run off the Cape tip; the rumors anent the forthcoming mystery car, the Model A Ford and so it went. And why a bit of trivia of such unimportance should stick in our mind we can't say, but here it is.

We'd been visiting with relatives in Dorchester, had our bed rocked by an explosion in nearby Milton where sympathizers of Sacco and Venzetti had attempted to blow up the house of the judge on the case. Next morning, anxious to get back to Truro, we arose early to meet Roger Burhoe, who had driven up to the Hub in Bill L'Engle's venerable Model T station wagon, accompanied by a few of our mutual friends. Off we putted, along the South Shore, with Roger obeying all the traffic laws and the hand throttle of the T at a cautious half quadrant. Jokingly, we proposed to hop out and help the T over the steep Plymouth hills. Stopped for a leg stretch at the canal, where we skipped stones in the water and gawked at the big vessels fighting the swift current.

Eventually we arrived in Yarmouthport, in those days a gem of a Cape village with huge elms shading the main street, quaint shops and authentic Cape homes, cheek by jowl. Attracted by a sign advertising ICE CREAM, TOBACCO GOODS, NOTIONS on a building owned by one Hallett, we persuaded Roger to brake up to that door and rushed in for refreshments. And while the other lads were waiting for their college ices to be built by a dour, silent old man behind the soda fountain, we strolled about, inspecting the store. And there in the window—here's the punch line—was a skunk, expertly mounted on a stand with a blasted tree limb, staring out at the public.

We'd seen many a skunk in our day, and had in fact, been sprayed on occasion. But they had all been clad in rough wiry fur of black and white, in varying proportions. But this creature unless our aging brain cells play tricks on us, was a rich, solid *brown*. One of our hand-carved birds or half hull ship models to anyone from up-Cape who can either verify or disclaim our tall tale.

Grim reminders of our own advancement in age comes often these days in the form of a question from folks who read our column. "How in tarnation," they want to know, "do you remember thus and so?" We make no claim to a photographic memory or total recall, but events of our youthful days in Truro often come back to us with the presenting of a simple query. For instance, yesterday evening at the Marshall birthday gala, brother Leo Marshall, a hale, handsome, recent octogenarian, braced us over the hors d'oeuvre table. "Do you remember my Uncle Manuel's blacksmith shop down in the square?" he queried us. Before he could sample his cheese dip, we were describing the gray-shingled shop, with its sliding barn doors and its smoke-blackened interior, and the interesting assortment of wagon parts and fractured tools, rusted plowshares and myriad other farm machinery. Satisfied with our brief sketch, Leo wandered off to chat with the beautiful ladies, while we sipped at our ginger ale and reminisced.

The Blacksmith shop had been abandoned when we moved to Truro in 1926, but the building could be entered with a bit of manipulation on a side door. Ernie Snow, our closet neighbor, acted as our guide first time we prowled through the ramshackle building, and he helped us find numerous treasures. A seaclam rake with a broken tong, waiting for the magic welding touch of Manuel Marshall that would never come; a wagon wheel to replace the dished affair on Ernie's Dad, Ed's Democrat wagon a mite rotten in the hub, and in need of a new iron tire but repairable, given the time. Here, in this pile of scrap iron and half-forged artifacts, an occasional horse shoe nail, the large stud heads embossed with a royal crown, trade mark of the manufacturer. You could bend those nails around a piece of pipe, file off the excess pointed steel, and fashion for yourself a reasonable facsimile of a ring. There were two occasions when you took the ring off'n your finger: when you were about to milk the cows, the metal was cold, and often a mite rough, so's to raise objections from the usually placid bovine; and again, when you got into a serious dispute on the school playground, the other kids would yell at you, "Take off the ring. We don't want any harm done here."

One day we discovered, on an overhead rafter, a long-handled tool with a pad-like rasp on the business end. Ernie explained it was a tooth file, used to grind down any proturberances on a hoss's worn molars so's he wouldn't bite his tongue—to promote general oral hygiene for the nag. He took it home, we recall, and converted it to another use. Ernie's dad, it appeared used to re-tap his son's shoes, and often the long nails he used penetrated the inner sole. It was quite difficult to peen the offending nails over so Ernie guessed as how the offending points could be reached with the rasp and filed down instanter.

In that era, Phat Francis lived across the street in his Square Deal general store with his elderly mother. The building offered no sanitary facilities, except for a crude chemical toilet, which Phat eschewed, he being an outdoors man of sorts. Consequently, he studied the land across the street, selected a sheltered spot in the lucust grove abaft the Lupien property, and improvised an al fresco loo by simply nailing a stout two-by-four between two suitable spaced locusts. Worked fine, weather permitting until the day one of the local wags, who claimed he'd been bested in a business deal with Phat, snuck up the valley, pried the two-by-four loose with a claw, hacksawed the spikes so's they barely protruded through the wood, and then tucked the wood back in place. The results were predictable, almost immediate, and evident from the general behavior and facial expressions on the face of Truro's ex-postmaster. "There's a reward of two packages of Piedmont cigarettes for the fellow who can tell me who messed with my outdoor, ah-ah-ah," here he hesitated for the proper word, finally ending up with the universal Portuguese "casinha." Needless to say, no one ever collected the reward. Memories, memories. . . .

Distraught and sympathetic with Shebnah's constant digging and chewing at the host of fleas that have been using him for a free boarding house all summer long, and this despite our own home remedies such as baths, combing and personal inspections, we fetched him off, reluctant and struggling, to an up-Cape pet shop this past week. What the little cuss lacks in intelligence and obedience, he makes up for in cunning and instinct. He recognized the kennel building instanter, and proceded to punish every bit of shrubbery within reach of his leash. (How does the greenery ever survive in like locations?) He said hello to a couple of black mongrels waiting in line, allowed himself finally to be conducted to the bathroom where a young lady attendant was clipping a dog that could have been Sheb's twin down to his bare hide, while a second gal was industriously lathering a Lab-type canine in a fancy green plastic tub. We almost envied the dog, so contented did he look, and with soap dangerously near his eyes, yet. We cautioned Sheb to stay on his good behavior, told him we'd be back after shopping to pick him up, and off we went.

Took Mother almost two hours to replenish the larder. (They kept changing the prices, and besides, shopping is a social event for me—I meet so many of my friends in the checkout line.) All we can say is that we had devoured every word in the weekly paper display, including the immortal prose of our dear friend Henry Morgan in the Chatham sheet, had sampled all the cheese at the counter and scrounged several handouts of a new brand of pizza from a nice lady whom we convinced our repeat trips were to fetch sample freebees to our wife, now in the ice cream aisle over yonder. (She always gets hungry while she's shopping.) We bought our ticket for the Massachusetts Megabucks, requesting that the beauteous lady behind the machine insert our ticket with her left hand, bring us luck, we explained. She was nice enough to do so, despite snide remarks from the man in back of us, who was, at the same time, making a small circle with his forefinger in the vicinity of his right temple. (Won't he be ashamed of himself tomorrow morning when he reads about the Truro ex-town clerk who will spend a portion of his new wealth buying a Porsche Turbo with a retractable steering wheel to accommodate those of generous girth and tooling right up over the Sagamore Bridge for his first trip across the canal in years?)

We finally managed to herd our bride through the checkout line, loaded the groceries in the car, drove back and picked up a happy, clean, and we hoped, flealess dog. Dragged Sheb past the yews and the rhododendrons at which he was casting a malevolent eye, put him in the back seat.

We hadn't driven more than a hundred yards when—up, the left hind foot to explore the left ear, up the right hind foot to rake the rib cage, bend on the spine so's he could reach the base of his tail. Sheb must have left some fleas behind in the Honda, we reason. Guess we'll have to wait for frigid weather and increase his daily patrols so the dern fleas will freeze to death on his hide—or perhaps a quick dunk in Isaac Rich's brook to drown the cusses.

Shortly before dawn this morning came the sound of a sudden downpour, accompanied by tremendous gusts of wind. Our locust trees groaned, and the old Cape Cod house creaked in all its timbers, and a loose blind rattled in frenetic, arhythmic beat. We rose a mite prematurely, closed open windows here and there, flicked the light switches, and prepared a light matutinal repast (we're dieting—lost nigh on to 10 pounds the first fortnight) and inspected the countryside in the first light of day. Locust leaves showered down, mingling with the rain; limbs scattered on the wet green sod; brilliant hues of meadow shrubbery flashing through the more sombre greens of upland rumcherry and alder and the clump of quivering aspen between our house and Jack Kelley's. The rain was short-lived, but the half-gale continued even as we drove our faithful Honda through deep puddles and scudding leaves to early Mass in Wellfleet. On the way home, we detoured by way of Pamet Harbor, there to join a convoy of cars bearing storm watchers like ourself. Boats remaining in the harbor faced sou'west, tugging at their mooring lines, swinging pendulum fashion against their painters in a wild, yet measured dance set by the howling wind. The moderate chop in the basin increased in size as it neared the mouth of the channel, where big whitecaps marked the rush of the tide along shore. And gulls fought the air currents, occasionally plunging into the lead-gray water to seize some tasty morsel. A wild day indeed; wind has shifted due west, temperature is a chill 46 degrees, and we're burning electricity in broad daylight, so overcast is the sky, with our home correspondingly gloomy.

There's a feeling akin to putting one's shoes on the wrong foot that comes to us when we write our column out of cycle, as we must when the holidays foreshorten the publishing deadline. We started to organize our thoughts last evening, when we took Shebnah out for his nocturnal perambulation of the property lines. Stretched our neck to observe the sky and like to slipped and fell on a thin skin of frozen snow abaft the trumpet vine. The stars were far and few between—tiny windows of light in an otherwise thinly overcast sky. Wind as calm as a schoolmarm's demeanor. Thin red line a mite under the freezing point. And silent as—but wait a second—comes the mournful, measured call of a hoot-owl from across the river, high on Dyer's range. And Sheb sniffs the air and growls deep in his throat, and circles the nearest locust tree, searching for an alien canine scent. Early to bed and when we arise in the dark hours this morning, we find the thin red line a bit lower in the glass, the caul of gray still covering the sky, and still nary a whisper of a breeze. We could set our clock by Jackie Kelley's first trip to the P.O. in his Brewster green sportster—quarter after the hour of six. After his passage, however, you could lay a prize wristwatch on the blacktop and it would be safe from traffic damage until breakfast time. So we perform our matutinal ablutions, work up a middlin' hearty breakfast of poached eggs upon bagels (hens were generous this week), watch from the corner of our eye as the day lightens, ever so slowly, on a valley scene of blended browns and grays and faded reds and pewter of the fresh crick. To anyone else but us the view might well be monotonous this time of year, but we love every blade of poor man's grass, every sere cattail wand, every gnarled locust bole. Carpe Diem—enjoy the day.

Our Christmas depression seems a wee bit lower than in recent years. We've gotten to the point we accept the grim reminders of advancing age: the receding hair line, the midriff paunch, the lagging step; the tendency to study the obits in the daily paper; putting off the heavier chores of cutting wood and mowing grass and shoveling snow in favor of the more sedentary hobby of whittling (feller can do a bit of pondering as he carves through the beautiful pine or teak or mahogany). In a recent session as we laid sandpaper to a freshly carved great blue heron (have to make the bird in two pieces, carefully glued, so's the neck will have cross grain to strengthen it) we got to thinking about Christmas past, when we shared bitter-sweet emotions with friends and family, some of them long gone, resting in the quiet of Gross Hill's burying grounds.

One year—during the war, it was—we were caroling with our townsfolk at town hall on a beautiful December afternoon. Biggest Christmas tree you ever saw graced the auditorium and Dode Kimball, he of the big belly and stentorous voice, clad in his Santa suit, holding the tots on his lap. And, when the heat became oppressive and some little brat stretched his patience to the limit, he said in a sotto voce you could hear yards away (Dode was a habitual cusser): "Don't you think you've asked for enough Gawl-Blammed-Sumbit toys?" And the beauteous young widow, Eleanor Ingraham, seated at the piano, responded to a request to play a carol familiar to few of the local folks.

Tiny Worthington promptly moved up to the battered upright and bellowed out in her clipped English—knew every word of the beautiful music. And when she'd finished, she turned to us and said, with a tear in her eye, "Reminds me of the Christmas some years ago, when Johnnie and Toppie were kids, and they crept downstairs as John and I were decorating the tree, and they looked so beautiful in their Dr. Denton jammies, and my gawd, how I miss my old man." (Her Air Force officer husband, John, was ferrying bombers overseas. More misty eyes for this sentimental Irishman.) And so it goes. The Christmas morning when the Benson brothers, Iver and Carl, asked Snowie and this slightly exhausted reporter (we'd been to one of the famed Benson smorgasbords the night before) if we'd like to go with them as they delivered a present to a local kid, Kim Boyd, seriously ill abed at his North Pamet home. The look on that lad's face and the poignancy of the occasion still brings tears to our eyes.

Many of our Christmas holidays have seen this mixture of warmth, happiness and sadness. Hope they'll let us play a few carols at the Orleans rest and convalescent home over the holidays. Helps us bring it all together.

NINETEEN EIGHTY-EIGHT

1988

A feller could run out of superlatives trying to describe this glorious winter day. Sun as bright as a newly minted coin with just enough innocent appearing cotton white clouds to relieve the monotony of a pale blue sky. The faintest whisper of a breeze from the southwest, barometer high and holding steady, and the thin red line of our shaded back porch thermometer inching up onto 50 degrees, up 10 notches since breakfast time. The sod underfoot is soggy, and you'd be hard put to find enough soiled snow in the most hidden, sunless spots to fashion a midget snowman. The fresh crick gives back the sunlight from its pewter surface, and the ordinary drab bottle green of the scrub pines is a welcome blob of color on winter's sere palette of browns and grays. Even with our woodstove getting a well-deserved rest, the house is warm from the generous sun on the southern windows. Our child bride saw a huge bird soaring over our property this morning—hawk of some sort—and that's why our chickens are strangely silent. Hope it doesn't affect their egg-laying habits. In all, a beautiful winter day.

The drug scene, with its violence, corruption, and waste of human life makes us avoid the TV screen and the screaming headlines—and compare this blot on our culture with the only illicit institution that even faintly resembles it, back in our day—the Prohibition Era. Lord knows we had our share of bootleg booze in the '20s and early '30s. Mysterious trucks roaring down the highway in the dark hours of night, an occasional boatload of burlap-baled hooch smuggled into some sheltered harbor—a hierarchy of operators ranging from the importers to the runners, to the local bootleggers. But in retrospect, it seems that the bootleggers were not of the same vicious, murdering ilk of current dope dealers.

You got caught by the Coast Guard, or the state police or the local police, and you took your lumps—for the most part. Avoiding arrest was the better procedure. "Don't sell to a stranger," John Lucas used to advise. "No free drinks to customers—makes your tongue loose," were the cryptic words of Captain Joe Francis. And Earl Cushing, a distributor well up on the pecking list, used to tell his customers to "hide your stock in a safe place." But once an officer of the law caught you in a sale, justice moved quickly and with certainty. A hearing before Judge Welsh, producing of the incriminating evidence—a pint of Black Rod or Belgian Alcohol—witness to the passing of marked money, and before you could say Obadiah Brown, the judge would slam down his gavel and send the offender, depending on past record, to the slammer in Barnstable.

An oft told yarn in our family tells how a distant relative, by name Barney Curran, found a way to beat the rap, as it were. Barney had arrived in Boston from his native sod at the beginning of the Prohibition Era. Worked for the city, digging graves, among other assignments, and the nature of his work undoubtedly increased his desire for a bit of poteen at day's end. And one night, having indulged beyond his normal capacity, he fell asleep on the railroad tracks in West Roxbury—woke up in the City Hospital days later minus his legs, but, being a robust feller, he was healed and out on the street instanter. A friend had a pair of leather cups fashioned for Barney so's the poor man could shuffle around a bit, and when it appeared his laboring days were over, his buddies got together and set him up in the bootleg business. They rented an abandoned store in Roxbury, hired a doorman, stocked it with pure Belgian alkie, and proudly displayed the premises to Barney. Barney himself devised a foolproof plan to spoil any raids by the revenuers. "I'll sit up here on the ledge av the sink," said he, "with two pitchers bayside me, one av them with the alkie, t'other with a bit uv sulfa napthol and if one av thim plainsclothesmen manages to get by the doorman, I'll pour the two pitchers into the sink, the stuff will mix quicker'n a wink, and they'll have no evidence at all."

Well, sir, Barney's strategy worked fine. Half a dozen times he had to do his mixing routine, and the frustrated cops could produce no pure evidence. But at long last a young, dedicated member of the dry squad outwitted the old Irishman. Snuck in the back door, he did, while his cohorts were distracting the attention of the doorman with a mock raid, and when Barney finally realized what was going on, and quick dumped the two pitchers, the young lawman fished out a big red bandanna from his pocket, and swooped down on the sink, and managed to get the bandanna soaked with pure alkie before it could mix. Barney spent the next few months on Long Island, in the city cooler.

On a recent TV talk show, we were interested to learn from a young Russian immigrant, that some of the things he found strange and interesting in this great land of ours included fast foods, ready-made clothes, especially blue denim jeans, eardrum-blasting portable radios, and boughten toilet paper. We Americans have a tendency to accept casually things which are considered a luxury in other cultures. But back to the last mentioned item. Had our Russian friend visited the Narrow Land back in the '20s and in subsequent decades, he'd not have found so many varieties of what we now genteelly refer to as bathroom tissue. There were a few brands that came in roll form, purchased by the more affluent folks, including the summer colonists, at Eben Paine's store. But the stuff couldn't be compared with today's cotton-soft, tinted, and slightly perfumed product.

To make a comparison. In the late '20s, the school committee of Truro, in response to parental pressure and firm proddings from Dr. Goff, the county health agent, authorized the razing of the original privy on its site amidst a clump of beachplum bushes just a hop skip and jump from the state highway. A new duplex toilet was added to the west wall of Wilder Grammar, semi free-standing, connected to the school by a sort of breezeway, with a narrow hallway that soon became a place for brief meetings of the pupils—they'd pass notes here, or exchange a sandwich or a slab of chewing gum, or perhaps homework to be copied. When it came time for the purchasing agent of the school committee to stock up on supplies, a new item was added to the list. In addition to the usual pencils, paper, pens, bibs, blotters, ink, and (rarely) a few new textbooks, the committee decided to adapt to the modernization theme of the addition by ordering some toilet paper, replacing the time-honored out-of-date mail order catalogues and weekly papers. (The catalogues had been perused so often that they were pre-crumpled, as it were. And they still made good reading, despite the missing pages.) The effete new specialty item came in bundles; ecru in color, coarse in texture, and you could sometimes actually see tiny wood splinters woven into the paper. But the biggest problem facing the committee had to do with the correct amount to buy. The bundles were labeled "Guaranteed Count, 1000 sheets." And it took considerable figuring, factoring in such things as projected student enrollment, frequency of visits, the occasional sudden draft through the open window that could lift the sheets from their wire hook and scatter them like autumn leaves. In due time a compromise was reached, supplies received and put to use. The darn tissue never did last a whole school year. So the Sears, Roebuck and the Montgomery Ward and the Charles Williams tomes were brought back to the scene and acted as supplements to the boughten product. The committee did, however, insist that certain sections of the catalogues be torn out before use. Take out the ladies' unmentionables, was the order to the school janitor. They shouldn't see women's corsets until they're 21—and/or married.

★ ★ ★

Truro's April Fool Club—yrs. truly, president, by virtue of seniority—will individually celebrate their birthdays on Good Friday this year. Other members in good standing are neighbors George Mooney and Paul Endich. Henry Morgan is an honorary member because of the closeness of his birthday—March 31 (almost midnight, according to Henry). Happy returns of the day to all.

Our tiny town was shocked last week to learn of the sudden tragic death of Joe and Ellie Schoonejongen in a one-car accident on the Maine Interstate. The well-known couple were on their way to a wedding when Ellie, driving, apparently either fell asleep or suffered a blackout. We remember the first time we met the Schoonies—at town hall it was, back in the '50s, and when we had difficulty recalling the spelling of the interesting Dutch name, Ellie spoke up and pointed out the monicker was easier to spell than her maiden name—Jankowski, if memory serves. We mourned the tragic death of their son, Herman, and found them a burial plot in Pine Grove Cemetery; thanked them for their generosity and thoughtfulness when they dropped by our house to slip a going away present to son Terry, bound for his stint in the Army. Presented them with one of our carved shorebirds and when Joe noticed we hadn't signed the carving, he asked us to do so. "Give the piece more value," he pointed out. "In years to come we'll look at that bird and think of you." And now we're thinking of Joe and Ellie—ave atque vale, old friends.

Conversations with our older brother Paul at the Orleans Convalescent Home often turn into mutual challenges of memory power. Paul is four years older than we are, but on occasion we can stump him. On our last visit we stopped by the kitchen to swipe one of those delicious corn muffins baked by a pretty young lady on the kitchen staff, detoured by the rec room and banged out a chorus of "Somewhere Over the Rainbow" (it was that kind of morning) while brother Paul was finishing his toilette. In response to his usual—"What's going on in Truro?"—we gave a digested version of local news. A pause, then, "Bet you don't remember the names of three horses in town: Ed Snow's mare, Ezra Hopkins' gelding, and that big work horse down at C. W. Snow's."

Easy as falling off a willow log. "Daisy, Sam, and Nig, in that order," we replied. Our turn. "Name the swimming hole in the Pamet where Naylor Hatch used to store some of his eel boxes." Duck soup to the *frère aine*. "Why Monroe's Landing, of course. Just back of Marm Yate's house. Shin up the bank a bit and you'd be at the terminus of the old Bridge Road, where the foot bridge used to cross the Pamet to what is now Holsbery Square. Remember the cold spring that used to bubble out of the sand? Freeze your toes off if you stood there for five minutes."

Then, "Bet you can't list—say—five brands of cigarettes not now on the market, that were popular in our day." A non-smoker should put such things out of his mind, but how could one ever forget such packages as Murad, Fatima (Turkish connections were emphasized, back then), Perfection (purple package, stronger than a he-goat), Piedmont, named for a mountain range somewhere down in tobacco country, and for the imported touch, how about English Ovals—oval they were, and they came packed in a flat 50 tin—elegant as all get-out.

Our deal. "When we moved into the Dahl house, up on Corey Hill, can you rattle off a list of treasures we found in the attic?" Like taking candy from a child. "There was a set of bent wire furniture from Miz Dahl's defunct soda shop, down in the square. Incidentally, before you ask me, her two children were named Sigrid and Trilby. A wheelchair used by her late husband we tried to convert into a bicycle, but Ma wouldn't let us take the thing apart—thought it would be bad luck to wreck an invalid's property. Original sign post identifying the highway through Truro. Located next to Austin Rose's store north end of Wilder's Dyke—but the sign was inaccurate. King's Highway, it said, but we all know that the ancient way is at least a mile and a half to eastward."

And so it went. How would you associate the following Truro folks, matching them up with their favorite automobiles? C. Arnold Slade—Packard Twin Six; the good Doctors Washburn, Thatcher, and Abbe—Nash owners all, and mostly touring car models, got more fresh air that way. David Snow, Hudson, to be sure—gas-guzzler, reputed to be the favorite auto of gangsters—but a prestige car, and much superior to its little brother, the Essex, driven by Dave's brother, Horace. Wallace Smith always drove an obscure model for which he never could get parts—among them Dort, the Star, and the Overland. But our visiting hour is over, and off we go, with a covetous eye on the kitchen table—but the muffins are gone, and so are our memories.

Sorry we missed the 60th wedding anniversary of one of our favorite couples, Joe and Mary Peters, of Ryder's Pond on the town line. Joe was our teacher-principal at the old Wilder School, and we taught with Mary much later at Wellfleet Consolidated. Had it not been for a summer complaint, we'd have wormed our way next to Joe at the gala and asked him if he remembered the time our calf shuffled into the coatroom at Wilder and, even as we were reciting the states and capitals, gummed her way through an assortment of sheepskin lined coats. Could Joe, we'd like to know, still umpire a fast moving game of scrub baseball down in the Holler across Depot Road? Those odors that used to scent the entire classroom at lunch time as the kids opened their ethnic goodies: linguica tucked in a bun, cold mashed baked bean sandwiches, spiced preserves from sour pickles to melon rinds. And apart from the food, how about the acrid tang of homemade mustard plasters in flu season, and the strong smell of tar-based lotions when head lice made their annual rounds. Memories, memories, and yes, we still recall that the capital of Vermont is Montpelier—North Dakota, Bismark; South Dakota, Pierre; Wisconsin, Madison—but the Carolinas are hazy, Joe. Ad multo annos, dear friends, and thanks for our association over the years.

We South Pamet folks are patiently waiting for friend and neighbor Mary Gray to return from her long sojourn at Mt. Auburn Hospital, where she has successfully undergone heart surgery. The beauteous Gwennie Kinkead has a stock of balloons on hand; Jackie Kelley will string streamers from the tallest locust trees, and we hope to come out of temporary retirement and render a chorus or two of "For She's a Jolly Good Fellow" on the valve trombone.

Most of the trees and shrubs in our yard have special meaning to us, if not a specific name. Nice way to commemorate special birthdays, wedding anniversaries, the spot where a special pet lies buried, perhaps even a trip to the hospital. We got to thinking the other day as we perambulated the area of the front yard, about some of the growing things and what they represented.

Biggest of all, of course, is the Atkins Maple. Not the genus Atkins, but named for the now-razed house in Provincetown once owned by the Atkins family. (The old lady became a bit eccentric in her dotage, kept uncounted cats on the premises. Sumner Horton sent us down there to cut the jungle-high grass, and we purloined three maple whips, one of which thrived on our front lawn.) There's a pale pink rose bush that marks the 25th anniversary of our wedding; we dug the hole simultaneously with our lamp post, given us the same day. There are three or four lilac bushes marking minor events: the day Shebnah was delivered to us (1977) if memory serves; and a big, skewed locust we ran over with our Model A the morning son Michael was born. In the excitement of the delivery we debated whether to uproot the mangled trunk or save 'er. Tall as our house eaves, it is. The needle spruce were hand delivered to us from the state of

New Hampshire by our closest friend, Fred W. Davis, only inches high. Now they form a beautiful, protective windbreak big enough to hide a herd of goats, and every tree bears loving memories of Capt. Fred.

Then there was an autumn afternoon when we were giving the lawn a final mowing, and a car purred into our driveway, and out stepped Steve Kinzer, neighbor over on North Pamet, accompanied by a short, dark, heavy-browed, shady-bearded man, together with a handsome little feller who was feasting his eyes on the beautiful scenery of the Pamet Valley. "Mike Dukakis, candidate for governor of the Commonwealth, and his son John," Steve made the introductions. And as we slowly strode across the lawn, we talked politics, especially those of the county. Got to about where our fire king maple stands, to the point where we realized a final handshake and vows of loyalty (politicians are always in a bit of a hurry) were in order, when around the corner of the house came our liver and white springer spaniel, Dolce. Dolce made friends with our guests instanter, lapping hands and sniffing in friendly manner at their ankles. "Why I remember this dog," said the governor-to-be. "Piece in the paper about him last winter. Your son Mike saved him from drowning when he fell through the ice." Care to make a wager on whom we're voting for come November? And we're carving a plaque, "Mike Dukakis Stood Here."

Got to thinking, this morning in the sauna-like conditions of Our Lady of Lourdes, about our duties in herding the worshipers into the pews. Folks all have their individual preferences. Some like to sit up front, probably to hear the Lord's word, but also to enjoy the feeble breezes from the pedestal-mounted fans. Others prefer the rear pews—nearest the door for a quick exit soon's the good Father intones the final blessing. There are those who like to sit about midway of the church, and with our best wishes—hope they catch a breath of moving air from the tiny windows. But for goodness' sake, lady, don't settle in the space nearest the aisle. Sometimes it seems we need the services of an electric animal prod to—but you get the idea.

We took the violin—this'd be back in grade school days, and our teacher was the late Josephine Patterson, a busty, short-tempered hacker at strings, but a good lady at the keyboard. With much practice by the light of the old Aladdin lamp, and assiduous study of the instrument and the appropriate printed exercises, we managed to conquer the scale of G. But on the open tones our hand-me-down violin used to squeal horribly, no matter how we held the bow, or tensioned it against the strings. We wanted to abandon that cussed instrument, but our sainted mother insisted we stay with it. "You're left-handed naturally, and I should think it's easier for you to finger that board—besides, I had a cousin in Boston, the North End, who could play a mandolin like a professional. Never took a lesson either."

One afternoon we were loafing down at C. W. Snow's barn, and Horace Pop Snow came clanking up in his Ford T truck, his day's work finished. "Whatsa matter, boy? You look lower than a barnacle on a boat bottom." We told him the story of our failure on the fiddle. Squawks—squeals, sounded like those pigs down in the sty when they're hungry. "I gorry, boy, maybe you ain't using the right resin." (He pronounced it rozzin.) "Now we got a barrel of it here in the corner, use it to make the drive belts on our machinery take a good hold on the pulleys. Them big pumps in the windmill tower? Thet saw mill with the big gas engine? Belts all well rubbed with rozzin. Never slip. Take a lump home and rub it on your bow, and maybe it'll help." Help our left eyebrow! The poor violin squawked worse'n ever. Next time we met Pop we mildly registered a complaint. "Oh, forgot to tell you. We also use that rozzin to rub on pigs' hides, after we've butchered 'em. Scald'em, scrape 'em, and the hide looks as though it had a fresh shave. You don't suppose there's any connection, do you?" Great kidder, was Pop. And shortly thereafter, Irv Tripp found a valve cornet in his attic (Civil War relic) and we found we could get a tone out of the battered instrument, even though we handled the keys right handed. The violin is still in our family—our granddaughter Heather draws beautiful tones from the instrument. Wonder what kind of resin she uses?

Chatting with brother Paul in the Orleans Convalescent and Retirement Home last week, we picked up a yarn he'd gotten from a fellow patient, the affable, congenial, prototype Yankee Easthamer, Clayton Horton. (We like Uncle Clayton first rate.) It seems that during the Boston police strike in the first decade of this century, Silent Cal Coolidge, governor of the Commonwealth, decreed that no one had any right to strike and endanger the lives and safety of the public. He therefore summoned the National Guard from all over the state to the beleaguered city, swore them into active duty, and had them assigned to various posts in the Hub. Men from every county in Massachusetts answered the call. Among them Uncle Clayton Horton, then a brash country lad of 16.

Clayton could do all things expected of an Eastham lad. Pound a nail, saw a board and make 'er fit. Dig a ditch, clean out a privy, plant a turnip field, cut asparagus and pick strawberries. He could hitch up a team of horses to a wagon, a mower, or a rake or cultivator. Nestle his head against a cow's flank and milk fast as any man in the neighborhood. And come winter, he'd drive to the nearest family wood lot and knock down wagon load after wagon load of pitch pine, drive it back to the family farm and stow it for drying. And evenings, on orders of their strict Yankee father, the Horton boys, Lester, Walter and Clayton, would be expected to buck up half a cord of wood apiece, to "settle their supper and keep 'em out of mischief." Made them sleep good, too.

Well, sir, Boston and this pseudo military duty was a hoss of a different color. The huge city was completely foreign to Uncle Clayton as would have been London or Paris. Coming from a town where byroads were known as roads or ways, Washington and Boylston streets with their busy traffic by day, and, for gosh sakes, street lights at night, were from another planet. But for a dollar per day, and the excitement of escaping the routine of household chores, he was willing to serve his stint. "Issued me a uniform, they did. Cut my hair down to a baldy sour style. Assigned me to the armory in the South End. Just about got to sleep that first night, when this big, red-faced, leather-lunged sergeant comes trotting in and bellows out, 'Hit the deck, you farmers. We got work to do. Latrine's over there, mess table through that door. On the Double.'" First two orders carried out, Clayton lined up with his squad, to be shortly berated by the beefy sergeant. "Get yourself a rifle from that rack." Fait accompli. The weapon felt awkward in Clayton's hands, and he screwed up courage to address a question to the sergeant: "All the guns we have down Eastham have hammers on 'em. You pull them back to cock the . . ." He was interrupted by a roar from the sergeant. "How'd you like a pitchfork to carry as an arm? And where in tarnation is Eastham?"

The canal bridges never looked so good to poor Clayton when his enlistment was completed. "Even then it looked as though fate was hindering my trip home. Dern drawbridge was open and got stuck in that position for half an hour."

Seems to be a late run of stripers off the backshore. This, of course, means activity in the harbor, where folks in waders are industriously scratching for sand eels, favorite bait of the anglers. We spent our share of time back in the good old days, combing the lily pads of most of the local ponds with our Sears, Roebuck $1.50 telescopic bait rod. Salt water fishing in those days attracted but few fishermen to our ocean beaches—and the biggest finned creature we ever caught was a red perch, 11-plus inches long, which, unhappily, tasted a bit muddy when we had our sainted mother pan fry it.

We almost gave up the sport when we hooked a sizable cat fish one lovely, sun-red evening at Slough Pond, and the poor creature mewed like a tortured baby as we hauled it up on the beach. We carefully extracted the barb and shooed it back into the limpid waters of the pond. Our good friend and mentor, George Buckingham, fishing next to us, said, "They say they're good eating—but I'm glad you let him go." In later years we favored the barbless hook—fun to catch them but more fun to let them go, became our motto. But there was one monster we had designs on—a huge carp that lived in the fresh Pamet somewhere around Fratus' Bend, which frequently swam lazily down-crick to the turn back of Ed Snow's house, attracted quite probably by the edible garbage which the Snows occasionally dropped in the shallow channel.

First time we ever saw him we couldn't believe our eyes—compared to the chubs, and the white perch and the summer eels of the crick, this fellow was a giant. With just a touch of hyperbole, we'd say he was the length of a baseball bat, big around as a 10-quart bucket. His whiskers were pencil thick, but there was no way to judge their length because they were constantly in motion, receiving messages, we guessed, as to water temperature, strength of current, and neighboring fish. His dorsal fin stood up like a catboat sail, and the lower section of his body was covered with bronze tinted scales, and his bug eyes protruded from his head like the headlamps of the then-popular Franklin automobile.

Those of us who were intrigued by the possibility of catching the carp—Ernie Snow, our brother Paul, Waldo Buster Brown, Herbie Gray—pooled our fishing know-how and sifted the sundry ideas. Couldn't stretch a seine across the crick and block the area, because this would require a license from town hall—available only at the time of the herring run. Besides, we reluctantly agreed this would be unsportsmanlike. Like shootin' fish in a barrel. Bait and dangle a stout hook in the water? Bread dough was the legendary bait for carp, but this clever fish simply sucked the dough from the hook and went his merry way. Dipnet, the size we used to bail out the herring or alewives in the spring? That contraption would accommodate the fish only up to his gill covers.

Finally, Buster came up with an idea: why not use an ordinary eel spear? With those needle-sharp tangs and the stout blade in the middle, handle fashioned from an old deepwell pump rod, with plenty of reach—easy as pumpkin pie. But when we had prepared the spear, and took turns poised on the bank, taking careful aim at the carp, who was casually slurping down a salt pork rind or whatever, we soon learned one of the basic rules of optics—things under water ain't where they're supposed to be. The water surface bends the line of vision so that a straight line to the target actually leads you astray. The only feller actually to strike the carp, and probably by accident—Herbie Gray—had the spear bounce off the fish's iron hard scales, and our prey made a leisurely turn to port and headed back to Fratus' Bend, unbowed, and not even bloody.

A persistent, thin gray caul has worked its way in from the bay on a mere breath of a sou'west breeze. Temperature is a warm 60 degrees, and the air is a mite damp. Barometer middle of the quadrant and holding steady. Our Pamet Valley is the usual microcosm of fall colors. Peach and orange, and glaring traffic yellow, together with the usual muted background of dying-coal bayberry and the still-green alder. Myriad Michaelmas daisies peek from the busy undergrowth, and goldenrod burgeons out on the meadow. Our Atkins maple has but a tinge of gold on its crown, and our locusts stubbornly cling to their fading, ovate leaves. On our way home from early Mass this morning we made the usual detour via Pamet Harbor. The string of buoys that separates the swimming area from the basin proper is strung along the parking area, awaiting winter storage. A scattered group of fishermen ploughing up from the flats, laden, we hope, with sandeels. Next stop for them is undoubtedly Ballston Beach, where they'll use all their skills to hook a lunker striper or vicious blue.

With a bit of mea culpa, we admit that there are moments at Mass in Wellfleet when our thought track gets a mite out of routine, and we start to study the worshipers, from our advantageous position at the rear of the chapel. The neatly coifed head of Dotty Rose—northeast gale wouldn't put one hair out of position. Young mother name of Suggs, with the big mane of shiny brown. Ernie Rose, who still sports a full cover, has 10 years on us. But bald pates attract us, mostly because they seem to show, at least in part, the personality of the owner. There's the patch, of course, with the promise of more to come—or is it go? The receding temples, like the tides at Pamet Harbor, and finally, the pure tonsure, wherein a dam-like band of hair seems to prevent the alopecia from descending any further on the cranium.

Handsome, friendly Bob Koch is our favorite in this latter style. He's usually only a few pews down from us and he usually selects a seat where the sun beats in through the stained glass windows and makes interesting patterns on the bare area. When he makes the slightest move, a kaleidoscope effect occurs—a touch of blue here, a thin strip of red, sometimes excerpts from the dedicatory inscription on the window "Gift of. . . ." Then we add another dimension to our Sunday game. We've always opined as how two persons can communicate if a bridge of willpower and concentration is built up. But it's no fair telling your subject in advance you're going to send him a message. Couple of weeks ago after the collection, we focused in on Bob's pate. Concentrated on a small area two inches above his collar line, and sent him the strongest message we could muster. "Calling in, Bob. Do you read?" Waited a few seconds, repeated the message in stronger mental volume. Then, strange to behold, a pattern of wrinkles appeared on the target area. "Hi, Tom," it read, plain as any block print. We've not had, in the interim, the chance to verify Bob's end of the ESP. Perhaps we could work up a vaudeville act together. Limit: seven characters per transmission.

It's been a week since our child bride fell in the back yard while wooing the chickens with stale bread, and cracked her radius at the wrist. She's in a cast, complains constantly about her lack of complete mobility, and grudgingly assigns various household tasks to us—preparation of gourmet meals, hanging out the laundry (we opt for pinning the T-shirts by the shoulders, evoking screams of anguish from our helpmate), vacuuming the rugs (whatever prompts us to try to catch Sheb's tail in the nozzle, irking the bride no end), and making the beds—sheet and quilt and electric blanket over or under the pillows? Whichever choice we make will be wrong. We'll talk with Dr. Eldredge, the bone man in Hyannis, on her next appointment, and have him convince her that domestic disagreements slow the healing process. Then we'll come home and hang the socks by their cuffs and mother's girdles by the legs, not the waistband.

For several years before the present Sacred Heart Church was built here in Truro (previous to 1900) Catholic services, on a flexible scale, were held at the home of Miz Rooster Brown, the present Kelky house—the nickname is lost in past history—a devoted Portuguese lady who enjoyed playing hostess to her fellow Azoreans newly moved to this country. They tell the story of one spring evening, with a full moon lighting the valley, that the Portuguese priest from Provincetown, Father Manuel Terra, had arranged for Lenten devotions at the Brown house. Word was spread about the neighborhood, to the Marshalls and the Deluzes and the Fishers and the Castle Road Grays, and the Josephs, up the road a piece, that this religious occasion called for a good attendance. There might, the good priest advised, be a venial sin punishment for those without a good excuse for being absent. In consequence, the Brown house was crowded that night—keeping room, parlor and the two downstairs bedrooms were jammed to the walls with an assortment of farmers, fishermen, and their spouses, whispering together in their musical tongue, the men freshly shaven, the ladies togged out in their Sunday best.

Promptly at 7:30 Father Terra threaded his way through a scattering of horse-drawn Democrat wagons, parked his ancient Buick next the kitchen door, and, selecting two of the Joseph brothers as altar boys, entered the

house-turned-church. He led the group in the customary hymns, performed the solemn elevation of the Host, then launched into one of his
familiar sermons, known to be long but inspiring—mostly in Portuguese,
but with occasional English phrases interjected to familiarize his parish
members with their adopted tongue.

The good father was particularly impressed with the odors that perme-
ated the Brown house, and he made this the subject of his sermon. He
likened the sweet smell of the bayberry candles on the impromptu altar to
sundry biblical incenses—sniffed at the strong odor of bay rum evaporating
from sun-tanned cheeks, and found it good—made mention of the odors of
sundry sachets secreted in the copious undergarments of the ladies, and
finally, giving each of his altar boys an encouraging pat on the head, he
summed up his homily by telling all hands they had been visited by "De
odor of Sanctity," even including the rather strong undertone of Mayo's
dark plug tobacco tucked away in several pants pockets.

Meantime, by purest coincidence, it so happened that Captain John H.
Rich, next-door neighbor to Rooster Brown, had decided to perform a
spring task that was almost ritualistic. For it was Captain Rich's habit to
visit the privies of his close neighbors, as well as his own, on appropriate
moonlit spring evenings, and, armed with a long handle shovel and his
sturdy wheelbarrow, clean out the sundry vaults. The product yielded was
deposited on the good farmer's cucumber patch, and produced the biggest,
best quality fruit in town. Poor Captain Rich was deafer 'n a haddock and
he was too busy to notice the gathering next door. Father Terra had
departed the scene just in time, but the bulk of the congregation arrived,
some on foot, some in Democrat wagons, at the Rich driveway just as John
was trundling his overloaded wheelbarrow to the garden site. "Whew,"
growled Depot Road John Marshall to his brother Manuel, "don't smell
much like the odor of sanctity, does it?"

Our sainted mother, Isabelle Rose (later Kane, of course), was born in the
latter part of the 1880's in the North End of Boston of Portuguese
parentage. Her father was an engineer on the T-Wharf tugboats, and he
allowed his second daughter (there was an older sister, Etta, whom we
loved beyond the telling) to attend the local school system through the
eighth grade, probably the equivalent of a high school education today. Ma
had done exceptionally well in school. In addition, she had picked up scraps
of Yiddish, Italian and other middle European languages from her play-
mates; she was neat and efficient-appearing in her tight-corseted waistline
and her pugged, black hair. Her hands were quick and accurate and she was

gifted with a phenomenal memory. So when she applied for a job with the phone company, she was hired instanter. Until the day she died, she always handled numerals in the style she had been taught by the phone company— 3 was thurrrree, 9 was ny-un, final consonants were clear as a bell, and proper names and company titles properly pronounced. Well, sir, Ma was on the job only a few months when her excellent performance at the switchboard came to the attention of the supervisor, and she was promoted to chief operator. In this position, she had her own switchboard to take care of—complicated long distance or emergency calls, but she also had to keep an eye on her girls. When one of them hesitated over the maze of plugs and sockets, it was Ma's duty to slip from her stool, race down the aisle and correct the matter. "The party wants Doctor Curran?" she'd whisper in her operator's ear. "That's Talbot Wun, WunWun Eight Thrrreee Nyun," fait accompli. (Doctor Curran in later years was to deliver both this scribe and an older brother, Paul.)

Somewhere in the records of the New England Telephone Company there must be an honor roll of faithful employees. And Ma's name must be high on the records. For she was on duty the day of the famous Original Chelsea Fire. The switchboard began to light up early in the day. And Ma and her girls were frantically processing calls, calls for assistance from neighboring fire departments by the beleaguered Chelsea smoke eaters. Horse-drawn wagons from the junkie district clogged the streets. Fire apparatus, sweating horses straining at the traces, iron-tired wheels shooting sparks from the curb stones, sought available hydrants as they beat a forced retreat from the blaze.

One by one the trunk lines in the office went out of service. And one by one, the chief operator sent her girls packing. The roar of the gigantic blaze drew closer to the exchange, the building next door exploded into flames, and smoke began to fill the working place. The last remaining operator dashed up to Ma and screamed, "Let's get out of here," and Ma, finally losing her composure, placed a call to her supervisor on the last remaining line, and received permission to leave the sinking ship, as it were. Grabbed her pocket book, scurried for the door, and from long force of habit, in accordance with company regs, locked it behind her. She no sooner reached the street than an obliging junk man yanked his nag to a stop and helped her up to a seat beside him. Perhaps that's why, in later years, when the local junkie in Dorchester (the clan O'Caghan moved to that blue collar area after Ma's marriage to our Dad, Tom Kane) used to drive down Armandine Street chanting "raaags and bottles," Ma would always manage to find something for him. God bless you, Ma, many jewels in your crown.

POSTSCRIPT

January, 1989

To my editors, and to faithful readers afar and abroad:

After some 40-odd years of writing "My Pamet" for the *Provincetown Advocate* and the Orleans *Cape Codder* newspapers, the time has come to put aside the tools of the trade, cover up the faithful Royal for the last time, and say good-bye to a host of friends, many of whom have been kind enough to drop by our South Pamet home or write us, saying they have enjoyed our weekly stint. For the kindnesses, thanks most sincerely.

To our editors, Duane Steele and Mal Hobbs, thanks for the space, and for your patience when we put your copywriters to work untangling a participle or un-splitting an infinitive. We admit to being the world's worst typist. I have tried over the years to keep my column non-political and inoffensive to all of my fellow citizens. If I have erred in this policy, I herewith offer my deepest apologies.

I shall miss chronicling the weather as seen through the eyes of a transplanted native . . . dropping tidbits that might interest the local reader, and spinning yarns about those picturesque old Yankees I once knew, about my beloved Portuguese neighbors, about the colonists to whom I have grown close over the years. Some of the yarns may have seemed a bit apocryphal, others ripe with hyperbole. In any event I have offered them for your reading enjoyment and I hope you have enjoyed them as much in the reading as I have in the writing.

Finally, I wish to thank most sincerely the men of the Truro Rescue Squad, who came to the Kane house last week at a time we needed them most. They performed their professional duties with skill, speed, and courtesy. On our local squad, Tamson Garran of the PD, Al Oakie Souza, Captain Bob White, and Tommy Prada, joined by neighbor Jack Kelley. The crew of the LCAA consisted of Clem and Ursula Silva and Doug Trumbo. If we've omitted any titles it's because there was confusion in my mind, and a bit of apprehension. Thanks, men, for a job well done.

So it's with a lump in the throat and a tear in the eye that we say: Au 'voir and three-o!

INDEX

OF NAMES